TEACHER RESOURCE BO

Ready® Common Core

5 Reading INSTRUCTION

Teacher Resource Book

Program Advisors

Katharine Garcia-Vance, Ed. D., PK-12 District Second Language Program Coordinator, Alief ISD and Assistant Professor at University of St. Thomas

Giovanna Grijalva, Ed.D, Academic Associate, Arizona State University

Adria Klein, Ph.D., Professor Emerita, California State University at San Bernardino

Albert Steven Lozano, Associate Professor of Education, Sacramento State College of Education

Margarita Pinkos, Ed.D., West Palm Beach, FL

Teacher Reviewers

Crystal Bailey, Math Impact Teacher, Eastern Guilford Middle School, Guilford County Schools, Gibsonville, NC

Leslie Blauman, Classroom Teacher, Cherry Hills Village Elementary, Cherry Creek School District, Cherry Hills Village, CO

Max Brand, Reading Specialist, Indian Run Elementary, Dublin City School District, Dublin, OH

Kathy Briguet, Retired Curriculum Coordinator for K-12 Literacy, Forest Lake Area Schools, Forest Lake, MN; Adjunct Instructor, Reading Instruction in the Elementary Grades, University of Minnesota, Minneapolis, MN

Helen Comba, Supervisor of Basic Skills & Language Arts, School District of the Chathams, Chatham, NJ

Cindy Dean, Classroom Teacher, Mt. Diablo Unified School District, Concord, CA

Jennifer Geaber, Kingston Hill Academy Charter School, South Kingstown, RI

Bill Laraway, Classroom Teacher, Silver Oak Elementary, Evergreen School District,San Jose, CA

Susie Legg, Elementary Curriculum Coordinator, Kansas City Public Schools, Kansas City, KS

Sarah Levine, Classroom Teacher, Springhurst Elementary School, Dobbs Ferry School District, Dobbs Ferry, NY

Nicole Peirce, Classroom Teacher, Eleanor Roosevelt Elementary, Pennsbury School District, Morrisville, PA

Donna Phillips, Classroom Teacher, Farmington R-7 School District, Farmington, MO

Kari Ross, Reading Specialist, MN

Sunita Sangari, Math Coach, PS/MS 29, New York City Public Schools, New York, NY

Shannon Tsuruda, Classroom Teacher, Mt. Diablo Unified School District, Concord, CA

Acknowledgments

Vice President of Product Development: Adam Berkin

Editorial Director: Katherine Rossetti

Executive Editor: William Kelleher

Editorial: Melissa Brown, Karen Casey, Anne Cullen, Carmela Fazzino-Farah, John Ham, Susan James, Joan Krensky, Charles McQuillen, Sheila Mehegan, Maura Piazza, Daniel Smith

Project Manager: Audra Bailey

Cover Design: Matt Pollock

Cover Illustrator: O'Lamar Gibson

Design/Production: William Gillis, Mark Nodland, Ed Scanlon, Jennifer Sorenson, Jeremy Spiegel

ISBN 978-1-4957-0584-7

North Billerica, MA 01862

15 14 13 12 11 10 9 8 7 6 5 4 3 2

Table of Contents

Table of Contents

Reading Lessons

*Standards in **boldface** are the focus standards that address major lesson content.*

Reading Lessons, *continued*

Standards in ***boldface*** *are the focus standards that address major lesson content.*

Table of Contents

*Standards in **boldface** are the focus standards that address major lesson content.*

Language Handbook

Teacher Resources

Welcome to *Ready® Reading*

Ready Reading is a rigorous standards-based program that builds strong, independent readers through instruction and practice with high-interest, complex informational and literary texts.

Rigor that is reachable

Built from scratch to meet Common Core expectations, *Ready Reading* provides a powerful combination of complex texts and rigorous instruction.

- Instruction is organized around a confidence-building, **gradual release of responsibility** model.
- A consistent **Read, Think, Talk, Write instructional model** fosters engagement and builds student autonomy.
- **Close reading habits** are taught through authentic, complex texts that reach across the content areas.

Support that simplifies

Offering step-by-step guidance and embedded teacher support, *Ready Reading's* teacher tools are easy to implement and support powerful, effective teaching.

- A comprehensive **Teacher Resource Book** provides point-of-use strategies and routines, and tips that support best-practice teaching.
- A nimble **Online Teacher Toolbox** offers a virtual filing cabinet of instructional resources to support teaching throughout the year.

Meet Our *Ready*® ELA Authors

The *Ready* program provides practical classroom instruction based on proven literacy research. Guidance from the distinguished *Ready* authorship team continues to shape the program.

James W. Cunningham, Ph.D.

Awards & Key Positions

- Text Complexity Committee for the CCSS in English Language Arts
- Reading Hall of Fame
- National Reading Conference Board of Directors

Research Focus

- Text complexity
- Reading diagnosis
- Reading comprehension
- Writing (K–8)

Maureen McLaughlin, Ed.D.

Awards & Key Positions

- Past President, International Reading Association (IRA)
- IRA Common Core Standards Committee
- IRA Outstanding Teacher Educator in Reading

Research Focus

- Reading comprehension
- Reading across the content areas
- Close Reading (focus on middle grades)
- New literacies

Brenda Overturf, Ed.D.

Awards & Key Positions

- Co-Chair, IRA Common Core State Standards Committee
- Former District Director K–12 Reading Curriculum and Assessment
- International Reading Association Board of Directors

Research Focus

- Vocabulary
- Designing & implementing literacy frameworks
- Reading across the content areas
- Standards-based instruction

D. Ray Reutzel, Ph.D.

Awards & Key Positions

- Literacy Researchers Association Board of Directors
- International Reading Association Board of Directors
- Reading Hall of Fame
- John C. Manning Public School Service Award

Research Focus

- Informational text
- Reading comprehension
- Reading assessment
- RTI—at-risk children
- Fluency

Program Components

Ready® *Reading*

- The **Student Instruction Book** delivers a deep study of each Literature and Informational Reading Standard with highly-engaging, complex texts from a wide range of genres.
- The **Teacher Resource Book** provides the point-of-use guidance and embedded teacher support needed for teaching every step of every lesson.
- The **Student Assessment Book** (PARCC, SBAC, or National) offers full-length assessments that mirror the format, question type, and rigor of state tests, including tech-enhanced item types.

Ready® *Writing*

- The **Student Instruction Book** provides explicit instruction in opinion, informative/explanatory, and narrative writing. Engaging source texts provided at point of use span a range of on-level science and social studies topics and support evidence-based writing.
- The **Teacher Resource Book** provides the point-of-use guidance and embedded teacher support needed for teaching every step of every lesson.

Ready Reading Instruction and Assessments and *Ready Writing* Instruction are available on the Online Teacher Toolbox.

***Ready®* Online Teacher Toolbox**

(Teacher-Toolbox.com)

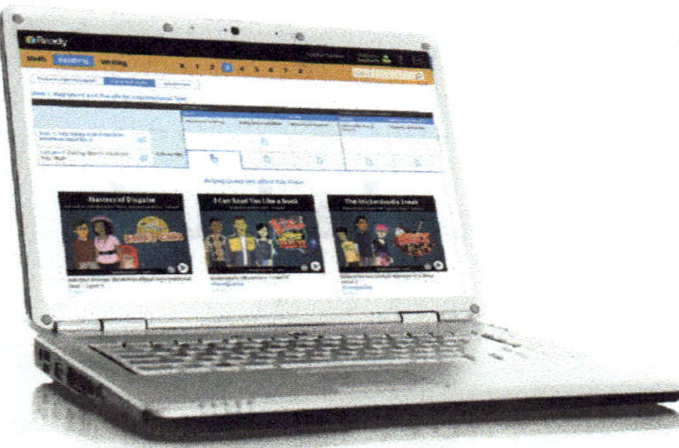

The easy-to-use **Online Teacher Toolbox** is a virtual filing cabinet of instructional resources designed to address the needs of all learners and differentiate instruction.

- Complete access to all K–8 content,
- Interactive Tutorials,
- *Ready* Instruction Prerequisite Lesson PDFs, and
- Tools for Instruction.

i-Ready®

(i-Ready.com)

i-Ready combines an adaptive diagnostic and growth measure, targeted assessment of grade-level standards, and individualized online instruction in a single program.

- ***i-Ready* Diagnostic** delivers a comprehensive understanding of each student's unique needs across a K-12 continuum and is proven to predict performance on state assessments.
- ***i-Ready* Standards Mastery** provides specific insight into students' mastery of individual, grade-level standards.
- ***i-Ready* data** shape each student's personalized instruction plan, prescribing a tailored combination of online instruction and downloadable, teacher-led lessons for each student.

World's Worst Pet

(Vocabulary Development App)

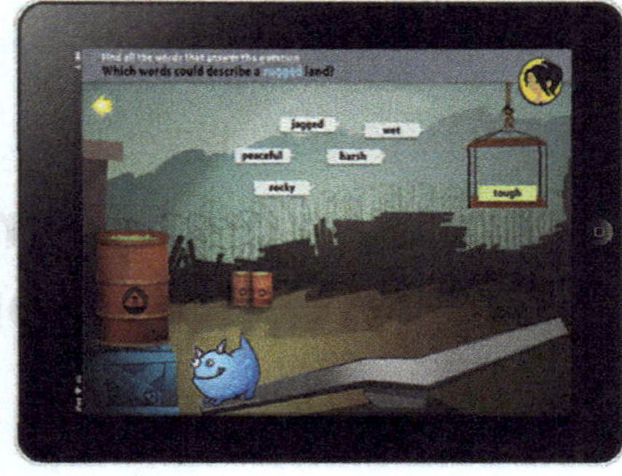

World's Worst Pet is a free i-Pad game app that provides robust practice to develop the Tier 2 vocabulary required to become a successful reader.

Using *Ready*® with *i-Ready*®: Program Overview

Whether using the *i-Ready*®/*Ready*® blended program or *Ready* as a stand-alone program, you have the flexibility to meet all your instruction and assessment needs.

Diagnose and Monitor

Adaptive Diagnostic and Growth Monitoring

i-Ready® Diagnostic

45–60 minutes, 3 times a year

Adaptive diagnostic designed to collect a broad spectrum of information on student ability to identify where students are struggling, measure growth across a student's career, and plan instructional paths with a single measurement tool

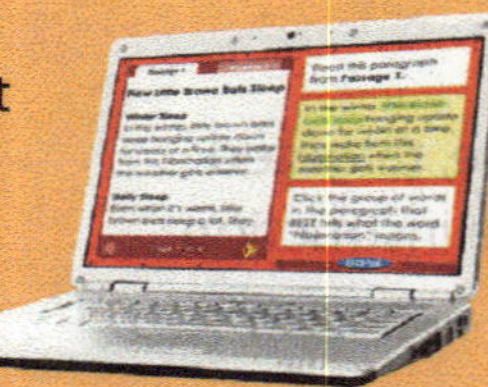

Standards Mastery Monitoring

i-Ready® Standards Mastery

10–15 minutes per standard

Our new Standards Mastery tool provides targeted insight into student's mastery of individual, grade-level standards.

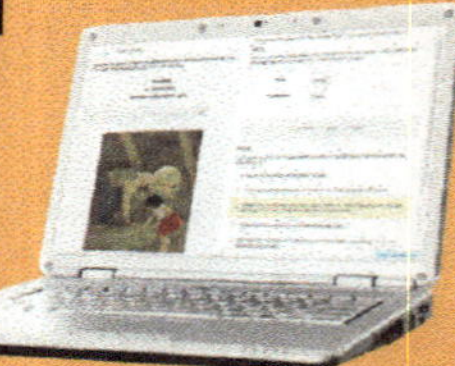

Alternatively, the following *Ready* assessment tools can be used instead of *i-Ready*.

- **Growth Monitoring:** *Ready Assessments* (PARCC, SBAC, or National)
- **Standards Mastery Monitoring:** *Ready* Instruction Interim Assessments

Instruct

Whole Class Instruction

Ready® Books and Online Teacher Toolbox

Small Group Differentiation

Ready® Online Teacher Toolbox

Personalized Learning and Intervention

i-Ready® Instruction

Instruct
Ready® Reading

45–60 min per day,
1 lesson per week

Teacher-led whole and small group reading instruction following a gradual-release model

Instruct
Ready® Writing

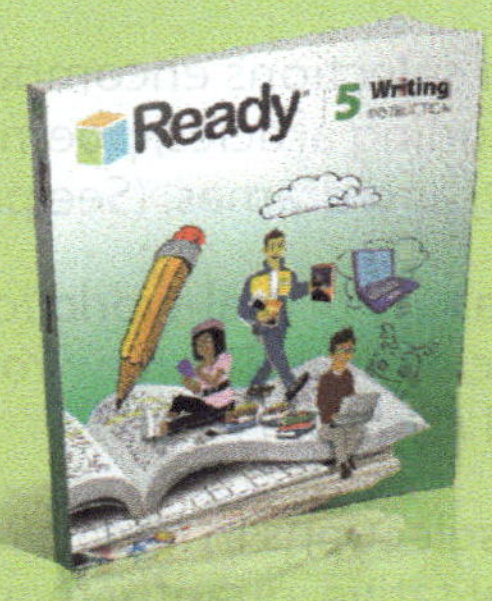

45 min per day
15 days per lesson

Teacher-led whole and small group writing instruction following a gradual-release model

Reteach
Ready® Instruction Prerequisite Lesson PDFs

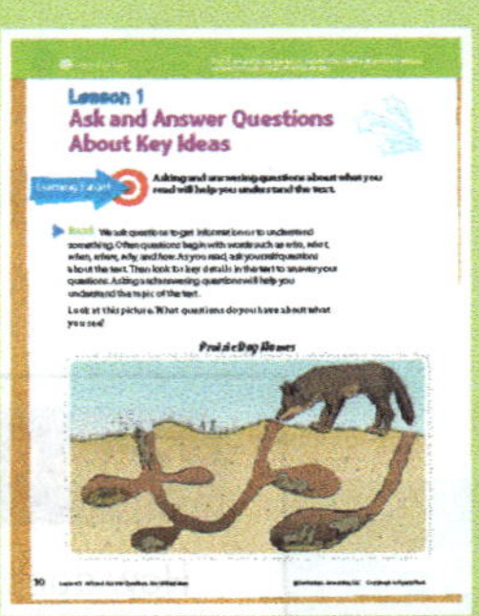

45–90 min per day,
1 lesson per week

Teacher-led in-depth instruction using *Ready* lessons from earlier grades to review prerequisite concepts or fill in gaps in student knowledge

Teacher-Led Activity
Tools for Instruction PDFs

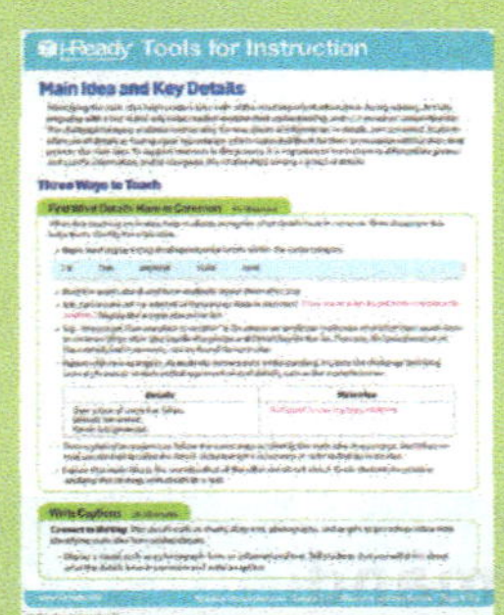

20–30 min per activity

Teacher-led activities for use with small groups of students requiring additional instruction on a prerequisite or on-level skill

Online Instruction
i-Ready® Instruction

At least 45 min per week

Animated, interactive lessons that allow students to work independently on their personalized online instructional plan

Vocabulary Development
World's Worst Pet i-Pad App

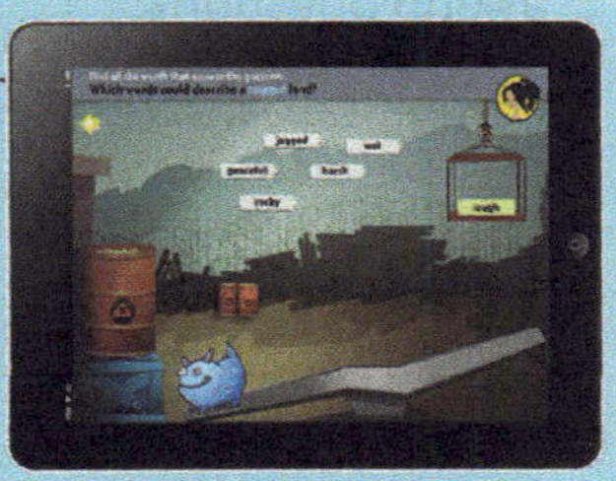

Optional 30–45 min per week

Targeted vocabulary development through multiple exposures and robust practice

Answering the Demands of the Reading Standards

Common Core standards have raised the rigor of reading instruction in several important ways. *Ready® Reading* was developed to support teachers in implementing these new demands.

Demand: Read complex texts from a range of genres

Ready Reading **provides a broad range of high-quality informational and literary texts.**

- Text selections encompass a range of genres and text types, including articles, poems, history text, technical text, scientific text, and dramas. (See page A18 for a complete list of text types.)
- A variety of real-world formats include newspaper and magazine articles from *The New York Times, National Geographic for Kids,* and *Highlights*.
- All selections in *Ready Reading* have been evaluated to address qualitative, quantitative, and reader-task criteria to ensure grade-level appropriateness.

Demand: Read closely and cite text-based evidence

Ready Reading **teaches students to read and reread to deepen understanding of text.**

- Every lesson contains activities requiring close reading, rereading, and frequent interactions with text.
- Close Reader Habits cultivate reading behaviors that successful readers employ, including marking text, taking notes, and asking questions.
- Partner talk and responsive-writing activities require students to cite text-based evidence.

Close Reader Habits

How does each bicycle model improve upon the model before it? Reread the article. **Underline** details that tell *why* each model was an improvement.

Talk

3 Based on information in the text, what changes to bicycle designs came about in the 1800s? What can you conclude about why the designs kept changing?

Write

4 **Short Response** Explain how the design of the bicycle was improved in the 1800s and why the changes were necessary. Use details from the text to support your answer. Use the space provided on page 31 to write your answer.

Demand: Build content knowledge

Ready Reading's **thematically organized reading selections build content area knowledge.**

- Thematically linked selections focus on grade-appropriate science and social studies topics, such as communities, westward expansion, and scientific discoveries. (See page A18 for a complete list of themes.)
- Theme activities in the Teacher Resource Book highlight relationships between topics and deepen content knowledge.
- As students read and write within these themes, they deepen their knowledge of academic vocabulary and domain-specific language.

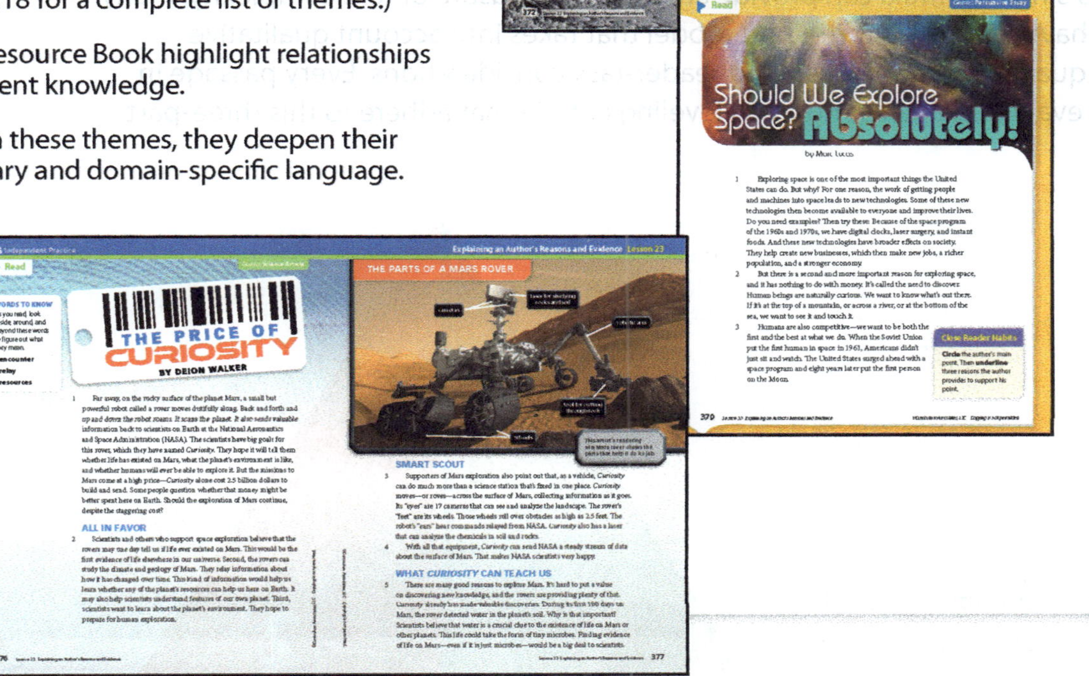

Demand: Integrate ELA instruction and apply academic vocabulary

Ready Reading **teaches reading standards through connected tasks that integrate writing, speaking and listening, and language standards.**

- The consistent *Read, Think, Talk, Write* instructional model integrates multiple modalities into every lesson.
- Students learn to use the academic vocabulary of the standard to facilitate discussion and deepen understanding of the text.
- Students demonstrate understanding and comprehension of text through collaborative discussions and writing.

Complex and Engaging Texts

Research has shown that over the past 50 years the texts students encounter in school have decreased in complexity and that college textbooks and professional journals have also become more complex. To be college and career ready, students need to encounter appropriately complex text starting in elementary school, progressively developing their language skills and conceptual knowledge. *Ready Reading* helps meet this challenge with engaging texts of appropriate complexity at each grade level.

Text Complexity in *Ready Reading*

Because no single formula can provide an accurate measure of text complexity, many educators have adopted a three-part model that takes into account qualitative measures, quantitative measures, and reader-task considerations. Every passage in *Ready* was evaluated against rigorous leveling criteria that adhere to this three-part model.

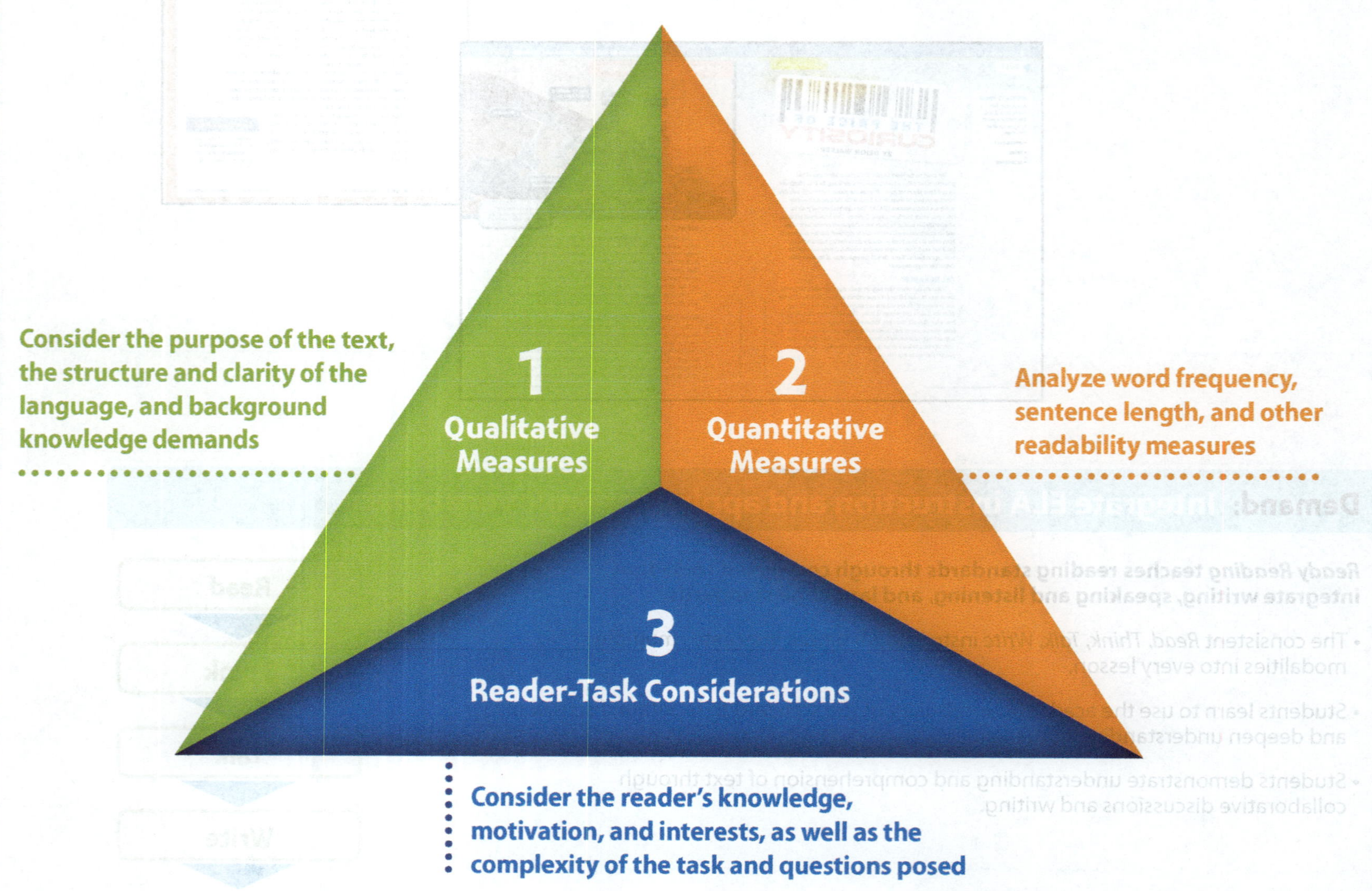

Ready Reading motivates students with high-interest text

Research has shown that students' reading levels vary depending on their interest in a text (Duke et al., 2011). The texts in *Ready Reading* were selected and designed with the understanding that students are more willing to approach more complex text when they are personally invested in what they are reading.

- **Authentic texts from a range of literary and informational genres**
  Drawing from celebrated authors including Henry Wadsworth Longfellow, Mary Hoffman, and Eileen Spinelli, and popular children's magazines, including *Cobblestone, Appleseeds,* and *Science News for Kids, Ready Reading* offers a wide range of compelling texts that address the diverse interests of young readers.
- **Student-friendly, interdisciplinary topics**
  Oftentimes celebrating the curious and the unexpected, thematically organized texts explore content-area topics through a student-centered lens.
- **Contemporary design elements and dynamic visuals**
  Engaging design, illustrations, photographs, maps, and other text features grab and hold students' interest, while supporting comprehension.
- **Instructional approaches that involve and engage**
  Activities accompanying each selection involve students in collaborative discussions and analysis that encourage personal investment and reflection.

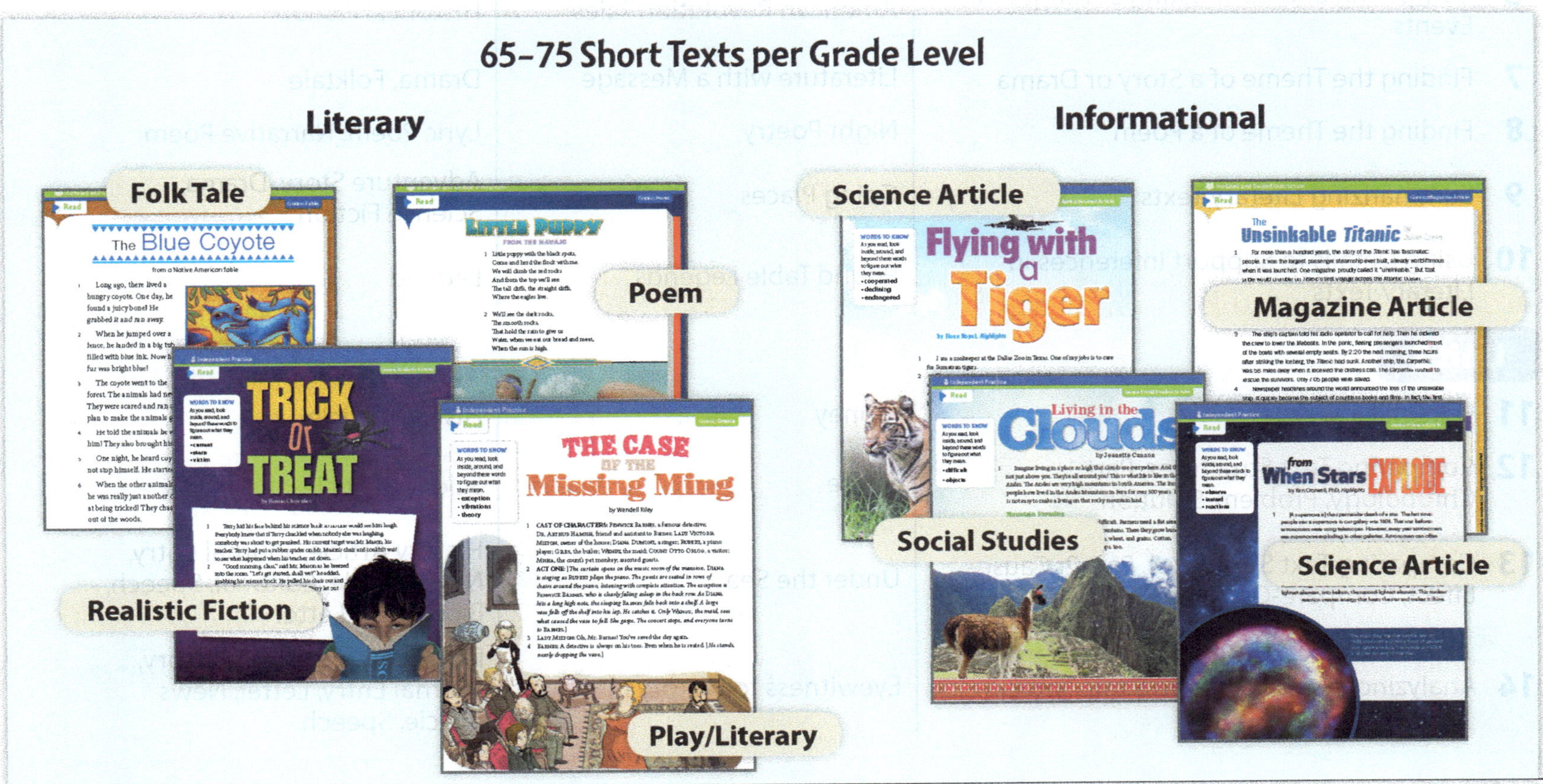

Genres and Themes in *Ready*®

To succeed in college and the world outside the classroom, students must master reading a wide range of literary and informational texts. *Ready*® ensures students read rich texts linked in meaningful ways by including a variety of genres and by organizing each lesson under a theme. The following chart shows the themes and genres for the grade 5 lessons.

Lesson		Theme	Genres
Unit 1			
1	Finding Main Ideas and Details	Stars and Planets	Science Text, Science Article
2	Summarizing Informational Texts	Cultural Mosaic	Biography, Interview
3	Using Details to Support Inferences	Adventures and Discovery	Biography, History Article
4a	Explaining Relationships in Scientific and Technical Texts	It's Electric	Science Text, Technical Text
4b	Explaining Relationships in Historical Texts	Ancient African Kingdoms	History Article, Eyewitness Account
Unit 2			
5	Comparing and Contrasting Characters in Drama	Familiar Characters	Drama
6	Comparing and Contrasting Settings and Events	American Revolution Tales	Historical Fiction
7	Finding the Theme of a Story or Drama	Literature with a Message	Drama, Folktale
8	Finding the Theme of a Poem	Night Poetry	Lyric Poem, Narrative Poem
9	Summarizing Literary Texts	Going Places	Adventure Story, Drama, Science Fiction
10	Using Details to Support Inferences in Literary Texts	Round Table Legends	Legend
Unit 3			
11	Unfamiliar Words	Money	History Article
12	Comparing Text Structures, Part 1: Chronology, Problem-Solution	Space	Science Article
13	Comparing Text Structures, Part 2: Cause-Effect, Compare-Contrast	Under the Sea	History Article, Journal Entry, News Article, Editorial, Speech, Biography, Letter
14	Analyzing Accounts of the Same Topic	Eyewitness to History	Biography, Editorial, History, Journal Entry, Letter, News Article, Speech

3 passages per theme

Ready Reading offers three reading passages per lesson. By repeatedly revisiting and building on academic vocabulary and concepts, these thematically-organized readings deepen cross-curricular knowledge. These three passages from Grade 4 Lesson 2, Understanding Historical Texts, explore the theme of transportation history. There are over 75 short texts in Grade 5. Half are fiction and half are nonfiction.

Lesson	Theme	Genres
Unit 4		
15 Language and Meaning	Nature	Lyric Poem, Realistic Fiction, Fantasy
16 Understanding Literary Structure	Laughter	Drama, Narrative Poem
17 Point of View	Native Voices	Poem, Realistic Fiction, Legend
Unit 5		
18 Finding Information from Multiple Sources	Human and Animal Communication	Science Text, Science Article
19 Understanding Supporting Evidence	Code Communication	History Article
20 Using Multiple Sources for Writing and Speaking	Electronic Communication	History Text, Science Text, Science Article, History Article, Magazine Article
Unit 6		
21 Analyzing Visual Elements in Literary Texts	Picturing Literature	Fable, Lyric Poem, Myth
22 Comparing and Contrasting Stories in the Same Genre	Similar Stories	Fable, Mystery, Adventure Story

Close Reader Habits

To become college and career ready, students need to develop the habits of close readers to independently unpack the evidence found in complex texts. *Ready Reading* was designed to teach these close reading skills and practices.

Short, Rich, Complex Texts

Short texts are one of the best ways to introduce close reading habits because they allow for multiple readings and let students practice a skill across the entire text (Fisher et al. 2012; Boyles 2012). To this end, *Ready* provides a library of short texts that merit multiple readings.

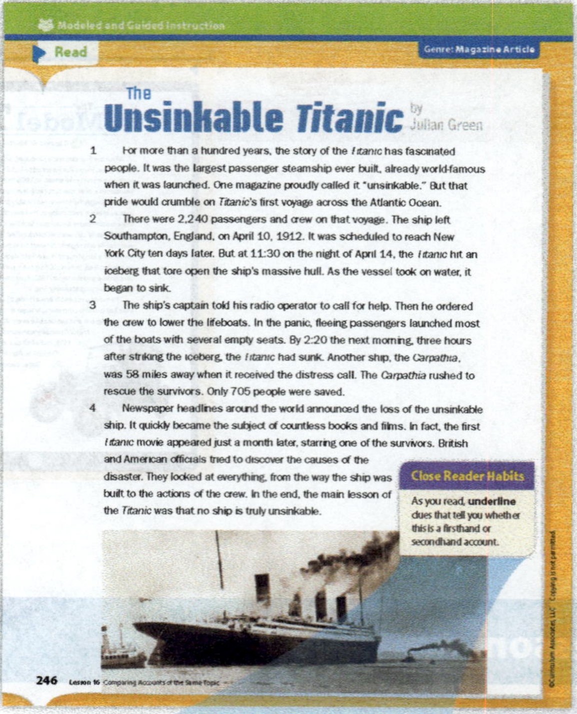

Modeled and Guided Instruction

Read

Genre: Magazine Article

The **Unsinkable *Titanic*** by Julian Green

1 For more than a hundred years, the story of the *Titanic* has fascinated people. It was the largest passenger steamship ever built, already world-famous when it was launched. One magazine proudly called it "unsinkable." But that pride would crumble on *Titanic*'s first voyage across the Atlantic Ocean.

2 There were 2,240 passengers and crew on that voyage. The ship left Southampton, England, on April 10, 1912. It was scheduled to reach New York City ten days later. But at 11:30 on the night of April 14, the *Titanic* hit an iceberg that tore open the ship's massive hull. As the vessel took on water, it began to sink.

3 The ship's captain told his radio operator to call for help. Then he ordered the crew to lower the lifeboats. In the panic, fleeing passengers launched most of the boats with several empty seats. By 2:20 the next morning, three hours after striking the iceberg, the *Titanic* had sunk. Another ship, the *Carpathia*, was 58 miles away when it received the distress call. The *Carpathia* rushed to rescue the survivors. Only 705 people were saved.

4 Newspaper headlines around the world announced the loss of the unsinkable ship. It quickly became the subject of countless books and films. In fact, the first *Titanic* movie appeared just a month later, starring one of the survivors. British and American officials tried to discover the causes of the disaster. They looked at everything, from the way the ship was built to the actions of the crew. In the end, the main lesson of the *Titanic* was that no ship is truly unsinkable.

Close Reader Habits

As you read, **underline** clues that tell you whether this is a firsthand or secondhand account.

246 Lesson 16 Comparing Accounts of the Same Topic

©Curriculum Associates, LLC Copying is not permitted.

Multiple Readings

Close reading requires a willingness to reread a text to understand its deeper meanings (Reutzel 2015). To cultivate this habit, *Ready* lessons require students to read a text multiple times. First, they read for literal comprehension. Then students reread the text to identify relevant text evidence and deepen understanding.

Close Reader Habits

As you read, **underline** clues that tell you whether this is a firsthand or secondhand account.

Annotate and Collect Text-Based Evidence

Using mark-up strategies to identify text-based evidence is a fundamental close reading practice (Fisher et al. 2012). To help students identify significant text details, the Close Reader Habits that accompany *Ready*'s reading selections guide them to use mark-up strategies as they analyze a text. Graphic organizers help students to organize the evidence they collect.

Teaching for Transfer

Students must take what they learn from the study of one text and apply it to the next. *Ready*'s gradual-release model encourages this transfer by gradually removing scaffolds, and cultivating self-direction. See pages A30–A55 to see how *Ready Reading* implements these metacognitive strategies.

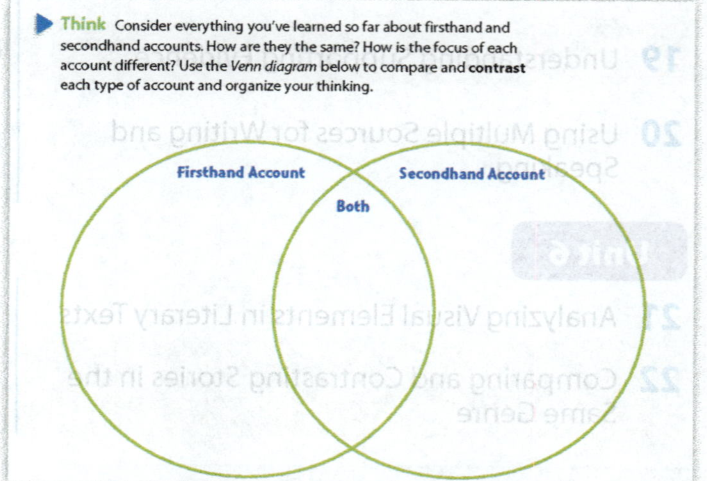

Think Consider everything you've learned so far about firsthand and secondhand accounts. How are they the same? How is the focus of each account different? Use the *Venn diagram* below to compare and **contrast** each type of account and organize your thinking.

Vocabulary Development

Research documents the reciprocal relationship between vocabulary knowledge and reading comprehension (Beck et al. 2002; Graves 2000). Building on this research, *Ready Reading* provides a two-part approach to vocabulary instruction. The words and phrases in Academic Talk focus on the language of instruction. Words to Know focuses on selection-level vocabulary.

Academic Talk Words – The Language of Instruction

One of the best ways to teach students new vocabulary is by introducing the words through an explicit and consistent instructional sequence (Feldman & Kinsella 2008) and then applying them in authentic discussions and writing activities. Academic Talk introduces and reinforces vocabulary that is aligned to the ELA standards and that students are likely to encounter on a standards-based assessment. Each lesson introduces a list of key words tied directly to the lesson objective. These terms are strategically revisited in discussions and writing assignments, building familiarity and expanding their use. These terms are introduced and reinforced by the Academic Talk Routine. See page A48.

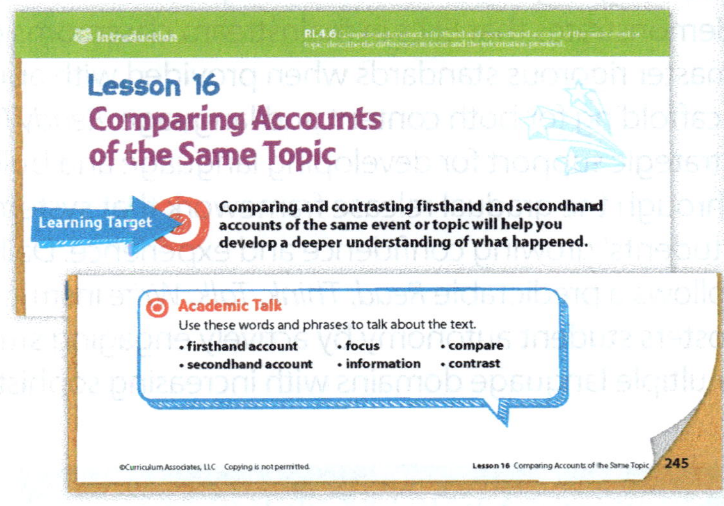

Words to Know – Selection-Level Vocabulary

During Independent Practice, students practice word learning strategies with a longer text. The Words to Know are either general academic words (sometimes called Tier 2) that are found across a variety of texts, or are domain-specific words (sometimes called Tier 3) that are mostly found in content-area texts. The Words to Know Box alerts students to key terms that are important in comprehending the text. Students then read with a heightened sense of awareness of the terms, anticipating the need to look inside, around, and beyond the words for their meanings.

WORDS TO KNOW

As you read, look inside, around, and beyond these words to figure out what they mean.

- **launch**
- **brilliant**
- **atmosphere**

Word Learning Strategies Since teachers cannot provide specific instruction for all the words students do not know, they need to teach students strategies to help them figure out word meanings. These word learning strategies include using context clues, identifying the meanings of word parts, and using reference materials such as dictionaries and glossaries (Edwards et al. 2004; Graves 2006). *Ready Reading*'s Teacher Resource Book provides point-of-use instruction of these word learning strategies. These strategies are reinforced by the Word Learning Routine. See page A48.

Word Learning Strategy
Use Context Clues

- Reread paragraph 1. Direct students' attention to the phrase *reasonably priced* in the next-to-last sentence.
  What do you think the phrase *reasonably priced* means?
  What word is a clue that helps you figure out the meaning?
- Guide students to find the synonym *cheaper*. Explain that *cheaper* helps them understand that *reasonably priced* means "not very expensive."
- Remind students that when they come to an unknown word or phrase, they can look at the surrounding words for a clue to the meaning. One type of context clue is a synonym, or word with a similar meaning.

L.4.4a

Word Learning Strategy
Analyze Word Parts

- Reread paragraph 2. Direct students' attention to the words *sailor* and *leader*. Ask:
  What does a *sailor* do?
  What does a *leader* do?
- Guide students to understand that the word part *-or* or *-er* at the end of a noun signals that the word means "a person who ______." For example, a *sailor* is "a person who sails."
- Have students practice attaching the suffix to other words such as *paint*, *teach*, *invent*, etc. Have them define each word as "a person who ______."

L.5.4b

Addressing English Language Learners

English Language Learners (ELLs) face the double challenge of meeting grade-level academic expectations while simultaneously acquiring English. Research in best practices consistently demonstrates that ELLs in mainstream classrooms can and will master rigorous standards when provided with appropriate scaffolding for both content and language. *Ready Reading* integrates strategic support for developing language and building meaning through the gradual release framework that systematically builds on students' growing confidence and experience. Daily instruction follows a predictable *Read, Think, Talk, Write* instructional model that fosters student autonomy by actively engaging students in using multiple language domains with increasing sophistication.

> "ELLs can and will master rigorous standards when provided with appropriate scaffolding for both content and language."

Supporting English Language Learners in Building Meaning

Recognizing the essential learning needs of English Language Learners, *Ready* supports ELLs in accessing content by establishing learning objectives, building background, frontloading vocabulary, and using visual aids.

Establish Learning Objectives

Research shows that effective instruction for ELLs should be grounded in clear learning objectives that are shared and clarified with students (Echevarría 2012). To this end, the program includes the following instructional features:

- **Learning Target** Each lesson introduces learning objectives written in student-friendly language, which are then revisited throughout the lesson.
- **Lesson Introduction** The TRB provides instructional support for students to understand key academic vocabulary and concepts they will need throughout the lesson.
- **Wrap Up** An end-of-lesson recap asks students to explain how the Learning Target helped them access and better understand grade-level text.

Build Background

ELLs bring to our classrooms richness and diversity in spoken languages and cultural backgrounds, as well as educational experiences. (Alliance For Excellent Education 2012). To make vocabulary and content meaningful, it is essential for effective ELL instruction to build on students' prior knowledge.

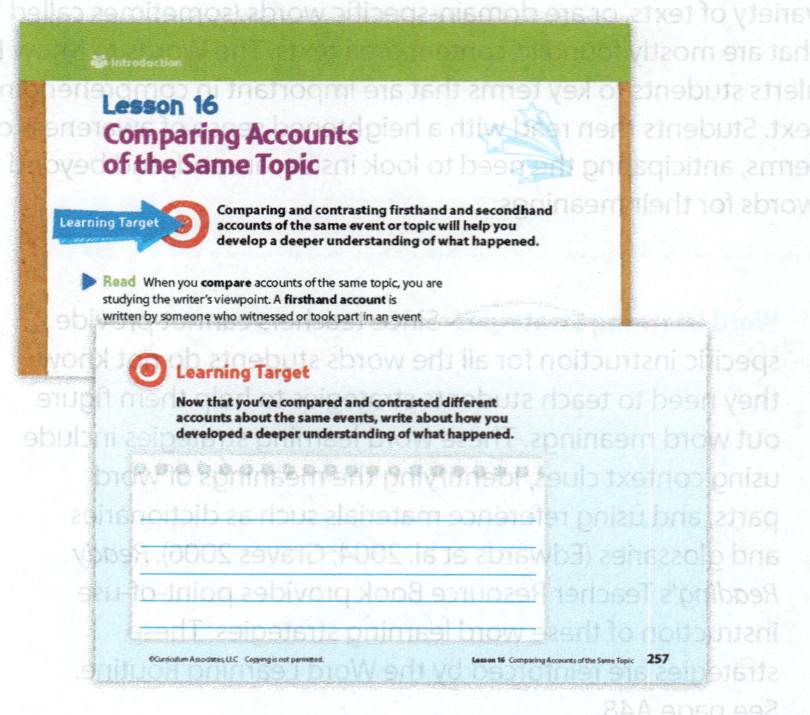

To build on students' prior knowledge, *Ready Reading* includes the following instructional supports:

- **Introduction** Each lesson introduces a new learning target through student-centered, real-life examples that build on familiar experiences.
- **Thematically-Organized Readings** Each thematically organized lesson in *Ready Reading* deepens content-area knowledge by repeatedly revisiting and building on academic vocabulary and concepts.
- **Talk** This regular feature helps all students practice sharing their thoughts and using new vocabulary in collaborative, low-pressure peer discussion, reducing an ELL's affective filter, or inner critic.
- **TRB Strategies** Instructional strategies range from direct instruction and modeling to cognate-recognition and collaborative activities to provide support as students access new words and language skills.

Frontload Concepts and Academic Language

Strategically exposing learners to the vocabulary, concepts, and skills they will later practice and apply sets up all learners, especially ELLs, for success (Beck 2002). Studies also show that vocabulary development is enhanced when students receive multiple exposures to key words and concepts (August, Carlo, Dressler, and Snow 2005). *Ready Reading* provides the following support:

- **Academic Talk** Students are exposed to key academic language at the start of each lesson. Each lesson fosters familiarity and understanding of the language of instruction by explicitly teaching and strategically revisiting key academic terms.
- **TRB Strategies** Specific instructional strategies are provided for ELLs to introduce both the academic language and the key domain-specific vocabulary students will need to unlock a given passage.

Use Visual Aids and Multiple Forms of Representation

Multimodal instruction can anticipate and accommodate the needs of ELLs with diverse backgrounds (CAST 2011; McLaughlin 2012). In addition, studies show that graphic organizers can help make relationships between concepts and skills apparent to students (Janzen 2008; McLaughlin 2012). *Ready Reading* includes:

- **Graphic Organizers** Used as thinking tools and included in every lesson, graphic organizers help ELLs visualize how a text's ideas and evidence are organized and help them organize their own thinking about a text.
- **Instructional Visuals** A rich number of photographs, illustrations, and other visuals build interest and ensure comprehension, offering ELLs another entry point into a text. Instructional strategies throughout the TRB provide support for teachers in using the Student Book visuals to deepen understanding and build comprehension.

> **ELL English Language Learners**
> **Develop Language**
>
> **Idioms** Help students comprehend a key story event by making sure they understand the expression *lose track of.*
>
> - Ask students to name things people often lose or misplace temporarily. Examples include objects such as keys, cell phones, or eyeglasses. Explain that people might say they *lost track of* these items.
> - Help students understand that people can lose track of other things, too. For example, you might say, "I *lost track of* what I wanted to say," if you were interrupted while you were talking, or "I *lost track of* the time while I was texting and missed the bus." Using examples like these, guide students to arrive at the meaning of "forget" for *lose track of.*

Supporting English Language Development

Ready Reading integrates content knowledge to help ELLs build their vocabulary in meaningful, content-rich contexts.

Apply Independent Word Learning Strategies

To successfully understand complex texts, students need to be able to figure out the meanings of new words, based on their knowledge about how words work in English (Hiebert and Pearson 2014). To foster this, the *Ready Reading* Teacher Resource Book offers word learning strategies that involve learners in using context clues, word parts, and reference tools to unlock the meaning of words they don't know.

Engage in Focused Language Study

Depending on an ELL's first language, grammar and syntax can create unique hurdles to comprehension. To help address these linguistic challenges, targeted ELL activities in the TRB explicitly teach idioms and grammar strategies. The **Language Handbook** provides additional language skill development with scaffolded lessons that specifically address the Common Core Language Standards.

Supporting Research

Ready® Reading is grounded in the leading research on literacy instruction from the *Ready* ELA authors—James W. Cunningham, Maureen McLaughlin, Brenda Overturf, and D. Ray Reutzel—and other literacy experts.

Ready® Uses …	Examples	Research Says …
Gradual Release of Responsibility		
Scaffolded instruction is the gradual withdrawal of instructional support as students become more proficient.	Instruction in ***Ready*** gradually releases responsibility from teacher to student. Each reading strategy is first modeled by the teacher and then practiced by students together. Finally, students demonstrate understanding through independent practice.	*"According to Vygotsky, a student should be taught within his or her zone of proximal development, which is the level at which the student can learn with the support of the knowledgeable other. As the student's understanding increases, the support from more knowledgeable other decreases, and the student takes on more responsibility."* —McLaughlin and Overturf, 2013, p. 67
Integrated ELA Instruction		
The processes of communication (reading, writing, listening, and speaking) are closely connected. This connection should be reflected in literacy instruction.	***Ready*** uses a consistent *Read, Think, Talk, Write* instructional path that integrates Speaking and Listening, Writing, and Language standards throughout every reading lesson.	*"The ELA Standards were built on an integrated model of literacy and designed to be connected and interwoven . . . . The expectation is that the CCSS should not be taught in isolation; rather they should be integrated when planning instruction and assessment."* —McLaughlin, 2015, pp. 156–157
Collaborative Learning		
Students work with partners or in small groups to achieve a goal.	***Ready*** provides many opportunities for students to work together in collaborative pairs or groups. The **Talk** activity in each lesson step promotes sharing and expanding upon each other's ideas. In **Guided Practice**, students work together to reread the text and identify evidence.	*". . . Collaboration results in students obtaining greater insights into the thinking process of others around a text."* —Reutzel and Cooter, 2011, p. 279

***Ready®* Uses …**	**Examples**	**Research Says …**
Predictable Structures and Routines		
With a consistent structure and routines, students know what is expected of them in each step and across the lesson.	Each step of a *Ready* lesson has the consistent structure of *Read, Think, Talk, Write* Four step-by-step routines support key activities throughout each lesson: **Academic Talk, Word Learning, Partner Talk,** and **Response Writing.**	"*Providing predictable routines for students supports learning. Not only does student behavior improve, but students also show greater engagement with learning and achieve at higher levels when they can predict the instructional routines in a classroom.*" —Kern and Clemens, 2007, pp. 65–75
Tapping Prior Knowledge		
Prior knowledge includes the experiences and knowledge a student brings to a task. Tapping prior knowledge activates students' awareness of this knowledge and enables them to connect it to new information.	The Introduction of each *Ready* lesson connects the target standard to students' own experiences through familiar, real-life examples.	"*Activating students' background knowledge (i.e., opening the relevant schema 'file folders' in children's brains) in preparation for reading is critical for promoting reading comprehension.*" —Reutzel and Cooter, 2012, p. 274
Metacognitive Strategies		
Metacognition is awareness of one's own thought processes or reasoning.	In *Ready*, the teacher models each standard with a **Think Aloud**, demonstrating the metacognitive strategies employed in applying the standard. As students answer questions about the text, they explain the thinking behind their responses. At the end of each lesson, students reflect back on the lesson goal and on what they have learned.	"*Thinking about one's thinking is essential for pairing the known with the unknown (Donovan and Bransford, 2005). . . . Further, their [Cross and Paris, 1988, p. 131] work . . . found that instruction about metacognitive thinking led to increased comprehension and performance. . . .*" —Fisher, Frey, and Lapp, 2012, pp. 81–82
Close Reading		
Close reading involves repeated reading and discussion of text in order to deepen understanding.	In *Ready*, students read each passage at least twice: first to understand what it says; then to analyze it to find evidence that will support discussions and writing about the text. Close Reader Habits in the Student Book guide students in identifying and marking up evidence.	"*Deep understanding, and writing in response to that understanding, begins with close reading and discussion of texts.*" —Fisher and Frey, 2014, p. 34

Supporting Research, *continued*

***Ready*® Uses ...**	**Examples**	**Research Says ...**
Complex Text		
To be college and career ready, students need to encounter appropriately complex text, starting in elementary school, progressively developing their language skills and conceptual knowledge.	Every text in ***Ready*** was evaluated against rigorous leveling criteria that adhere to a three-part model that takes into account qualitative measures, quantitative measures, and reader-task considerations. See p. A16 of this document for more information on these criteria.	*"To grow, our students must read lots, and more specifically, they must read lots of 'complex' texts—texts that offer them new language, new knowledge, and new modes of thought."* —Adams, 2009, p. 182
Text-Based Evidence		
Questions that are text-dependent can be answered only by using information contained in the text itself, not personal opinion or background knowledge.	In ***Ready***, the items in each Think section are dependent on information from the text. Talk and Write prompts require students to cite evidence from the text.	*"One of the major instructional shifts in the ELA standards is that students are expected to provide text-based answers to text-dependent questions. . . . To meet this expectation, we need to create text-dependent questions and facilitate close reading lessons that engage students in rigorous text-based conversations."* —McLaughlin, 2015, p. 150
Variety of Genres		
Motivating, high-interest text in a variety of genres keeps students interested and engaged.	The rich assortment of reading selections in ***Ready*** encompass a range of literary and informational genres and text types. Texts include authentic magazine articles from publications such as *National Geographic for Kids*, *Cobblestones*, and *Highlights*.	*"A student who is motivated to read something can far exceed our expectations of what he or she should be capable of reading."* —Fisher, Frey, and Lapp, 2012, p. 79
Building Content Knowledge		
Reading multiple texts on a single topic builds knowledge and an increasingly deeper understanding of the topic.	***Ready's*** thematic organization builds cross-curricular knowledge. Reading selections in each lesson are thematically linked and focus on grade-appropriate science and social studies topics.	*"Linking literacy instruction and content area learning is beneficial for students' literacy development."* —Cervetti and Hiebert, 2015

Ready® Uses ...	Examples	Research Says ...
Graphic Organizers		
Graphic organizers are thinking tools that help students to visualize relationships among structural elements in a text and organize their own thinking.	A graphic organizer is introduced at the beginning of each ***Ready*** lesson. Students use it throughout the lesson to organize their ideas prior to partner discussions and writing tasks.	*"Readers who understand the organizational patterns or text structures an author has used in producing an expository text recall more from their reading than readers who do not. The National Reading Panel has strongly recommended the use of graphic organizers as a comprehension strategy for which there is abundant scientific evidence of effectiveness."* —Reutzel and Cooter, 2011, p. 355.
Academic Talk		
Academic Talk refers to words and phrases that relate directly to the standard or lesson objective.	**Academic Talk** words are introduced at the beginning of each ***Ready*** lesson, using a consistent Academic Talk Routine. Students are prompted and encouraged to use the words in discussion throughout the lesson.	*"Students should interact with their peers and their teachers using academic language and argumentation skills as they discuss the text."* —Fisher and Frey, 2015, p. 4
Vocabulary Strategies		
A strategic approach to analyzing unfamiliar words makes students successful, independent word learners.	***Ready*** teaches students a three-step Word Learning Routine: use word parts; use context; use reference sources. The strategy is reinforced in every lesson, and students apply it independently in **Independent Practice** (See pp. A50–A51 for more details.)	*The Common Core State Standards recognize the importance of vocabulary to aid comprehension through a focus on meaning and adding new words to students' vocabulary banks."* —Cunningham and Cunningham, 2015
Response to Writing		
When students write about what they read, they demonstrate what they have learned in the lesson and also explore their own thinking about the text.	Each step of a ***Ready*** lesson concludes with a Write activity. Students respond to a prompt, returning to the text for evidence to support their response.	*"The act of composing helps organize our thoughts and think aloud about new ideas. It also helps us internalize learning. . . . Writing is not only used to show what students know; it is also a tool for thinking and learning deeply."* —Overturf, 2015

Depth of Knowledge Levels in *Ready*®

The following table shows the *Ready*® lessons and sections with higher-complexity items, as measured by Webb's Depth of Knowledge (DOK) index. See page TR37 for a chart that describes the behaviors and skills involved in each DOK level.

Depth of Knowledge Levels for Higher-Rigor Items in *Ready*

Lesson	Section	Item	DOK
1	Modeled and Guided Instruction	3	3
1	Guided Practice	4	3
1	Independent Practice	4	3
2	Modeled and Guided Instruction	3	3
2	Guided Practice	5	3
2	Independent Practice	6	3
3	Guided Practice	3	3
3	Modeled and Guided Instruction	3	3
3	Independent Practice	5	3
3	Independent Practice	6	3
4a	Modeled and Guided Instruction	3	3
4a	Guided Practice	1	3
4a	Guided Practice	3	3
4a	Independent Practice	1	3
4a	Independent Practice	3	3
4a	Independent Practice	5	3
4b	Modeled and Guided Instruction	3	3
4b	Guided Practice	3	3
4b	Independent Practice	4	4
4b	Independent Practice	5	4
4b	Independent Practice	1	3
4b	Independent Practice	3	3
Unit 1	Interim Assessment	2	3
Unit 1	Interim Assessment	5	3
Unit 1	Interim Assessment	6	3
Unit 1	Interim Assessment	9	4
5	Modeled and Guided Instruction	3	3
5	Modeled and Guided Instruction	3	3
5	Independent Practice	2	3
5	Independent Practice	5	3
6	Modeled and Guided Instruction	3	3
6	Guided Practice	3	3
6	Independent Practice	1	3
6	Independent Practice	4	3
6	Independent Practice	5	3
7	Modeled and Guided Instruction	3	3
7	Guided Practice	3	3
7	Independent Practice	4	3
8	Modeled and Guided Instruction	3	3
8	Guided Practice	3	3
8	Independent Practice	3	3
8	Independent Practice	5	3
9	Modeled and Guided Instruction	3	3
9	Guided Practice	3	3
9	Independent Practice	2	3
9	Independent Practice	3	3
9	Independent Practice	6	3
10	Modeled and Guided Instruction	1	3
10	Guided Practice	1	3
10	Guided Practice	4	3
10	Independent Practice	1	3
10	Independent Practice	3	3
10	Independent Practice	5	3
Unit 2	Interim Assessment	9	3
12	Modeled and Guided Instruction	3	3
12	Guided Practice	2	3
12	Guided Practice	5	3
12	Independent Practice	1	3
12	Independent Practice	4	3
13	Modeled and Guided Instruction	3	3
13	Guided Practice	1	3
13	Guided Practice	2	3
13	Guided Practice	5	3
13	Independent Practice	1	3
13	Independent Practice	2	3
13	Independent Practice	4	3
14	Modeled and Guided Instruction	3	3
14	Guided Practice	1	3

Lesson	Section	Item	DOK
14	Guided Practice	4	3
14	Independent Practice	5	4
14	Independent Practice	4	3
Unit 3	Interim Assessment	4A	3
Unit 3	Interim Assessment	4B	3
Unit 3	Interim Assessment	5	3
Unit 3	Interim Assessment	6	4
Unit 3	Interim Assessment	7	3
Unit 3	Interim Assessment	8	3
Unit 3	Interim Assessment	9	4
15	Modeled and Guided Instruction	3	3
15	Guided Practice	3	3
15	Independent Practice	5	3
16	Modeled and Guided Instruction	3	3
16	Guided Practice	1	3
16	Guided Practice	3	3
16	Independent Practice	2	3
16	Independent Practice	3	3
16	Independent Practice	5	3
16	Independent Practice	6	3
17	Modeled and Guided Instruction	3	3
17	Guided Practice	1	3
17	Guided Practice	3	3
17	Independent Practice	1	3
17	Independent Practice	3	3
17	Independent Practice	4	3
17	Independent Practice	5	3
Unit 4	Interim Assessment	1	3
Unit 4	Interim Assessment	2	3
Unit 4	Interim Assessment	5	3
Unit 4	Interim Assessment	8	3
Unit 4	Interim Assessment	9	3
18	Modeled and Guided Instruction	3	3
18	Guided Practice	1	3
18	Guided Practice	2	3
18	Guided Practice	5	3
18	Independent Practice	1	3
18	Independent Practice	4	3
18	Independent Practice	5	3
19	Modeled and Guided Instruction	3	3
19	Guided Practice	1	3
19	Guided Practice	3	3
19	Independent Practice	3	3
19	Independent Practice	5	3
20	Modeled and Guided Instruction	3	4
20	Guided Practice	1	4
20	Guided Practice	2	4
20	Guided Practice	3	4
20	Guided Practice	5	4
20	Independent Practice	1	4
20	Independent Practice	3	4
20	Independent Practice	5	4
Unit 5	Interim Assessment	4A	3
Unit 5	Interim Assessment	4B	3
Unit 5	Interim Assessment	7	3
Unit 5	Interim Assessment	9	3
21	Modeled and Guided Instruction	3	3
21	Guided Practice	3	3
21	Independent Practice	2	3
21	Independent Practice	4	3
21	Independent Practice	5	3
22	Modeled and Guided Instruction	3	3
22	Guided Practice	1	3
22	Guided Practice	2	3
22	Guided Practice	3	3
22	Guided Practice	5	3
22	Independent Practice	2	3
22	Independent Practice	3	3
22	Independent Practice	4	3
22	Independent Practice	5	3
22	Independent Practice	6	3
Unit 6	Interim Assessment	3	3
Unit 6	Interim Assessment	5	3
Unit 6	Interim Assessment	6	3
Unit 6	Interim Assessment	7	3
Unit 6	Interim Assessment	8A	3
Unit 6	Interim Assessment	8B	3
Unit 6	Interim Assessment	10	3
Unit 6	Interim Assessment	11	3

Instructional Models that Foster Engagement

Ready® lessons follow the gradual-release model that transfers responsibility for the learning process from teacher to student. By the end of a lesson, students have the ability and confidence to independently apply the lesson's standard.

Week-long Gradual Release of Responsibility

	Teacher Role	Student Role
Introduction Day 1	Set goals and objectives and introduce lesson content	Make connections
Modeled and Guided Instruction Day 2	Model with a think aloud and encourage pairs of students to participate	Participate as the teacher models. Collaborate with partners in thinking, talking, and writing about the text.
Guided Practice Day 3	Provide support	Collaborate with partners to read and apply the standard to a new text
Independent Practice Days 4 and 5	Support as needed	Independently apply the strategies to meet the lesson's standard

Daily instruction in *Ready Reading* follows a consistent *Read, Think, Talk, Write* instructional model that fosters engagement and builds student autonomy.

The *Read, Think, Talk, Write* Model for Daily Instruction

Read

Students read selections multiple times for different purposes. The first read focuses on reading to determine what the text says. In subsequent reads, students analyze and evaluate the text for deeper meaning and to develop critical-thinking skills.

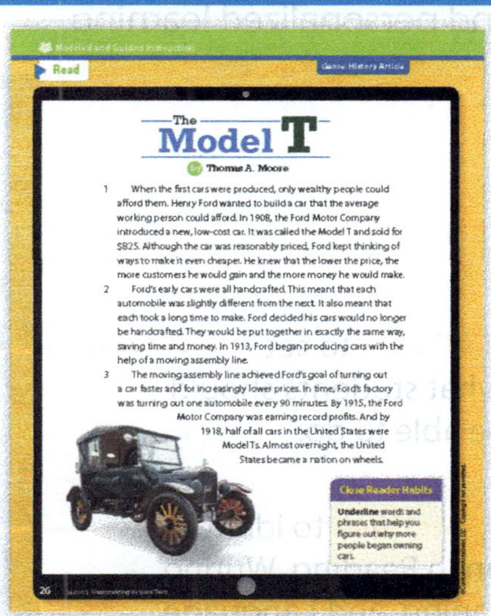
Modeled and Guided Instruction

Read

Genre: History Article

The Model T

by Thomas A. Moore

1 When the first cars were produced, only wealthy people could afford them. Henry Ford wanted to build a car that the average working person could afford. In 1908, the Ford Motor Company introduced a new, low-cost car. It was called the Model T and sold for $825. Although the car was reasonably priced, Ford kept thinking of ways to make it even cheaper. He knew that the lower the price, the more customers he would gain and the more money he would make.

2 Ford's early cars were all handcrafted. This meant that each automobile was slightly different from the next. It also meant that each took a long time to make. Ford decided his cars would no longer be handcrafted. They would be put together in exactly the same way, saving time and money. In 1913, Ford began producing cars with the help of a moving assembly line.

3 The moving assembly line achieved Ford's goal of turning out a car faster and for increasingly lower prices. In time, Ford's factory was turning out one automobile every 90 minutes. By 1915, the Ford Motor Company was earning record profits. And by 1918, half of all cars in the United States were Model Ts. Almost overnight, the United States became a nation on wheels.

Close Reader Habits

Underline words and phrases that help you figure out why more people began owning cars.

26

Think

During the Think stage of daily instruction, students unpack the text, using a graphic organizer to analyze the text's structure and evidence.

Talk

Through meaningful activities, students interact with their peers to discuss the text, clarify their thinking, and, thereby, continue to deepen their understanding of the text.

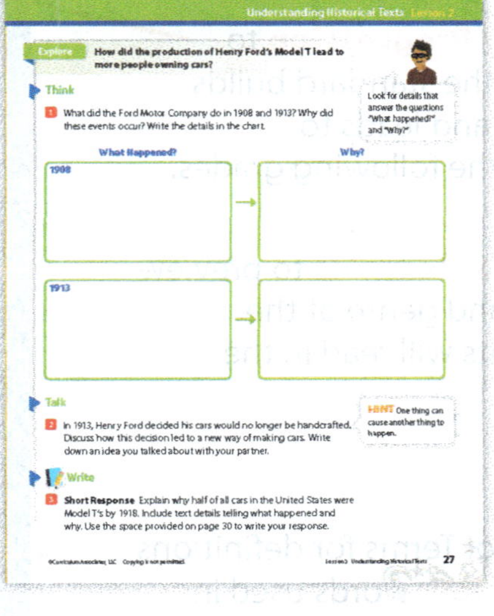
Understanding Historical Texts Lesson 2

Explore **How did the production of Henry Ford's Model T lead to more people owning cars?**

Think

1 What did the Ford Motor Company do in 1908 and 1913? Why did these events occur? Write the details in the chart.

Look for details that answer the questions "What happened?" and "Why?"

What Happened?	Why?
1908	
1913	

Talk

2 In 1913, Henry Ford decided his cars would no longer be handcrafted. Discuss how this decision led to a new way of making cars. Write down an idea you talked about with your partner.

HINT One thing can cause another thing to happen.

Write

3 **Short Response** Explain why half of all cars in the United States were Model T's by 1918. Include text details telling what happened and why. Use the space provided on page 30 to write your response.

©Curriculum Associates, LLC Copying is not permitted. Lesson 2 Understanding Historical Texts 27

Write

Each day's instruction wraps up with a writing activity. Through short- and extended-response writing prompts, students demonstrate their understanding of the text and learning target.

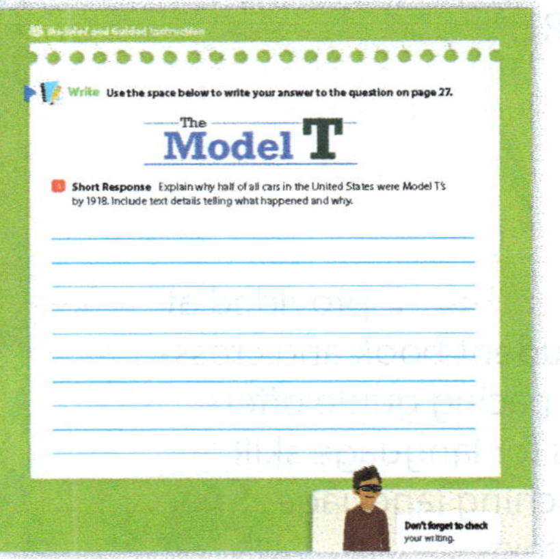
Modeled and Guided Instruction

Write Use the space below to write your answer to the question on page 27.

The Model T

3 **Short Response** Explain why half of all cars in the United States were Model T's by 1918. Include text details telling what happened and why.

Don't forget to check your writing.

Teacher Resource Book: Lesson Overview

Use the information on these pages to plan whole class instruction, small group differentiation, and personalized learning.

Use the **Standards Focus** to set expectations for what students should understand and be able to do.

Use the **Lesson Objectives** to identify goals for the lesson in Reading, Writing, Speaking and Listening, and Language.

Use the **Learning Progression** to understand how the standard builds on prior learning and leads to expectations for the following grades.

Use **Lesson Text Selections** to preview the title, author, and genre of the selections students will read in the lesson.

Use the Glossary of Terms for definitions of the **Academic Talk** words used in the lesson. The Glossary of Terms begins on page TR2.

The **Language Handbook** provided at the back of the student book and cross-referenced in this pacing guide offers additional lessons for language skill development, teaching language instruction in context.

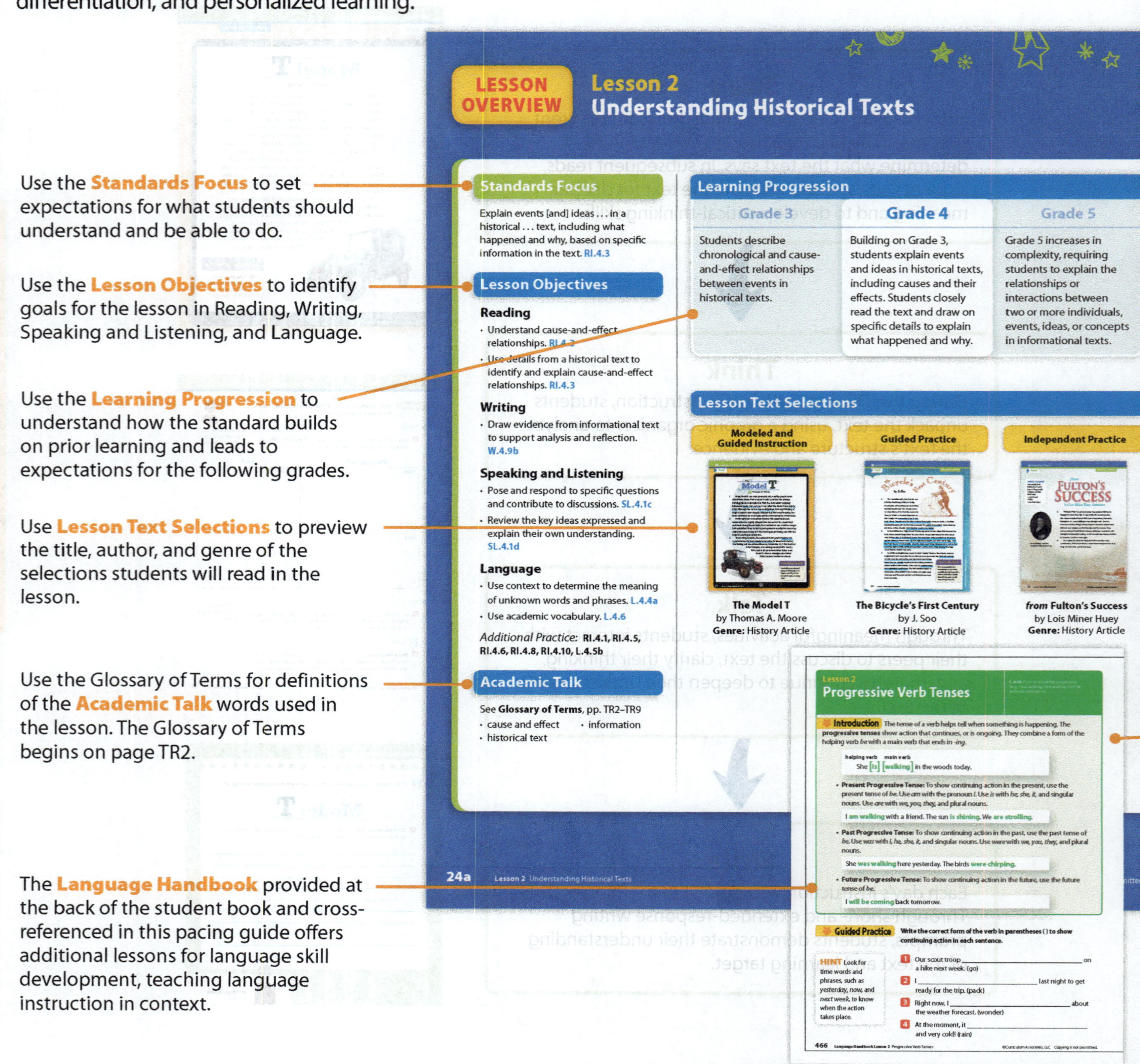

LESSON OVERVIEW

Lesson 2

Understanding Historical Texts

Standards Focus

Explain events [and] ideas . . . in a historical . . . text, including what happened and why, based on specific information in the text. RI.4.3

Lesson Objectives

Reading

- Understand cause-and-effect relationships. RI.4.3
- Use details from a historical text to identify and explain cause-and-effect relationships. RI.4.3

Writing

- Draw evidence from informational text to support analysis and reflection. W.4.9b

Speaking and Listening

- Pose and respond to specific questions and contribute to discussions. SL.4.1c
- Review the key ideas expressed and explain their own understanding. SL.4.1d

Language

- Use context to determine the meaning of unknown words and phrases. L.4.4a
- Use academic vocabulary. L.4.6

Additional Practice: RI.4.1, RI.4.5, RI.4.6, RI.4.8, RI.4.10, L.4.5b

Academic Talk

See **Glossary of Terms**, pp. TR2–TR9

- cause and effect
- information
- historical text

Learning Progression

Grade 3	Grade 4	Grade 5
Students describe chronological and cause-and-effect relationships between events in historical texts.	Building on Grade 3, students explain events and ideas in historical texts, including causes and their effects. Students closely read the text and draw on specific details to explain what happened and why.	Grade 5 increases in complexity, requiring students to explain the relationships or interactions between two or more individuals, events, ideas, or concepts in informational texts.

Lesson Text Selections

Modeled and Guided Instruction	Guided Practice	Independent Practice
The Model T by Thomas A. Moore **Genre:** History Article	**The Bicycle's First Century** by J. Soo **Genre:** History Article	*from* **Fulton's Success** by Lois Miner Huey **Genre:** History Article

24a Lesson 2 Understanding Historical Texts

Lesson 2

Progressive Verb Tenses

Introduction The tense of a verb helps tell when something is happening. The **progressive tenses** show action that continues, or is ongoing. They combine a form of the helping verb *be* with a main verb that ends in *-ing*.

helping verb main verb

She [is] [walking] in the woods today.

- **Present Progressive Tense:** To show continuing action in the present, use the present tense of *be*. Use *am* with the pronoun *I*. Use *is* with *he, she, it,* and singular nouns. Use *are* with *we, you, they,* and plural nouns.

I **am walking** with a friend. The sun **is shining**. We **are strolling**.

- **Past Progressive Tense:** To show continuing action in the past, use the past tense of *be*. Use *was* with *I, he, she, it,* and singular nouns. Use *were* with *we, you, they,* and plural nouns.

She **was walking** here yesterday. The birds **were chirping**.

- **Future Progressive Tense:** To show continuing action in the future, use the future tense of *be*.

I **will be coming** back tomorrow.

Guided Practice Write the correct form of the verb in parentheses ( ) to show continuing action in each sentence.

HINT Look for time words and phrases, such as *yesterday, now,* and *next week,* to know when the action takes place.

1. Our scout troop ______ on a hike next week. (go)
2. I ______ last night to get ready for the trip. (pack)
3. Right now, I ______ about the weather forecast. (wonder)
4. At the moment, it ______ and very cold! (rain)

466 Language Handbook Lesson 2 Progressive Verb Tenses

Teacher Resource Book

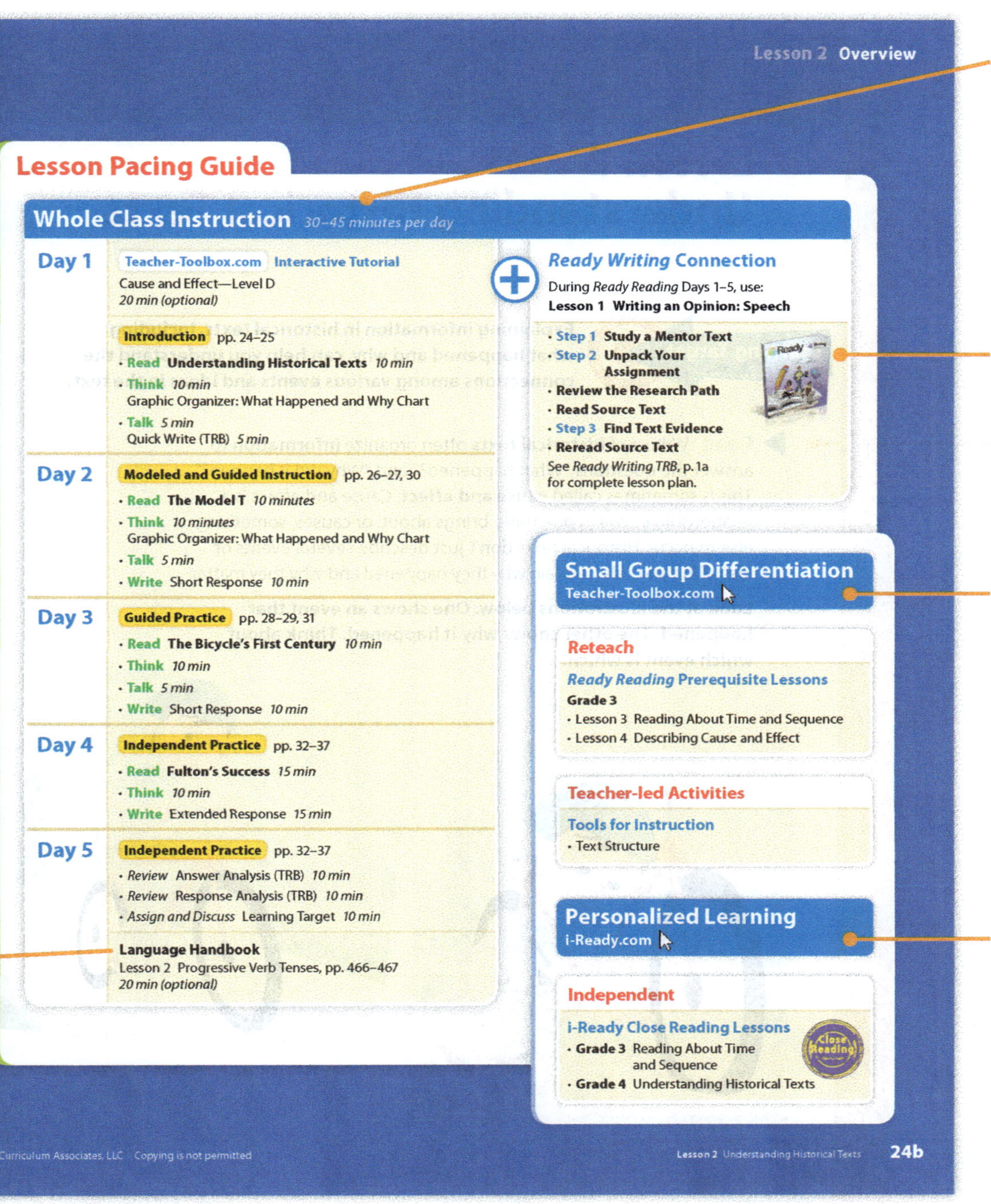
Lesson 2 Overview

Lesson Pacing Guide

Whole Class Instruction *30–45 minutes per day*

Day 1
Teacher-Toolbox.com Interactive Tutorial
Cause and Effect—Level D
20 min (optional)

Introduction pp. 24–25
- Read **Understanding Historical Texts** *10 min*
- Think *10 min*
  Graphic Organizer: What Happened and Why Chart
- Talk *5 min*
  Quick Write (TRB) *5 min*

Day 2
Modeled and Guided Instruction pp. 26–27, 30
- Read **The Model T** *10 minutes*
- Think *10 minutes*
  Graphic Organizer: What Happened and Why Chart
- Talk *5 min*
- Write Short Response *10 min*

Day 3
Guided Practice pp. 28–29, 31
- Read **The Bicycle's First Century** *10 min*
- Think *10 min*
- Talk *5 min*
- Write Short Response *10 min*

Day 4
Independent Practice pp. 32–37
- Read **Fulton's Success** *15 min*
- Think *10 min*
- Write Extended Response *15 min*

Day 5
Independent Practice pp. 32–37
- *Review* Answer Analysis (TRB) *10 min*
- *Review* Response Analysis (TRB) *10 min*
- *Assign and Discuss* Learning Target *10 min*

Language Handbook
Lesson 2 Progressive Verb Tenses, pp. 466–467
20 min (optional)

***Ready Writing* Connection**
During *Ready Reading* Days 1–5, use:
Lesson 1 Writing an Opinion: Speech
- Step 1 **Study a Mentor Text**
- Step 2 **Unpack Your Assignment**
- **Review the Research Path**
- **Read Source Text**
- Step 3 **Find Text Evidence**
- **Reread Source Text**

See *Ready Writing TRB*, p. 1a for complete lesson plan.

Small Group Differentiation
Teacher-Toolbox.com

Reteach
Ready Reading **Prerequisite Lessons**
Grade 3
- Lesson 3 Reading About Time and Sequence
- Lesson 4 Describing Cause and Effect

Teacher-led Activities
Tools for Instruction
- Text Structure

Personalized Learning
i-Ready.com

Independent
i-Ready Close Reading Lessons
- **Grade 3** Reading About Time and Sequence
- **Grade 4** Understanding Historical Texts

©Curriculum Associates, LLC Copying is not permitted

Lesson 2 Understanding Historical Texts 24b

Plan teacher-led **whole class instruction**, following *Ready's* gradual-release model. An optional Interactive Tutorial in the Teacher Toolbox offers an additional way to launch the lesson. Teacher-led Language Handbook lessons can be used to reinforce and extend specific language skills.

When appropriate, related ***Ready Writing*** lessons are highlighted at point of use. These writing lessons are designed to integrate with *Ready's* themes and skills.

Plan **small group differentiation**, using *Ready Instruction* lessons from earlier grades to review prerequisite concepts and teacher-led Tools for Instruction activities for small groups.

Plan students' **personalized learning**, using *i-Ready* Close Reading Lessons to engage with additional challenging and high-quality texts.

The *i-Ready* Close Reading Lessons, *Ready* Writing, and the Online Teacher Toolbox are available as an optional purchase.

Student Book: Introduction

Students explore the goals for the lesson, connect what they will learn to their own knowledge and experiences, and learn key terms and concepts.

Read *(whole class)*

Teacher's Role Begin by introducing the **Learning Target**, which sets a goal for the lesson. Read the introductory text, and discuss what students will learn in the lesson. Use the **Academic Talk Routine** (pp. A48–A49) to introduce words and phrases students will need to know to talk about the text and the standard. Discuss the example with students, and ensure that they understand its connection to the Learning Target.

Students' Role Develop an understanding of the lesson concept. Consider how the skill relates to their own lives or builds on prior learning.

Introduction

RI.4.3 Explain events [and] ideas . . . in a historical . . . text, including what happened and why, based on specific information in the text.

Lesson 2
Understanding Historical Texts

Learning Target

Explaining information in historical texts, including what happened and why, can help you understand the connections among various events and ideas in the text.

Read Writers of **historical texts** often organize **information** to answer the questions "What happened?" and "Why did it happen?" This is sometimes called **cause and effect**. Cause and effect is a relationship in which one thing brings about, or causes, something else to occur. Historical texts don't just describe several events or ideas. The texts also explain why they happened and why they matter.

Look at the illustrations below. One shows an event that happened. The other shows why it happened. Think about which event is which.

24 **Lesson 2** Understanding Historical Texts

Student Instruction Book

Theme: Transportation History Lesson 2

Think Consider what you've learned about causes and effects and why writers use them to organize their writing. Remember, understanding what happened and why helps you understand what happens around you every day.

In the chart below, describe what happened in the first illustration. Then explain why the event happened.

What Happened?	→	Why?

Talk Share your chart with a partner.

- Based on the events in the illustrations, what do you think the boy will do next?
- Explain why the boy will do that next.

Academic Talk

Use these words and phrases to talk about the text.

- **cause and effect**
- **information**
- **historical text**

Lesson 2 Understanding Historical Texts 25

Think *(whole class/partner)*

Teacher's Role Introduce the **graphic organizer** to students as a tool for collecting text evidence and organizing their thinking. Direct students to complete the diagram or chart. As partners work, circulate to provide assistance.

Students' Role Work in pairs on the graphic organizer to organize their thoughts and demonstrate learning.

Talk *(partner)*

Students' Role Talk with a partner to clarify thinking about what they have learned.

Teacher's Role Use the **Talk Routine** (pp. A52–A53) to promote good discussion habits. Circulate during partner discussions to provide support and clarify misunderstandings. Have students respond to the **Quick Write** prompt in the Teacher Resource Book and independently apply the new strategy or concept. Wrap up by inviting students to use the Academic Talk words to share what they have learned.

Student Book: Modeled and Guided Instruction

Students begin to unpack the standard and apply it to a text with teacher modeling and guidance.

Read *(independent and partner)*

Teacher's Role

First read: Introduce the passage and ask students to practice effective prereading habits, such as reflecting on the title and looking at the pictures and illustrations. Then ask students to read the passage silently for understanding.

Second read: Read the **Explore** question, which sets a purpose for rereading. Model how to reread for information to answer the question, using the **Think Aloud** in the Teacher Resource Book and the **Close Reader Habits** on the Student Book page to identify and mark specific details.

Students' Role Read independently first for understanding. For the second reading, begin by reading aloud the Close Reader Habits. Then, after the teacher models how to respond to the prompt, mark up the text, rereading and analyzing part of the text with a partner.

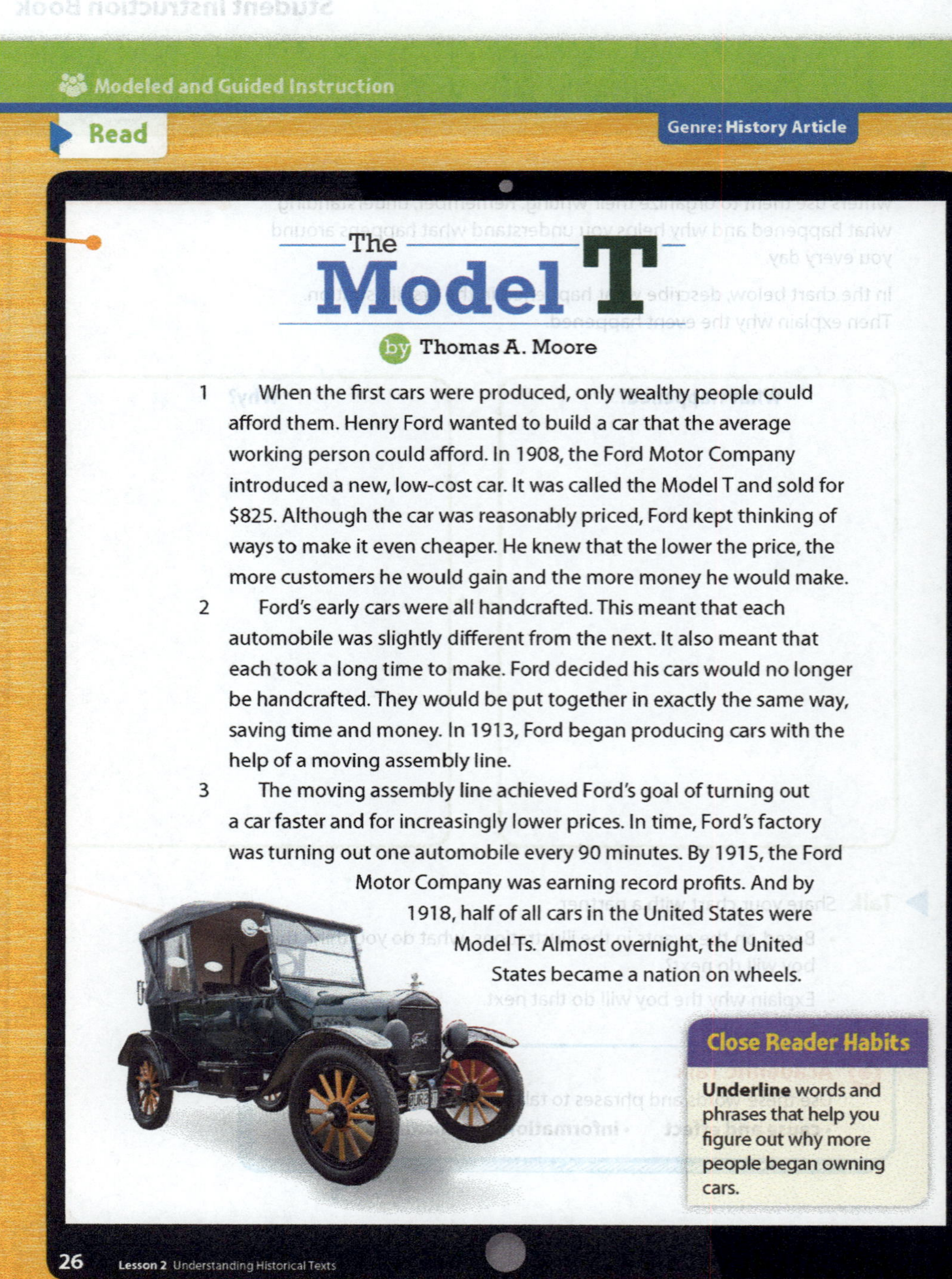

Modeled and Guided Instruction

Read

Genre: History Article

The Model T

by Thomas A. Moore

1 When the first cars were produced, only wealthy people could afford them. Henry Ford wanted to build a car that the average working person could afford. In 1908, the Ford Motor Company introduced a new, low-cost car. It was called the Model T and sold for $825. Although the car was reasonably priced, Ford kept thinking of ways to make it even cheaper. He knew that the lower the price, the more customers he would gain and the more money he would make.

2 Ford's early cars were all handcrafted. This meant that each automobile was slightly different from the next. It also meant that each took a long time to make. Ford decided his cars would no longer be handcrafted. They would be put together in exactly the same way, saving time and money. In 1913, Ford began producing cars with the help of a moving assembly line.

3 The moving assembly line achieved Ford's goal of turning out a car faster and for increasingly lower prices. In time, Ford's factory was turning out one automobile every 90 minutes. By 1915, the Ford Motor Company was earning record profits. And by 1918, half of all cars in the United States were Model Ts. Almost overnight, the United States became a nation on wheels.

Close Reader Habits

Underline words and phrases that help you figure out why more people began owning cars.

26 Lesson 2 Understanding Historical Texts

Student Instruction Book

Understanding Historical Texts Lesson 2

Explore **How did the production of Henry Ford's Model T lead to more people owning cars?**

Look for details that answer the questions "What happened?" and "Why?"

Think

1 What did the Ford Motor Company do in 1908 and 1913? Why did these events occur? Write the details in the chart.

What Happened?		Why?
1908	→	
1913	→	

Talk

2 In 1913, Henry Ford decided his cars would no longer be handcrafted. Discuss how this decision led to a new way of making cars. Write down an idea you talked about with your partner.

HINT One thing can cause another thing to happen.

Write

3 **Short Response** Explain why half of all cars in the United States were Model T's by 1918. Include text details telling what happened and why. Use the space provided on page 30 to write your response.

Think *(whole class and partner)*

Teacher's Role Model how to use the graphic organizer to structure thinking, using evidence from the text. Then ask students to work with partners to complete it.

Students' Role Complete the graphic organizer with a partner to organize the evidence they identified in the text. This prepares them to engage in Talk and Write.

Talk *(partner)*

Students' Role Share their thinking with partners and "rehearse" their ideas before putting them into writing.

Teacher's Role Remind students of the **Talk Routine** (pp. A52–A53). Circulate, providing support as needed.

Write *(independent)*

Students' Role Use the text evidence they've already identified to write a short response.

Teacher's Role Make sure students understand the prompt and know where to write their response. Show students how the **Response-Writing Routine** (pp. A54–A55) can help them craft a short response. Use **Review Responses** in the Teacher Resource Book to evaluate and discuss completed responses. Wrap up by asking students to recall the learning target and share how the new strategy or concept helped them better understand the article.

Student Book: Guided Practice

Students work collaboratively, with guidance from the teacher, to practice the standard.

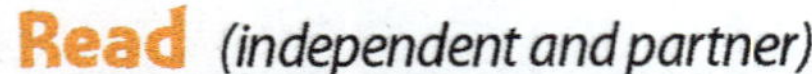

Read *(independent and partner)*

Teacher's Role Gradually decrease the amount of support you provide. Have students independently read the passage and then work with partners to reread it and complete the Think and Talk activities. Encourage them to use the **Close Reader Habits** to mark up the text.

Students' Role Read independently to understand the passage, using the **Word Learning Routine** (pp. A50–A51) to determine the meanings of unfamiliar words. Then reread with a partner. Use the question embedded in the **Close Reader Habits** to establish a purpose for rereading. Last, find and mark up evidence to meet that purpose.

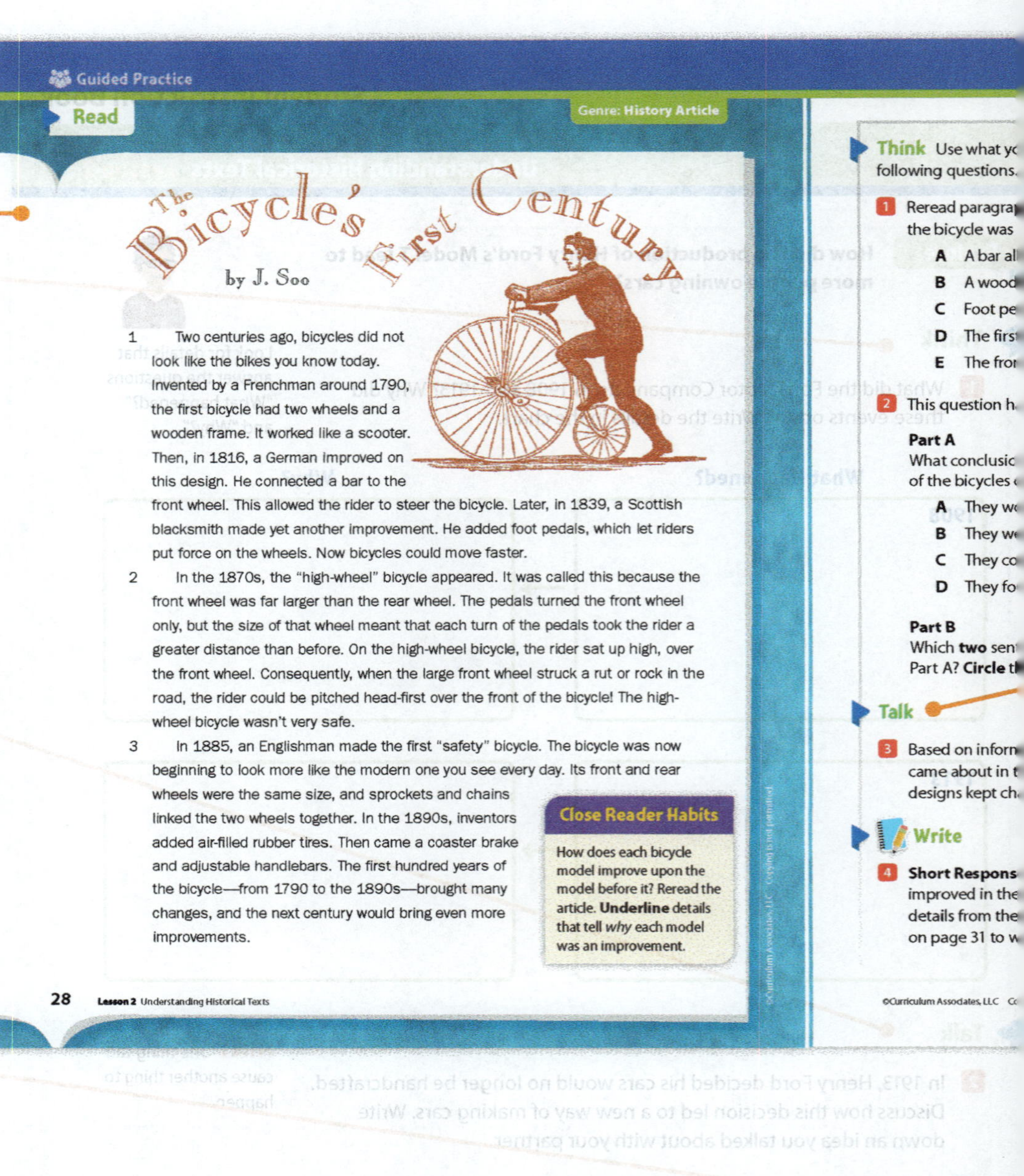

Guided Practice

Read

Genre: History Article

The Bicycle's First Century

by J. Soo

1 Two centuries ago, bicycles did not look like the bikes you know today. Invented by a Frenchman around 1790, the first bicycle had two wheels and a wooden frame. It worked like a scooter. Then, in 1816, a German improved on this design. He connected a bar to the front wheel. This allowed the rider to steer the bicycle. Later, in 1839, a Scottish blacksmith made yet another improvement. He added foot pedals, which let riders put force on the wheels. Now bicycles could move faster.

2 In the 1870s, the "high-wheel" bicycle appeared. It was called this because the front wheel was far larger than the rear wheel. The pedals turned the front wheel only, but the size of that wheel meant that each turn of the pedals took the rider a greater distance than before. On the high-wheel bicycle, the rider sat up high, over the front wheel. Consequently, when the large front wheel struck a rut or rock in the road, the rider could be pitched head-first over the front of the bicycle! The high-wheel bicycle wasn't very safe.

3 In 1885, an Englishman made the first "safety" bicycle. The bicycle was now beginning to look more like the modern one you see every day. Its front and rear wheels were the same size, and sprockets and chains linked the two wheels together. In the 1890s, inventors added air-filled rubber tires. Then came a coaster brake and adjustable handlebars. The first hundred years of the bicycle—from 1790 to the 1890s—brought many changes, and the next century would bring even more improvements.

Close Reader Habits

How does each bicycle model improve upon the model before it? Reread the article. **Underline** details that tell *why* each model was an improvement.

28 Lesson 2 Understanding Historical Texts

Think Use what yo following questions.

1 Reread paragra the bicycle was

A A bar al
B A wood
C Foot pe
D The firs
E The fron

2 This question h

Part A
What conclusio of the bicycles

A They w
B They w
C They co
D They fo

Part B
Which **two** sen Part A? **Circle** t

Talk

3 Based on inform came about in t designs kept ch

Write

4 **Short Respons** improved in the details from the on page 31 to w

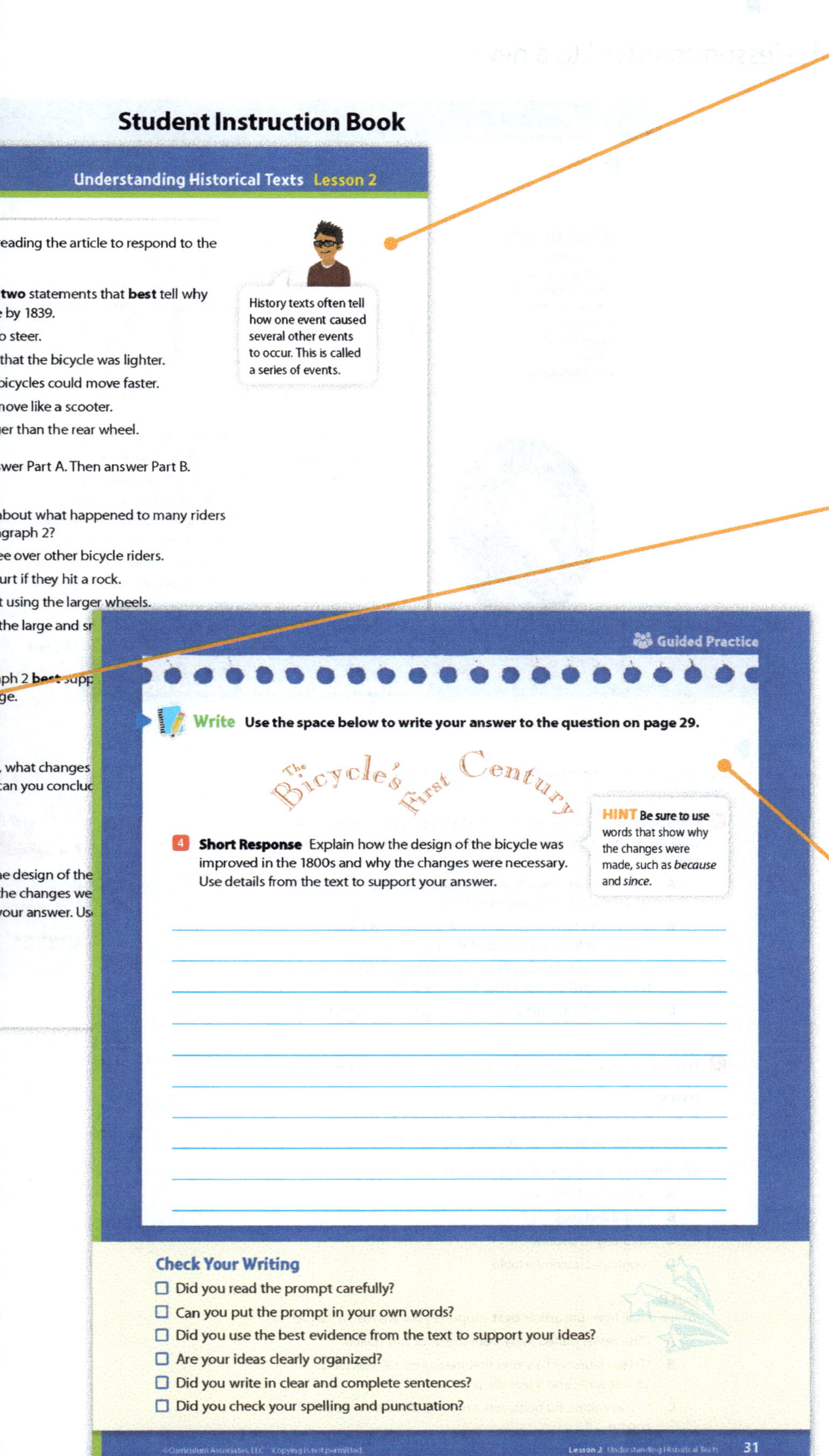
Student Instruction Book

Understanding Historical Texts Lesson 2

…reading the article to respond to the…

…**two** statements that **best** tell why …e by 1839.

…o steer.

…that the bicycle was lighter.

…bicycles could move faster.

…nove like a scooter.

…ger than the rear wheel.

…swer Part A. Then answer Part B.

…about what happened to many riders …agraph 2?

…ee over other bicycle riders.

…urt if they hit a rock.

…t using the larger wheels.

…the large and sm…

…aph 2 **best** supp… …ge.

…, what changes …can you conclu…

…he design of the …the changes we… …your answer. Us…

History texts often tell how one event caused several other events to occur. This is called a series of events.

Guided Practice

Write Use the space below to write your answer to the question on page 29.

The Bicycle's First Century

4 **Short Response** Explain how the design of the bicycle was improved in the 1800s and why the changes were necessary. Use details from the text to support your answer.

HINT Be sure to use words that show why the changes were made, such as *because* and *since*.

Check Your Writing

- ☐ Did you read the prompt carefully?
- ☐ Can you put the prompt in your own words?
- ☐ Did you use the best evidence from the text to support your ideas?
- ☐ Are your ideas clearly organized?
- ☐ Did you write in clear and complete sentences?
- ☐ Did you check your spelling and punctuation?

©Curriculum Associates, LLC Copying is not permitted. Lesson 2: Understanding Historical Texts 31

Think *(whole class and partner)*

Teacher's Role Assign partners to complete the practice items together. When they have finished, use the **Answer Analysis** in the Teacher Resource Book to discuss correct and incorrect responses and the reasons for them.

Students' Role Work together to complete the items, referring back to the passage for specific evidence. The **Reading Buddy tip** provides additional information about the standard or the genre.

Talk *(partner)*

Students' Role Engage in discussion with a partner to clarify their ideas about the text and gain new understandings.

Teacher's Role Circulate during student discussions to provide support and clarify misunderstandings. Use the **Monitor Understanding** if/then strategy in the Teacher Resource Book to identify and address challenges students typically face.

Write *(independent)*

Students' Role Respond to the prompt, using the evidence they identified in rereading and discussing the text and completing the practice items. The **Hint** gives guidance without giving away the answer. The **Response-Writing Routine** (pp. A54–A55) offers a step-by-step strategy for crafting a response. Use Check Your Writing to self-evaluate.

Teacher's Role Use **Review Responses** and **Sample Responses** in the Teacher Resource Book to help students evaluate their completed responses. Wrap up by asking students to recall the Learning Target and explain how the new strategy or concept helps them understand the passage.

Student Book: Independent Practice

Students take ownership of their learning and apply the lesson standard to a new and longer text.

Read *(independent)*

Teacher's Role Introduce the passage and the task, and make sure students understand what they are to do. Remind them to apply the new skills and strategies they have learned. To support comprehension and increase access for English Language Learners, encourage students to use text and graphic features, such as photos and maps. For students who may have difficulty reading the passage independently, use the **Monitor Understanding** suggestions in the Teacher Resource Book.

Students' Role Demonstrate independently what they have learned in the lesson. As they read, they use the **Word Learning Routine** (pp. A50–A51) to determine the meanings of the **Words to Know**. Check definitions by using the Glossary in the back of the Student Book.

Think *(independent)*

Students' Role Apply the lesson standard as they complete assessment items similar to those they will encounter on standardized tests, including multi-part questions, questions with multiple correct answers, constructed responses, and written responses.

Teacher's Role Use **Answer Analysis** in the Teacher Resource Book to discuss student's correct and incorrect responses and provide constructive feedback.

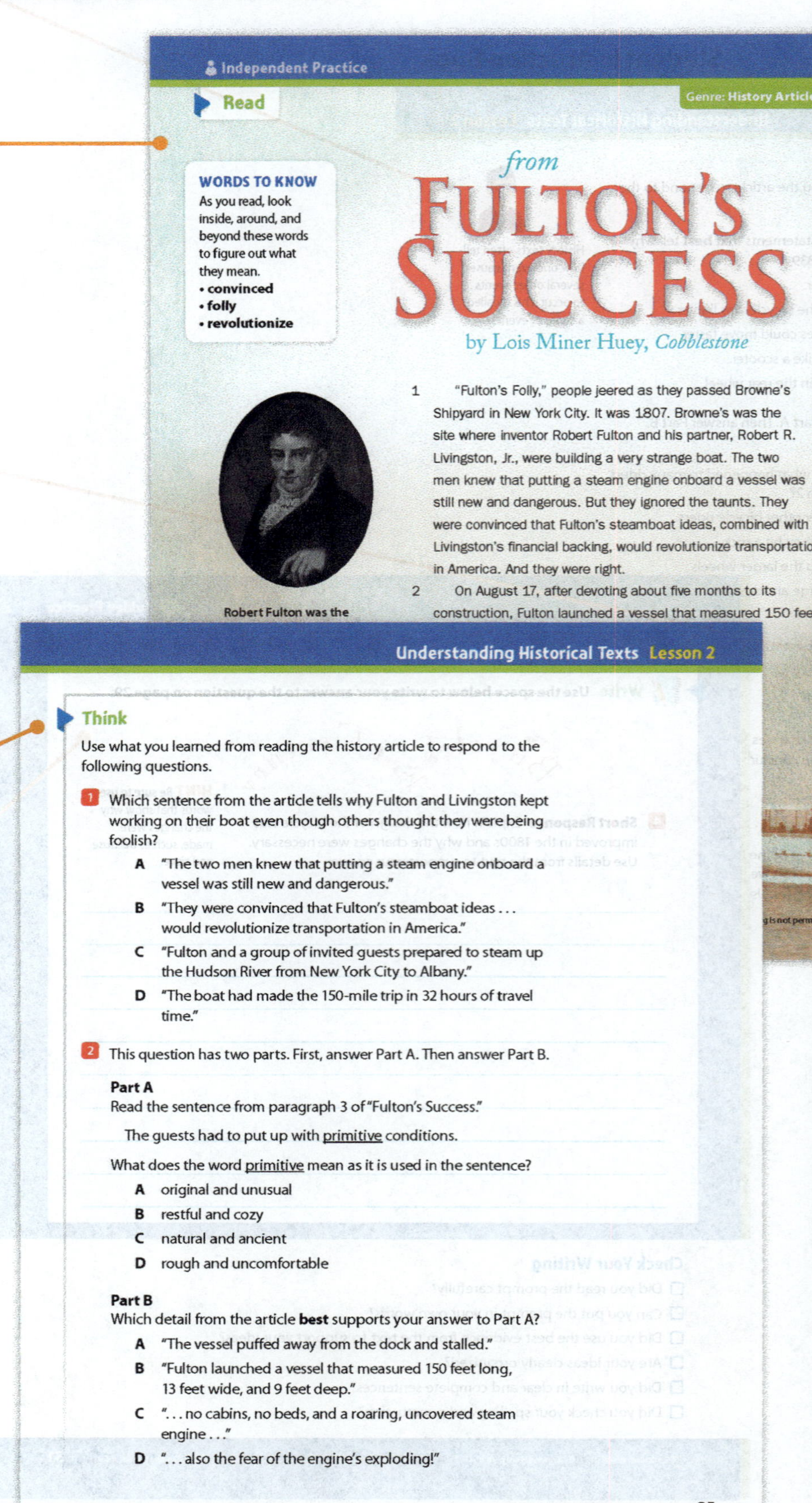

Independent Practice

Read

Genre: History Article

WORDS TO KNOW
As you read, look inside, around, and beyond these words to figure out what they mean.
• convinced
• folly
• revolutionize

from
FULTON'S SUCCESS
by Lois Miner Huey, *Cobblestone*

1 "Fulton's Folly," people jeered as they passed Browne's Shipyard in New York City. It was 1807. Browne's was the site where inventor Robert Fulton and his partner, Robert R. Livingston, Jr., were building a very strange boat. The two men knew that putting a steam engine onboard a vessel was still new and dangerous. But they ignored the taunts. They were convinced that Fulton's steamboat ideas, combined with Livingston's financial backing, would revolutionize transportation in America. And they were right.

2 On August 17, after devoting about five months to its construction, Fulton launched a vessel that measured 150 feet

Robert Fulton was the

Understanding Historical Texts Lesson 2

Think

Use what you learned from reading the history article to respond to the following questions.

1 Which sentence from the article tells why Fulton and Livingston kept working on their boat even though others thought they were being foolish?

A "The two men knew that putting a steam engine onboard a vessel was still new and dangerous."

B "They were convinced that Fulton's steamboat ideas . . . would revolutionize transportation in America."

C "Fulton and a group of invited guests prepared to steam up the Hudson River from New York City to Albany."

D "The boat had made the 150-mile trip in 32 hours of travel time."

2 This question has two parts. First, answer Part A. Then answer Part B.

Part A
Read the sentence from paragraph 3 of "Fulton's Success."

The guests had to put up with primitive conditions.

What does the word primitive mean as it is used in the sentence?

A original and unusual
B restful and cozy
C natural and ancient
D rough and uncomfortable

Part B
Which detail from the article **best** supports your answer to Part A?

A "The vessel puffed away from the dock and stalled."
B "Fulton launched a vessel that measured 150 feet long, 13 feet wide, and 9 feet deep."
C ". . . no cabins, no beds, and a roaring, uncovered steam engine . . ."
D ". . . also the fear of the engine's exploding!"

©Curriculum Associates, LLC Copying is not permitted. Lesson 2 Understanding Historical Texts 35

Student Instruction Book

Understanding Historical Texts Lesson 2

3 Fulton and a group of invited guests prepared to steam up the Hudson River from New York City to Albany. Albany is the state capital. The guests had to put up with primitive conditions. There were no cabins, no beds, and a roaring, uncovered steam engine mounted in the center of the boat. There was also the fear of the engine's exploding!

4 They cast off at 1 P.M. The vessel puffed away from the dock and stalled. The passengers' whispering turned into loud mumbles, which eventually gave way to shouts of dismay. Sensing their fear, Fulton promised to return to the dock if he could not fix the problem.

5 After a short time, there was a huge blast of smoke. Once again, the boat churned upriver. It was described as looking like a giant teakettle. The vessel's engine let off steam and rained down sparks that sizzled in the water. The noise was deafening, but the boat was moving. The passengers cheered. The boat chugged upstream against the tide at a fast four to five miles per hour. It easily passed sailing ships and fishing craft.

Fulton's route up the Hudson River from New York City to Albany

Independent Practice

3 This question has two parts. First, answer Part A. Then answer Part B.

Part A
Which statement **best** explains why some people who saw Fulton's boat steaming up the Hudson River were terrified?

- **A** They were excited about Fulton's strange new invention.
- **B** The new steamboat looked and sounded dangerous.
- **C** The people were upset that they were not allowed to ride on the steamboat.
- **D** The steamboat was oddly shaped and easily passed the other boats on the river.

Part B
Underline **three** sentences from paragraph 5 that **best** support your answer in Part A.

After a short time, there was a huge blast of smoke. Once again, the boat churned upriver. It was described as looking like a giant teakettle. The vessel's engine let off steam and rained down sparks that sizzled in the water. The noise was deafening, but the boat was moving. The passengers cheered. The boat chugged upstream against the tide at a fast four to five miles per hour. It easily passed sailing ships and fishing craft.

Write

What conclusion can be drawn about why the steamboat was known as "Fulton's Folly" and how it became "Fulton's Success"? Reread the text. **Underline** details that show the reasons the steamboat was a success.

4 **Plan Your Response** First, identify why the steamboat was originally called "Fulton's Folly." Then identify what turned it into a success. Use a chart to help organize your thoughts by explaining "What happened?" and "Why?"

5 **Write an Extended Response** Use evidence from the text and the information in your chart to describe why the steamboat was called "Fulton's Folly" and how it eventually became "Fulton's Success."

36 Lesson 2 Understanding Historical Texts ©Curriculum Associates, LLC Copyin

Write *(independent)*

Students' Role Complete either a short or extended response. For extended response, students use the support provided to plan their writing. They will apply the skills developed throughout the lesson, including using a graphic organizer as a thinking and planning tool. Student responses should also draw on their new understanding of the Learning Target and apply the Academic Talk terms. The **Response-Writing Routine** (pp. A54–A55) offers step-by-step support in crafting a written response.

Teacher's Role Use the **2-Point Writing Rubric** on p. TR10 of the Teacher Resource Book to review the criteria students will use to evaluate their work. When students are finished, have them share their responses with a partner or in small groups.

Learning Target

In this lesson, you learned different ways that historical texts may answer the questions "What happened?" and "Why?" Now explain how this understanding about causes and effects can help you as you read other historical texts.

 Lesson 2 Understanding Historical Texts 37

Meeting New Expectations & Best Practices

What Ready® Reading Instruction Looks Like

How to Implement Ready® Reading

Teacher Resource Book

Point-of-use professional development and step-by-step instruction support best-practice teaching.

Get Started explains what students will be doing in this particular step of the lesson.

The Teacher Resource Book lesson follows the **Read, Think, Talk, Write** structure of the Student Book lesson. Side-column notes provide instructional support for each step.

Call outs highlight when to use the teaching strategies below the facsimiles of the Student Book pages.

Tips offer point-of-use professional development.

Lesson 2 Understanding Historical Texts

Modeled and Guided Instruction

Get Started

Today you will read an article about an important development in transportation history. First, you'll read to understand what the author says. Then you'll read to analyze details about key events that happened and why.

Read

- Read aloud the title of the article and call attention to the photo. Guide students to an understanding that the article is about an old-fashioned car called the Model T.
- Have students read the article independently. Tell them to place a check mark above any confusing words and phrases as they read. Remind students to look inside, around, and beyond each unknown word or phrase to help them figure out its meaning.
- When students have finished reading, clarify the meanings of words and phrases they still find confusing. Then use the questions below to check understanding. Encourage students to identify details in the text that support their answers.

  What was the Model T? *(a new, low-cost car)*

  Who do you think Henry Ford was? *(a man who built cars)*

  What is the article mostly about? *(Henry Ford's development of the Model T)*

English Language Learners

Word Learning Strategy

Explore

- Read aloud the Explore question at the top of p. 27 to set the purpose for the second read. Tell students they will need to take a closer look at cause-and-effect relationships to answer this question.
- Have students read aloud the Close Reader Habit on the lower right of p. 26.

TIP Tell students that signal words such as *because* and *consequently* can help them connect causes and effects. However, more often they will have to make an inference, or educated guess, to link what happened and why.

Modeled and Guided Instruction

Read — Genre: History Article

The Model T

by Thomas A. Moore

1 When the first cars were produced, only wealthy people could afford them. Henry Ford wanted to build a car that the average working person could afford. In 1908, the Ford Motor Company introduced a new, low-cost car. It was called the Model T and sold for $825. Although the car was reasonably priced, Ford kept thinking of ways to make it even cheaper. He knew that the lower the price, the more customers he would gain and the more money he would make.

2 Ford's early cars were all handcrafted. This meant that each automobile was slightly different from the next. It also meant that each took a long time to make. Ford decided his cars would no longer be handcrafted. They would be put together in exactly the same way, saving time and money. In 1913, Ford began producing cars with the help of a moving assembly line.

3 The moving assembly line achieved Ford's goal of turning out a car faster and for increasingly lower prices. In time, Ford's factory was turning out one automobile every 90 minutes. By 1915, the Ford Motor Company was earning record profits. And by 1918, half of all cars in the United States were Model Ts. Almost overnight, the United States became a nation on wheels.

Close Reader Habits

Underline words and phrases that help you figure out why more people began owning cars.

26

English Language Learners

Build Meaning

Build Background Help students to understand what an assembly line is.

- Show students images or a video of a product being passed from one worker to another in a factory until the product is finished. Have students say as much as they can about what they see.
- Use total physical response to reinforce understanding. Have two teams complete a simple task such as moving books from one table to another. Have the first team move the books one at a time. Then have the second team move the books using an "assembly line" to pass the books from one to another. Have students say why the second way was faster.

Word Learning Strategy

Use Context Clues

- Reread paragraph 1. Direct students' attention to the phrase *reasonably priced* in the next-to-last sentence.

  What do you think the phrase *reasonably priced* means?

  What word is a clue that helps you figure out the meaning?
- Guide students to find the synonym *cheaper*. Explain that *cheaper* helps them understand that *reasonably priced* means "not very expensive."
- Remind students that when they come to an unknown word or phrase, they can look at the surrounding words for a clue to the meaning. One type of context clue is a synonym, or word with a similar meaning. **L.4.4a**

Teacher Resource Book

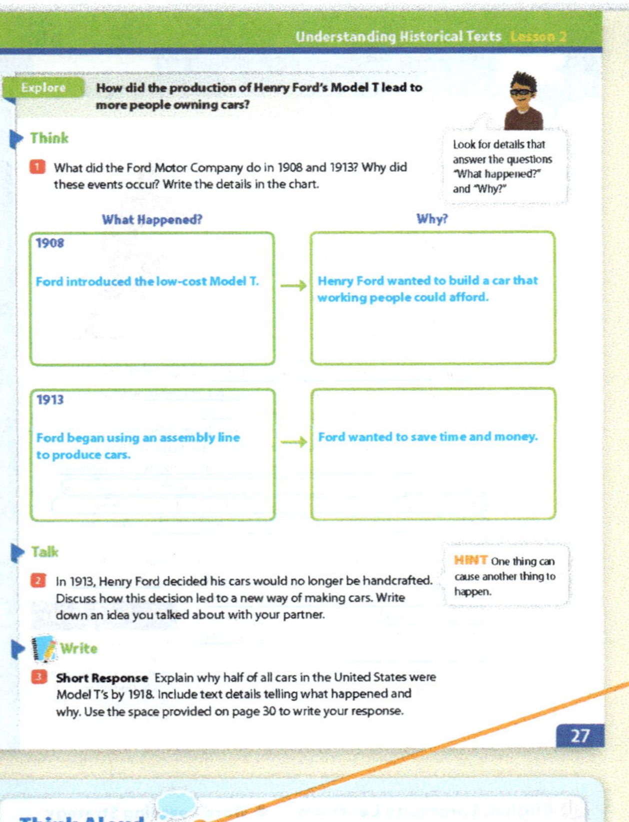

Understanding Historical Texts Lesson 2

Explore How did the production of Henry Ford's Model T lead to more people owning cars?

Think

1 What did the Ford Motor Company do in 1908 and 1913? Why did these events occur? Write the details in the chart.

Look for details that answer the questions "What happened?" and "Why?"

What Happened?	Why?
1908 Ford introduced the low-cost Model T.	Henry Ford wanted to build a car that working people could afford.
1913 Ford began using an assembly line to produce cars.	Ford wanted to save time and money.

Talk

2 In 1913, Henry Ford decided his cars would no longer be handcrafted. Discuss how this decision led to a new way of making cars. Write down an idea you talked about with your partner.

HINT One thing can cause another thing to happen.

Write

3 **Short Response** Explain why half of all cars in the United States were Model T's by 1918. Include text details telling what happened and why. Use the space provided on page 30 to write your response.

27

Think Aloud

- The first event happened in 1908. I find that date in the third sentence. I read that in 1908, the Ford Motor Company introduced a new, low-cost car called the Model T. I'll write that event in the What Happened? box.
- I need to go back to the text to figure out why the Ford Motor Company introduced the low-cost car. I know that a cause is often described before its effect. So, I'll look at the first two sentences for the cause.
- The second sentence answers the question why: "Henry Ford wanted to build a car that the average working person could afford." Using the Close Reader Habit, I'll underline that detail in the text and then add it to the Why? box.
- When I put the two details together, I understand their relationship. *The Ford Motor Company introduced the low-cost Model T because Henry Ford wanted to build a car that the average working person could afford.*

Lesson 2

Think

- Read aloud the Think section. Explain to students that you will reread the first paragraph of the article. Then you will model how to find text evidence to fill in the chart. Use the **Think Aloud** below to guide your modeling.
- Revisit the Explore question. Guide students to determine that they need to look for more details.
- Encourage students to work with a partner to continue rereading the passage and to complete the chart. Remind students that the Buddy Tip will help them find the information they need.
- Ask volunteers to share their completed charts.
- Guide students to see that one event led to the other. First, Ford produced the affordable Model T so average people could own cars. That led to Ford introducing the assembly line to produce more cars quickly and cheaply.

Talk

- Read aloud the Talk prompt.
- Have partners respond to the prompt. Use the Talk Routine on pp. A52–A53.
- Circulate to check that students are discussing and taking notes about what happened *because* Henry Ford decided to no longer make handcrafted cars.

Write

- Ask a volunteer to read aloud the Write prompt.
- Invite a few students to tell what the prompt is asking them to do.
- Make sure students understand that they need to explain the reasons why car owners were mostly buying Model Ts by 1918. Point out that details in their charts will support their writing.
- Have students turn to p. 30 to write their responses.
- Use Review Responses on p. 30 to assess students' writing.

Wrap Up

- Ask students to recall the Learning Target. Have them explain how knowing what happened and why it happened helped them better understand this history article.

In Modeled and Guided Instruction, a **Think Aloud** supports the teacher in explicitly modeling how to reread the text and apply the Close Reader Habits.

Every step of the lesson concludes with a **Wrap Up** that reminds students of the Learning Target and encourages them to reflect on what they have learned so far.

Teacher Resource Book

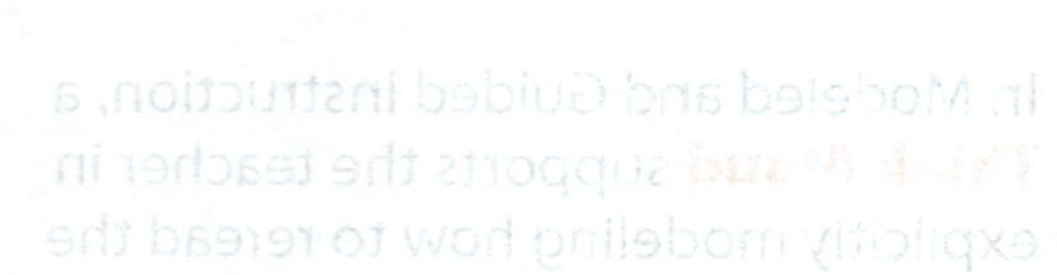

Lesson 2 Understanding Historical Texts

Guided Practice

Get Started

Today you will read another article related to transportation history. First, you will read to understand what the article is about. Then you will reread with a partner to analyze cause-and-effect relationships.

Read

- Read aloud the title of the passage. Ask if anyone knows what the word *century* means. Establish that a century is a period of 100 years.
- Have students predict what the article will be about based on the title and the illustration.
- **Read to Understand** Have students read the article independently. Tell students to place a check mark above any confusing words or phrases as they read. Remind students to look inside, around, and beyond each unknown word or phrase to help them figure out its meaning. Use the Word Learning Routine on pp. A50–A51.
- When students have finished reading, clarify the meanings of words and phrases they still find confusing. Then use the questions below to check understanding. Encourage students to identify details in the text that support their answers.

  What parts did the first bicycle have? *(two wheels and a wooden frame)*

  What did the high-wheel bicycle look like? *(It had a very big front wheel with a seat over it.)*

  How was the safety bicycle like a modern bicycle? *(The two wheels were the same size, and sprockets and chains linked them together.)*

  What is the article mostly about? *(It is about the invention and development of the bicycle.)*

English Language Learners

Word Learning Strategy

- **Read to Analyze** Read aloud the Close Reader Habit on the lower right of p. 28 to set the purpose for the second read. Then have students reread the article with a partner and discuss any questions they might have.

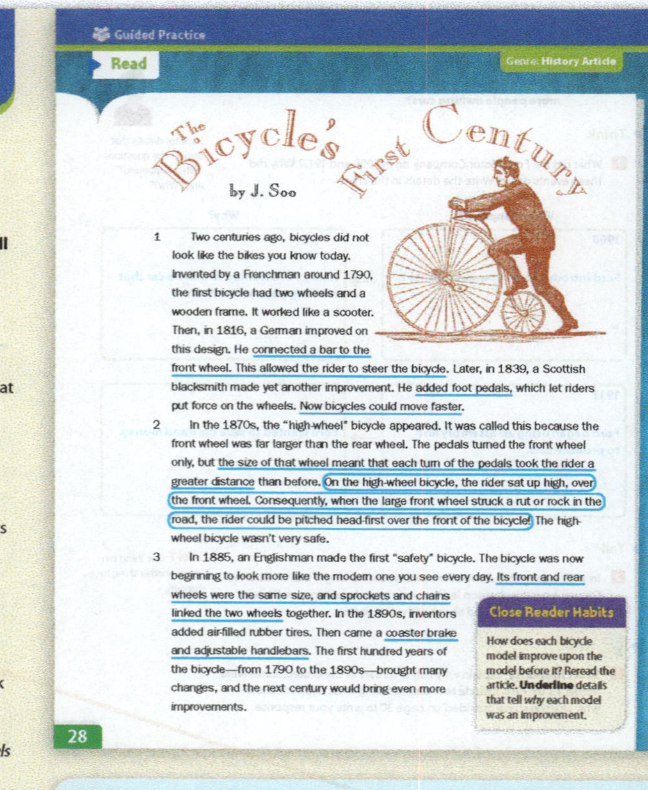

Guided Practice

Read

Genre: History Article

The Bicycle's First Century

by J. Soo

1 Two centuries ago, bicycles did not look like the bikes you know today. Invented by a Frenchman around 1790, the first bicycle had two wheels and a wooden frame. It worked like a scooter. Then, in 1816, a German improved on this design. He connected a bar to the front wheel. This allowed the rider to steer the bicycle. Later, in 1839, a Scottish blacksmith made yet another improvement. He added foot pedals, which let riders put force on the wheels. Now bicycles could move faster.

2 In the 1870s, the "high-wheel" bicycle appeared. It was called this because the front wheel was far larger than the rear wheel. The pedals turned the front wheel only, but the size of that wheel meant that each turn of the pedals took the rider a greater distance than before. On the high-wheel bicycle, the rider sat up high, over the front wheel. Consequently, when the large front wheel struck a rut or rock in the road, the rider could be pitched head-first over the front of the bicycle! The high-wheel bicycle wasn't very safe.

3 In 1885, an Englishman made the first "safety" bicycle. The bicycle was now beginning to look more like the modern one you see every day. Its front and rear wheels were the same size, and sprockets and chains linked the two wheels together. In the 1890s, inventors added air-filled rubber tires. Then came a coaster brake and adjustable handlebars. The first hundred years of the bicycle—from 1790 to the 1890s—brought many changes, and the next century would bring even more improvements.

Close Reader Habits

How does each bicycle model improve upon the model before it? Reread the article. **Underline** details that tell *why* each model was an improvement.

28

English Language Learners

Develop Language

Concept Vocabulary Show some pictures of old-fashioned and modern bicycles downloaded from the Internet.

- Have students say as much as they can about what they see in the pictures. As students talk, supply any needed vocabulary, such as *wheels, tires, handlebars, pedals, brakes, chain, sprocket.*
- Ask students to order the pictures chronologically and to speculate about how each new model was an improvement over previous models.

Word Learning Strategy

Use Context Clues

- Draw students' attention to paragraph 2. Read aloud the sentence with the word *pitched*. Tell students to think about the words around *pitched* to help them figure out its meaning.

  What does the word *pitched* means as it is used in this sentence? *(suddenly thrown forward)*

  What words in the sentence help you figure out the meaning? *(head-first over the front of the bicycle)*

- Explain that many words, like *pitched*, have more than one meaning. The meaning depends on how the word is used in the text. L.4.4a

28 Lesson 2 Understanding Historical Texts

Support for **English Language Learners** employs research-based strategies to build meaning and language knowledge. Features include building background, unpacking figurative language, and connecting to cognates.

The **Word Learning Strategy** teaches students a systematic approach to figuring out unknown words on their own by looking inside the word (word parts), around the word (context clues), and beyond the word (reference sources).

Teacher Resource Book

Think Use what you learned from reading the article to respond to the following questions.

History texts often tell how one event caused several other events to occur. This is called a series of events.

1. Reread paragraph 1. Choose the **two** statements that **best** tell why the bicycle was a better machine by 1839.
   - (A) A bar allowed the rider to steer.
   - B A wooden frame meant that the bicycle was lighter.
   - (C) Foot pedals meant that bicycles could move faster.
   - D The first bicycles could move like a scooter.
   - E The front wheel was larger than the rear wheel.

2. This question has two parts. Answer Part A. Then answer Part B.

   Part A
   What conclusion can you draw about what happened to many riders of the bicycles described in paragraph 2?
   - A They would be able to see over other bicycle riders.
   - (B) They were likely to get hurt if they hit a rock.
   - C They could not go as fast using the larger wheels.
   - D They found ways to link the large and small wheels together.

   Part B
   Which **two** sentences in paragraph 2 **best** support the answer to Part A? **Circle** them in the passage.

Talk

3. Based on information in the text, what changes to bicycle designs came about in the 1800s? What can you conclude about why the designs kept changing?

Write

4. **Short Response** Explain how the design of the bicycle was improved in the 1800s and why the changes were necessary. Use details from the text to support your answer. Use the space provided on page 31 to write your answer.

HINT Be sure to use words that show why the changes were made, such as *because* and *since*.

29

● Integrating Standards

Use the following questions to further students' understanding of the article:

- **How was the first bicycle different from the bicycle that was developed 100 years later? How was it the same?** *(The first bicycle did not have a handlebar, foot pedals, brakes, sprockets and chains, or air-filled rubber tires. Like the bicycle of the 1890s, it did have two wheels the same size.)*
  DOK 2 **RI.4.1**
- **How does the author organize information in this article?** *(The author presents information in time order, beginning with an event that took place in 1790 and ending with events in the 1890s. This structure helps the reader understand how the bicycle changed over time.)*
  DOK 3 **RI.4.5**

● Monitor Understanding

If... students have difficulty making a conclusion about why designs kept changing,

then... tell them to think of the specific cause of each change. For example, a bar was added in 1816 because you couldn't steer a bicycle. Then ask, What quality or qualities of bicycles got better because of all these design changes? For example, did each change improve the bicycle's appearance, performance, safety, or cost?

Lesson 2

Think

- Have students work with a partner to complete items 1 and 2. Draw attention to the boldface words **two**, **best**, and **circle**.

TIP If students have trouble answering these questions, have them turn each question into a statement. For example: *The bicycle was a better machine by 1839 because ...*

Answer Analysis
When students have finished, discuss correct and incorrect responses.

1. **The correct choices are A and C.** The text states that the steering bar and the foot pedals improved the bicycle.
   - **B** and **D** do not reflect improvements. The original bicycle had a wooden frame and worked like a scooter.
   - **E** describes a bicycle built after 1839.

   DOK 2

2. **Part A**
   The correct choice is B. Riders would likely be pitched over the high front wheel if they hit an obstruction in the road.
   - **A** might be true, but no text details support it.
   - **C** and **D** are not supported by text details.

   Part B
   See the circled sentences in paragraph 2 on page 28.
   DOK 3

● Integrating Standards

Talk

- Have partners discuss the prompt.
- Provide copies of the chart on p. TR15 so students can organize the ideas they discuss.
- Circulate to clarify misunderstandings.

● Monitor Understanding

Write

- See p. 31 for instructional guidance.

Wrap Up

- Ask students to recall the Learning Target. Have them explain how identifying causal relationships helped them better understand this history article.

To help students respond to questions with multiple correct answers, **Answer Analysis** explains correct and incorrect responses and the reasons for them.

Integrating Standards offers questions that further students' understanding. The reference codes below each prompt highlight the Depth of Knowledge level and the non-target standard addressed by the questions.

The if/then format of the **Monitor Understanding** teaching strategy identifies typical challenges students face and provides concrete suggestions for differentiating instruction.

Ongoing Opportunities to Monitor Understanding

i-Ready and *Ready® Reading* provide a comprehensive assessment system, as shown below and on pages A12–A13. The *Ready Reading* Student Book and Teacher Resource Book include practical, easy-to-use progress-monitoring tools as shown on the table to the right.

Diagnose

Use *i-Ready Diagnostic* to **diagnose individual student skill levels** and identify instructional needs.

Monitor Understanding

Use the informal assessment tools in the *Ready* Student Book and Teacher Resource Book to **inform ongoing instruction.**

Assess Mastery

Use *i-Ready Standards Mastery* or *Ready Unit Interim Assessments* to **evaluate student mastery of content** at the lesson and unit level.

Measure Growth

Use *i-Ready Diagnostic* or *Ready Assessments* to **track student progress toward end-of-year goals.**

Tool	What it does	How to use it
Student Book		
Think, Talk	Encourage students to collaborate in applying the lesson standard and sharing ideas about the text.	Observe students as they participate in these activities and respond with targeted strategies and activities to support individual needs.
Write	Provides an opportunity for students to respond independently to a writing prompt about the text.	
Independent Practice	Provides opportunities for students to demonstrate understanding as they apply the lesson standard to a new text.	
Learning Target (end of lesson)	Serves as an "exit ticket" at the end of the lesson for students to reflect on what they have learned.	
Teacher Resource Book		
Monitor Understanding	Provides a quick if/then diagnostic for students who are having difficulty and offers specific remediation strategies.	Use to identify individual student needs and provide immediate support.
Answer Analysis	For multiple-choice items, provides an explanation of why each answer choice is correct or incorrect.	Discuss correct and incorrect answers with students to help them understand the reasons for their errors.
Writing Rubric	Helps the teacher evaluate students' short and extended responses.	Score extended response essays; then share with students to help them understand how to improve their writing.

Ready Reading Classroom Routines

The following four routines—*Academic Talk, Word Learning, Talk,* and *Response-Writing*—support a successful implementation of *Ready Reading*. Each routine is used in every lesson and is referenced at point of use in the Teacher Resource Book. The goal is for these routines to become so ingrained that students use them on a regular basis. Before students can use these routines independently, they will need to understand their purpose and how the routines function, so allot time at the beginning of the year to "teach" each routine.

Academic Talk Routine

What is Academic Talk?

In *Ready Reading*, Academic Talk is the vocabulary that aligns to the ELA standards and that students may encounter on standards-based assessments.

When to Use

- Use this routine when you are presenting the Academic Talk words and phrases in the Lesson Introduction.
- Refer to the Academic Talk words and phrases whenever you are discussing the lesson selections. Remind students to use these terms in the class discussions and when they are responding to writing prompts to demonstrate understanding of the text.

Why It Matters

- Students need to be familiar with the academic language used to discuss a text and the way it is structured.
- Students may encounter words and phrases such as these on standards-based assessments.
- Students need to be able to use academic terms in written responses.

What the Research Says

- *"Some words are clearly 'linchpin words' required for reading and writing across genres. These words, such as main idea, sequence, context, and definition, are used to describe and engage in the very processes of reading and writing, and so may be thought of as process words."* (Blachowicz et al. 2013)

Management Tips

- Provide examples of each word or phrase.
- Review the terms before you introduce each *Talk* prompt in the lesson. Remind students to use the terms in discussion. Listen to students' discussions to ensure they are using and pronouncing the words and phrases correctly.
- Consider having students keep an Academic Talk Journal or e-Journal in which they record the academic terms with notes they write to help them remember what the terms mean or how they are used.

1 Academic Talk Routine

1. **Read the Academic Talk Words and Phrases.**
   Look at the Academic Talk box in your book. Listen as your teacher explains the words and phrases. Ask for clarification if you don't understand any terms.

   - Write each word or phrase on individual cards.
   - Point to each word or phrase.
   - Define each word or phrase as you read it aloud. See the *Glossary of Terms*, pp. TR2–TR9 for definitions. Provide an example sentence for each word.
   - Post the words and phrases on an *Academic Talk Word Bank*.

2. **Read the Introduction.**
   Circle the Academic Talk words and phrases as you read them in your book.

   As you read the Learning Target and the Introduction with students, stop when you come to each Academic Talk term. Show the word card again or emphasize the word by rereading.

3. **Practice the Academic Talk Words and Phrases.**
   Challenge yourself to use the words and phrases three to four times in today's discussions.

   Listen to students' discussions to make certain they use and understand the words and phrases.

4. **Use the Academic Talk Words and Phrases.**
   Throughout the lesson, use the words and phrases when you talk or write about a text.

   - Revisit the Academic Talk terms at the beginning and end of each step in the lesson.
   - Encourage students to use the terms as they talk about texts with their peers.

Post this routine on an anchor chart for students.

2 Word Learning Routine

When to Use

- Students should use this routine when they encounter words or phrases in a text that they don't know.
- Point-of-use instruction in the Teacher Resource Book directs teachers to remind students to use the word learning strategies when they encounter unfamiliar words.
- A Words to Know feature box that appears in the Independent Practice of each student lesson reminds students to use these strategies.

Why It Matters

The majority of new words students acquire are learned by encountering them in texts. This Word Learning Routine will help students:

- Determine the meaning of unknown and unfamiliar words and phrases they encounter in texts.
- Expand their vocabulary.
- Apply their word learning skills as they become independent readers and learners.

What the Research Says

- *"Teachers need to use a variety of teaching techniques to develop indirect word-learning strategies such as using context clues, identifying word parts, and dictionary use to help students figure out word meanings on their own."* (Edwards et al. 2004)
- *"Students need to master word-learning strategies using context, using word parts, and using the dictionary. Although native English speakers must also learn these strategies, word-learning strategies are particularly important for English Language Learners because they have so many words to learn."* (August et al. 2005)

Management Tips

- **Post** the three steps on an anchor chart and review them frequently:
  1. Look **inside** the word or phrase.
  2. Look **around** the word or phrase.
  3. Look **beyond** the word or phrase.
- **Use sentence starters** such as these to build word awareness:
  - *I have heard the word used before in talking about…*
  - *The word sounds like it could have something to do with…*

2

Word Learning Routine

Use the following steps to figure out unfamiliar words. If you figure out what the word means, continue reading. If not, then try the next step.

1. **Say the Word or Phrase Aloud.**
   Circle the word or phrase that you find confusing. Read the sentence aloud.

   Teach students to circle the word or phrase that they find confusing and say it aloud.

2. **Look Inside the Word or Phrase.**
   Look for familiar word parts, such as prefixes, suffixes, and root words.
   Try breaking the word into smaller parts.
   Can you figure out a meaning from the word parts you know?

   - Model looking for meaningful parts, such as prefixes, suffixes, and roots, including Greek and Latin roots.
   - Make it visual by breaking the word into smaller parts.

raindrop	rain + drop
photosynthesis	photo + synthesis
unprofitable	un + profit + able

3. **Look Around the Word or Phrase.**
   Look for clues in the words or sentences around the word or phrase you don't know and the context of the paragraph.

   - Look for clues in the context of the sentence or paragraph.
   - Look for text features, such as bold face text, captions, and visuals.

4. **Look Beyond the Word or Phrase.**
   Look for the meaning of the word or phrase in a dictionary, glossary, or thesaurus.

   Look for the meaning of the word in a dictionary, glossary, or thesaurus. When modeling how to use a dictionary, note that many words have multiple meanings and that students still need to use context to identify the best definition.

5. **Check the Meaning.**
   Ask yourself, "Does this meaning make sense in the sentence?"

   Model for students how to check to make certain the meaning makes sense in the context of the phrase, sentence, and topic of the selection. Ask yourself, *"Does this word meaning make sense in the sentence?"*.

Post this routine on an anchor chart for students.

3 Talk Routine

When to Use

Use the Talk Routine during the Talk step of the Introduction, Modeled and Guided Instruction, and Guided Practice sections of each lesson.

Why It Matters

Opportunities for short collaborative discussions are an integral step of *Ready Reading's* research-based *Read, Think, Talk, Write* instructional model. These opportunities help students:

- Use higher-order thinking skills.
- Deepen and extend comprehension of a text.
- Build knowledge by listening to and understanding other's perspectives.
- Stay engaged, focused, and motivated.

What the Research Says

- *"Classroom talk is an important component of students' learning. When we cultivate it, we help students learn to problem solve and use strategies that may inspire others."* (McLaughlin 2015)
- *"Engaged student talk is not enough. We must help students talk to deepen their thinking and prepare for what the 21st century needs: a population that can talk, think, and learn from and with one another."* (Nemecek et al. 2014)

Management Tips

To promote good discussion habits, you may wish to:

Create classroom discussion guidelines:

- **Look** at your partner.
- **Listen** carefully to your partner.
- **Ask questions** if you don't understand.
- **Be flexible** and **respect** others' ideas.
- **Contribute** your ideas.

Post sentence starters for students.

- **Express active listening.**
  - *I was confused when you said…*
  - *I would like to talk more about…*
- **Share thinking.**
  - *I found evidence here in on page…*
  - *I infer that…because the text states…*
- **Ask clarifying questions.**
  - *What do you mean when you say…? Why do you think that?*
  - *Can you tell me where you saw that in the text?*
- **Disagree or agree respectfully.**
  - *The text says something different to me. In this section, I think…*
  - *I agree/disagree with…because…*

3 Talk Routine

1. **Read the Prompt.**
   Take turns with your partner reading the prompt to make sure you understand the topic of your discussion.

2. **Respond and Prove.**
   Use evidence from the text in your response.

3. **Listen and Build.**
   Listen carefully to what your partner says. Ask him or her to explain their thinking and where they found their evidence. Identify connections to their ideas or evidence.

4. **Share Your Understandings.**
   Together with your partner, be prepared to tell your class what you learned from the text and your discussion.

Post this routine on an anchor chart for students.

Have students read the entire prompt. Make sure they understand what they are being asked to discuss. Ask a few of them to restate the prompt in their own words. If needed, clarify any misconceptions before students begin their discussion.

TIP: *At the beginning of the school year, set clear expectations on what needs to be accomplished during discussion time.*

Tell students that when they respond to the *Talk* prompt, they need to use evidence from the text to support their ideas and understanding of the text.

Explain to students that they should share their ideas with their partner. They then should think about their partner's ideas and try to build on them to deepen their own thinking.

Invite students to share their ideas and learning with the class.

4 Response-Writing Routine

When to Use

Use the Response-Writing Routine during the *Write* step of Modeled and Guided Instruction, Guided Practice, and Independent Practice of each *Ready* lesson.

Why It Matters

Opportunities for writing are an integral step in *Ready Reading's* research-based *Read, Think, Talk, Write* instructional path. These opportunities help students:

- Demonstrate their understanding of the target standard.
- Make connections between reading and writing by building on the *Read, Think,* and *Talk* steps.
- Communicate the knowledge students have gained by reading and talking.
- Respond to a variety of on-demand prompts.

What the Research Says

- *"The act of composing helps organize our thoughts and think aloud about new ideas. It also helps us internalize learning."* (Overturf 2015)
- *"Reading and writing are inextricably linked, so writing is a natural part of reading instruction. Writing from sources, writing text-based answers, and engaging in brief research tasks can lead to writing to explore ideas and demonstrate learning in social studies, science, and other content areas."* (McLaughlin & Overturf 2013)

Management Tips

- Display sentence starters students can incorporate into their writing such as:
  - *In the text, the author says…*
  - *The text states…*
  - *According to the text…*
  - *This detail shows…*
  - *This example from the text proves that…*
- Display a list of transition words and phrases students can use to connect sentences and paragraphs, such as *first, finally, for example, because, however, as a result.*
- Explain to students that they can test their understanding of a prompt by asking themselves questions such as:
  - *What topic am I writing about?*
  - *What am I supposed to do?*
  - *How much evidence do I need to include?*
- Circulate to observe students' writing in order to provide supportive feedback or instructional assistance. Use questions such as:
  - *Have you answered every part of the prompt? Show me where.*
  - *What evidence have you included? Is it enough? If you need more evidence, what can you do?*
  - *Are all of your sentences complete?*

4 Response-Writing Routine

1. **Read and Analyze the Prompt.**
Identify and circle key words and phrases that tell what you should do. Underline words or phrases that indicate evidence you need to provide. Say the prompt in your own words to be sure you understand it.

2. **Gather Text Evidence.**
Support your writing with evidence from the text.

3. **Organize Ideas and Evidence.**
Use a graphic organizer to help you organize your ideas before you begin writing.

4. **Write the Response.**
Use the information you gathered from the text and talked about with your partner to answer the prompt.

5. **Evaluate Your Response.**
Revise to make it clearer or to add more text evidence. Fix any mistakes. Together with your partner, tell your class what you learned from the text and your discussion.

Post this routine on an anchor chart for students.

Have students read the entire prompt. Help them unpack it by circling words and phrases that state directions, such as *describe, explain, compare,* and *contrast.* Underline the words and phrases that show what information they need to provide. Model restating the prompt in one's own words.

Remind students to return to the markups they made during the *Read* step and the answers and ideas developed in *Think* and *Talk*. Emphasize that students should keep in mind the topic and include only evidence that is related to the prompt.

Encourage students to arrange their ideas and evidence in a logical order, such as chronologically or beginning with the most important piece of evidence. Point out that the Hints in the Student Book sometimes provide suggestions for organization.

Have students write their responses, using the evidence they identified and the order they chose. Tell them that they can revise their responses later, if needed, and check for mistakes.

Remind students to use the Check Your Writing checklist on the Modeled and Guided Instruction and Guided Practice writing pages of the Student Book. For Independent Practice, have students use the 2-Point Writing Rubric on p. TR10 of the Teacher Resource Book.

Pacing *Ready*® *Reading*

Ready Reading provides a full year of instruction. A lesson-specific planning guide appears on the opening spread of each lesson in the Teacher Resource Book, suggesting the amount of time to spend on each part of the reading lesson.

Monthly Pacing Guide Grade 5

Month	*Ready* Instruction Lesson	Days	Language Handbook Lesson (allow 20 minutes per lesson)
September	Assessment 1 or *i-Ready* Diagnostic	2	–
	L1 Finding Main Ideas and Details	5	15
	L2 Summarizing Informational Texts	5	16
October	L3 Using Details to Support Inferences	5	17
	L4a Explaining Relationships in Scientific and Technical Texts	5	18
	L4b Explaining Relationships in Historical Texts	5	19
	Unit 1 Interim Assessment or *i-Ready* Standards Mastery	1	–
November	L5 Comparing and Contrasting Characters in Drama	5	20
	L6 Comparing and Contrasting Settings and Events	5	21
	L7 Finding the Theme of a Story or Drama	5	22
	L8 Finding the Theme of a Poem	5	1
December	L9 Summarizing Literary Texts	5	2
	L10 Using Details to Support Inferences in Literary Texts	5	3
	Unit 2 Interim Assessment or *i-Ready* Standards Mastery	1	–
January	L11 Unfamiliar Words	5	4
	L12 Comparing Text Structures, Part 1: Chronology, Problem-Solution	5	6
	L13 Comparing Text Structures, Part 2: Cause-Effect, Compare-Contrast	5	6
	L14 Analyzing Accounts of the Same Topic	5	7
February	Unit 3 Interim Assessment or *i-Ready* Standards Mastery	1	–
	Assessment 2 or *i-Ready* Diagnostic	2	–
	L15 Language and Meaning	5	8
	L16 Understanding Literary Structure	5	9
March	L17 Point of View	5	10
	Unit 4 Interim Assessment or *i-Ready* Standards Mastery	1	–
	L18 Finding Information from Multiple Sources	5	11
	L19 Understanding Supporting Evidence	5	12
April	L20 Using Multiple Sources for Writing and Speaking	5	13
	Unit 5 Interim Assessment or *i-Ready* Standards Mastery	1	–
	L21 Using Multiple Sources for Writing and Speaking	5	14
	L22 Comparing and Contrasting Stories in the Same Genre	5	–
May	Unit 6 Interim Assessment or *i-Ready* Standards Mastery	1	–
	Assessment 3 or *i-Ready* Diagnostic	2	–

Weekly Pacing Guide 1 lesson per week

Day 1

Teacher-Toolbox.com Interactive Tutorial
Supporting Inferences About Informational Text—Level E
20 min (optional)

Introduction pp. 38–39
- **Read** **Using Details to Support Inferences** *10 min*
- **Think** *10 min*
  Graphic Organizer: Three-Column Chart
- **Talk** *5 min*
  Quick Write (TRB) *5 min*

Day 2

Modeled and Guided Instruction pp. 40–41, 44
- **Read** **Zheng He** *10 min*
- **Think** *10 min*
  Graphic Organizer: Three-Column Chart
- **Talk** *5 min*
- **Write** Short Response *10 min*

Day 3

Guided Practice pp. 42–43, 45
- **Read** **Firsts in Flight** *10 min*
- **Think** *10 min*
- **Talk** *5 min*
- **Write** Short Response *10 min*

Day 4

Independent Practice pp. 46–51
- **Read** **Treasures of the Tomb** *10 min*
- **Think** *10 min*
- **Write** Short Response *10 min*

Day 5

Independent Practice pp. 46–51
- *Review* Answer Analysis (TRB) *10 min*
- *Review* Response Analysis (TRB) *10 min*
- *Assign and Discuss* Learning Target *10 min*

Language Handbook
Lesson 17 Using a Dictionary or Glossary, pp. 470–471
20 min (optional)

Daily Pacing 30–45 minutes a day

Read *10 min*	Students read a passage twice, first independently for comprehension, then with a partner to find text evidence.
Think *10 min*	Students unpack the text, using a graphic organizer to analyze the text's structure, organization, and evidence.
Talk *5 min*	Students solidify their thinking through discussions and practice applying key terms and concepts.
Write *10–15 min*	Students independently reflect on the day's learning through short- and extended-response essays.

Instruction for each section of the lesson follows a similar *Read, Think, Talk, Write* instructional model. The chart above shows the structure and goals for one part of the lesson.

Ready® Reading + Writing = Fully Integrated Instruction

Ready® Reading

With *Ready Reading,* you can give your students instruction that addresses the rigor of the new reading standards in a highly supportive way.

Ready Reading builds strong, independent readers through instruction and practice with high-interest, complex informational and literary texts and is a rigorous standards-based program. Each lesson focuses on one standard, or part of one standard.

+ *Ready® Writing*

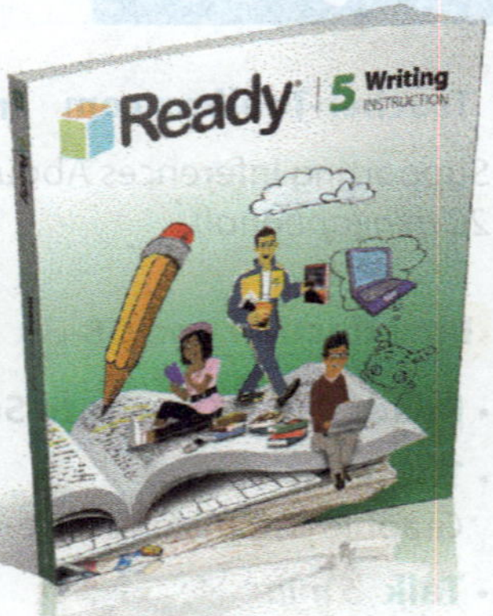

With *Ready Writing,* you can teach your students to meet the rigorous expectations of the new writing standards as they become confident, competent writers.

Six lessons at each grade provide in-depth instruction in the following writing types: opinion, informative/explanatory, and narrative. The new demands for writing to sources and using text-based evidence is facilitated by Source Texts that are embedded right into the Student Book, with explicit systematic instruction for teachers—all in one place.

Common Core State Standards

Together, *Ready Reading* and *Ready Writing* provide complete coverage of Common Core State Standards for Reading, Writing, and Language, as well as many of the related standards for Speaking and Listening.

Ready Reading	*Ready Writing*
All Standards for Reading Literature and Informational Text	All Writing Standards
All Language Standards	All Language Standards
Appropriate Writing and Speaking/Listening Standards	Appropriate Reading and Speaking/Listening Standards

Ready Writing was designed to work with *Ready Reading*. Writing lessons are sequenced to follow the themes and skills of *Ready Reading* lessons. The pacing chart below shows when to teach a writing lesson when you are using both programs.

Ready Writing Grade 5

Lesson 1
Writing an Opinion: Letter to the Editor

Lesson 2
Writing to Inform: Article

Lesson 3
Writing a Narrative: Legend

Lesson 4
Writing to Analyze Literature: Essay

Lesson 5
Writing to Inform: Book Chapter

Lesson 6
Writing an Opinion: Speech

Ready Reading Grade 5

Unit 1 Key Ideas and Details in Informational Text

Lesson 1 Finding Main Ideas and Details
Lesson 2 Summarizing Informational Texts
Lesson 3 Using Details to Support Inferences
Lesson 4a Explaining Relationships in Scientific and Technical Texts
Lesson 4b Explaining Relationships in Historical Texts

Unit 2 Key Ideas and Details in Literature

Lesson 5 Comparing and Contrasting Characters in Drama
Lesson 6 Comparing and Contrasting Settings and Events
Lesson 7 Finding the Theme of a Story or Drama
Lesson 8 Finding the Theme of a Poem
Lesson 9 Summarizing Literary Texts
Lesson 10 Using Details to Support Inferences in Literary Texts

Unit 3 Craft and Structure in Informational Text

Lesson 11 Unfamiliar Words
Lesson 12 Comparing Text Structures, Part 1: Chronology, Problem–Solution
Lesson 13 Comparing Text Structures, Part 2: Cause–Effect, Compare–Contrast
Lesson 14 Analyzing Accounts of the Same Topic

Unit 4 Craft and Structure in Literature

Lesson 15 Language and Meaning
Lesson 16 Understanding Literary Structure
Lesson 17 Point of View

Unit 5 Integration of Knowledge and Ideas in Informational Text

Lesson 18 Finding Information from Multiple Sources
Lesson 19 Understanding Supporting Evidence
Lesson 20 Using Multiple Sources for Writing and Speaking

Unit 6 Integration of Knowledge and Ideas in Literature

Lesson 21 Analyzing Visual Elements in Literary Texts
Lesson 22 Comparing and Contrasting Stories in the Same Genre

Unit 1

Key Ideas and Details in Informational Text

Key Ideas and Details in Informational Text

One of the easiest ways to draw a person is by drawing a stick figure. These show you just enough information to help you see what the person is doing. Stick figures are a little like **main ideas**: They provide the most important information but very few details. In the drawing on this page, the dark stick figure shows the main idea: A person is cooking something over a fire. But the rest of the drawing, in lighter print, shows all the **details** that support the main idea. It provides the viewer with details about the camper and her activity. These details, like the details in informational text, support the main idea of the illustration.

In this unit, you'll learn how to use key ideas to determine the main idea of an informational text. You'll also use key ideas to summarize texts, to make inferences, and to make connections between people, events, and ideas.

Self Check

Before starting this unit, check off the skills you know below. As you complete each lesson, see how many more skills you can check off!

I can:	Before this unit	After this unit
determine two or more main ideas of informational texts and explain how key details support the main ideas.	☐	☐
summarize an informational text.	☐	☐
refer to details and examples when explaining and inferring what a text says.	☐	☐
explain relationships between individuals, events, and ideas in informational texts.	☐	☐

8

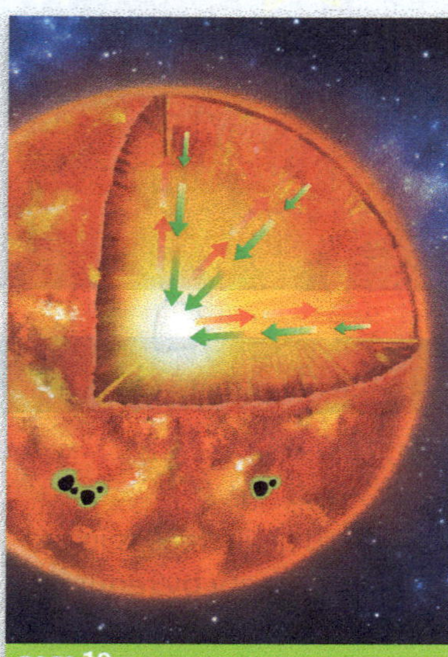
page 19

page 26

page 32

page 60

page 47

page 66

At a Glance

- These two pages introduce students to the skills and strategies they will learn in this unit.
- The checklist allows them to see what skills they will be learning and take ownership of their progress.
- The visual table of contents gives a graphic preview of the passages in the unit.

Step by Step

- Explain to students that they are going to begin a new unit of lessons. Tell them that in all the lessons in this unit they will be learning about key ideas and details in informational text.
- Have the class read together the introduction to the unit in their books. Invite and respond to comments and questions, if any.
- Then take a few minutes to have each student independently read through the list of skills.
- Ask students to consider each skill and check the box if it is a skill they think they already have. Tell students that they may have worked on similar skills in the past, but these skills go deeper than before.
- Engage students in a brief discussion about the skills. Invite students to comment on which ones they would most like to learn, or which ones seem similar or related to something they already know. Remind them that the goal is to be able to check off one skill at a time until they have them all checked.
- Invite students to look at the graphics and predict what the passages will be about.

LESSON OVERVIEW

Lesson 1
Finding Main Ideas and Details

Standards Focus

Determine two or more main ideas of a text and explain how they are supported by key details . . . RI.5.2

Lesson Objectives

Reading

- Identify two or more main ideas in a text. RI.5.2
- Explain how two or more main ideas are supported by key details in a text. RI.5.2
- Identify which details support which main idea. RI.5.2

Writing

- Draw evidence from informational texts to support analysis and reflection. W.5.9b

Speaking and Listening

- Pose and respond to specific questions and contribute to discussions. SL.5.1c
- Review the key ideas expressed and draw conclusions. SL.5.1d

Language

- Use context as a clue to the meaning of a word or phrase. L.5.4a
- Acquire and use academic and domain-specific words and phrases. L.5.6

Additional Practice: **RI.5.1, RI.5.3, RI.5.4, RI.5.8**

Academic Talk

See **Glossary of Terms**, pp. TR2–TR9

- main idea
- key detail
- detail
- support
- topic

Learning Progression

Grade 4	Grade 5	Grade 6
Students identify one main idea of a text and explain how it is supported by key details.	Building on Grade 4, students broaden their understanding of the main idea to see that texts can have several major ideas and that each paragraph of a text may have a main idea.	Grade 6 increases in complexity by requiring students to add up the most important details of a text to find the central idea. Students develop an understanding of how all the details in a text work together, not just key details, to convey the central idea.

Lesson Text Selections

Modeled and Guided Instruction

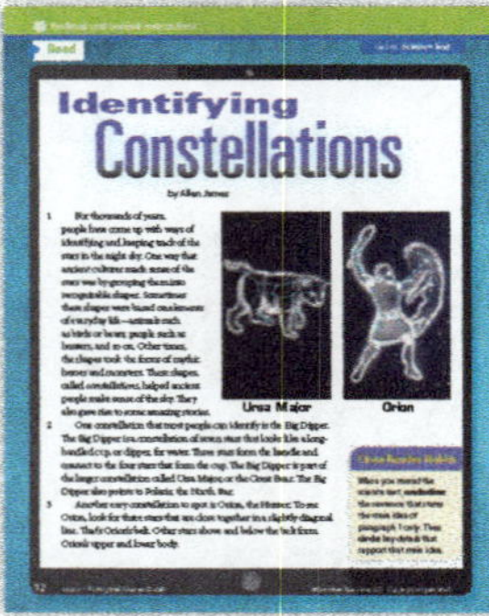

Identifying Constellations
by Allen James
Genre: Science Text

Guided Practice

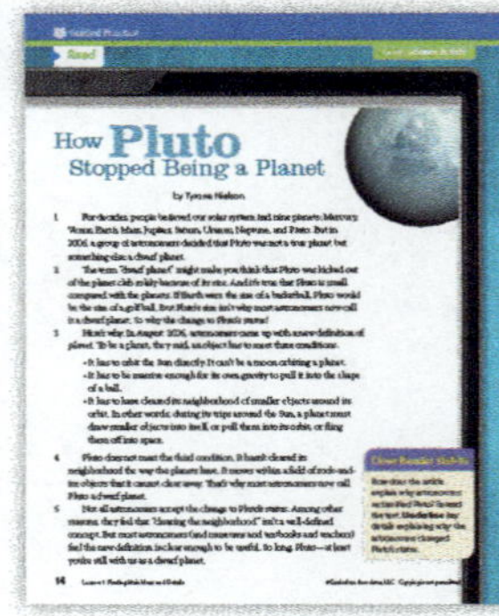

How Pluto Stopped Being a Planet
by Tyrone Nielson
Genre: Science Article

Independent Practice

When Stars Explode
by Ken Croswell, Ph.D.
Genre: Science Article

Lesson Pacing Guide

Whole Class Instruction *30–45 minutes per day*

Day 1

Teacher-Toolbox.com **Interactive Tutorial**
Finding Main Ideas and Details in Informational Texts—Level E
20 min (optional)

Introduction pp. 10–11
- **Read** **Finding Main Ideas and Details** *10 min*
- **Think** *10 min*
  Graphic Organizer: Main Idea Organizer
- **Talk** *5 min*
  Quick Write (TRB) *5 min*

Day 2

Modeled and Guided Instruction pp. 12–13, 16
- **Read** **Identifying Constellations** *10 min*
- **Think** *10 min*
  Graphic Organizer: Main Idea Organizer
- **Talk** *5 min*
- **Write** Short Response *10 min*

Day 3

Guided Practice pp. 14–15, 17
- **Read** **How Pluto Stopped Being a Planet** *10 min*
- **Think** *10 min*
- **Talk** *5 min*
- **Write** Short Response *10 min*

Day 4

Independent Practice pp. 18–23
- **Read** **When Stars Explode** *15 min*
- **Think** *10 min*
- **Write** Short Response *10 min*

Day 5

Independent Practice pp. 18–23
- *Review* Answer Analysis (TRB) *10 min*
- *Review* Response Analysis (TRB) *10 min*
- *Assign and Discuss* Learning Target *10 min*

Language Handbook
Lesson 15 Using Context Clues, pp. 466–467
20 min (optional)

Small Group Differentiation
Teacher-Toolbox.com

Reteach

***Ready Reading* Prerequisite Lesson**
- **Grade 4** Lesson 1 Finding Main Ideas and Details

Teacher-led Activities

Tools for Instruction
- Main Idea and Supporting Details

Personalized Learning
i-Ready.com

Independent

***i-Ready* Close Reading Lessons**
- **Grade 4** Finding Main Ideas and Details

- **Grade 5** Finding Main Ideas and Details

Introduction

Get Started

- Explain to students that in this lesson they will read several science texts and work to determine the main idea and key details of each text.
- Tap into what students already know about main ideas and key details. Invite them to share some strategies they have used to determine the main idea. *(Read the title, review the introduction and conclusion, think about what all the paragraphs have in common.)*
- Guide students to recognize that a passage can have more than one main idea. For example:

  Remember the passage we read about the moon landing? The main idea—the most important point—of the whole text was that it was the result of many inventions and years of preparation. But each paragraph had a different main idea that gave information about one part of the bigger topic. For example, the invention of *Apollo 11*'s powerful rockets was the main idea of the second paragraph.
- Focus students' attention on the Learning Target. Read it aloud to set the purpose for the lesson.
- Display the Academic Talk words and phrases. Tell students to listen for these terms and their meanings as you work through the lesson together. Use the Academic Talk Routine on pp. A48–A49.

English Language Learners

Genre Focus

Read

- Read aloud the Read section as students follow along. Restate to reinforce:

  Each passage has a topic, or subject. The main idea is the most important idea about the topic in the passage. Each main idea is supported by examples, facts, and information that are known as *key details*.
- Have students read the passage carefully to figure out the main idea and key details. Encourage them to consider how the photograph supports the main idea.

Introduction

RL5.2 Determine two or more main ideas of a text and explain how they are supported by key details.

Lesson 1
Finding Main Ideas and Details

Figuring out the main ideas of a text and the key details supporting them is necessary for understanding that text.

Read A **topic** is what a passage is about. A **main idea** is an important idea about that topic. Short passages usually develop just one main idea. Long passages often have two or more main ideas.

A passage's **details** are the facts, examples, and other information stated in the text. The details that help explain a main idea are called **key details**. We sometimes say that key details **support** main ideas.

Read the passage below. Underline what you think is the main idea. Then look for key details that help explain it.

At some point in your life you've probably looked up, gazed at the moon, and studied it in wonder. Throughout time, the moon has inspired many people. In 1801, Ludwig van Beethoven composed a piano piece called "Moonlight Sonata." Later, in 1889, Vincent van Gogh painted *The Starry Night*. In this painting, swirls of white and yellow create a halo around the moon. In 2011, Marilyn Singer wrote a book called *A Full Moon Is Rising* about how people all over the world celebrate the moon. The next time you gaze upon the moon, maybe you'll be inspired by it, too!

10

English Language Learners
Develop Language

Concept Vocabulary Review that one meaning of *main* is "most important." Have students complete this sentence frame: "One of the main streets in our community is ________."

- Next review one meaning of *support*, "to show to be true." Have students complete this sentence frame: "Her report card ________ her claim that she is a good student."
- Guide students to combine the meanings of both words to define the target skill. "Since *main* means 'most important,' the *main idea* is the most important idea. Since *support* means 'to show to be true,' a *supporting detail* must be a detail that shows the main idea to be true."

Genre Focus
Science Texts

Explain to students that throughout this lesson, they will read texts about science topics. Science texts are informational texts. Their purpose is to inform readers about discoveries in science and to explain science concepts.

Science texts are based on facts. The details in these texts give specific, measurable, and provable answers to the questions *who, what, when, where, why,* and *how*. Photos, diagrams, and other visual aids are also common.

Provide some examples of science texts, such as Seymour Simons's *The Sun* or *The Moon*. Then ask students to name other science texts they've read. Be sure they don't confuse informational science texts with science fiction, which is a literary genre.

Think Consider what you have read about main ideas and key details. In the *main idea organizer* below, write down one sentence from the passage you think states the main idea. Then write down two key details that develop the main idea.

Main Idea
Throughout time, the moon has inspired many people.

Key Detail	Key Detail	Key Detail
Beethoven's "Moonlight Sonata" was composed in 1801.	In 1889, the artist van Gogh painted *The Starry Night* with a halo around the moon.	The 2011 book *A Full Moon Is Rising*, by Marilyn Singer, is about celebrations of the moon around the world.

Talk Share your organizer with a partner.

- Did you both choose the same sentence for your main idea?
- Why do you think the sentence you chose, and not some other sentence, is the main idea?
- Do all three key details support the sentence you believe is the main idea? How do you know?

Academic Talk
Use these words and phrases to talk about the text.

- main idea
- key detail
- detail
- support
- topic

Monitor Understanding

If... students struggle to identify main ideas and supporting details,

then... provide an example. Say: "Tonight I have to write a science report and study for a history quiz. Then I have to read two poems. I have a lot of homework to do."

- **Which sentence summarizes what this short explanation is about?** *("I have a lot of homework to do.")*
- **What are three details that support, or give examples of, lots of homework?** *(write a science report, study for a history quiz, read two poems)*

Ask students to provide examples of main ideas and details from other aspects of their everyday lives. For example, if the main idea of a news story states which team won a ball game, what might the supporting details consist of?

Think

- Have students read aloud the Think section. Explain that the main idea organizer will help them collect their ideas and evidence.
- Have partners complete the organizer. Remind students to look for a sentence in the passage that directly states the main idea.
- As students work, circulate and provide assistance as needed.
- Ask volunteers to share what they wrote in their organizers.
- Make sure students can identify which key details in the paragraph support the main idea that the moon has inspired many people.

Talk

- Read aloud the Talk prompts.
- Have partners discuss the reasons for their choice of main idea. Make sure students explain why they chose the key details they did.
- Ask volunteers to share their ideas.

Quick Write Have students write a response to the following prompt:

Think about a person, place, or thing that inspires you. Name the source of your inspiration, and then write supporting details that explain how and why it inspires you.

Ask students to share their responses.

Wrap Up

- Invite students to share what they've learned so far. Encourage them to use the Academic Talk words and phrases in their explanations.
- Explain to students that science texts are almost always organized according to main ideas and supporting details because, in science, statements have to be supported by evidence.

In the next section, we'll read a science text about the stars. Finding main ideas and details will help you organize and remember the information that you read. As you read, keep asking "What is the text mostly about?"

Monitor Understanding

Modeled and Guided Instruction

Get Started

Today you will read a science text about the stars. First you'll read to understand what the text is about. Then you'll read to find main ideas and key details.

Read

- Read aloud the title of the text and call attention to the pictures. Based on the pictures, ask students to define *constellation*.
- Have students read the text independently. Tell them to place a check mark above any confusing words and phrases as they read. Encourage students to look inside, around, and beyond each unknown word to help them figure out its meaning. Use the Word Learning Routine on pp. A50–A51.
- When students have finished reading, clarify the meanings of words and phrases they still find confusing. Then use the questions below to check understanding. Encourage students to identify details in the text that support their answers.

  How did ancient cultures make sense of the stars? *(by grouping them into recognizable shapes)*

  Which constellation is part of a larger constellation called Ursa Major? *(the Big Dipper)*

  What is one way to find the constellation Orion? *(Look for the three stars that form his belt.)*

English Language Learners

- **Word Learning Strategy**

Explore

- Read aloud the Explore question at the top of p. 13 to set the purpose for the second read. Tell students they will need to look for related information in the text to answer this question.
- Have students read aloud the Close Reader Habit on p. 12.

> **TIP** Explain that the main idea is not always stated directly. To find the main idea, students should think about the topic of the text and ask, "What does the author want readers to understand after reading this?"

Modeled and Guided Instruction

Read — Genre: Science Text

Identifying Constellations

by Allen James

Ursa Major

Orion

1 For thousands of years, people have come up with ways of identifying and keeping track of the stars in the night sky. One way that ancient cultures made sense of the stars was by grouping them into recognizable shapes. Sometimes these shapes were based on elements of everyday life—animals such as birds or bears, people such as hunters, and so on. Other times, the shapes took the forms of mythic heroes and monsters. These shapes, called *constellations*, helped ancient people make sense of the sky. They also gave rise to some amazing stories.

2 One constellation that most people can identify is the Big Dipper. The Big Dipper is a constellation of seven stars that looks like a long-handled cup, or dipper, for water. Three stars form the handle and connect to the four stars that form the cup. The Big Dipper is part of the larger constellation called Ursa Major, or the Great Bear. The Big Dipper also points to Polaris, the North Star.

3 Another easy constellation to spot is Orion, the Hunter. To see Orion, look for three stars that are close together in a slightly diagonal line. That's Orion's belt. Other stars above and below the belt form Orion's upper and lower body.

Close Reader Habits

When you reread the science text, **underline** the sentence that states the main idea of paragraph 1 only. Then **circle** key details that support that main idea.

12

English Language Learners

Develop Language

Cognates Read aloud the title of the passage. Have speakers of Latin-based languages identify words for *identify* and *constellation* in their first languages. Invite students to share their understanding of these terms.

- Explain that these words are *cognates*, or words in two languages that share a similar spelling, meaning, and sometimes, pronunciation. Discuss with students how recognizing cognates can help them when they read in English.
- Encourage students to identify other cognates from the text, including *elements*, *forms*, and *animals*.

Word Learning Strategy

Look Inside, Around, and Beyond

- Explain that when readers encounter challenging words, they can look *inside*, *around*, and *beyond* the words to determine their meaning.
- Tell students that looking *inside* a word means looking at its parts: word roots, base words, prefixes, and suffixes.
- Or they can look *around* the word: check the context. How is it used in the sentence? What clues are nearby in the text, pictures, or text features?
- Finally, they can go *beyond* the text and check a dictionary or other resource to find the meaning. **L.5.4**

Explore What is the main idea of paragraph 1? What key details support that main idea?

The main idea of a paragraph isn't always the first sentence. Sometimes the main idea appears later in the paragraph.

Think

1 Complete this main idea organizer for paragraph 1 only.

Main Idea
To make sense of the sky, ancient people grouped stars into shapes called constellations.

Key Detail	Key Detail	Key Detail
Some constellations are based on objects and creatures from everyday life.	Some constellations are based on mythic heroes and monsters.	People made stories based on the constellations.

Talk

2 Share your organizers. Do you agree about the main idea of paragraph 1? What did you write for your key details? If necessary, revise your organizers.

Write

3 **Short Response** What is the main idea of paragraph 1? How do the key details support that main idea? Use the space provided on page 16 to write your answer.

HINT Include the name of the passage, and remember that you're writing only about paragraph 1.

Think Aloud

- I'm looking for the main idea, a statement that says or sums up what paragraph 1 is about.
- One strategy I can use is to review the paragraph and ask what each sentence is about. That should help me choose the most important sentence.
- The first sentence is about people identifying and keeping track of the stars. The next sentence is about grouping stars into shapes. Then there are three sentences with details about the shapes, including the fact that the shapes are called *constellations*. The last sentence is about stories.
- When I summarize what each sentence is about, I can see that most of the sentences in this paragraph are about different types of constellations. The main idea must be that constellations are around because ancient people grouped the stars to make sense of what they saw in the night sky. I'll use the next-to-last sentence in paragraph 1 for the main idea: "These shapes, called *constellations*, helped ancient people make sense of the sky."

Think

- Read aloud the Think section. Explain to students that you will model how to find text evidence to fill in part of the main idea organizer. Use the **Think Aloud** below to guide your modeling.
- Revisit the Explore question. Guide students to determine that they need to look for more details, using the Close Reader Habit.
- Encourage them to work with a partner to continue rereading the passage and complete the organizer. Remind them that the Buddy Tip will help them find the information they need.
- Ask volunteers to share their completed organizers.
- Have students check to make sure that each key detail they have chosen supports the main idea of paragraph 1.

Talk

- Read aloud the Talk prompt.
- Have partners respond to the prompt. Use the Talk Routine on pp. A52–A53.
- Circulate to check that students are discussing how they determined the main idea and key details of the paragraph. Make sure they explain how they know the details are key details.

Write

- Ask a volunteer to read aloud the Write prompt.
- Invite a few students to tell what the prompt is asking them to do.
- Make sure students understand that they need to restate three key details from the text that support the main idea of paragraph 1.
- Have students turn to p. 16 to write their responses.
- Use Review Responses on p. 16 to assess students' writing.

Wrap Up

- Ask students to recall the Learning Target. Have them explain how identifying the main idea helps them to classify the most important details in the text and to understand what the text is about.

Guided Practice

Get Started

Today you will read a science article. First you will read to understand what the article is about. Then you will reread with a partner to identify main ideas and supporting details.

Read

- Read aloud the title of the article. Have students restate the title in the form of a question (*How did Pluto stop being a planet?*) and then look for the answer as they read the passage.
- **Read to Understand** Have students read the article independently. Tell them to place a check mark above any confusing words and phrases as they read. Remind students to look inside, around, and beyond each unknown word to help them figure out its meaning. Use the Word Learning Routine on pp. A50–A51.
- When students have finished reading, clarify the meanings of words and phrases they still find confusing. Then use the questions below to check understanding. Encourage students to identify details in the text that support their answers.

  How many planets do astronomers now think our solar system has? *(eight)*

  What event led astronomers to re-count the planets? *(In 2006, astronomers came up with a new definition of* planet.*)*

  What force keeps Pluto in orbit and makes it into a ball? *(gravity)*

  What is Pluto called now? *(a dwarf planet)*

 **English Language Learners**

● **Word Learning Strategy**

- **Read to Analyze** Read aloud the Close Reader Habit on p. 14 to set the purpose for the second read. Then have students reread the article with a partner and discuss any questions they might have.

Guided Practice

Read — Genre: Science Article

How Pluto Stopped Being a Planet

by Tyrone Nielson

1 For decades, people believed our solar system had nine planets: Mercury, Venus, Earth, Mars, Jupiter, Saturn, Uranus, Neptune, and Pluto. But in 2006, a group of astronomers decided that Pluto was not a true planet but something else: a dwarf planet.

2 The term "dwarf planet" might make you think that Pluto was kicked out of the planet club solely because of its size. And it's true that Pluto is small compared with the planets. If Earth were the size of a basketball, Pluto would be the size of a golf ball. But Pluto's size isn't why most astronomers now call it a dwarf planet. So why the change to Pluto's status?

3 Here's why. In August 2006, astronomers came up with a new definition of *planet*. To be a planet, they said, an object has to meet three conditions.

- It has to orbit the Sun directly. It can't be a moon orbiting a planet.
- It has to be massive enough for its own gravity to pull it into the shape of a ball.
- It has to have cleared its neighborhood of smaller objects around its orbit. In other words, during its trips around the Sun, a planet must draw smaller objects into itself, or pull them into its orbit, or fling them off into space.

4 Pluto does not meet the third condition. It hasn't cleared its neighborhood the way the planets have. It moves within a field of rock-and-ice objects that it cannot clear away. That's why most astronomers now call Pluto a dwarf planet.

5 Not all astronomers accept the change to Pluto's status. Among other reasons, they feel that "clearing the neighborhood" isn't a well-defined concept. But most astronomers (and museums and textbooks and teachers) feel the new definition is clear enough to be useful. So long, Pluto—at least you're still with us as a dwarf planet.

Close Reader Habits

How does the article explain why astronomers reclassified Pluto? Reread the text. **Underline** key details explaining why the astronomers changed Pluto's status.

14

English Language Learners

Build Meaning

Visual Aid Reread paragraphs 3 and 4 and point to the phrase *cleared its neighborhood.* Prompt students to define *neighbors* and *neighborhood.*

- Use illustrations or gestures, such as clearing objects from a desk or a set table and a cleared table, to illustrate the meaning of *clear.* Place an object that stands for Pluto on the desk and ask students to place other objects in Pluto's neighborhood. Then have them clear the objects from Pluto's neighborhood.
- Have students reread paragraph 4 and identify the objects that are not being cleared from Pluto's neighborhood. *(rocks and ice)*

● Word Learning Strategy

Use Context Clues

- Point out the word *status* at the end of paragraph 2.

  What does the word *status* mean in this sentence?

- Guide students to look for context clues in the surrounding words and sentences.

  What happened to Pluto's *status*? *(It changed.)*

  Describe the change. *(Pluto went from being a planet to a dwarf planet.)*

- Guide students to determine that *status* means "position or degree of importance." Ask students to use *status* to explain what happened to Pluto in their own words.

L.5.4a

Think Use what you learned from reading the science article to respond to the following questions.

Many science articles are about new discoveries or changes to old ideas. Like any informational text, a science article has one or more main ideas supported by key details.

1 This question has two parts. Answer Part A. Then answer Part B.

Part A
What is the main idea of the science article by Tyrone Nielson?

- A A group of astronomers decided that Pluto is a dwarf planet.
- B Pluto is large enough to be a moon but too small to be a planet.
- C Many astronomers are pleased that Pluto is not a planet anymore.
- D Some astronomers still believe Pluto should be called a planet.

Part B
Which statement from the text **best** supports the answer to Part A?

- A "For decades, people believed our solar system had nine planets. . . ."
- B "And it's true that Pluto is small compared with the planets."
- C "In August 2006, astronomers came up with a new definition of *planet*."
- D "It has to be massive enough for its own gravity to pull it into the shape of a ball."

2 Which of these is **most clearly** a key detail of the passage?

- A "And it's true that Pluto is small compared with the planets."
- B "If Earth were the size of a basketball, Pluto would be the size of a golf ball."
- C "It hasn't cleared its neighborhood the way the planets have."
- D "Not all astronomers accept the change to Pluto's status."

Talk

3 What is the main idea of paragraph 3? What key details support it? Use the organizer on page 17 to organize your information.

Write

4 **Short Response** Use the information in your organizer to explain how the key details you identified support the main idea of paragraph 3. Use the space provided on page 17 to write your answer.

HINT Don't just identify the key details. Also say how they support the main idea.

Integrating Standards

Use the following questions to further students' understanding of the article.

- **Explain the conflict among astronomers over Pluto's reclassification.** *(Some astronomers feel that the idea of "clearing the neighborhood" isn't well defined or clear enough. Others feel that the new classification is "clear enough to be useful.")*
  DOK 3 RI.5.1, RI.5.3
- **How does the author support his claim that Pluto was not "kicked out of the planet club solely because of its size."** *(He gives information about the three conditions a planet must meet to be classified as a planet. Then he explains that Pluto does not meet one of these conditions.)*
  DOK 3 RI.5.8

Monitor Understanding

If... students have difficulty finding text evidence to answer item 3,

then... lead them to recognize that the phrase "Here's why" is a clue that important information will follow. Guide students to summarize the reason why Pluto is no longer considered a planet, and explain that their answer is the main idea statement.

Think

- Have students work with a partner to complete items 1 and 2. Note that item 1 has two parts.

TIP Remind students that the title of a text often gives a clue about its main idea.

Answer Analysis

When students have finished, discuss correct and incorrect responses.

1 **Part A**
The correct choice is A. This idea is restated throughout the passage. **B** and **C** are not supported by the text. **D** is a small detail.

Part B
The correct choice is C. This tells what the astronomers decided. **A, B,** and **D** are not the strongest evidence.
DOK 2

2 **The correct choice is C.** This is the reason Pluto is now called a dwarf planet. **A, B,** and **D** do not directly develop or support the main idea of the passage.
DOK 2

- **Integrating Standards**

Talk

- Have partners discuss the prompt. Remind students to support their ideas with text details.
- Circulate to clarify misunderstandings.

- **Monitor Understanding**

Write

- Ask a volunteer to read aloud the Write prompt.
- Invite students to tell what the prompt is asking them to do. Make sure they understand that they should only focus on paragraph 3.
- Call attention to the HINT.
- Have students turn to p. 17 to write their responses.
- Use Review Responses on p. 17 to assess writing.

Wrap Up

- Ask students to recall the Learning Target. Have them explain how finding the main idea and supporting details helped them understand why Pluto is no longer a planet.

Modeled and Guided Instruction

Write

- Remember to use the Response–Writing Routine on pp. A54–A55.

Review Responses

After students complete the writing activity, help them evaluate their responses.

3 Responses may vary but key details should support the main idea that people have come up with ways to identify the stars. See the sample response on the student book page. ***DOK 3***

Write Use the space below to write your answer to the question on page 13.

Identifying Constellations

HINT Include the name of the passage, and remember that you're writing only about paragraph 1.

3 **Short Response** What is the main idea of paragraph 1? How do the key details support that main idea?

Sample response: In "Identifying Constellations," the main idea of paragraph 1 is that ancient people grouped the stars into shapes called *constellations* to make sense of the sky. The key details support the main idea by helping the reader understand what a constellation is. For example, a constellation can be a shape based on everyday life. Or, a constellation can be a shape based on a hero or monster. A third key detail also tells us that people made stories based on constellations. These key details support the main idea by helping readers better understand what a constellation is.

Check Your Writing

- ☐ Did you read the prompt carefully?
- ☐ Did you put the prompt in your own words?
- ☐ Did you use the best evidence from the text to support your ideas?
- ☐ Are your ideas clearly organized?
- ☐ Did you write in clear and complete sentences?
- ☐ Did you check your spelling and punctuation?

16

Scaffolding Support for Reluctant Writers

If students are having a difficult time getting started, use the strategies below. Work individually with struggling students, or have students work with partners.

- Circle the verbs in the prompt that tell you what to do, such as *describe*, *explain*, or *compare*.
- Underline words and phrases in the prompt that show what information you need to provide in your response, such as *causes*, *reasons*, or *character traits*.
- Talk about the details from the text that you will include in your response.
- Explain aloud how you will respond to the prompt.

How Pluto Stopped Being a Planet

3 **Use the main idea organizer below to organize your information.**

Main Idea		
Key Detail	**Key Detail**	**Key Detail**

Write Use the space below to write your answer to the question on page 15.

4 **Short Response** Use the information in your organizer to explain how the key details you identified support the main idea of paragraph 3.

HINT Don't just identify the key details. Also say how they support the main idea.

In "How Pluto Stopped Being a Planet," the main idea of paragraph 3 is that an object must meet three conditions to be a planet. The key details are that the object must orbit the Sun directly, must be massive enough for its gravity to pull it into a ball, and must be able to "clear the neighborhood," or remove objects from its orbit. These three key details support the main idea by helping the reader better understand why some objects are considered planets and some, like Pluto, are not.

Teacher Notes

Talk

3 Students should use the main idea organizer to record their thoughts and evidence.

Write

- Remember to use the Response–Writing Routine on pp. A54–A55.

Review Responses

After students complete the writing activity, help them evaluate their responses.

4 Responses may vary but key details should support the main idea that most astronomers think Pluto does not meet one of three conditions for being a planet. See the sample response on the student book page. ***DOK 3***

Independent Practice

Get Started

Today you are going to read a science article that explains a complex series of events. Identifying main ideas and key details can help you understand how this scientific process works.

- Ask a volunteer to explain why identifying main ideas and key details will help readers understand scientific texts. Encourage students to use the Academic Talk words and phrases in their responses.

English Language Learners

Read

You are going to read the science article independently and use what you have learned to think and write about the text. As you read, remember to notice key details, identify what the details have in common, and find the main ideas that the key details support.

- Read aloud the title of the passage, and then encourage students to preview the text, paying close attention to the diagrams.
- Call attention to the Words to Know in the upper left of p. 18.
- If students need support in reading the passage, you may wish to use the Monitor Understanding suggestions.
- When students have finished, have them complete the Think and Write sections.

● **Monitor Understanding**

Independent Practice

Read

Genre: Science Article

WORDS TO KNOW
As you read, look inside, around, and beyond these words to figure out what they mean.
- **observe**
- **inward**
- **reactions**

from When Stars EXPLODE

by Ken Croswell, PhD, *Highlights*

1 [A supernova is] the spectacular death of a star. The last time people saw a supernova in our galaxy was 1604. That was before astronomers were using telescopes. However, every year astronomers see supernovae exploding in other galaxies. Astronomers can often observe such supernovae for months before they fade from view.

2 Most supernovae—that's the plural of supernova and pronounced SOO-per-NOO-vee—come from massive stars. Antares is a massive star. Such a star is born with more than eight times the mass of the Sun.

3 When a massive star is young, it is hot, bright, and blue. Its center makes energy the same way the Sun does: by changing hydrogen, the lightest element, into helium, the second-lightest element. This nuclear reaction creates energy that heats the star and makes it shine.

The exploding star that people saw in 1604 produced a glowing cloud of gas and dust called a *nebula*. The nebula at the left is all that remains of that star.

18

English Language Learners

Build Meaning

Background Knowledge To support students who are likely to struggle with the complexity of language and concepts in this article, you may wish to tap prior knowledge and provide context prior to reading.

- Read aloud the title of the article. Invite students to share the words for *stars* and *explode* in their first languages. Have them tell in their own words what this title means. Explain that *supernova* is the word for an exploded star.
- Take a picture walk through the article. Look at the diagrams, and ask students to describe what they see.
- If possible, show a NASA video of a supernova. This will help give students a point of reference as they learn all of the terminology associated with supernovae.

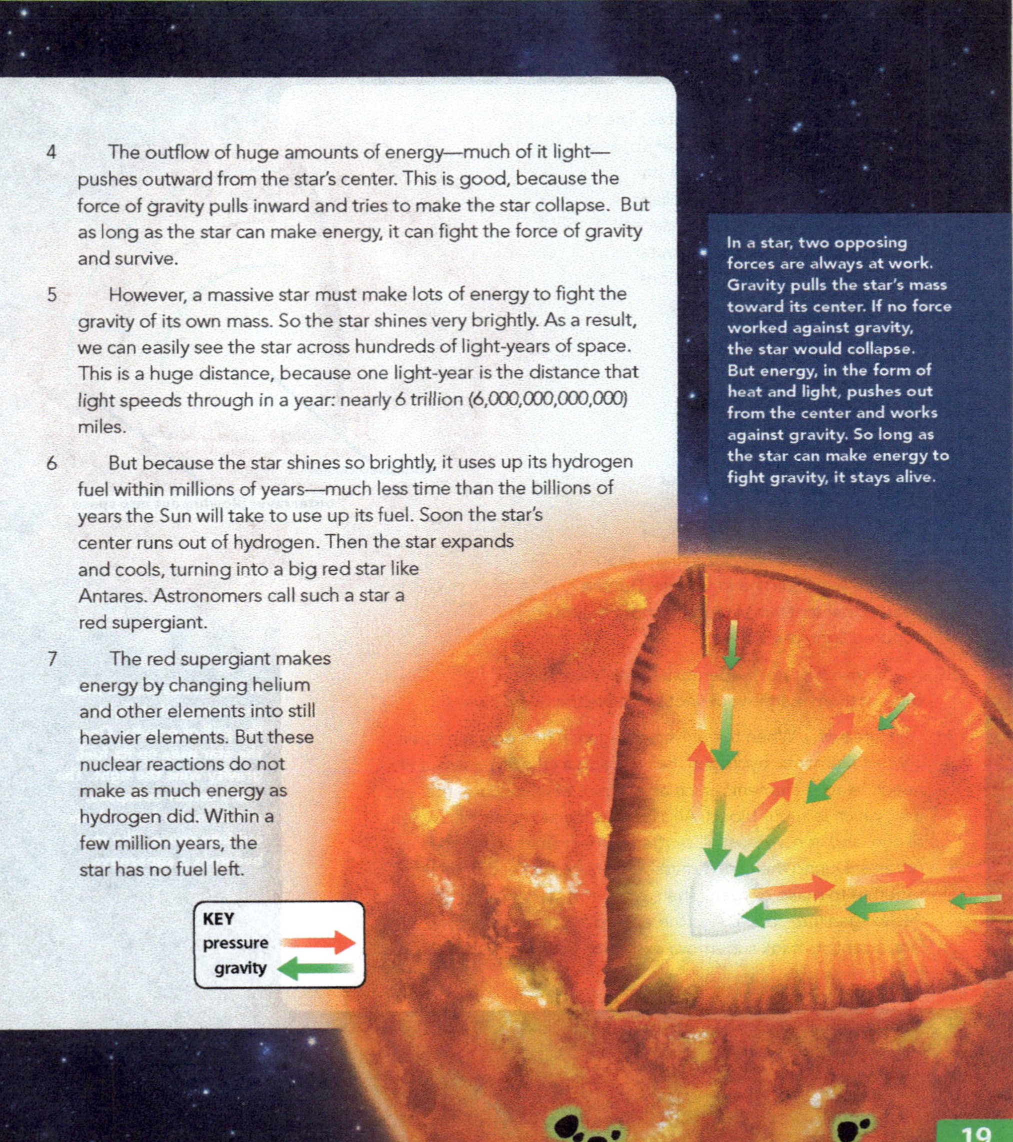

4 The outflow of huge amounts of energy—much of it light—pushes outward from the star's center. This is good, because the force of gravity pulls inward and tries to make the star collapse. But as long as the star can make energy, it can fight the force of gravity and survive.

5 However, a massive star must make lots of energy to fight the gravity of its own mass. So the star shines very brightly. As a result, we can easily see the star across hundreds of light-years of space. This is a huge distance, because one light-year is the distance that light speeds through in a year: nearly 6 trillion (6,000,000,000,000) miles.

6 But because the star shines so brightly, it uses up its hydrogen fuel within millions of years—much less time than the billions of years the Sun will take to use up its fuel. Soon the star's center runs out of hydrogen. Then the star expands and cools, turning into a big red star like Antares. Astronomers call such a star a red supergiant.

7 The red supergiant makes energy by changing helium and other elements into still heavier elements. But these nuclear reactions do not make as much energy as hydrogen did. Within a few million years, the star has no fuel left.

In a star, two opposing forces are always at work. Gravity pulls the star's mass toward its center. If no force worked against gravity, the star would collapse. But energy, in the form of heat and light, pushes out from the center and works against gravity. So long as the star can make energy to fight gravity, it stays alive.

Monitor Understanding

If... students struggle to read and understand the passage,

then... use these scaffolding suggestions:

Question the Text Preview the text by asking the following questions:

- **Based on the title and the diagrams, what do you predict the article will be about?**
- **What questions do you have about the text?**

Vocabulary Support Define words that may interfere with comprehension, such as *mass, massive, energy*, and *elements*.

Read Aloud Read aloud the text with students. You could also have students chorally read the text in a small group.

Check Understanding Use the questions below to check understanding. Encourage students to cite details in the text that support their answers.

- **When does a supernova take place?** *(when a massive star explodes)*
- **What is the article mostly about?** *(the process by which a massive star expands and then explodes, forming a supernova)*

Independent Practice

Integrating Standards

After students have read the article, use these questions to discuss it with them.

- **What process does this scientific text describe?** *(This text describes how a giant star builds mass until it explodes, forming a supernova.)*
  DOK 1 **RI.5.1**
- **What is the definition of a light-year? What is another way a light-year can be expressed?** *(A light-year is a measurement of distance. It is the distance that light travels in one year. Another way to express a light-year is nearly 6 trillion miles per year.)*
  DOK 2 **RI.5.4**
- **What details help you infer that life would not exist were it not for supernovae?** *(The last paragraph says that "life needs heavier elements, such as oxygen… and iron." It goes on to say that "almost all oxygen came from massive stars." So, I can infer that before supernovae, life didn't exist because the elements needed for life didn't exist. Therefore supernovae must be necessary for life to exist.)*
  DOK 2 **RI.5.1**
- **What evidence does the author present for his claim that the sun will never blow up?** *(The claim is supported by evidence that most supernovae come from massive stars, and the sun is not a massive star.)*
  DOK 3 **RI.5.8**

● **Theme Connection**

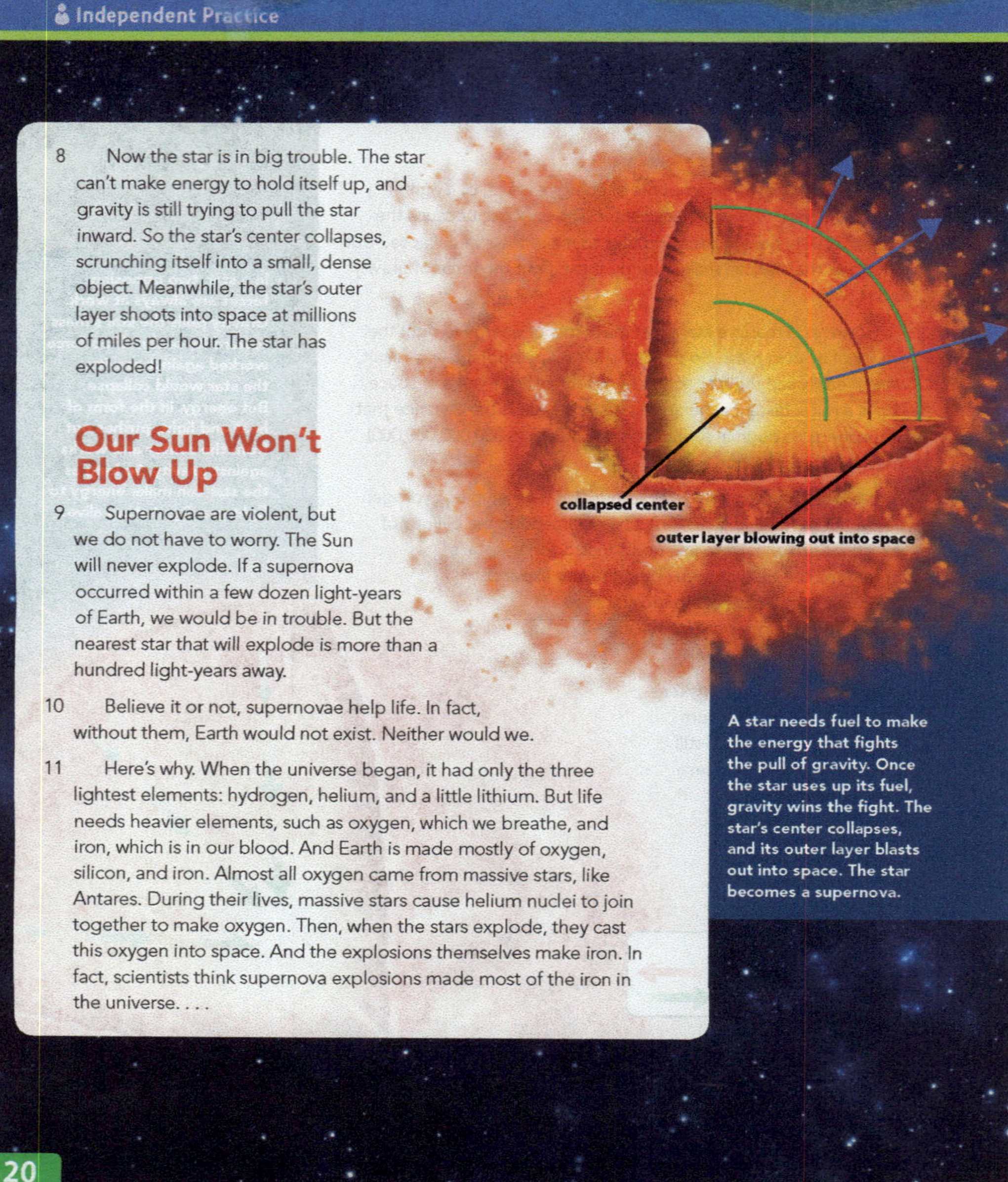

8 Now the star is in big trouble. The star can't make energy to hold itself up, and gravity is still trying to pull the star inward. So the star's center collapses, scrunching itself into a small, dense object. Meanwhile, the star's outer layer shoots into space at millions of miles per hour. The star has exploded!

Our Sun Won't Blow Up

9 Supernovae are violent, but we do not have to worry. The Sun will never explode. If a supernova occurred within a few dozen light-years of Earth, we would be in trouble. But the nearest star that will explode is more than a hundred light-years away.

10 Believe it or not, supernovae help life. In fact, without them, Earth would not exist. Neither would we.

11 Here's why. When the universe began, it had only the three lightest elements: hydrogen, helium, and a little lithium. But life needs heavier elements, such as oxygen, which we breathe, and iron, which is in our blood. And Earth is made mostly of oxygen, silicon, and iron. Almost all oxygen came from massive stars, like Antares. During their lives, massive stars cause helium nuclei to join together to make oxygen. Then, when the stars explode, they cast this oxygen into space. And the explosions themselves make iron. In fact, scientists think supernova explosions made most of the iron in the universe. . . .

A star needs fuel to make the energy that fights the pull of gravity. Once the star uses up its fuel, gravity wins the fight. The star's center collapses, and its outer layer blasts out into space. The star becomes a supernova.

20

● **Theme Connection**

- Remind students that the theme of this lesson is Stars and Planets.
- Ask students to explain how each article in this lesson relates to the theme.
- Have them jot down at least one main idea that they learned from one or more of the articles, along with at least two key details that support each main idea.
- Have students form groups to compare their notes and compile organizers of the main ideas and key details in this lesson. Display the organizers in the classroom.

Think Use what you learned from reading the science article to respond to the following questions.

1 This question has two parts. First, answer Part A. Then answer Part B.

Part A
What are **two** main ideas of the article by Ken Croswell?

- **(A)** Supernovae are violent explosions of stars.
- **B** Astronomers did not always use telescopes.
- **C** Astronomers can see supernovae for months.
- **(D)** Stars make energy through nuclear reactions.
- **E** Stars produce light that travels across the universe.
- **F** Supernovae are interesting for astronomers to study.

Part B
Which **two** sentences from the article **best** support the answer to Part A?

- **A** "The last time people saw a supernova in our galaxy was 1604."
- **B** "That was before astronomers were using telescopes."
- **C** "Such a star is born with more than eight times the mass of the Sun."
- **(D)** "Its center makes energy the same way the Sun does: by changing hydrogen, the lightest element, into helium, the second-lightest element."
- **E** "As a result, we can easily see the star across hundreds of light-years of space."
- **(F)** "If a supernova occurred within a few dozen light-years of Earth, we would be in trouble."

2 Read the following sentence from the text.

> But as long as the star can make energy, it can fight the force of gravity and survive.

Which dictionary entry **best** defines energy?

- **A** physical strength
- **B** hydrogen and helium gas
- **C** heavy metals that increase weight
- **(D)** power that comes from heat

21

Monitor Understanding

If... students struggle to complete the items,

then... you may wish to use the following suggestions:

Read Aloud Activities

- As you read, have students note any unfamiliar words or phrases. Clarify any misunderstandings.
- Discuss each item with students to make certain they understand the expectation.

Reread the Text

- Have students complete a main idea organizer as they reread.
- Have partners summarize the text.

Think

- Use the Monitor Understanding suggestions to support students in completing items 1–3.

Monitor Understanding

Answer Analysis

When students have finished, discuss correct and incorrect responses.

1 **Part A**

The correct choices are A and D. A is a main idea because the entire passage is about supernovae. **D** is a main idea because nuclear reactions are fundamental to how all stars function and why some stars explode as supernovae.

- **B, C, E,** and **F** are supporting details. They are not main ideas because they are not further supported or developed by any other details in the passage.

DOK 2 **RI.5.2**

Part B

The correct choices are D and F. D is a key detail supporting the main idea stated in Part A, Choice D, about nuclear reactions. This key detail describes the nuclear reaction that takes place within a star. **F** is a key detail supporting the main idea stated in Part A, Choice A, about supernovae being violent explosions of stars. This key detail provides an example of the intensity of that violence.

- **A, B, C,** and **E** are all incorrect because they are not key details that directly support the main ideas that appear in Part A.

2 **The correct choice is D.** In the sentence context, the star is creating power to fight gravity and survive.

- **A, B,** and **C** are not reasonable definitions of energy and are not supported by the context of the sentence.

DOK 1 **RI.5.2**

Independent Practice

3 **See the answers on the student book page.** Discuss students' responses to make sure they understand the main ideas and key details. Remind students that this item simulates drag-and-drop items they may see on a computer-based assessment.

***DOK 2* RI.5.2**

3 In the chart below, only **two** sentences are actually main ideas of the article. Identify those main ideas. Copy them in the rows titled "Main Idea 1" and "Main Idea 2" in the charts at the bottom of the page.

Possible Main Ideas	
In 1604, a supernova exploded.	Antares is a massive star.
Supernovae make important elements.	Only some stars will become supernovae.
Astronomers did not always use telescopes.	Hydrogen is the lightest element.

Now study this chart. It contains supporting details from the article. Choose **one** detail that **best** supports **each** main idea you chose. In the charts at the bottom of the page, write each detail below the main idea it supports.

Possible Supporting Details	
"The last time people saw a supernova in our galaxy was 1604."	"And the explosions themselves produce iron."
"However, every year astronomers see supernovae exploding in other galaxies."	"The outflow of huge amounts of energy—much of it light—pushes outward from the star's center."
"The Sun will never explode."	"This nuclear reaction creates energy that heats the star and makes it shine."

Main Idea 1	**Supernovae make important elements.**
Supporting Detail	**"And the explosions themselves produce iron."**

Main Idea 2	**Only some stars will become supernovae.**
Supporting Detail	**"The Sun will never explode."**

22

Monitor Understanding

If... students don't understand the writing task,

then... read aloud the writing prompt. Use the following questions to help students get started.

- **What is the prompt asking you to write about?**
- **Do you need to reread the text to find more information?**
- **How will you identify the information you need to include?**

- Have partners talk about how they will organize their responses.
- Provide a graphic organizer to assist students, if needed.

 Write

4 **Short Response** Reread paragraphs 6, 7, and 8. What is the author's main idea in these paragraphs? Use key details from these paragraphs to support your answer.

Sample response: The author's main idea is that a massive star shines very brightly, but it lives and dies quickly compared to other stars. Shining brightly uses up the hydrogen fuel inside the star. The center of the star begins to run out of the fuel. It expands and cools. Eventually it collapses and explodes.

 Learning Target

In this lesson, you determined the main ideas of texts and explained how key details supported them. Describe how these skills will help you understand other informational texts.

Responses will vary, but students should recognize that identifying main ideas and explaining how key details support them helps them develop a deeper understanding of the text.

4 2-Point Writing Rubric

Points	Focus	Evidence	Organization
2	My answer does exactly what the prompt asked me to do.	My answer is supported with plenty of details from the text.	My ideas are clear and in a logical order.
1	Some of my answer does not relate to the prompt.	My answer is missing some important details from the text.	Some of my ideas are unclear and out of order.
0	My answer does not make sense.	My answer does not have any details from the text.	My ideas are unclear and not in any order.

Write

- Tell students that using what they read, they will plan and compose a short response to the writing prompt.

Monitor Understanding

Review Responses

After students have completed each part of the writing activity, help them evaluate their responses.

4 Display or pass out copies of the reproducible **2-Point Writing Rubric** on p. TR10. Have students use the rubric to individually assess their writing and revise as needed.

When students have finished their revisions, evaluate their responses. Answers will vary but should summarize the process by which a supernova forms. See the sample response on the student book page.

DOK 3 **RI.5.2, W.5.9b**

Wrap Up

Learning Target

- Have each student respond in writing to the Learning Target prompt.
- When students have finished, have them share their responses. This may be done with a partner, in small groups, or as a whole class.

Lesson 2
Summarizing Informational Texts

Standards Focus

. . . summarize the text. RI.5.2

Lesson Objectives

Reading

- Identify main ideas and key details. RI.5.2
- Use main ideas and key details to summarize a text. RI.5.2

Writing

- Draw evidence from informational texts to support analysis and reflection. W.5.9b

Speaking and Listening

- Pose and respond to specific questions and contribute to discussions. SL.5.1c
- Review the key ideas expressed and draw conclusions. SL.5.1d

Language

- Use context as a clue to the meaning of a word or phrase. L.5.4a
- Acquire and use academic and domain-specific words and phrases. L.5.6

Additional Practice: **RI.5.1, RI.5.3, RI.5.4, RI.5.7, RI.5.9, SL.5.1, L.5.5b**

Academic Talk

See **Glossary of Terms**, pp. TR2–TR9

- main idea
- key detail
- summarize

Learning Progression

Grade 4	Grade 5	Grade 6
Students synthesize information to produce a summary of key details.	Building on Grade 4, students determine the main idea and details of a text to produce a summary.	Grade 6 increases in complexity by requiring students to bring together two or more main ideas and use key details and sequencing when summarizing a text.

Lesson Text Selections

Modeled and Guided Instruction

A Portrait of Frida Kahlo
by Gene Erskine
Genre: Biography

Guided Practice

Cesar Chavez
by José Hernandez
Genre: Biography

Independent Practice

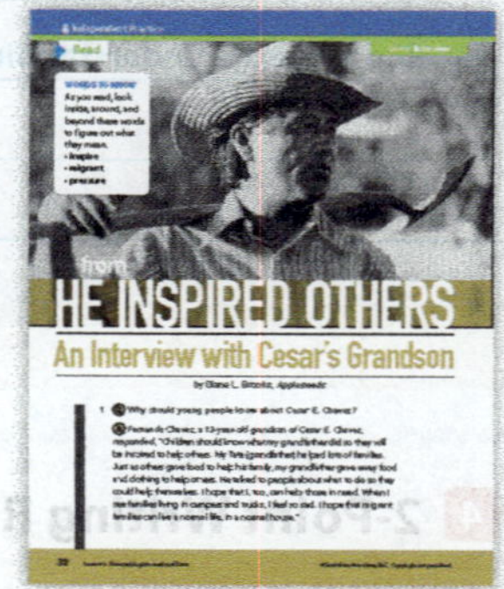

He Inspired Others: An Interview with Cesar's Grandson
by Diane L. Brooks
Genre: Interview

Lesson Pacing Guide

Whole Class Instruction *30–45 minutes per day*

Day 1

Teacher-Toolbox.com **Interactive Tutorial**
Summarize—Level E
20 min (optional)

Introduction pp. 24–25
- **Read** **Summarizing Informational Texts** *10 min*
- **Think** *10 min*
  Graphic Organizer: Main Idea Organizer
- **Talk** *5 min*
  Quick Write (TRB) *5 min*

Day 2

Modeled and Guided Instruction pp. 26–27, 30
- **Read** **A Portrait of Frida Kahlo** *10 min*
- **Think** *10 min*
  Graphic Organizer: Main Idea Organizer
- **Talk** *5 min*
- **Write** Short Response *10 min*

Day 3

Guided Practice pp. 28–29, 31
- **Read** **Cesar Chavez** *10 min*
- **Think** *10 min*
- **Talk** *5 min*
- **Write** Short Response *10 min*

Day 4

Independent Practice pp. 32–37
- **Read** **He Inspired Others: An Interview with Cesar's Grandson** *15 min*
- **Think** *10 min*
- **Write** Short Response *10 min*

Day 5

Independent Practice pp. 32–37
- *Review* Answer Analysis (TRB) *10 min*
- *Review* Response Analysis (TRB) *10 min*
- *Assign and Discuss* Learning Target *10 min*

Language Handbook
Lesson 16 Greek and Latin Word Parts, pp. 468–469
20 min (optional)

Ready Writing Connection

During *Ready Reading* Days 1–5, use:
Lesson 1 Writing an Opinion: Letter to the Editor

- **Step 1 Study a Mentor Text**
- **Step 2 Unpack Your Assignment**
- **Review the Research Path**
- **Read Source Text**
- **Step 3 Find Text Evidence**
- **Reread Source Text**

See *Ready Writing TRB*, p. 1a for complete lesson plan.

Small Group Differentiation
Teacher-Toolbox.com

Reteach

***Ready Reading* Prerequisite Lesson**
- **Grade 4** Lesson 5 Summarizing Informational Texts

Teacher-led Activities

Tools for Instruction
- Summarize Informational Text

Personalized Learning
i-Ready.com

Independent

i-Ready Close Reading Lessons

- **Grade 4** Summarizing Informational Texts
- **Grade 5** Summarizing Informational Texts

Introduction

Get Started

- Explain to students that in this lesson they will read passages about people who made a big cultural impact, and they will use main ideas and key details to summarize the texts.
- Use a familiar example to review the concept of summarizing. Guide students to recall that a good summary is brief and includes only the most important ideas and details. Explain:

  When you tell a friend about an event, such as a soccer game, you tell only the most important details. You might say, "The team was losing until the very end, when they scored two goals to win the game." You would leave out less important details like what time the game started and ended.
- Focus students' attention on the Learning Target. Read it aloud to set the purpose for the lesson.
- Display the Academic Talk words and phrases. Tell students to listen for these terms and their meanings as you work through the lesson together. Use the Academic Talk Routine on pp. A48–A49.

English Language Learners

- Genre Focus

Read

- Read aloud the Read section as students follow along. Restate to reinforce:

  When you read informational texts, it's helpful to pause and think about what information is really important. You can ask yourself what a paragraph or a section of the text is mostly about. Identifying the main idea and key details will help you summarize the text, or tell about it briefly in your own words.
- Have students read the passage. Remind them to think carefully about the most important details they would include in a summary.

Introduction RI.5.2

Lesson 2
Summarizing Informational Texts

Identifying the main idea and key details in a text will help you summarize it. Summarizing a text helps you better understand it.

Read When you tell your friends about a soccer game, you don't want to bore them with every detail. Instead, you tell only the most important events, leaving out the parts that aren't necessary for understanding what happened.

Similarly, when you **summarize** a text, you should use your own words to tell a short but complete version of that text. Include only the **main idea** (the big idea) and the **key details** that say more about the main idea.

Read the passage below. Identify what the passage is about.

LET'S PLAY FUTEBOL!

The most popular sport in Brazil is futebol, also known as soccer. As of 2015, the Brazilian national team has won the World Cup more times than any other country. Brazil is known for its many champion soccer players, including Pelé, often called the best soccer player ever. Most Brazilian cities, towns, schools, and neighborhoods have local soccer teams. In Brazil, children quickly turn any open space or patch of dirt into a soccer field.

24

English Language Learners

Build Meaning

Background Knowledge Provide context about the game of soccer that students could not learn from reading the passage. Explain:

Soccer is a game played on a field by two teams. Each team tries to kick a ball into the other team's net.

- Use visual aids such as photographs or a brief video to illustrate, and invite students to share their understanding of or experience with the game.
- Explain that the World Cup is a series of games played by the best soccer teams in the world. It happens every four years. The World Cup champion is the best soccer team in the world.
- Point out cognates for the terms *national* and *champion*. Ask students to provide meanings for each word.

Genre Focus

Interview

Explain that during Independent Practice, students will read a type of informational text called an interview. An interview is a recorded conversation between two people. One person asks questions and the other person answers them.

Interviews are often seen on TV news, when a journalist speaks with another person to get that person's opinions about events or issues. In magazines, interviews often appear in written form. The interviewer's questions are printed along with the answers of the person being interviewed.

Provide some examples of interviews printed in magazines, such as *Time* or *Newsweek*, or clips from interviews on local news.

Think Consider what you've learned so far about summarizing a text. In the *main idea organizer* below, add two key details from the passage "Let's Play Futebol!" Then use the organizer to complete the summary of the passage.

Main Idea
Soccer is the most popular sport in Brazil.

First Key Detail	Second Key Detail	Third Key Detail
The Brazilian national soccer team is a world champion.	Brazil is known for its champion soccer players like Pelé.	Brazilian cities, towns, and neighborhoods all have soccer teams.

Summary: Soccer is the most popular sport in Brazil. For example, the Brazilian national soccer team is a world champion. In addition, Brazil is known for its champion soccer players like Pelé. Cities, towns, schools, and neighborhoods all have soccer teams.

Talk Share your main idea organizer and summary with a partner.

- What relationships do you see between your organizers and summaries?
- Do your second and third key details develop the main idea? How do you know?
- Could any key details in the organizer be stated differently?

Academic Talk
Use these words and phrases to talk about the text.
- main idea
- key detail
- summarize

Monitor Understanding

If... students struggle to identify the main idea and key details, **then...** provide a visual aid. Display a picture with many details, such as two teams in action. Ask:

- **What is this picture all about?** *(a soccer game)*
- **What key details help you understand the main idea?** *(One player kicks a soccer ball. The players wear uniforms. There is a goal at the end of the field.)*
- **Describe what is happening in the picture.** *(Two teams are playing soccer, and one player is kicking the ball toward the goal.)*

Explain to students that by telling the important details of what is happening in the picture, they are giving a summary of the events. Ask students to provide example summaries based on pictures displayed in the classroom or pictures chosen for this purpose.

Think

- Have students read aloud the Think section. Explain that the main idea organizer will help them record their ideas.
- Have partners complete the main idea organizer. Remind students that each key detail must tell more about the main idea.
- As students work, circulate and provide assistance as needed.
- Ask volunteers to share what they wrote in their main idea organizers. Then have students complete the summary.
- Make certain students understand that a summary includes the main idea and key details. It should be short and stated in their own words.

Talk

- Read aloud the Talk prompts.
- Have partners discuss why the summary needs to contain all these details to make sense.
- Ask volunteers to share their ideas.

Quick Write Have students write a response to the following prompt:

Think about an interesting or unusual experience you had recently. Summarize your experience by telling the main idea and key details of what happened.

Ask students to share their responses.

Wrap Up

- Invite students to share what they've learned so far. Encourage them to use the Academic Talk words and phrases in their explanations.
- Remind students that when they read informational texts, they should look for important ideas and details. These will help them summarize information and better understand and remember what they read.

In the next section, we'll read a biography and practice summarizing the information. Summarizing helps you pick out the main idea and key details that are important to remember.

Monitor Understanding

Modeled and Guided Instruction

Get Started

Today you will read a biography. First, you'll read to find the main idea and key details. Then you will work to summarize the most important ideas in your own words.

Read

- Read aloud the title of the passage and call attention to the illustration. Invite students to share their understanding of the word *portrait*.
- Have students read the article independently. Tell them to place a check mark above any confusing words and phrases as they read. Remind students to look inside, around, and beyond each unknown word to help them figure out its meaning. Use the Word Learning Routine on pp. A50–A51.
- When students have finished reading, clarify the meanings of words and phrases they still find confusing. Then use the questions below to check understanding. Encourage students to identify details in the text that support their answers.

  Who was Frida Kahlo? *(an artist)*

  How did Kahlo communicate her feelings and ideas? *(She expressed her pain and some of the events in her life through her self-portraits.)*

  Why did Kahlo begin to paint self-portraits? *(She was alone most of the time after her accident and she was the subject she knew best.)*

English Language Learners

● Word Learning Strategy

Explore

- Read aloud the Explore question at the top of p. 27 to set the purpose for the second read. Tell students they will need to take a closer look at what the details are mostly about to answer this question.
- Have students read aloud the Close Reader Habit on p. 26.

TIP Suggest that students distinguish important details from unimportant ones by asking themselves, "Would my summary make sense if I left out this detail?"

Modeled and Guided Instruction

Read Genre: Biography

A Portrait of FRIDA KAHLO

by Gene Erskine

1 In September 1925, a bus in Mexico City was in a terrible accident. One passenger, an 18-year-old woman, was hurt so badly that she had to stay in bed for three months. Looking for a task to occupy her mind, she decided to paint pictures. This is how Frida Kahlo, one of the most famous Mexican artists of the 20th century, began her career.

2 Kahlo produced more than 150 paintings during her life. Of those, 55 were self-portraits, for which she is best known. In the paintings, Kahlo has brown skin, black hair, thick eyebrows, and a faint mustache. She often wears brightly colored traditional Mexican blouses and skirts. She usually gazes confidently at the viewer. Kahlo explained, "I paint myself because I am so often alone and because I am the subject I know best."

3 For Kahlo, a self-portrait was a way to communicate ideas. For example, Kahlo's injuries from the bus accident left her in pain all her life. So, some of her self-portraits express this discomfort. Others depict events in her life. For instance, in the early 1930s, Kahlo lived in the United States. She was homesick, so she painted herself standing between Mexican flowers and buildings on one side and American factories and skyscrapers on the other. The painting showed how she felt: torn between where she was living and where she wanted to be. Not all of Kahlo's self-portraits have such a clear message. Some are like painted dreams, with Kahlo before tropical plants and surrounded by spider monkeys, parrots, and cats. For Kahlo, a self-portrait could express whatever she wanted.

4 Frida Kahlo died in 1954. During her life, she had traveled the world, impressed famous artists, and taught painting to college students in Mexico. As she told her students, "To paint is the most terrific thing that there is, but to do it well is very difficult." Lovers of her art believe that Frida Kahlo painted very well, indeed.

Close Reader Habits

When you reread the biography, **underline** key details that develop the main idea about Kahlo and her art.

26

English Language Learners

Build Language

- **Concept Vocabulary** Display images of famous self-portraits that are available online, such as Kahlo's *Self Portrait with Thorn Necklace and Hummingbird* or Pablo Picasso's 1901 *Self-Portrait.* Display accompanying photographs of the artist who is the subject of each portrait. Have students describe what they see and together determine a meaning for *self-portrait.*
- Invite students to share their experiences with seeing or creating art. Emphasize that quite often, art represents the artist's feelings or ideas. Have them tell what they learned about the ideas or feelings in some of Kahlo's paintings from "A Portrait of Frida Kahlo."

● Word Learning Strategy

Use Context Clues

- Direct students' attention to the line "I am the subject I know best" in paragraph 2.

  What are some meanings of *subject*? Guide students to define *subject* as "a course of study" or "a person or thing being focused on or discussed."

  What does *subject* mean here?
- Prompt students to test both definitions in the sentence and ask themselves, "Does the meaning make sense?" They should understand that in this sentence, the word *subject* refers to Frida Kahlo, the person who is the focus of the painting.

  L.5.4a

Explore What is most important to know about Frida Kahlo and her art?

Some texts state a main idea directly. Other texts let the reader figure it out from the details.

Think

1 Complete the main idea organizer below. Include three key details that you underlined in the passage.

Main Idea

Frida Kahlo, a famous Mexican artist, is best known for her self-portraits.

First Key Detail	Second Key Detail	Third Key Detail
When Kahlo had to stay in bed after an accident, she was alone much of the time and began painting.	She painted self-portraits because she was the subject she knew best.	Some self-portraits convey her physical discomfort and life events, but others are like painted dreams.

Talk

2 Share your organizers. Do you agree about the main idea of the passage? What about the key details? Make any changes to your organizers that will help you write an accurate and complete summary.

Write

3 **Short Response** Summarize what you learned about Frida Kahlo and her art. Include key details from the text in your summary. Use the space provided on page 30 to write your answer.

HINT Link key details to the main idea by using phrases such as "for example" and "for instance."

27

Think Aloud

- To answer the Explore question, I need to figure out which details are the most important about Frida Kahlo and her art.
- Sentences in a paragraph work together to develop an idea, so let me reread the whole first paragraph.
- The last sentence in paragraph 1 really catches my attention. "This is how Frida Kahlo, one of the most famous Mexican artists of the 20th century, began her career." That seems really important! So which details in this paragraph lead up to this statement?
- There is a smaller detail in each sentence before that one: there was a bus accident; a young woman was forced to stay in bed for three months; she painted to occupy her mind. Together, these details tell me how Frida began her famous career. In the box for *First Key Detail*, I'll write "When Kahlo had to stay in bed after an accident, she was alone much of the time and began painting." Notice how I combined and restated all of those smaller details into one.

Think

- Read aloud the Think section. Explain that you will model how to find text evidence to fill in part of the main idea organizer. Use the **Think Aloud** below to guide your modeling.
- Revisit the Explore question. Guide students to determine that they need to look for more details, using the Close Reader Habit.
- Encourage students to work with a partner to continue rereading the passage and complete the main idea organizer. Remind them to read the Buddy Tip.
- Ask volunteers to share their completed charts.
- Guide students to see that it is often necessary to determine the important details first and then figure out what they have in common to determine the main idea.

Talk

- Read aloud the Talk prompt.
- Have partners respond to the prompt. Use the Talk Routine on pp. A52–A53.
- Circulate to check that students are comparing their main ideas about Frida Kahlo and key details that tell why she began painting, why she painted self-portraits, and what her self-portraits show.

Write

- Ask a volunteer to read aloud the Write prompt.
- Invite a few students to tell what the prompt is asking them to do.
- Make sure students understand that they need to summarize what they learned in their own words, based on the details from their main idea organizer.
- Have students turn to p. 30 to write their response.
- Use Review Responses on p. 30 to assess students' writing.

Wrap Up

- Ask students to recall the Learning Target. Have them explain how identifying the main idea and key details helped them summarize this biography.

Guided Practice

Get Started

Today you will read another biography. First you will read to understand what the text is about. Then you will reread with a partner to summarize the main idea and key details.

Read

- Read aloud the title of the passage. Remind students that biographies are usually about people who have done something important or extraordinary in their lives.
- **Read to Understand** Have students read the article independently. Tell them to place a check mark above any confusing words and phrases as they read. Remind students to look inside, around, and beyond each unknown word to help them figure out its meaning. Use the Word Learning Routine on pp. A50–A51.
- When students have finished reading, clarify the meanings of words and phrases they still find confusing. Then use the questions below to check understanding. Encourage students to identify details in the text that support their answers.

  Who was Cesar Chavez? *(Cesar Chavez was an important labor leader who grew up in a family of migrant workers. He worked hard to improve the lives of farm workers.)*

  Why did Chavez want to organize farm workers? *(He wanted to get them to work together for higher pay and safer working conditions.)*

  How did Chavez try to bring about nonviolent change? *(He fasted and organized strikes, marches, and boycotts.)*

● **Word Learning Strategy**

- **Read to Analyze** Read aloud the Close Reader Habit on p. 28 to set the purpose for the second read. Then have students reread the biography with a partner and discuss any questions they might have.

TIP To help students who have difficulty distinguishing the main idea, guide them to stop after each paragraph and ask themselves what the paragraph was mostly about.

Guided Practice

Read

Genre: Biography

CESAR CHAVEZ

by José Hernandez

1 Cesar Estrada Chavez was an important labor leader. He fought for the rights of migrant farm workers in the United States. Chavez knew firsthand of the many hardships farm workers faced. When Chavez was a young boy, his family lost their farm during the Great Depression. The Chavez family became migrant workers, toiling side by side for long hours in the fields. At night, they slept in a tent or outside. Like other migrant workers, they moved from farm to farm, following the harvest seasons of the vineyards and fruit orchards in California.

2 In 1962, Chavez founded the National Farm Workers Association (NFWA) to fight for *La Causa*—the cause. By organizing farm workers into a union, Chavez hoped to increase their wages. He also hoped to improve working conditions and safety for farm workers. Chavez strongly believed that this cause could be achieved. In fact, his motto was "Yes, it can be done!"

3 Chavez believed in bringing about change in nonviolent ways. He fasted, or went without eating, to bring attention to the poor treatment of farm workers. He organized strikes and marches. He also organized boycotts, which urged people to stop buying certain products. Two of Chavez's most effective boycotts were against grapes and lettuce. When people stopped buying grapes and lettuce, the boycotts put economic pressure on the growers. These boycotts also brought attention to the plight of migrant farm workers. Because of Chavez's dedicated efforts, migrant farm workers received better pay and working conditions.

Close Reader Habits

What did Chavez do to improve conditions for migrant workers? Reread the biography. **Underline** key details that show what he did.

28

English Language Learners

Develop Language

Multiple-meaning Words Call attention to the expression "fought for the rights" in paragraph 1.

- Point out that *right* can be an adjective, a noun, or a verb. Invite students to share known meanings of the word, such as "correct" (e.g., That is the right answer.) and "the opposite of left" (e.g., Hold out your right hand.) Clarify that these are both adjectives.
- Explain that when used as a noun, a *right* is something one deserves to have, no matter what. To demonstrate, provide some familiar examples of rights, such as the right to education or free speech.
- Have students explain what rights Caesar Chavez fought for.

● Word Learning Strategy

Use Context Clues

- Read aloud the last sentence in paragraph 1.

  What does the word *migrant* mean here? *(a person who moves from one place to another when the seasons change)*

  What clues help you figure out the meaning? *("they moved from farm to farm, following the harvest seasons")*

- Explain that the meaning of unfamiliar words can often be figured out by using the *context*, or other words in the sentence or in the surrounding sentences. In this example, Chavez is compared to other migrant workers who moved around.

L.5.4a

Think Use what you learned from reading the biography to respond to the following questions.

A summary of a biography includes only key details of a person's life. To decide which details to use, choose the ones that develop the main idea of the biography.

1 Which statement is **most** important to include in a summary of the passage "Cesar Chavez"?

A Like other migrant workers, Chavez moved from farm to farm.
B The Chavez family often slept in a tent or outdoors at night.
C "Yes, it can be done!" was Chavez's motto.
(D) Chavez brought about change in nonviolent ways.

2 Select the **two** sentences that should be included in a summary of paragraph 1.

(A) Chavez was an important labor leader.
B Chavez had a difficult childhood.
C As a boy, Chavez often slept in a tent or outside.
D The Chavez family followed the harvest seasons in California.
(E) Chavez fought for the rights of farm workers.
F Chavez worked hard after his family lost their farm.

3 Which is **most** important to put in a summary of how Chavez helped others?

A ". . . his family lost their farm. . . ."
B ". . . they moved from farm to farm. . . ."
C ". . . strongly believed that this cause could be achieved."
(D) ". . . migrant farm workers received better pay. . . ."

Talk

4 What is the main idea of the passage? What key details develop that main idea? Use the organizer on page 31 to gather your information.

Write

5 **Short Response** Summarize the passage. Include key details from your organizer in your summary. Use the space provided on page 31 to write your answer.

HINT Make sure you have figured out the main idea of the *whole* passage.

29

Integrating Standards

Use these questions to further students' understanding of the text.

- **How did Chavez's background influence his decision to help migrant farm workers?** *(He grew up in a family of migrant farm workers, so he understood their hardships.)* **DOK 2 RI.5.3**
- **Why were boycotts against grapes and lettuce an effective way to bring about change?** *(When people stopped buying grapes and lettuce, the farmers who grew those crops couldn't make money. This motivated the farmers to hear the workers' demands.)* **DOK 3 RI.5.1**

Monitor Understanding

If... students have difficulty determining the main idea,

then... create a three-column chart with the headings *Paragraph 1, Paragraph 2,* and *Paragraph 3.* Invite students to reread each paragraph and identify key details. Record them in the appropriate column.

Work with students to look across the columns and find similarities. Help them see that information in each column pertains to Chavez's mission to improve the lives and working conditions of migrant farm workers. Reinforce that this is the main idea of the passage.

Think

- Have students work with a partner to complete items 1–3. Draw attention to the boldface words in each item.

Answer Analysis

When students have finished, discuss correct and incorrect responses.

1 **The correct choice is D.** It sums up how Chavez brought about change.

- **A, B,** and **C** present details from the text but are not key details that develop the main idea.

DOK 2

2 **The correct choices are A and E.** They describe Chavez's importance to the labor movement.

- **B, C, D,** and **F** are all details in the biography, but they do not directly relate to how Chavez inspired others and fought for workers' rights.

DOK 2

3 **The correct choice is D.** This detail shows the outcome of Chavez's efforts to help others.

- **A, B,** and **C** are important details about Chavez's life but they do not support the main idea of how he helped people.

DOK 2

- **Integrating Standards**

Talk

- Have partners discuss the prompt. Emphasize that students should support their ideas with text details.
- Circulate to clarify misunderstandings.

- **Monitor Understanding**

Write

- See p. 31 for instructional guidance.

Wrap Up

- Ask students to recall the Learning Target. Have them explain how identifying the main idea and key details helped them summarize this text.

Modeled and Guided Instruction

Write

- Remember to use the Response-Writing Routine on pp. A54–A55.

Review Responses

After students complete the writing activity, help them evaluate their responses.

3 Responses may vary but should include the main idea and key details from the biography of Frida Kahlo. See the sample response on the student book page.
DOK 3

Write Use the space below to write your answer to the question on page 27.

A Portrait of FRIDA KAHLO

HINT Link key details to the main idea by using phrases such as "for example" and "for instance."

3 **Short Response** Summarize what you learned about Frida Kahlo and her art. Include key details from the text in your summary.

Sample response: Frida Kahlo, a famous Mexican artist, is best known for her self-portraits. When Kahlo had to stay in bed after an accident, she was alone much of the time and began painting. She painted self-portraits because she was the subject she knew best. For example, some self-portraits convey her physical discomfort and life events. But others are like painted dreams. For instance, she shows herself in front of tropical plants and surrounded by animals such as spider monkeys and parrots.

Check Your Writing

- ☐ Did you read the prompt carefully?
- ☐ Did you put the prompt in your own words?
- ☐ Did you use the best evidence from the text to support your ideas?
- ☐ Are your ideas clearly organized?
- ☐ Did you write in clear and complete sentences?
- ☐ Did you check your spelling and punctuation?

30

Scaffolding Support for Reluctant Writers

If students are having a difficult time getting started, use the strategies below. Work individually with struggling students, or have students work with partners.

- Circle the verbs in the prompt that tell you what to do, such as *describe*, *explain*, or *compare*.
- Underline words and phrases in the prompt that show what information you need to provide in your response, such as *causes*, *reasons*, or *character traits*.
- Talk about the details from the text that you will include in your response.
- Explain aloud how you will respond to the prompt.

CESAR CHAVEZ

4 Use the main idea organizer below to organize your ideas and evidence.

Main Idea		
First Key Detail	Second Key Detail	Third Key Detail

Write Use the space below to write your answer to the question on page 29.

HINT Make sure you have figured out the main idea of the *whole* passage.

5 **Short Response** Summarize the passage. Include key details from your organizer in your summary.

Sample response: Cesar Chavez was an important leader in the fight for the rights of migrant farm workers. He understood the hardships migrant workers faced because he had been a migrant worker. He started a labor union to work for better pay and safer conditions for farm workers. He helped bring about change in nonviolent ways.

Teacher Notes

Talk

4 Students should use the organizer to record their thoughts and evidence.

Write

- Ask a volunteer to read aloud the Write prompt.
- Invite students to tell what the prompt is asking them to do. Make sure they understand that they need to retell the main idea in their own words and use key details from their organizers to support the main idea.
- Call attention to the HINT.
- Remember to use the Response-Writing Routine on pp. A54–A55.

Review Responses

After students complete the writing activity, help them evaluate their responses.

5 Responses may vary but should show an understanding of Cesar Chavez's effect on the labor movement and organization of farm workers for better pay and working conditions. See the sample response on the student book page.
DOK 3

Independent Practice

Get Started

Today you are going to read an interview with Cesar Chavez's grandson and use what you have learned about identifying the main idea and key details to help you summarize the text.

- Ask a volunteer to explain why summarizing helps readers better understand informational texts. Encourage students to use the Academic Talk words and phrases in their response.

 **English Language Learners**

Read

You are going to read the interview independently and use what you have learned to think and write about the text. As you read, remember to look closely at the key details in order to identify the main idea.

- Read aloud the title of the interview and then encourage students to preview the text, paying close attention to the photographs, captions, and the question-and-answer format.
- Call attention to the Words to Know in the upper left of p. 32.
- If students need support in reading the passage, you may wish to use the Monitor Understanding suggestions.
- When students have finished, have them complete the Think and Write sections.

● **Monitor Understanding**

Independent Practice

Read

Genre: Interview

WORDS TO KNOW
As you read, look inside, around, and beyond these words to figure out what they mean.
- **inspire**
- **migrant**
- **pressure**

from
HE INSPIRED OTHERS
An Interview with Cesar's Grandson
by Diane L. Brooks, *Appleseeds*

1 **Q Why should young people know about Cesar E. Chavez?**

A *Fernando Chavez, a 13-year-old grandson of Cesar E. Chavez, responded,* "Children should know what my grandfather did so they will be inspired to help others. My Tata (grandfather) helped lots of families. Just as others gave food to help his family, my grandfather gave away food and clothing to help others. He talked to people about what to do so they could help themselves. I hope that I, too, can help those in need. When I see families living in campers and trucks, I feel so sad. I hope that migrant families can live a normal life, in a normal house."

32

 **English Language Learners**

Build Meaning

Text Features Guide students to preview the interview "He Inspired Others." Have them point out text features that can help them understand the text, such as the photographs, boldface type, and captions.

Discuss what is unusual about the way this text is organized. Make sure students understand that the interviewer asked the questions, and the answers are Fernando Chavez's responses. Then ask:

- **What do you predict the interview will be about?**
- **What questions do you have about the text?**

List students' questions, and encourage them to seek answers to these questions as they read.

2 Q **What do you remember about your grandfather?**

A "I had a birthday, then just three days after, Grandfather died. Many, many people came to pray and give final thanks for all that he had done for them. My dad reminds me that on that day, I took my sandwich and went to eat it by his graveside; my last moments with Tata. My family and I really miss him, especially at Christmastime. Tata loved being with his (33) grandchildren. My grandfather also loved his dogs. He had two German shepherds, guard dogs, called Huelga (the Spanish word for "strike") and Boycott, and later, another named Oso. They are buried near him."

3 Q **What stories do you remember about Cesar E. Chavez?**

A "I remember stories about my grandfather's courage and bravery. He gave a lot of speeches, and he helped a lot of people. There were stories about hard work in the fields, and terrible things like farmers with guns, people trying to tear the Union apart, and racism—people yelling names. I'm grateful that I don't have to go through that. These stories make me want to stand up and do something when I am older and braver. I will stand up! But I have also learned from my grandfather that the best way to solve a problem is to talk it out. These stories mean a lot to me, and I'm inspired to help those who go through tough times. And there are still problems—people with no place to live, boycotts, and problems with contracts between farmers and workers."

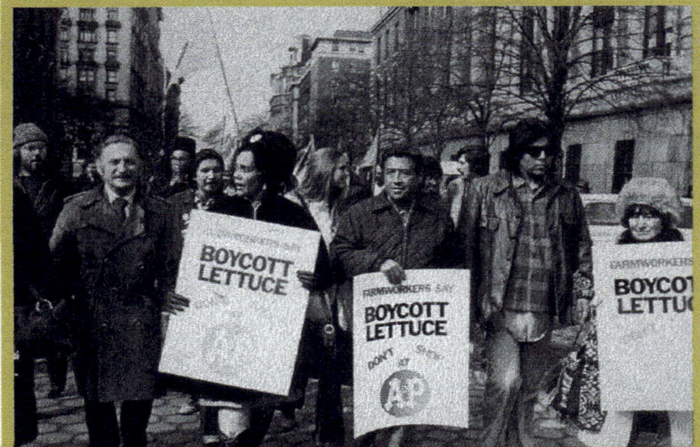

Cesar Chavez and Coretta Scott King (the wife of Martin Luther King, Jr.) lead a march in New York City in 1973.

Monitor Understanding

If... students struggle to read and understand the passage,
then... use these scaffolding suggestions:

Question the Text Preview the text by asking the following questions:

- **What types of text features has the author included?** *(photographs, boldface type, symbols for questions and answers, and captions)*
- **What do you predict the interview will be about?**
- **What questions do you have about the text?**

Vocabulary Support Define words that may interfere with comprehension, such as *racism*, *boycott*, and *contracts*.

Read Aloud Read aloud the text with students. You could also have students chorally read the text in a small group.

Check Understanding Use the questions below to check understanding. Encourage students to cite details in the text that support their answers.

- **Who is Fernando Chavez?** *(the grandson of Cesar Chavez)*
- **What does he remember about his grandfather?** *(stories of his courage and bravery)*
- **Why do the stories mean so much to Fernando?** *(The stories have inspired him to help others.)*

Independent Practice

Integrating Standards

After students have read the interview, use these questions to discuss the interview with them.

- **Explain why Fernando Chavez admires his grandfather. Use details from "Cesar Chavez" and "He Inspired Others" to support your answer.**

  (Fernando Chavez admires his grandfather because of the way he helped others. Cesar Chavez fasted and organized strikes, marches, and boycotts to bring "attention to the plight of migrant farm workers." Fernando was proud that his grandfather "gave away food and clothing to help others.")
  DOK 3 RI.5.9
- **What does Fernando mean when he says, "it puts a lot of pressure on me," on p. 34?**

  (He is describing how having a famous grandfather affects his behavior. It pressures, or forces, him to make sure he acts in an honorable way, too.)
  DOK 2 RI.5.4, L.5.5b
- **How does the text under the heading "About Fernando Chavez" on p. 34 add to the interview?**

  (The text provides personal information about the person being interviewed as well as the interviewer's thoughts and opinions. It helps readers better understand the author's purpose.)
  DOK 2 RI.5.7
- **Discuss in small groups: Suppose you were interviewing Fernando Chavez. What are some questions you might ask? Use details from the text to predict how Fernando might respond to the questions.**

  (Discussions will vary. Encourage students to consider what they might want to learn about Cesar Chavez from someone who knew him, as well as what else they might want to learn about Fernando or his family members. Guide them to use the text to understand Fernando's point of view and to formulate possible responses from Fernando.)
  DOK 3 SL.5.1

● **Theme Connection**

4 Ⓠ **What is it like to be the grandson of a famous person, and the son of a father who continues to work for "the cause"?**

Ⓐ "It feels good, and I'm proud that my grandfather is in history books. But it puts a lot of pressure on me—I can't put a bad name on my grandfather or my family. I know that I need to stay under control."

About Fernando Chavez

Fernando Chavez turned 13 years old in 2001. With his two brothers and one sister, he lives with his family in La Paz, a small community near Bakersfield, California. His father, Paul F. Chavez, was the sixth of the eight children of Cesar and Helen Chavez.

The author of this interview thinks that "staying under control" is good advice for anyone. She also learned that Fernando has many traits of his courageous grandfather—respect, responsibility, and caring.

This sculpture, titled *Cesar Marching to Sacramento*, is in Cesar Chavez Park in Sacramento, California.

● Theme Connection

- Remind students that the theme of this lesson is Cultural Mosaic.
- Discuss some of the reasons why Frida Kahlo and Cesar Chavez became notable historical figures—specifically, how they each made important contributions to culture and society.
- Encourage students to use details from each passage to support their responses.

Think Use what you learned from reading the interview to respond to the following questions.

1 Which sentence is the **best** summary of why Fernando Chavez thinks young people should know about Cesar Chavez?

A Young people should know about Cesar Chavez because he was Fernando's grandfather.

(B) Young people should know about Cesar Chavez so that they can be inspired to help others like he did.

C Young people should know about Cesar Chavez because he organized a union for farm workers.

D Young people should know about Cesar Chavez because it makes Fernando sad to see migrant families without homes.

2 Select the **two** sentences that should be included in a summary of Fernando's answer to the second interview question.

A Fernando's grandfather named his dogs Strike and Boycott.

(B) When Fernando's grandfather died, many people came to give thanks for all that he had done for them.

(C) Fernando and his family miss Tata, especially at Christmas.

D Fernando's grandfather had two guard dogs that are buried near his grave.

E Tata had thirty-three grandchildren, and he loved all of them.

F Tata died just three days after Fernando's birthday.

3 Which statement **best** summarizes Fernando's answer to the third interview question?

(A) Chavez was brave.

B Chavez gave speeches.

C Chavez worked in the fields.

D Chavez held boycotts.

Monitor Understanding

If... students struggle to complete the items,

then... you may wish to use the following suggestions:

Read Aloud Activities

- As you read, have students note any unfamiliar words or phrases. Clarify any misunderstandings.
- Discuss each item with students to make certain they understand the expectation.

Reread the Text

- Have students complete a main idea organizer as they reread.

Think

- Use the Monitor Understanding suggestions to support students in completing items 1–5.

Monitor Understanding

Answer Analysis

When students have finished, discuss correct and incorrect responses.

1 **The correct choice is B.** This is the only choice directly supported by Fernando's response in the interview.

- **A** alone is not a good reason for young people to know about Chavez.
- **C** is plausible, but it does not give the best summary of why Fernando thinks young people should know about Chavez.
- **D** is not supported by text details.

DOK 2 **RI.5.2**

2 **The correct choices are B and C.** They retell the ideas that people respected Chavez and that Fernando misses him.

- **A** and **D** only refer to Chavez's dogs; they do not develop the main idea and therefore are not key details.
- **E** is about Chavez's grandchildren and is unrelated to his work for the rights of migrant workers.
- **F** is not an important detail to include in a summary.

DOK 2 **RI.5.2**

3 **The correct choice is A.** The third interview question is about Chavez's bravery.

- **B, C,** and **D** are details, not summaries.

DOK 2 **RI.5.2**

Independent Practice

4 **Part A**

The correct choice is D. This is the only answer stating that Chavez's actions inspired Fernando to help people.

- **A** only tells who Fernando is.
- **B** and **C** are minor details, not summaries.

Part B

The correct choice is B. This choice relates to the main idea that stories of Chavez's courage inspired Fernando.

- **A, C,** and **D** do not develop the main idea.

DOK 2 RI.5.2

5 **The correct choice is B.** The prefix *con-* means "together."

- **A** is a meaning for the prefix *in-*, *dis-*, or *un-*.
- **C** is a meaning for the prefix *pre-*.
- **D** is a meaning for the prefix *in-*.

DOK 1 L.5.4b

4 This question has two parts. First, answer Part A. Then answer Part B.

Part A

Which statement **best** summarizes the main idea of the interview?

A Fernando is the grandson of Cesar Chavez, a famous leader in the labor movement.

B Fernando remembers his last moments with his Tata at the side of his grave.

C Fernando feels very sad because many migrant workers do not live in regular houses but in campers and trucks.

(D) Fernando wants to help others when he grows up because stories about his grandfather have inspired him.

Part B

Which detail from the text **best** supports your answer to Part A?

A "I'm grateful that I don't have to go through that."

(B) "These stories make me want to stand up and do something when I am older and braver."

C "When I see families living in campers and trucks, I feel so sad."

D "My family and I really miss him, especially at Christmastime."

5 Read the sentence from paragraph 3.

> And there are still problems—people with no place to live, boycotts, and problems with contracts between farmers and workers.

What does the prefix *con-* in the word contracts mean?

A not

(B) together

C before

D into

Monitor Understanding

If... students don't understand the writing task,

then... read aloud the writing prompt. Use the following questions to help students get started.

- **What is the prompt asking you to write about?**
- **Do you need to reread the text to find more information?**
- **How will you identify the information you need to include?**

- Have partners talk about how they will organize their responses.
- Provide a graphic organizer to assist students, if needed.

Write

6 **Short Response** Summarize Fernando's message about his grandfather, Cesar E. Chavez. Use details from the text to support your summary.

Sample response: In an interview about Cesar Chavez, his grandson Fernando says young people should know about Chavez and his work because it will inspire them to help others. Fernando and his family are proud of how Chavez helped migrant families live better lives. Fernando says he hopes that when he is older, he will be courageous like his grandfather was and help people to solve problems in a peaceful way.

Learning Target

In this lesson, you summarized texts by identifying their main ideas and key details. Explain how summarizing is a skill you can use to better understand other informational texts you read.

Responses will vary, but students should mention ways that summarizing a text's main ideas and key details helps them locate, comprehend, and retain the most important information in the text.

37

6 2-Point Writing Rubric

Points	Focus	Evidence	Organization
2	My answer does exactly what the prompt asked me to do.	My answer is supported with plenty of details from the text.	My ideas are clear and in a logical order.
1	Some of my answer does not relate to the prompt.	My answer is missing some important details from the text.	Some of my ideas are unclear and out of order.
0	My answer does not make sense.	My answer does not have any details from the text.	My ideas are unclear and not in any order.

Write

- Tell students that using what they read, they will plan and compose a short response to the writing prompt.

● **Monitor Understanding**

Review Responses

After students have completed each part of the writing activity, help them evaluate their responses.

6 Display or pass out copies of the reproducible **2-Point Writing Rubric** on p. TR10. Have students use the rubric to individually assess their writing and revise as needed.

When students have finished their revisions, evaluate their responses. Answers will vary but should show that Fernando's message was about his grandfather's courage in working for migrant families and the inspiration it gives young people to help others. See the sample response.

DOK 3 **RI.5.2, W.5.9b**

Wrap Up

Learning Target

- Have each student respond in writing to the Learning Target prompt.
- When students have finished, have them share their responses. This may be done with a partner, in small groups, or as a whole class.

Lesson 3
Using Details to Support Inferences

Standards Focus

Quote accurately from a text when explaining what the text says explicitly and when drawing inferences from the text. **RI.5.1**

Lesson Objectives

Reading

- Use details and examples from a text when explaining what the text says. **RI.5.1**
- Use details and examples from a text along with personal knowledge when explaining inferences drawn from the text. **RI.5.1**

Writing

- Draw evidence from informational texts to support analysis and reflection. **W.5.9b**

Speaking and Listening

- Pose and respond to specific questions and contribute to discussions. **SL.5.1c**
- Review the key ideas expressed and draw conclusions. **SL.5.1d**

Language

- Use Greek and Latin affixes and roots as clues to the meaning of a word. **L.5.4b**
- Acquire and use academic and domain-specific words and phrases. **L.5.6**

Additional Practice: **RI.5.2, RI.5.4, RI.5.5, RI.5.6, RI.5.8, L.5.4a, L.5.5b**

Academic Talk

See **Glossary of Terms**, pp. TR2–TR9

- inference
- quote
- explicit meaning
- evidence

Learning Progression

Grade 4	Grade 5	Grade 6
Students refer to details and examples in the text to support their inferences.	Building on Grade 4, students not only refer to the text but also quote from it when making inferences. This helps to prepare students for the analysis required at Grade 6.	Grade 6 increases in complexity by requiring students to cite textual evidence to support analysis of a text, not just inferences.

Lesson Text Selections

Modeled and Guided Instruction

Zheng He
by Marcus Lim
Genre: Biography

Guided Practice

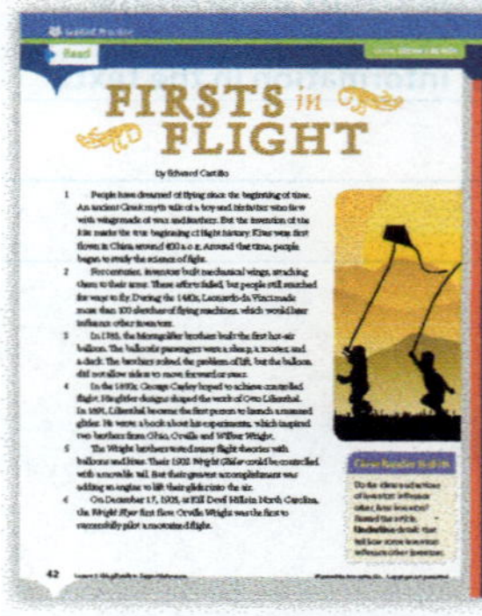

Firsts in Flight
by Edward Castillo
Genre: History Article

Independent Practice

Treasures of the Tomb
by Sean Price
Genre: History Article

Lesson Pacing Guide

Whole Class Instruction *30–45 minutes per day*

Day 1

Teacher-Toolbox.com **Interactive Tutorial**
Supporting Inferences About Informational Text—Level E
20 min (optional)

Introduction pp. 38–39
- **Read** **Using Details to Support Inferences** *10 min*
- **Think** *10 min*
  Graphic Organizer: Three-Column Chart
- **Talk** *5 min*
  Quick Write (TRB) *5 min*

Day 2

Modeled and Guided Instruction pp. 40–41, 44
- **Read** **Zheng He** *10 min*
- **Think** *10 min*
  Graphic Organizer: Three-Column Chart
- **Talk** *5 min*
- **Write** Short Response *10 min*

Day 3

Guided Practice pp. 42–43, 45
- **Read** **Firsts in Flight** *10 min*
- **Think** *10 min*
- **Talk** *5 min*
- **Write** Short Response *10 min*

Day 4

Independent Practice pp. 46–51
- **Read** **Treasures of the Tomb** *15 min*
- **Think** *10 min*
- **Write** Short Response *10 min*

Day 5

Independent Practice pp. 46–51
- *Review* Answer Analysis (TRB) *10 min*
- *Review* Response Analysis (TRB) *10 min*
- *Assign and Discuss* Learning Target *10 min*

Language Handbook
Lesson 17 Using a Dictionary or Glossary, pp. 470–471
20 min (optional)

Ready Writing Connection

During *Ready Reading* Days 1–5, use:
Lesson 1 Writing an Opinion: Letter to the Editor

- **Think It Through**
- **Step 4 Organize Your Evidence**
- **Step 5 Draft**

See *Ready Writing TRB*, p. 1a for complete lesson plan.

Small Group Differentiation

Teacher-Toolbox.com

Reteach

***Ready Reading* Prerequisite Lesson**
- **Grade 4** Lesson 6 Supporting Inferences About Informational Texts

Teacher-led Activities

Tools for Instruction
- Cite Textual Evidence
- Make Inferences

Personalized Learning

i-Ready.com

Independent

i-Ready Close Reading Lessons
- **Grade 4** Supporting Inferences About Informational Texts
- **Grade 5** Using Details to Support Inferences

Introduction

Get Started

- Explain to students that in this lesson they will read information about adventures and discoveries. They will make inferences from what they read and support those inferences with evidence.
- Ask students where they've heard the term *evidence* before. Together recall that evidence is used in detective stories or courtroom trials. Explain that just like detectives, students will look for evidence to support their conclusions about what they read. Review that details such as facts and examples are pieces of evidence.
- Tap into what students already know about inferences. For example, discuss how they know that it will probably rain today. Explain:

  When we have clues, such as a dark sky with lightning and thunder, we can use what we know from our experience to figure out what will happen. In this case, we can make an informed guess, or an inference, that it will rain soon.
- Focus students' attention on the Learning Target. Read it aloud to set the purpose for the lesson.
- Display the Academic Talk words and phrases. Tell students to listen for these words and their meanings as you work through the lesson together. Use the Academic Talk Routine on pp. A48–A49.

● Genre Focus

Read

- Read aloud the Read section as students follow along. Restate to reinforce:

  When you read informational texts, you can use the explicit meaning, or what is stated directly, along with your experience to make inferences. To explain your inferences, use evidence in the text and quote the text accurately.
- Direct students' attention to the cartoon. Tell them to look for clues in the picture to figure out the answer to the question in the speech bubble.

Introduction

RI.5.1 Quote accurately from a text when explaining what the text says explicitly and when drawing inferences from the text.

Lesson 3
Using Details to Support Inferences

When you make an inference about a text, you can support it with quotes from that text.

Read When you read, you can look for **explicit meanings**, which the author states directly. You can also use what you already know and details from the text to come up with your own ideas about what the author is saying. This is called making **inferences**.

You should always be able to support an inference with **evidence**. **Quotes** from the text are a strong form of evidence.

Look at the picture below. Make an inference about what just happened. Then circle any evidence in the picture that supports your inference.

38

English Language Learners
Develop Language

Concept Vocabulary To talk about inferences, students should be able to use the words *evidence* and *experience*.

- Help students identify cognates for each term in their first languages. Have them share, in English, their understanding of the meaning of each term.
- Together, determine that *evidence* means "support" or "proof of something" and that *experience* means "what you know from what you have seen or learned."
- Model using each term in academic sentences, and invite students to share examples of their own.

● Genre Focus
Biography

Explain that in Modeled and Guided Instruction, students will read a biography. A biography is a type of informational text that tells about all or part of a person's life. Biographies usually tell:

- When and where the person was born
- Why the person is important
- What special events happened during the person's lifetime

Point out the distinction between a biography and autobiography, which is a person telling his or her own story.

Encourage students to name some examples of biographies they've read.

Think What have you learned about making inferences? Use the chart below to help you develop and support an inference about what happened to the boy's steak.

What's in the Image (Evidence)	What I Know (Experience)	My Inference
• a boy is wondering where his steak went • a dog is on the floor below the table • the dog is asleep, looks happy, and is drooling • there is a bone next to him	• Dogs eat meat, including steak. • An animal that eats too much can get sleepy. • It's unclear what else in the picture could possibly have taken away the meat.	I think the dog ate the steak.

Talk Share your chart with a partner.

- Did you both make the same inference?
- Did you both select the same evidence in column one?
- What information did you each add to column two?

Academic Talk

Use these words and phrases to talk about the text.

- inference
- explicit meaning
- quote
- evidence

39

Think

- Have students read aloud the Think section. Explain that the chart will help them organize their thinking.
- Have partners complete the chart. Remind students to use the clues in the picture along with their own experience to make an inference.
- As students work, circulate and provide assistance as needed.
- Ask volunteers to share what they wrote in their charts.
- Make certain students understand that inferences are not just guesses. They must be supported by text evidence.

Talk

- Read aloud the Talk prompts.
- Have partners discuss what happened to the steak and why they think so.
- Ask volunteers to share their ideas.

Quick Write Have students write a response to the following prompt:

Describe a time when you had a hunch, or suspicion, about something. Explain what you suspected and why you thought so.

Ask students to share their responses.

Wrap Up

- Invite students to share what they've learned so far. Encourage them to use the Academic Talk words and phrases in their explanations.
- Tell students that when they read informational texts, they can make inferences to figure out parts of a text that are not explicitly stated.

In the next section, we'll read a biography. We'll use the evidence that is explicitly, or directly, stated in the text along with our own experience to make inferences.

● **Monitor Understanding**

● Monitor Understanding

If... students struggle to make inferences,

then... demonstrate with an example. Have students consider the following evidence and make an inference:

- A cat has been sitting in front of a window all afternoon.
- It's spring and there's a tree with leaves outside the window.
- You have heard chirping and twittering coming from outside.
- What inference can you make? *(A bird is nesting in the tree.)*

Ask students to provide their own clues and have volunteers make inferences based on the evidence. Remind students that solid inferences are based on good evidence, not just experience.

Modeled and Guided Instruction

Get Started

Today you will read a biography about an important person in history. First, you'll read to understand what it is about. Then you'll read to identify evidence that supports your inferences about the text.

Read

- Read aloud the title of the biography. Have students repeat it after you to learn the correct pronunciation (Jung Huh).
- Have students read the biography independently. Tell them to place a check mark above any confusing words and phrases as they read. Remind students to look inside, around, and beyond each unknown word to help them figure out its meaning. Use the Word Learning Routine on pp. A50–A51.
- When students have finished reading, clarify the meanings of words and phrases they still find confusing. Then use the questions below to check understanding. Encourage students to identify details in the text that support their answers.

  Who was Zheng He? *(a Chinese admiral and explorer in the early 1400s)*

  What did Zheng He do? *(He traded Chinese goods for goods from foreign lands.)*

  Why was Zheng He important? *(He introduced China to the world and brought knowledge about the world back to China.)*

- Word Learning Strategy

Explore

- Read aloud the Explore question at the top of p. 41 to set the purpose for the second read. Tell students they will need to take a closer look at details in the text to answer this question.
- Have students read aloud the Close Reader Habit on p. 40.

> **TIP** Remind students that experience also includes what they have learned before. Encourage them to think of famous explorers or traders and compare those events to Zheng He's account.

Modeled and Guided Instruction

Read

Genre: Biography

Zheng He

by Marcus Lim

1 The year is 1405. The place is China, where the Yangtze River empties into the Pacific Ocean. Floating on the river is the mightiest fleet the world has ever seen—more than 300 boats with nearly 30,000 sailors. The largest ships, called Treasure Ships, are more than 400 feet long—far larger than the greatest European boats of the day. The ships will sail the Indian Ocean, visiting ports along the lands we know as Indonesia, India, and Africa. Who commands this fleet? Admiral Zheng He.

2 Born in 1371, Zheng He (pronounced Jung Huh) was forced to join the Chinese army at age 10. He became not just a soldier and sailor but also a diplomat[1] speaking with foreigners on behalf of the Chinese government. That is why Zheng He was made leader of the fleet. Not only could he represent his government politely—he could also back up his politeness with force.

3 So why did China send Zheng He and his fleet to sea? In the early 1400s, China was growing rich and hungered for goods from faraway lands. To feed that hunger, the government built its fleet. But although Zheng He was a military man, his fleet came to trade, not to conquer. When they left Chinese shores, the Treasure Boats were heavy with silk and porcelain and jade. They returned laden with foreign goods: wood, gold, spices, and medicines. They even brought back odd animals—what we now call ostriches, zebras, camels, and giraffes. Zheng He took China out into the world, and he brought the world back to China.

4 Zheng He died in 1433 during his seventh voyage. For reasons not fully clear, a new emperor stopped the trading expeditions and ordered records of Zheng He's travels destroyed. But enough information remains to make one fact clear: Zheng He was one of the most marvelous sailors of his age.

[1] diplomat: a person who travels abroad on behalf of a government

Close Reader Habits

When you reread the biography, **circle** words that tell the roles Zheng He played, and **underline** evidence of how his travels might have changed the world.

40

English Language Learners

Develop Language

Figurative Language Read aloud the second and third sentences in paragraph 3, and ask:

Does this mean the country was hungry, as in, it wanted food?

- Guide students to understand that the author is giving China, a country, the characteristics of a human. The effect is to show that people in China very much wanted things they could get from other lands.
- Repeat the exercise with the last sentence of paragraph 3. Use the examples in the paragraph to help students understand how Zheng He introduced China to other parts of the world, and vice versa.

Word Learning Strategy

Analyze Word Parts

- Reread paragraph 2. Direct students' attention to the words *sailor* and *leader*. Ask:

  What does a *sailor* do?

  What does a *leader* do?

- Guide students to understand that the word part *-or* or *-er* at the end of a verb signals that the word means "a person who ____." For example, a *sailor* is "a person who sails."
- Have students practice attaching the suffix to other words such as *paint, teach, invent,* etc. Have them define each word as "a person who ______."

L.5.4b

Explore What inference can you make about how Zheng He affected the world's knowledge of China?

For the "What I Know" column, think about the roles leaders, diplomats, and traders play in the world.

Think

1 Complete the chart below with quotes and details from the text. It will help you support your inferences with textual evidence.

What's in the Text (Evidence)	What I Know (Experience)	My Inference
Zheng He: • commanded "the mightiest fleet the world" ever saw • "not just a soldier and sailor but also a diplomat" • "fleet came to trade, not to conquer" • took seven voyages along the coasts of Africa and Asia over almost 30 years	• A person who does everything the text describes must have had some effect on the world. • Diplomats are people who visit other places and talk with other people. • Trade is an activity that leads to people learning about each other.	The world's knowledge of China probably increased because of Zheng He's travels.

Talk

2 Share your charts. Did your partner provide evidence in "What I Know" that you didn't? If so, what was it? Add details to your chart if needed.

Write

3 **Short Response** What inference can be drawn about how Zheng He affected the world's knowledge about China? Support your answer with quotes from the passage. Use the space provided on page 44 to write your answer.

HINT First, state your inference. Then provide quotes from the text to support it.

Think Aloud

- The Explore question asks me to figure out how Zheng He affected, or influenced, the world's knowledge of China. I'm going to go back and reread to find evidence to answer the question.
- The first paragraph tells me when and where the events take place. It also tells me about the "mightiest fleet the world has ever seen." What's so impressive about this fleet? I read that it has more than 300 boats the largest of which are much larger than any European boats. These ships will sail to different ports in Indonesia, India, and Africa.
- At the end of the paragraph I read that Admiral Zheng He commands, or is in charge of, that entire fleet. This is a clue that he was a very important person.
- I will continue reading find more evidence about how Zheng He affected the world's knowledge of China, but first I'm going to add a detail to the first column of the chart. I'll write "commanded the 'mightiest fleet the world has ever seen.'" I'll put quotation marks around the exact words from the text.

Think

- Read aloud the Think section. Explain to students that you will model how to find text evidence to fill in part of the chart. Use the **Think Aloud** below to guide your modeling.
- Revisit the Explore question. Guide students to determine that they need to look for more details, using the Close Reader Habit.
- Encourage students to work with a partner to continue rereading the passage and complete the chart. Remind them to read the Buddy Tip.
- Ask volunteers to share their completed charts.
- Guide students to see that they can quote from the text to support inferences. Emphasize that quotes are a strong and reliable form of evidence.

Talk

- Read aloud the Talk prompt.
- Have partners respond to the prompt. Use the Talk Routine on pp. A52–A53.
- Circulate to check that students are discussing and writing text evidence in addition to their own experience.

Write

- Ask a volunteer to read aloud the Write prompt.
- Invite a few students to tell what the prompt is asking them to do.
- Make sure students understand that they need to make an inference about Zheng He's effect on the world's knowledge about China.
- Have students turn to p. 44 to write their response.
- Use Review Responses on p. 44 to assess students' writing.

Wrap Up

- Ask students to recall the Learning Target. Have them explain how using what was stated in the text along with their own experience helped them better understand this biography.

Guided Practice

Get Started

Today you will read a history article related to adventures and discovery. First you will read to understand what the article is about. Then you will reread with a partner to make inferences and support them with evidence.

Read

- Read aloud the title of the article. Ask a volunteer to explain what the word *flight* means. Establish that a *flight* is a trip through the air.
- Have students predict what the article will be about based on the title and the illustration.
- **Read to Understand** Have students read the article independently. Tell them to place a check mark above any confusing words and phrases as they read. Remind students to look inside, around, and beyond each unknown word or phrase to help them figure out its meaning. Use the Word Learning Routine on pp. A50–A51.
- When students have finished reading, clarify the meanings of words and phrases they still find confusing. Then use the questions below to check understanding. Encourage students to identify details in the text that support their answers.

  Who flew the first kites? *(people in China)*

  How did Leonardo da Vinci contribute to flight history? *(He made sketches of flying machines that influenced many other inventors.)*

  What was the difference between the first hot-air balloon and Otto Lilienthal's glider? *(The first hot-air balloon couldn't be controlled, but Lilienthal designed a glider that a person could fly.)*

  What is the article mostly about? *(It is about the history of flying machines and their inventors.)*

English Language Learners

Word Learning Strategy

- **Read to Analyze** Read aloud the Close Reader Habit on p. 42 to set the purpose for the second read. Then have students reread the article with a partner and discuss any questions they might have.

Guided Practice

Read

Genre: History Article

FIRSTS in FLIGHT

by Edward Castillo

1 People have dreamed of flying since the beginning of time. An ancient Greek myth tells of a boy and his father who flew with wings made of wax and feathers. But the invention of the kite marks the true beginning of flight history. Kites were first flown in China around 400 B.C.E. Around that time, people began to study the science of flight.

2 For centuries, inventors built mechanical wings, attaching them to their arms. These efforts failed, but people still searched for ways to fly. During the 1480s, Leonardo da Vinci made more than 100 sketches of flying machines, which would later influence other inventors.

3 In 1783, the Montgolfier brothers built the first hot-air balloon. The balloon's passengers were a sheep, a rooster, and a duck. The brothers solved the problem of lift, but the balloon did not allow riders to move forward or steer.

4 In the 1850s, George Cayley hoped to achieve controlled flight. His glider designs shaped the work of Otto Lilienthal. In 1891, Lilienthal became the first person to launch a manned glider. He wrote a book about his experiments, which inspired two brothers from Ohio, Orville and Wilbur Wright.

5 The Wright brothers tested many flight theories with balloons and kites. Their 1902 *Wright Glider* could be controlled with a movable tail. But their greatest accomplishment was adding an engine to lift their glider into the air.

6 On December 17, 1903, at Kill Devil Hills in North Carolina, the *Wright Flyer* first flew. Orville Wright was the first to successfully pilot a motorized flight.

Close Reader Habits

Do the ideas and actions of inventors influence other, later inventors? Reread the article. **Underline** details that tell how some inventors influence other inventors.

42

English Language Learners

Build Meaning

Visual Aids Download and display some pictures of Leonardo da Vinci's flying machine sketches, the Montgolfier brothers' hot-air balloon, Cayley's glider designs, Lilienthal's glider, and the *Wright Flyer.* Have students describe the early inventions, and supply any needed vocabulary, such as *inventor, controlled, glider, designs, inspired, theories,* and *engine.*

- Have students put the pictures in order and explain how each invention was an improvement on the previous one.

Word Learning Strategy

Analyze Word Parts

- Draw students' attention to the word *mechanical* in paragraph 2. Write the word on the board and underline the Greek root *mech.*
- Ask students to look for context clues in the paragraph that tell the meaning of *mechanical.* Guide them to see the reference to "flying machines" in the last sentence.
- Explain that the Greek root *mech* means "machine." When students see this root, they should think about how the word relates to machinery. Invite students to tell how "mechanical wings" relates to machinery.

L.5.4b

Think Use what you learned from reading the history article to respond to the following questions.

Use quotes to support your inferences. Otherwise, your inferences will seem like guesses.

1 This question has two parts. Answer Part A. Then answer Part B.

Part A

Which inference is **best** supported by the passage?

- (A) Inventors learn from the work of others.
- B Inventing is much easier than it used to be.
- C Most inventors try to keep their ideas from being stolen.
- D Some inventors are geniuses who don't need help from others.

Part B

Which **two** sentences from the text **best** illustrate the inference in Part A?

- A "People have dreamed of flying since the beginning of time."
- B "In 1783, the Montgolfier brothers built the first hot-air balloon."
- (C) "His glider designs shaped the work of Otto Lilienthal."
- D "In 1891, Lilienthal became the first person to launch a manned glider."
- (E) "He wrote a book about his experiments, which inspired two brothers from Ohio, Orville and Wilbur Wright."
- F "Orville Wright was the first to successfully pilot a motorized flight."

Talk

2 The technology of flight improved greatly in less than 150 years. What evidence from the passage supports this idea? Use the chart on page 45 to collect quotes from the passage and organize your thinking.

Write

3 **Short Response** What evidence from the passage supports the idea that the technology of flight improved greatly in less than 150 years? Use quotes from the passage in your response. Use the space provided on page 45 to write your answer.

HINT First, restate the idea from the question. Then provide the evidence supporting that idea.

Integrating Standards

Use the following questions to further students' understanding of the article.

- **"The Wright brothers *tested* many flight *theories* with balloons and kites." Use context clues to explain the meaning of *tested* and *theories*.** Tested *means "tried out a machine to see if it works," and* theories *are "ideas to explain events before they are known or proven.")*
  DOK 2 RI.5.4, L.5.4a
- **Contrast the organization of "Firsts in Flight" with the organization of "Zheng He."** *("Zheng He" is organized by cause-and-effect to show how he influenced the world. "Firsts in Flight" is told in chronological order.)*
  DOK 3 RI.5.5

Monitor Understanding

If... students have difficulty with item 2,

then... guide them to make a time line of events from the passage. As they record each invention, have students make a note about the way in which it was improved from the previous version.

Think

- Have students work with a partner to complete item 1. Draw attention to the boldface words **best** in Part A and **two** and **best** in Part B.

TIP Remind students that their inferences should be based on text evidence and not their opinions.

Answer Analysis

When students have finished, discuss correct and incorrect responses.

1 **Part A**

The correct choice is A. Cayley's work influenced Lilienthal, who inspired the Wright brothers.

- **B, C,** and **D** are not supported by the text.

Part B

The correct choices are C and E.

- **A, B, D,** and **F** are unrelated to the inference that inventors learned from the work of earlier inventors.

DOK 2

Integrating Standards

Talk

- Have partners discuss the prompt.
- Circulate to clarify misunderstandings.

Monitor Understanding

Write

- Ask a volunteer to read aloud the Write prompt.
- Invite students to tell what the prompt is asking them to do. Make sure they understand that they need to provide direct quotes as evidence.
- Call attention to the HINT.
- Have students turn to p. 45 to write their response.
- Use Review Responses on p. 45 to assess students' writing.

Wrap Up

- Ask students to recall the Learning Target. Have them explain how making inferences helped them to better understand this history article.

Modeled and Guided Instruction

Write

- Remember to use the Response–Writing Routine on pp. A54–A55.

Review Responses

After students complete the writing activity, help them evaluate their responses.

3 Responses may vary but should include that Zheng He probably greatly influenced the world's knowledge of China because he traded goods in foreign lands throughout Asia and Africa. See the sample response on the student book page.
DOK 3

Write Use the space below to write your answer to the question on page 41.

Zheng He

HINT First, state your inference. Then provide quotes from the text to support it.

3 **Short Response** What inference can be drawn about how Zheng He affected the world's knowledge about China? Support your answer with quotes from the passage.

Sample response: Zheng He probably greatly increased the world's knowledge about China. For example, in 1405, Zheng He commanded "the mightiest fleet" the world had ever seen. This mighty fleet told the world of China's naval might. In addition, Zheng He was "not just a soldier and sailor but also a diplomat." This means that Zheng He spoke for the Chinese government when meeting foreigners. And, because his "fleet came to trade, not to conquer," people throughout Asia and Africa probably learned more about China through its goods. For all these reasons, Zheng He probably greatly increased the world's knowledge about China.

Don't forget to check your writing.

Check Your Writing

- ☐ Did you read the prompt carefully?
- ☐ Did you put the prompt in your own words?
- ☐ Did you use the best evidence from the text to support your ideas?
- ☐ Are your ideas clearly organized?
- ☐ Did you write in clear and complete sentences?
- ☐ Did you check your spelling and punctuation?

Scaffolding Support for Reluctant Writers

If students are having a difficult time getting started, use the strategies below. Work individually with struggling students, or have students work with partners.

- Circle the verbs in the prompt that tell you what to do, such as *describe*, *explain*, or *compare*.
- Underline words and phrases in the prompt that show what information you need to provide in your response, such as *causes*, *reasons*, or *character traits*.
- Talk about the details from the text that you will include in your response.
- Explain aloud how you will respond to the prompt.

FIRSTS in FLIGHT

2 **Use the chart below to organize your ideas and your evidence.**

What's in the Text (Evidence)	What I Know (Experience)	My Inference

Write **Use the space below to write your answer to the question on page 43.**

3 **Short Response** What evidence from the passage supports the idea that the technology of flight improved greatly in less than 150 years? Use quotes from the passage in your response.

HINT First, restate the idea from the question. Then provide the evidence supporting that idea.

Sample response: "First in Flight" contains evidence that the technology of flight improved greatly in less than 150 years. Between 400 B.C.E. and 1783, flight wasn't possible. But in 1783, the Montgolfier brothers made a hot-air balloon that "solved the problem of lift." So now people could rise in the air, "but the balloon did not allow riders to move forward or steer." During the 1800s and early 1900s, George Cayley, Otto Lilienthal, and the Wright brothers solved the problems of forward movement, steering, and powered flight. So, for more than 2,000 years, humans could not fly at all—and then, in less than 150 years, humans developed fully powered flight.

Teacher Notes

Talk

2 Students should use the chart to organize their thoughts and evidence.

Write

- Remember to use the Response-Writing Routine on pp. A54–A55.

Review Responses

After students complete the writing activity, help them evaluate their responses.

3 Responses may vary but should show an understanding that inventors continued to build on the work of those who came before them. See the sample response on the student book page.
DOK 3

Independent Practice

Get Started

Today you are going to read a history article and use what you have learned about making and supporting inferences to understand the text more deeply.

- Ask a volunteer to explain why making inferences based on text evidence will help readers better understand history texts. Encourage students to use the Academic Talk words and phrases in their response.

 **English Language Learners**

Read

You are going to read the history article independently and use what you have learned to think and write about the text. As you read, remember to look closely at the text and make inferences using the text evidence and your own knowledge and experience.

- Read aloud the title of the article and then encourage students to preview the text, paying close attention to the photographs and captions.
- Call attention to the Words to Know in the upper left of p. 46.
- If students need support in reading the article, you may wish to use the Monitor Understanding suggestions.
- When students have finished, have them complete the Think and Write sections.

● **Monitor Understanding**

Read

Genre: History Article

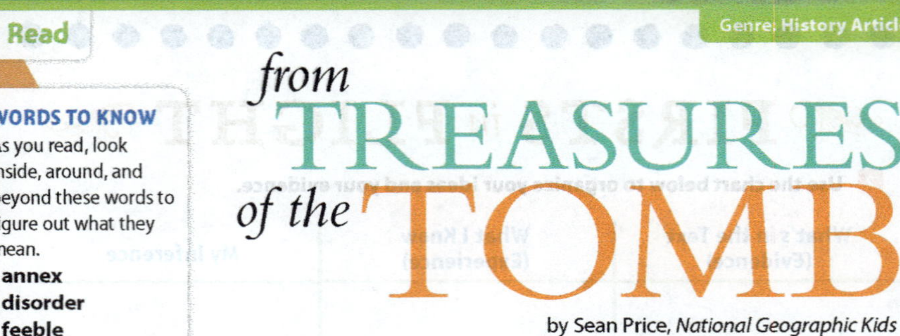

from TREASURES of the TOMB

by Sean Price, *National Geographic Kids*

WORDS TO KNOW
As you read, look inside, around, and beyond these words to figure out what they mean.
- **annex**
- **disorder**
- **feeble**

DISCOVERING KING TUT'S INCREDIBLE RICHES

1 It's pitch black. His hands trembling, British archaeologist Howard Carter makes a small hole in the tomb's second door. He inserts a candle. Next to him, Lord Carnarvon blurts out, "Can you see anything?" After a moment of stunned silence, Carter replies, "Yes, wonderful things."

2 What Carter sees looks like the inside of a giant treasure chest. Gold gleams everywhere! There are glittering statues, a throne, and fabulous golden beds with posts shaped like the heads of wild animals. Precious items are heaped all over the room. A mound of chariot parts fills one corner.

3 It has taken five years of digging in Egypt's Valley of the Kings—a graveyard for ancient Egypt's richest kings—and $500,000 (in today's money) of British millionaire Lord Carnarvon's cash, but Carter has hit the jackpot. He has discovered the tomb of Tutankhamun (often called Tut for short). Tut had become pharaoh at age nine and died just ten years later around 1323 B.C.

This photograph shows Lord Carnarvon (left) and Howard Carter (right). Lord Carnarvon provided much of the money that supported Carter's searches, one of which led to the discovery of Tutankhamun's tomb.

46

English Language Learners

Build Meaning

Background Knowledge To help students fully understand what the archaeologists discover inside the tomb of Tutankhamun, provide them with appropriate context on Egyptian burial rituals.

Explain that Egyptians believed there was a life after death, called the *afterlife.* Part of making sure the dead had a good afterlife was using chemicals and other methods to keep the body from breaking down. The end result was a *mummy.* The mummy's body was kept in a cool, dark, airless place called a *tomb.*

Another part of ensuring a good afterlife was filling the tomb with everything the person might want or need, including food, tools, and riches. The tombs of pharaohs and other royalty had several *chambers,* or rooms full of goods for the afterlife.

4 Carter, Lord Carnarvon, and two others enter the cluttered first room, which they call the antechamber. Under a bed with posts in the shape of hippopotamus heads, Lord Carnarvon finds the entrance to another room. Soon known as the annex, this tiny chamber holds more than 2,000 everyday objects. They include boomerangs, shields, a box containing eye makeup, and 116 baskets of food. Some of the piles reach nearly six feet high! When Carter clears the annex out later, his workers are suspended by ropes at first to keep from stepping on things.

5 The disorder in the annex indicates ancient grave robbers had looted the tomb. They left behind footprints and a bundle of Tut's gold finger-rings hurriedly wrapped in cloth. Luckily, they'd been caught and the tomb resealed. That was more than 3,000 years ago.

6 The explorers are fascinated by two tall statues in the antechamber showing Tut dressed in gold. The figures seem to be guarding yet another room. Sweltering in the heat, the group crawls through a hole created by the ancient robbers. Before them stands a huge wooden box, or shrine, that glitters with a layer of gold. This room must be Tut's burial chamber! At the very center of the shrine is a carved sarcophagus, or stone coffin. Inside it are three nested coffins, each one more richly decorated than the one before. Inside the last coffin, made of solid gold, lies the mummy of Tutankhamun. A 22-pound gold mask covers its head and shoulders. A collar made from 171 separate gold pieces rests on the mummy's chest. It wears gold sandals on its feet.

7 On one side of the burial chamber is an open doorway. It reveals the fourth room of the tomb, this one so full of riches that Carter dubs it the treasury. Towering over the other objects is a gold-covered shrine protected by statues of goddesses. The shrine holds Tut's liver, lungs, stomach, and intestines. Each vital organ is preserved, wrapped in linen, and placed in its very own small coffin.

8 Today about 2.5 million people visit Egypt's Cairo Museum each year to see Tut's treasures on display. The ancient Egyptians believed that "to speak the name of the dead is to make them live again." If that is true, Tutankhamun certainly lives on.

This mask made of gold and gems covered the head and shoulders of the mummy of Tutankhamun.

Monitor Understanding

If... students struggle to read and understand the passage,

then... use these scaffolding suggestions:

Question the Text Preview the text by asking the following questions:

- **Based on the title and photographs, what do you predict the article will be about?**
- **What questions do you have about the text?**

Vocabulary Support Define words that may interfere with comprehension, such as *archaeologist* and *pharaoh*.

Read Aloud Read aloud the text with students. You could also have students chorally read the text in a small group.

Check Understanding Use the questions below to check understanding. Encourage students to cite details in the text that support their answers.

- **Who was Tutankhamun?** *(a pharaoh in ancient Egypt)*
- **What did Howard Carter and Lord Carnarvon discover in the tomb?** *(King Tut's treasures and his mummy with a gold mask over his head and shoulders)*
- **What is the article mostly about?** *(the discovery of King Tut's tomb)*

Independent Practice

Integrating Standards

After students have read the passage, use these questions to discuss the text with them.

- **What does the author mean by "Carter has hit the jackpot" in paragraph 3? How does this expression show the author's feelings about the explorers' discovery?**
  (The author means that Carter has discovered something highly valuable by digging to find Tut's tomb. The author clearly values the discovery because he describes the artifacts as "precious items" and "treasures.")
  DOK 3 RI.5.4, L.5.5b
- **In paragraphs 10 and 11, there are different views of Lord Carnarvon's death and King Tut's "curse." Describe the differences between the newspapers' and the author's points of view.**
  (In paragraph 10, the newspapers reported that Lord Carnarvon died because of King Tut's curse. Yet, in paragraph 11, the author points out that there are reasonable explanations for his death.)
  DOK 2 RI.5.6
- **The author titled the passage "Treasures of the Tomb." What reasons or evidence does the author provide that the tomb held treasures?**
  (The author writes "Gold gleams everywhere!" The tomb has Tut's gold finger-rings, statues of Tut dressed in gold, and a solid gold coffin. The mummy wears a mask, necklace, and sandals of gold. The fourth room of the tomb has so many valuable items that Carter calls it the "treasury.")
  DOK 3 RI.5.8
- **Summarize the main idea of paragraphs 9–12.**
  (The main idea of the section "Curse of the Mummy" is that many people believed the men who disturbed the tomb were cursed because Lord Carnarvon died suddenly, his dog died, and the lights of Cairo went out. However, only 6 out of 26 of the people who were present when the tomb was opened died during the next 10 years.)
  DOK 2 RI.5.2

Theme Connection

This photo shows the city of Cairo as it appeared around the time of Lord Carnarvon's unexpected death. Because he died shortly after the opening of Tutankhamun's tomb, some newspapers claimed that a curse caused Carnarvon's death.

CURSE OF THE MUMMY

9 On April 5, 1923, Lord Carnarvon died suddenly in Egypt. At that same moment, lights went out all over Cairo. In England, Lord Carnarvon's dog, Susie, howled and died.

10 Newspapers claimed that these events were caused by King Tut's "curse." According to the newspapers, Tut's burial chamber contained a warning: "Death shall come on swift wings to him that toucheth the tomb of the Pharaoh."

11 It was a chilling story. But was it true? Actually, there was no warning in Tut's tomb. The papers made up that part. Skeptics[1] say the events have other explanations. Lord Carnarvon had been in poor health for years. Cairo's feeble electric system caused lights to wink out all the time. And dogs sometimes do die unexpectedly.

12 Only 6 of the 26 people who saw the opening of Tut's burial chamber died within the next ten years. Howard Carter, who should have been the most cursed of all, lived until 1939—17 years after coming face-to-face with Tutankhamun's mummy.

[1] **Skeptics:** people who doubt and have disbelief

Theme Connection

- Remind students that the theme of this lesson is Adventures and Discovery.
- Display a web organizer with the title "Zheng He" in the center oval. Attach surrounding ovals.
  What important facts and ideas did you learn about adventures and discovery from the text?
- Add students' responses to the organizer. Repeat with web organizers for "Firsts in Flight" and "Treasures of the Tomb." Then summarize.
  How do all the passages in this lesson relate to the theme of adventures and discovery?

Think Use what you learned from reading the history article to respond to the following questions.

1 Which sentence from the article **best** supports the inference that one custom of the ancient Egyptians was to preserve bodies after death?

A "A mound of chariot parts fills one corner."
B "Soon known as the annex, this tiny chamber holds more than 2,000 everyday objects."
C "A collar made from 171 separate gold pieces rests on the mummy's chest."
(D) "The shrine holds Tut's liver, lungs, stomach, and intestines."

2 This question has two parts. First, answer Part A. Then answer Part B.

Part A
What is the meaning of suspended as it is used in paragraph 4 of the article?

A floated
B swung
(C) carried
D waited

Part B
Which phrase from paragraph 4 helps the reader understand the meaning of suspended?

A ". . . Carter clears the annex out later, . . ."
(B) ". . . by ropes. . . ."
C ". . . which they call the antechamber."
D ". . . a box containing eye makeup, and 116 baskets of food."

3 Which paragraph **best** supports the idea that finding King Tutankhamun's tomb required a lot of time and money?

(A) paragraph 3
B paragraph 5
C paragraph 9
D paragraph 12

● **Monitor Understanding**

If... students struggle to complete the items,
then... you may wish to use the following suggestions:

Read Aloud Activities

- As you read, have students note any unfamiliar words or phrases. Clarify any misunderstandings.
- Discuss each item with students to make certain they understand the expectation.

Reread the Text

- Have students complete an inference chart as they reread.
- Have partners summarize the text.

Think

- Use the Monitor Understanding suggestions to support students in completing items 1–5.

● **Monitor Understanding**

Answer Analysis

When students have finished, discuss correct and incorrect responses.

1 **The correct choice is D.** This is the only answer that relates to the ancient Egyptians' interest in and ability to preserve bodies.

- **A** and **B** do not relate to the Egyptians' treatment of bodies.
- **C** mentions jewelry that was placed on the mummy's chest but does not have to do with how the Egyptians preserved his body.

DOK 2 RI.5.1

2 **Part A**

The correct choice is C. The workers must be carried by ropes in order to avoid breaking the objects piled up in the tomb.

- **A, B,** and **D** show definitions for *suspended,* but none of the definitions make sense in the context.

Part B

The correct choice is B. The phrase "by ropes" is a clue to the word *suspended* meaning "carried."

- **A, C,** and **D** are not phrases that help readers understand the word *suspended* or that could be substituted in the sentence.

DOK 1 L.5.4a

3 **The correct choice is A.** This is the only paragraph that explicitly refers to the time (five years) and money ($500,000 in today's money) spent searching.

- **B, C,** and **D** are incorrect, although these paragraphs mention time in some way ("3,000 years ago," "April 5, 1923," and "17 years," respectively), such references are unrelated to how long it took to find King Tutankhamun's tomb and say nothing about money.

DOK 1 RI.5.1

Independent Practice

4 **Part A**

The correct choice is B. The text provides reasonable explanations as to why these events probably happened by coincidence.

- **A** and **C** suggest that the author believes the "curse" could affect events, but the author questions that idea by asking, ". . . was it true?"
- **D** gives information that cannot be inferred from the article.

Part B

The correct choices are B and F. Both are examples that show the author did not believe that a "curse" brought on the disasters.

- **A, C, D,** and **E** all suggest a connection between King Tut's curse and the events.

DOK 2 RI.5.1

5 **Students should underline the following sentence:** "Soon known as the annex, this tiny chamber holds more than 2,000 everyday objects."

DOK 3 RI.5.1

4 This question has two parts. First, answer Part A. Then answer Part B.

Part A

What can you infer about the author's point of view regarding the events of April 5, 1923, described in paragraph 9?

A The events prove that King Tut's "curse" was real.

(B) The events probably were a coincidence.

C The events served as a warning about entering the tomb.

D The events should have been investigated as crimes.

Part B

Which **two** sentences from the article **best** illustrate the inference you made in Part A?

A "On April 5, 1923, Lord Carnarvon died suddenly in Egypt."

(B) "Lord Carnarvon had been in poor health for years."

C "Newspapers claimed that these events were caused by King Tut's 'curse.'"

D "It was a chilling story."

E "In England, Lord Carnarvon's dog, Susie, howled and died."

(F) "Actually, there was no warning in Tut's tomb."

5 Read the sentence and the directions that follow.

The ancient Egyptians believed they could take the things they used in their daily lives with them to the grave.

Underline the sentence from the paragraph below that **best** shows this idea.

Carter, Lord Carnarvon, and two others enter the cluttered first room, which they call the antechamber. Under a bed with posts in the shape of hippopotamus heads, Lord Carnarvon finds the entrance to another room. Soon known as the annex, this tiny chamber holds more than 2,000 everyday objects. They include boomerangs, shields, a box containing eye makeup, and 116 baskets of food. Some of the piles reach nearly six feet high! When Carter clears the annex out later, his workers are suspended by ropes at first to keep from stepping on things.

Monitor Understanding

If... students don't understand the writing task,

then... read aloud the writing prompt. Use the following questions to help students get started.

- **What is the prompt asking you to write about?**
- **Do you need to reread the text to find more information?**
- **How will you identify the information you need to include?**

- Have partners talk about how they will organize their responses.
- Provide a graphic organizer to assist students, if needed.

 Write

6 **Short Response** What inference can be drawn about how ancient Egyptians felt about the bodies and belongings of their dead pharaohs? Support your answer with evidence from the text.

Sample response: We can infer that the ancient Egyptians respected their pharaohs because they took care to hide, preserve, and decorate King Tut's body and tomb. First, the tomb was well-hidden and made up of a maze of rooms. Second, the king's body was carefully preserved. Finally, Tut's mummy was decorated and surrounded by gold and precious objects. These details all support the idea that the ancient Egyptians respected their pharaohs.

Learning Target

In this lesson, you practiced making inferences and supporting them with quotes from the text. Explain how these skills can help you develop a better understanding of any informational text you read.

Responses will vary, but students should explain that making inferences and supporting them with quotations from the text will provide a far deeper understanding of what the text is telling them.

6 2-Point Writing Rubric

Points	Focus	Evidence	Organization
2	My answer does exactly what the prompt asked me to do.	My answer is supported with plenty of details from the text.	My ideas are clear and in a logical order.
1	Some of my answer does not relate to the prompt.	My answer is missing some important details from the text.	Some of my ideas are unclear and out of order.
0	My answer does not make sense.	My answer does not have any details from the text.	My ideas are unclear and not in any order.

Write

- Tell students that using what they read, they will compose a short response to the writing prompt.

Monitor Understanding

Review Responses

After students have completed each part of the writing activity, help them evaluate their responses.

6 Display or pass out copies of the reproducible **2-Point Writing Rubric** on p. TR10. Have students use the rubric to individually assess their writing and revise as needed.

When students have finished their revisions, evaluate their responses. Answers will vary but should show that the ancient Egyptians respected Tutankhamun, preserved his body in a hidden tomb, and believed that King Tut should have his treasures of gold with him in the tomb. Their responses should include evidence from the text. See the sample response on the student book page.

DOK 3 **RI.5.1, W.5.9b**

Wrap Up

Learning Target

- Have each student respond in writing to the Learning Target prompt.
- When students have finished, have them share their responses. This may be done with a partner, in small groups, or as a whole class.

LESSON OVERVIEW

Lesson 4a Explaining Relationships in Scientific and Technical Texts

Standards Focus

Explain the relationships or interactions between two or more . . . events, ideas, or concepts in a . . . scientific or technical text. RI.5.3

Lesson Objectives

Reading

- Identify relationships between two or more events, ideas, or concepts in a scientific or technical text. RI.5.3
- Explain relationships between two or more events, ideas, or concepts in a scientific or technical text. RI.5.3

Writing

- Draw evidence from informational texts to support analysis and reflection. W.5.9b

Speaking and Listening

- Pose and respond to specific questions and contribute to discussions. SL.5.1c
- Review the key ideas expressed and draw conclusions. SL.5.1d

Language

- Use context as a clue to the meaning of a word or phrase. L.5.4a
- Acquire and use academic and domain-specific words and phrases. L.5.6

Additional Practice: **RI.5.1, RI.5.2, RI.5.5, RI.5.7, RI.5.8**

Academic Talk

See **Glossary of Terms**, pp. TR2–TR9

- relationship
- interaction
- scientific text
- technical text

Learning Progression

Grade 4	Grade 5	Grade 6
Students explain events, procedures, ideas, or concepts in a scientific or technical text, including what happened and why, based on specific information in the text.	Building on Grade 4, students draw on specific details to explain the relationships between events, ideas, or concepts in a scientific or technical text. The inclusion of scientific concepts and technical procedures points to CCSS's focus on academic and domain-specific knowledge.	Grade 6 increases in complexity by requiring students to analyze in detail how a key individual, event, or idea is introduced, illustrated, and elaborated in a text (e.g., through examples).

Lesson Text Selections

Modeled and Guided Instruction

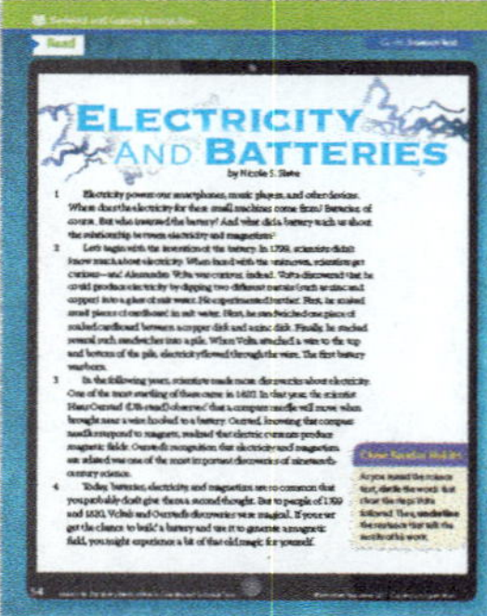

Electricity and Batteries
by Nicole S. Slate
Genre: Science Text

Guided Practice

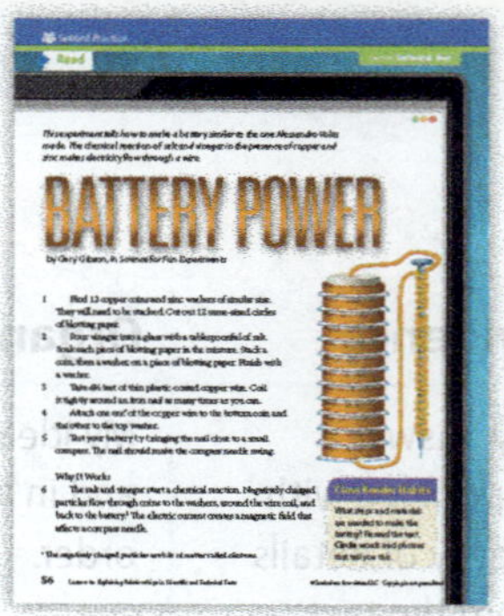

Battery Power
by Gary Gibson
Genre: Technical Text

Independent Practice

Hydroelectric Power
by the United States Geological Survey
Genre: Technical Text

Lesson Pacing Guide

Whole Class Instruction *30–45 minutes per day*

Day 1

Teacher-Toolbox.com **Interactive Tutorial**
Explaining Relationships in Informational Texts—Level E
20 min (optional)

Introduction pp. 52–53

- **Read** **Explaining Relationships in Scientific and Technical Texts** *10 min*
- **Think** *10 min*
  Graphic Organizer: Sequence Chart
- **Talk** *5 min*
  Quick Write (TRB) *5 min*

Day 2

Modeled and Guided Instruction pp. 54–55, 58

- **Read** **Electricity and Batteries** *10 min*
- **Think** *10 min*
  Graphic Organizer: Sequence Chart
- **Talk** *5 min*
- **Write** Short Response *10 min*

Day 3

Guided Practice pp. 56–57, 59

- **Read** **Battery Power** *10 min*
- **Think** *10 min*
- **Talk** *5 min*
- **Write** Short Response *10 min*

Day 4

Independent Practice pp. 60–65

- **Read** **Hydroelectric Power** *15 min*
- **Think** *10 min*
- **Write** Short Response *10 min*

Day 5

Independent Practice pp. 60–65

- *Review* Answer Analysis (TRB) *10 min*
- *Review* Response Analysis (TRB) *10 min*
- *Assign and Discuss* Learning Target *10 min*

Language Handbook
Lesson 18 Figurative Language, pp. 472–473
20 min (optional)

Ready Writing Connection

During *Ready Reading* Days 1–5, use:
Lesson 1 Writing an Opinion: Letter to the Editor

- **Steps 6 and 7 Revise**
- **Step 8 Edit**
- **Prepare to Publish**
- **Collaborate**
- **Present**

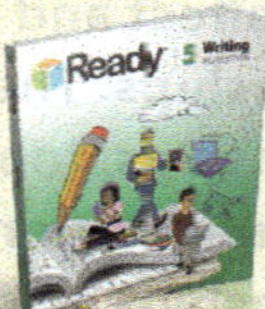

See *Ready Writing TRB*, p. 1a for complete lesson plan.

Small Group Differentiation

Teacher-Toolbox.com

Reteach

***Ready Reading* Prerequisite Lessons**
Grade 4
- Lesson 3 Understanding Technical Texts
- Lesson 4 Understanding Scientific Texts

Teacher-led Activities

Tools for Instruction
- Text Structure

Personalized Learning

i-Ready.com

Independent

i-Ready Close Reading Lesson
- **Grade 5** Explaining Relationships in Scientific and Technical Texts

Introduction

Get Started

- Explain to students that in this lesson they will read informational texts about electricity. As they read, they will identify and explain relationships between and among ideas and events.
- Ask students to state the meaning of *relationship*. Guide them to define it as "the connection between two or more things." Review:

  You are probably already familiar with cause–effect and compare–contrast relationships. There are other types of relationships, too, like steps in a process or problem–solution. When we think about relationships in a text, we think about how two or more details are connected.
- Work with students to review familiar examples of each type of relationship: a recipe has steps in a process; an FAQ guide has problems and solutions. Encourage students to offer their own examples.
- Focus students' attention on the Learning Target. Read it aloud to set the purpose for the lesson.
- Display the Academic Talk words and phrases. Tell students to listen for these terms and their meanings as you work through the lesson together. Use the Academic Talk Routine on pp. A48–A49.

English Language Learners

Genre Focus

Read

- Read aloud the Read section as students follow along. Restate to reinforce:

  There is an important difference between scientific texts and technical texts. A scientific text teaches you facts and ideas about our natural world. A technical text—like a set of instructions—teaches you how something works, or how to use, make, or do something.
- Have students read the passage. Remind them to underline parts of the text that describe connections between events and ideas.

Introduction

RI.5.3 Explain the relationships or interactions between two or more . . . events, ideas, or concepts in a . . . scientific or technical text.

Lesson 4a
Explaining Relationships in Scientific and Technical Texts

Explaining the relationships or interactions between events and ideas will help you develop a deeper understanding of scientific or technical texts.

Read When you read **scientific texts**, you learn about the natural world. If you read about why lightning strikes or how electricity works, you're reading a scientific text. When you read **technical texts**, you are learning to make or do something. If you read the directions for using a cell phone, you are reading a technical text. Both scientific and technical texts describe the **relationships** and **interactions** between events, ideas, or concepts.

Read the passage. Underline any relationships or details that seem important.

ELECTRICITY IN MOTION

You're pretty familiar with what electricity can do. You flip a switch and a light bulb glows. You push a button and a fan whirs to life. Turning on an electric oven makes it heat up. But why do you get these results? What do a glowing light bulb, a spinning fan, and a hot oven have in common?

The answer is current electricity, or the steady flow of bits of matter called electrons. You can't see electrons. They're so small that even the best microscopes won't show one to you. But while electrons aren't visible, you can see the effects of their motion. Light bulbs, fans, ovens—all of these work because you've let the electrons flow.

52

English Language Learners

Develop Language

- **Academic Vocabulary** Clarify for students that *relationship* is a multiple-meaning word. Invite students to share known meanings of the word. *("the way two people know one another, as in family members"; "two people romantically involved")* Record students' definitions on the board.
- Underline the words or concepts that the definitions have in common. Guide students to see that all relationships have to do with two or more things being connected somehow.
- Connect this meaning to the academic language, reviewing terms such as *cause-and-effect, compare-contrast, sequence, process* and so forth.

Genre Focus

Technical Texts

Explain that in Guided Practice and Independent Practice, students will read technical texts. These types of informational texts often deal with subjects such as engineering, electronics, and architecture.

Typically, technical texts tell how things work or how to use, do, or make things. Examples include notes on scientific experiments, how-to manuals, directions, and procedures.

Technical texts often contain specialized vocabulary that is specific to the topic. For example, a recipe uses words like *cup, teaspoon, whip, grill, poach,* and *preheat.*

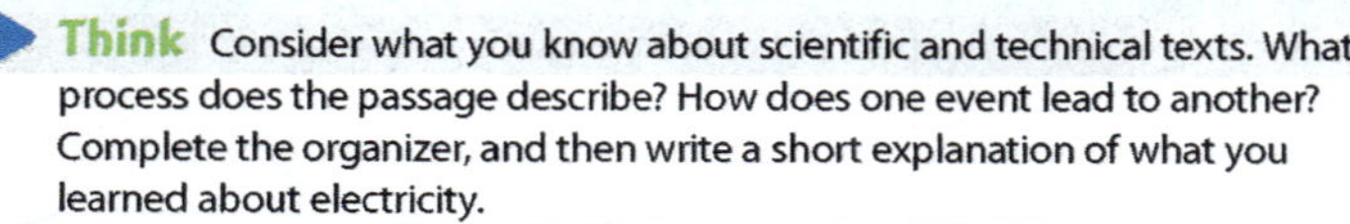

Think Consider what you know about scientific and technical texts. What process does the passage describe? How does one event lead to another? Complete the organizer, and then write a short explanation of what you learned about electricity.

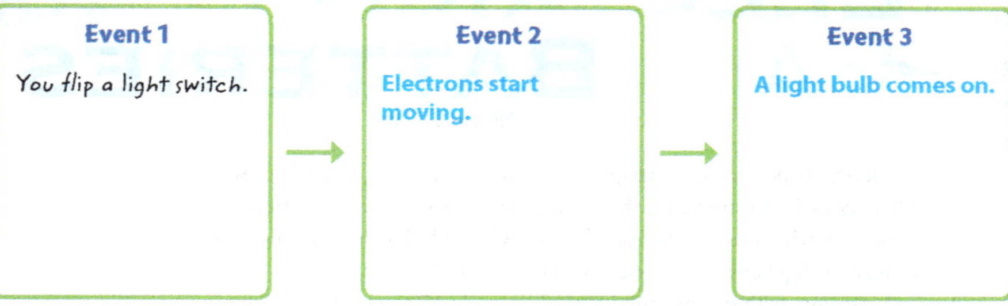

Event 1		Event 2		Event 3
You flip a light switch.	→	Electrons start moving.	→	A light bulb comes on.

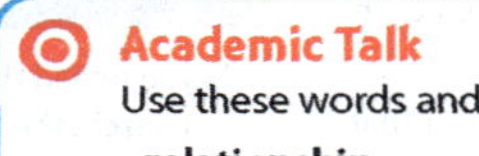

Explanation of the Process

By flipping a switch, you start the electrons moving. When the electrons are flowing, the light bulb shines. The electricity has given you light to see in a dark room.

Talk Share your explanation with a partner.

- What events do you include in your organizer?
- What kind of relationships do you see between one event and another?
- How does understanding one event help you understand another event?

Academic Talk
Use these words and phrases to talk about the text.

- relationship
- interaction
- scientific text
- technical text

53

Monitor Understanding

If... students struggle to identify relationships,

then... give an example. Tell students that yesterday you filled your teakettle with water, placed the kettle on the stove, and turned on the gas flame.

- **What do you think happened next?** *(The water in the teakettle boiled. The teakettle began to whistle.)*
- **Why did these events happen?** *(Heat causes water to boil and change to steam. When steam forces itself through the tiny hole in the cover over the teakettle's spout, it causes a whistling sound.)*

Ask students to provide their own examples.

Think

- Have students read aloud the Think section. Explain that the organizer will help them capture their thinking.
- Have partners complete the organizer. Remind students to use details from the passage to describe the events that happen as a result of flipping a light switch.
- As students work, circulate and provide assistance as needed.
- Ask volunteers to share what they wrote in their organizers.
- Make certain students understand that Event 1 causes Event 2 to happen, and Event 2 causes Event 3.

Talk

- Read aloud the Talk prompts.
- Have partners discuss and identify the type of relationship that exists between Events 1 and 2 and between Events 2 and 3. (*cause–effect*)
- Ask volunteers to share their ideas.

Quick Write Have students write a response to the following prompt:

Choose a process you go through each day, such as tying your shoes or getting ready for school. Write each step of the process and then explain why you go through the steps in the order you do.

Ask students to share their responses.

Wrap Up

- Invite students to share what they've learned so far. Encourage them to use the Academic Talk words and phrases in their explanations.
- Explain to students that when they read scientific and technical texts, they discover connections, relationships, and interactions among scientific events and ideas.

In the next section, you'll read about how electricity, batteries, and magnetism are related. Explaining these relationships will help you better understand the information in the text.

Monitor Understanding

Modeled and Guided Instruction

Get Started

Today you will read a science text. First, you'll read to understand the events that the author describes. Then you'll read to analyze connections between events and scientific ideas.

Read

- Read aloud the title of the text. Invite students to briefly share prior knowledge about what electricity and batteries are commonly used for.
- Have students read the text independently. Tell them to place a check mark above any confusing words and phrases as they read. Remind students to look inside, around, and beyond each unknown word to help them figure out its meaning. Use the Word Learning Routine on pp. A50–A51.
- When students have finished reading, clarify the meanings of words and phrases they still find confusing. Then use the questions below to check understanding. Encourage students to identify details in the text that support their answers.

  What materials did Volta use to create a battery? *(zinc and copper disks, salt water, cardboard, and wire)*

  What did Oersted discover? *(that electricity and magnetism are connected; that a compass needle reacts to the electrical current in a battery's wire)*

● **Word Learning Strategy**

Explore

- Read aloud the Explore question at the top of p. 55 to set the purpose for the second read. Tell students they will need to take a closer look at the connections between batteries and magnetism to answer this question.
- Have students read aloud the Close Reader Habit on p. 54.

TIP Tell students that often they will also need to make inferences, or educated guesses, to link events, facts, and ideas.

Read — Genre: Science Text

ELECTRICITY AND BATTERIES

by Nicole S. Slate

1 Electricity powers our smartphones, music players, and other devices. Where does the electricity for these small machines come from? Batteries, of course. But who invented the battery? And what did a battery teach us about the relationship between electricity and magnetism?

2 Let's begin with the invention of the battery. In 1799, scientists didn't know much about electricity. When faced with the unknown, scientists get curious—and Alessandro Volta was curious, indeed. Volta discovered that he could produce electricity by dipping two different metals (such as zinc and copper) into a glass of salt water. He experimented further. First, he soaked small pieces of cardboard in salt water. Next, he sandwiched one piece of soaked cardboard between a copper disk and a zinc disk. Finally, he stacked several such sandwiches into a pile. When Volta attached a wire to the top and bottom of the pile, electricity flowed through the wire. The first battery was born.

3 In the following years, scientists made more discoveries about electricity. One of the most startling of these came in 1820. In that year, the scientist Hans Oersted (UR-stead) observed that a compass needle will move when brought near a wire hooked to a battery. Oersted, knowing that compass needles respond to magnets, realized that electric currents produce magnetic fields. Oersted's recognition that electricity and magnetism are related was one of the most important discoveries of nineteenth-century science.

4 Today, batteries, electricity, and magnetism are so common that you probably don't give them a second thought. But to people of 1799 and 1820, Volta's and Oersted's discoveries were magical. If you ever get the chance to build a battery and use it to generate a magnetic field, you might experience a bit of that old magic for yourself.

Close Reader Habits

As you reread the science text, **circle** the words that show the steps Volta followed. Then, **underline** the sentence that tells the results of his work.

54

English Language Learners

Build Meaning

Visual Aids To help students understand the words *sandwiched* and *sandwiches* in the article, have them study the illustration on p. 56.

How is this like a sandwich? How is it like Volta's battery? *(A sandwich has stacks of ingredients. Volta's battery had stacks of different metals and soaked cardboard.)*

- Have students form trios and create hand "sandwiches." Student A places one hand flat on a desktop, B places a hand on top of A's hand, and C places a hand on top of B's. They then repeat the process to form an ABCABC "sandwich" of hands.

● Word Learning Strategy

Use Context Clues

- Direct students' attention to the word *devices* in the first sentence.

  What do you think *devices* means? What clues help you figure this out?
- Guide students to find the examples *smartphones* and *music players* as well as the synonymous phrase *small machines*. Help them infer that *device* can mean "a small machine." Have students name other battery-powered devices, such as watches and remote controls.
- Remind students that one type of context clue is a synonym, a word or phrase with a similar meaning. Another type is an example. **L.5.4a**

Explore How does explaining the discoveries of Volta and Oersted add to your understanding of electricity?

Paragraphs 2 and 3 don't just describe two discoveries. They tell you how the second one depended on the first.

Think

1 Complete this organizer for the important events in paragraphs 2 and 3.

Event 1		Event 2		Event 3
Volta put small pieces of cardboard between disks of copper and zinc and stacked several of them together.	→	Electricity flowed through a wire attached to the top and bottom of the stack, making a battery.	→	Oersted discovered that a compass needle moves if it is near a wire connected to a battery.

Talk

2 Share your organizers. Discuss the events you describe and how they are related. Revise your organizers as necessary.

Write

3 **Short Response** Explain how Volta's discovery led to Oersted's discovery. Use details from the text to support your answer. Use the space provided on page 58 to write your answer.

HINT Don't just describe what Volta and Oersted discovered. Explain how Oersted's discovery depended on Volta's.

Think Aloud

- Event 1 has already been provided in the organizer. It says that *Volta put small pieces of cardboard between disks of copper and zinc and stacked several of them together.*
- I need to go back to the text to figure out what happened immediately after Event 1.
- What happened as a result of Volta's idea to stack the metals and cardboard? The second-to-last sentence in paragraph 2 tells me the answer: "When Volta attached a wire to the top and bottom of the pile, electricity flowed through the wire." I'll write about electricity flowing in the *Event 2* box.

Think

- Read aloud the Think section. Explain to students that you will model how to find text evidence to fill in part of the organizer. Use the **Think Aloud** below to guide your modeling.
- Revisit the Explore question. Guide students to determine that they need to look for more details, using the Close Reader Habit.
- Encourage students to work with a partner to continue rereading the passage and complete the organizer. Remind them that the Buddy Tip will help them find the information they need.
- Ask volunteers to share their completed organizers.
- Guide students to see that the first two events led to the third. First, Volta invented a battery. As a result, Oersted discovered the connection between electricity and magnetism.

Talk

- Read aloud the Talk prompt.
- Have partners respond to the prompt. Use the Talk Routine on pp. A52–A53.
- Circulate to check that students are using details from their partners' organizers to improve their own.

Write

- Ask a volunteer to read aloud the Write prompt.
- Invite a few students to tell what the prompt is asking them to do.
- Make sure students understand that they need to show how Oersted's discovery was a result of Volta's invention.
- Have students turn to p. 58 to write their response.
- Use Review Responses on p. 58 to assess students' writing.

Wrap Up

- Ask students to recall the Learning Target. Have them explain how looking closely at relationships between events and interactions among materials (such as zinc, copper, salt water, cardboard, and wire) helped them better understand this scientific text.

Guided Practice

Get Started

Today you will read a technical text. First you will read to understand what the text is about. Then you will reread with a partner to make sure you fully understand the steps of the procedure.

Read

- Read aloud the short introduction and the title of the text. Have students predict what the text will be about based on the introduction, the genre, the title, and the illustration.
- **Read to Understand** Have students read the text independently. Tell them to place a check mark above any confusing words and phrases as they read. Remind students to look inside, around, and beyond each unknown word or phrase to help them figure out its meaning. Use the Word Learning Routine on pp. A50–A51.
- When students have finished reading, clarify the meanings of words and phrases they still find confusing. Then use the questions below to check understanding. Encourage students to identify details in the text that support their answers.

  What materials do you need to create this kind of battery? *(12 copper coins, 12 zinc washers, 12 circles of blotting paper, salt, vinegar, wire, and an iron nail)*

  Describe the stack that the instructions and the illustration tell you how to make. *(Stack a coin, then a washer, on a piece of blotting paper 12 times; end with a zinc washer on top.)*

  What should you do after you have created the stack of 36 items? *(Coil a long piece of wire many times around a nail. Attach the ends of the wire to the top washer and the bottom coin.)*

 **English Language Learners**

● **Word Learning Strategy**

- **Read to Analyze** Read aloud the Close Reader Habit on p. 56 to set the purpose for the second read. Then have students reread the text with a partner and discuss any questions they might have.

This experiment tells how to make a battery similar to the one Alessandro Volta made. The chemical reaction of salt and vinegar in the presence of copper and zinc makes electricity flow through a wire.

BATTERY POWER

by Gary Gibson, in *Science for Fun Experiments*

1 Find 12 copper coins and zinc washers of similar size. They will need to be stacked. Cut out 12 same-sized circles of blotting paper.

2 Pour vinegar into a glass with a tablespoonful of salt. Soak each piece of blotting paper in the mixture. Stack a coin, then a washer, on a piece of blotting paper. Finish with a washer.

3 Take 6½ feet of thin plastic-coated copper wire. Coil it tightly around an iron nail as many times as you can.

4 Attach one end of the copper wire to the bottom coin and the other to the top washer.

5 Test your battery by bringing the nail close to a small compass. The nail should make the compass needle swing.

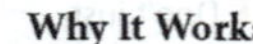

Why It Works

6 The salt and vinegar start a chemical reaction. Negatively charged particles flow through coins to the washers, around the wire coil, and back to the battery.[1] The electric current creates a magnetic field that affects a compass needle.

[1] The negatively charged particles are bits of matter called *electrons*.

Close Reader Habits

What steps and materials are needed to make the battery? Reread the text. **Circle** words and phrases that tell you this.

56

 **English Language Learners**

Develop Language

Act It Out Have students demonstrate and describe the meaning of the verbs *blot* and *coil*.

- Dribble some water on a desktop. Ask a volunteer to blot the water with a paper towel or tissue. Say, and have students repeat: **[Student] used a [paper towel] to blot the water. The [paper towel] soaked up the water.**
- Use the illustration on p. 56 and a coiling gesture to have students demonstrate and describe the meaning of *coil*. Encourage them to describe other coiled objects they know, such as a coiled rope or a coiled snake.

● **Word Learning Strategy**

Use Context Clues

- Point out the word *charged* in the last paragraph.

  What does the word *charged* means as it is used in this sentence? *(having an electric charge; containing flowing electrons)*

  What context clues help you figure out the meaning? *("particles flow through coins . . . and back to the battery"; "electric current"; "bits of matter called* electrons*")*

- Remind students that when they encounter multiple-meaning words, they should analyze how the word is used in the text to determine its correct meaning in that instance. **L.5.4a**

Think Use what you learned from reading the technical text to respond to the following questions.

Read all the directions to understand what you're making or doing. Then reread and picture what happens at each step.

1 This question has two parts. Answer Part A. Then answer Part B.

Part A
Which statement **best** describes how an electric current affects a compass?

- A The electric current goes from the wire into the compass.
- B The electric current works only with thin copper wire.
- (C) The electric current makes the compass needle move.
- D The electric current causes the nail to swing near the compass.

Part B
Which **two** sentences **best** show the relationship made in Part A?

- A "Pour vinegar into a glass with a tablespoonful of salt."
- B "Coil it tightly around an iron nail as many times as you can."
- C "Attach one end of the copper wire to the bottom coin and the other to the top washer."
- (D) "The nail should make the compass needle swing."
- E "The salt and vinegar start a chemical reaction."
- (F) "The electric current creates a magnetic field that affects a compass needle."

Talk

2 Reread the steps to make and test the battery. Why is it important to follow the steps in the order? What would happen if you didn't, or if you used different materials? Write notes from your discussion.

Write

3 **Short Response** Explain why it is important to follow the steps in order and use the proper materials. Use details from the text to support your answer. Use the space provided on page 59 to write your answer.

HINT Don't just describe the steps and materials. Explain why the steps and specific materials are necessary.

57

Integrating Standards

Use these questions to further students' understanding of the text.

- **Summarize the purpose of the experiment. Explain how you can tell whether the experiment is a success.** *(The purpose is to create a working battery. It is successful if the battery causes the needle of a compass to move.)*
  DOK 3 **RI.5.2**
- **How does the author organize information in this text?** *(The author lists the instructions in a sequence, beginning with the first step in the process and ending with the last step.)*
  DOK 3 **RI.5.5**

Monitor Understanding

If... students have difficulty answering Part B of item 1,

then... remind them that this answer depends on identifying the correct answer to Part A. To answer Part B, students should pick the two sentences that are most closely related to answer choice C of Part A, which reads "The electric current makes the compass needle move." Guide students to see that in Part B, sentences D and F relate most closely to this description because both mention the compass needle.

Think

- Have students work with a partner to complete item 1. Draw attention to the boldface words in each part.

TIP If students have trouble answering Part A, explain that the word *affects* means "causes to change in some way."

Answer Analysis

When students have finished, discuss correct and incorrect responses.

1 **Part A**
The correct choice is C.

- **A** and **B** do not tell how a battery's electric current affects a compass. **D** gives incorrect information—the nail does not swing.

Part B
The correct choices are D and F.

- **A, B, C,** and **E** are either unrelated or not closely related to the statement *The electric current makes the compass needle move.*

DOK 3

● **Monitor Understanding**

● **Integrating Standards**

Talk

- Have partners discuss the prompt. Emphasize that students should support their ideas with text details and take notes on their discussion.
- Circulate to clarify misunderstandings.

Write

- See p. 59 for instructional guidance.

Wrap Up

- Ask students to recall the Learning Target. Have them discuss the interactions among the battery's materials (the ways that the materials affect one another to produce an electric charge). Discuss how looking closely at these interactions helps them better understand this technical text.

Modeled and Guided Instruction

Write

- Remember to use the Response-Writing Routine on pp. A54–A55.

Review Responses

After students complete the writing activity, help them evaluate their responses.

3 Responses may vary but should show that students realize Oersted could not have observed a compass needle responding to a battery if the battery had not been invented. See the sample response on the student book page. ***DOK 3***

Write Use the space below to write your answer to the question on page 55.

ELECTRICITY AND BATTERIES

HINT Don't just describe what Volta and Oersted discovered. Explain how Oersted's discovery depended on Volta's.

3 **Short Response** Explain how Volta's discovery led to Oersted's discovery. Use details from the text to support your answer.

Sample response: When Alessandro Volta invented the battery in 1799, he produced an object that could make electricity flow through a wire. Years later, in 1820, Hans Oersted saw that the needle of a magnetic compass will move when brought near a wire hooked up to a battery. This observation suggested that electricity flowing through the wire could produce a magnetic force. This observation led Oersted to discover that the forces of electricity and magnetism are closely related. Without Volta's invention of the battery in 1799, Oersted might not have made his discovery about electricity and magnetism.

Don't forget to check your writing.

Scaffolding Support for Reluctant Writers

If students are having a difficult time getting started, use the strategies below. Work individually with struggling students, or have students work with partners.

- Circle the verbs in the prompt that tell you what to do, such as *describe*, *explain*, or *compare*.
- Underline words and phrases in the prompt that show what information you need to provide in your response, such as *causes*, *reasons*, or *character traits*.
- Talk about the details from the text that you will include in your response.
- Explain aloud how you will respond to the prompt.

Write Use the space below to write your answer to the question on page 57.

BATTERY POWER

3 **Short Response** Explain why it is important to follow the steps in order and use the proper materials. Use details from the text to support your answer.

HINT Don't just describe the steps and materials. Explain why the steps and specific materials are necessary.

Sample response: Following the steps in the order they appear in "Battery Power" produces a working battery. If a step is done out of order, then the experiment might fail. As for why specific materials are needed, the section "Why It Works" explains it. This section says that the salt and vinegar start a chemical reaction with the copper coins and zinc washers. This reaction lets "charged particles" flow, producing an electric current in the wire. If other sorts of materials are used, the chemical reaction might not happen and electricity won't flow. *(DOK 3)*

Check Your Writing

- ☐ Did you read the prompt carefully?
- ☐ Did you put the prompt in your own words?
- ☐ Did you use the best evidence from the text to support your ideas?
- ☐ Are your ideas clearly organized?
- ☐ Did you write in clear and complete sentences?
- ☐ Did you check your spelling and punctuation?

Teacher Notes

Write

- Ask a volunteer to read aloud the Write prompt.
- Invite students to tell what the prompt is asking them to do. Make sure they understand that they need to explain why getting the correct result *depends on using the proper materials and* following the order of the steps described.
- Call attention to the HINT.
- Remember to use the Response-Writing Routine on pp. A54–A55.

Review Responses

After students complete the writing activity, help them evaluate their responses.

3 Responses may vary but should demonstrate understanding that all the materials must be aligned precisely for the battery to work. See the sample response on the student book page. ***DOK 3***

Independent Practice

Get Started

Today you are going to read another technical text. As you read, look for relationships among steps in the process of using water to create electric power.

- Ask a volunteer to state why explaining relationships between steps in a process can help readers understand that process more deeply. Encourage students to use the Academic Talk words and phrases in their response.

 **English Language Learners**

Read

You are going to read the text independently and use what you have learned to think and write about the text. As you read, remember to look closely at details to identify the steps involved in creating hydroelectric power. Also pay attention to the relationships, or connections, between steps or events.

- Read aloud the title of the passage and then encourage students to preview the text, paying close attention to the photograph and the diagrams. Help students infer that the word part *hydro-* means "water."
- Call attention to the Words to Know in the upper left of p. 60.
- If students need support in reading the passage, you may wish to use the Monitor Understanding suggestions.
- When students have finished, have them complete the Think and Write sections.

● **Monitor Understanding**

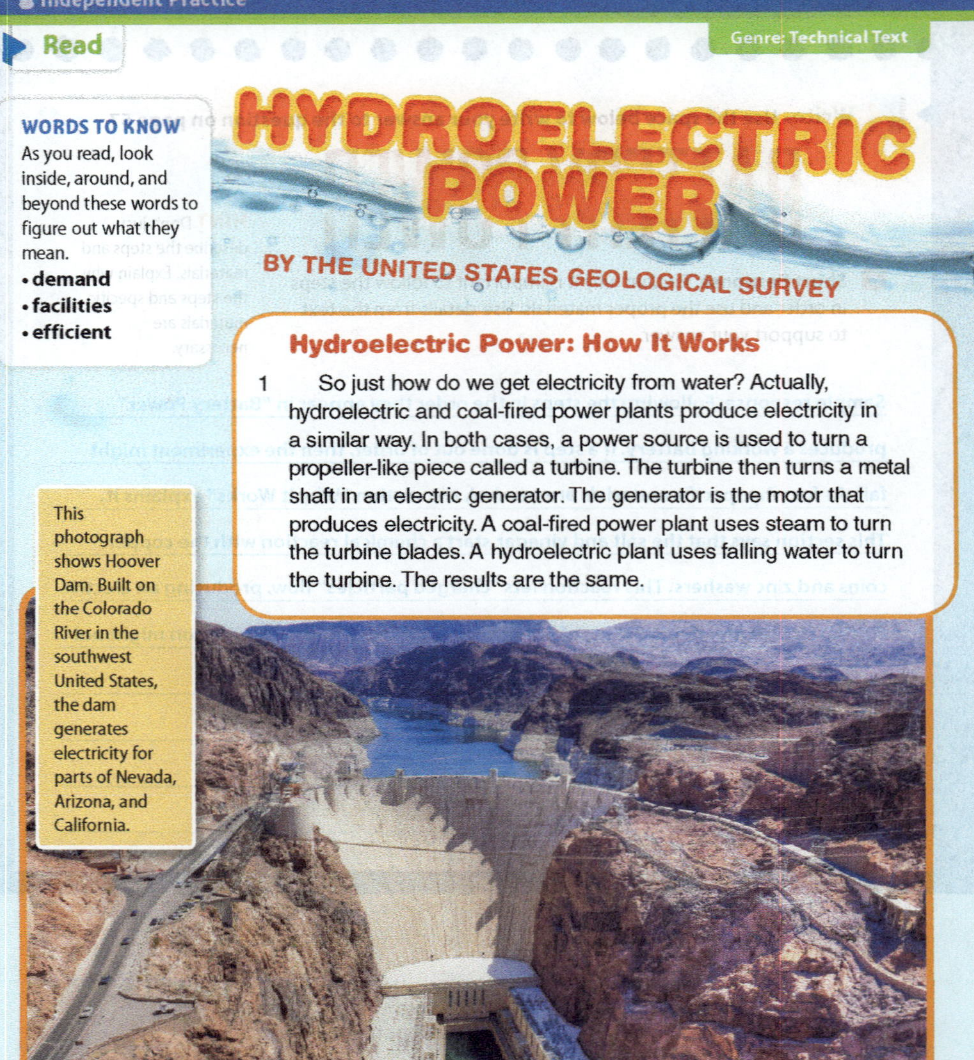
Independent Practice

Read

Genre: Technical Text

WORDS TO KNOW
As you read, look inside, around, and beyond these words to figure out what they mean.
- **demand**
- **facilities**
- **efficient**

HYDROELECTRIC POWER

BY THE UNITED STATES GEOLOGICAL SURVEY

Hydroelectric Power: How It Works

1 So just how do we get electricity from water? Actually, hydroelectric and coal-fired power plants produce electricity in a similar way. In both cases, a power source is used to turn a propeller-like piece called a turbine. The turbine then turns a metal shaft in an electric generator. The generator is the motor that produces electricity. A coal-fired power plant uses steam to turn the turbine blades. A hydroelectric plant uses falling water to turn the turbine. The results are the same.

This photograph shows Hoover Dam. Built on the Colorado River in the southwest United States, the dam generates electricity for parts of Nevada, Arizona, and California.

60

 **English Language Learners**

Build Meaning

Preview Illustrations Have students preview the visuals that accompany the text in "Hydroelectric Power." Begin by having them describe what they see in the photograph on p. 60. Then guide discussion with the following questions:

- **Where can you see water in the photograph?**
- **What structure is in front of the higher body of water in the photograph?**
- **Where do you see the same structure in the diagram on p. 61?**
- **What questions do you have about this structure?**

List students' questions. Then read aloud the first two sentences on p. 61 to make certain students have a firm understanding of the words *dam* and *reservoir*.

2 A typical hydroelectric dam is built on a large river with a large drop in elevation. The dam stores lots of water behind it in the reservoir. Near the bottom of the dam wall there is the water intake called a penstock. Gravity causes the water to fall through the penstock inside the dam. At the end of the penstock, there is a turbine propeller, which is turned by the moving water. The shaft from the turbine goes up into the generator, which produces the power.[1] Power lines connected to the generator carry electricity to your home and mine. The water continues past the propeller through the tailrace. The water then flows into the river, past the dam. By the way, it is not a good idea to be playing in the water right below a dam when water is released!

[1] For the generator to produce electricity, loops of wire must spin rapidly through force fields made by magnets.

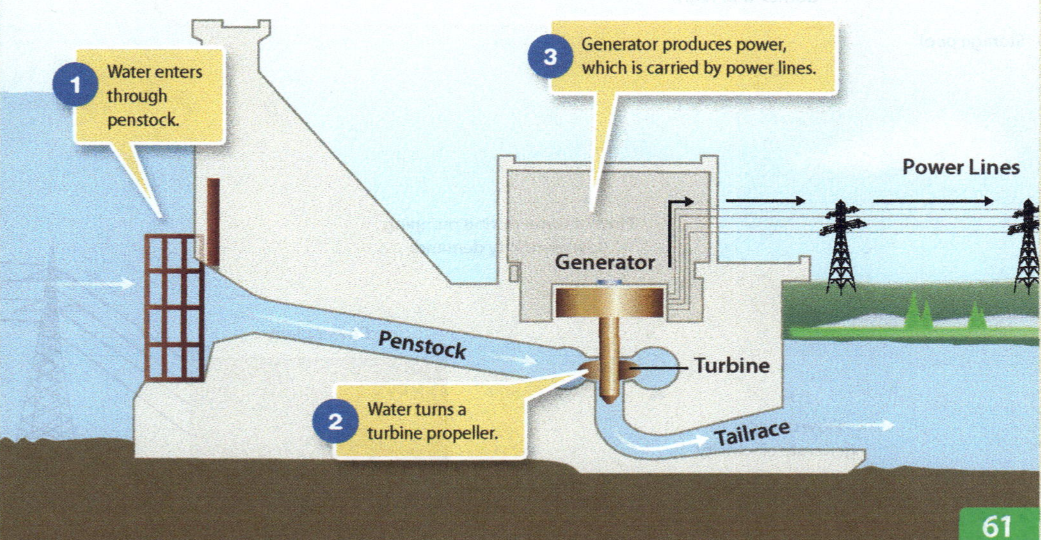

Monitor Understanding

If... students struggle to read and understand the passage, **then...** use these scaffolding suggestions:

Question the Text Preview the text by asking the following questions:

- **Based on the title and text features, what do you predict this text will be about?**
- **What questions do you have about the text?**

Vocabulary Support Define specialized terms that may interfere with comprehension, such as *coal-fired, power source, propeller, turbine, shaft,* and *generator.*

Read Aloud Read aloud the text with students. You could also have students chorally read the text in a small group.

Check Understanding Use the questions below to check understanding. Encourage students to cite details in the text and illustrations that support their answers.

- **What happens after moving water turns the propeller?** *(The moving propeller spins the turbine shaft in a generator.)*
- **Where does the electric power go after the generator creates it?** *(It travels over power lines to homes and businesses.)*
- **What is the text mainly about?** *(how people use huge dams to create hydroelectric power)*

Independent Practice

Integrating Standards

After students have read the text, use these questions to discuss the text with them.

- **Compare the photograph on p. 60 to the diagram on p. 61. Where in the photograph do you think the penstock and the tailrace are located?**
  (The penstock is probably located near the bottom of the water in the reservoir behind the dam; its entrance is probably near the bottom on the side of the dam that we cannot see in the photograph. The tailrace is probably located at the dam end of the rectangular pool shown at the bottom of the photograph.)
  DOK 3 RI.5.7
- **Reread the footnote on p. 61. What do you think causes the loops of wire to "spin rapidly through force fields"? Explain why you think your answer is correct.**
  (The force produced by the turbine's moving propeller and shaft probably causes the loops to spin. I think so because the text says, "The shaft from the turbine goes up into the generator, which produces the power." Then the footnote gives more details about how the generator creates power. I think the shaft spins inside the generator and causes the wire loops to spin.)
  DOK 3 RI.5.1
- **What reasons does the author use to show why pumped storage makes hydroelectric plants efficient?**
  (The author tells how hydroelectric plants are able to produce power differently at different times of the day. The plants store water in reserve pools when demand is low; they reuse this water to produce more power when demand is high.)
  DOK 3 RI.5.8

Theme Connection

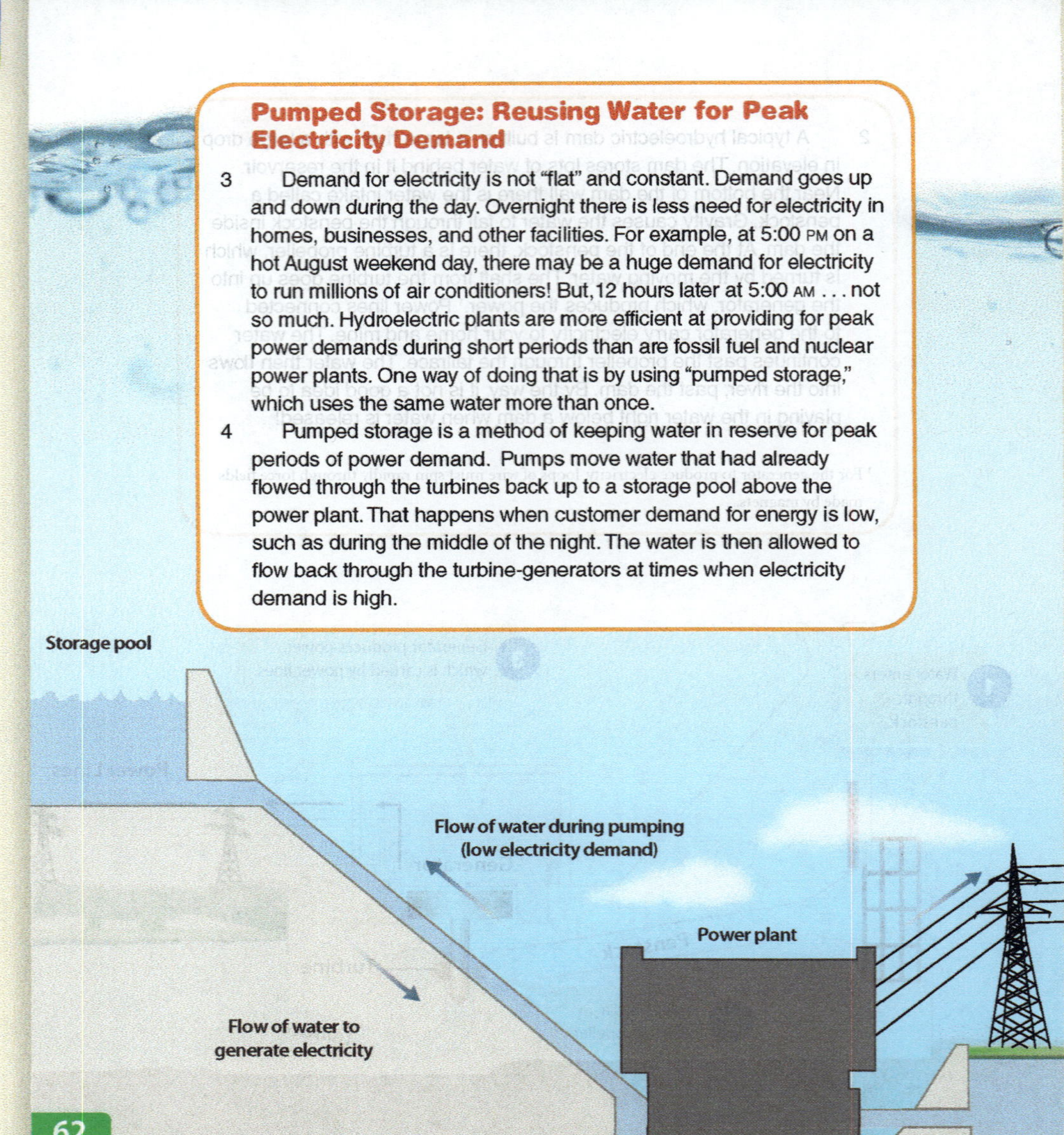

Independent Practice

Pumped Storage: Reusing Water for Peak Electricity Demand

3 Demand for electricity is not "flat" and constant. Demand goes up and down during the day. Overnight there is less need for electricity in homes, businesses, and other facilities. For example, at 5:00 PM on a hot August weekend day, there may be a huge demand for electricity to run millions of air conditioners! But, 12 hours later at 5:00 AM . . . not so much. Hydroelectric plants are more efficient at providing for peak power demands during short periods than are fossil fuel and nuclear power plants. One way of doing that is by using "pumped storage," which uses the same water more than once.

4 Pumped storage is a method of keeping water in reserve for peak periods of power demand. Pumps move water that had already flowed through the turbines back up to a storage pool above the power plant. That happens when customer demand for energy is low, such as during the middle of the night. The water is then allowed to flow back through the turbine-generators at times when electricity demand is high.

62

Theme Connection

- Remind students that the theme of this lesson is It's Electric.
- Display a four-column chart on a white board. Label each column with the passage titles, including "Introduction" for the short passage on p. 52.
- Ask students to recall facts and ideas they learned from each passage. List their responses in the appropriate column.
- Ask students to explain how all of the passages relate to the theme of electricity.

Think Use what you learned from reading the technical text to respond to the following questions.

1 The boxes below describe four events from "Hydroelectric Power." Two events are causes, one event is an effect, and one event results from that effect. The events are in no particular order.

Water is stored in response to changing demand.	People use more electricity in the day.	The demand on a power plant changes over time.	Electricity use drops at night.

Complete the diagram below by copying each event in the correct box.

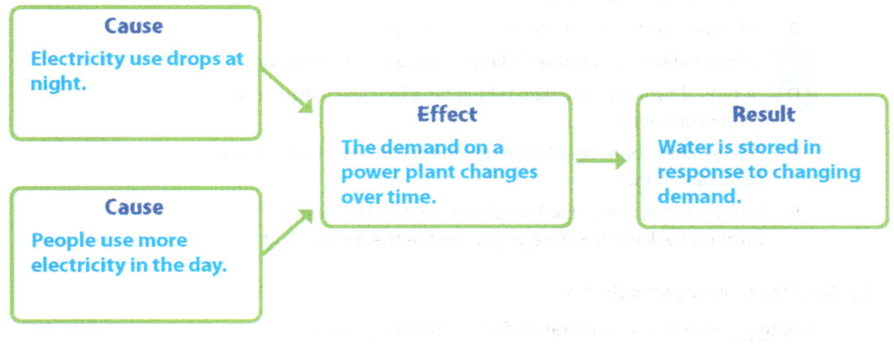

2 Which sentence describes a way hydroelectric plants are better than other power plants?

A "Actually, hydroelectric and coal-fired power plants produce electricity in a similar way."

B "A typical hydroelectric dam is built on a large river with a large drop in elevation."

C "Overnight there is less need for electricity in homes, businesses, and other facilities."

(D) "Hydroelectric plants are more efficient at providing for peak power demands during short periods than are fossil fuel and nuclear power plants."

63

Monitor Understanding

If... students struggle to complete the items,

then... you may wish to use the following suggestions:

Read Aloud Activities

- As you read, have students note any unfamiliar words or phrases. Clarify any misunderstandings.
- Discuss each item with students to make certain they understand the expectation.

Reread the Text

- Have students complete a *What Happens? and Why?* chart as they reread. For example: What Happens? *Water flows from the reservoir at the top of the dam into the penstock.* Why? *The penstock slants downhill, so gravity causes water to flow into the penstock and down, like a child sliding down a slide.*
- Have partners ask each other questions to clarify parts of the process that they do not understand.

Think

- Use the Monitor Understanding suggestions to support students in completing items 1–4.

Monitor Understanding

Answer Analysis

When students have finished, discuss correct and incorrect responses.

1 **See the answers on the student book page.** Discuss students' answers to make sure they understand which events lead to other events. Remind students that this item simulates drag-and-drop items they may see on a computer-based assessment.
DOK 3 RI.5.3

2 **The correct choice is D.** This is the only choice that clearly describes an advantage that hydroelectric plants have over other types of power plants.

- **A** only describes a similarity between hydroelectric and coal-fired power plants.
- **B** describes a characteristic of a hydroelectric plant, but it does not say whether that characteristic makes it better than other power plants.
- **C** does not describe power plants, just the facilities that rely on them to produce electricity.

DOK 1 RI.5.3

Independent Practice

3 **Part A**

The correct choice is C. This sentence provides the best summary of the process.

- **A** and **D** each describe only one aspect of the process.
- **B** is factual, but it describes a coal-fired electric plant, not a hydroelectric one.

Part B

The correct choices are C and D. These sentences are most closely related to answer choice C in Part A.

- **A, B, E,** and **F** are either unrelated or not very closely related to the statement in answer choice C in Part A.

***DOK 3* RI.5.3**

4 **The correct choice is C.** The quotation implies that a turbine "turns like a wheel."

- **A** is incorrect—a turbine is not a natural force; it is man-made.
- **B** is incorrect—a turbine is not an intake valve or a gate.
- **D** is incorrect—a turbine is part of a machine, but it does not carry things to different places.

***DOK 2* RI.5.4, L.5.4b**

3 This question has two parts. First, answer Part A. Then answer Part B.

Part A

Select the statement that **best** describes how water produces electricity.

- **A** Water is stored during periods when electricity is not needed.
- **B** A coal-fired power plant turns steam into electricity.
- **(C)** Moving water turns a turbine within a generator.
- **D** A penstock is needed to create electricity from water.

Part B

Which **two** sentences from the text **best** show the relationship described in Part A?

- **A** "Actually, hydroelectric and coal-fired power plants produce electricity in a similar way."
- **B** "The generator is the motor that produces electricity."
- **(C)** "A hydroelectric plant uses falling water to turn the turbine."
- **(D)** "A typical hydroelectric dam is built on a big river with a large drop in elevation."
- **E** "Power lines connected to the generator carry electricity to your home and mine."
- **F** "Pumps move water that had already flowed through the turbines back up to a storage pool above the power plant."

4 Read the sentence from the text.

The turbine then turns a metal shaft in an electric generator.

Which dictionary entry **best** defines turbine?

- **A** a natural force that causes things to fall
- **B** a gate for regulating the flow of water
- **(C)** an engine with a part that turns like a wheel
- **D** a machine for carrying things to different levels in a building

Monitor Understanding

If... students don't understand the writing task,

then... read aloud the writing prompt. Use the following questions to help students get started.

- **What is the prompt asking you to write about?**
- **Do you need to reread the text to find more information?**
- **How will you identify the information you need to include?**

- Have partners talk about how they will organize their responses.
- Provide a graphic organizer to assist students, if needed.

Write

5 **Short Response** Explain the role that gravity plays in a hydroelectric dam's ability to produce electricity. Use details from the text to support your answer.

Sample response: Gravity begins the whole process of creating electricity in a hydroelectric dam. Gravity causes water to move downward. Paragraph 2 explains, "gravity causes the water to fall through the penstock." Then the moving water turns the "turbine propeller." The turbine moves inside the generator, which produces electricity.

Learning Target

In this lesson, you practiced explaining the relationships and interactions between events and ideas in scientific and technical texts. Explain how your work has prepared you to read other scientific or technical texts.

Responses will vary, but students should identify that looking for and explaining the relationships or interactions of events and ideas helps them understand what scientific and technical texts are trying to tell them.

65

5 **2-Point Writing Rubric**

Points	Focus	Evidence	Organization
2	My answer does exactly what the prompt asked me to do.	My answer is supported with plenty of details from the text.	My ideas are clear and in a logical order.
1	Some of my answer does not relate to the prompt.	My answer is missing some important details from the text.	Some of my ideas are unclear and out of order.
0	My answer does not make sense.	My answer does not have any details from the text.	My ideas are unclear and not in any order.

Write

- Tell students that using what they read, they will compose a short response to the writing prompt.

Monitor Understanding

Review Responses

After students have completed the writing activity, help them evaluate their responses.

5 Display or pass out copies of the **2-Point Writing Rubric** on p. TR10. Have students use the rubric to individually assess their writing and revise as needed.

When students have finished their revisions, evaluate their responses. Answers will vary but should use details from the text to explain gravity's role. See the sample response.

DOK 3 **RI.5.3, W.5.9b**

Wrap Up

Learning Target

- Have each student respond in writing to the Learning Target prompt.
- When students have finished, have them share their responses. This may be done with a partner, in small groups, or as a whole class.

LESSON OVERVIEW

Lesson 4b Explaining Relationships in Historical Texts

Standards Focus

Explain the relationships or interactions between two or more individuals, events, [or] ideas . . . in a historical . . . text based on specific information in the text. RI.5.3

Lesson Objectives

Reading

- Identify relationships and interactions between two or more people, events, ideas, or concepts in a historical text. RI.5.3
- Explain relationships and interactions between two or more people, events, ideas, or concepts in a historical text. RI.5.3

Writing

- Draw evidence from informational texts to support analysis and reflection. W.5.9b

Speaking and Listening

- Pose and respond to specific questions and contribute to discussions. SL.5.1c
- Review the key ideas expressed and draw conclusions. SL.5.1d

Language

- Consult reference materials to determine the meaning of words. L.5.4c
- Acquire and use academic and domain-specific words and phrases. L.5.6

Additional Practice: **RI.5.1, RI.5.4, RI.5.8, RI.5.9, SL.5.1, L.5.4a**

Academic Talk

See **Glossary of Terms**, pp. TR2–TR9

- cause and effect
- ideas
- historical texts
- relationships

Learning Progression

Grade 4	Grade 5	Grade 6
Students explain events, ideas, or concepts in a historical text, including what happened and why, based on specific information in the text.	Building on Grade 4, students draw on specific details to explain the relationships or interactions among people, events, ideas, or concepts in a historical text.	Grade 6 increases in complexity by requiring students to analyze in detail how a key individual, event, or idea is introduced, illustrated, and elaborated in a text (e.g. through examples or anecdotes).

Lesson Text Selections

Modeled and Guided Instruction

Ancient Saharan Trade Routes
by Joris Maddrin
Genre: History Article

Guided Practice

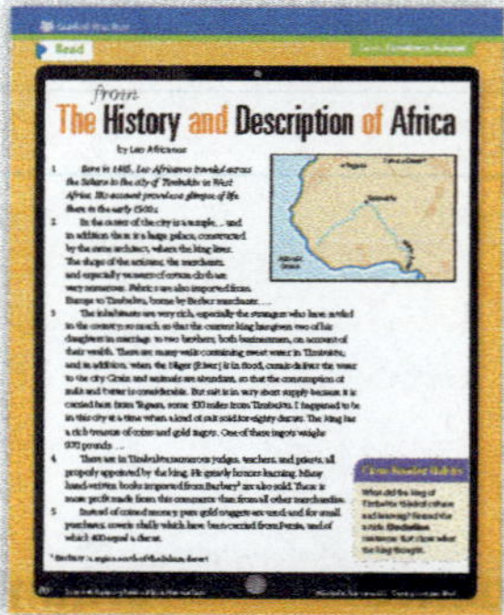

The History and Description of Africa
by Leo Africanus
Genre: Eyewitness Account

Independent Practice

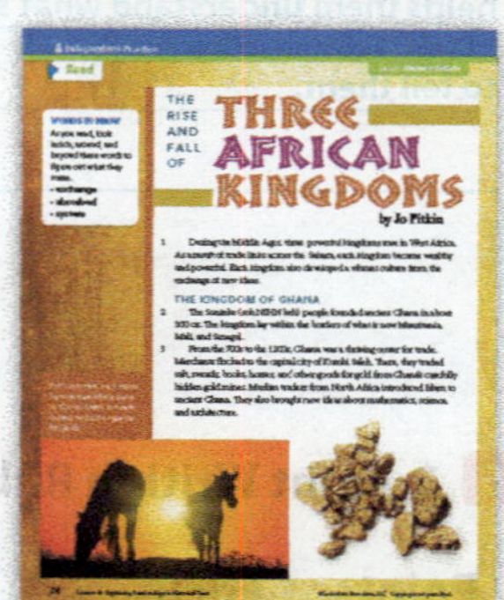

The Rise and Fall of Three African Kingdoms
by Jo Pitkin
Genre: History Article

Lesson Pacing Guide

Whole Class Instruction *30–45 minutes per day*

Day 1

Teacher-Toolbox.com **Interactive Tutorial**
Explaining Relationships in Informational Texts—Level E
20 min (optional)

Introduction pp. 66–67

- **Read** **Explaining Relationships in Historical Texts** *10 min*
- **Think** *10 min*
  Graphic Organizer: Cause-and-Effect Organizer
- **Talk** *5 min*
  Quick Write (TRB) *5 min*

Day 2

Modeled and Guided Instruction pp. 68–69, 72

- **Read** **Ancient Saharan Trade Routes** *10 min*
- **Think** *10 min*
  Graphic Organizer: Cause-and-Effect Organizer
- **Talk** *5 min*
- **Write** Short Response *10 min*

Day 3

Guided Practice pp. 70–71, 73

- **Read** **The History and Description of Africa** *10 min*
- **Think** *10 min*
- **Talk** *5 min*
- **Write** Short Response *10 min*

Day 4

Independent Practice pp. 74–79

- **Read** **The Rise and Fall of Three African Kingdoms** *15 min*
- **Think** *10 min*
- **Write** Extended Response *15 min*

Day 5

Independent Practice pp. 74–79

- *Review* Answer Analysis (TRB) *10 min*
- *Review* Response Analysis (TRB) *10 min*
- *Assign and Discuss* Learning Target *10 min*

Language Handbook
Lesson 19 Idioms, Adages, and Proverbs, pp. 474–475
20 min (optional)

Ready Writing Connection

During *Ready Reading* Days 1–5, use:
Lesson 2 Writing to Inform: Article

- **Step 1** **Study a Mentor Text**
- **Step 2** **Unpack Your Assignment**
- **Review the Research Path**
- **Read Source Text**
- **Step 3** **Find Text Evidence**
- **Reread Source Text**

See *Ready Writing TRB*, p. 32a for complete lesson plan.

Small Group Differentiation
Teacher-Toolbox.com

Reteach

***Ready Reading* Prerequisite Lesson**
- **Grade 4** Lesson 2 Understanding Historical Texts

Teacher-led Activities

Tools for Instruction
- Text Structure

Personalized Learning
i-Ready.com

Independent

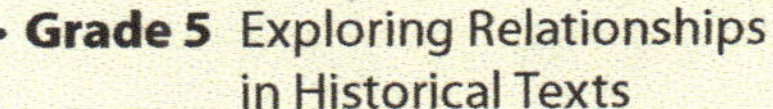
i-Ready Close Reading Lessons

- **Grade 4** Understanding Historical Texts
- **Grade 5** Exploring Relationships in Historical Texts

Get Started

- Explain to students that in this lesson they will read historical texts. They will make connections and explain cause-and-effect relationships between people, events, and ideas in history.
- Define *cause* and *effect,* using an example such as wind powering a sailing ship across the ocean. Prompt students to identify the wind filling the sails as the cause and the movement of the ship as the effect.
- Provide an example of cause-and-effect relationships in history, such as the first voyage of Christopher Columbus. Explain:

  Columbus believed the world was much smaller. This caused him to sail west from Spain, instead of east, to get to Asia. The effect of Columbus's voyage was unexpected. He reached the Americas instead of Asia.
- Focus students' attention on the Learning Target. Read it aloud to set the purpose for the lesson.
- Display the Academic Talk words and phrases. Tell students to listen for these terms and their meanings as you work through the lesson together. Use the Academic Talk Routine on pp. A48–A49.

English Language Learners

● **Genre Focus**

Read

- Read aloud the Read section as students follow along. Restate to reinforce:

  Historical texts include facts about important people, events, and ideas. Many historical texts explain what happened and why it happened. Sometimes one event has more than one cause or more than one effect.
- Direct students' attention to the passage, and have them read to identify what happened and why it happened.

RI.5.3 Explain the relationships or interactions between two or more individuals, events, [or] ideas . . . in a historical . . . text based on specific information in the text.

Lesson 4b
Explaining Relationships in Historical Texts

Explaining relationships between people, events, and ideas will help you understand what matters in historical texts.

Read When we read **historical texts**, we learn about people, events, and **ideas**. Some historical texts describe simple **cause-and-effect relationships** that tell what happened and why. Other historical texts explain how one cause led to many effects, or how several causes produced one important effect.

Read the passage below. As you do, try to identify relationships between causes and their effects.

During the Middle Ages, much of Africa was a mystery to Europeans. A few travelers, however, told tales of wealthy African kingdoms and endless supplies of gold. But was this true? Could fortunes be made there?

By the 1400s, improvements to European sailing ships made long ocean trips possible. So, Portuguese sailors began exploring along Africa's coastline. They set up trading posts in ports along the way, and other Europeans soon followed. This was because the Portuguese had discovered the stories to be true. Indeed, there was wealth to be had. Europeans could trade their goods for salt, spices, ivory, and yes, even gold!

English Language Learners
Develop Language

Concept Vocabulary To help students identify and talk about cause-and-effect relationships in the passage, encourage them to ask "why" as they read. Remind them that a *cause* is a reason why an event happened.

- Demonstrate with a simple example, such as, "James went to the store. He needed groceries."
- Model asking "why" to identify cause and effect. "Why did James go to the store? Because he needed groceries. His need for groceries was the cause, and his trip to the store was the effect."
- Have students ask and answer other "why" questions, based on their daily routines. Encourage them to name the cause and effect in each sentence pair.

● Genre Focus
Eyewitness Accounts

Explain that during Guided Practice, students will read one type of historical text called an eyewitness account. Help them infer the meaning of this text type from the word *eyewitness.*

Discuss the strengths and weaknesses of this genre. Students should recognize that people often experience or remember events differently and may have different reasons for telling the story or biases in the retelling.

Provide some examples of eyewitness accounts, such as *The Diary of Anne Frank.* Ask students to name others.

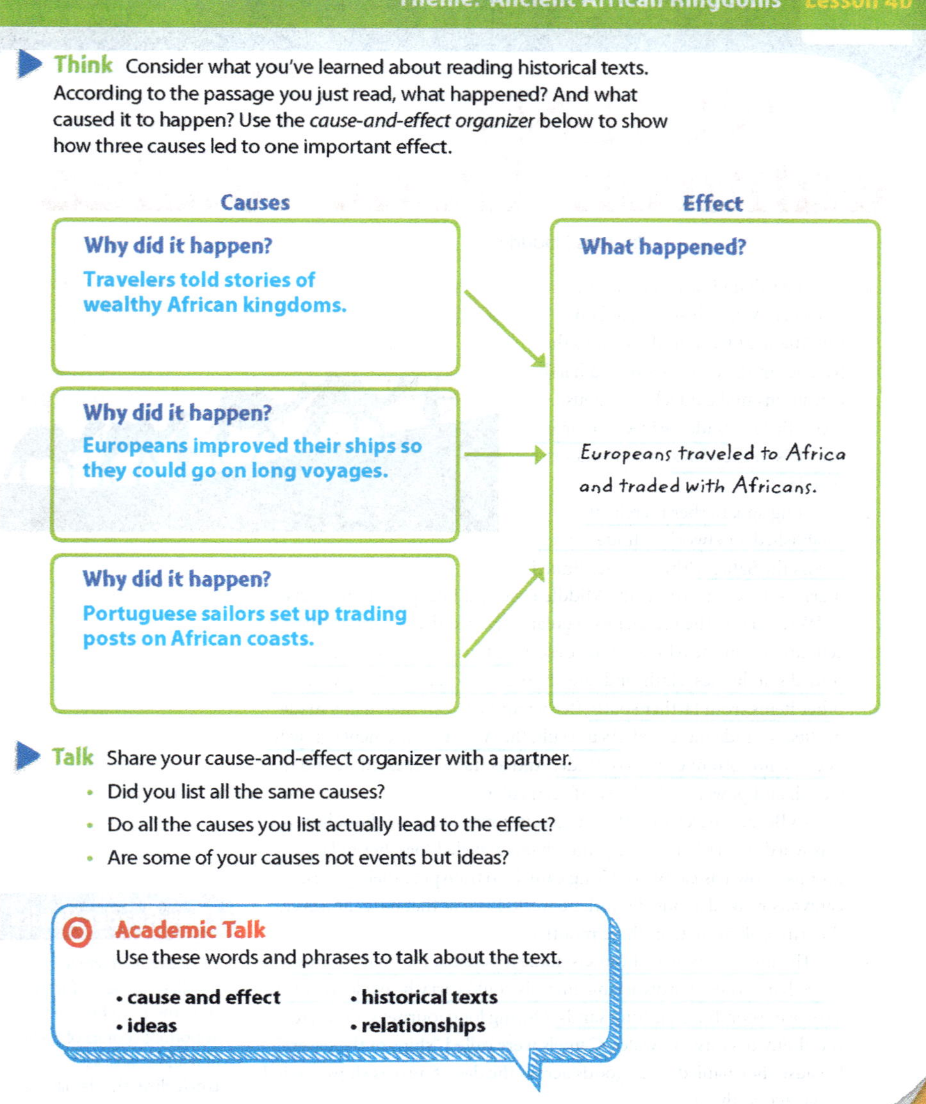

Theme: Ancient African Kingdoms Lesson 4b

Think Consider what you've learned about reading historical texts. According to the passage you just read, what happened? And what caused it to happen? Use the *cause-and-effect organizer* below to show how three causes led to one important effect.

Causes	Effect
Why did it happen? Travelers told stories of wealthy African kingdoms.	**What happened?** Europeans traveled to Africa and traded with Africans.
Why did it happen? Europeans improved their ships so they could go on long voyages.	
Why did it happen? Portuguese sailors set up trading posts on African coasts.	

Talk Share your cause-and-effect organizer with a partner.

- Did you list all the same causes?
- Do all the causes you list actually lead to the effect?
- Are some of your causes not events but ideas?

Academic Talk
Use these words and phrases to talk about the text.

- cause and effect
- ideas
- historical texts
- relationships

©Curriculum Associates, LLC Copying is not permitted.

67

Think

- Have students read aloud the Think section. Explain that the cause-and-effect organizer will help them organize the ideas in the passage.
- Have partners complete the organizer. Remind students to use the details in the passage to describe what happened and why it happened.
- As students work, circulate and provide assistance as needed.
- Ask volunteers to share what they wrote.
- Make certain students understand that what happened (the effect) is that Europeans traded with Africans and that this effect was the result of multiple causes.

Talk

- Read aloud the Talk prompts.
- Have partners discuss the causes that led to Europeans traveling to Africa. Encourage them to describe their ideas in *because* statements. The Europeans traveled . . . *because* . . .
- Ask volunteers to share their ideas.

Quick Write Have students write a response to the following prompt:

Think about a time when you did something nice for someone. Describe what you did. What caused you to do this nice thing? What were the effects of your actions?

Ask students to share their responses.

Monitor Understanding

If... students struggle to identify cause-and-effect relationships and sequences,

then... demonstrate an example. Ask students to clap when you say their names. Name several students. While they are clapping, call on other students to answer.

- **What caused the clapping?** *(You said their names.)*
- **What is the effect of the clapping?** *(The room is noisy.)*
- **The clapping caused the room to be noisy. What is the effect of the noisy room?** *(We can't hear anything else.)*

Ask students to provide other examples of how an effect becomes the cause of a different effect.

Wrap Up

- Invite students to share what they've learned so far. Encourage them to use the Academic Talk words and phrases in their explanations.
- Explain to students that when they read historical texts, they can discover the relationships, or connections, between each event.

Recognizing cause-and-effect relationships will help you understand the information in the text. You will also discover that events in history can have multiple causes, and each cause can have multiple effects. All the causes and effects together create our rich, complex history.

Monitor Understanding

Modeled and Guided Instruction

Get Started

Today you will read an article about ancient Africa. First, you'll read to understand what the author says. Then you'll read to analyze the relationships between people, events, and ideas.

Read

- Read aloud the title of the article and call attention to the photo. Encourage students to look for the words in the title as they read the article.
- Have students read the article independently. Tell them to place a check mark above any confusing words and phrases as they read. Remind students to look inside, around, and beyond each unknown word or phrase to help them figure out its meaning. Use the Word Learning Routine on pp. A50–A51.
- When students have finished reading, clarify the meanings of words and phrases they still find confusing. Then use the questions below to check understanding. Encourage students to identify details in the text that support their answers.

  Why did Berber merchants travel across the Sahara? *(to trade goods from North Africa, the Middle East, and Europe with West Africa)*

  What did the merchants trade? *(salt, horses, cloth, books, gold, metals, and spices)*

  What is the article mostly about? *(trade in West Africa and the Sahara Desert)*

 **English Language Learners**

● **Word Learning Strategy**

Explore

- Read aloud the Explore question at the top of p. 69 to set the purpose for the second read. Tell students they will need to identify cause-and-effect relationships to answer this question.
- Have students read aloud the Close Reader Habit on p. 68.

TIP To visually define *network of trade routes*, display a simple map of Africa and the Sahara Desert. Use a marker to illustrate some of the trade routes mentioned in the text.

Modeled and Guided Instruction

Read Genre: History Article

ANCIENT Saharan Trade Routes

by Joris Maddrin

1 The Sahara is a vast desert in northern Africa. It stretches from the Atlantic Ocean in the west to the Red Sea in the east. Its size and harsh conditions make travel hazardous. Nevertheless, trade thrived here from the 700s to the 1500s. It continues to this day.

2 Long ago, Berber merchants established a network of trade routes across the Sahara. These routes linked markets in North Africa, the Middle East, and Europe with markets in West Africa. The merchants regularly crossed the Sahara to African settlements on the fringes of the desert. In those settlements, they traded salt, horses, cloth, and later, books for gold, metals, spices, and other items from farther south. Berber and African merchants made profits, so trade increased. As a result, the African settlements grew to become important centers of trade. And as trade increased, so did the wealth and power of the West African rulers.

3 To Berber merchants, the dangerous journey across the Sahara was worth the risk. For safety, merchants traveled together in large groups known as caravans. Using camels to transport their goods, caravans walked about 200 miles a week. Even at that pace, however, the trip took more than three months.

4 The merchants' use of camels made it possible for them to cross the Sahara. These hardworking animals could carry heavy loads with ease over scorching, shifting sands. During long journeys, they had the ability to conserve water. Camels were called "ships of the desert" because they hauled trade goods across the desert, just as ships carried cargo across the sea.

Close Reader Habits

What events made it possible for West African settlements to become important centers of trade? Reread the article. **Underline** the details that seem most important.

68

English Language Learners

Build Meaning

Background Knowledge Guide students to an understanding of the term *Berber merchants* as well as their importance in trade with Africa.

- Draw attention to paragraph 2. Reread the first sentence aloud.
- Explain that Berber merchants were a group of people who traveled across northern and western Africa, and even into Europe, to trade. Not only did they trade goods, but they traded ideas with people across that area.
- Have students explain why the trade of ideas and language, as well as goods like cloth and gold, might be important.

● Word Learning Strategy

Use a Dictionary

- Direct students' attention to the word *established* in paragraph 2. Invite volunteers to share known or inferred meanings for the word. Then have students locate the word in a dictionary and read its various meanings.

  Which meaning makes sense in this sentence?

- Help students recognize that in this context, *established* means "to set up, or bring about on a permanent basis."
- Ask students to name organizations that were established more than 100 years ago, such as the U.S. government. **L.5.4c**

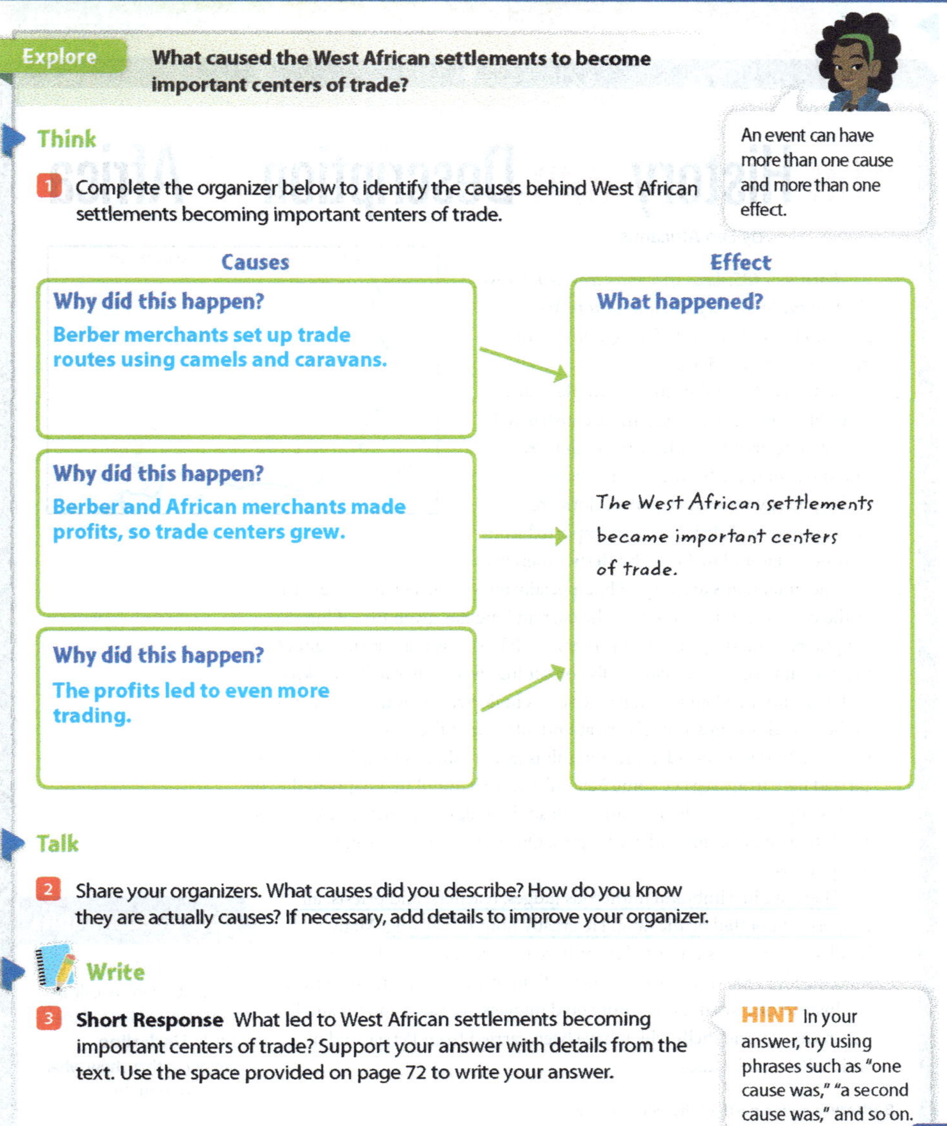

Explore What caused the West African settlements to become important centers of trade?

An event can have more than one cause and more than one effect.

Think

1 Complete the organizer below to identify the causes behind West African settlements becoming important centers of trade.

Causes	Effect
Why did this happen? Berber merchants set up trade routes using camels and caravans.	**What happened?** The West African settlements became important centers of trade.
Why did this happen? Berber and African merchants made profits, so trade centers grew.	
Why did this happen? The profits led to even more trading.	

Talk

2 Share your organizers. What causes did you describe? How do you know they are actually causes? If necessary, add details to improve your organizer.

Write

3 **Short Response** What led to West African settlements becoming important centers of trade? Support your answer with details from the text. Use the space provided on page 72 to write your answer.

HINT In your answer, try using phrases such as "one cause was," "a second cause was," and so on.

69

Think Aloud

- This graphic organizer tells me the effect, so I need to read closely to identify the causes. Each cause has to answer the question, "Why did West African settlements become important centers of trade?"
- First I'll skim to see where the text mentions West African settlements as important centers of trade. I see it near the bottom of the second paragraph: "As a result, the African settlements grew to become important centers of trade."
- "As a result" is a clue that the cause was stated in this paragraph. I'll reread it more carefully now. As I read each detail, I'll ask myself, "Does this tell me why West African settlements became important centers of trade?"
- The first detail states that the Berber merchants established trade routes across the Sahara. Without these trade routes, West African settlements could not have become important centers of trade. I'll underline this detail and add it to the organizer under "Causes."

Think

- Read aloud the Think section. Explain to students that you will model how to find text evidence to fill in part of the organizer. Use the **Think Aloud** below to guide your modeling.
- Revisit the Explore question. Guide students to determine that they need to look for more details, using the Close Reader Habit.
- Encourage students to work with a partner to continue rereading the passage and complete the organizer. Remind them to read the Buddy Tip.
- Ask volunteers to share their completed organizers.
- Guide students to see that causes and effects are linked in chains of events. Because Berber merchants established trade routes, both Berber and African merchants started to make profits. These profits caused trade to increase. All of these events led to West African settlements becoming important centers of trade.

Talk

- Read aloud the Talk prompt.
- Have partners respond to the prompt. Use the Talk Routine on pp. A52–A53.
- Circulate to check that students are discussing causes and writing reasons that West African settlements became important centers of trade.

Write

- Ask a volunteer to read aloud the Write prompt.
- Invite a few students to tell what the prompt is asking them to do.
- Make sure students understand that they need to explain specifically which people and events helped West African settlements become important centers of trade.
- Have students turn to p. 72 to write their response.
- Use Review Responses on p. 72 to assess students' writing.

Wrap Up

- Ask students to recall the Learning Target. Have them explain how knowing what happened and why it happened helped them better understand this article.

Guided Practice

Get Started

Today you will read another passage related to African history. First you will read to understand what the passage is about. Then you will reread with a partner to analyze cause-and-effect relationships.

Read

- Read aloud the title of the passage. Have students identify the writer's name. Point out the genre tab at the top of the page and review that Leo Africanus is telling about his own experiences.
- Have students predict what the passage will be about based on the title and the illustration.
- **Read to Understand** Have students read the passage independently. Tell them to place a check mark above any confusing words and phrases as they read. Remind students to look inside, around, and beyond each unknown word or phrase to help them figure out its meaning. Use the Word Learning Routine on pp. A50–A51.
- When students have finished reading, clarify the meanings of words and phrases they still find confusing. Then use the questions below to check understanding. Encourage students to identify details in the text that support their answers.

  Who is the writer, and when did he travel to Timbuktu? *(Leo Africanus traveled to Timbuktu in the early 1500s.)*

  How did Timbuktu receive goods from Europe? *(Berber merchants brought them.)*

  How does the writer describe the inhabitants of Timbuktu? *(He says they are very rich.)*

  What is the account mostly about? *(what life in the city of Timbuktu was like)*

English Language Learners

- Word Learning Strategy

- **Read to Analyze** Read aloud the Close Reader Habit on p. 70 to set the purpose for the second read. Then have students reread the passage with a partner and discuss any questions they might have.

Guided Practice

Read

Genre: Eyewitness Account

from

The History and Description of Africa

by Leo Africanus

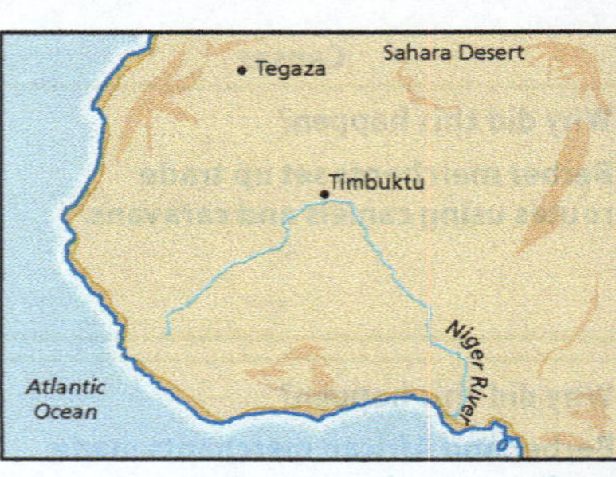

1 *Born in 1485, Leo Africanus traveled across the Sahara to the city of Timbuktu in West Africa. His account provides a glimpse of life there in the early 1500s.*

2 In the center of the city is a temple… and in addition there is a large palace, constructed by the same architect, where the king lives. The shops of the artisans, the merchants, and especially weavers of cotton cloth are very numerous. Fabrics are also imported from Europe to Timbuktu, borne by Berber merchants. …

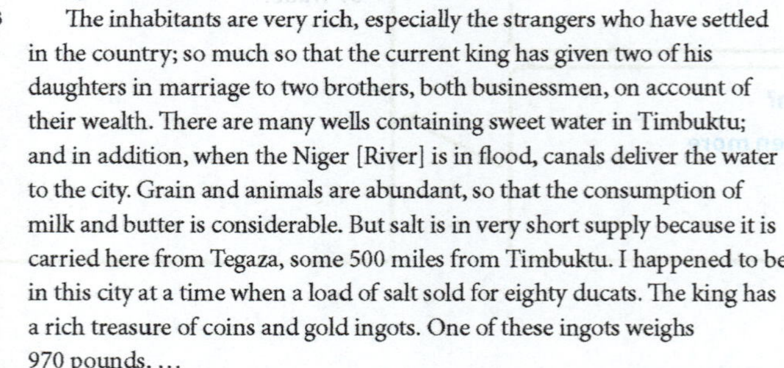

3 The inhabitants are very rich, especially the strangers who have settled in the country; so much so that the current king has given two of his daughters in marriage to two brothers, both businessmen, on account of their wealth. There are many wells containing sweet water in Timbuktu; and in addition, when the Niger [River] is in flood, canals deliver the water to the city. Grain and animals are abundant, so that the consumption of milk and butter is considerable. But salt is in very short supply because it is carried here from Tegaza, some 500 miles from Timbuktu. I happened to be in this city at a time when a load of salt sold for eighty ducats. The king has a rich treasure of coins and gold ingots. One of these ingots weighs 970 pounds. …

4 There are in Timbuktu numerous judges, teachers, and priests, all properly appointed by the king. He greatly honors learning. Many hand-written books imported from Barbary[1] are also sold. There is more profit made from this commerce than from all other merchandise.

5 Instead of coined money, pure gold nuggets are used; and for small purchases, cowrie shells which have been carried from Persia, and of which 400 equal a ducat.

[1] **Barbary:** a region north of the Sahara desert

Close Reader Habits

What did the king of Timbuktu think of culture and learning? Reread the article. **Underline** sentences that show what the king thought.

70

English Language Learners

Build Meaning

- **Cognates** Reread the first sentence of paragraph 2. Point out the word *temple*.
- Ask Spanish-speaking students (or speakers of other Latin-based languages) if they know the Spanish word for *temple (templo)*. Have them share the meaning of the word in English.
- Explain that these words are *cognates*, or words in two languages that share a similar spelling, meaning, and sometimes, pronunciation. Discuss with students how recognizing cognates can help them when they read in English.
- Call attention to other cognates in the passage, such as *palace, artisans, inhabitants*, and *abundant*.

Word Learning Strategy

Use a Dictionary

- Draw students' attention to words in this passage that are based on Latin and that begin with the prefix *con-* (Latin for "with"), including *constructed, containing, consumption*, and *considerable*. Have students deconstruct those words and define them according to their Latin roots, with the help of a dictionary.
- Encourage students to brainstorm other words beginning with the prefix *con-*. Discuss whether the meaning of the Latin prefix fits into the meaning of each word. Have students check each word in the dictionary.

L.5.4b, L.5.4c

Think Use what you learned from the eyewitness account to answer the following questions.

An eyewitness account gives the point of view of a writer who was there. Eyewitness accounts typically tell what the writer experienced.

1 The chart shows causes and effects from the text. Complete the chart by drawing Xs in the boxes to connect the causes with the effects. Some causes may have two effects.

Causes \ Effects	Timbuktu merchants became rich.	There were many judges, teachers, and priests.	Salt was imported from 500 miles away.
Berber merchants set up trade routes with Europe.	X		X
Grain and animals were plentiful, but salt was not.	X		X
The king respected education and learning.		X	

Talk

2 Based on Leo Africanus' account, what were two causes that led to Timbuktu becoming a center of culture and learning? Use the organizer on page 73 to gather evidence from the text.

Write

3 **Short Response** Use evidence from your organizer and the text to explain how Timbuktu became a center of culture and learning. Use the space provided on page 73 to write your answer.

HINT Use words and phrases such as "because" and "as a result" to show relationships.

• Integrating Standards

Use the following questions to further students' understanding of the passage.

- **What details support the inference that Leo Africanus was impressed with Timbuktu?** *(Africanus details the wealth and excess of resources. He describes weavers as "very numerous," inhabitants as "very rich," and grain and animals as "abundant.")* ***DOK 3*** **RI.5.1**
- **What do you learn from "Ancient Saharan Trade Routes" that helps you understand *The History and Description of Africa*?** *(The trading practices of the Berber merchants are important to understanding how the city of Timbuktu became a center of trade and learning.)* ***DOK 4*** **RI.5.9**

• Monitor Understanding

If... students have difficulty linking the causes and effects in item 1,

then... have them turn each effect into a question. For example, "Why did Timbuktu merchants become rich?" Students should review the text to find out which of the causes answers their question.

Think

- Have students work with a partner to complete item 1.

TIP Remind students that causes, effects, and other connections are often implied rather than stated. Tell students that sometimes they have to make an inference to understand how details are related.

Answer Analysis

When students have finished, discuss correct and incorrect responses.

1 **See the answers on the student book page.** ***DOK 2***

• Monitor Understanding

• Integrating Standards

Talk

- Have partners discuss the prompt. Emphasize that students should support their ideas with text details.
- Circulate to clarify misunderstandings.

Write

- Ask a volunteer to read aloud the Write prompt.
- Invite students to tell what the prompt is asking them to do. Make sure they understand that they need to list causes for Timbuktu becoming a center of culture and learning.
- Call attention to the HINT.
- Have students turn to p. 73 to write their response.
- Use Review Responses on p. 73 to assess students' writing.

Wrap Up

- Ask students to recall the Learning Target. Have them explain how understanding cause-and-effect relationships and sequences of events helped them better understand this eyewitness account.

Modeled and Guided Instruction

Write

- Remember to use the Response-Writing Routine on pp. A54–A55.

Review Responses

After students complete the writing activity, help them evaluate their responses.

3 Responses may vary but should explain that West African settlements became important centers of trade because of Berber merchants' trade routes in the Sahara. See the sample response on the student book page. **DOK 3**

Modeled and Guided Instruction

Write Use the space below to write your answer to the question on page 69.

ANCIENT Saharan Trade Routes

3 **Short Response** What led to West African settlements becoming important centers of trade? Support your answer with details from the text.

HINT In your answer, try using phrases such as "one cause was," "a second cause was," and so on.

Sample response: Several causes led to settlements in West Africa becoming important centers of trade. One cause was that Berber merchants set up trade routes in the Sahara using camels and caravans. A second cause was that both Berber and African merchants made profits from their trade, so trade centers grew. A third cause was that the profits made by Berber and African merchants led to even more trade. The result of these three causes working together was that West African settlements became important centers of trade.

Check Your Writing

- ☐ Did you read the prompt carefully?
- ☐ Did you put the prompt in your own words?
- ☐ Did you use the best evidence from the text to support your ideas?
- ☐ Are your ideas clearly organized?
- ☐ Did you write in clear and complete sentences?
- ☐ Did you check your spelling and punctuation?

72

Scaffolding Support for Reluctant Writers

If students are having a difficult time getting started, use the strategies below. Work individually with struggling students, or have students work with partners.

- Circle the verbs in the prompt that tell you what to do, such as *describe*, *explain*, or *compare*.
- Underline words and phrases in the prompt that show what information you need to provide in your response, such as *causes*, *reasons*, or *character traits*.
- Talk about the details from the text that you will include in your response.
- Explain aloud how you will respond to the prompt.

The History and Description of Africa

2 Use the cause-and-effect organizer below to organize your ideas and evidence.

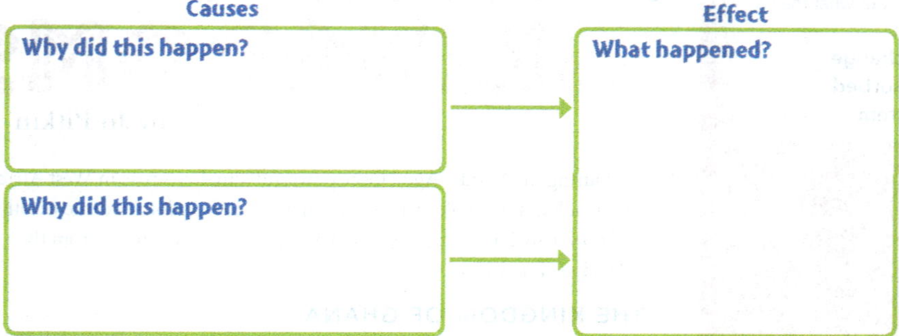

Write Use the space below to write your answer to the question on page 71.

HINT Use words and phrases such as "because" and "as a result" to show relationships.

3 **Short Response** Use evidence from your organizer and the text to explain how Timbuktu became a center of culture and learning.

Sample response: There were a couple of causes for why Timbuktu became a center of culture and learning. The first cause was that the king of Timbuktu greatly honored learning. As a result, he appointed many judges, teachers, and priests, who were all involved in Timbuktu's culture and learning. A second cause was that the trade in books imported from Barbary was more profitable than all other forms of commerce. Because the trade in books was profitable, many books came to Timbuktu, and books are an important part of culture and learning. As a result of these two causes, Timbuktu became an important center of culture and learning.

Teacher Notes

Talk

2 Students should use the cause-and-effect organizer to record their thoughts and evidence.

Write

- Remember to use the Response-Writing Routine on pp. A54–A55.

Review Responses

After students complete the writing activity, help them evaluate their responses.

3 Responses may vary but should explain that Timbuktu became a center of trade and learning because of successful trade and strong leadership. See the sample response on the student book page.
DOK 3

Independent Practice

Get Started

Today you are going to read a history article and use what you have learned about relationships between people, events, and ideas in history to explain what happened and why.

- Ask a volunteer to explain how connecting cause-and-effect chains of events can help readers understand a historical text. Encourage students to use the Academic Talk words and phrases in their responses.

 **English Language Learners**

Read

You are going to read the article independently and use what you have learned to think and write about the text. As you read, look for causes and their effects. Remember that one cause can have multiple effects, and that effects can in turn become causes of other events. Notice the dates and the names and locations of cities to make connections based on time and place.

- Read aloud the title of the passage and then encourage students to preview the text, paying close attention to the map.
- Call attention to the Words to Know in the upper left of p. 74.
- If students need support in reading the passage, you may wish to use the Monitor Understanding suggestions.
- When students have finished, have them complete the Think and Write sections.

● **Monitor Understanding**

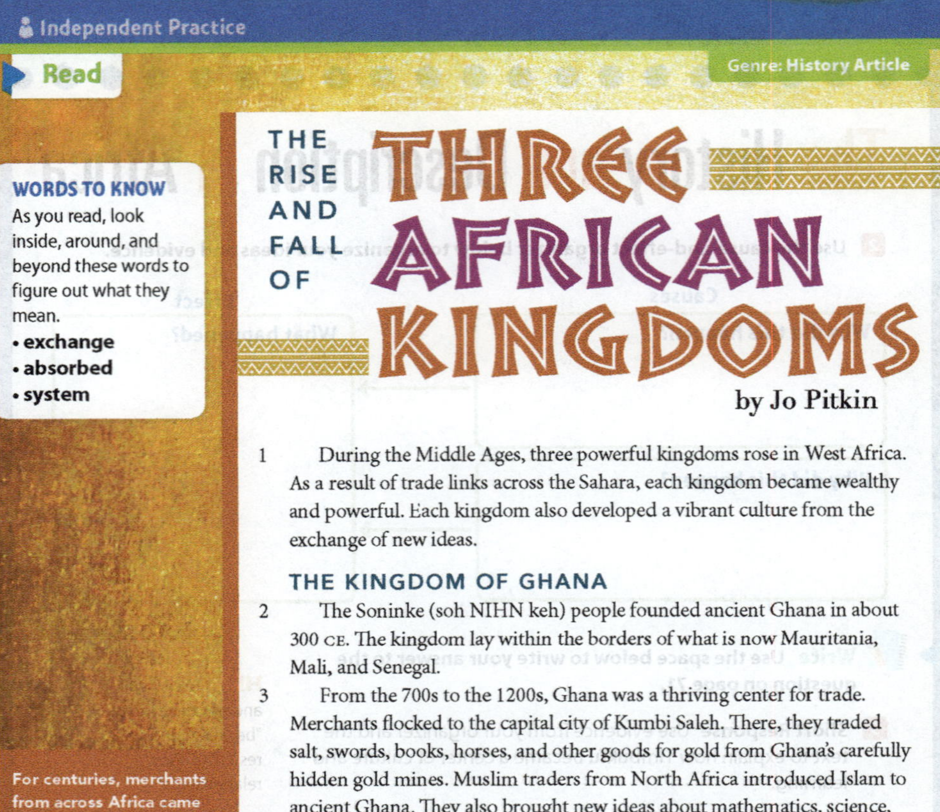

Independent Practice

Read

Genre: History Article

WORDS TO KNOW
As you read, look inside, around, and beyond these words to figure out what they mean.
- **exchange**
- **absorbed**
- **system**

THE RISE AND FALL OF THREE AFRICAN KINGDOMS

by Jo Pitkin

1 During the Middle Ages, three powerful kingdoms rose in West Africa. As a result of trade links across the Sahara, each kingdom became wealthy and powerful. Each kingdom also developed a vibrant culture from the exchange of new ideas.

THE KINGDOM OF GHANA

2 The Soninke (soh NIHN keh) people founded ancient Ghana in about 300 CE. The kingdom lay within the borders of what is now Mauritania, Mali, and Senegal.

3 From the 700s to the 1200s, Ghana was a thriving center for trade. Merchants flocked to the capital city of Kumbi Saleh. There, they traded salt, swords, books, horses, and other goods for gold from Ghana's carefully hidden gold mines. Muslim traders from North Africa introduced Islam to ancient Ghana. They also brought new ideas about mathematics, science, and architecture.

For centuries, merchants from across Africa came to Kumbi Saleh to trade horses and other goods for gold.

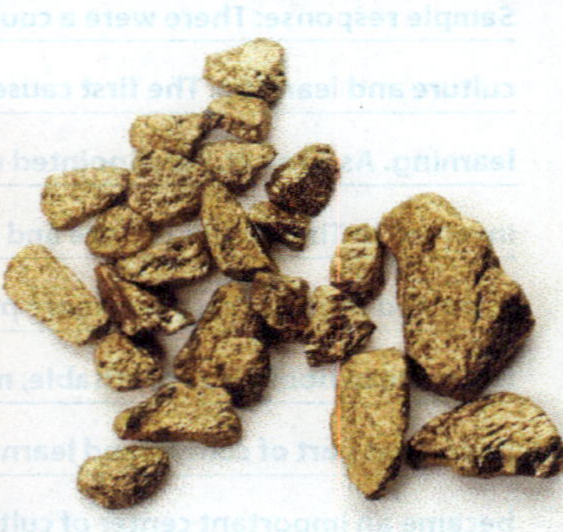

74

English Language Learners

Build Meaning

Text Features Have students preview "The Rise and Fall of Three African Kingdoms." Guide them to identify details on the map and in the photographs. Read aloud the captions and prompt discussion with the following questions:

- **What do you predict the passage will be about?** *(Students might predict that the article is about three kingdoms on the Saharan trade route that gained and lost power.)*
- **Based on what you have already read in this lesson, how do you think African kingdoms gained power? Why do you think that?** *(Students might infer that control of the trade in gold and salt helped the kingdoms gain power.)*

List students' responses. Then read aloud the first paragraph to make certain students have a firm understanding of the passage topic.

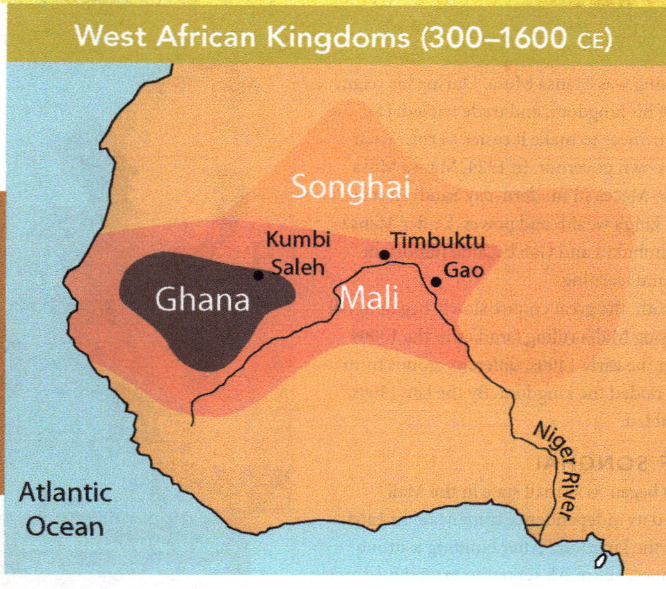

This map shows the locations of the kingdoms of Ghana, Mali, and Songhai. Ghana existed from roughly 300 to 1240 CE, but was then absorbed into the growing kingdom of Mali. Mali lasted until the late 1400s, when it was taken over by Songhai. Songhai fell in 1591.

4 Kings in Ghana helped the kingdom prosper. They controlled the gold trade and introduced a system of taxation. They taxed merchants for what they brought in and took out of the kingdom. The kings also founded an army that kept the merchants safe and protected the kingdom from invaders.

5 Ghana's empire reached its peak in the 11th century. Over the next 200 years, however, events weakened the kingdom. North African raiders repeatedly invaded Ghana. Smaller states under Ghana's control revolted. And Ghana suffered a terrible drought. By 1240, Ghana had lost its power and was absorbed into another thriving West African kingdom—Mali.

THE KINGDOM OF MALI

6 The kingdom of Mali was founded in the mid-1200s after Ghana collapsed. Its first ruler expanded the kingdom beyond the borders of Ghana and its gold fields. Mali grew to be three times the size of Ghana. At its height, Mali controlled both the gold trade and the salt trade in the north.

75

Monitor Understanding

If... students struggle to read and understand the passage, **then...** use these scaffolding suggestions:

Question the Text Preview the text by asking the following questions:

- **What types of text features has the author included?** *(photographs, captions, headings, and a map)*
- **Based on the title and the text features, what do you predict the article will be about?**
- **What questions do you have about the text?**

Vocabulary Support Define words that may interfere with comprehension, such as *vibrant, thriving, provinces,* and *empire.*

Read Aloud Read aloud the text with students. You could also have students chorally read the text in a small group.

Check Understanding Use the questions below to check understanding. Encourage students to cite details in the text that support their answers.

- **In what order did the three kingdoms rise and fall?** *(Ghana, Mali, Songhai)*
- **Who was Mansa Musa?** *(the most powerful ruler of the kingdom of Mali)*
- **What is the article mostly about?** *(three kingdoms that controlled much of West Africa over many centuries)*

Independent Practice

Integrating Standards

After students have read the passage, use these questions to discuss the passage with them.

- **What details help you infer that trade influenced Ghana's culture?** *(Paragraph 3 states, "Muslim traders from North Africa introduced Islam to ancient Ghana. They also brought new ideas about mathematics, science, and architecture." These details suggest that trade influenced the culture of ancient Ghana.)* **DOK 3 RI.5.1**
- **What is the meaning of the word *prosper* in paragraph 4? Which context clues in the passage help you determine the meaning?** *(The word prosper means "to succeed or become wealthy." The phrases "controlled the gold trade" and "introduced a system of taxation" provide clues about the meaning of the word in this context.)* **DOK 2 RI.5.4, L.5.4a**
- **What evidence supports the author's claim that Mansa Musa was Mali's most powerful king?** *(The author shows how Mansa Musa expanded his kingdom, tripled trade, and divided Mali into provinces to make it easier to rule. Following his death, the empire of Mali began to fall apart. All of these examples are evidence of Mansa Musa's great power as a king.)* **DOK 3 RI.5.8**
- **Discuss in small groups: How were Ghana, Mali, and Songhai similar and different?** *(Discussions will vary. Remind students to make comparisons, draw conclusions, and make inferences based on the information in the text. For similarities, students should identify that Ghana, Mali, and Songhai each took control of the gold trade. After Ghana fell, Mali expanded its territory. Songhai did the same thing at its height. For differences, students should recognize that Mali took control of the salt trade but Ghana and Songhai did not, and that only Songhai developed a system of laws.)* **DOK 3 SL.5.1**

● **Theme Connection**

7 Mali's most powerful king was Mansa Musa. During his reign, he extended the borders of his kingdom, and trade tripled. He divided his empire into provinces to make it easier to rule. Each province was headed by its own governor. In 1324, Mansa Musa made a religious journey to Mecca in modern-day Saudi Arabia. This drew attention to the king's wealth and power. Under Mansa Musa's rule, the cities of Timbuktu and Gao became important centers of Islamic culture and learning.

8 After Mansa Musa's death, the great empire slowly began to fall apart. Power struggles among Mali's ruling families in the 1300s weakened the kingdom. In the early 1400s, different groups from the north, south, and east raided the kingdom. By the late 1400s, the Mali empire had crumbled.

This is an image of Mansa Musa, the most powerful king of Mali. It comes from a map made around 1375. His crown and staff represent his royal power, and the golden nugget he holds indicates his great wealth.

THE KINGDOM OF SONGHAI

9 Songhai (song HIGH) began as a small state in the Mali empire. In 1340, it declared its independence from Mali. In 1464, Sunni Ali became ruler of the kingdom. After building a strong army and fleets of war canoes, Sunni Ali set out to extend his empire. He conquered Timbuktu in 1468. Then he captured what was left of the Mali territories. Now the Songhai kingdom was larger than the old empires of Ghana and Mali combined.

10 Muhammad Touré was one of Sunni Ali's generals. He ruled Songhai from 1493 to 1528. He increased the size of the empire yet again. Touré also created a new system of laws and found new ways to boost trade. By encouraging the study of mathematics and science, the king made Timbuktu into a center of learning once more.

11 Like Ghana and Mali, Songhai controlled trade routes and rich sources of gold. Yet the Songhai empire eventually fell. Power struggles erupted among leaders of different provinces. Then war broke out. Finally, Moroccan soldiers with guns invaded Songhai in 1591, defeating Songhai troops armed with swords, spears, and bows and arrows. The provinces were split up into small states, bringing the mighty Songhai empire to an end.

● Theme Connection

- Remind students that the theme of this lesson is Ancient African Kingdoms.
- Display a four-column chart. Label the columns "Introduction," "Ancient Saharan Trade Routes," "The History and Description of Africa," and "The Rise and Fall of Three African Kingdoms."
- Ask students to recall facts and ideas about ancient Africa that they learned from each passage. List their responses in the appropriate column.
- Have students draw lines to connect details that appear in more than one passage. Encourage them to connect events by causes and effects and to compare the times and places in which events took place.

Think

Use what you learned from reading the history article to answer the following questions.

1 This question has two parts. First, answer Part A. Then answer Part B.

Part A

Which of the following **best** explains why the kingdom of Mali eventually fell apart?

- A It lacked safe trade routes for merchants.
- B It failed to hide the location of its gold mines.
- (C) It was weakened by attacks from outside its borders.
- D It was split up into smaller provinces ruled by governors.

Part B

Choose the sentence that **best** supports the answer in Part A.

- A "Its first ruler expanded the kingdom beyond the borders of Ghana and its gold fields."
- B "At its height, Mali controlled both the gold trade and the salt trade in the north."
- C "In 1324, Mansa Musa made a religious journey to Mecca in modern-day Saudi Arabia."
- (D) "In the early 1400s, different groups from the north, south, and east raided the kingdom."

2 Read the sentence from the text.

Muslim traders from North Africa <u>introduced</u> Islam to ancient Ghana.

What does the prefix *intro-* in the word <u>introduced</u> mean?

- (A) to the inside
- B away from
- C yet again
- D in between

Monitor Understanding

If... students struggle to complete the items,

then... you may wish to use the following suggestions:

Read Aloud Activities

- As you read, have students note any unfamiliar words or phrases. Clarify any misunderstandings.
- Discuss each item with students to make certain they understand the expectation.

Reread the Text

- Have students complete a cause-and-effect organizer as they reread.
- Have partners summarize the text.

Think

- Use the Monitor Understanding suggestions to support students in completing items 1–3.

Monitor Understanding

Answer Analysis

- When students have finished, discuss correct and incorrect responses.

1 **Part A**

The correct choice is C. This is the reason stated in the passage for the fall of Mali.

- **A** and **B** are not supported by any details in the text.
- **D** is incorrect because, although it's true that Mansa Musa divided Mali into smaller provinces ruled by governors, the relationship between this fact and the fall of Mali is not supported by the text.

Part B

The correct choice is D. This sentence explains why Mali eventually fell apart.

- **A** tells why Mali grew strong.
- **B** is a fact about the territory Mali controlled at its height.
- **C** is a detail about Mansa Musa and how he drew attention to his kingdom abroad.

DOK 3 RI.5.3

2 **The correct choice is A.**

- **B** is incorrect because a prefix meaning *away* would be *ex-*.
- **C** is incorrect because a prefix meaning *again* would be *re-*.
- **D** is incorrect because a prefix meaning *between* would be *inter-*.

DOK 1 L.5.4b

Independent Practice

3 **Correct Answers:**
Cause: Controlled the gold trade Ghana, Mali, Songhai

- Gold mines were an important resource for all three kingdoms.

Cause: Controlled the salt trade Mali

- Mali controlled the salt trade at its height, but the passage does not mention this fact for the other two kingdoms.

Cause: Had a strong army Ghana, Songhai

- Ghana and Songhai had strong armies. Students might reasonably infer that Mali also had a strong army, but the article does not explicitly state that fact.

Cause: Had a system of laws Songhai

- The passage mentions this fact only in relation to Songhai, not the other two kingdoms.

DOK 3 **RI.5.3**

Write

- Tell students that using what they read, they will plan and compose an extended response to the writing prompt. Have students create a table with two columns and three rows, like the one shown on page 79.

Monitor Understanding

Review Responses

After students have completed each part of the writing activity, help them evaluate their responses.

4 Display the **Sample Response** for the planning chart shown on the next page. Have students compare their charts with the sample. Are they missing any information?
DOK 4 **RI.5.3**

5 Display or pass out copies of the reproducible **2-Point Writing Rubric** on p. TR10. Have students use the rubric to individually assess their writing and revise as needed.

When students have finished their revisions, evaluate their responses. Answers will vary but should include details from the text about the rise and fall of all three kingdoms.
DOK 4 **RI.5.3, W.5.9b**

3 The chart shows causes and effects that are stated in the text. Complete the chart by drawing Xs in the boxes to connect the causes with the effects. Some causes may have more than one effect.

	Effects		
Causes	Ghana grew wealthy and powerful.	Mali grew wealthy and powerful.	Songhai grew wealthy and powerful.
Controlled the gold trade	X	X	X
Controlled the salt trade		X	
Had a strong army	X		X
Had a system of laws			X

Write

What can you conclude about why Ghana, Mali, and Songhai grew powerful and eventually fell? Reread the passage. Underline specific causes that led to each kingdom's rise and fall. Then answer items 4 and 5.

4 **Plan Your Response** What are the causes of the rise and fall of Ghana, Mali, and Songhai? Use an organizer to gather evidence from the text.

5 **Write an Extended Response** Use evidence from the text and information from your organizer to explain why Ghana, Mali, and Songhai rose and fell.

Responses will vary, but a top-scoring response will clearly identify causes and effects of the rise and fall of each kingdom: Ghana, Mali, and Songhai. Students will use details from the text to support their explanations of events.

Monitor Understanding

If... students don't understand the writing task,

then... read aloud the writing prompt. Use the following questions to help students get started.

- **What is the prompt asking you to write about?**
- **Do you need to reread the text to find more information?**
- **How will you identify the information you need to include?**

- Have partners talk about how they will organize their responses.

Learning Target

In this lesson, you explained the relationships between people, events, and ideas in different historical texts. Describe how doing so will help you better understand historical texts.

Responses will vary, but students should identify ways that explaining relationships in historical texts will help them understand how and why events in history happen.

Wrap Up

Learning Target

- Have each student respond in writing to the Learning Target prompt.
- When students have finished, have them share their responses. This may be done with a partner, in small groups, or as a whole class.

4 Sample Response

	Causes of Rise	Causes of Fall
Ghana	Trade, strong kings, gold mines, system of taxation, strong army	Raiders invaded, small states revolted, terrible drought
Mali	Large territory, gold and salt, tripled trade, divided territory, center of culture and learning	Power struggles; invaders from north, south, and east
Songhai	Strong king, Sunni Ali; strong army and navy; large territory; laws; trade; arts and sciences	Power struggles among leaders, war, foreign invaders with superior weapons

5 Writing Rubric

Points	Focus	Evidence	Organization
2	My answer does exactly what the prompt asked me to do.	My answer is supported with plenty of details from the text.	My ideas are clear and in a logical order.
1	Some of my answer does not relate to the prompt.	My answer is missing some important details from the text.	Some of my ideas are unclear and out of order.
0	My answer does not make sense.	My answer does not have any details from the text.	My ideas are unclear and not in any order.

Assessment

Get Started

Today you are going to read a historical article. You will use what you have learned in this unit to understand what you are reading.

- Ask students to recall what they have learned, such as asking and answering questions, looking for connections between events, and the main idea in a text.
- Encourage students to use the Academic Talk words and phrases from the unit's lessons in their response.

Read

You are going to read the article independently and use what you have learned to think and write about the text.

- Ask a student to read aloud the title of the passage.
- Encourage students to preview the text, paying close attention to the photographs, captions, and map.
- Remind students to look inside, around, and beyond when they encounter unfamiliar words. Use the Word Learning Routine on pp. A50–A51.
- When students have finished, have them complete the Think and Write sections.

Read

Genre: History Article

Read the history article. Then answer the questions that follow.

A Time of Discovery and Rediscovery

by Nancy Day, *Calliope*

1 Italy had awakened from a thousand-year slumber, or so it seemed to fifteenth-century Italians. They felt that the fifth-century sacking of Rome by invading tribes was the bitter pill that had put the world to sleep. They began to call the centuries that followed the Dark Ages. The time period in which they lived was the Renaissance, or "rebirth." Was their comparison fair? Historians disagree. What is clear is that the Renaissance was a remarkable time of discovery and rediscovery that changed the world.

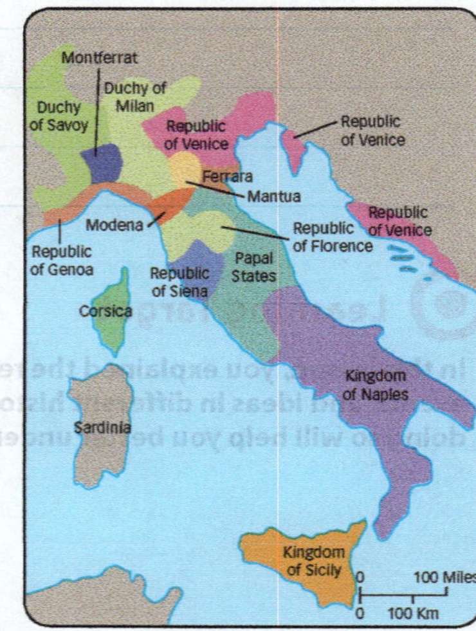

Renaissance Italy

2 In 1347, a merchant ship sailed from Crimea on the Black Sea to Sicily. Onboard were rats infested with fleas that carried a disease called the plague. Soon after, the plague swept through Italy and the rest of Europe. It killed more than one-third of the population. Cities shrank, production slowed, and prices dropped. Rather than give in to low grain prices, Italians switched to more profitable products such as wine, oil, and cheese. As wool exports fell, they turned to silk. Gradually, Italy began to specialize in luxuries such as artistic metalwork, fine leather, and beautiful furniture.

3 The northern Italian city-states, including Venice, Milan, and Florence, prospered. So did the Papal States of central Italy and the kingdoms of Naples and Sicily to the south. Money bought education for the privileged few. Learning had previously focused on religious studies. It expanded to include grammar, rhetoric, history, poetry, and moral philosophy. Wealthy Italians thought that these subjects would lead to a greater understanding of human nature and give them an advantage in business.

4 Renaissance Italians turned to ancient Rome as the model for a great civilization. Lawyers studied Roman law. Others discovered the joy of reading classical books. They became interested in poetry, history, and philosophy. Before long, scholars were rediscovering Greek and Roman art, science, and literature.

5 In the Middle Ages, the Church had taught people to think about the afterlife. During the Renaissance, people wanted to enjoy life on earth. Enthusiasm for games, sports, and entertainment blossomed. Music flourished.

6 Individual expression and accomplishment became important. The fourteenth-century Italian poet and scholar Petrarch spent countless hours studying ancient texts. He left a detailed record of his thoughts and activities. The ideal was to be well-rounded. A "Renaissance man" was supposed to be skilled in all the arts and sciences. A perfect example was Leonardo da Vinci. He was a painter, sculptor, architect, musician, engineer, and scientist.

7 Interest in humanity brought realism to art. The great sculptor Donatello, while working on a particularly lifelike work, was heard saying to the stone, "Speak then! Why will you not speak!" Painters drew everyday people in natural settings and faces that showed each individual's personality and emotions.

8 Art stimulated interest in anatomy, mathematics, and even physics. Leonardo's famous flying machine, for example, was designed to make a decorative angel flap its wings when pulled through the streets during Carnival. Leonardo also studied anatomy by dissecting human bodies. This enabled him to draw detailed studies of human figures.

Leonardo's flying machine

9 The Renaissance achievement that had the greatest effect on the modern world was the printing press. It was invented by a German craftsman named Johannes Gutenberg around 1455. The press revolutionized education and standardized language. Before the printing press, books were reproduced by

Teacher Notes

hand. As a result, few were readily available, and they were very expensive. With the invention of printing, the number of books in circulation increased. The cost of a book decreased. As more and more people bought books, the ideas of the Renaissance spread quickly.

10 Italy was located in the heart of the greatest trading area of the time. It became the center not only of trade but also of art, culture, and ideas. By the end of the fifteenth century, the Renaissance had spread to Germany. From there it spread to France, England, and Spain.

Gutenberg's printing press

11 Not everyone experienced a Renaissance. Most women had few liberties. A fourteenth-century merchant expressed the common attitude toward the female gender: "If you have women in your house, keep them shut up as much as possible and return home very often and keep them in fear and trembling." Laborers, servants, tradesmen, and apprentices also had little say in the rules that controlled their lives. In addition, they were poor and illiterate.

12 As the decades passed, the artistic, cultural, scientific, and intellectual achievements of the period between 1350 and 1550 gradually affected all levels of society. For scholars, philosophers, and artists of the time, the Renaissance led Western civilization from the Middle Ages to modern times.

Teacher Notes

Think

1 Choose the **two** main ideas and write them in each empty box labeled "Main Idea." Then choose **one** detail that best supports **each** main idea. Write each detail in the box under the Main Idea it supports.

Possible Main Ideas

The plague nearly destroyed Italy's economy.
Renaissance women had less freedom than men.
The effects of the Renaissance are still felt today.
Renaissance Italy was the center of trade as well as culture.
Both arts and sciences flourished during the Renaissance.
Italy prospered when it began selling different products.

Possible Supporting Details

"Gradually, Italy began to specialize in luxuries such as artistic metalwork, fine leather, and beautiful furniture."
"By the end of the fifteenth century, the Renaissance had spread to Germany."
"Before long, scholars were rediscovering Greek and Roman art, science, and literature."
"Cities shrank, production slowed, and prices dropped."
"The press revolutionized education and standardized language."
"If you have women in your house, keep them shut up. . . ."

Main Idea 1	Main Idea 2
The effects of the Renaissance are still felt today.	Both arts and sciences flourished during the Renaissance.

Supporting Detail	Supporting Detail
"The press revolutionized education and standardized language."	"Before long, scholars were rediscovering Greek and Roman art, science, and literature."

Teacher Notes

Answer Analysis

When students have completed the Interim Assessment, discuss correct and incorrect responses.

1 **See the answers on the student book page.**
***DOK 2* RI.5.2**

Assessment

2 **See the answers on the student book page.**

DOK 3 **RI.5.3**

3 **Students should underline the word lifelike.** The paragraph provides an example of the realism in Renaissance art, and *lifelike* serves to restate the meaning.

DOK 2 **RI.5.4, L.5.4a**

2 The chart shows causes and effects that are stated in the text. Complete the chart by drawing Xs in the boxes to connect the causes with the effects. Some causes may have more than one effect.

	Effects		
Causes	**Renaissance ideas spread.**	**Education expanded.**	**Old knowledge became valued.**
Gutenberg invented the printing press.	X	X	
Italian states and kingdoms grew wealthy.		X	
Italy was a great center of trade.	X		
Italians looked back to ancient Rome.			X

3 **Read the sentence and the directions that follow.**

Interest in humanity brought realism to art.

Underline the word in the paragraph that **best** explains the meaning of the word realism.

The great sculptor Donatello, while working on a particularly lifelike work, was heard saying to the stone, "Speak then! Why will you not speak!" Painters drew everyday people in natural settings and faces that showed each individual's personality and emotions.

Teacher Notes

4 This question has two parts. First, answer Part A. Then answer Part B.

Part A
According to the article, why was Leonardo da Vinci a perfect example of a "Renaissance man"?

A He had a great enthusiasm for games and sports.
(B) He was skilled in all areas of the arts and sciences.
C He designed and built a famous flying machine.
D He wanted more people to study anatomy and science.

Part B
Which sentence from the article **best** supports the answer to Part A?

A "He left a detailed record of his thoughts and activities."
(B) "He was a painter, sculptor, architect, musician, engineer, and scientist."
C "Leonardo's famous flying machine, for example, was designed to make a decorative angel flap its wings when pulled through the streets during Carnival."
D "Leonardo also studied anatomy by dissecting human bodies."

5 Read these sentences from the passage.

> Renaissance Italians turned to ancient Rome as the model for a great civilization. . . . Before long, scholars were rediscovering Greek and Roman art, science, and literature.

Based on these sentences, what can you infer about the Renaissance?

A The Renaissance made Italians wish they had lived in a different time.
B The Renaissance helped the Italian people become more civil and cultured.
C The Renaissance in Italy introduced new and old ideas from the Greeks and Romans.
(D) The Renaissance in Italy was influenced by ancient Greek and Roman ideas.

4 Part A

The correct choice is B. The passage states that a "'Renaissance man' was supposed to be skilled in all the arts and sciences."

- **A** is incorrect because the passage does not state that Leonardo was interested in games and sports.
- **C** correctly states that Leonardo designed a famous flying machine, but this does not explain why he was the perfect "Renaissance man."
- **D** is incorrect because the passage never states that Leonardo wanted more people to study anatomy and science.

Part B

The correct choice is B. This list of occupations shows that Leonardo was a master of many fields of study.

- **A** is not one of the requirements of a "Renaissance man."
- **C** demonstrates only one of Leonardo's talents.
- **D** shows that Leonardo was interested in science, but a "Renaissance man" had to pursue the arts, as well.

DOK 1 **RI.5.2**

5 **The correct choice is D.** Scholars of the Renaissance era studied Greek and Roman arts and sciences, which influenced the development of their own ideas.

- **A** is incorrect because the text never states that Renaissance Italians longed to live in earlier Greek and Roman times.
- **B** suggests that Italians were not previously civil and cultured, which is not supported by the text.
- **C** is incorrect because no new Greek and Roman ideas were introduced during the Renaissance.

DOK 3 **RI.5.1**

6 **See the answers on the student book page.**

***DOK 3* RI.5.3**

6 Using the list of events in the article, complete the diagram to show a cause, its effects, and then the response.

Italians began making wine, oil, and cheese.	The price of grain dropped.
The population of cities fell.	The plague swept across Europe.
Production slowed down.	

Cause: The plague swept across Europe.

Effect: The price of grain dropped.

Effect: The population of cities fell.

Effect: Production slowed down.

Response: Italians began making wine, oil, and cheese.

Teacher Notes

7 This question has two parts. First, answer Part A. Then answer Part B.

Part A
How did the printing press change people's lives?

- **A** It had little effect, as most people never learned how to read.
- **(B)** More people could afford to read books, and Renaissance ideas spread.
- **C** It had a positive effect on people who studied human anatomy.
- **D** More people were exposed to printed songs, and Renaissance music spread.

Part B
Which paragraph provides evidence to support the answer to Part A?

- **(A)** paragraph 9
- **B** paragraph 10
- **C** paragraph 11
- **D** paragraph 12

8 Read the paragraph and the directions that follow.

In the Middle Ages, the Church had taught people to think about the afterlife. During the Renaissance, people wanted to enjoy life on earth. Enthusiasm for games, sports, and entertainment blossomed. Music flourished.

Which statement **best** describes the main idea of the paragraph?

- **A** Some of the new inventions of the Renaissance include music, sports, and games.
- **B** The Church taught a different message in the Renaissance than it did in the Middle Ages.
- **C** In the Renaissance, people lost interest in the Church's teachings about the afterlife.
- **(D)** Changing values led Renaissance people to seek out various ways to entertain themselves.

7 **Part A**

The correct choice is B. Paragraph 9 states, "The press revolutionized education and standardized language."

- **A** is incorrect because paragraph 9 states that the printing press had "the greatest effect on the modern world."
- **C** is not mentioned in the passage.
- **D** is incorrect because Renaissance songs are never discussed in relation to the printing press.

Part B

The correct choice is A. This paragraph states that with the invention of the printing press, "the number of books in circulation increased, and the cost of a book decreased. As more and more people bought books, the ideas of the Renaissance spread quickly."

- **B** discusses Italy's place as the center of Renaissance trade, art, and cuture.
- **C** explains that women and the working class had less opportunity to explore Renaissance ideas.
- **D** describes the lasting effects of the Renaissance as a whole.

DOK 1 **RI.5.3**

8 **The correct choice is D.** The paragraph states that Renaissance people began to think more about their earthly lives than they had in the Middle Ages, which led to more leisure activities.

- **A** is incorrect because music, sports, and games were not invented in the Renaissance.
- **B** is not supported by the passage, which only states what the Church taught in the Middle Ages.
- **C** does not appear in the passage.

DOK 2 **RI.5.2**

Assessment

Write

Review Responses

9 After students have completed the Interim Assessment, evaluate their responses to the Extended Response using the **4-Point Writing Rubric** below.

Answers will vary but should show that students understand that the plague led to the Renaissance because the survivors were forced to produce different goods, which in turn made them wealthy enough to pursue education, art, and leisure. See the sample response on the student book page.

***DOK 4* RI.5.3**

Write

9 **Extended Response** Based on information in the article, how did the spread of the plague lead to the developments of the Renaissance?

In your answer, be sure to

- tell what effects the plague had in Italy
- tell how Italians responded to those effects
- tell how their response made the Renaissance possible
- use details from the passage in your answer

Check your writing for correct spelling, grammar, capitalization, and punctuation.

Sample response: The plague led to the Renaissance because it forced Italy to make important changes. As the passage says, the plague "killed more than one-third of the population." With fewer people, "production slowed, and prices dropped." In response to these problems, Italians had to start making higher-priced goods like wine and silk. These new products made Italy rich. As people grew wealthy, they could afford more education for their children. It was expanding education that led to the Renaissance. But without the plague, Italians would have kept selling grain. They might never have gotten rich enough to buy the education that made the Renaissance possible.

4-Point Writing Rubric

All three criteria must be satisfied in order for a response to gain full points.

Points	Focus	Evidence	Organization
4	The response demonstrates a full understanding of the prompt and provides accurate analysis.	The response supports the analysis with generous textual evidence.	Ideas are consistently presented in a purposeful and logical order.
3	The response demonstrates a good understanding of the prompt and provides mostly accurate analysis.	The response supports the analysis with adequate textual evidence.	Ideas are generally presented in a purposeful and logical order, although some ideas may be unclear or out of order.
2	The response demonstrates a general understanding of the prompt and provides some accurate analysis but includes inaccurate descriptions or explanations.	The response supports the analysis with limited textual evidence but does not reference the text explicitly.	Some ideas are presented in a purposeful and logical order, but others are unclear or out of order.
1	The response demonstrates a limited understanding of the prompt and provides limited analysis with significant inaccuracies.	The response may use textual evidence, but it does not support the analysis and does not reference the text explicitly.	Most ideas are not presented in a purposeful and logical order.
0	The response does not demonstrate understanding of the prompt.	Ideas are not supported with reference to textual evidence.	The response does not present ideas in a purposeful or logical order.

Review Unit Opener Self-Check

Ask students to complete the unit self-check on page 8 of the student book. Then have them discuss the items in the self-check with a partner. Encourage students to give each other examples from the lessons that show where they really began to understand the skill.

Finally, bring students together for a whole-class discussion. Ask them how knowing these skills have helped make them better readers. Remind them to use their Academic Talk words.

Unit 2

Key Ideas and Details in Literature

Key Ideas and Details in Literature

Have you ever heard comments like these? "You are just like your brother!" or "You're just like your cousin!" Of course you're not *just like* anyone. You're unique, but you are probably similar to some of your family members. Maybe you look alike, or act the same way when you're angry.

Characters within stories can be like relatives. They're similar enough to be compared and different enough to be contrasted. Good readers know that comparing and contrasting characters within stories will help them better understand what they read.

In this unit, you'll learn how to pay attention to the kinds of **key ideas** and **details** that can help you compare and contrast characters, settings, and events within stories, plays, and poems. You'll learn to pay attention to details that will help you determine the theme, or main message, of a selection. You'll also learn which of these details are important to include in a summary.

✓ Self Check

Before starting this unit, check off the skills you know below. As you complete each lesson, see how many more skills you can check off!

I can:	Before this unit	After this unit
compare and contrast characters and how they interact based on details in stories and plays.	☐	☐
use details to compare and contrast settings and events in stories and plays.	☐	☐
determine a theme of a story, drama, or poem.	☐	☐
explain how a theme is supported by details, including how characters respond to challenges.	☐	☐
summarize stories and plays.	☐	☐
support inferences with quotes and specific details.	☐	☐

90

page 102

page 114

page 129

page 143

page 152

page 156

page 171

91

At a Glance

- These two pages introduce students to the skills and strategies they will learn in this unit.
- The checklist allows them to see what skills they will be learning and take ownership of their progress.
- The visual table of contents gives a graphic preview of the passages in the unit.

Step by Step

- Explain to students that they are going to begin a new unit of lessons. Tell them that in all the lessons in this unit they will be learning about key ideas and details in literature.
- Have the class read together the introduction to the unit in their books. Invite and respond to comments and questions, if any.
- Then take a few minutes to have each student independently read through the list of skills.
- Ask students to consider each skill and check the box if it is a skill they think they already have. Tell students that they may have worked on similar skills in the past, but these skills go deeper than before.
- Engage students in a brief discussion about the skills. Invite students to comment on which ones they would most like to learn, or which ones seem similar or related to something they already know. Remind them that the goal is to be able to check off one skill at a time until they have them all checked.
- Invite students to look at the graphics and predict what the passages will be about.

Lesson 5
Comparing and Contrasting Characters in Drama

Standards Focus

Compare and contrast two or more characters . . . in a . . . drama, drawing on specific details in the texts (e.g., how characters interact). RL.5.3

Lesson Objectives

Reading

- Use details in a drama to describe characters. RL.5.3
- Use details to compare and contrast characters' motivations, feelings, and behaviors. RL.5.3

Writing

- Draw evidence from literary texts to support analysis and reflection. W.5.9a

Speaking and Listening

- Pose and respond to specific questions and contribute to discussions. SL.5.1c
- Review the key ideas expressed and draw conclusions. SL.5.1d

Language

- Use context as a clue to the meaning of a word or phrase. L.5.4a
- Acquire and use academic and domain-specific words and phrases. L.5.6

Additional Practice: **RL.5.1, RL.5.2, RL.5.4, RL.5.5, SL.5.1, L.5.4a, L.5.5c**

Academic Talk

See **Glossary of Terms**, pp. TR2–TR9

- compare
- stage directions
- contrast
- drama
- dialogue

Learning Progression

Grade 4	Grade 5	Grade 6
Students describe a character, setting, or event in a story or drama, drawing on specific details in the text.	Building on the Grade 4 standard, students compare and contrast two or more characters, settings, or events in a story or drama. By describing how characters interact or settings are different from one another, students will explore these elements in greater detail and better understand the text.	At Grade 6, the standard adds complexity by requiring students to describe characters in the relation to the plot. They identify how a story's or drama's plot unfolds in a series of episodes and how the characters respond or change as the plot moves toward a resolution.

Lesson Text Selections

Modeled and Guided Instruction

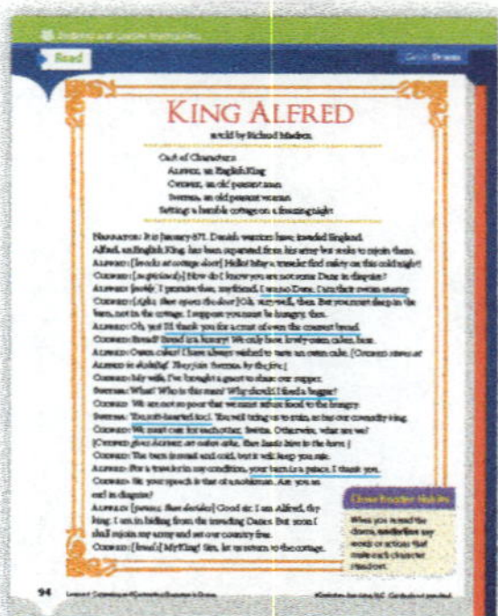

King Alfred
retold by Richard Madsen
Genre: Drama

Guided Practice

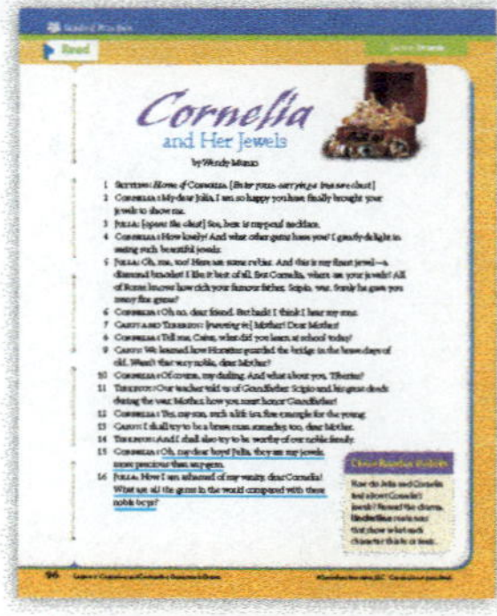

Cornelia and Her Jewels
by Wendy Munro
Genre: Drama

Independent Practice

Amelia
by Louise Rozett
Genre: Drama

Lesson Pacing Guide

Whole Class Instruction *30–45 minutes per day*

Day 1

Teacher-Toolbox.com **Interactive Tutorial**
Comparing and Contrasting Characters—Level E
20 min (optional)

Introduction pp. 92–93

- **Read** **Comparing and Contrasting Characters in Drama** *10 min*
- **Think** *10 min*
  Graphic Organizer: Venn Diagram
- **Talk** *5 min*
  Quick Write (TRB) *5 min*

Day 2

Modeled and Guided Instruction pp. 94–95, 98

- **Read** **King Alfred** *10 min*
- **Think** *10 min*
  Graphic Organizer: Venn Diagram
- **Talk** *5 min*
- **Write** Short Response *10 min*

Day 3

Guided Practice pp. 96–97, 99

- **Read** **Cornelia and Her Jewels** *10 min*
- **Think** *10 min*
- **Talk** *5 min*
- **Write** Short Response *10 min*

Day 4

Independent Practice pp. 100–105

- **Read** **Amelia** *15 min*
- **Think** *10 min*
- **Write** Short Response *10 min*

Day 5

Independent Practice pp. 100–105

- *Review* Answer Analysis (TRB) *10 min*
- *Review* Response Analysis (TRB) *10 min*
- *Assign and Discuss* Learning Target *10 min*

Language Handbook
Lesson 20 Synonyms and Antonyms, pp. 476–477
20 min (optional)

Ready Writing Connection

During *Ready Reading* Days 1–5, use:
Lesson 2 Writing to Inform: Article

- **Think It Through**
- **Step 4 Organize Your Evidence**
- **Step 5 Draft**

See *Ready Writing TRB*, p. 32a for complete lesson plan.

Small Group Differentiation

Teacher-Toolbox.com

Reteach

***Ready Reading* Prerequisite Lesson**

- **Grade 4** Lesson 7 Describing Characters in Plays

Teacher-led Activities

Tools for Instruction

- Analyze Characters

Personalized Learning

i-Ready.com

Independent

i-Ready Close Reading Lessons

- **Grade 4** Describing Characters in Plays
- **Grade 5** Comparing and Contrasting Characters in Drama

Get Started

- Explain to students that in this lesson they will read short dramas and compare and contrast the characters in each drama.
- Review what students already know about comparison and contrast. For example, choose two animals such as a lion and a dog. Invite students to share ways that the animals are alike and different. Record their responses in a Venn diagram.
- Tell students that they can compare and contrast characters in the same way. Review with students what details they look for when they describe characters. *(thoughts, words, actions)* Explain:

  We can compare what characters think, do, and say. We can compare their motivations—what causes them to do what they do. Sometimes, we can also compare what they look like. Comparing characters helps us learn more about each character and the meaning of the story.
- Focus students' attention on the Learning Target. Read it aloud to set the purpose for the lesson.
- Display the Academic Talk words and phrases. Tell students to listen for these terms and their meanings as you work through the lesson together. Use the Academic Talk Routine on pp. A48–A49.

English Language Learners

Genre Focus

Read

- Read aloud the Read section as students follow along. Restate to reinforce:

  Dialogue tells how characters think and feel. Stage directions show what characters do. Together, these can help you figure out traits, such as shyness or cleverness, which you can use to compare and contrast characters.
- Direct students' attention to the illustration. Prompt them to notice how the characters in the illustration are the same and how they are different.

Lesson 5
Comparing and Contrasting Characters in Drama

Learning Target **When you compare and contrast what characters in a drama do and say, you can better understand how they move the story along.**

Read In a **drama**, or play, you can learn about characters by reading or listening to the spoken **dialogue** between the characters. You can also read the **stage directions**, which are short notes that tell what a character is doing on stage.

You can get to know characters better by **comparing** and **contrasting** them. Identify what the characters do and say to each other, how they act, and how they look.

Read the cartoon below. Think about what the girl and boy look like, how they act, and how they interact with each other.

English Language Learners

Develop Language

Concept Vocabulary To compare and contrast, students should be able to join sentences and sentence parts with conjunctions such as *and, but, also, both . . . and,* and *neither . . . nor.*

- Demonstrate with simple examples, such as "I have a large desk. Carla has a small desk. Ben has a small desk." Use students' names and point to desks.
- Ask students to identify which desks are alike and which are different.
- Model combining the sentences with *but* and *both . . . and.* "I have a large desk, *but* Carla has a small one. *Both* Carla *and* Ben have small desks."
- Have students give examples of their own, then repeat the same procedure with *neither . . . nor.*

Genre Focus

Drama

Drama is a genre that includes plays. A play is one type of drama.

Plays are stories that are acted out on stage. They have characters, one or more settings, and a plot. The text of a play is called a *script.* Scripts include stage directions that tell how the actors should speak, move, or behave.

Provide some examples of dramas, such as plays based on *Jack and the Beanstalk* or *Stellaluna.* Then ask students to name other plays they have read or seen.

Think What have you learned about comparing and contrasting characters? How are the boy and girl in the cartoon similar and different? What do they say and do? Use the *Venn diagram* to compare and contrast the characters.

Girl Only	Both	Boy Only
Traits Confident, organized **Actions / Interactions** Sits up straight, ready to work Suggests a topic, asks the boy his thoughts	In the same class Must complete the same assignment React to the teacher	**Traits** Unsure, disorganized **Actions / Interactions** Leans over; has bored, tired, or unhappy expression Replies with a negative comment

Talk Share your Venn diagram with a partner.

- What details from the cartoon did you use to compare and contrast the boy and the girl?
- How did your comparison help you better understand each character?
- How do you think the characters will interact next?

Academic Talk
Use these words and phrases to talk about the text.

- **compare**
- **contrast**
- **drama**
- **stage directions**
- **dialogue**

93

Think

- Have students read aloud the Think section. Explain that the Venn diagram will help them organize their thinking.
- Have partners complete the Venn diagram. Model how to identify a character trait.

  I can tell that the girl is confident by the way she talks and acts. Confidence is a character trait.
- As students work, circulate and provide assistance as needed.
- Ask volunteers to share what they wrote in their Venn diagrams.
- Make certain students understand that details that tell about the boy only, and details that tell about the girl only, are contrasts. Details that tell about both the boy and the girl are comparisons.

Talk

- Read aloud the Talk prompts.
- Have partners discuss the characters' traits, actions, and interactions.
- Ask volunteers to share their ideas.

Quick Write Have students write a response to the following prompt:

Think of two characters from your favorite story, game, television show, or movie. Tell how the characters are alike and different, using at least one trait word to describe each character.

Ask students to share their responses.

Monitor Understanding

If... students struggle to identify character traits,
then... brainstorm a list of words used to describe what people are like, such as *curious, brave,* and *shy*. Ask:

- **What might a curious person say?** *("What's in there?" "I wonder how that works.")*
- **How might a curious person behave?** *(looking around, taking things apart, excited to learn more)*

Invite students to answer the questions for other words on the list. Emphasize that character traits are inferred from characters' words and actions.

Wrap Up

- Invite students to share what they've learned so far. Encourage them to use the Academic Talk words and phrases in their explanations. Also invite them to use the words *traits, same, different, but,* and *also.*
- Explain to students that when they read dramas, they will often be comparing and contrasting characters' words, actions, and traits.

  In the next section, we'll read a drama set more than a thousand years ago. Comparing and contrasting the characters' words, actions, and interactions will help us to learn more about each character's traits and motivations.

● Monitor Understanding

Modeled and Guided Instruction

Get Started

Today you will read a play set long ago. First, you'll read to understand what happens. Then you'll read to compare and contrast the characters.

Read

- Read aloud the title of the play and call attention to the cast of characters and the setting. Guide students to an understanding that the play is about King Alfred and his interactions with Cudred and Switha.
- Have students read the play independently. Tell them to place a check mark above any confusing words and phrases as they read. Remind students to look inside, around, and beyond each unknown word to help them figure out its meaning. Use the Word Learning Routine on pp. A50–A51.
- When students have finished reading, clarify the meanings of words and phrases they still find confusing. Then use the questions below to check understanding. Encourage students to identify details in the text that support their answers.

  What does King Alfred want? *(He wants food and a place to sleep.)*

  What does Cudred give him? *(an oaten cake and a place to sleep in the barn)*

  How does the play end? *(Alfred says he is king, so Cudred welcomes him inside.)*

English Language Learners

Word Learning Strategy

Explore

- Read aloud the Explore question at the top of p. 95 to set the purpose for the second read. Tell students they will need to take a closer look at each character's words, actions, and traits to answer this question.
- Have students read aloud the Close Reader Habit on p. 94.

TIP As needed, review the relationships that help reveal traits in the long-ago setting of the story: a king is far more important than a peasant, and a peasant might even fear a king; bread is more of a luxury than an oaten cake.

Modeled and Guided Instruction

Read

Genre: Drama

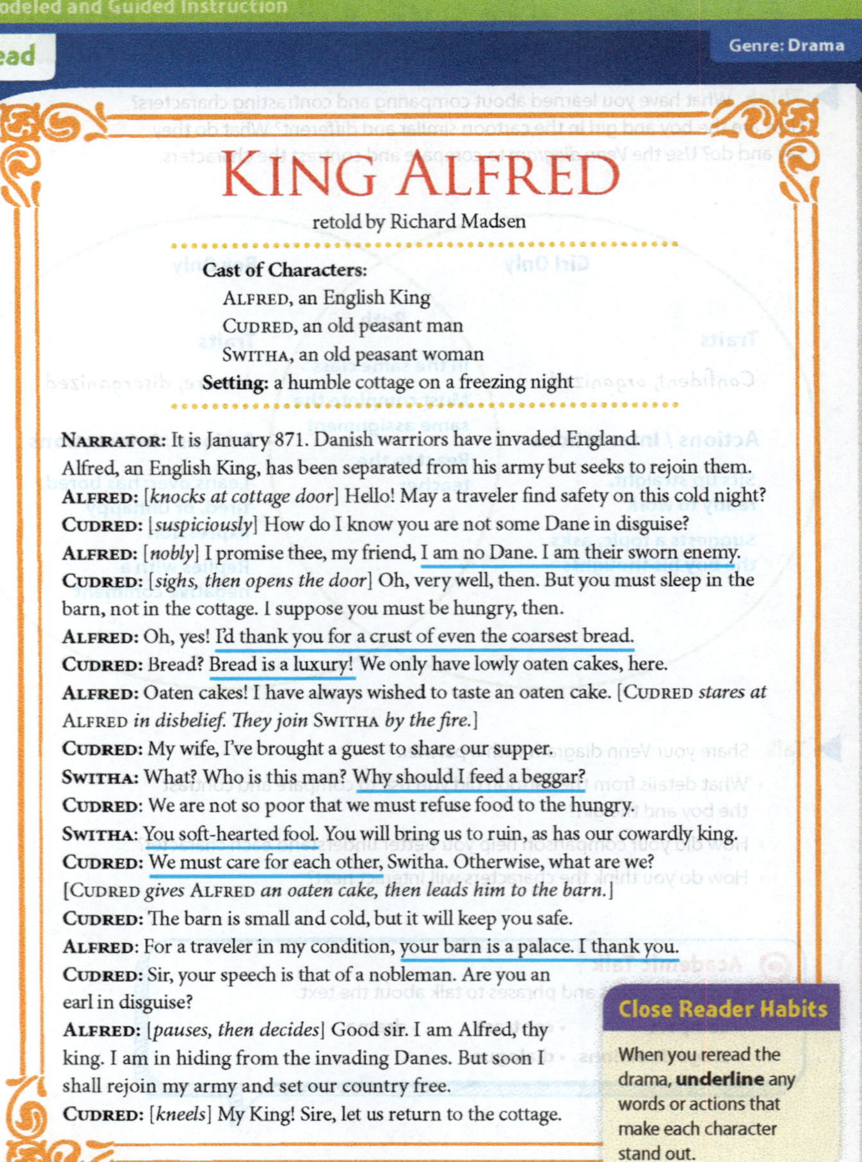

KING ALFRED

retold by Richard Madsen

Cast of Characters:

ALFRED, an English King

CUDRED, an old peasant man

SWITHA, an old peasant woman

Setting: a humble cottage on a freezing night

NARRATOR: It is January 871. Danish warriors have invaded England. Alfred, an English King, has been separated from his army but seeks to rejoin them.

ALFRED: [*knocks at cottage door*] Hello! May a traveler find safety on this cold night?

CUDRED: [*suspiciously*] How do I know you are not some Dane in disguise?

ALFRED: [*nobly*] I promise thee, my friend, I am no Dane. I am their sworn enemy.

CUDRED: [*sighs, then opens the door*] Oh, very well, then. But you must sleep in the barn, not in the cottage. I suppose you must be hungry, then.

ALFRED: Oh, yes! I'd thank you for a crust of even the coarsest bread.

CUDRED: Bread? Bread is a luxury! We only have lowly oaten cakes, here.

ALFRED: Oaten cakes! I have always wished to taste an oaten cake. [CUDRED *stares at* ALFRED *in disbelief. They join* SWITHA *by the fire.*]

CUDRED: My wife, I've brought a guest to share our supper.

SWITHA: What? Who is this man? Why should I feed a beggar?

CUDRED: We are not so poor that we must refuse food to the hungry.

SWITHA: You soft-hearted fool. You will bring us to ruin, as has our cowardly king.

CUDRED: We must care for each other, Switha. Otherwise, what are we?

[CUDRED *gives* ALFRED *an oaten cake, then leads him to the barn.*]

CUDRED: The barn is small and cold, but it will keep you safe.

ALFRED: For a traveler in my condition, your barn is a palace. I thank you.

CUDRED: Sir, your speech is that of a nobleman. Are you an earl in disguise?

ALFRED: [*pauses, then decides*] Good sir. I am Alfred, thy king. I am in hiding from the invading Danes. But soon I shall rejoin my army and set our country free.

CUDRED: [*kneels*] My King! Sire, let us return to the cottage.

Close Reader Habits

When you reread the drama, **underline** any words or actions that make each character stand out.

94

English Language Learners

Build Meaning

Prior Knowledge Show images of a peasant and a king. Ask students to name these people in their native languages. Guide them to describe common traits of each person, based on what they know.

- Work with students to transfer their understanding into English words, including *king, peasant, rich, poor, powerful,* and *humble.* Have students take turns creating sentences containing these words.

Word Learning Strategy

Use Context Clues

- Reread the lines about oaten cakes in the middle of the play. Explain that students can use context clues to figure out what these are.

  What words around *oaten cakes* tell you what they are not? *(They are not a "luxury" like bread. "Only" suggests that oaten cakes are of lesser quality than other foods.)*

  What do the details tell you about what *oaten cakes* are? *(They are "lowly"; a poor man's substitute for bread.)*

- Remind students that antonyms are one type of context clue. Antonyms tell what the word is not, making it easier to figure out what the word is. **L.5.4a, L.5.5c**

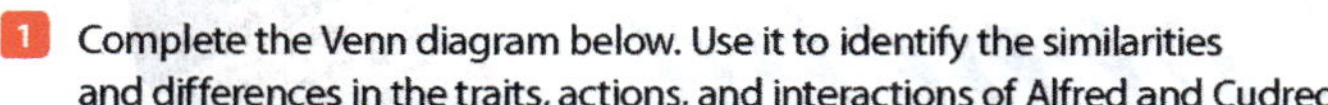

Explore In what ways are Alfred and Cudred similar and different?

Think

1 Complete the Venn diagram below. Use it to identify the similarities and differences in the traits, actions, and interactions of Alfred and Cudred.

Alfred Only

Traits
Noble, thankful
Actions / Interactions
Says he is an enemy of the Danes, separated from his army, gratefully accepts place to sleep in barn
Disguises himself, then tells Cudred who he is; hears negative things about himself

Both

Traits
Englishmen
Dislike the Danes
Polite
Humble

Cudred Only

Traits
Generous, welcoming
Actions / Interactions
Gets Switha to give Alfred bread, gives Alfred a place to stay
Tells Switha they must care about others, gives Alfred a place inside after learning he's the king

Talk

2 How would Alfred's interactions with Cudred have been different had Alfred not told the truth about who he is? Based on your discussion, decide whether you need to add or change any details in your diagram.

Write

3 **Short Response** Compare and contrast Alfred's and Cudred's traits, actions, and interactions. Include **two** details from the drama in your answer. Use the space provided on page 98 to write your answer.

HINT One way to start a compare–contrast answer is to tell how the characters are similar.

95

Think Aloud

- This Venn diagram will help me compare and contrast King Alfred and Cudred based on their traits, actions, and interactions, or what characters say and do to each other.
- I will read closely to find details about each character's traits. When Cudred questions Alfred's motives to come in, Alfred calls him "my friend" and promises that he is not a Dane in disguise. The stage direction notes that Alfred says this *nobly*. I do think this behavior is noble.
- Now I'll look at details about Cudred. Although Cudred has little food, he gives food to a stranger. He says, "We are not so poor that we must refuse food to the hungry." This is a generous action.
- Because these traits are different, I will write *Noble* in the "Alfred Only" section, and *Generous* in the "Cudred Only" section.

Think

- Read aloud the Think section. Explain to students that you will model how to find text evidence to fill in part of the Venn diagram. Use the Think Aloud below to guide your modeling.
- Revisit the Explore question. Guide students to determine that they need to look for more details, using the Close Reader Habit.
- Encourage students to work with a partner to continue rereading the passage and complete the Venn diagram. Point out that the Buddy Tip will help students compare and contrast the characters.
- Ask volunteers to share their completed Venn diagrams.
- Guide students to see that Alfred and Cudred are different because of their social status, but they are similar too. Both dislike the Danes, and both are polite, good people.

Talk

- Read aloud the Talk prompt.
- Have partners respond to the prompt. Use the Talk Routine on pp. A52–A53.
- Circulate to check that students are discussing how the interactions between the characters would have differed if Alfred had not revealed his true identity.

Write

- Ask a volunteer to read aloud the Write prompt.
- Invite a few students to tell what the prompt is asking them to do.
- Make sure students understand that they need to compare and contrast what the characters say and do, as well as their traits.
- Have students turn to p. 98 to write their responses.
- Use Review Responses on p. 98 to assess students' writing.

Wrap Up

- Ask students to recall the Learning Target. Have them explain how comparing and contrasting two main characters helped them better understand the characters and what the play is about.

Guided Practice

Get Started

Today you will read another play. First you will read to understand what happens. Then you will reread with a partner to compare and contrast the characters.

Read

- Read aloud the title of the play. Ask if anyone knows what *jewels* are. Guide students to connect to the more familiar word *jewelry*.
- Have students predict what the play will be about based on the title and the illustration.
- **Read to Understand** Have students read the play independently. Tell them to place a check mark above any confusing words and phrases as they read. Remind students to look inside, around, and beyond each unknown word or phrase to help them figure out its meaning. Use the Word Learning Routine on pp. A50–A51.
- When students have finished reading, clarify the meanings of words and phrases they still find confusing. Then use the questions below to check understanding. Encourage students to identify details in the text that support their answers.

  Name the setting and the characters. *(Cornelia's home; Julia, Cornelia, and Cornelia's sons, Caius and Tiberius)*

  What are Cornelia and Julia talking about at the beginning of the play? *(Julia's beautiful jewels)*

  Why are Caius and Tiberius excited? *(They are talking about the interesting things they learned in school that day.)*

  What jewels does Cornelia have? *(She says that her sons are her jewels.)*

English Language Learners

Word Learning Strategy

- **Read to Analyze** Read aloud the Close Reader Habit on p. 96 to set the purpose for the second read. Then have students reread the play with a partner and discuss any questions they might have.

TIP Explain that the thoughts and feelings of characters may change as they interact with other characters. Have students think about how Julia's feelings change.

Guided Practice

Read

Genre: Drama

Cornelia and Her Jewels

by Wendy Munro

1 **Setting:** *Home of* Cornelia [*Enter* Julia *carrying a treasure chest.*]

2 **Cornelia:** My dear Julia, I am so happy you have finally brought your jewels to show me.

3 **Julia:** [*opens the chest*] See, here is my pearl necklace.

4 **Cornelia:** How lovely! And what other gems have you? I greatly delight in seeing such beautiful jewels.

5 **Julia:** Oh, me, too! Here are some rubies. And this is my finest jewel—a diamond bracelet! I like it best of all. But Cornelia, where are your jewels? All of Rome knows how rich your famous father, Scipio, was. Surely he gave you many fine gems?

6 **Cornelia:** Oh no, dear friend. But hark! I think I hear my sons.

7 **Caius and Tiberius:** [*running in*] Mother! Dear Mother!

8 **Cornelia:** Tell me, Caius, what did you learn at school today?

9 **Caius:** We learned how Horatius guarded the bridge in the brave days of old. Wasn't that very noble, dear Mother?

10 **Cornelia:** Of course, my darling. And what about you, Tiberius?

11 **Tiberius:** Our teacher told us of Grandfather Scipio and his great deeds during the war. Mother, how you must honor Grandfather!

12 **Cornelia:** Yes, my son, such a life is a fine example for the young.

13 **Caius:** I shall try to be a brave man someday, too, dear Mother.

14 **Tiberius:** And I shall also try to be worthy of our noble family.

15 **Cornelia:** Oh, my dear boys! Julia, they are my jewels, more precious than any gem.

16 **Julia:** How I am ashamed of my vanity, dear Cornelia! What are all the gems in the world compared with these noble boys?

Close Reader Habits

How do Julia and Cornelia feel about Cornelia's jewels? Reread the drama. **Underline** sentences that show what each character thinks or feels.

96

English Language Learners

Build Meaning

Background Knowledge Make a concept map with *Valuable Things* in the center. Explain that this play is partly about valuable things called *jewels*. Cluster the jewels in the play around one side of the map: *pearls, rubies, diamonds*.

- Brainstorm some valuable things that people cannot touch, such as *love, friendship,* and *honesty*.
- As they read, ask students to think about what is the most valuable thing to Cornelia.
- After students read, have them add valuable things from the play to the opposite side of the concept map. Invite students to summarize what the map shows.

Word Learning Strategy

Use Context Clues

- Draw students' attention to the word *vanity* in line 16. Encourage them to think about the words around *vanity* to figure out its meaning.

  What does the word *ashamed* tell you about the meaning of *vanity*? (Vanity *is something to feel bad about. It is not good. It is negative.)*

  How do Julia's words and actions make her guilty of vanity? *(She values her jewels, or her things. But there are more important things to value.)*
- Guide students to express that *vanity* can mean "caring too much about one's appearance or possessions." Invite volunteers to use *vanity* in a sentence about the passage.

L.5.4a

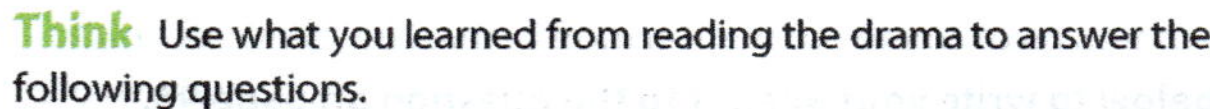

Think Use what you learned from reading the drama to answer the following questions.

A *drama* is also called a play. Like stories, plays include characters, settings, and a plot. The text of a play, called a *script*, uses stage directions. Stage directions tell actors how to move, speak, and act.

1 Which comparisons of Julia and Cornelia are true? Select **two** options.

- A Julia thinks jewels are fun to admire; Cornelia does not.
- B Julia is from a noble family; Cornelia is not.
- (C) Julia does not talk about her children; Cornelia does.
- D Julia believes history is important; Cornelia does not.
- (E) Julia has many fine gems and jewelry; Cornelia does not.
- F Julia is impressed by Cornelia's sons; Cornelia is not.

2 This question has two parts. Answer Part A. Then answer Part B.

Part A
How are Caius and Tiberius **most** similar?

- A They like learning how Horatius guarded a bridge long ago.
- B They enjoy history more than any other subject at school.
- (C) They respect their grandfather and want to be like him.
- D They think Horatius and Scipio were equally brave.

Part B
What sentence from the play **best** supports the answer in Part A?

- A "We learned how Horatius guarded the bridge in the brave days of old."
- B "Wasn't that very noble, dear Mother?"
- (C) "I shall try to be a brave man someday, too, dear Mother."
- D "What are all the gems in the world compared with these noble boys?"

Talk

3 Describe how Cornelia and Julia each feel about Cornelia's jewels.

Write

4 **Short Response** Use evidence from the text to describe how Julia and Cornelia each feel about Cornelia's jewels. Use the space provided on page 99 to write your answer.

HINT Sometimes two characters are more similar than they are different.

97

Think

- Have students work with a partner to complete items 1 and 2. Draw attention to the boldface words **two, most,** and **best** in the items.

Answer Analysis

When students have finished, discuss each response.

1 **The correct choices are C and E.** Julia shows off her jewels, while Cornelia claims that her sons are her jewels.

- **A, B, D,** and **F** are not consistent with the details in the drama.

DOK 2

2 **Part A The correct choice is C.**

- **A** is incorrect because Caius mentions Horatius. **B** and **D** are not supported by details in the drama.

Part B The correct choice is C. Caius says that he wants to be like his Grandfather Scipio.

- **A** and **B** quote Caius talking about Horatius, not Scipio. **D** quotes Julia talking about her boys, and it is not about the boys' feelings about Scipio.

DOK 2

- **Monitor Understanding**
- **Integrating Standards**

Talk

- Have partners discuss the prompt. Emphasize that students should support their ideas with text details.
- Provide copies of the Venn diagram on p. TR24 so students can record their information.
- Circulate to clarify misunderstandings.

Write

- See p. 99 for instructional guidance.

Wrap Up

Ask students to recall the Learning Target and explain how comparing and contrasting characters' actions helps them better understand a story or play.

Integrating Standards

Use the following questions to further students' understanding of the play.

- **What is one theme of the play? Use details from the text to support your answer.** *(Family is more valuable than objects are. Cornelia's last line sums up this theme: "Oh, my dear boys! Julia, they are my jewels, more precious than any gem.")*
  DOK 3 RL.5.2
- **How does Julia's point of view change?** *(In the beginning, Julia is only concerned with gems and wealth. By the end of the play, Julia recognizes that her possessions aren't as important as family is.)*
  DOK 3 RL.5.1

Monitor Understanding

If... students have difficulty finding the answer to item 2,

then... make a chart with two column headings, *Caius* and *Tiberius* and two side headings, *Says* and *Means*. Review each line of dialogue spoken by the boys; record it; then ask students to tell in their own words what it means. Note that the word *too* in the target evidence for Part B means "like my brother" and/or "like my grandfather."

Modeled and Guided Instruction

Write

- Remember to use the Response-Writing Routine on pp. A54–A55.

Review Responses

After students complete the writing activity, help them evaluate their responses.

3 Responses may vary but should show an understanding of the character traits of both Alfred and Cudred. Responses should also compare and contrast the characters using details, dialogue, and stage directions from the play. See the sample response on the student book page.
DOK 3

Write **Use the space below to write your answer to the question on page 95.**

KING ALFRED

HINT One way to start a compare–contrast answer is to tell how the characters are similar.

3 **Short Response** Compare and contrast Alfred's and Cudred's traits, actions, and interactions. Include **two** details from the drama in your answer.

Sample response: Alfred and Cudred are both polite, humble, and respectful characters. Even when Cudred is afraid the stranger at his door might be an enemy, he opens the door anyway. Alfred gratefully accepts the oaten cakes, even though he is used to better food. Alfred doesn't show anger when he overhears Switha's comment about how "cowardly" their king is. When Cudred tells Switha that all people "must care for each other," he shows kindness. When Alfred finally reveals that he is the king, his actions show that he respects his subjects. Cudred's actions also show that he respects the king when he invites Alfred into his home.

Don't forget to check your writing.

Scaffolding Support for Reluctant Writers

If students are having a difficult time getting started, use the strategies below. Work individually with struggling students, or have students work with partners.

- Circle the verbs in the prompt that tell you what to do, such as *describe*, *explain*, or *compare*.
- Underline words and phrases in the prompt that show what information you need to provide in your response, such as *causes*, *reasons*, or *character traits*.
- Talk about the details from the text that you will include in your response.
- Explain aloud how you will respond to the prompt.

Write Use the space below to write your answer to the question on page 97.

4 **Short Response** Use evidence from the text to describe how Julia and Cornelia each feel about Cornelia's jewels.

HINT Sometimes two characters are more similar than they are different.

Sample response: Cornelia describes her sons as being her jewels, and she says they are "more precious than any gem." Julia asks, "What are all the gems in the world compared with these noble boys?" Both women feel Cornelia's boys are more precious than jewels.

Check Your Writing

- ☐ Did you read the prompt carefully?
- ☐ Did you put the prompt in your own words?
- ☐ Did you use the best evidence from the text to support your ideas?
- ☐ Are your ideas clearly organized?
- ☐ Did you write in clear and complete sentences?
- ☐ Did you check your spelling and punctuation?

Teacher Notes

Write

- Ask a volunteer to read aloud the Write prompt.
- Invite students to tell what the prompt is asking them to do. Make sure students understand that they need to include both Julia's and Cornelia's feelings.
- Call attention to the HINT.
- Remember to use the Response-Writing Routine on pp. A54–A55.

Review Responses

After students complete the writing activity, help them evaluate their responses.

4 Responses may vary but should show an understanding of how Julia values objects and Cornelia values her sons, as well as how Julia's feelings change once Cornelia shares her feelings about what she values. See the sample response on the student book page. ***DOK 2***

Independent Practice

Get Started

Today you are going to read a play and use what you have learned about comparing and contrasting characters in drama.

- Ask a volunteer to explain how comparing and contrasting characters helps readers better understand dramas. Encourage students to use the Academic Talk words and phrases in their responses.

 **English Language Learners**

Read

You are going to read the drama independently and use what you have learned to think and write about the text. As you read, remember to look closely at the characters' words, actions, and traits.

- Read aloud the title of the play and then encourage students to preview the text, paying close attention to the photographs and captions.
- Call attention to the Words to Know in the upper left of p. 100.
- If students need support in reading the passage, you may wish to use the Monitor Understanding suggestions.
- When students have finished, have them complete the Think and Write sections.

● **Monitor Understanding**

Read

Genre: Drama

WORDS TO KNOW
As you read, look inside, around, and beyond these words to figure out what they mean.

- **regarded**
- **sensation**
- **determined**

by Louise Rozett, *Junior Scholastic*

1 **PROLOGUE**

2 **Prologue Narrator:** In 1920, Amelia Earhart took her first ride in an airplane and fell in love with flying. She was 23. Flying was extremely dangerous in those days and considered a man's job. Earhart decided to take lessons anyway. Within a few years, she was regarded as one of the country's best female pilots. In 1927, when a young man named Charles Lindbergh flew solo across the Atlantic Ocean and became an overnight sensation, Earhart was ready to make her mark too.

3 **SCENE 1**

4 **Narrator A:** It is 1928. Earhart is in New York City to meet with George Palmer Putnam, who has just published a book by Lindbergh. Putnam is looking for a female pilot to fly across the Atlantic.

5 **Amelia Earhart:** Pleased to meet you, Mr. Putnam.

6 **George Palmer Putnam:** I'll get right to the point, Miss Earhart. I'm told that you want to fly the Atlantic. Why?

7 **Earhart:** Why does a man ride a horse?

8 **Putnam:** Three women have died attempting the flight. If you make it, you'd be the first.

9 **Earhart:** I have a fondness for firsts, Mr. Putnam.

A photograph of George Palmer Putnam and Amelia Earhart in 1935.

English Language Learners

Develop Language

Academic Vocabulary Point out the word *Prologue* in Line 1. Ask students if they can determine what it means, based on its position in the text and the information it contains. Guide them to understand that a *prologue* is an introduction. It sometimes helps to tell the five Ws—*who, what, when, where, why*—about a play or story.

Who is the prologue mainly about? *(Amelia Earhart)*

What did Earhart do in 1920? *(In 1920, Earhart took her first ride in an airplane.)*

Point out the word *narrator*. Explain that this play has a prologue narrator and other narrators. As they read, ask students to think about what information each narrator tells.

Teacher Notes

10 **Narrator B:** Putnam explains that Earhart will become famous. But there's a catch.

11 **Putnam:** Bill Stultz will be the pilot. You'll be aboard.

12 **Earhart:** As a passenger?

13 **Putnam:** But you'd still be the first woman to fly across the Atlantic. People will remember it as your flight.

14 **Earhart:** My fraud, you mean! My dream is to fly the Atlantic, Mr. Putnam, but not like this.

15 **Putnam:** Think about it, Miss Earhart. This could win you more chances to fly.

16 **SCENE 2**

17 **Narrator C:** Swayed by the prospect of future opportunities, Earhart agrees to Putnam's plan. The pilot is to be Stultz, with Slim Gordon as navigator. Earhart is "commander" of the flight in name only.

18 **Narrator D:** On June 17, 1928, the trio is in Newfoundland, Canada, ready to depart for the transatlantic flight to Ireland. But . . .

19 **Bill Stultz:** We've got a problem. This seaplane won't take off from the harbor.

20 **Narrator E:** A determined Earhart reduces the amount of fuel they are carrying. This makes the plane lighter. Finally, it soars.

21 **Stultz:** Well done!

In June 1928, Earhart, Slim Gordon, and Bill Stultz flew this plane, named *Friendship*, across the Atlantic Ocean. This photo shows the plane off the coast of Wales, a country on the island of Great Britain.

101

Monitor Understanding

If... students struggle to read and understand the drama,
then... use these scaffolding suggestions:

Question the Text Preview the text by asking the following questions:

- **Based on the title and the text features, what do you predict the play will be about?**
- **What questions do you have about the text?**

Vocabulary Support Define words and phrases that may interfere with comprehension, such as *make her mark*, *fraud*, and *swayed*.

Read Aloud Read aloud the text with students. You could also have students chorally read the text in a small group.

Check Understanding Use the questions below to check understanding. Encourage students to cite details in the text that support their answers.

- **In Scene 1, what does Putnam want Earhart to do?** *(fly across the Atlantic as a passenger)*
- **Why does Earhart protest?** *(She does not want to be famous for flying as a passenger. She calls it a fraud.)*
- **What happens in Scene 2?** *(Earhart flies across the ocean with two men. She is not the pilot. They land safely in Wales.)*

Independent Practice

Integrating Standards

After students have read the passage, use these questions to discuss it with them.

- **What details help you infer that Earhart believed Putnam's plan would one day help her fly the Atlantic as a pilot?**

  (At the beginning of Scene 2, the narrator says, "Swayed by the prospect of future opportunities, Earhart agrees to Putnam's plan." Since she was swayed by his idea, she agreed with him and believed the flight would help her in her future.)

  DOK 3 RL.5.1

- **What does *prospect* mean as it is used by Narrator C at the start of Scene 2? Which context clues help you determine the meaning?**

  (The clues "could win you more chances" and "future opportunities" help me understand that prospect *means " a chance of something happening.")*

  DOK 2 RL.5.4, L.5.4a

- **Work with a partner or a small group to summarize Scene 1 and Scene 2.**

  (Summaries will vary. Sample response: In Scene 1, Earhart and Putnam discuss Earhart flying across the Atlantic as a passenger. Earhart wants to be the pilot. Scene 2: Earhart flies with Stultz and Gordon across the Atlantic. They run into some problems, but Earhart pushes them on, and they make it across the ocean.)

  DOK 2 RL.5.2

- **Discuss how Scene 2 builds on the information in Scene 1, or how Scene 1 helps you understand Scene 2.**

  (Discussions will vary. Students should recognize that Scene 1 is a discussion about the flight that happens in Scene 2. Scene 2 also builds on the reader's understanding of the character Amelia Earhart from Scene 2, especially her desire to be a pilot, not a passenger. Scene 1 sets up this information. Remind students to ask one another questions to clarify each other's points.)

  DOK 3 RL.5.5, SL.5.1

22 **Narrator A:** Things are fine—until the radio goes out somewhere over the ocean. In these early days of aviation, equipment is unreliable.

23 **Stultz:** We have no way to figure out wind speed or where, exactly, we are.

24 **Slim Gordon:** We've been flying for 19 hours. We have one hour of fuel left.

25 **Stultz:** If we land on the water now, we might get rescued.

26 **Earhart:** But we'll have failed. That's not an option.

27 **Gordon:** Wait. What's that?

28 **Stultz:** Land! We've got land!

29 **Narrator B:** The plane touches down on the water near a small port town. News of its arrival spreads quickly. By the time the trio reaches shore, hundreds of people have turned out, applauding and singing.

30 **Earhart:** Is it Irish tradition to greet newcomers with song?

31 **Reporter 1:** I couldn't say, Miss Earhart. This is Wales!

32 **Reporter 2:** Are you proud to be the first woman to fly the Atlantic?

33 **Earhart:** I was just a passenger. But a woman will do this one day. This flight will get women thinking, I hope.

34 **Reporter 1:** What has it got you thinking, Miss Earhart?

35 **Earhart:** That there's more to life than being a passenger.

This photograph shows Earhart on June 19, 1928, a day after her plane landed in Wales. Slim Gordon, wearing goggles, is on her left. Bill Stultz is on her right.

Think Use what you learned from reading the drama to answer the following questions.

1 Based on how Earhart and Putnam act in the first scene, which of the following **best** describes how these characters are different?

A Earhart enjoys flying more than Putnam does.

B Earhart avoids danger more than Putnam does.

(C) Earhart is more concerned about fraud than Putnam is.

D Earhart is less interested in future flights than Putnam is.

2 This question has two parts. First, answer Part A. Then answer Part B.

Part A
Which of the following describes how Earhart's behavior during the flight differs from that of Stultz?

A Earhart remains determined, but Stultz gives up completely and lands the plane in the water.

(B) Earhart remains determined, but Stultz strongly suggests landing in the water and getting rescued.

C Earhart wants to give up, but Stultz insists on trying to get the radio to work before landing.

D Earhart realizes that they must land, but Stultz insists that failure is not an option for them.

Part B
Choose **two** pieces of evidence from the text that **best** support the answer in Part A.

A "STULTZ: We've got a problem. This seaplane won't take off from the harbor."

B "STULTZ: We have no way to figure out wind speed or where, exactly, we are."

(C) "STULTZ: If we land on water now, we might get rescued."

(D) "EARHART: But we'll have failed. That's not an option."

E "EARHART: I was just a passenger. But a woman will do this one day."

F "EARHART: That there's more to life than being a passenger."

Monitor Understanding

If... students struggle to complete the items,

then... you may wish to use the following suggestions:

Read Aloud Activities

- As you read, have students note any unfamiliar words or phrases. Clarify any misunderstandings.
- Discuss each item with students to make certain they understand the expectation.

Reread the Text

- Have students complete a Venn diagram for each scene as they reread. Have them compare and contrast Earhart and Putnam in the first Venn diagram and Earhart and Stultz in the second.
- Have partners summarize the text.

Think

- Use the Monitor Understanding suggestions to support students in completing items 1–4.

Monitor Understanding

Answer Analysis

- When students have finished, discuss correct and incorrect responses.

1 **The correct choice is C.** Earhart describes the flight as "my fraud" and is upset at Putnam's plan. Putnam thinks it will lead to more chances for Earhart to fly.

- **A** is incorrect because there are no details to describe Putnam's enjoyment of flying.
- **B** is incorrect because Earhart does not avoid the danger.
- **D** is not the best answer because the play does not explicitly mention Earhart's interest in future flights. There is not enough information to make a comparison.

DOK 2 **RL.5.3**

2 **Part A**

The correct choice is B. Stultz says, "If we land on the water now, we might get rescued." He is willing to give up. Earhart is not. She says, "We'll have failed. That's not an option."

- **A** is incorrect because they land the plane only after seeing land.
- **C** is incorrect because at no moment in the play does Earhart want to give up.
- **D** is incorrect because Stultz is the one who says they should land in the water and give up, while Earhart is the one who insists failure is not an option.

Part B

The correct choices are C and D. Stultz is ready to land on water and get rescued, while Earhart will not accept failure as an option.

- **A** is a detail about their takeoff, not their landing.
- **B** is a statement from Stultz about what is going on with the equipment, not an opinion about what should be done.
- **E** and **F** indicate Earhart's desire to control both her own plane and her own life, not to be a passenger in either instance.

DOK 3 **RL.5.3**

Independent Practice

3 **See the correct answer on the student book page.** Make sure students understand which descriptions apply to each character and why. Explain to students that this item simulates drag-and-drop items they will see on computer-based assessments.

***DOK 2* RL.5.3**

4 **Part A**

The correct choice is B. The context clue in the drama is "until the radio goes out" the equipment worked.

- **A** is incorrect because something that is unreliable might still be occasionally useful.
- **C** and **D** may be facts about the radio, but they are not the meaning of "unreliable."

Part B

The correct choice is C. The radio going out is a demonstration of it being not dependable, or unreliable.

- **A** refers to removing fuel from the plane; it does not support the context of "unreliable."
- **B** indicates everything is going well, the opposite of "unreliable."
- **D** is unrelated to the equipment being either reliable or unreliable.

***DOK 2* L.5.4a**

3 In this activity, you will compare the characters of Earhart and Putnam. First, select **one** word that describes Earhart and **one** word that describes Putnam. Copy those words in the column labeled "Description." Then complete the chart by copying one quotation that provides evidence for **each** description.

Descriptions
daring
gentle
scared
convincing

Evidence
"This could win you more chances to fly."
"But we'll have failed. That's not an option."
"But there's a catch."
"I have a fondness for firsts, Mr. Putnam."

Character	Description	Evidence
Earhart	daring	"I have a fondness for firsts, Mr. Putnam."
Putnam	convincing	"This could win you more chances to fly."

4 This question has two parts. First, answer Part A. Then answer Part B.

Part A

Read this sentence from "Amelia."

In these early days of aviation, equipment is unreliable.

What does the word unreliable mean as it is used in the sentence?

- **A** not useful
- **B** not dependable
- **C** easily broken
- **D** barely modern

Part B

Which detail from the drama **best** supports the answer to Part A?

- **A** "This makes the plane lighter."
- **B** "Things are fine. . . ."
- **C** ". . . until the radio goes out. . . ."
- **D** "The plane touches down on the water. . . ."

Monitor Understanding

If... students don't understand the writing task,

then... read aloud the writing prompt. Use the following questions to help students get started.

- **What is the prompt asking you to write about?**
- **Do you need to reread the text to find more information?**
- **How will you identify the information you need to include?**

- Have partners talk about how they will organize their responses.
- Provide a graphic organizer to assist students, if needed.

Write

5 **Short Response** The drama states that Earhart was "commander" of the flight in name only. In what ways was Earhart as much in command of the flight as Stultz and Gordon? Use at least **two** details from the drama that support your response.

Sample response: Even though the play says Earhart was "commander" in name only, she makes some important decisions that affect the flight. When there is a problem taking off, Earhart reduces the amount of fuel so the plane is lighter. When the radio goes out and they are low on fuel, Earhart tells the men that failure is not an option. They keep flying until they see land. Earhart is a commanding presence on board.

Learning Target

In this lesson, you compared and contrasted what characters did and said in dramas. Explain how you can use this skill to better understand how dramas tell their stories.

Responses will vary. Students should recognize that comparing and contrasting characters allow them to better understand what each character is like, how the characters relate to each other, and why they are important to the events of the story.

5 2-Point Writing Rubric

Points	Focus	Evidence	Organization
2	My answer does exactly what the prompt asked me to do.	My answer is supported with plenty of details from the text.	My ideas are clear and in a logical order.
1	Some of my answer does not relate to the prompt.	My answer is missing some important details from the text.	Some of my ideas are unclear and out of order.
0	My answer does not make sense.	My answer does not have any details from the text.	My ideas are unclear and not in any order.

Write

- Tell students that using what they read, they will compose a short response to the writing prompt.

Monitor Understanding

Review Responses

After students have completed each part of the writing activity, help them evaluate their responses.

5 Display or pass out copies of the reproducible **2-Point Writing Rubric** on p. TR10. Have students use the rubric to individually assess their writing and revise as needed.

When students have finished their revisions, evaluate their responses. Responses will vary but should show that Earhart took charge and was "in command," at least at times. Answers should also include comparisons and contrasts with Stultz and Gordon. See the sample response on the student book page.

DOK 3 RL.5.3, W.5.9a

Wrap Up

Learning Target

- Have each student respond in writing to the Learning Target prompt.
- When students have finished, have them share their responses. This may be done with a partner, in small groups, or as a whole class.

LESSON OVERVIEW

Lesson 6
Comparing and Contrasting Settings and Events

Standards Focus

Compare and contrast two or more . . . settings or events in a story . . . drawing on specific details in the texts . . . RL.5.3

Lesson Objectives

Reading

- Use details in a story or drama to describe settings and events. RL.5.3
- Use details to compare and contrast two or more settings and events in a story or drama. RL.5.3

Writing

- Draw evidence from literary texts to support analysis and reflection. W.5.9a

Speaking and Listening

- Pose and respond to specific questions and contribute to discussions. SL.5.1c
- Review the key ideas expressed and draw conclusions. SL.5.1d

Language

- Use context as a clue to the meaning of a word or phrase. L.5.4a
- Acquire and use academic and domain-specific words and phrases. L.5.6

Additional Practice: **RL.5.1, RL.5.2, RL.5.4, RL.5.6**

Academic Talk

See **Glossary of Terms**, pp. TR2–TR9

- compare
- event
- contrast
- details
- setting

Learning Progression

Grade 4	Grade 5	Grade 6
Students describe a character, setting, or event in a story or drama, drawing on specific details in the text.	Building on the Grade 4 standard, students compare and contrast two or more characters, settings, or events in a story or drama. By describing how characters interact or settings or events are different from one another, students will describe these elements in greater detail and better understand the text.	At Grade 6, the standard adds complexity by requiring students to describe characters in the relation to the plot. They identify how a story's or drama's plot unfolds in a series of episodes and how the characters respond or change as the plot moves toward a resolution.

Lesson Text Selections

Modeled and Guided Instruction

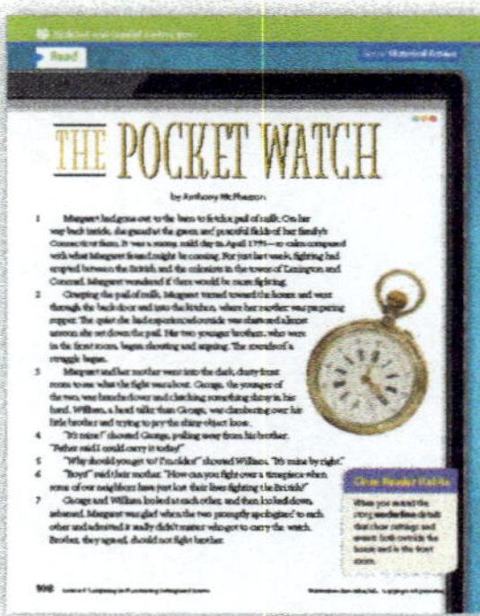

The Pocket Watch
by Anthony McPherson
Genre: Historical Fiction

Guided Practice

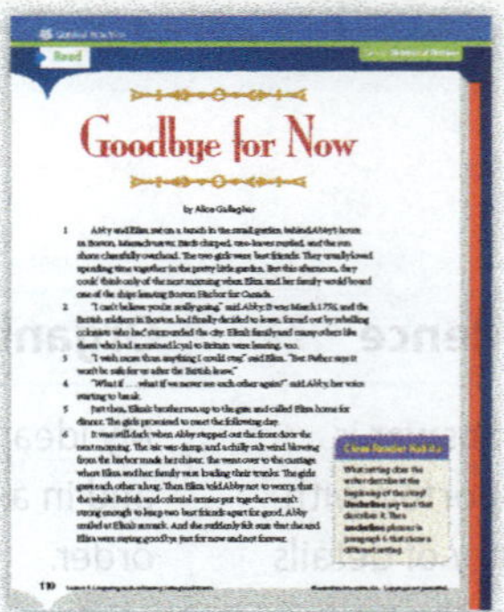

Goodbye for Now
by Alice Gallagher
Genre: Historical Fiction

Independent Practice

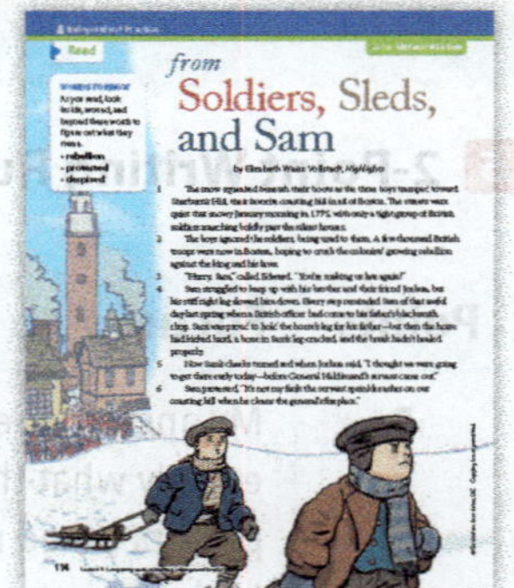

Soldiers, Sleds, and Sam
by Elizabeth Weiss Vollstadt
Genre: Historical Fiction

Lesson Pacing Guide

Whole Class Instruction *30–45 minutes per day*

Day 1

Teacher-Toolbox.com **Interactive Tutorial**
Story Structure—Level E
20 min (optional)

Introduction pp. 106–107

- **Read** **Comparing and Contrasting Settings and Events** *10 min*
- **Think** *10 min*
  Graphic Organizer: Two-Column Chart
- **Talk** *5 min*
  Quick Write (TRB) *5 min*

Day 2

Modeled and Guided Instruction pp. 108–109, 112

- **Read** **The Pocket Watch** *10 min*
- **Think** *10 min*
  Graphic Organizer: Two-Column Chart
- **Talk** *5 min*
- **Write** Short Response *10 min*

Day 3

Guided Practice pp. 110–111, 113

- **Read** **Goodbye for Now** *10 min*
- **Think** *10 min*
- **Talk** *5 min*
- **Write** Short Response *10 min*

Day 4

Independent Practice pp. 114–119

- **Read** **Soldiers, Sleds, and Sam** *15 min*
- **Think** *10 min*
- **Write** Extended Response *15 min*

Day 5

Independent Practice pp. 114–119

- *Review* Answer Analysis (TRB) *10 min*
- *Review* Response Analysis (TRB) *10 min*
- *Assign and Discuss* Learning Target *10 min*

Language Handbook
Lesson 21 Homographs, pp. 478–479
20 min (optional)

Ready Writing Connection

During *Ready Reading* Days 1–5, use:
Lesson 2 Writing to Inform: Article

- **Steps 6 and 7** **Revise**
- **Step 8** **Edit**
- **Prepare to Publish**
- **Collaborate**
- **Present**

See *Ready Writing TRB*, p. 32a for complete lesson plan.

Small Group Differentiation

Teacher-Toolbox.com

Reteach

***Ready Reading* Prerequisite Lesson**

- **Grade 4** Lesson 8 Describing Settings and Events in Stories

Teacher-led Activities

Tools for Instruction

- Analyze Story Elements

Personalized Learning

i-Ready.com

Independent

i-Ready Close Reading Lessons

- **Grade 4** Describing Settings and Events in Stories
- **Grade 5** Comparing and Contrasting Settings and Events

Introduction

Get Started

- Explain to students that in this lesson they will read several historical fiction pieces. They will compare and contrast the settings and events within each piece in order to better understand the story.
- Remind students that to compare and contrast, they must think about how things are alike and different.
- Invite students to share the meanings of *setting* and *events,* along with some examples from familiar stories. Use students' examples to point out that most stories have more than one setting and more than one event.
- Help students understand how comparing and contrasting settings and events can highlight important details. Say:

  During your school day, you spend time in the classroom, in the library, in the cafeteria, and on the playground. What does each of these settings look like? What happens there? How do you feel when you're there? Do you behave the same way in each place? The setting in your life can have a big impact on you and what happens to you. The same is true for characters in a story.
- Emphasize that comparing and contrasting settings and events in a story can help readers understand important details about characters and plot.
- Focus students' attention on the Learning Target. Read it aloud to set the purpose for the lesson.
- Display the Academic Talk words. Tell students to listen for these words and their meanings as you work through the lesson together. Use the Academic Talk Routine on pp. A48–A49.

 **English Language Learners**

● **Genre Focus**

Read

- Read aloud the Read section as students follow along. Restate to reinforce:

  When you compare and contrast settings and events, you notice what is alike and different. These details can help you make important inferences about characters and plot in a story.
- Direct students' attention to the photographs. Have them study the images closely to compare and contrast the settings and events.

Introduction

RL.5.3 Compare and contrast two or more . . . settings, or events in a story . . . drawing on specific details in the texts. . . .

Lesson 6
Comparing and Contrasting Settings and Events

Using details to compare and contrast settings or events in a story will help you better understand what that story is about.

Read The **setting** is when and where a story takes place. When you **compare** and **contrast** settings, you consider how the scenes are alike and different. When you compare and contrast **events,** you consider how the things that happen are similar or different. Looking at the **details** will help you see the similarities and differences.

Compare and contrast these two settings and events from the movie *The Wizard of Oz.* In the photographs, look for details about the place and what is happening.

106

English Language Learners

Build Meaning

Background Knowledge Help familiarize students with the film *The Wizard of Oz.*

Explain that the main character, Dorothy, lives on a farm in Kansas. One day, a tornado picks up Dorothy's house with Dorothy inside. The house lands in a strange and magical land. Dorothy asks how she can get home and she is told to follow the yellow brick road to Emerald City, where she must ask the Wizard of Oz for help.

On the way, Dorothy meets a tin man, a scarecrow, and a cowardly lion. They travel together until they reach Emerald City, where Dorothy finally learns how to get home. She wakes up back in her bed in Kansas.

● **Genre Focus**

Historical Fiction

Historical fiction is literature that is set in the past. It may be about real people, real events, a real time period, or any combination of those. While the details and situations are realistic to the time period, parts of the story, such as dialogue and some characters, may be made-up.

Historical fiction is not meant to be used as an informational text, but it can often shed light on the mood and tone of historical eras by allowing readers to feel as if they're witnessing events firsthand.

Give examples of historical fiction texts, such as *Little House on the Prairie* and *Esperanza Rising.*

Think What have you learned so far about comparing and contrasting settings and events? Complete the chart below with details about the setting and event in each photograph.

Left Photo	Right Photo
Where: A farm in Kansas	**Where:** The Land of Oz
Setting: • a barnyard with animals • a tree, a fence, and distant fields • all is gray, cloudy, gloomy	**Setting:** • in the woods • a house with flowers in the background • all is colorful, beautiful
Event: • A girl is holding a dog. • The girl is talking or singing to herself.	**Event:** • The girl from the first picture and a man dressed as a scarecrow are listening to a man in a metal suit talk or sing. • The man in the metal suit seems sad about something.

Talk Share your chart with a partner.

- What are the similarities and differences in the settings and events?
- What details from the pictures did you use to figure out the settings and events?
- Did you describe the settings and events in the same way?

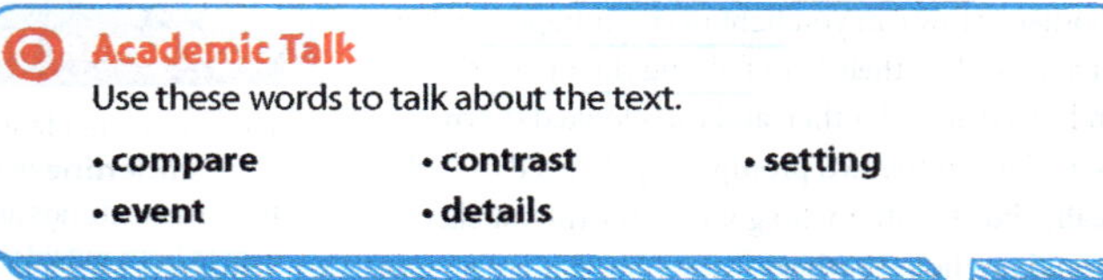

Academic Talk
Use these words to talk about the text.

- compare
- contrast
- setting
- event
- details

Monitor Understanding

If... students struggle to identify settings and events,

then... provide an example. Say: "This classroom is the setting where learning takes place."

- **In a story or drama, what details would show that the setting is a classroom?** *(desks, whiteboard, posters, books)*
- **What events might take place in a classroom?** *(answering questions, taking a quiz, reading a story, solving math problems)*

Repeat the activity with other examples, such as a movie theater, a mall, and a house. Work with students to brainstorm descriptive details and possible events for each setting.

Think

- Have students read aloud the Think section. Explain that the chart will help them organize the details in each photograph.
- Have partners complete the chart. Remind students to look carefully at each picture and think about where the characters are and what they are doing. Provide assistance as needed.
- Ask volunteers to share what they wrote in their charts.
- Make sure students understand that sometimes determining a setting or event involves making an inference based on the details provided.

Talk

- Read aloud the Talk prompts.
- Have partners discuss the similarities and differences between the settings and events.
- Ask volunteers to share their ideas.

Quick Write Have students write a response to the following prompt:

> **Imagine being at your best friend's house and then imagine being at school. Compare and contrast the settings and events in these two scenarios.**

Ask students to share their responses.

Wrap Up

- Invite students to share what they've learned so far. Encourage them to use the Academic Talk words in their explanations.
- Remind students that by comparing and contrasting settings and events in a story, they can learn more about each of those elements, as well as how they influence the characters and the plot.

  Next, we'll read historical fiction stories that are set during the American Revolution. Noticing details about settings and events in each story will give you a better understanding of what the stories are about.

● **Monitor Understanding**

Modeled and Guided Instruction

Get Started

Today you will read a historical fiction story. First, you'll read to understand what the story is about. Then you'll read to analyze the settings and events so you can compare and contrast them.

Read

- Read aloud the title of the story and call attention to the picture. Ask students to define *pocket watch.*
- Have students read the story independently. Tell them to place a check mark above any confusing words and phrases as they read. Remind students to look inside, around, and beyond each unknown word or phrase to help them figure out its meaning. Use the Word Learning Routine on pp. A50–A51.
- When students have finished reading, clarify the meanings of words and phrases they still find confusing. Then use the questions below to check understanding. Encourage students to identify details in the text that support their answers.

  What is the setting of the story? *(April, 1775, on a farm in Connecticut)*

  What are the brothers fighting over? *(which of them gets to carry Father's pocket watch that day)*

  What is the story mostly about? *(A family agrees that it isn't right to fight over silly issues when a real war is going on.)*

English Language Learners

- **Word Learning Strategy**

Explore

- Read aloud the Explore question at the top of p. 109 to set the purpose for the second read. Tell students they will need to take a closer look at the description of each setting to answer this question.
- Have students read aloud the Close Reader Habit on p. 108.

> **TIP** Encourage students to look at each scene from Margaret's point of view and notice what she sees, thinks, and feels. They should ask themselves, *How does the setting match Margaret's feelings?*

Modeled and Guided Instruction

Read

Genre: Historical Fiction

THE POCKET WATCH

by Anthony McPherson

1 Margaret had gone out to the barn to fetch a pail of milk. On her way back inside, she gazed at the green and peaceful fields of her family's Connecticut farm. It was a sunny, mild day in April 1775—so calm compared with what Margaret feared might be coming. For just last week, fighting had erupted between the British and the colonists in the towns of Lexington and Concord. Margaret wondered if there would be more fighting.

2 Grasping the pail of milk, Margaret turned toward the house and went through the back door and into the kitchen, where her mother was preparing supper. The quiet she had experienced outside was shattered almost as soon she set down the pail. Her two younger brothers, who were in the front room, began shouting and arguing. The sounds of a struggle began.

3 Margaret and her mother went into the dark, dusty front room to see what the fight was about. George, the younger of the two, was hunched over and clutching something shiny in his hand. William, a head taller than George, was clambering over his little brother and trying to pry the shiny object loose.

4 "It's mine!" shouted George, pulling away from his brother. "Father said I could carry it today!"

5 "Why should you get to? I'm older!" shouted William. "It's mine by right."

6 "Boys!" said their mother. "How can you fight over a timepiece when some of our neighbors have just lost their lives fighting the British?"

7 George and William looked at each other, and then looked down, ashamed. Margaret was glad when the two promptly apologized to each other and admitted it really didn't matter who got to carry the watch. Brother, they agreed, should not fight brother.

Close Reader Habits

When you reread the story, **underline** details that show settings and events both outside the house and in the front room.

108

English Language Learners

Develop Language

Concept Vocabulary Draw a concept map to help students understand the shifts between settings and events.

- Ask students to tell where Margaret is first *(outside on the farm).* Record the answer and brainstorm words that describe this setting, such as *green, peaceful,* and *calm.* Then have students describe what is happening in this setting. Add their descriptions to the map.
- Repeat with the second setting. Have students describe the setting as well as the events taking place there. Define or clarify words as needed.
- Work with students to compare and contrast the settings. Help them see the relationship between each setting and the events described.

Word Learning Strategy

Use Context Clues

- Reread paragraph 1. Direct students' attention to the word *erupted.*

  What do you think *erupted* means?

  What clues help you figure out its meaning?

- Guide students to identify *fighting* as the thing that had erupted. Then reread the previous sentence: "so calm, compared with what Margaret feared might be coming." Help students recognize that *erupted* is an antonym for *calm.*
- Together determine that *erupted* means "broke out" or "burst forth suddenly." Ask students to tell what else erupts in this story. *(the brothers' argument)*

L.5.4a

Explore How do the settings in "The Pocket Watch" add to your understanding of the story?

Include details when you compare and contrast settings.

Think

1 Complete the chart by comparing the setting and events of paragraph 1 with the setting and events of paragraphs 3 through 6.

Paragraph 1	Paragraphs 3–6
Where: barn and view of fields	**Where:** house front room
Setting: • a sunny April day in 1775 on a farm in Connecticut	**Setting:** • dark and dusty
Events: • Margaret walks back to the house with a pail of milk. • She sees the "peaceful fields" surrounding the farm.	**Events:** • The boys are arguing over who will carry their father's watch. • The boys regret their fighting when they are reminded by their mother that neighbors have lost their lives in the fight with British soldiers.

Talk

2 Writers choose settings to fit particular events. Discuss how the two settings help you imagine the events you describe in your chart.

Write

3 **Short Response** Compare and contrast the main settings of "The Pocket Watch." Use details to describe their similarities and differences. Use the space provided on page 112 to write your answer.

HINT Try using terms such as *alike, unlike, similar, different,* and *in contrast* in your response.

Think Aloud

- I'm looking for details about the settings and events in this story so I can better understand what the story is about.
- The chart heads indicate that I need to find settings and events in paragraph 1 and in paragraphs 3–6. I'll start with paragraph 1. The first sentence gives me a strong clue about the setting. Margaret is fetching a pail of milk from the barn. From this detail I know that the setting is on a farm, because that's where barns are located.
- The rest of the first paragraph gives some explicit details about the setting. The narrator mentions the "Connecticut farm" and tells that it is a "sunny, mild day in April 1775." That takes care of both where and when the story take place. I'm going to write those details under *Setting* in the chart.

Think

- Read aloud the Think section. Explain to students that you will model how to find text evidence to fill in part of the chart. Use the **Think Aloud** below to guide your modeling.
- Revisit the Explore question. Guide students to determine that they need to look for more details, using the Close Reader Habit.
- Encourage students to work with a partner to continue rereading the passage and complete the chart. Remind them that the Buddy Tip will help them choose which details to write in the chart.
- Ask volunteers to share their completed charts.
- Have students check to make sure they have compared and contrasted details about the setting and events only.

Talk

- Read aloud the Talk prompt.
- Have partners respond to the prompt. Use the Talk Routine on pp. A52–A53.
- Circulate to check that students are discussing both *what* the details in the text tell them about the setting, as well as *how* those details help them picture what is happening in the story.

Write

- Ask a volunteer to read aloud the Write prompt.
- Invite a few students to tell what the prompt is asking them to do.
- Make sure students understand that they should tell how the settings are both similar and different, not just one or the other.
- Have students turn to p. 112 to write their response.
- Use Review Responses on p. 112 to assess students' writing.

Wrap Up

- Ask students to recall the Learning Target. Have them explain how comparing and contrasting settings and events helped them better understand what the story is about.

Guided Practice

Get Started

Today you will read another piece of historical fiction that takes place during the American Revolution. First you will read to understand what happens in the story. Then you will reread with a partner to compare and contrast details about settings and events.

Read

- Read aloud the title of the passage. Ask students to predict what they think the story will be about.
- **Read to Understand** Have students read the story independently. Tell them to place a check mark above any confusing words and phrases as they read. Remind students to look inside, around, and beyond each unknown word to help them figure out its meaning. Use the Word Learning Routine on pp. A50–A51.
- When students have finished reading, clarify the meanings of words and phrases they still find confusing. Then use the questions below to check understanding. Encourage students to identify details in the text that support their answers.

  When and where does the opening scene take place? *(in a small garden behind Abby's house in Boston, Massachusetts; March 1776)*

  Why does Eliza have to leave? *(Eliza's family have remained loyal to the British, but the British soldiers are leaving and it won't be safe for them to stay.)*

  What is the story mostly about? *(two young friends have to part when one of the friends leaves Boston for Canada)*

English Language Learners

● **Word Learning Strategy**

- **Read to Analyze** Read aloud the Close Reader Habit on p. 110 to set the purpose for the second read. Then have students reread the story with a partner and discuss any questions they might have.

Guided Practice

Read

Genre: Historical Fiction

Goodbye for Now

by Alice Gallagher

1 Abby and Eliza sat on a bench in the small garden behind Abby's house in Boston, Massachusetts. Birds chirped, tree-leaves rustled, and the sun shone cheerfully overhead. The two girls were best friends. They usually loved spending time together in the pretty little garden. But this afternoon, they could think only of the next morning when Eliza and her family would board one of the ships leaving Boston Harbor for Canada.

2 "I can't believe you're really going," said Abby. It was March 1776, and the British soldiers in Boston had finally decided to leave, forced out by rebelling colonists who had surrounded the city. Eliza's family and many others like them who had remained loyal to Britain were leaving, too.

3 "I wish more than anything I could stay," said Eliza. "But Father says it won't be safe for us after the British leave."

4 "What if . . . what if we never see each other again?" said Abby, her voice starting to break.

5 Just then, Eliza's brother ran up to the gate and called Eliza home for dinner. The girls promised to meet the following day.

6 It was still dark when Abby stepped out the front door the next morning. The air was damp, and a chilly salt wind blowing from the harbor made her shiver. She went over to the carriage where Eliza and her family were loading their trunks. The girls gave each other a hug. Then Eliza told Abby not to worry, that the whole British and colonial armies put together weren't strong enough to keep two best friends apart for good. Abby smiled at Eliza's remark. And she suddenly felt sure that she and Eliza were saying goodbye just for now and not forever.

Close Reader Habits

What setting does the writer describe at the beginning of the story? **Underline** any text that describes it. Then **underline** phrases in paragraph 6 that show a different setting.

110

English Language Learners

Build Meaning

- **Background Knowledge** Use a map to point out the location of the original thirteen colonies and Great Britain. Explain that a *colony* is "a group of people who leave their homeland for a new place but are still ruled by the place they left." In this case, the colonists left Great Britain and settled in America, but still had to follow British laws.
- After some time, the colonists grew tired of being under British control and wanted to be free. This began a war called the American Revolution, which lasted more than five years. The colonists won their freedom, and the United States of America was born.

● Word Learning Strategy

Use Context Clues

- Reread paragraph 4 and point out the phrase *starting to break.*
- **What does the word *break* mean in this context? What clues help you figure out the meaning?**
- Guide students to recognize that Abby's voice is starting to break, and therefore a *break* is something that can be heard. Point out the three periods in Abby's dialogue, which show that she has to pause and begin her sentence again because she is upset.
- Work with students to define *break* in this context as "to become shaky or unstable."

L.5.4a, RL.5.4

Think Use what you learned from reading the story to answer the following questions.

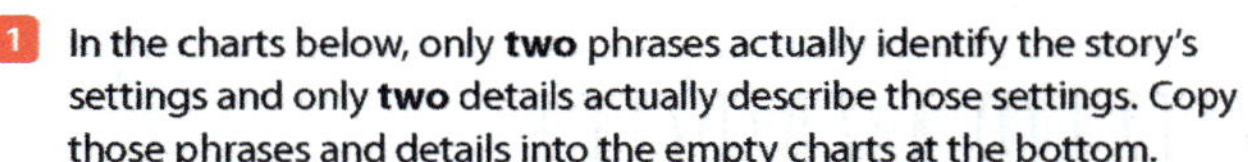

1 In the charts below, only **two** phrases actually identify the story's settings and only **two** details actually describe those settings. Copy those phrases and details into the empty charts at the bottom.

Descriptive details help you picture both settings and events.

Possible Settings
Boston Harbor
a bench in a garden
outside a house in the morning
a ship leaving for Canada

Possible Details
"the sun shone cheerfully overhead"
"board one of the ships"
"called Eliza home for dinner"
"a chilly salt wind blowing"

First Setting	a bench in a garden
Detail	"the sun shone cheerfully overhead"

Second Setting	outside a house in the morning
Detail	"a chilly salt wind blowing"

Talk

2 What happens in paragraphs 1 through 4? What happens in paragraph 6? Use the chart on page 113 to record any details from the passage that can help you answer those questions.

Write

3 **Short Response** Compare and contrast the event occurring in paragraphs 1 through 4 with the event occurring in paragraph 6. Use the space provided on page 113 to write your answer.

HINT First, describe the events. Then tell how they are similar. Finally, tell how they are different.

111

● Integrating Standards

Use the following questions to further students' understanding of the story.

- **What inference can you make about Abby's family's loyalty?** *(Because Eliza's family is leaving the colonies and Abby's is not, the reader can infer that Abby's family is loyal to the rebels and not the British.)*
  DOK 3 **RL.5.1**
- **What is a possible theme of the story? What details help you identify it?** *(A possible theme is that good friends can remain friends in spite of challenges. The theme is clear from paragraph 6, when the girls promise to stay friends even though they'll be apart for a while.)*
  DOK 2 **RL.5.2**

● Monitor Understanding

If... students have difficulty finding text evidence to answer item 2,

then... have them use a Venn diagram. Label the left circle *Paragraphs 1–4* and the right circle *Paragraph 6*. Have students fill in the diagram in response to the following questions:

- **Where are the girls?**
- **What is happening?**
- **How do the girls feel?**

Students should use the answers to these questions to help them compare and contrast the events.

Think

- Have students work with a partner to complete item 1. Draw attention to the boldface word **two**.

TIP If students struggle to identify different settings within the story, guide them to look for transition words and phrases that indicate a change in time or place.

Answer Analysis

When students have finished, discuss correct and incorrect responses.

1 **See the answers on the student book page.** Discuss students' responses with them. Remind students that this item simulates a drag-and-drop item they might encounter on a computer-based assessment.
DOK 2

● **Integrating Standards**

Talk

- Have partners discuss the prompt. Emphasize that students should support their ideas with text details.
- Circulate to clarify misunderstandings.

● **Monitor Understanding**

Write

- Ask a volunteer to read aloud the Write prompt.
- Invite students to tell what the prompt is asking them to do. Make sure they understand that something important changes from the beginning of the story to the end.
- Call attention to the HINT.
- Have students turn to p. 113 to write their response.
- Use Review Responses on p. 113 to assess students' writing.

Wrap Up

- Ask students to recall the Learning Target. Have them explain how comparing and contrasting the settings and events in the story helped them understand more about the meaning of the story.

Write

- Remember to use the Response–Writing Routine on pp. A54–A55.

Review Responses

After students complete the writing activity, help them evaluate their responses.

3 Responses may vary but key details should support the comparisons between the paragraphs—specifically the contrast between the calm, peaceful outdoors and the dark, chaotic indoors. See the sample response on the student book page.
DOK 3

 **Write** Use the space below to write your answer to the question on page 109.

THE POCKET WATCH

3 **Short Response** Compare and contrast the main settings of "The Pocket Watch." Use details to describe their similarities and differences.

HINT Try using terms such as *alike, unlike, similar, different,* and *in contrast* in your response.

Sample response: Both settings in "The Pocket Watch" are alike in being located on a Connecticut farm in April 1775, but those settings are very different. Paragraph 1 describes an outdoor setting. The day is "sunny" and "mild" and "calm," and the fields are "green and peaceful." In contrast, paragraphs 3 through 6 describe an indoor setting of a "dark, dusty" front room. Unlike the outdoor setting, the room is not "mild" or "calm." Instead, it is the site of a noisy fight between two brothers.

Don't forget to check your writing.

Check Your Writing

- ☐ Did you read the prompt carefully?
- ☐ Did you put the prompt in your own words?
- ☐ Did you use the best evidence from the text to support your ideas?
- ☐ Are your ideas clearly organized?
- ☐ Did you write in clear and complete sentences?
- ☐ Did you check your spelling and punctuation?

Scaffolding Support for Reluctant Writers

If students are having a difficult time getting started, use the strategies below. Work individually with struggling students, or have students work with partners.

- Circle the verbs in the prompt that tell you what to do, such as *describe*, *explain*, or *compare*.
- Underline words and phrases in the prompt that show what information you need to provide in your response, such as *causes*, *reasons*, or *character traits*.
- Talk about the details from the text that you will include in your response.
- Explain aloud how you will respond to the prompt.

Goodbye for Now

2 Use the chart below to organize your ideas and details.

Event in Paragraphs 1–4	Event in Paragraph 6

 **Write** Use the space below to write your answer to the question on page 111.

HINT First, describe the events. Then tell how they are similar. Finally, tell how they are different.

3 **Short Response** Compare and contrast the event occurring in paragraphs 1 through 4 with the event occurring in paragraph 6.

Sample response: In paragraphs 1 through 4 of "Goodbye for Now," the event is that Abby and Eliza talk about Eliza getting ready to leave Boston for Canada. In paragraph 6, the event is that Abby and Eliza say goodbye to each other. These events are similar in two ways. Both show Abby and Eliza's interactions. Both focus on the fact that Eliza has to leave. But the events are also different. Paragraphs 1 through 4 focus on the girls' sadness at being separated and their concern that they might not see each other again. Paragraph 6, in contrast, focuses not on the girls' sadness or concern but on how sure Abby feels that she will see Eliza again.

Teacher Notes

Guided Practice

Talk

2 Students should use the chart to organize their thoughts and evidence.

Write

- Remember to use the Response–Writing Routine on pp. A54–A55.

Review Responses

After students complete the writing activity, help them evaluate their responses.

3 Responses may vary but should compare and contrast details from the first day in the garden and the next morning at the gate. See the sample response on the student book page. ***DOK 3***

Independent Practice

Get Started

Today you are going to read another story that takes place during the American Revolution. Comparing and contrasting the settings and events in the story can help you better understand what the story is about.

- Ask a volunteer to explain how comparing and contrasting details about settings and events can help readers better understand what a story is about. Encourage students to use the Academic Talk words in their response.

English Language Learners

Read

You are going to read the story independently and use what you have learned to think and write about the text. As you read, look for details that tell when and where each scene is set, and note what happens in each scene.

- Read aloud the title of the passage and then encourage students to preview the text, paying close attention to the illustrations.
- Call attention to the Words to Know in the upper left of p. 114.
- If students need support in reading the passage, you may wish to use the Monitor Understanding suggestions.
- When students have finished, have them complete the Think and Write sections.

Independent Practice

Read

Genre: Historical Fiction

WORDS TO KNOW
As you read, look inside, around, and beyond these words to figure out what they mean.
- **rebellion**
- **protested**
- **despised**

from Soldiers, Sleds, and Sam

by Elizabeth Weiss Vollstadt, *Highlights*

1 The snow squeaked beneath their boots as the three boys tramped toward Sherburn's Hill, their favorite coasting hill in all of Boston. The streets were quiet that snowy January morning in 1775, with only a tight group of British soldiers marching boldly past the silent houses.

2 The boys ignored the soldiers, being used to them. A few thousand British troops were now in Boston, hoping to crush the colonists' growing rebellion against the king and his laws.

3 "Hurry, Sam," called Edward. "You're making us late again!"

4 Sam struggled to keep up with his brother and their friend Joshua, but his stiff right leg slowed him down. Every step reminded Sam of that awful day last spring when a British officer had come to his father's blacksmith shop. Sam was proud to hold the horse's leg for his father—but then the horse had kicked hard, a bone in Sam's leg cracked, and the break hadn't healed properly.

5 Now Sam's cheeks turned red when Joshua said, "I thought we were going to get there early today—before General Haldimand's servant came out."

6 Sam protested, "It's not my fault the servant sprinkles ashes on our coasting hill when he cleans the general's fireplace."

114

English Language Learners

Build Meaning

Preview Illustrations Have pairs of students work together to preview the illustrations and label as many elements as they can. Encourage students to look closely at details in the foreground and the background, as well as details about characters' facial expressions and body language.

- When students have finished, discuss each illustration as a group. Use students' responses to point out synonyms, and help them make connections to words in the text such as *soldier, sled, servant,* and *ash*.
- Invite students to predict what the story will be about, based on the title and the illustrations.

7 Joshua looked up and groaned, "Oh no, late again." A man was standing in the middle of Sherburn's Hill, trampling the snow and scattering ashes.

8 "Well, that's it," said Edward, kicking the sled. "If we'd gotten here sooner, we could have had a few good runs before he ruined our hill."

9 "Sure could have," said Joshua, looking at Sam. "Next time he stays home."

10 Sam jammed his icy fingers into his pockets and lifted his chin. "I may be slow," he finally said, "but I'm not afraid of the Redcoats. I'll get the servant to stop."

11 The two older boys hooted with laughter. "You?" said Joshua. "What can you do?"

12 "I'll—" Sam hesitated. What could he do? Then he looked at the servant again and said, "I'll tell him to scatter the ashes someplace else."

13 He started to limp up the hill, Edward and Joshua following. The cold wind bit into Sam's cheeks, but he kept going until he reached the servant.

14 "Please, sir," Sam said, "I . . . I'd like to make a request." Sam wanted to run, but he had come too far. "Could you scatter the ashes someplace else? They ruin the snow and we can't coast."

15 The servant laughed, but it wasn't a happy sound. "It is not for colonist children to tell the British army what to do. Now run along before I—"

16 Sam didn't hear the rest, as Edward grabbed his arm and pulled him away.

17 "Come on," he said.

18 Sam followed Edward and Joshua. How he despised that servant! Coasting was the one time his bad leg didn't matter. "Stop!" Sam called suddenly. "I'm going to see General Haldimand himself."

19 "Then you're going alone," said Joshua. "He'll never listen to us."

20 Edward looked at Joshua. "We'd better stay with Sam," he said. "Ma will blame me if anything happens to him."

Monitor Understanding

If... students struggle to read and understand the passage, **then...** use these scaffolding suggestions:

Question the Text Preview the text by asking the following questions:

- **Based on the title and illustrations, what do you predict the story will be about?**
- **What questions do you have about the story?**

Vocabulary Support Define words that may interfere with comprehension, such as *coasting, rebellion,* and *trampling.*

Read Aloud Read aloud the text with students. You could also have students chorally read the text in a small group.

Check Understanding Use the questions below to check understanding. Encourage students to cite details in the text that support their answers.

- **What details establish the setting?** *(The setting is Boston in winter. The details are snow, cold, sledding, and icy fingers.)*
- **What problem do the children face?** *(The servant ruins their sledding hill by scattering ashes on the snow.)*
- **How does Sam solve the problem?** *(He speaks with General Haldimand directly. The General honors his request.)*

Independent Practice

Integrating Standards

After students have read the story, use these questions to discuss the story with them.

- **What details help you infer that people in Boston did not welcome the British soldiers?**
  (Paragraphs 1 and 2 describe British soldiers "marching boldly past the silent houses" as well as the British troops in Boston "hoping to crush the colonists' growing rebellion." In paragraph 25, the general admits that there are bad feelings between the army and the people.)
  DOK 2 RL.5.1
- **How does the narrator's point of view affect the way the events in this story are told?**
  (This story has a third-person narrator who tells each character's words and actions, but also shares Sam's thoughts and feelings. This affects the way the story is told: readers learn that Sam is brave despite being scared, and also that he is determined.)
  DOK 3 RL.5.6
- **The author says that Sam "stood his ground." What does this mean, and what details from both the indoor and outdoor scenes help develop this meaning?**
  (It means that Sam bravely faced a challenge and didn't back down. In the outdoor scene, we learn that Sam has been injured by a British soldier's horse. In spite of that, he is the only one of the three boys who has the nerve to talk to the servant. He remains brave during the indoor scene, when he reminds the general that "we are free citizens of Boston.")
  DOK 3 RL.5.4
- **What is one theme of this story? Use details from both the outdoor and indoor settings to support your answer.**
  (One possible theme is "Stand up for what you believe in." Sam and the boys don't think it is right for the servant to scatter ashes on the hill. Sam stands up to the servant and then the general, making himself be heard. He finds the bravery inside to do what the other boys cannot and ends up being a hero to the other boys.)
  DOK 3 RL.5.2

● **Theme Connection**

21 Sam headed for the general's house. He could feel his heart—thump . . . thump . . . thump—like the steady beat of a drum. He stopped at the heavy wooden door, his knees shaking. But he lifted his hand, made a fist, and pounded as hard as he could. A young soldier opened the door.

22 "Who is it, private?" a voice boomed from inside. "Let them in and close the door! The wind will blow my fire out!" The three boys crowded into the hall to find a big man in a red uniform standing in a doorway. "I'm General Haldimand," the man said. He led them into his office. Flames leaped about in a huge stone fireplace.

23 Sam swallowed. "Well, sir . . ." he began. He told the general about the hill and the servant. "We are free citizens of Boston," he said, "and you have no right to destroy our hill."

24 General Haldimand frowned, and Edward tugged at Sam's sleeve. "Let's go," he whispered, but this time Sam stood his ground. For ten long seconds, no one moved.

25 Then the general raised his hands. "You win, my lad," he said, smiling. "There are already bad feelings between our army and the people of Boston. I shall not add to them, and I will give orders that my servant repair the damage and no longer scatter ashes on your hill."

26 Back outside, Joshua and Edward whooped and shouted in the falling snow. Edward draped his arm around Sam's shoulder, and Joshua patted Sam on the back. "You can have the first coast tomorrow," he said.

27 Sam's eyes shone. His sled would fly faster than anyone's! The boys tramped home together through the snow, and no one told Sam to hurry up—not once.

116

● Theme Connection

- Remind students that the theme of this lesson is American Revolution Tales. Review that each passage in this lesson is set during the American Revolution.
- Write the title of each passage on the board, and invite students to share details they learned or inferred about the American Revolution from each passage. Emphasize that they may give facts, such as the time and place of the Revolution, or they may give details such as the way the Revolution affected people.
- Use the notes to discuss ways in which the Historical Fiction genre is helpful for learning about a certain place or time in history.

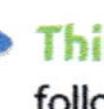

Think Use what you learned from reading the story to answer the following questions.

1 This question has two parts. First, answer Part A. Then answer Part B.

Part A
How is the setting of the boys' meeting with the servant different from the setting of their meeting with the general?

- **A** The boys meet with the servant during the early morning but meet with the general in the afternoon.
- **B** The boys meet with the servant at the general's house but meet with the general in the blacksmith shop of Sam's father.
- **(C)** The boys meet with the servant outside in the cold but meet with the general inside his house in front of a warm fire.
- **D** The boys meet with the servant on Sherburn's Hill but meet with the general at the camp of the British soldiers.

Part B
Choose **one** detail that describes the scene between the boys and the servant and **one** detail that describes the scene between the boys and the general.

- **A** "The snow squeaked beneath their boots as the three boys tramped toward Sherburn's Hill, their favorite coasting hill in all of Boston."
- **B** "Every step reminded Sam of that awful day last spring when a British officer had come to his father's blacksmith shop."
- **(C)** "The cold wind bit into Sam's cheeks, but he kept going until he reached the servant."
- **D** "He stopped at the heavy wooden door, his knees shaking."
- **(E)** "Flames leaped about in a huge stone fireplace."
- **F** "Back outside, Joshua and Edward whooped and shouted in the falling snow."

● Monitor Understanding

If... students struggle to complete the items,

then... you may wish to use the following suggestions:

Read Aloud Activities

- As you read, have students note any unfamiliar words or phrases. Clarify any misunderstandings.
- Discuss each item with students to make certain they understand the expectation.

Reread the Text

- Have students complete a graphic organizer as they reread.
- Have partners summarize the text to one another.

Think

Use the Monitor Understanding suggestions to support students in completing items 1–3.

● **Monitor Understanding**

Answer Analysis

When students have finished, discuss correct and incorrect responses.

1 Part A

The correct choice is C. This is the only answer that is supported by details from the text.

- **A** is incorrect because the boys meet with the general in the morning as well.
- **B** and **D** are incorrect because they do not describe scenes from the story.

Part B

The correct choices are C and E. C supports the cold setting of Sherburn's Hill, where Sam spoke to the servant. **E** supports the setting of the general's house with the warm fire.

- **A** happens before the boys meet with the servant in the morning.
- **B** happens in the spring of the previous year.
- **D** describes the scene before Sam talks to the general.
- **F** describes the boys' reaction after Sam talks to the general.

DOK 3 RL.5.3

Independent Practice

2 Students should circle the word *trampling*. This most closely matches the definition provided.
DOK 2 RL.5.4, L.5.4c

3 **The correct choice is A.** The hill is cold, a fact suggested by the snow and Sam jamming "icy fingers" in his pockets. The general's house is warm, as suggested by the flames leaping about "in a huge stone fireplace."

- **B** is incorrect because the general's house does not seem welcoming at first.
- **C** is incorrect because the hill is not clean and the general's house is not dirty.
- **D** is incorrect because the hill is not warm and the general's house is not cold.

DOK 2 RL.5.3

Write

- Tell students that, using what they read, they will plan and compose an extended response to the writing prompt. Provide copies of the Venn diagram on p. TR24.

Monitor Understanding

Review Responses

After students have completed each part of the writing activity, help them evaluate their responses.

4 Display the **Sample Response** for the Venn diagram on the next page. Have students compare their diagrams with the sample. Are they missing any information?
DOK 3 RL.5.3

5 Display or pass out copies of the reproducible **2-Point Writing Rubric** on p. TR10. Have students use the rubric to individually assess their writing and revise as needed.

When students have finished their revisions, evaluate their responses. Answers will vary but should include details that show how the servant scoffed at Sam and his friends, while the general was kind and courteous. They should also show how Sam was brave when facing both men.
DOK 3 RL.5.3, W.5.9a

Independent Practice

2 First, read the following dictionary definition. Then complete the task.

destroying by stepping on and crushing with the feet

Circle the word in the sentences below that **most closely** matches the definition provided.

Joshua looked up and groaned, "Oh no, late again." A man was standing in the middle of Sherburn's Hill, trampling the snow and scattering ashes.

3 Which statement **best** compares the two main settings of the story?

- **(A)** The hill is freezing, and the general's house is warm.
- **B** The hill is dirty, and the general's house is welcoming.
- **C** The hill is clean, and the general's house is dirty.
- **D** The hill is sunny and warm, and the general's house is dark and cold.

Write

Sam talks to both the servant and General Haldimand about the ashes on Sherburn's Hill. Compare and contrast Sam's interactions with the two men and the outcomes of each interaction. Include details from the story to support your response to numbers 4 and 5.

4 **Plan Your Response** What are the similarities and differences between Sam's interactions with the servant and Sam's interactions with General Haldimand? How are the outcomes of the interactions different? Use a Venn diagram to organize your thoughts and evidence before you write.

5 **Write an Extended Response** Use evidence from the story and information from your Venn diagram to compare and contrast Sam's interactions with the servant to his interactions with General Haldimand.

Responses will vary. A top-scoring response will describe the similarities and differences between Sam's interactions with the servant and with General Haldimand, including a comparison of the outcomes of those interactions.

118

Monitor Understanding

If... students don't understand the writing task,

then... read aloud the writing prompt. Use the following questions to help students get started.

- **What is the prompt asking you to write about?**
- **Do you need to reread the text to find more information?**
- **How will you identify the information you need to include?**
- Have partners talk about how they will organize their responses.

Learning Target

In this lesson, you compared and contrasted two or more settings or events in stories. Explain how doing so will help you better understand other stories you read.

Responses will vary, but students should identify ways that details reveal comparisons and contrasts in settings and events. Paying such close attention to particular settings and events in stories will help them better understand those stories.

119

Wrap Up

Learning Target

- Have each student respond in writing to the Learning Target prompt.
- When students have finished, have them share their responses. This may be done with a partner, in small groups, or as a whole class.

4 Sample Response

Sam's Interaction with the Servant	Alike	Sam's Interaction with the General
• Sam asks timidly. • The servant is rude and threatens Sam. • Sam runs away without getting what he wants.	Sam is polite, but frightened. He overcomes his fear.	• Sam is firm about what he wants. • The general is polite. • Sam gets what he wants.

5 2-Point Writing Rubric

Points	Focus	Evidence	Organization
2	My answer does exactly what the prompt asked me to do.	My answer is supported with plenty of details from the text.	My ideas are clear and in a logical order.
1	Some of my answer does not relate to the prompt.	My answer is missing some important details from the text.	Some of my ideas are unclear and out of order.
0	My answer does not make sense.	My answer does not have any details from the text.	My ideas are unclear and not in any order.

Lesson 7
Finding the Theme of a Story or Drama

Standards Focus

Determine a theme of a story, drama . . . from details in the text, including how characters in a story or drama respond to challenges. . . . RL.5.2

Lesson Objectives

Reading

- Identify the theme of a story or drama from details in the text. RL.5.2
- Explore how details about characters support the theme, including details about how characters respond to challenges. RL.5.2

Writing

- Draw evidence from literary texts to support analysis and reflection. W.5.9a

Speaking and Listening

- Pose and respond to specific questions and contribute to discussions. SL.5.1c
- Review the key ideas expressed and draw conclusions. SL.5.1d

Language

- Use context as a clue to the meaning of a word or phrase. L.5.4a
- Acquire and use academic and domain-specific words and phrases. L.5.6

Additional Practice: **RL.5.3, RL.5.4, RL.5.5, RL.5.6**

Academic Talk

See **Glossary of Terms**, pp. TR2–TR9

- theme
- details
- challenge
- characters

Learning Progression

Grade 4	Grade 5	Grade 6
Students determine a theme from key details in the text.	Building on Grade 4, students consider the characters' actions and how they respond to challenges when determining the theme.	Grade 6 increases in complexity by requiring students to focus on the central idea of a text, in addition to the theme, and explain how it is conveyed through particular details in the text.

Lesson Text Selections

Modeled and Guided Instruction

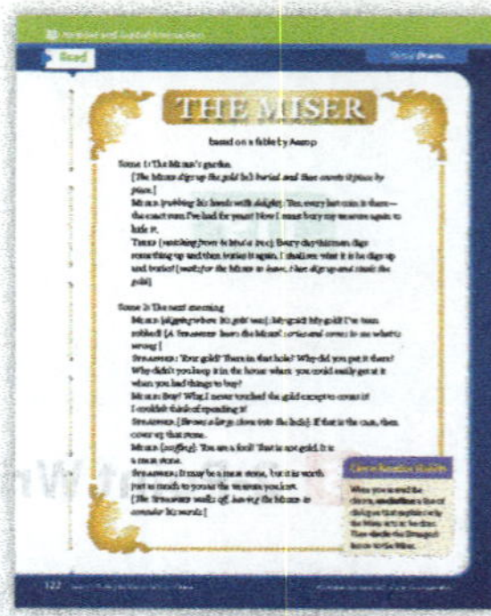

The Miser
based on a fable by Aesop
Genre: Drama

Guided Practice

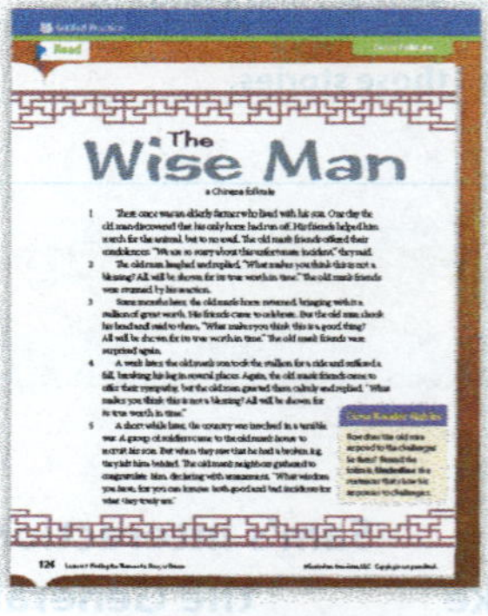

The Wise Man
a Chinese folktale
Genre: Folktale

Independent Practice

The Bell of Atri
retold by Jane Carey
Genre: Folktale

Lesson Pacing Guide

Whole Class Instruction *30–45 minutes per day*

Day 1

Teacher-Toolbox.com **Interactive Tutorial**
Identifying Theme—Level E
20 min (optional)

Introduction pp. 120–121
- **Read** **Finding the Theme of a Story or Drama** *10 min*
- **Think** *10 min*
  Graphic Organizer: Theme Organizer
- **Talk** *5 min*
  Quick Write (TRB) *5 min*

Day 2

Modeled and Guided Instruction pp. 122–123, 126
- **Read** **The Miser** *10 min*
- **Think** *10 min*
  Graphic Organizer: Theme Organizer
- **Talk** *5 min*
- **Write** Short Response *10 min*

Day 3

Guided Practice pp. 124–125, 127
- **Read** **The Wise Man** *10 min*
- **Think** *10 min*
- **Talk** *5 min*
- **Write** Short Response *10 min*

Day 4

Independent Practice pp. 128–133
- **Read** **The Bell of Atri** *15 min*
- **Think** *10 min*
- **Write** Short Response *10 min*

Day 5

Independent Practice pp. 128–133
- *Review* Answer Analysis (TRB) *10 min*
- *Review* Response Analysis (TRB) *10 min*
- *Assign and Discuss* Learning Target *10 min*

Language Handbook
Lesson 22 Using a Thesaurus, pp. 480–481
20 min (optional)

Small Group Differentiation
Teacher-Toolbox.com

Reteach

Ready Reading **Prerequisite Lesson**
- **Grade 4** Lesson 9 Determining the Theme of a Story

Teacher-led Activities

Tools for Instruction
- Determine Theme

Personalized Learning
i-Ready.com

Independent

i-Ready Close Reading Lessons

- **Grade 4** Determining the Theme of a Story
- **Grade 5** Finding the Theme of a Story

Introduction

Get Started

- Explain to students that in this lesson they will read different types of literary text and analyze them to find their themes.
- Tap into what students already know about theme. For example, make three statements, such as "The boy made a discovery," "Oranges contain vitamin C," and "Honesty is the best policy," and ask which one is a theme, and why.
- Guide students to answer that "Honesty is the best policy" is a theme. Explain:

  A theme is a message or idea about life. It is not an event, a series of events, or a plot. It is not a simple fact or the topic of a story. Instead, it's an idea that's worth thinking about and relating to.
- Focus students' attention on the Learning Target. Read it aloud to set the purpose for the lesson.
- Display the Academic Talk words. Tell students to listen for these words and their meanings as you work through the lesson together. Use the Academic Talk Routine on pp. A48–A49.

English Language Learners

● Genre Focus

Read

- Read aloud the Read section as students follow along. Restate to reinforce:

  Usually, a story or drama doesn't state the theme. Instead, readers interpret the theme by using details about the characters and how they meet and respond to challenges.
- Remind students that to understand characters in stories and plays, they need to analyze their words, actions, and interactions.
- Direct students' attention to the cartoon panels. Explain that even though the topic is "making the soccer team," the theme is not about soccer. Instead, it is a message readers should infer based on details about the girl who tries out for the team. Tell students to study the details in both pictures to figure what message the author is trying to communicate.

Introduction

RL.5.2 Determine a theme of a story, drama . . . from details in the text, including how characters in a story or drama respond to challenges.

Lesson 7
Finding the Theme of a Story or Drama

Understanding characters in stories and dramas, including how they respond to challenges, helps you understand the themes of such texts.

Read In a fictional text, a **theme** is a lesson about life that an author wants readers to understand. For example, a fictional text might present the lesson that loyalty to friends is important. Or, it might develop the idea that living a full life sometimes means taking risks. Themes are always developed by a text's **details**.

One way to determine a theme is to look at how **characters** respond to **challenges**. A challenge is a problem a character must face.

In the cartoon below, what challenge does the girl face? How does she respond to it? What does that tell you about the theme?

120

English Language Learners

Develop Language

Concept Vocabulary Help students learn word families related to theme.

- Use *challenges* as a naming word. Work with students to give a definition, such as "problems to solve" or "things that are hard to do." Then say the describing word *challenging*. Have students define it. Ask what is challenging in the cartoon.
- Repeat with *respond to*. Ask students to define the word in terms of challenges *(meet, act on, try to overcome)*. Write and say *response*. Have students define it and give examples. Make a web with *Responses to Challenges* in the center, and record students' examples.

● Genre Focus

Folktales

Explain that during Guided Practice and Independent Practice, students will be reading folktales. This type of literary text began as a story that was told by word of mouth, until eventually it was written down. Most folktales teach a lesson or explain something in the natural world. Characters may be ordinary or superhuman.

Provide an example of a folktale such as "The Little Red Hen." Invite students to name other folktales they have read, and discuss whether each folktale teaches a lesson or explains something about the world.

Think What have you learned about identifying the theme of a fictional text? Use the organizer below to help you identify the characters, setting, and character experiences that develop the theme.

Characters	Setting
an adult and a girl	the soccer tryouts

Character Experiences
The girl is excited about trying out for the team. When she doesn't make the team, she's confident that she'll make it next time with more practice.

Theme
If you don't succeed at first, keep trying.

Talk Share your organizer with a partner.

- Did you write down the same character experiences?
- How did the main character react to the challenge?
- Did you arrive at roughly the same theme?

Academic Talk
Use these words to talk about the text.

- theme
- details
- challenge
- characters

Monitor Understanding

If... students struggle to understand how challenges become themes,

then... brainstorm a list of things students would like to change or do, such as getting better grades, being a better big sister, learning to swim, mastering the guitar, and so on:

- **Why are all these things challenges?** *(They are problems to solve or difficult things to do.)*
- **How could you respond to the challenges?** *(Answers will vary but may include reading more, practicing, being more patient, listening to the instructor, getting help, and so on.)*

Record students' answers and then work with them to recast their answers as statements of theme, such as *Practice makes perfect; Patience is a good quality; Listen to/Learn from people who can help you; Always keep trying;* and so on.

Think

- Have students read aloud the Think section. Explain that the organizer will help them collect their ideas.
- Have partners complete the organizer. Remind students that they have to interpret the theme based on the details.
- As students work, circulate and provide assistance as needed.
- Ask volunteers to share what they wrote in their organizers.
- Make certain students understand that the theme is related to the challenge the character faced and her response to it.

Talk

- Read aloud the Talk prompts.
- Have partners discuss how one theme can be stated in different ways. For example, this theme could also be "Don't give up" or "Keep a good attitude."
- Ask volunteers to share their ideas.

Quick Write Have students write a response to the following prompt:

> **Think about a challenge you have had to overcome. What happened? What lesson about life did you learn from overcoming this challenge?**

Ask students to share their responses.

Wrap Up

- Invite students to share what they've learned so far. Encourage them to use the Academic Talk words in their explanations.
- Explain to students that stories and dramas they read will have at least one theme. Sometimes, the theme will be stated at the end of the story. Most of the time, however, students will have to use details in the story to figure out the message about life that the story or play conveys.

In the next section, we'll read a drama. We'll analyze the way characters respond to challenges and use this to interpret the theme.

Monitor Understanding

Modeled and Guided Instruction

Get Started

Today you will read a play called "The Miser." First you'll read to understand what happens. Then you'll read to analyze, or interpret, the theme.

Read

- Read aloud the title of the drama. Ask students what a *miser* is. Guide them to define it as a person who cares too much about his or her money and does not ever want to spend it.
- Have students read the drama independently. Tell them to place a check mark above any confusing words and phrases as they read. Remind students to look inside, around, and beyond each unknown word to help them figure out its meaning. Use the Word Learning Routine on pp. A50–A51.
- When students have finished reading, clarify the meanings of words and phrases they still find confusing. Then use the questions below to check understanding. Encourage students to identify details in the text that support their answers.

  What does the Miser do every day? *(He digs up his money and then buries it again.)*

  What happens to the Miser's money? *(The Thief steals it.)*

  What does the Stranger try to teach the Miser? *(His money didn't do him any good.)*

English Language Learners

Word Learning Strategy

Explore

- Read aloud the Explore question at the top of p. 123 to set the purpose for the second read. Tell students they will need to take a closer look at what happens to the money and, most of all, the stranger's words to the miser, to interpret the theme.
- Have students read aloud the Close Reader Habit on p. 122.

> **TIP** Remind students that a theme can often be a lesson that someone in the story learns. Have students analyze characters' actions and reactions to figure out the lesson the main character learns (or fails to learn).

Modeled and Guided Instruction

Read Genre: Drama

THE MISER

based on a fable by Aesop

Scene 1: The MISER's garden

[*The* MISER *digs up the gold he's buried and then counts it piece by piece.*]

MISER [*rubbing his hands with delight*]: Yes, every last coin is there—the exact sum I've had for years! Now I must bury my treasure again to hide it.

THIEF [*watching from behind a tree*]: Every day this man digs something up and then buries it again. I shall see what it is he digs up and buries! [*waits for the* MISER *to leave, then digs up and steals the gold*]

Scene 2: The next morning

MISER [*digging where his gold was*]: My gold! My gold! I've been robbed! [*A* STRANGER *hears the* MISER*'s cries and comes to see what is wrong.*]

STRANGER: Your gold? There in that hole? Why did you put it there? Why didn't you keep it in the house where you could easily get at it when you had things to buy?

MISER: Buy? Why, I never touched the gold except to count it! I couldn't think of spending it!

STRANGER [*throws a large stone into the hole*]: If that is the case, then cover up that stone.

MISER [*scoffing*]: You are a fool! That is not gold. It is a mere stone.

STRANGER: It may be a mere stone, but it is worth just as much to you as the treasure you lost.

[*The* STRANGER *walks off, leaving the* MISER *to consider his words.*]

Close Reader Habits

When you reread the drama, **underline** a line of dialogue that explains why the Miser acts as he does. Then **circle** the Stranger's lesson to the Miser.

122

English Language Learners

Build Meaning

Act It Out To help students develop a rich understanding of the characters in this drama, conduct a Reader's Theater.

- Ask three volunteers who understand the story well to perform the play in pantomime gestures. Assign one role each to the Miser, the Thief, and the Stranger. Remind them that they cannot use words, but they should use facial expressions and body movements.
- As the students act out the scenes, invite language learners to describe what is happening. Ask follow-up questions such as, "How is the Miser feeling? How can you tell?"
- At the end of the play, invite students to summarize what happened.

Word Learning Strategy

Use Context Clues

- Direct students' attention to the word *mere* in the last line of the play.

  What do you think *mere* means? What context clue helps you figure out the meaning?

- Guide students to find the antonym context clue for *mere stone*: "that is not gold." Explain that *mere* suggests only a stone, or nothing more than a stone.
- Remind students that when they come to an unknown word or phrase, they can look at the surrounding words for a clue to the meaning. One type of context clue is an antonym, or word or phrase with an opposite, or nearly opposite, meaning.

L.5.4a

Explore What is the theme of "The Miser"?

Think

1 Complete this organizer by identifying the details of the drama.

Think about how the characters interact to figure out the theme of the drama.

Characters
The Miser, a Thief, and a Stranger

Setting
The Miser's garden over two days

Character Experiences
The Miser refuses to spend any of his money. He keeps his wealth buried where it doesn't benefit anyone. Then the Thief takes it. The Stranger tells him that, if he never did anything with his treasure, it's no better than a stone.

Theme
If you don't use your wealth, you might as well not have it.

Talk

2 Discuss how you figured out the theme of the drama. If you identify more details that you'd like to add to your organizer, do so now.

Write

3 **Short Response** Describe the theme of the drama. Explain which details develop the theme. Use details from the organizer in your response. Use the space provided on page 126 to write your answer.

HINT In your answer, identify how the characters behave or interact with each other.

123

Think Aloud

- To find the theme of "The Miser," I'll go back to the text and first learn more about the characters and the setting.
- The play is called "The Miser," and I see from scanning the play that the Miser is one of the people who speaks most. I think he's the main character. But I can also see that there are characters called "Thief" and "Stranger." I'll put those names in the diagram under *Characters*.
- Now I'll try to figure out the setting. I'll start by rereading Scene 1. Right at the top of the text, I can see a description of the scene. It says Scene 1 takes place in the Miser's garden. Then the stage direction tells me he's digging in the garden. I'll scan to see what happens later, just to see if the setting changes in Scene 2. When I read the boldface description, I see that the place hasn't changed, but it's now the next morning. So I know this play takes place in the garden across two days. I'll write that detail in the chart under *Setting*.

Lesson 7

Think

- Read aloud the Think section. Explain to students that you will model how to find text evidence to fill in part of the chart. Use the **Think Aloud** below to guide your modeling.
- Revisit the Explore question. Guide students to determine that they need to look for more details, using the Close Reader Habit.
- Encourage students to work with a partner to continue rereading the passage and complete the organizer. Remind students that the Buddy Tip will help them focus on the key characters, especially the Stranger and the Miser.
- Ask volunteers to share their completed organizers.
- Guide students to see how, in this case, someone (the Stranger) actually teaches the lesson of the story. Ask where in the story the theme becomes clear. Note that themes often become clear at the end of stories.

Talk

- Read aloud the Talk prompt.
- Have partners respond to the prompt. Use the Talk Routine on pp. A52–A53.
- Circulate to check that students are discussing how they figured out the theme.

Write

- Ask a volunteer to read aloud the Write prompt.
- Invite a few students to tell what the prompt is asking them to do.
- Make sure students understand that they need to state the theme and also explain how details in their organizers helped them interpret the theme.
- Have students turn to p. 126 to write their response.
- Use Review Responses on p. 126 to assess students' writing.

Wrap Up

- Ask students to recall the Learning Target. Have them explain how finding the theme helps them better understand and relate to a drama.

Guided Practice

Get Started

Today you will read a Chinese folktale called "The Wise Man." First, you will read to find out what happens. Then you will reread with a partner to find the theme.

Read

- Read aloud the title of the folktale. Invite students to tell the meaning of *wise*. *("Having information or good judgement.")*
- **Read to Understand** Have students read the story independently. Tell them to place a check mark above any confusing words and phrases as they read. Remind students to look inside, around, and beyond each unknown word or phrase to help them figure out its meaning. Use the Word Learning Routine on pp. A50–A51.
- When students have finished reading, clarify the meanings of words and phrases they still find confusing. Then use the questions below to check understanding. Encourage students to identify details in the text that support their answers.

  How does the old man come to have a stallion "of great worth"? *(The horse that ran away returns home with it.)*

  What is the old man's attitude about the stallion? *(He does not celebrate. He says the worth of the stallion will become clear later.)*

  What happens to the old man's son? *(He falls off the stallion and breaks his leg.)*

  How does the old man react to his son's accident? *(He is calm about it. He suggests that it could be a blessing.)*

  How does the son's accident turn out to be a blessing? *(When there is a war, the son cannot go to fight because of his injury.)*

English Language Learners

● Word Learning Strategy

- **Read to Analyze** Read aloud the Close Reader Habit on p. 124 to set the purpose for the second read. Then have students reread the story with a partner and discuss any questions they might have.

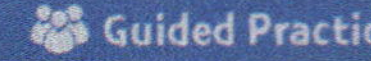

Guided Practice

Read

Genre: Folktale

The Wise Man

a Chinese folktale

1 There once was an elderly farmer who lived with his son. One day the old man discovered that his only horse had run off. His friends helped him search for the animal, but to no avail. The old man's friends offered their condolences. "We are so sorry about this unfortunate incident," they said.

2 The old man laughed and replied, "What makes you think this is not a blessing? All will be shown for its true worth in time." The old man's friends were stunned by his reaction.

3 Some months later, the old man's horse returned, bringing with it a stallion of great worth. His friends came to celebrate. But the old man shook his head and said to them, "What makes you think this is a good thing? All will be shown for its true worth in time." The old man's friends were surprised again.

4 A week later, the old man's son took the stallion for a ride and suffered a fall, breaking his leg in several places. Again, the old man's friends came to offer their sympathy, but the old man greeted them calmly and replied, "What makes you think this is not a blessing? All will be shown for its true worth in time."

5 A short while later, the country was involved in a terrible war. A group of soldiers came to the old man's house to recruit his son. But when they saw that he had a broken leg, they left him behind. The old man's neighbors gathered to congratulate him, declaring with amazement, "What wisdom you have, for you can foresee both good and bad incidents for what they truly are."

Close Reader Habits

How does the old man respond to the challenges he faces? Reread the folktale. **Underline** the sentences that show his responses to challenges.

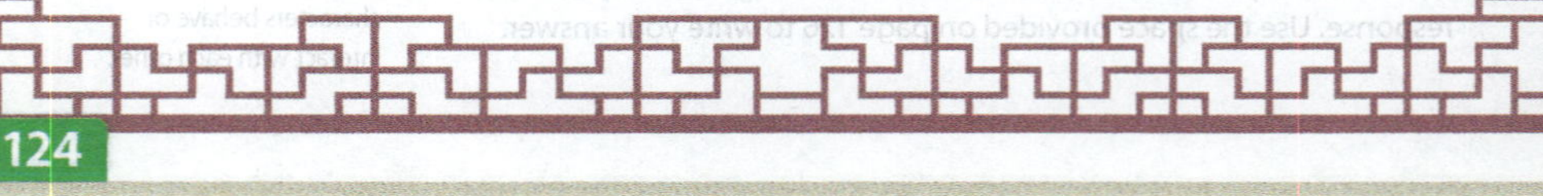

124

English Language Learners

Build Meaning

Syntax Point out that old stories often have irregular syntax. Write on the board "All will be shown for its true worth in time." Then add slashes to chunk the text. Reread the chunks: "All will be shown | for its true worth | in time." Guide students to paraphrase each chunk.

What's another way to say "All will be shown"? *(Everything will become clear.)*

What does "in time" mean in this sentence? *(after some time passes, later)*

- Have students paraphrase the whole sentence, encouraging them to change its order if it makes sense.

● Word Learning Strategy

Use Context Clues

- Point to the word *condolences* in paragraph 1.

  What does *condolences* mean as it is used in this sentence? *(words that show the speaker is sorry about bad luck, a loss, or other pain or suffering)*

  What context clues help you figure out the meaning? *("We are so sorry . . .")*

- Repeat with *incident* in the same paragraph, eliciting the meaning "something that happened." Have students identify the relevant context clue: the man's only horse had run off.
- Encourage students to use each word in their own sentences to demonstrate understanding.

L.5.4a

Think Use what you learned from reading the folktale to respond to the following questions.

A folktale is a story told again and again over generations of people. Many folktales teach lessons or have messages.

1 This question has two parts. Answer Part A. Then answer Part B.

Part A
How do the actions of the old man's friends contribute to the theme of the story?

- **A** They want to celebrate with the old man.
- **(B)** They jump to conclusions about what events are blessings and misfortunes.
- **C** They are glad because the old man's son does not have to go to war.
- **D** They are confused by the old man's happiness.

Part B
Which detail from the folktale **best** supports the answer to Part A?

- **(A)** "The old man's friends offered their condolences. 'We are so sorry about this unfortunate incident,' they said."
- **B** "The old man's friends were stunned by his reaction."
- **C** "Some months later, the old man's horse returned, bringing with it a stallion of great worth."
- **D** "A group of soldiers came to the old man's house to recruit his son."

Talk

2 What is the theme of the passage? Use details from the passage to support your answer. Use the organizer on page 127 to identify the characters, setting, theme, and evidence for the theme.

Write

3 **Short Response** Use the information in your organizer to determine the theme of the folktale. Use details from the passage to support your response. Use the space provided on page 127 to write your answer.

HINT Be sure to say how the old man responds to events and interacts with his friends.

125

● Integrating Standards

Use the following questions to further students' understanding of the folktale.

- **Compare and contrast how the old man and his friends react to his horse running off.** *(When the horse runs off, the old man and his friends both search for the horse. The friends say they are sorry about the old man's loss. In contrast, the old man says, "What makes you think this is not a blessing?")*
DOK 2 **RL.5.3**
- **How does each scene in the story help show how the old man and his neighbors are different?** *(In each scene, the neighbors judge each event to be good or bad, but the old man does not rush to judgments and always says the same thing: let's wait and see what this really means.)*
DOK 3 **RL.5.5**

● Monitor Understanding

If... students have trouble answering item 1, Part B,

then... verify that students chose the correct answer to item 1, Part A (choice B). Then have students narrow down the answer choices for those that logically have to do with the old man's friends (choices A and B). Next, have them think about which choice makes the most sense to support the idea that the friends "jump to conclusions about what events are blessings and misfortunes."

Think

- Have students work with a partner to complete item 1. Draw attention to the boldface word **best** in Part B.

TIP If students have trouble answering Part A, remind them to look for what the characters learn or realize by the end of the story.

Answer Analysis

When students have finished, discuss correct and incorrect responses.

1 Part A
The correct choice is B.

- **A** is only half of the way the friends contribute to the theme, since they also want to commiserate with the old man. **C** is a minor detail. **D** is not supported by story evidence.

Part B
The correct choice is A. The friends jump to the conclusion that the old man wants to be comforted after his horse runs away.

- **B** is evidence of the friends being confused about why the old man doesn't come to the same conclusions they do. **C** and **D** have nothing to do with the actions of the friends.

DOK 2

● **Monitor Understanding**

● **Integrating Standards**

Talk

- Have partners discuss the prompt. Emphasize that students should support their ideas with text details.
- Circulate to clarify misunderstandings.

Write

- See p. 127 for instructional guidance.

Wrap Up

- Ask students to recall the Learning Target. Have them explain how identifying the theme helped them better understand and appreciate the folktale.

Modeled and Guided Instruction

Write

- Remember to use the Response-Writing Routine on pp. A54–A55.

Review Responses

After students complete the writing activity, help them evaluate their responses.

3 Responses may vary but should show an understanding that the theme of the folktale is that never enjoying your wealth is like having no wealth at all. Students should give examples about the Miser's behavior around his obsession with his coins and his grief over losing them. The Stranger uses a useless rock to teach the Miser that wealth not spent is not wealth. See the sample response on the student book page. ***DOK 3***

Write Use the space below to write your answer to the question on page 123.

THE MISER

HINT In your answer, identify how the characters behave or interact with each other.

3 **Short Response** Describe the theme of the drama. Explain which details develop the theme. Use the details from the organizer in your response.

Sample response: The theme of "The Miser" is this: If you don't use the wealth you have, you might as well not have any wealth at all. The drama develops this theme through events and character interactions. First, we learn that the Miser buries his treasure in his garden and checks on it every day. But then the Thief sees the Miser bury the treasure and steals it when the Miser isn't around. When the Miser realizes that his treasure is gone, a passing Stranger provides him with a lesson—that buried wealth is no better than a buried rock. It is through these events and character interactions that "The Miser" develops its theme.

Check Your Writing

- ☐ Did you read the prompt carefully?
- ☐ Did you put the prompt in your own words?
- ☐ Did you use the best evidence from the text to support your ideas?
- ☐ Are your ideas clearly organized?
- ☐ Did you write in clear and complete sentences?
- ☐ Did you check your spelling and punctuation?

126

Scaffolding Support for Reluctant Writers

If students are having a difficult time getting started, use the strategies below. Work individually with struggling students, or have students work with partners.

- Circle the verbs in the prompt that tell you what to do, such as *describe*, *explain*, or *compare*.
- Underline words and phrases in the prompt that show what information you need to provide in your response, such as *causes*, *reasons*, or *character traits*.
- Talk about the details from the text that you will include in your response.
- Explain aloud how you will respond to the prompt.

Guided Practice

The Wise Man

2 Use the graphic organizer below to organize your ideas and evidence.

Characters	Setting

Character Experiences

Theme

Write Use the space below to write your answer to the question on page 125.

HINT Be sure to say how the old man responds to events and interacts with his friends.

3 **Short Response** Use the information in your organizer to determine the theme of the folktale. Use details from the passage to support your response.

Sample response: The theme of "The Wise Man" is that a person should not judge events too quickly. Both the events in the story and the old man's responses develop this theme. For example, the old man's horse runs off. His friends say it is "unfortunate," but it later returns with a stallion, which was good. Every time something happened, the old man responded not by judging whether the events were good or bad, but by saying that their true value will be revealed in time.

127

Teacher Notes

Guided Practice

Talk

2 Students should use the organizer to record their thoughts and evidence.

Write

- Ask a volunteer to read aloud the Write prompt.
- Invite students to tell what the prompt is asking them to do. Make sure they understand that they need to tell the theme as well as provide events that show the theme.
- Call attention to the HINT.
- Remember to use the Response-Writing Routine on pp. A54–A55.

Review Responses

After students complete the writing activity, help them evaluate their responses.

3 Responses may vary but should show an understanding that the theme of the folktale is that you should not rush to judgment about whether an event is good or bad. When the old man loses his horse and his son breaks his leg, these events turn out to be blessings because the man gains a stallion and his son does not have to go to war. Yet, the event of getting a new horse is not a positive event because it results in his son having an accident. See the sample response on the student book page. *DOK 3*

Independent Practice

Get Started

Today you are going to read a folktale called "The Bell of Atri." You will use what you have learned about finding the theme to determine the folktale's message about life.

- Ask a volunteer to explain how finding the theme will help readers to better understand and appreciate folktales. Encourage students to use the Academic Talk words in their response.

English Language Learners

Read

You are going to read the folktale independently and use what you have learned to think and write about the story. As you read, remember to look closely at the details in the story to identify the characters and their response to events.

- Read aloud the title of the folktale and then encourage students to preview the text, paying close attention to the illustrations.
- Call attention to the Words to Know in the upper left of p. 128.
- If students need support in reading the folktale, you may wish to use the Monitor Understanding suggestions.
- When students have finished, have them complete the Think and Write sections.

● **Monitor Understanding**

Read

Genre: Folktale

WORDS TO KNOW
As you read, look inside, around, and beyond these words to figure out what they mean.
- **justice**
- **judgment**

The Bell of Atri

retold by Jane Carey

1 Atri is the name of a little town in Italy. A long time ago, the King of Atri had a large bell hung up in a tower in the marketplace. A rope that reached almost to the ground was fastened to the bell so that even the smallest child could ring the bell by pulling upon this rope. All the men, women, and children of Atri came down to the marketplace to look at the bell. It was a very pretty bell, and it was polished until it looked as bright and yellow as the sun.

2 "My people," said the king, "do you see this beautiful bell? It is the bell of justice. If any of you is wronged at any time, you may come and ring the bell. Then the judges shall come together at once, hear your case, and give you justice. Rich and poor, old and young, all alike may come, but you must not pull the rope unless you know you have been wronged."

3 Many years passed, and many times did the bell ring out to call the judges together. Many wrongs were righted and many ill-doers punished. At last the rope, worn and broken, became so short that only a tall man could reach it. "This will never do," said the judges one day. "What if a child should be wronged? He or she could not reach the bell to ring it." They gave orders that a new rope should be put on the bell, but there was not a rope to be found in all of Atri. They would have to send across the mountains for one, and it would be many days before it could be brought.

4 "Let me fix it," said a man who stood by. He ran to his garden and soon came back with a long grapevine. He climbed up and fastened it to the bell. The slender vine, with its leaves and tendrils still upon it, trailed to the ground. The judges thought it to be a very good rope.

128

English Language Learners

Develop Language

Concept Vocabulary Develop a concept map for the word *justice*. Invite students to share cognates for the term in their first languages. Then invite them to share their ideas about what justice is, who gives and receives it, and why we need it. Write their words in the concept map, organizing them into subclusters such as *people, reasons,* and *events*.

Integrate passage vocabulary with students' explanations. For example, if students say *judges,* say, "Yes, judges 'hear your case'" (p. 128). Or say, "Yes, justice punishes 'ill-doers'" (p.128). Or say, "Yes, someone 'is wronged' (p. 128), so there is a 'judgment'" (p. 131). Add more words and phrases to the appropriate subclusters. Have students summarize what the concept map says about justice, one subcluster at a time.

Have pairs use the concept map to write several sentences about what justice is. Invite volunteers to share their best sentences, and write them on the board.

5 Now, on the hillside above the village, there lived a man who had once been a brave knight. In his youth, he had fought in many a battle. His best friend had been his horse—a strong, noble steed that had borne him safe through danger. But the knight, when he grew older, cared no more to ride into battle and cared no more to do brave deeds. He thought of nothing but gold and became a miser. Day after day, he sat among his bags of money and planned how he might get more, and day after day, his horse stood in his bare stall, half starved and miserable.

6 "What is the use of that lazy steed?" said the knight to himself one morning. "It costs more to keep him than he is worth. I might sell him, but there is not a man who wants him. I will let him fend for himself." So the brave old horse was turned out to find what he could on the barren hillside. Weak and sick, he strolled along the dusty roads, glad to find a blade of grass or a thistle.

7 One hot afternoon, the horse wandered into town. Not a person was there, for the heat had driven them all indoors. It wasn't long before the poor beast saw the grapevine that hung from the bell, the leaves and tendrils upon it still fresh and green. What a fine dinner they would be for a starving horse! He stretched his neck and took one of the tender morsels in his mouth, but it was hard to break it from the vine. He pulled at it, and the great bell began to ring.

8 The judges put on their robes and went out through the hot streets to the marketplace, where they saw the old horse nibbling at the vine. "Ha!" cried one. "It is the knight's steed. He has come to call for justice, for his master, as everybody knows, has treated him shamefully."

Monitor Understanding

If… students struggle to read and understand the passage,

then… use these scaffolding suggestions:

Question the Text Preview the text by asking the following questions:

- **Based on the title and illustrations, what do you predict the folktale will be about?**
- **What questions do you have about the story?**

Vocabulary Support Define words that may interfere with comprehension, such as *vine* and *tendrils*.

Read Aloud Read aloud the text with students. You could also have students chorally read the text in a small group.

Check Understanding Use the questions below to check understanding. Encourage students to cite details in the text that support their answers.

- **How did the knight change?** *(He had once been brave, but when he got old, he thought only of gold. He also got rid of his horse, who was once his best friend.)*
- **What happens to the horse?** *(He gets weak and sick.)*
- **The horse has a happy ending. What is it?** *(He finds food in the town of Atri. He also receives justice there.)*

Independent Practice

Integrating Standards

After students have read the folktale, use these questions to discuss it with them.

- **In paragraph 5, the story describes the horse as a "noble steed that had borne [the knight] safe through danger." What does *borne* mean? Which context clues in the paragraph help you figure out this meaning?**

  (Borne means "carried." The context clue "ride into battle" helps me understand that borne *has to do with the horse carrying the knight safely through danger.)*

  DOK 2 RL.5.4, L.5.4a

- **What is the narrator's point of view about the horse? What might be different if the story were told from the knight's point of view?**

  (The narrator says that the "horse stood in his bare stall, half starved and neglected." These words make readers feel sorry for the horse. If the story were told from the knight's point of view, then the reader might sympathize a bit more with the knight instead of judging him as a bad character.)

  DOK 3 RL.5.6

- **What causes the change from a short rope on the bell to a long vine? How does this affect what happens with the horse?**

  (The short rope is changed because children can't reach it, and justice is supposed to be "for all." When the longer vine is fastened to the bell, it has tendrils growing on it that the horse can eat. Eating them causes the bell to ring, and the ringing of the bell eventually leads to food and justice for the horse.)

  DOK 2 RL.5.3

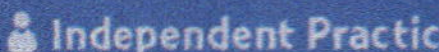
Independent Practice

9 Meanwhile a crowd had gathered, eager to learn what cause the judges were about to try. When they saw the horse, everyone stood still in wonder. Then all were ready to tell how they had seen him wandering the hills, uncared for and unfed.

10 The judges ordered the knight to be brought before them. And when he came, they bade him stand and hear their judgment. "This horse has served you well," they said. "He has saved you from many a peril. He has helped you gain your wealth. Therefore, we order that half your gold shall be set aside to buy him shelter and food, a green pasture where he may graze, and a warm stall to comfort him in his old age."

11 The knight hung his head and grieved to lose his gold, but the people shouted with joy, and the horse was led away to his new stall and a dinner such as he had not had in many a day.

130

Theme Connection

- Remind students that the theme of this lesson is Literature with a Message.
- Review each passage from this lesson and ask students to state one or more messages conveyed by the passage. Discuss whether these themes have been present in any other stories, plays, or poems the students have read.

Think Use what you learned from reading the folktale to respond to the following questions.

1 This question has two parts. First, answer Part A. Then answer Part B.

Part A
How are the events in paragraphs 1, 2, and 3 important to one of the themes of the story?

A They show that townspeople are concerned about whether children can seek justice.
B They show that judges must be very wise in order to provide justice for everyone.
C They show that the bell's new rope must come from far away, across the mountains.
(D) They show that the town's leaders want everyone to have equal access to justice.

Part B
Which **two** sentences from the story provide the **best** support for the answer in Part A?

(A) "A rope that reached almost to the ground was fastened to the bell so that even the smallest child could ring the bell by pulling upon this rope."
B "It was a very pretty bell, and it was polished until it looked as bright and yellow as the sun."
(C) "'If any of you is wronged at any time, you may come and ring the bell.'"
D "Many years passed, and many times did the bell ring out to call the judges together."
E "At last the rope, worn and broken, became so short that only a tall man could reach it."
F "They would have to send across the mountains for one, and it would be many days before it could be brought."

Think

- Use the Monitor Understanding suggestions to support students in completing items 1–3.

● **Monitor Understanding**

Answer Analysis

When students have finished, discuss correct and incorrect responses.

1 **Part A**
The correct choice is D. The first three paragraphs focus on the bell and its rope being long enough for even a child to pull in order to beg for justice. This connects to the theme of fair treatment for all (even horses).

- **A, B,** and **C** are true, but do not relate to a theme. **B** is also not supported by the details in paragraphs 1–3.

Part B
The correct choices are A and C. These details show that the bell's purpose is to provide justice for all, even for a small child.

- **B** and **D** are both details about the bell, but the sentences are not relevant to the theme.
- **E** and **F** discuss how the bell came to need a new rope over time, but these details are not relevant to the theme.

***DOK 2* RL.5.2**

● **Monitor Understanding**

If... students struggle to complete the items,

then... you may wish to use the following suggestions:

Read Aloud Activities

- As you read, have students note any unfamiliar words or phrases. Clarify any misunderstandings.
- Discuss each item with students to make certain they understand the expectation.

Reread the Text

- Have students complete a graphic organizer as they reread.
- Have partners summarize the text.

Independent Practice

2 **Part A**

The correct choice is C. The knight's actions show that wealth should be used to help those who have been loyal friends.

- **A** is not supported by details in the passage.
- **B** is not the lesson taught by the detail of the knight turning his horse out to run wild.
- **D** is incorrect because the knight's behavior is viewed negatively the community.

Part B

The correct choice is D. The detail supports the theme that wealth should be used to help those in need.

- **A** is a detail about how badly the knight has treated his horse.
- **B** is a detail about what the horse went through.
- **C** is a detail about how the judges brought the knight to stand before them.

DOK 2 **RL.5.2**

3 **The correct choice is A.** The details in the sentence indicate that the horse is in very bad shape and is unhappy.

- **B** is incorrect because the horse is not greedy, just in need of food for survival.
- **C** is incorrect because the horse is hungry, but that fits better as the meaning of *starved* than of *miserable*.
- **D** is incorrect because, although the horse is loyal, loyalty is not conveyed by the word *miserable*.

DOK 2 **RL.5.4, L.5.4a**

Independent Practice

2 This question has two parts. First, answer Part A. Then answer Part B.

Part A

How do the knight's actions contribute to a theme of the story?

- **A** His decision to appear in front of the judges shows that it is brave to stand up for yourself.
- **B** His treatment of his horse demonstrates that animals should be allowed to roam freely.
- **(C)** His choices show that wealth should be used to help those who have been loyal friends.
- **D** His actions show that a person can behave poorly but still be respected in the community.

Part B

Which detail from the story **best** supports the answer to Part A?

- **A** ". . . his master, as everybody knows, has treated him shamefully.'"
- **B** ". . . they had seen him wandering the hills, uncared for and unfed."
- **C** ". . . they bade him stand and hear their judgment."
- **(D)** "'Therefore, we order that half your gold shall be set aside to buy him shelter and food, . . .'"

3 Read the sentence from the text. Then answer the question.

> Day after day, he sat among his bags of money and planned how he might get more, and day after day, his horse stood in his bare stall, half starved and <u>miserable</u>.

What does the use of the word <u>miserable</u> suggest?

- **(A)** The horse is unhappy.
- **B** The horse is greedy.
- **C** The horse is hungry.
- **D** The horse is loyal.

132

● Monitor Understanding

If... students don't understand the writing task,

then... read aloud the writing prompt. Use the following questions to help students get started.

- **What is the prompt asking you to write about?**
- **Do you need to reread the text to find more information?**
- **How will you identify the information you need to include?**

- Have partners talk about how they will organize their responses.
- Provide a graphic organizer to assist students, if needed.

 Write

4 **Short Response** One theme of "The Bell of Atri" is that you should help those who have helped you. Write a paragraph that explains how the theme of the story is shown through the characters' actions and their responses to events.

Sample response: The story expresses the theme "Help those who have helped you" because this is a lesson the knight learns. The judges tell the knight that the horse "has helped you gain your wealth." Even more importantly, the horse has saved the knight's life. They punish the knight for not helping the horse by ordering that "half [his] gold shall be set aside" for the horse. If the knight had taken care of his horse, then he would not have gotten punished and been made to give up half his gold.

 Learning Target

In this lesson, you determined the themes of fictional texts. Explain how the skills you practiced will help you figure out the themes of fictional texts you read in the future.

Responses will vary, but students should recognize that identifying the details in a text, such as how the characters in a story or drama interact and respond to challenges, helps them understand the theme or the deeper meaning of the story.

4 **2-Point Writing Rubric**

Points	Focus	Evidence	Organization
2	My answer does exactly what the prompt asked me to do.	My answer is supported with plenty of details from the text.	My ideas are clear and in a logical order.
1	Some of my answer does not relate to the prompt.	My answer is missing some important details from the text.	Some of my ideas are unclear and out of order.
0	My answer does not make sense.	My answer does not have any details from the text.	My ideas are unclear and not in any order.

Write

- Tell students that using what they read, they will compose a short response to the writing prompt.

Monitor Understanding

Review Responses

After students have completed each part of the writing activity, help them evaluate their responses.

4 Display or pass out copies of the reproducible **2-Point Writing Rubric** on p. TR10. Have students use the rubric to individually assess their writing and revise as needed.

When students have finished their revisions, evaluate their responses. Answers will vary but should include that judges tell the knight the horse "has helped you gain your wealth." Even more important, the horse has saved the knight's life. They punish the knight for not helping the horse by ordering that "half [his] gold shall be set aside" for the horse. See the sample response on the student book page. ***DOK 3* RL.5.2, W.5.9a**

Wrap Up

Learning Target

- Have each student respond in writing to the Learning Target prompt.
- When students have finished, have them share their responses. This may be done with a partner, in small groups, or as a whole class.

Lesson 8
Finding the Theme of a Poem

Standards Focus

Determine a theme of a . . . poem from details in the text, including how the speaker in a poem reflects upon a topic. . . . **RL.5.2**

Lesson Objectives

Reading

- Identify the speaker of a poem. **RL.5.2**
- Distinguish main idea from theme by understanding that theme is the larger message of a text. **RL.5.2**
- Describe how the speaker reflects on a topic in a poem. **RL.5.2**

Writing

- Draw evidence from literary texts to support analysis and reflection. **W.5.9a**

Speaking and Listening

- Pose and respond to specific questions and contribute to discussions. **SL.5.1c**
- Review the key ideas expressed and draw conclusions. **SL.5.1d**

Language

- Use Greek and Latin affixes and roots as clues to the meaning of a word. **L.5.4b**
- Acquire and use academic and domain-specific words and phrases. **L.5.6**

Additional Practice: **RL.5.1, RL.5.3, RL.5.4, RL.5.6**

Academic Talk

See **Glossary of Terms**, pp. TR2–TR9

- theme
- topic
- speaker
- reflect

Learning Progression

Grade 4	Grade 5	Grade 6
Students determine a theme from key details in the text.	Building on Grade 4, students determine the theme of a poem from text details, including how the speaker in a poem reflects on a topic.	Grade 6 increases in complexity by focusing on the central idea of a text, in addition to the theme, and requiring students to explain how it is conveyed through particular details in the text.

Lesson Text Selections

Modeled and Guided Instruction

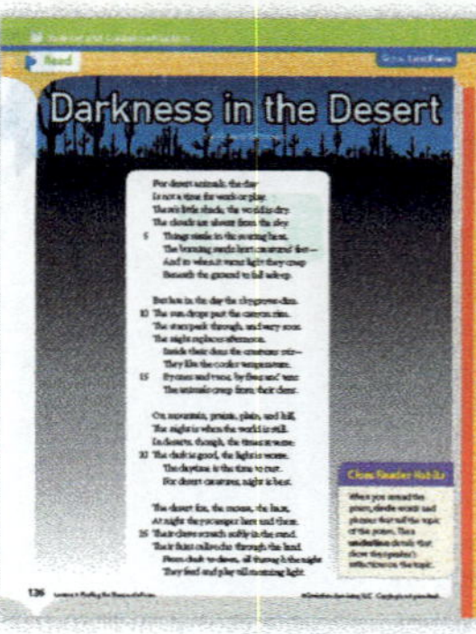

Darkness in the Desert
by Morena Sommers
Genre: Lyric Poem

Guided Practice

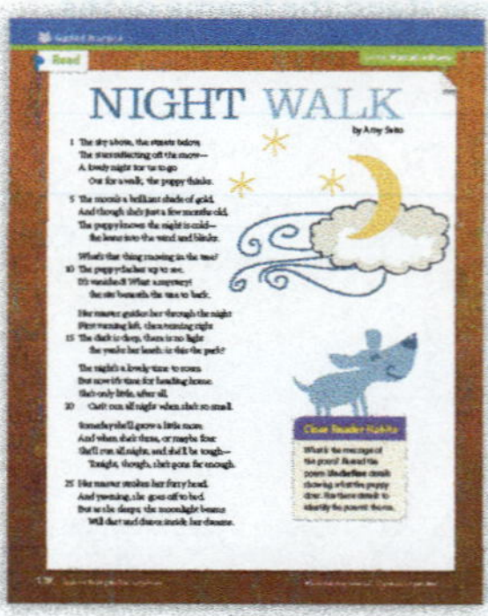

Night Walk
by Amy Saito
Genre: Narrative Poem

Independent Practice

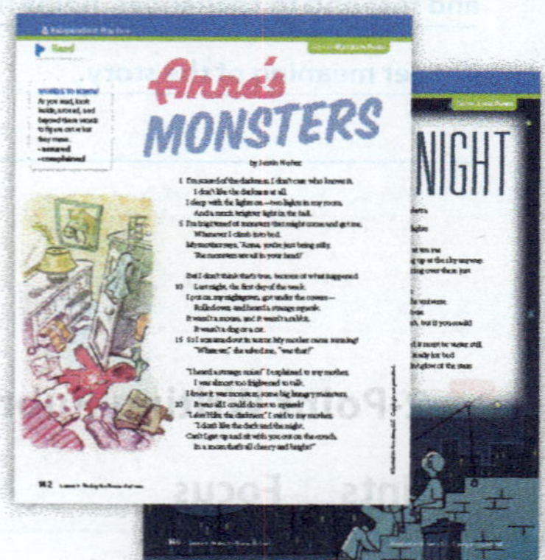

Anna's Monsters
by Justin Nuñez
Genre: Narrative Poem

Summer Night
by Bianca Cappeletta
Genre: Lyric Poem

Lesson Pacing Guide

Whole Class Instruction *30–45 minutes per day*

Day 1

Teacher-Toolbox.com **Interactive Tutorial**
Identifying Theme—Level E
20 min (optional)

Introduction pp. 134–135

- **Read** **Finding the Theme of a Poem** *10 min*
- **Think** *10 min*
  Graphic Organizer: Four-Column Chart
- **Talk** *5 min*
  Quick Write (TRB) *5 min*

Day 2

Modeled and Guided Instruction pp. 136–137, 140

- **Read** **Darkness in the Desert** *10 min*
- **Think** *10 min*
  Graphic Organizer: Four-Column Chart
- **Talk** *5 min*
- **Write** Short Response *10 min*

Day 3

Guided Practice pp. 138–139, 141

- **Read** **Night Walk** *10 min*
- **Think** *10 min*
- **Talk** *5 min*
- **Write** Short Response *10 min*

Day 4

Independent Practice pp. 142–147

- **Read**
  Anna's Monsters *15 min*
  Summer Night *5 min*
- **Think** *10 min*
- **Write** Short Response *10 min*

Day 5

Independent Practice pp. 142–147

- *Review* Answer Analysis (TRB) *10 min*
- *Review* Response Analysis (TRB) *10 min*
- *Assign and Discuss* Learning Target *10 min*

Language Handbook
Lesson 1 Coordinating and Subordinating Conjunctions, pp. 438–439
20 min (optional)

Small Group Differentiation
Teacher-Toolbox.com

Reteach

***Ready Reading* Prerequisite Lesson**

- **Grade 4** Lesson 10 Determining the Theme of a Poem

Teacher-led Activities

Tools for Instruction

- Determine Theme

Personalized Learning
i-Ready.com

Independent

***i-Ready* Close Reading Lessons**

- **Grade 4** Determining the Theme of a Poem
- **Grade 5** Finding the Theme of a Poem

Get Started

- Explain to students that in this lesson they will read poetry about nighttime and analyze to find the topic and theme of each poem.
- Remind students that the *topic* is what a story or poem is about. To determine *theme*, readers must combine details from the text with their own experiences to make an inference. Review that a theme is a message the author wants readers to understand.
- Prompt students to distinguish between topics and themes. Display "The Star-Spangled Banner" or another poem that is familiar to students. Explain:

  The topic of the poem is the flag flying during a battle. But what is the theme? The speaker's words are filled with pride ("what so proudly we hailed"; "so gallantly streaming") because he saw "that our flag was still there." From his feeling and our own knowledge, we can infer that the theme, or message, is that our nation is strong and mighty.
- Focus students' attention on the Learning Target. Read it aloud to set the purpose for the lesson.
- Display the Academic Talk words. Tell students to listen for these words and their meanings as you work through the lesson together. Use the Academic Talk Routine on pp. A48–A49.

 **English Language Learners**

● **Genre Focus**

Read

- Read aloud the Read section as students follow along. Restate to reinforce:

  When you read a poem, pay attention to the details that show the speaker's thoughts or feelings about the topic. This will help you figure out the poem's theme.
- Direct students' attention to the comic strip. Have them study the details in each panel to figure out the theme.

Lesson 8
Finding the Theme of a Poem

Studying how a poet reflects upon a topic and the details she includes will help you identify the theme of a poem.

Read Poems can express feelings and ideas on many **topics**. The **speaker** in a poem **reflects** on a topic by saying what he or she thinks and feels about it. You can use these reflections and other details in a poem to figure out that poem's message, or **theme**.

Identify the theme of this comic strip by studying what the characters say and do. Also think about how the comic strip ends.

English Language Learners

Develop Language

Academic Vocabulary Tell students that poetry has a special vocabulary that is different from stories.

- Draw a two-column chart on the board with the headings *Stories* and *Poems*. Ask who writes a story and who writes a poem. Record *author* and *poet* in the correct columns.
- Next ask who tells a story. Guide students to provide the term *narrator*, and then explain that a poem is told by the *speaker*. The speaker may or may not be the poet, just like the narrator of a story may or may not be the author.
- Continue with the terms *stanza/paragraph* and *line/sentence*. Keep the chart posted for reference.

● Genre Focus

Poetry

Poetry uses language in creative ways to express ideas and describe experiences. Common features of poetry include:

- **Stanzas**—groups of lines
- **Rhymes**—words that end in the same sounds
- **Rhythm**—the pattern of beats, or stressed syllables, in lines of poetry
- **Imagery**—descriptive language that helps readers picture the subject

Ask students to give examples of poems they know, such as "Where the Sidewalk Ends," by Shel Silverstein.

Think What have you learned so far about using details to identify a theme? Complete the chart below, filling it out with details from the comic strip.

What Do the Characters Say?	What Do the Characters Do?	How Does the Comic Strip End?	What Is the Theme?
One person is stressed; the other person says he can help.	They sit and watch the sun set and the stars come out.	The girl is no longer stressed.	Night can ease the worries of the day.

Talk Share your chart with a partner.

- What is the topic of the comic strip?
- Did you describe in the same way what the friends say and do? How about the ending?
- Do the details you found support the theme? How do you know?

Academic Talk
Use these words to talk about the text.

- theme
- topics
- speaker
- reflect

135

Monitor Understanding

If... students struggle to identify theme,

then... have them think about an episode of a television show they like. Explain that episodes are often based on a central message. When students have thought of an episode, ask them to think about the following ideas:

- **What was the problem?**
- **How was the problem solved?**
- **Did any of the characters change their behavior or way of thinking?**
- **Did anyone learn a lesson?**

Point out that often the characters will state the theme by expressing the lesson they have learned. In poems, however, readers usually have to ask themselves these question to figure out the message on their own.

Think

- Have students read aloud the Think section. Explain that the chart will help them organize their thinking.
- Have partners complete the chart, thinking carefully about what the characters do (and do not do) and say, and what happens as a result.
- As students work, circulate and provide assistance as needed.
- Ask volunteers to share what they wrote in their charts.
- Make certain students understand that the theme is not stated directly in the comic strip. Readers must consider the characters' interactions, as well as what happened, to infer the theme.

Talk

- Read aloud the Talk prompts.
- Have partners discuss their interpretations of the comic strip. Students should identify how the characters' actions (such as sitting quietly) and words (such as "I needed that") reveal the theme.
- Ask volunteers to share their ideas.

Quick Write Have students write a response to the following prompt:

> **Think about a time when you learned an important lesson from something that happened to you or a character in a story. Describe what happened, and explain the lesson you learned as a result.**

Ask students to share their responses.

Wrap Up

- Invite students to share what they've learned so far. Encourage them to use the Academic Talk words in their explanations.
- Explain to students that when they read poetry they should pay close attention to the speaker's reflections, or thoughts, on a topic.

 In the next part of the lesson, we'll read a poem about nighttime. We'll read carefully to find details that show the poem's theme.

Monitor Understanding

Modeled and Guided Instruction

Get Started

Today you will read a lyric poem—a poem that sounds like a song. First, you'll read to understand what the poem is about. Then you'll read to analyze the poem's theme.

Read

- Read aloud the title of the poem. Invite students to predict what it will be about.
- Have students read the poem independently. Tell them to place a check mark above any confusing words and phrases as they read. Remind students to look inside, around, and beyond each unknown word to help them figure out its meaning. Use the Word Learning Routine on pp. A50–A51.
- When students have finished reading, clarify the meanings of words and phrases they still find confusing. Then use the questions below to check understanding. Encourage students to identify details in the text that support their answers.

  What creatures are the subjects of this poem? *(desert animals)*

  How does the speaker describe the desert during the day? *("little shade," "dry," "sizzle," "searing heat")*

  How do the animals' actions during the day compare to their actions at night? *(The animals sleep during the day and "scamper," "feed and play" at night.)*

 **English Language Learners**

● **Word Learning Strategy**

Explore

- Read aloud the Explore question at the top of p. 137 to set the purpose for the second read. Tell students they will need to take a closer look at how the speaker reflects on, or shares thoughts and feelings about, the topic in order to discover the poem's theme.
- Have students read aloud the Close Reader Habit on p. 136.

> **TIP** Remind students that poets use words that appeal to the senses to make a strong impression on readers. As students read, have them find words that tell how things look, sound, and feel.

Modeled and Guided Instruction

Read

Genre: Lyric Poem

Darkness in the Desert

by Morena Sommers

For desert animals, the day
Is not a time for work or play.
There's little shade; the world is dry.
The clouds are absent from the sky.
Things sizzle in the searing heat,
The burning sands hurt creatures' feet—
And so when it turns light they creep
Beneath the ground to fall asleep.

But late in the day the sky grows dim.
The sun drops past the canyon rim.
The stars peek through, and very soon
The night replaces afternoon.
Inside their dens the creatures stir—
They like the cooler temperature.
By ones and twos, by fives and tens
The animals creep from their dens.

On mountain, prairie, plain, and hill,
The night is when the world is still.
In deserts, though, the times reverse:
The dark is good, the light is worse.
The daytime is the time to rest.
For desert creatures, night is best.

The desert fox, the mouse, the hare,
At night they scamper here and there.
Their claws scratch softly in the sand.
Their faint calls echo through the land.
From dusk to dawn, all through the night
They feed and play till morning light.

Close Reader Habits

When you reread the poem, **circle** words and phrases that tell the topic of the poem. Then **underline** details that show the speaker's reflections on the topic.

136

 **English Language Learners**

Build Meaning

Descriptive Language Point to the phrase "when it turns light" in line 7. Ask students to read the first stanza and find a word that means the same as that phrase *(day)*.

- Then have students read the first line of the second stanza to find the phrase with the opposite meaning *("the sky grows dim")*. Explain the meaning of *dim*, providing a visual aid if possible.
- Guide students to see that the poem moves from day to night. The poet uses descriptive language to help readers see, hear, and feel the details in the desert. Discuss examples of descriptive language in the poem.

● **Word Learning Strategy**

Use Context Clues

- Read aloud line 5 of the poem: "Things sizzle in the searing heat."

  What do *sizzle* and *searing* mean? What clues can you use to figure out the meanings?

- Guide students to reread the first stanza (lines 1–8). Have them locate the time of day *(daytime)*, the conditions *(sunny, dry)*, and the effect on living things *(the burning sands hurt creatures' feet.)*
- Point out that *sizzle* is an example of onomatopoeia and guide students to determine that it means "to cook with a hissing sound," while *searing* means "burning."
- Discuss with students how these descriptive words add imagery and create mood.

L.5.4a

Explore What details in the poem "Darkness in the Desert" develop its theme?

Think

1 Complete the chart below. Identify the poem's topic, the details that develop the topic, and the speaker's reflections on the topic. Use this information to determine the theme of the poem.

Look for evidence of what the speaker thinks about day and night in the desert.

What Is the Topic of the Poem?	What Are the Details About the Topic?	What Are the Speaker's Reflections on the Topic?	What Is the Theme of the Poem?
How animals respond to day and night in the desert	"desert animals," "day," "when it turns light they creep / Beneath the ground to fall asleep," "night," "animals creep from their dens"	"In deserts, though, the times reverse: / The dark is good, the light is worse. / The daytime is the time to rest. / For desert creatures, night is best."	For some, the night is a better time than the day.

Talk

2 Share your charts. Did you and your partner identify the same theme? What details did you use to support your understanding of the poem's theme? If necessary, return to your chart to change or add details.

Write

3 **Short Response** What is the theme of the poem "Darkness in the Desert"? Use examples from the poem and your chart to support your response. Use the space provided on page 140 to write your answer.

HINT Start your response by stating the theme in one sentence.

137

Think Aloud

- To answer the Explore question, I need to look carefully at the details in the poem to figure out its theme. The first column in the chart asks me to name the topic of the poem. I'll reread to figure out what the poem is about.
- The first stanza is about how hot the desert is and how the animals won't "work or play" outside during the day because the hot sand will "hurt creatures' feet."
- The second stanza shifts. Now it's nighttime, and the animals start coming out. I'll keep reading to make sure I've learned all there is to know about the topic of this poem. In the fourth stanza, I finally learn what the animals do when they come out: they feed, play, and call to each other.
- In the *Topic* column of the chart, I'm going to write that the poem is about how animals respond to day and night in the desert.

Think

- Read aloud the Think section. Explain to students that you will model how to find text evidence to fill in part of the chart. Use the **Think Aloud** below to guide your modeling.
- Revisit the Explore question. Guide students to determine that they need to look for more details, using the Close Reader Habit.
- Encourage students to work with a partner to continue rereading the passage and complete the chart. Remind them that the Buddy Tip will help them find the information they need.
- Ask volunteers to share their completed charts.
- Guide students to find words that appeal to the senses, such as words that describe temperature, and note how these words make them feel. Remind them that they are looking for evidence of what the speaker thinks and feels.

Talk

- Read aloud the Talk prompt.
- Have partners respond to the prompt. Use the Talk Routine on pp. A52–A53.
- Circulate to check that students are discussing and writing about the speaker's reflection on nighttime in the desert.

Write

- Ask a volunteer to read aloud the Write prompt.
- Invite a few students to tell what the prompt is asking them to do.
- Make sure students understand that they need to state the theme in a single sentence and then support that idea with evidence from the poem.
- Have students turn to p. 140 to write their response.
- Use Review Responses on p. 140 to assess students' writing.

Wrap Up

- Ask students to recall the Learning Target. Have them explain how analyzing details in the poem helped them understand the theme.

Guided Practice

Get Started

Today you will read another poem that is set at night. First, you will read to understand what the poem is about. Then you will reread to analyze the poem's theme.

Read

- Read aloud the title of the poem and the genre (narrative poem). Explain that a narrative poem tells a story.
- Have students predict what the poem will be about, based on the title and the illustration.
- **Read to Understand** Have students read the poem independently. Tell them to place a check mark above any confusing words and phrases as they read. Remind students to look inside, around, and beyond each unknown word or phrase to help them figure out its meaning. Use the Word Learning Routine on pp. A50–A51.
- When students have finished reading, clarify the meanings of words and phrases they still find confusing. Then use the questions below to check understanding. Encourage students to identify details in the text that support their answers.

  What happens in the poem? *(A person takes a puppy out for a walk at night.)*

  At what time of year does the poem take place? *(Winter, because there's snow on the ground and it's cold.)*

  Whose thoughts does the speaker tell about? Explain your answer. *(The speaker tells the puppy's thoughts by giving details like "It's vanished! What a mystery!")*

English Language Learners

- **Word Learning Strategy**

- **Read to Analyze** Read aloud the Close Reader Habit on p. 138 to set the purpose for the second read. Then have students reread the poem with a partner and discuss any questions they might have.

Guided Practice

Read

Genre: Narrative Poem

NIGHT WALK

by Amy Saito

The sky above, the streets below,
The stars reflecting off the snow—
A lovely night for us to go
Out for a walk, the puppy thinks.

The moon's a brilliant shade of gold,
And though she's just a few months old,
The puppy knows the night is cold—
She leans into the wind and blinks.

What's that thing moving in the tree?
The puppy dashes up to see.
It's vanished! What a mystery!
She sits beneath the tree to bark.

Her master guides her through the night
First turning left, then turning right
The dark is deep, there is no light
She yanks her leash: is this the park?

The night's a lovely time to roam
But now it's time for heading home.
She's only little, after all,
Can't run all night when she's so small.

Someday she'll grow a little more
And when she's three, or maybe four
She'll run all night, and she'll be tough—
Tonight, though, she's gone far enough.

Her master strokes her furry head,
And yawning, she goes off to bed.
But as she sleeps, the moonlight beams
Will dart and dance inside her dreams.

Close Reader Habits

What is the message of the poem? Reread the poem. **Underline** details showing what the puppy does. Use these details to identify the poem's theme.

138

English Language Learners

Build Meaning

Rhythm Help students understand that poets often "play" with language and text structure, using unusual organization or punctuation to fit a particular rhythm or emphasize an idea.

- Read aloud the first stanza, emphasizing the rhythm of the verse. If possible, provide a visual aid of a street at night in wintertime to identify the details.
- Invite volunteers to read aloud the remaining verses. Guide them to use the correct rhythm. Have students discuss what is happening after each verse.

Word Learning Strategy

Analyze Word Parts

- Point out the word *reflecting* in line 2. Work with students to break it into three parts: *re-* | *flect* | *-ing*.
- Begin with the prefix *re-*. Invite students to brainstorm other words containing this prefix, such as *return, review, repay*. Determine that the prefix means "again" or "back."
- Explain that *flect* is a Latin root that means "to bend." Review that *-ing* signals the progressive tense of a verb, which means it is an ongoing action.
- Together, determine that *reflecting* means the starlight is bending back, or bouncing off of the snow. Use a mirror to demonstrate a reflection. **L.5.4b**

Think Use what you learned from reading the poem to answer the following questions.

A narrative poem tells a story. Identifying how characters respond to events will help you figure out the theme of the poem.

1 This question has two parts. Answer Part A. Then answer Part B.

Part A
How are the events in stanzas three and four important to the theme of the poem?

A The events show it is a good night for a walk.
(B) The events show that puppy is young and active.
C The events show the speaker is the puppy's master.
D The events show that the night is dark and dangerous.

Part B
Select **one** choice from **each** stanza that **best** supports the answer to Part A.

A "What's that thing moving in the tree?" (stanza three)
(B) "The puppy dashes up to see." (stanza three)
C ". . . sits beneath the tree. . . ." (stanza three)
D "Her master guides her. . . ." (stanza four)
E ". . . there is no light . . ." (stanza four)
(F) "She yanks her leash: . . ." (stanza four)

Talk

2 What details in the poem can help you identify the topic and the theme of "Night Walk"? Use the chart on page 141 to record such details.

HINT Think about the speaker's reflections on how the puppy will change over time.

Write

3 **Short Response** Describe the topic and the theme of the poem "Night Walk." Use details from the poem and your chart to support your response. Use the space provided on page 141 to write your answer.

139

Think

- Have students work with a partner to complete item 1. Draw attention to the boldface words in Part B.

TIP Encourage students to reread stanzas three and four against each answer choice to decide which choices are irrelevant.

Answer Analysis

When students have finished, discuss correct and incorrect responses.

1 **Part A**
The correct choice is B. A young, active puppy is being taken for a walk.

- **A** is incorrect because these details are in stanza one. **C** is incorrect because the speaker talks about the puppy's master in the third person. **D** is not supported by text details.

Part B
The correct choices are B and F. They both show the puppy is young and active.

- **A** is not about the puppy's activity. **C** describes the puppy being still. **D** is about how the puppy's master guides the walk, not the puppy. **E** is about the darkness, not the puppy's activity.

DOK 2

● **Integrating Standards**

Talk

- Have partners discuss the prompt. Emphasize that students should support their ideas with text details.
- Circulate to clarify misunderstandings.

● **Monitor Understanding**

Write

- See p. 141 for instructional guidance.

Wrap Up

- Ask students to recall the Learning Target. Have them explain how analyzing the speaker's reflections about the night walk helped them understand the theme of the poem.

● **Integrating Standards**

Use the following questions to further students' understanding of the poem.

- **What example of personification (giving a nonliving thing human qualities) can you find in the last lines of the poem?** *(Moonlight is given the human traits of being able to "dart and dance" inside the puppy's dreams.)*
DOK 2 **RL.5.4**
- **What is the speaker's point of view, and how does it affect the story told in the poem?** *(The speaker is a third-person narrator who sees all the action and tells the reader about what the puppy is doing and thinking.)*
DOK 3 **RL.5.6**

● **Monitor Understanding**

If... students have difficulty finding text evidence to answer item 2,

then... suggest that they revisit the title to complete the first column *(What Is the Topic of the Poem?)*. Then have them reread the poem line by line to add details to the second column. As they list each detail, have students ask whether it gives more information about the topic or whether it conveys the poet's feelings or ideas.

Modeled and Guided Instruction

Write

- Remember to use the Response-Writing Routine on pp. A54–A55.

Review Responses

After students complete the writing activity, help them evaluate their responses.

3 Responses may vary but should show an understanding of the topic (desert animals' nighttime behavior) as well as the theme of the poem (for some, night is a better time than day). See the sample response on the student book page.
DOK 3

Modeled and Guided Instruction

Write Use the space below to write your answer to the question on page 137.

Darkness in the Desert

3 **Short Response** What is the theme of the poem "Darkness in the Desert"? Use examples from the poem and your chart to support your response.

HINT Start your response by stating the theme in one sentence.

Sample response: The theme is that for some, the night is a better time than the day. The speaker notes that desert animals are busy at night. They come out of their dens to play after dark, they call to each other, and they find food and water. The speaker says, "The desert fox, the mouse, the hare, / At night they scamper here and there." During the day, in contrast, desert animals go underground to sleep and escape the hot temperatures. The speaker's reflection that "The dark is good, the light is worse" for desert creatures sums up the theme of the poem.

Don't forget to check your writing.

Check Your Writing

- ☐ Did you read the prompt carefully?
- ☐ Did you put the prompt in your own words?
- ☐ Did you use the best evidence from the text to support your ideas?
- ☐ Are your ideas clearly organized?
- ☐ Did you write in clear and complete sentences?
- ☐ Did you check your spelling and punctuation?

140

Scaffolding Support for Reluctant Writers

If students are having a difficult time getting started, use the strategies below. Work individually with struggling students, or have students work with partners.

- Circle the verbs in the prompt that tell you what to do, such as *describe*, *explain*, or *compare*.
- Underline words and phrases in the prompt that show what information you need to provide in your response, such as *causes*, *reasons*, or *character traits*.
- Talk about the details from the text that you will include in your response.
- Explain aloud how you will respond to the prompt.

NIGHT WALK

2 Use the chart below to organize your ideas.

What Is the Topic of the Poem?	What Are the Details About the Topic?	What Are the Speaker's Reflections on the Topic?	What Is the Theme of the Poem?

Write Use the space below to write your answer to the question on page 139.

3 **Short Response** Describe the topic and the theme of the poem "Night Walk." Use details from the poem and your chart to support your response.

Sample response: The topic of the poem is the puppy's excitement on her night walk. The theme is that the exciting experiences of youth improve with age. This theme is supported by details about the puppy. She is happy to dash around, but she gets tired when the walk has taken her "far enough." The speaker reflects that the puppy "can't run all night when she's so small," but when she's older she'll be "tough" and able to do more.

Teacher Notes

Talk

2 Students should use the chart to organize their thoughts and evidence.

Write

- Ask a volunteer to read aloud the Write prompt.
- Invite students to tell what the prompt is asking them to do. Make sure they understand that they need to use details from the poem to support their statements of theme.
- Call attention to the HINT.
- Remember to use the Response-Writing Routine on pp. A54–A55.

Review Responses

After students complete the writing activity, help them evaluate their responses.

3 Responses may vary but should make a clear distinction between topic and theme. The response should include details about the puppy's behavior as well the reflections of the speaker. Statements of theme should include the idea that the puppy will change as it grows. See the sample response on the student book page. *DOK 3*

Independent Practice

Get Started

Today you are going to read two more poems about nighttime and use what you have learned about determining the theme of a poem.

- Ask a volunteer to explain why studying details in this poem will help readers understand the story and discover the theme. Encourage students to use the Academic Talk words in their response.

 **English Language Learners**

Read

You are going to read both poems independently and use what you have learned to think and write about the texts. As you read, remember to look closely at the details in the texts to identify the topics and themes.

- Read aloud the title of the first poem and then encourage students to preview the text, paying close attention to the illustrations.
- Call attention to the Words to Know in the upper left of p. 142.
- If students need support in reading the poem, you may wish to use the Monitor Understanding suggestions.
- When students have finished reading the first poem, have them complete the Think section. Explain that they will then read the second poem and complete the Write section.

● **Monitor Understanding**

Read

Genre: Narrative Poem

WORDS TO KNOW
As you read, look inside, around, and beyond these words to figure out what they mean.
- **assured**
- **complained**

Anna's MONSTERS

by Justin Nuñez

I'm scared of the darkness, I don't care who knows it,
I don't like the darkness at all.
I sleep with the lights on—two lights in my room,
And a much brighter light in the hall.
I'm frightened of monsters that might come and get me,
Whenever I climb into bed.
My mother says, "Anna, you're just being silly,
The monsters are all in your head!"

But I don't think that's true, because of what happened
Last night, the first day of the week.
I put on my nightgown, got under the covers—
Rolled over, and heard a strange squeak.
It wasn't a mouse, and it wasn't a rabbit,
It wasn't a dog or a cat.
So I screamed out in terror. My mother came running!
"Whatever," she asked me, "was that?"

"I heard a strange noise!" I explained to my mother,
I was almost too frightened to talk.
I *knew* it was monsters, some big hungry monsters,
It was all I could do not to squawk!
"I *don't* like the darkness," I said to my mother,
"I don't like the dark and the night.
Can't I get up and sit with you out on the couch,
In a room that's all cheery and bright?"

142

 **English Language Learners**

Build Meaning

Listen Actively Remind students that poetry is meant to be heard. Hearing a poem read aloud can help them understand some of its meaning and decide the mood, or the way the poet wants readers to feel.

- Tell students to listen actively as you read aloud each stanza. As they listen, they should write an emotion word or draw a face beside the stanza to show how Anna (the speaker) and her mother are feeling.
- Preview the text, looking for punctuation marks and other indicators of intonation. Point to the italicized words in stanzas 3–5, and explain that these words are meant to be emphasized, or read with a stronger voice.

"Oh, *Anna*," Mom said, and she looked at me sadly.
"Do we need to go through this once *more*?
Last night you assured me that you saw a monster—
It turned out to be socks on the floor."
"But this one was real!" I complained to my mother.
"I heard it squeak loudly and clear!
I don't like the darkness, the monsters will eat me—
Don't let them come anywhere near!"

My mother explained that the noises weren't monsters;
She showed me some interesting things.
For example, I learned that my bed makes a squeak
When you push down too hard on the springs.
So there *weren't* any monsters, they didn't exist,
And I *know* that my mother was right…
But what if those monsters that never existed
Come into my bedroom tonight?

Integrating Standards

After students have read the poem, use these questions to discuss the poem with them.

- **How does the speaker's point of view affect the reader's understanding of what happens?**
  (The poem is presented from Anna's point of view so it tells what Anna is thinking and feeling. That helps the reader understand Anna's behavior.)
  DOK 3 RL.5.6
- **Where is Anna's mother while Anna is trying to get to sleep? Quote a line from the poem to support your answer.**
  (Her mother is in the living room. In the third stanza, Anna asks, "Can't I get up and sit with you out on the couch / In a room that's all cheery and bright?")
  DOK 2 RL.5.1
- **In line 25, what inference can you make about why Anna's mother looks at her sadly? Use quotes from the poem to support your answer.**
  (Anna's mother is sad because Anna has done this before. The question "Do we need to go through this once more?" supports that idea. So do the next lines, when her mother reminds her that the previous monster "turned out to be socks on the floor.")
  DOK 3 RL.5.1, RL.5.3
- **Do you think Anna is still afraid of monsters at the end of the poem? What events in the poem support your opinion?**
  (Responses will vary, but students may say that at the beginning of the poem, it's clear that Anna is genuinely afraid of the dark and has an imagination lively enough to imagine monsters. The events in the last stanza show that Anna knows that monsters do not exist and that she should not be afraid but she still is, at least a little.)
  DOK 3 RL.5.1, RL.5.3

● Monitor Understanding

If… students struggle to read and understand "Anna's Monsters":
then… use these scaffolding suggestions:

Question the Text Preview the text by asking the following questions:

- **Based on the title and illustrations, what do you predict the poem will be about?**
- **What questions do you have about the poem?**

Vocabulary Support Define words that may interfere with comprehension, such as *frightened* and *terror*.

Read Aloud Read aloud the text with students. You could also have students chorally read the text in a small group.

Check Understanding Use the questions below to check understanding. Encourage students to cite details in the text that support their answers.

- **Who is the speaker of this poem?**
  (a girl named Anna)
- **What sights and sounds does the speaker think come from monsters?**
  (squeaks, strange noises, dark shapes)
- **What are the real explanations for what the speaker sees and hears?**
  (The squeaks are made by the bed, and the monsters turn out to be socks on the floor.)

Independent Practice

Think

- Use the Monitor Understanding suggestions to support students in completing items 1–4.

● **Monitor Understanding**

Answer Analysis

When students have finished, discuss correct and incorrect responses.

1 Part A

The correct choice is C. Anna's mother is trying to convince her that the noises she hears are not monsters but her imagination at work.

- **A** is incorrect because Anna's mother is not saying that the monsters are easy to see.
- **B** is incorrect because imaginary monsters can't attack a person.
- **D** is not supported by the text.

Part B

The correct choice is D. Anna's mother wants to convince Anna that there are no monsters in her room by calling her "silly."

- Choices **A, B,** and **C** show Anna's fear, but these do not show that the fear is only in her mind.

DOK 2 **RL.5.4, L.5.4a**

2 The correct choice is C. It explains that although Anna's mother has demonstrated that monsters are not real, Anna's fears have not entirely gone away.

- **A** is incorrect because there is no evidence that Anna is afraid of the quiet. She is afraid of noises.
- **B** is not supported by evidence in the text.
- **D** is incorrect because Anna is not finding it easy to get over her fear of the dark.

DOK 2 **RL.5.2**

● **Theme Connection**

Think Use what you learned from reading the poem to answer the following questions.

1 This question has two parts. First, answer Part A. Then answer Part B.

Part A
Read the line from the first stanza of the poem.

The monsters are <u>all in your head</u>!

Which phrase **best** states the meaning of <u>all in your head</u>?

A easy to see
B ready to attack you
(C) only imagined
D giving you a headache

Part B
Which detail in the first stanza **best** helps the reader understand the meaning of <u>all in your head</u>?

A "I'm scared of the darkness, . . ."
B "I sleep with the lights on, . . ."
C "Whenever I climb into bed."
(D) "'Anna, you're just being silly, . . ."

2 Which statement **best** summarizes the speaker's message about fears?

A For most people, nighttime is scary because it is dark and quiet and nobody is awake.
B Many people are much too fearful, and some are even afraid of their own surroundings.
(C) It can be hard to stop being afraid, even when someone proves that what you fear is not real.
D It is easy to get over a fear once someone shows you that your fear is based on something that is not real.

● Theme Connection

- Remind students that the theme of this lesson is Night Poetry.
- Display a three-column chart. Label each column with a poem title from this lesson.
- Beneath each title, have students list the topic and theme of the poem.
- Lead a class discussion comparing the poems in terms of topics, themes, point of view, and use of language. Students should also compare the features of lyric and narrative poems. Ask students to explain how the poems relate to the theme of Night Poetry.

3 This question has two parts. First, answer Part A. Then answer Part B.

Part A
How are the events in stanzas two and three important to the poem's theme?

A These events show Anna doesn't like the dark of night because that is when she sees the monsters.

B These events show Anna remembers it was last night that she heard a squeak.

C These events show Anna's mother comes running in fear when Anna screams.

(D) These events show Anna believes that monsters make the noises that scare her in the dark.

Part B
Select **one** choice from **each** stanza that **best** supports the answer to Part A.

A ". . . because of what happened. . . ." (stanza two)

(B) ". . . I screamed out in terror." (stanza two)

C ". . . 'Whatever,' she asked me, 'was that?'" (stanza two)

(D) "I *knew* it was monsters, . . ." (stanza three)

E "It was all I could do. . . ." (stanza three)

F ". . . a room that's all cheery and bright?" (stanza three)

4 Which line from the poem **best** summarizes a theme of the poem?

(A) "'The monsters are all in your head!'" (line 8)

B "Rolled over, and heard a strange squeak." (line 12)

C "So I screamed out in terror. My mother came running!" (line 15)

D "'I *don't* like the darkness,' I said to my mother," (line 21)

Monitor Understanding

If... students struggle to complete the items,
then... you may wish to use the following suggestions:

Read Aloud Activities

- As you read, have students note any unfamiliar words or phrases. Clarify any misunderstandings.
- Discuss each item with students to make certain they understand the expectation.

Reread the Text

- Have students create a four-column chart to organize their thoughts and evidence.
- Have partners summarize the poem.

3 **Part A**

The correct choice is D. Anna was terrified and she screamed after hearing a squeak. She says she heard a "strange noise" and "*knew* it was monsters, some big hungry monsters, . . ."

- **A** is incorrect because Anna thinks the noises are monsters based on what she hears, not what she sees.
- **B** and **C** are both details from stanza one, and they do not develop the theme of the poem.

Part B

The correct choices are B and D. They support the ideas that Anna screamed because she was terrified and that she really believes the noises are made by monsters.

- **A** and **C** are details that do not directly point to the theme of the poem.
- **E** and **F** do not support the idea that Anna is sure she heard monsters.

DOK 3 **RL.5.2**

4 **The correct choice is A.** A theme of the poem is that what we fear is not necessarily real. Anna's mother is trying to impart this lesson to her, even if Anna does not accept it.

- **B** shows what causes Anna's fear in the poem, not a lesson about her fear.
- **C** and **D** show Anna's reactions to her fear, but they do not tell a lesson about her fear.

DOK 2 **RL.5.2**

Independent Practice

Get Started

Now you will read the second poem about nighttime and use what you have learned about finding the topic and theme to write about the poem. As you read, remember to look closely at the details that show the speaker's thoughts and feelings about the topic.

English Language Learners

Read

- Read aloud the title of the poem and encourage students to preview the text, paying close attention to the illustration.
- Call attention to the Words to Know in the upper left of p. 146.
- Have students read the poem independently. If any students need support, you may wish to use the following questions to check understanding.

  What are Ben and Louie doing? *(They are sitting outside looking up at the stars.)*

  What are Ben and Louie thinking about as they look up at the sky? *(They think about traveling to the edge of the universe and about how vast the universe is.)*

  Why can't Ben and Louie go inside and get ready for bed? *(It's just "too wonderful" looking up at the sky.)*

- When students have finished, have them complete the Write section.

Independent Practice

Read

Genre: Lyric Poem

WORDS TO KNOW
As you read, look inside, around, and beyond these words to figure out what they mean.
- **hovering**
- **vaster**

SUMMER NIGHT

by Bianca Cappeletta

The city is full of streetlights, stoplights, floodlights
 making it hard to see the stars
But Ben and Louie are out this summer night at ten PM
 in front of their apartment building, peering up at the sky anyway.
Ben asks if that's the constellation Orion hovering over there just
 above that billboard
Louie shrugs because he doesn't know for sure
He asks how many light-years to the edge of the universe
 and what's beyond the edge when you get there
if you could get there (which you probably can't, but if you *could*)
Ben says he doesn't know for sure either
It's a vast place, the universe, but what's beyond it must be vaster still
And they know they should go inside and get ready for bed
 but it's too wonderful out here below the faint glow of the stars
  and they just can't

146

English Language Learners

Build Meaning

Preview the Text Have students look carefully at the title of the poem and the illustration. Prior to reading, invite volunteers to share what is happening in the photo, and what they predict the poem will be about.

- Call attention to some words in the poem that are cognates for speakers of Latin-based languages, such as *constellation, universe,* and *vast*. Have students explain the meanings of these words, and provide supporting vocabulary as needed.

Write Use what you learned from reading "Summer Night" to answer the following question.

5 **Short Response** What is the theme of the poem "Summer Night"? Use details from the poem to support your answer.

Sample response: The theme is that the universe is wonderful and limitless. When Louie asks what is beyond the "edge of the universe," Ben says he doesn't know because the universe is "a vast place," and "what's beyond it must be vaster still." Ben also says they should go inside, but they "just can't" because the "glow of the stars" outside is "too wonderful."

Learning Target

In this lesson, you used details from poems to identify their themes. Explain why this activity is important for understanding poetry in general.

Responses will vary, but students should identify ways that using details in the poem, including how the speaker reflects on a topic, helped them develop a better understanding of the poems they read. They should also point out how they can apply this understanding to other poems they read.

Write

- Tell students that using what they read, they will plan and compose a short response to the writing prompt.

● **Monitor Understanding**

Review Responses

After students have completed each part of the writing activity, help them evaluate their responses.

5 Display or pass out copies of the reproducible **2-Point Writing Rubric** on p. TR10. Have students use the rubric to individually assess their writing and revise as needed.

When students have finished their revisions, evaluate their responses. Answers will vary but should reflect the sense of wonder felt by Ben and Louie. Responses should also include direct quotation of words, phrases, and lines in the poem. *DOK 3* **RL.5.2, W.5.9a**

Wrap Up

Learning Target

- Have each student respond in writing to the Learning Target prompt.
- When students have finished, have them share their responses. This may be done with a partner, in small groups, or as a whole class.

● **Monitor Understanding**

If... students don't understand the writing task, **then...** read aloud the writing prompt. Use the following questions to help students get started.

- **What is the prompt asking you to write about?**
- **Do you need to reread the text to find more information?**
- **How will you identify the information you need to include?**

- Have partners talk about how they will organize their responses.
- Provide a graphic organizer to assist students, if needed.

5 **2-Point Writing Rubric**

Points	Focus	Evidence	Organization
2	My answer does exactly what the prompt asked me to do.	My answer is supported with plenty of details from the text.	My ideas are clear and in a logical order.
1	Some of my answer does not relate to the prompt.	My answer is missing some important details from the text.	Some of my ideas are unclear and out of order.
0	My answer does not make sense.	My answer does not have any details from the text.	My ideas are unclear and not in any order.

Lesson 9
Summarizing Literary Texts

Standards Focus

. . . summarize the text. RL.5.2

Lesson Objectives

Reading

- Identify the main characters, settings, and events of a story or drama. RL.5.2
- Distinguish important story events and details. RL.5.2
- Use key elements of a story to create a summary. RL.5.2

Writing

- Draw evidence from literary texts to support analysis and reflection. W.5.9a

Speaking and Listening

- Pose and respond to specific questions and contribute to discussions. SL.5.1c
- Review the key ideas expressed and draw conclusions. SL.5.1d

Language

- Use context as a clue to the meaning of a word or phrase. L.5.4a
- Acquire and use academic and domain-specific words and phrases. L.5.6

Additional Practice: **RL.5.3, RL.5.4, RL.5.5, RL.5.6, L.5.4a**

Academic Talk

See **Glossary of Terms**, pp. TR2–TR9

- key detail
- summarize

Learning Progression

Grade 4	Grade 5	Grade 6
Students closely read a text to synthesize important information and infer a larger meaning from a summary of key details.	Building on Grade 4, students understand that characters' actions and speakers' feelings are clues that reveal the theme of a story, drama, or poem. Students continue to summarize a text by synthesizing key details.	Grade 6 increases in complexity by requiring students to synthesize and infer a larger meaning (theme and central idea) from key details. Grade 6 requires students to exclude opinions and judgments from summaries.

Lesson Text Selections

Modeled and Guided Instruction

The Adventures of Montgomery May
by Anna Blum
Genre: Adventure Story

Guided Practice

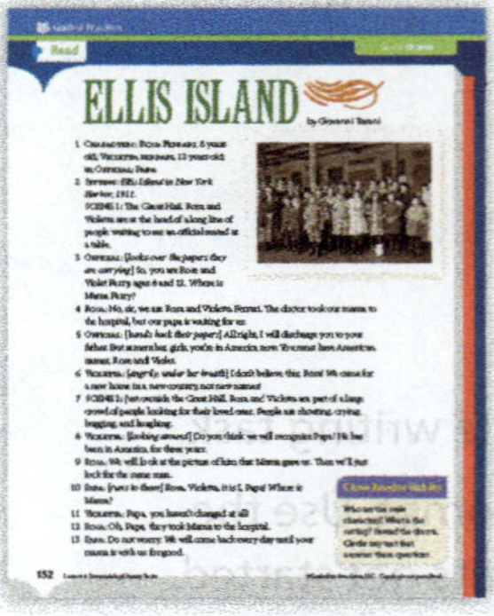

Ellis Island
by Giovanni Tesani
Genre: Drama

Independent Practice

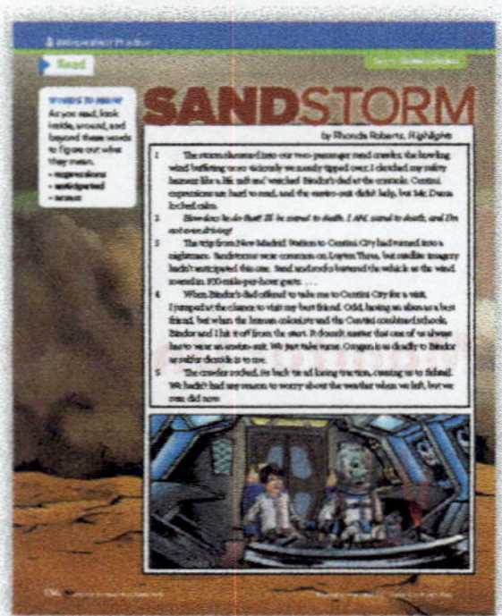

Sandstorm
by Rhonda Roberts
Genre: Science Fiction

Lesson Pacing Guide

Whole Class Instruction *30–45 minutes per day*

Day 1

Teacher-Toolbox.com **Interactive Tutorial**
Summarizing a Story—Level E
20 min (optional)

Introduction pp. 148–149

- **Read** **Summarizing Literary Texts** *10 min*
- **Think** *10 min*
  Graphic Organizer: Summary Organizer
- **Talk** *5 min*
  Quick Write (TRB) *5 min*

Day 2

Modeled and Guided Instruction pp. 150–151, 154

- **Read** **The Adventures of Montgomery May** *10 min*
- **Think** *10 min*
  Graphic Organizer: Summary Organizer
- **Talk** *5 min*
- **Write** Short Response *10 min*

Day 3

Guided Practice pp. 152–153, 155

- **Read** **Ellis Island** *10 min*
- **Think** *10 min*
- **Talk** *5 min*
- **Write** Short Response *10 min*

Day 4

Independent Practice pp. 156–161

- **Read** **Sandstorm** *15 min*
- **Think** *10 min*
- **Write** Short Response *10 min*

Day 5

Independent Practice pp. 156–161

- *Review* Answer Analysis (TRB) *10 min*
- *Review* Response Analysis (TRB) *10 min*
- *Assign and Discuss* Learning Target *10 min*

Language Handbook
Lesson 2 Prepositions and Prepositional Phrases, pp. 440–441
20 min (optional)

Small Group Differentiation

Teacher-Toolbox.com

Reteach

***Ready Reading* Prerequisite Lesson**

- **Grade 4** Lesson 11 Summarizing Literary Texts

Teacher-led Activities

Tools for Instruction

- Summarize Literary Text

Personalized Learning

i-Ready.com

Independent

i-Ready Close Reading Lessons

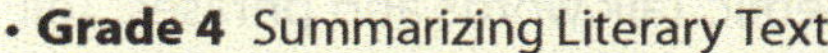
- **Grade 4** Summarizing Literary Texts

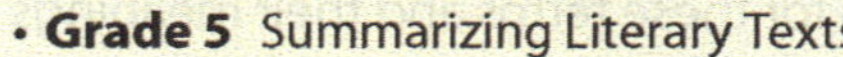
- **Grade 5** Summarizing Literary Texts

Introduction

Get Started

- Explain to students that in this lesson they will read stories about travels and adventures. After reading each story, they will summarize it.
- Review with students the story elements needed for a thorough retelling. Guide them to identify characters, settings, events, and often, a problem to solve.
- Connect this to the concept of summarizing. For example, have students imagine that a relative has asked about what they did during school vacation.
- Point out that the relative does not want to know everything about what happened each day—just some highlights, or main events. Explain:

  I might say: "I went camping with my friend Miko's family in New Hampshire." That tells where I was and who was there. Next I'd sum up the exciting events, saying: "We hiked up Mt. Washington, Miko's dad took us river rafting, and we made a big campfire on the last night." Notice how I covered the most important parts of the trip, but left out smaller details like what time we arrived.
- Focus students' attention on the Learning Target. Read it aloud to set the purpose for the lesson.
- Display the Academic Talk words and phrases. Tell students to listen for these terms and their meanings as you work through the lesson together. Use the Academic Talk Routine on pp. A48–A49.

● **Genre Focus**

Read

- Read aloud the Read section as students follow along. Restate to reinforce:

  When you summarize a story, you mention only the most important details about the characters, setting, main problem, and events. A good summary is short. However, it includes every piece of information needed to understand what the story is about.
- Have students read the passage. Remind them to pay attention to the key details they will need to summarize the story.

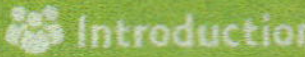

Introduction RL.5.2 summarize the text.

Lesson 9
Summarizing Literary Texts

Identifying and summarizing key details will help you develop a deeper understanding of any literary text you read.

Read When you **summarize** a story or drama, you briefly retell its **key details.** Key details are those that are most important about the characters, the setting, the main problem, and the events.

Read the story below. Identify the key details related to the characters, setting, main problem, and events.

The Legend of Hua Mulan

"Beloved daughter," said the old man. "Do not do this."

The young woman shook her head. "You are too old to serve. My brother is but a child. I am the only one fit to fight." And so she put on men's clothing, left her village, and joined the army.

At first the soldiers teased her. "The boy is so short! No hair on his face! No strength in those arms!" And all they said was true, but she was stubborn and cunning. Her will and her wits won their respect. Soon, the soldiers recognized her bravery and her brilliance in battle.

For twelve years, she fought alongside the men. But then the war ended, and the soldiers brought her home. After greeting her family, she disappeared into their house. Shortly, a woman in a dress emerged.

"Who are you?" asked the soldiers. "Where is our fighter?"

"I am Hua Mulan," she said, "and you are my brothers in arms."

All was silent. Then one soldier smiled. Others joined him. And then the army let loose a cheer like none the village would ever hear again.

English Language Learners

Build Meaning

Prior Knowledge Make certain that students understand the concept of story elements: character, setting, problem, events, conclusion.

- Write each word on chart paper. Invite students to identify cognates of *problem, events,* and *conclusion* as applicable in their first languages. Discuss the meaning of each word with students, and come to a consensus on a definition for each term.
- Choose a short, familiar story such as a fairy tale, and work with students to name each of the story elements for that story. Record them beside their labels.

● Genre Focus

Science Fiction

Explain that during Independent Practice, students will read a science fiction story. Science fiction is usually based on real-life scientific facts or theories combined with details from the author's imagination. While these stories are usually futuristic fantasies filled with unexpected phonemena, they tend to also include details that seem realistic and familiar.

Provide some examples of science fiction, such as *Star Wars* or *A Wrinkle in Time*. Then ask students to name other science fiction they've read or seen.

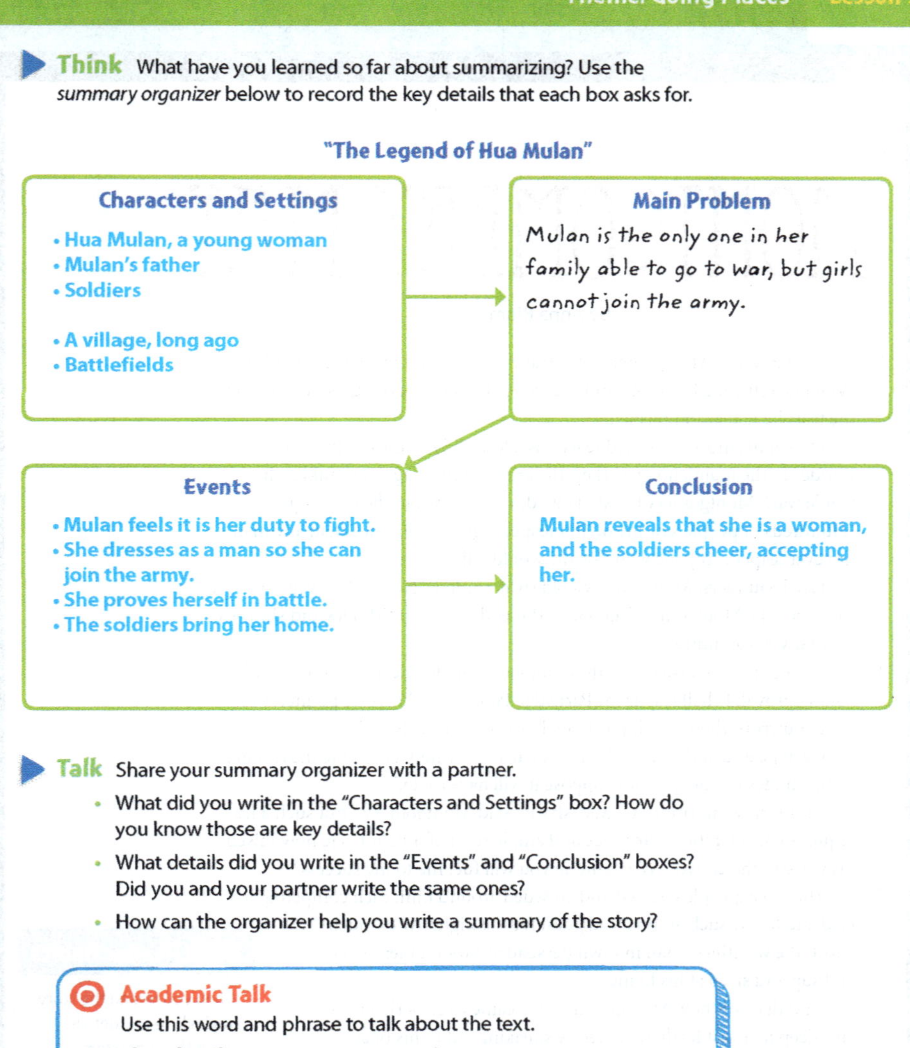

Think What have you learned so far about summarizing? Use the *summary organizer* below to record the key details that each box asks for.

"The Legend of Hua Mulan"

Characters and Settings
- Hua Mulan, a young woman
- Mulan's father
- Soldiers
- A village, long ago
- Battlefields

Main Problem
Mulan is the only one in her family able to go to war, but girls cannot join the army.

Events
- Mulan feels it is her duty to fight.
- She dresses as a man so she can join the army.
- She proves herself in battle.
- The soldiers bring her home.

Conclusion
Mulan reveals that she is a woman, and the soldiers cheer, accepting her.

Talk Share your summary organizer with a partner.
- What did you write in the "Characters and Settings" box? How do you know those are key details?
- What details did you write in the "Events" and "Conclusion" boxes? Did you and your partner write the same ones?
- How can the organizer help you write a summary of the story?

Academic Talk
Use this word and phrase to talk about the text.
- key detail
- summarize

Monitor Understanding

If... students struggle to understand summarizing,
then... scaffold with an example. Read aloud a brief version of a fairy tale such as "The Three Little Pigs." Ask:

- **When and where does the story happen?** *(once upon a time in a village)*
- **Who are the main characters?** *(the three pigs and the wolf)*
- **What is the main problem?** *(The wolf wants to catch and eat the pigs.)*
- **What happens first?** *(The wolf blows down the straw house and the pig goes to hide in the stick house.)*
- **What happens next?** *(The wolf blows down the stick house and the pigs go to hide in the brick house.)*
- **What happens last?** *(The wolf tries to blow down the brick house but he cannot.)*

Invite volunteers to add up all the details into a brief summary.

Think

- Have students read aloud the Think section. Explain that the summary organizer will help them capture each of the main story elements.
- Have partners complete their summary organizers. Remind students to include only main events in the *Events* box.
- As students work, circulate and provide assistance as needed.
- Ask volunteers to share what they wrote in their summary organizers.
- Make sure students understand that while a summary should be brief, it should include every detail needed to understand what the story is mainly about.

Talk

- Read aloud the Talk prompts.
- Have partners compare and contrast what they wrote in their organizers.
- Ask volunteers to share their ideas.

Quick Write Have students write a response to the following prompt:

Think of a day when you did something really fun. Summarize the day, telling where you were, who was there, and a few important things that happened.

Ask students to share their responses.

Wrap Up

- Invite students to share what they've learned so far. Encourage them to use the Academic Talk words and phrases in their explanations.
- Explain that summarizing stories can help students remember the most important events and determine the story's theme.

In the next section, we'll read a story about one man's adventures. Summarizing the story will help us remember the most important details about it and understand its meaning.

Monitor Understanding

Modeled and Guided Instruction

Get Started

Today you will read a story about one man's adventures. First, you'll read to understand the plot. Then you'll read to identify key details to include in a summary of the story.

Read

- Read aloud the title of the story and call attention to the picture of a ship's wheel. Invite students to predict what the story will be about.
- Have students read the story independently. Tell them to place a check mark above any confusing words and phrases as they read. Remind students to look inside, around, and beyond each unknown word to help them figure out its meaning. Use the Word Learning Routine on pp. A50–A51.
- When students have finished reading, clarify the meanings of words and phrases they still find confusing. Then use the questions below to check understanding. Encourage students to identify details in the text that support their answers.

  What does Montgomery May say was his greatest accomplishment? *(a leap from the island of Rhodes to the mainland of Turkey)*

  What does Cecil challenge Montgomery to do? *(show how far he can jump)*

  How does the story end? *(Montgomery sneaks out at sunrise.)*

 English Language Learners

● Word Learning Strategy

Explore

- Read aloud the Explore question at the top of p. 151 to set the purpose for the second read. Tell students they will need to take a closer look at the story elements to answer this question.
- Have students read aloud the Close Reader Habit on p. 150.

TIP Students might wish to use small annotations such as *Ch*, *S*, *E*, and *Con* to keep track of each story element they underline.

Modeled and Guided Instruction

Read

Genre: Adventure Story

The Adventures of MONTGOMERY MAY

by Anna Blum

1 For ten years, Montgomery May traveled the world in a battered old ship. When he returned home, he told everyone about the adventures he'd had and the feats he had accomplished.

2 One of his most renowned feats was a leap. "I leaped from the island of Rhodes to the mainland of Turkey, the great sea nipping at my ankles the whole way," Montgomery boasted one day to a crowd in the town square. "Hundreds of people saw me do it. I leaped a greater distance than any man has ever leaped. Anyone who saw me would tell you so."

3 Cecil Saunders, Montgomery's old rival, smiled. "No need to wait for those people, Montgomery," he said. "Pretend you are in Rhodes and show us how far you can jump."

4 Montgomery paused for only a moment. "Gladly, Cecil. If it meets with your approval, I shall leap from Partridge Point"—and here he pointed to a rocky outcrop where his ship was anchored—"to Isla's Island."

5 Cecil peered at the black dot far out at sea. "Hmph. Not quite the distance from Rhodes to Turkey, but I suppose it will have to do."

6 "Tomorrow morning at 7 A.M. sharp," said Montgomery. "But such a leap requires considerable sustenance and ample rest beforehand." He now raised his voice to the crowd. "Who among you will fuel me to my success?"

7 The townspeople cheered and crowded around him, each competing to feed and house such an honored guest for the night. After much effort, the wealthiest man in town persuaded Montgomery to come and sup and sleep at his home.

8 And that was how Montgomery May came to eat a rich meal and sleep in a vast featherbed before sneaking out to his boat at 6 A.M. and sailing into the sunrise—doubtless to have more adventures and accomplish more feats.

Close Reader Habits

When you reread the story, **underline** key details about the characters, setting, problem, events, and conclusion.

150

English Language Learners

Develop Language

Act It Out Reread paragraph 2, and call attention to the word *boasted*, noting that it is the past tense of the word *boast*. Invite volunteers to share ideas about its meaning, based on context clues or their own experiences.

- Demonstrate the meaning using inflection and body language. Say, "I tell." Then state matter-of-factly, "I am a teacher." Next say, "I boast." Place your hands on your hips, puff your chest, and exclaim, "I am the best teacher ever!"
- Invite students to compare and contrast your demonstrations. Guide them to infer that *boast* means "to speak proudly about oneself, or to brag."
- Have students demonstrate their own examples of boasting.

● Word Learning Strategy

Use Context Clues

- Direct students' attention to the word *feats* in paragraphs 1 and 2. Explain that it is a plural of the word *feat*.

  Which clues help you figure out the meaning of *feat*?
- Guide students to find the words *accomplished* and *boasted* and discuss their meanings. Help students infer that a *feat* is an "amazing accomplishment, deed, or action."
- Remind students that when they come to an unknown word or phrase, they can look at nearby words and phrases for clues to the meaning. **L.5.4a**

Explore What details should you include in a summary of this story?

Think

1 Complete the summary organizer with key details from the text.

When choosing details, ask: Does my reader really need this detail?

"The Adventures of Montgomery May"

Characters and Settings
- Montgomery May, a world traveler
- Cecil Saunders, his rival
- A town square in a seaport village

Main Problem
Cecil challenges Montgomery to demonstrate his jumping ability.

Events
- Montgomery brags about his ability to jump.
- Cecil challenges him to jump.
- Montgomery says he will jump to an island at 7 A.M.

Conclusion
Montgomery sails away at 6 A.M., avoiding the need to prove his boast.

Talk

2 Imagine you witnessed the events of this story and want to tell a friend what happened. What details would be most important for your friend to know? If necessary, add or delete details from your organizer.

Write

3 **Short Response** Write a summary of the story. Use key details from the text in your summary. Use the space provided on page 154 to write your answer.

HINT After writing, imagine you've never read the story. Then read your summary. Does it give only the details needed to understand the story?

Think Aloud

- The Explore question wants me to identify the details I should include in my summary. I'll start with "Characters and Settings."
- I'll go back to the story and look for names. I know from the title that the story is about Montgomery May. I'll write his name and keep reading. Here is Cecil Saunders, called "Montgomery's old rival." Because the author told us how Montgomery knows this character, I think he is important. I'll add him to the organizer, too.
- Now I'll look for information about the setting. Here it says that Montgomery May "returned home." I'm not sure where "home" is though, so I'll keep reading. Here it says he's "in the town square." This town must be near the sea, because Montgomery's boat is docked there. I'll write "a town square in a seaport village."

Think

- Read aloud the Think section. Explain that you will model how to find text evidence to fill in part of the summary organizer. Use the **Think Aloud** below to guide your modeling.
- Revisit the Explore question. Encourage students to work with a partner to continue rereading the passage and complete the summary organizer, using their markup from the Close Reader Habit.
- Remind students that the Buddy Tip will help them find the information they need.
- Ask volunteers to share their completed organizers.
- Guide students to see that a summary is a restatement of the basic story elements.

Talk

- Read aloud the Talk prompt.
- Have partners respond to the prompt. Use the Talk Routine on pp. A52–A53.
- Circulate to check that students are discussing which details to include and which to leave out, making changes to their organizers as needed.

Write

- Ask a volunteer to read aloud the Write prompt.
- Invite a few students to tell what the prompt is asking them to do.
- Make sure students understand that their summary needs to be composed of complete sentences. The sentences should flow together like a paragraph, and the details should be organized logically.
- Have students turn to p. 154 to write their response.
- Use Review Responses on p. 154 to assess students' writing.

Wrap Up

- Ask students to recall the Learning Target. Have them explain how identifying and summarizing key details helped them to better understand the meaning of the story.

Guided Practice

Get Started

Today you will read a drama, or a play. First you will read to understand what happens to the characters. Then you will reread with a partner to summarize the drama.

Read

- Read aloud the title of the drama. Ask if anyone knows what Ellis Island was used for in the early 1900s.
- Have students predict what the drama will be about based on the title and the photograph.
- **Read to Understand** Have students read the drama independently. Tell them to place a check mark above any confusing words and phrases as they read. Remind students to look inside, around, and beyond each unknown word to help them figure out its meaning. Use the Word Learning Routine on pp. A50–A51.
- When students have finished reading, clarify the meanings of words and phrases they still find confusing. Then use the questions below to check understanding. Encourage students to identify details in the text that support their answers.

  Why are Rosa and Violetta alone at first? *(Their mama is in the hospital. Papa is waiting for them.)*

  Why does the official want to change their names? *(to make them sound more American)*

  What does Papa say that makes the two girls feel better? *(They will come back every day until Mama is allowed to leave Ellis Island with them.)*

English Language Learners

Word Learning Strategy

- **Read to Analyze** Read aloud the Close Reader Habit on p. 152 to set the purpose for the second read. Then have students reread the drama with a partner and discuss any questions they might have.

> **TIP** Inform students that during this era, most European immigrants had to undergo health examinations at Ellis Island before they were allowed onto the U.S. mainland.

Guided Practice

Read

Genre: Drama

ELLIS ISLAND

by Giovanni Tesani

1 Characters: Rosa Ferrari, 8 years old; Violetta Ferrari, 12 years old; an Official; Papa

2 Setting: *Ellis Island in New York Harbor, 1911.*

SCENE 1: The Great Hall. Rosa and Violetta are at the head of a long line of people waiting to see an official seated at a table.

3 Official: *[looks over the papers they are carrying]* So, you are Rose and Violet Ferry, ages 8 and 12. Where is Mama Ferry?

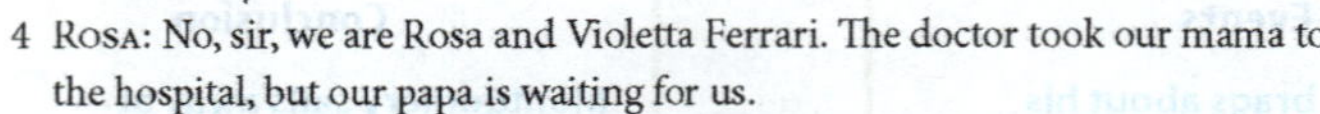

4 Rosa: No, sir, we are Rosa and Violetta Ferrari. The doctor took our mama to the hospital, but our papa is waiting for us.

5 Official: *[hands back their papers]* All right, I will discharge you to your father. But remember, girls, you're in America now. You must have American names, Rose and Violet.

6 Violetta: *[angrily, under her breath]* I don't believe this, Rosa! We came for a new home in a new country, not new names!

7 **SCENE 2:** Just outside the Great Hall. Rosa and Violetta are part of a large crowd of people looking for their loved ones. People are shouting, crying, hugging, and laughing.

8 Violetta: *[looking around]* Do you think we will recognize Papa? He has been in America for three years.

9 Rosa: We will look at the picture of him that Mama gave us. Then we'll just look for the same man.

10 Papa: *[runs to them]* Rosa, Violetta, it is I, Papa! Where is Mama?

11 Violetta: Papa, you haven't changed at all!

12 Rosa: Oh, Papa, they took Mama to the hospital.

13 Papa: Do not worry. We will come back every day until your mama is with us for good.

Close Reader Habits

Who are the main characters? What is the setting? Reread the drama. **Circle** any text that answers these questions.

152

English Language Learners

Build Meaning

Background Knowledge If students need additional context to understand the drama, say:

Ellis Island is a place near the Statue of Liberty, close to New York City. From 1892–1954, it was a place where immigrants, or people moving to the United States, were allowed to enter the country if they were healthy and not in trouble with the law.

- Share key terms related to immigration, such as *admit, discharge, inspection,* and *citizen.*
- Invite students to restate what is happening in this drama, using these terms.

Word Learning Strategy

Use Context Clues

- Point to the word *Official* in the cast of characters. Guide students to think about what this character does in order to figure out the word's meaning.

  What does the *Official* do in Scene 1? *(He reads over the girls' papers; he gives the girls new, American names.)*

  Based on his actions, what kind of person is an official? *(An official is someone who is in charge, or who makes decisions.)*
- Call attention to the root *office-*, noting the letter change. Discuss the relationship between *office* and a person in charge.
- Ask students to name examples of other officials.

L.5.4a, L.5.4b

Think Use what you learned from reading the drama to respond to the following questions.

Many dramas are split into scenes that occur in different settings. Dramas also have stage directions that tell readers what the characters do or feel.

1 This question has two parts. Answer Part A. Then answer Part B.

Part A

Which pair of sentences provides the **best** summary of Scene 1?

A Rosa is 8 years old and Violetta is 12 years old. The doctor took their mother to the hospital, and they are waiting to see an official on Ellis Island.

B The official questions Rosa and Violetta. Then he sends them to find their father.

(C) Rosa and Violetta have arrived on Ellis Island. An official questions them, gives them American names, and releases them.

D The official takes Rosa and Violetta's mother to the hospital. Then he gives them American names and takes them to find their father.

Part B

Which **two** sentences from the drama **best** support the answer to Part A?

A "Where is Mama Ferry?"

B "The doctor took our mama to the hospital, but our papa is waiting for us."

C "No sir, we are Rosa and Violetta Ferrari."

(D) "All right, I will discharge you to your father."

(E) "You must have American names, Rose and Violet."

F "I don't believe this, Rosa!"

Talk

2 Summarize Scene 2. Use the summary organizer on page 155 to record the key details related to the problem, the events, and the conclusion of the scene.

Write

3 **Short Response** Use the information from your summary organizer to summarize Scene 2. Use the space provided on page 155 to write your answer.

HINT After writing, read your summary. Do you need to add or cut details?

153

Integrating Standards

Use these questions to further students' understanding of the drama.

- **How do events in Scene 2 build on events from Scene 1?** *(In Scene 1, the official says he will discharge the girls to their father. In Scene 2, they are reunited with their father.)* *DOK 3* RL.5.5
- **What clues help you understand what *recognize* means?** *(Rosa says, "We will look at the picture . . . [t]hen we'll just look for the same man." This clue helps me figure out that to recognize someone means "to know what he or she looks like.")* *DOK 2* RL.5.4, L.5.4a

Monitor Understanding

If... students have difficulty completing item 2,

then... clarify that often, characters in stories can face many small challenges, or problems. Explain that students should think about all the events together to identify the big problem. Discuss the difference between the smaller problem in Scene 2 (the girls worrying about recognizing Papa) and the bigger problem (Mama being in the hospital).

Think

- Have students work with a partner to complete item 1. Draw attention to the boldface words.

TIP If students have trouble answering item 1, guide them to eliminate answers that give too much or too little information. For example, in Part A, choice A describes only part of the scene.

Answer Analysis

When students have finished, discuss correct and incorrect responses.

1 **Part A**

The correct choice is C. It briefly tells the characters, setting, and some events in Scene 1.

- **A** and **B** are incorrect because they leave out the important detail of the official changing the girls' names.
- **D** is incorrect because the official does not take the girls' mother to the hospital.

Part B

The correct choices are D and E. D shows the girls are being released. E captures the event of the girls' names being changed.

- **A, B, C,** and **F** are not key details required to develop a meaningful summary of Scene 1.

DOK 2

Integrating Standards

Talk

- Have partners discuss the prompt. Emphasize that students should support their ideas with text details.
- Circulate to clarify misunderstandings.

Monitor Understanding

Write

- See p. 155 for instructional guidance.

Wrap Up

- Ask students to recall the Learning Target. Have them explain how summarizing the drama helped them understand what happened and what it was about.

Modeled and Guided Instruction

Write

- Remember to use the Response-Writing Routine on pp. A54–A55.

Review Responses

After students complete the writing activity, help them evaluate their responses.

3 Responses may vary but should correctly and concisely identify the characters, setting, problem, main events, and conclusion. See the sample response on the student book page. **DOK 3**

Modeled and Guided Instruction

Write Use the space below to write your answer to the question on page 151.

The Adventures of MONTGOMERY MAY

HINT After writing, imagine you've never read the story. Then read your summary. Does it give only the details needed to understand the story?

3 **Short Response** Write a summary of the story. Use key details from the text in your summary.

Sample response: Montgomery May returns to his village from years at sea. He brags he jumped from Rhodes to Turkey. His rival, Cecil, asks him to prove he can jump that far. Montgomery says he will jump to an island the next day, at 7 A.M. Montgomery then sails off at 6 A.M., avoiding having to actually make the jump.

Check Your Writing

Don't forget to check your writing.

- ☐ Did you read the prompt carefully?
- ☐ Did you put the prompt in your own words?
- ☐ Did you use the best evidence from the text to support your ideas?
- ☐ Are your ideas clearly organized?
- ☐ Did you write in clear and complete sentences?
- ☐ Did you check your spelling and punctuation?

154

Scaffolding Support for Reluctant Writers

If students are having a difficult time getting started, use the strategies below. Work individually with struggling students, or have students work with partners.

- Circle the verbs in the prompt that tell you what to do, such as *describe*, *explain*, or *compare*.
- Underline words and phrases in the prompt that show what information you need to provide in your response, such as *causes*, *reasons*, or *character traits*.
- Talk about the details from the text that you will include in your response.
- Explain aloud how you will respond to the prompt.

ELLIS ISLAND

2 Use the summary organizer below to organize your ideas.

Scene 2 of *Ellis Island*

Characters and Settings	→	Main Problem
Events	→	**Conclusion**

Write Use the space below to write your answer to the question on page 153.

3 **Short Response** Use the information from your summary organizer to summarize Scene 2.

HINT After writing, read your summary. Do you need to add or cut details?

Sample response: Rosa and Violetta are in a crowd of people and looking for their father. When Papa sees the girls, he runs to them. Rosa tells him Mama is in the hospital, but he reassures them she will be back with them.

Teacher Notes

 **Guided Practice**

Talk

2 Students should use the summary organizer to record their thoughts and evidence.

Write

- Ask a volunteer to read aloud the Write prompt.
- Invite students to tell what the prompt is asking them to do. Make sure they understand that they need to use their own words in the summary, rather than an exact restating of the drama.
- Call attention to the HINT.
- Remember to use the Response-Writing Routine on pp. A54–A55.

Review Responses

After students complete the writing activity, help them evaluate their responses.

3 Responses may vary but should include key details about the problem, the events, and the conclusion of Scene 2. See the sample response on the student book page.

DOK 3

Independent Practice

Get Started

Today you are going to read a science fiction story and use what you have learned about identifying key details to summarize the story.

- Ask a volunteer to review the story elements that belong in a summary, including characters and settings, events, problems, and conclusion. Encourage students to use the Academic Talk words and phrases in their response.

 **English Language Learners**

Read

You are going to read the story independently and use what you have learned to think and write about the text. As you read, remember to look for key details about characters, settings, the main problem, key events, and the story's ending. You will use these details to summarize the story.

- Read aloud the title of the story and then encourage students to preview the text, paying close attention to the title and illustrations.
- Call attention to the Words to Know in the upper left of p. 156.
- If students need support in reading the story, you may wish to use the Monitor Understanding suggestions.
- When students have finished, have them complete the Think and Write sections.

● **Monitor Understanding**

Read

Genre: Science Fiction

WORDS TO KNOW
As you read, look inside, around, and beyond these words to figure out what they mean.
- **expressions**
- **anticipated**
- **assess**

SANDSTORM

by Rhonda Roberts, *Highlights*

1 The storm slammed into our two-passenger sand crawler, the howling wind buffeting us so viciously we nearly tipped over. I clutched my safety harness like a life raft and watched Bindor's dad at the controls. Centini expressions are hard to read, and the enviro-suit didn't help, but Mr. Dama looked calm.

2 *How does he do that? I'd be scared to death. I AM scared to death, and I'm not even driving!*

3 The trip from New Madrid Station to Centini City had turned into a nightmare. Sandstorms were common on Luyten Three, but satellite imagery hadn't anticipated this one. Sand and rocks battered the vehicle as the wind roared in 100-mile-per-hour gusts. . . .

4 When Bindor's dad offered to take me to Centini City for a visit, I jumped at the chance to visit my best friend. Odd, having an alien as a best friend, but when the human colonists and the Centini combined schools, Bindor and I hit it off from the start. It doesn't matter that one of us always has to wear an enviro-suit. We just take turns. Oxygen is as deadly to Bindor as sulfur dioxide is to me.

5 The crawler rocked, its back tread losing traction, causing us to fishtail. We hadn't had any reason to worry about the weather when we left, but we sure did now.

156

English Language Learners
Build Meaning

Preview Illustrations Have students preview "Sandstorm" by looking through the illustrations. Have them point out details that can help them identify key story elements, such as the characters, the setting, and the problem. Ask:

- **How are the two main characters different from each other?** *(One is a boy and the other is an alien.)*
- **Where does the story look like it takes place?** *(on a spaceship)*
- **What do you think the characters' problem is?** *(The alien looks hurt. The boy looks like he is stuck.)*

Have students correct or confirm their predictions as they read the story.

Teacher Notes

6 Mr. Dama said something I didn't catch. Before I could ask him to repeat what he'd said, a tremendous gust flipped us over. We tumbled end over end for what seemed like forever.

7 When we stopped, I was dangling upside down, held in midair by my safety harness. The air smelled like a locker room after a really tough game, and I felt as if I'd just ridden the new Black Hole ride at Cosmic Adventureland. I looked over at Mr. Dama. What I saw made my heart skip a beat. Mr. Dama's safety harness had broken loose. He was crumpled in a corner of the cabin, motionless.

8 "Mr. Dama!" Fumbling with the latch, I finally released my harness and sprawled onto the roof of the crawler, which was now our floor. "Mr. Dama!" I crawled toward him, then froze. I heard the sound that brought fear into the heart of every colonist—the whistle of atmosphere leaking from an enviro-suit.

9 Mr. Dama had worn his suit so I wouldn't have to. *If he loses his suit atmosphere, he'll die. If too much of the sulfur dioxide in his suit vents into the cabin, I'll die.*

10 I felt as if icy hands were choking me. *What am I going to do? I can't handle this!* I took a ragged breath. *What is it that Mrs. Nadale always says in Emergency Preparedness Class?* I could barely remember my own name, let alone emergency procedures. *1. Stay calm. Too late for that! 2. Assess the situation. OK. We've crashed, and my best friend's dad is going to die if I don't do something. 3. Take stock of your resources.*

Monitor Understanding

If... students struggle to read and understand the passage,

then... use these scaffolding suggestions:

Question the Text Preview the story by asking the following questions:

- **Based on the title and illustrations, what do you predict the story will be about?**
- **What questions do you have about the story?**

Vocabulary Support Define words and phrases that may interfere with comprehension, such as *satellite imagery* and *sulfur dioxide*.

Read Aloud Read aloud the text with students. You could also have students chorally read the text in a small group.

Check Understanding Use the questions below to check understanding. Encourage students to cite details in the text that support their answers.

- **Who is Mr. Dama?** *(the father of Jason's friend, Bindor)*
- **When a human and a Centini are together, why does one of them have to wear an enviro-suit?** *(The gas that each of them breathes is poisonous to the other.)*
- **How does Jason save Mr. Dama's life?** *(by patching Mr. Dama's leaking enviro-suit and giving him more Centini air)*

Independent Practice

Integrating Standards

After students have read the story, use these questions to discuss it with them.

- **At the story's end, how does Bindor's opinion of Jason compare to Jason's opinion of himself?** *(Bindor thinks Jason is a hero, but Jason downplays his own role and calls Mr. Dama the real hero because he remained calm.)*
  ***DOK 3* RL.5.3**
- **How would the story be different if it were told from Mr. Dama's point of view?** *(Sample response: The story would not focus on Jason's thoughts, feelings, and actions. Mr. Dama might concentrate on the challenges of controlling the vehicle and then describe what it feels like to be injured. He might tell how relieved and thankful he feels that Jason saved his life.)*
  ***DOK 3* RL.5.6**
- **In paragraph 1, as Jason and Mr. Dama drive through the sandstorm, to what does Jason compare his safety harness? What do the two items have in common?** *(Jason compares his safety harness to a life raft. A safety harness and a life raft both protect people in a dangerous situation.)*
  ***DOK 2* RL.5.4, L.5.4a**
- **Determine one theme of "Sandstorm." Use text evidence to support your answer.** *(Sample response: One theme of "Sandstorm" is "Real heroes choose courage over fear." After the accident, the text shows several times when Jason is afraid—"What I saw made my heart skip a beat; I felt as if icy hands were choking me; I could barely remember my own name; I was shaking all over."—but he does not let fear keep him from saving Mr. Dama's life. He tells Mr. Dama, "Everything is going to be OK, sir!" even though he is still shaking. When Bindor calls Jason a hero, Jason will not take the credit.)*
  ***DOK 3* RL.5.2**

● Theme Connection

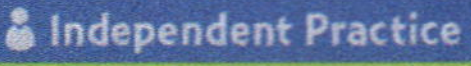

Independent Practice

11 I searched the jumbled mess until I found my backpack, and I pulled out the emergency kit I take everywhere. *I'll never gripe about carrying it again, Mom, I promise.*

12 *4. Form a strategy and act on it.*

13 It seemed to take forever to use materials from my kit to patch Mr. Dama's suit. A search of the cabin yielded a spare bottle of Centini air, and I topped off his tank.

14 What a relief when Mr. Dama groaned and looked up at me!

15 "Everything is going to be OK, sir!" I tried to smile, but I was shaking all over. Fortunately, the radio was still working and I was able to get through to Centini City for help.

16 At the hospital, it was my turn to wear the enviro-suit. Bindor whacked me on the shoulder, nearly knocking me down. "You're a hero, Jason!"

17 "Nah, your dad's the hero, Bindor. You should've seen how calm he was, driving in that storm. He was great." . . .

18 Mr. Dama set his hands on my shoulders. His eyes were serious. "Jason, you saved my life. What can I do to repay you?"

19 I grinned. "How about telling Mrs. Nadale I paid attention in Emergency Preparedness Class!"

158

● Theme Connection

- Remind students that the theme of this lesson is Going Places.
- Display a four-column chart on a white board. Label each column with the story titles from this lesson, including "The Legend of Hua Mulan."
- Ask students to recall where the main characters traveled in each story. List responses in the appropriate column.
- Ask students to determine how all of the stories relate to the themes of travel, adventure, and overcoming challenges.

Think Use what you learned from reading the science-fiction story to respond to the following questions.

1 Which sentence **best** summarizes how Jason reacts after the crawler crashes?

- A He gives in to the urge to panic.
- (B) He deals with the situation as best he can.
- C He imagines what it will be like to be a hero.
- D He goes looking for his backpack.

2 Select the **three** sentences that should be included in a summary of paragraphs 1 through 9 of the story.

- A Jason, a human, and Bindor, a Centini, are best friends despite being very different.
- (B) Jason is on a trip to visit his best friend when fierce winds blow his craft around.
- C Imagery from the weather satellites did not predict the sandstorm on Luyten Three.
- D Jason hangs on to his safety harness, and Mr. Dama works the sand crawler's controls.
- (E) Jason is scared of how powerful the sandstorm is, but Mr. Dama, the driver, seems calm.
- F Mr. Dama says something, but Jason doesn't hear it.
- (G) After a gust flips the crawler over, Jason hears a leak from Mr. Dama's suit and realizes they could die.

3 Which of these **best** explains why Jason's emergency kit is a key detail?

- A It contains a bottle of Centini air.
- B Jason complains about carrying it.
- C It gives Jason a place to store items.
- (D) Jason uses it to save Mr. Dama's life.

● Monitor Understanding

If... students struggle to complete the items,

then... you may wish to use the following suggestions:

Read Aloud Activities

- As you read, have students note any unfamiliar words or phrases. Clarify any misunderstandings.
- Discuss each item with students to make certain they understand the expectation.

Reread the Text

- Have students complete a story map or summary organizer as they reread.

Think

- Use the Monitor Understanding suggestions to support students in completing items 1–5.

● **Monitor Understanding**

Answer Analysis

When students have finished, discuss correct and incorrect responses.

1 **The correct choice is B.** It summarizes Jason's thoughts and actions after the accident.

- **A** is incorrect because Jason does not panic.
- **C** is incorrect because Jason does not spend time imagining himself as a hero.
- **D** is an action Jason takes, but it is only one part of his overall reaction, which is to deal with the situation as best he can.

DOK 2 **RL.5.2**

2 **The correct choices are B, E, and G.** These sentences state key details about the characters, setting, problem, and events.

- **A** describes Jason's friendship with Bindor. This is an important idea in the story, but it doesn't need to be included in a summary of paragraphs 1–9.
- **C, D,** and **F** describe less important details about the events.

DOK 3 **RL.5.2**

3 **The correct choice is D.** The emergency kit is a key detail because it contains the air that lets Jason save Mr. Dama's life. Without the kit, the story would have ended very differently.

- **A** is incorrect because, although it is true that the kit contains a bottle of Centini air, this statement by itself does not explain why the kit is a key detail.
- **B** is incorrect because, although Jason thinks, *"I'll never gripe about carrying it again,"* he is grateful for the kit during the events of the story.
- **C** is incorrect because, although it is true that the kit gives Jason a place to store items, this statement does not explain why the kit is a key detail.

DOK 3 **RL.5.2**

Independent Practice

4 **Part A**

The correct choice is A. The atmosphere is the gas leaking from Mr. Dama's suit.

- **B** is incorrect because what Jason hears is a "whistle," and water does not whistle.
- **C** is incorrect because the whistle, not the atmosphere itself, is the sound.
- **D** is incorrect because, while the suit provides protection, it is not "protection" that is leaking from the suit.

Part B

The correct choice is D. The spare bottle contains Centini air, which is a type of gas, and Jason uses it to replace the atmosphere leaking from Mr. Dama's suit.

- **A** and **B** are incorrect because the "wind" mentioned in both refers to the atmosphere outside of the sand crawler, not the atmosphere leaking from Mr. Dama's suit.
- **C** is incorrect because, although the emergency kit has a container of the atmosphere Mr. Dama needs to survive, this sentence does not provide that information.

DOK 2 **L.5.4a**

5 **The correct choice is D.** The entire story illustrates how Jason had to stay calm and think so that Mr. Dama would not die.

- **A, B,** and **C** are incorrect because they are minor ideas that appear only in isolated parts of the story.

DOK 2 **RL.5.2**

4 This question has two parts. First, answer Part A. Then answer Part B.

Part A

Read this sentence from paragraph 8.

I heard the sound that brought fear into the heart of every colonist—the whistle of atmosphere leaking from an enviro-suit.

What does the word atmosphere mean as it is used in the sentence?

- **A** gas (circled)
- **B** water
- **C** sound
- **D** protection

Part B

Which detail from the story provides the **best** clue for the meaning of the word atmosphere?

- **A** "The storm slammed into our two-passenger sand crawler, the howling wind buffeting us so viciously we nearly tipped over."
- **B** "Sand and rocks battered the vehicle as the wind roared in 100-mile-per-hour gusts. . . ."
- **C** "I searched the jumbled mess until I found my backpack, and I pulled out the emergency kit I take everywhere."
- **D** "A search of the cabin yielded a spare bottle of Centini air, and I topped off his tank." (circled)

5 Which statement **best** summarizes the main idea of the text?

- **A** New experiences sometimes bring danger.
- **B** It is important to take care of the people you care for.
- **C** People from very different backgrounds can be friends.
- **D** In an emergency, stay calm and think before taking action. (circled)

160

Monitor Understanding

If... students don't understand the writing task,

then... read aloud the writing prompt. Use the following questions to help students get started.

- **What is the prompt asking you to write about?**
- **Do you need to reread the text to find more information?**
- **How will you identify the information you need to include?**

- Have partners talk about how they will organize their responses.
- Provide a graphic organizer to assist students, such as a summary organizer, if needed.

Write

6 **Short Response** Summarize what happens **after** Jason realizes that Mr. Dama's enviro-suit is leaking. Use key details from the text in your summary.

Sample response: Jason knows that Mr. Dama's suit is leaking atmosphere and that this will result in Mr. Dama's death as well as his own. He panics, but then remembers his teacher's Emergency Preparedness Class and makes a plan. He patches Mr. Dama's suit, then provides Mr. Dama with Centini air to breathe. Mr. Dama revives, and Jason calls Centini City for help. At the hospital, Mr. Dama thanks Jason for saving his life.

In this lesson, you identified key details in literary texts to summarize those texts. Explain how summarizing literary texts can help you better understand them.

Responses will vary, but students should recognize that identifying the key details helps them focus on what to include in a summary and better understand and retain the most important parts of what they read.

161

6 **2-Point Writing Rubric**

Points	Focus	Evidence	Organization
2	My answer does exactly what the prompt asked me to do.	My answer is supported with plenty of details from the text.	My ideas are clear and in a logical order.
1	Some of my answer does not relate to the prompt.	My answer is missing some important details from the text.	Some of my ideas are unclear and out of order.
0	My answer does not make sense.	My answer does not have any details from the text.	My ideas are unclear and not in any order.

Write

- Tell students that using what they read, they will plan and compose a short response to the writing prompt.

● **Monitor Understanding**

Review Responses

After students have completed each part of the writing activity, help them evaluate their responses.

6 Display or pass out copies of the reproducible **2-Point Writing Rubric** on p. TR10. Have students use the rubric to individually assess their writing and revise as needed.

When students have finished their revisions, evaluate their responses. Answers will vary but should cover the most important events that occur in the last part of the story. See the sample response.

DOK 3 **RL.5.2, W.5.9a**

Wrap Up

Learning Target

- Have each student respond in writing to the Learning Target prompt.
- When students have finished, have them share their responses. This may be done with a partner, in small groups, or as a whole class.

Lesson 10
Using Details to Support Inferences in Literary Texts

Standards Focus

Quote accurately from a text when explaining what the text says explicitly and when drawing inferences from the text. **RL.5.1**

Lesson Objectives

Reading

- Use details and examples from a text when explaining what the text says. **RL.5.1**
- Use details and examples from a text along with personal knowledge when explaining inferences drawn from the text. **RL.5.1**

Writing

- Draw evidence from literary texts to support analysis and reflection. **W.5.9a**

Speaking and Listening

- Pose and respond to specific questions and contribute to discussions. **SL.5.1c**
- Review the key ideas expressed and draw conclusions. **SL.5.1d**

Language

- Use context as a clue to the meaning of a word or phrase. **L.5.4a**
- Acquire and use academic and domain-specific words and phrases. **L.5.6**

Additional Practice: **RL.5.2, RL.5.3, RL.5.4, RL.5.6, RL.5.9, L.5.5b**

Academic Talk

See **Glossary of Terms**, pp. TR2–TR9

- explicit meaning
- quotes
- inference
- evidence

Learning Progression

Grade 4	Grade 5	Grade 6
Students refer to details and examples in the text to support their inferences.	Building on Grade 4, students not only refer to the text but quote accurately from it when making inferences. This helps to prepare students for the analysis required at Grade 6.	Grade 6 increases in complexity by requiring students to cite textual evidence to support analysis of a text, not just inferences.

Lesson Text Selections

Modeled and Guided Instruction

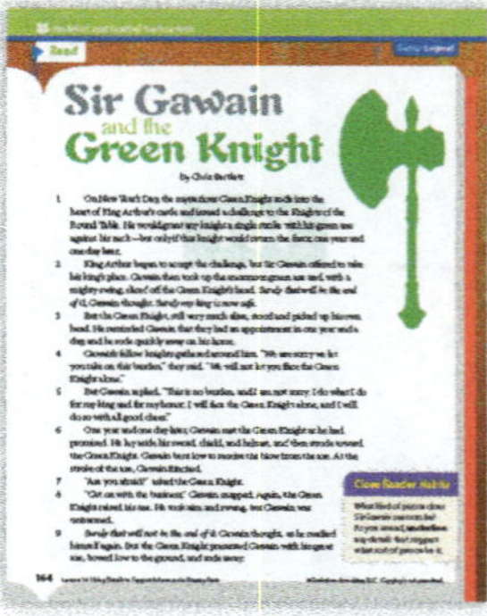

Sir Gawain and the Green Knight
by Chris Bartlett
Genre: Legend

Guided Practice

The Story of Sir Gareth & Lynette
by Maude L. Radford
Genre: Legend

Independent Practice

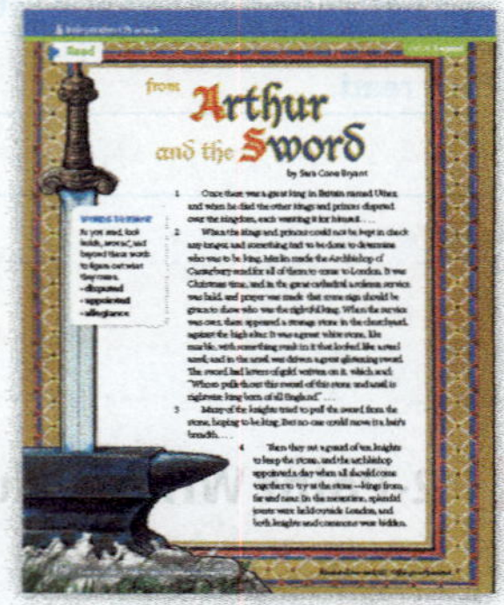

Arthur and the Sword
by Sara Cone Bryant
Genre: Legend

Lesson Pacing Guide

Whole Class Instruction *30–45 minutes per day*

Day 1

Teacher-Toolbox.com **Interactive Tutorial**
Making Inferences About Literature—Level D
20 min (optional)

Introduction pp. 162–163

- **Read** **Using Details to Support Inferences in Literary Texts** *10 min*
- **Think** *10 min*
  Graphic Organizer: Three-Column Chart
- **Talk** *5 min*
  Quick Write (TRB) *5 min*

Day 2

Modeled and Guided Instruction pp. 164–165, 168

- **Read** **Sir Gawain and the Green Knight** *10 min*
- **Think** *10 min*
  Graphic Organizer: Three-Column Chart
- **Talk** *5 min*
- **Write** Short Response *10 min*

Day 3

Guided Practice pp. 166–167, 169

- **Read** **The Story of Sir Gareth & Lynette** *10 min*
- **Think** *10 min*
- **Talk** *5 min*
- **Write** Short Response *10 min*

Day 4

Independent Practice pp. 170–175

- **Read** **Arthur and the Sword** *15 min*
- **Think** *10 min*
- **Write** Short Response *10 min*

Day 5

Independent Practice pp. 170–175

- *Review* Answer Analysis (TRB) *10 min*
- *Review* Response Analysis (TRB) *10 min*
- *Assign and Discuss* Learning Target *10 min*

Language Handbook
Lesson 3 Interjections, pp. 442–443
20 min (optional)

Small Group Differentiation
Teacher-Toolbox.com

Reteach

***Ready Reading* Prerequisite Lesson**
- **Grade 4** Lesson 12 Supporting Inferences About Literary Texts

Teacher-led Activities

Tools for Instruction
- Cite Textual Evidence
- Make Inferences

Personalized Learning
i-Ready.com

Independent

i-Ready Close Reading Lessons

- **Grade 4** Supporting Inferences About Literary Texts

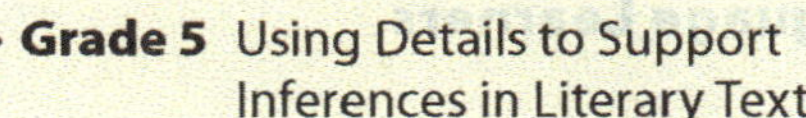

- **Grade 5** Using Details to Support Inferences in Literary Text

Introduction

Get Started

- Explain to students that in this lesson they will read legends about King Arthur and Knights of the Round Table. They will make inferences from what they read and support those inferences with text evidence.
- Remind students that an *inference* is an educated guess based on evidence and one's own knowledge and experience.
- Tap into what students already know about making inferences. For example, have them tell what they infer when they see and hear a fire truck go by. Have them share the reasons for their inferences.
- Guide students to distinguish between evidence and inferences. Explain:

  Earlier I saw a teacher talking to a group of students. The students all laughed. I didn't hear what the teacher said, but I can infer that it was funny. The students' laughter was my evidence, combined with knowing that people laugh when something is funny.
- Focus students' attention on the Learning Target. Read it aloud to set the purpose for the lesson.
- Display the Academic Talk words and phrases. Tell students to listen for these terms and their meanings as you work through the lesson together. Use the Academic Talk Routine on pp. A48–A49.

English Language Learners

Genre Focus

Read

- Read aloud the Read section as students follow along. Restate to reinforce:

  When an author does not state something explicitly, you need to make an inference to decide what is happening. Inferences about literature come from your own life experiences as well as what you have come across in other stories, television shows, or movies.
- Have students read the comic strip and make an inference about the woman's opinion. Remind them to circle the evidence that supports their inference.

Introduction

RL.5.1 Quote accurately from a text when explaining what the text says explicitly and when drawing inferences from the text.

Lesson 10
Using Details to Support Inferences in Literary Texts

Quoting directly from a text will help you support inferences about it and better understand the text.

Read In a literary text, the author may state something directly. A direct statement that is clear and complete has an **explicit meaning**. But authors aren't always direct. Sometimes we must infer what they mean. Making an **inference** means combining what we read with what we know from our experience.

Always support an inference with **evidence**. **Quotes** from a text are a strong form of evidence.

In the comic strip, circle anything that helps you infer what the woman thinks about the man's new recipe.

162

English Language Learners
Develop Language

- **Multiple-meaning Words** Explain that *quote* is used both as a noun and a verb. First define the noun ("one or more words repeated from another source") and explain that *quote* is actually a shorter form of *quotation*. Model using a quote from a familiar text, and have students use the words *quote* and *quotation* to explain what you are doing.
- Then define the verb ("to repeat words from another source"). Invite students to help you conjugate the verb *(quotes, quoted, will quote, quoting)* and guide them to practice using the forms of the verb in sentences related to supporting inferences.

Genre Focus
Legends

Explain that a legend is a story that has been passed down through several generations. Some legends were originally based on a historical location or event, but the stories have been repeated so often for so long that now they are mostly fictional.

Legends typically follow the deeds and acts of humans, rather than gods and goddesses. The main character is usually a hero, and the story demonstrates the character's admirable traits, such as bravery or honesty. Often legends include unusual events, such as tests of courage.

Have students share examples of legends they have read or heard.

Think What do you know about making inferences? Use the organizer below to help you develop and support an inference about how the new recipe tastes.

What's in the Image (Evidence)	What I Know (Experience)	My Inference
• A man is cooking. • He asks the woman to taste it. • She tastes it and makes a weird face. • The man looks worried about the woman's reaction.	• If a person makes a weird face after eating something, the food probably tastes bad.	• The woman thinks the food tastes terrible.

Talk Share your organizer with a partner.

- Did you both make the same inference?
- Did you both use the same information from the comic strip?
- Based on details in the comic strip, what can you infer will happen next?

Academic Talk

Use these words and phrases to talk about the text.

- explicit meaning
- inference
- evidence
- quotes

163

Monitor Understanding

If... students struggle to distinguish between evidence and experience,

then... provide an example.

- **Suppose I return the quizzes you took last week. Your friend looks at her quiz and smiles. What would you infer from that evidence?** *(She got a good grade on her quiz.)*
- **What evidence supports your inference?** *(She smiles just after reading her grade.)*
- **What in your own experience supports your inference?** *(I know that people usually smile when they get good news.)*

Ask students to provide their own examples of inferences drawn from evidence and general knowledge or experience.

Think

- Have students read aloud the Think section. Explain that the organizer will help them collect their thoughts and evidence.
- Have partners complete the organizer. Remind them to use evidence from the words and images in the comic strip to support their inferences.
- As students work, circulate and provide assistance as needed.
- Ask volunteers to share what they wrote.
- Make certain students understand that good inferences are based on both explicit evidence and their own knowledge and experience.

Talk

- Read aloud the Talk prompts.
- Have partners discuss what will probably happen next, and why.
- Ask volunteers to share their ideas.

Quick Write Have students write a response to the following prompt:

Think of a time when you or someone you know solved a mystery. Explain what the mystery was, what clues were used as evidence, and how those clues led to an inference that solved the mystery.

Ask students to share their responses.

Wrap Up

- Invite students to share what they've learned so far. Encourage them to use the Academic Talk words and phrases in their explanations.
- Explain to students that when they read stories, they can make inferences to better understand the author's meaning. Basing their inferences on both experience and evidence from the story will ensure that their inferences are not merely guesses.

In the next section, you will read a legend from the days of King Arthur. In order to fully understand what happens in the story, you will make inferences about the characters and plot. You will support these inferences with evidence from the text.

Monitor Understanding

Modeled and Guided Instruction

Get Started

Today you will read a legend about one of the Knights of the Round Table. First, you'll read to understand what the story is about. Then you'll read to analyze and make inferences about the story.

Read

- Read aloud the title of the legend and call attention to the illustration. Guide students to understand that it is an axe.
- Have students read the story independently. Tell them to place a check mark above any confusing words and phrases as they read. Remind students to look inside, around, and beyond each unknown word or phrase to help them figure out its meaning. Use the Word Learning Routine on pp. A50–A51.
- When students have finished reading, clarify the meanings of words and phrases they still find confusing. Then use the questions below to check understanding. Encourage students to identify details in the text that support their answers.

  What evidence shows that this story is a legend, not actual history? *("But the Green Knight, still very much alive, stood and picked up his own head.")*

  Why does Sir Gawain meet the Green Knight for the second time? *(He had made a promise.)*

  What does the Green Knight do at the end of the story? *(He gives Sir Gawain his axe and rides away.)*

 English Language Learners

● Word Learning Strategy

Explore

- Read aloud the Explore question at the top of p. 165 to set the purpose for the second read. Tell students they will need to take a closer look at what Sir Gawain says and does before they make inferences about him.
- Have students read aloud the Close Reader Habit on p. 164.

TIP Review with students the types of words that are used to describe someone's character, such as *bossy*, *clever*, and *kind*.

Modeled and Guided Instruction

Read

Genre: Legend

Sir Gawain and the Green Knight

by Chris Bartlett

1 On New Year's Day, the mysterious Green Knight rode into the heart of King Arthur's castle and issued a challenge to the Knights of the Round Table. He would grant any knight a single stroke with his green axe against his neck—but only if that knight would return the favor, one year and one day later.

2 King Arthur began to accept the challenge, but Sir Gawain offered to take his king's place. Gawain then took up the enormous green axe and, with a mighty swing, sliced off the Green Knight's head. *Surely that will be the end of it,* Gawain thought. *Surely my king is now safe.*

3 But the Green Knight, still very much alive, stood and picked up his own head. He reminded Gawain that they had an appointment in one year and a day, and he rode quickly away on his horse.

4 Gawain's fellow knights gathered around him. "We are sorry we let you take on this burden," they said. "We will not let you face the Green Knight alone."

5 But Gawain replied, "This is no burden, and I am not sorry. I do what I do for my king and for my honor. I will face the Green Knight alone, and I will do so with all good cheer."

6 One year and one day later, Gawain met the Green Knight as he had promised. He lay aside his sword, shield, and helmet, and then strode toward the Green Knight. Gawain bent low to receive the blow from the axe. At the stroke of the axe, Gawain flinched.

7 "Are you afraid?" asked the Green Knight.

8 "Get on with the business," Gawain snapped. Again, the Green Knight raised his axe. He took aim and swung, but Gawain was unharmed.

9 *Surely that will not be the end of it,* Gawain thought, as he readied himself again. But the Green Knight presented Gawain with his great axe, bowed low to the ground, and rode away.

Close Reader Habits

What kind of person does Sir Gawain seem to be? As you reread, **underline** any details that suggest what sort of person he is.

164

English Language Learners

Develop Language

Pronouns Copy the last sentence of paragraph 1 onto chart paper. Circle *He, his,* and *his*. Ask, "Who do these pronouns refer to?"

- Have students reread the paragraph and identify the two characters. Ask, "Which character does something?" *(the Green Knight)* "What did he do?" *(rode; issued)*. Discuss why King Arthur cannot be the subject. *(The sentence is not about him; he does not do anything.)*
- Remind students that the subject of a sentence may not always be named in the sentence. In these cases, students should look for the subject of the previous sentence and decide whether that subject makes sense in place of the pronouns.

● Word Learning Strategy

Use Context Clues

- Point out the phrase *take his king's place* in paragraph 2. Explain that *take the place* is a phrase with its own meaning. Students should not try to interpret the meanings of the individual words in the phrase.
- Have students read before and after the phrase to identify what was happening when Gawain took the king's place. *(King Arthur had accepted the challenge, but Sir Gawain faced the Green Knight instead.)*
- Guide students to define *take one's place* as "to take over a duty or role assigned to someone else." **L.5.4a, L.5.5b**

Explore Based on what Sir Gawain says and does, what inferences can you make about him?

Think

1 Complete this organizer with quotes and details from the text and what you already know. Such evidence will help you support your inferences.

Look for what Sir Gawain says, thinks, and does. Such details will support your inferences.

What's in the Text (Evidence)	What I Know (Experience)	My Inferences
• "Sir Gawain offered to take his king's place." • "Surely my king is now safe." • He is happy to protect his king and his honor. • Even when afraid, he keeps his promises.	• People who try to protect others are noble. • People who keep their promises are trustworthy. • People who do what they must when afraid are brave.	Sir Gawain is a noble, trustworthy, and brave person.

Talk

2 Discuss what Sir Gawain is like. Why do you think he offers to take King Arthur's place? What does Gawain think will happen when he meets the Green Knight again? Add or change quotes or details in your organizer as necessary.

Write

3 **Short Response** What inferences can you make about the kind of person Sir Gawain is? Support your answer with quotes and details from the story and your organizer. Use the space provided on page 168 to write your answer.

HINT Start by stating at least one of Gawain's traits. Then quote parts of the story that show those traits.

Think Aloud

- I'm going to go back into the text to look for evidence about what Sir Gawain says and does.
- In paragraph 1, the Green Knight issues a challenge. King Arthur starts to accept, but Sir Gawain offers to take the king's place. He picks up the axe and slices the head off the Green Knight.
- This detail definitely tells about Sir Gawain's character. He stepped in to protect his king. I'm going to write this quote in the *What's in the Text (Evidence)* column: "Sir Gawain offered to take his king's place." Notice I put the quote in quotation marks because I used the author's exact words.
- I've read many stories about knights, so I know that Sir Gawain is being noble, the way a knight is supposed to act. He is loyal. He is protecting his king. I'll make a note of that in the *What I Know (Experience)* column.
- As I keep reading the story, I will add more details about what Sir Gawain says and does so I can make a solid inference about him.

Think

- Read aloud the Think section. Explain to students that you will model how to find text evidence to fill in part of the organizer. Use the **Think Aloud** below to guide your modeling.
- Revisit the Explore question. Guide students to determine that they need to look for more details, using the Close Reader Habit.
- Encourage students to work with a partner to continue rereading the passage and complete the organizer. Remind them that the Buddy Tip will help them find the information they need.
- Ask volunteers to share their completed organizers.
- Have partners check each other's inferences to make sure they are supported by text evidence as well as personal experience.

Talk

- Read aloud the Talk prompt.
- Have partners respond to the prompt. Use the Talk Routine on pp. A52–A53.
- Circulate to check that students are supporting their inferences with details about Gawain only found in the text, and not guesses.

Write

- Ask a volunteer to read aloud the Write prompt.
- Invite a few students to tell what the prompt is asking them to do.
- Make sure students understand that they need to use text evidence as well as what they know about knights and people in general to make an inference about what kind of person Sir Gawain is.
- Have students turn to p. 168 to write their response.
- Use Review Responses on p. 168 to assess students' writing.

Wrap Up

- Ask students to recall the Learning Target. Have them explain how making well-supported inferences helped them better understand the story.

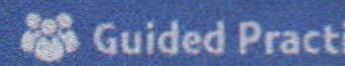

Guided Practice

Get Started

Today you will read a legend about another knight from King Arthur's Round Table, Sir Gareth. First, you will read to understand what the story is about. Then you'll read to analyze and make inferences about the story.

Read

- Read aloud the title of the legend, as well as the introductory text above it. Make sure students understand that Arthur is the same King Arthur from "Sir Gawain and the Green Knight."
- **Read to Understand** Have students read the story independently. Tell them to place a check mark above any confusing words and phrases as they read. Remind students to look inside, around, and beyond each unknown word or phrase to help them figure out its meaning. Use the Word Learning Routine on pp. A50–A51.
- When students have finished reading, clarify the meanings of words and phrases they still find confusing. Then use the questions below to check understanding. Encourage students to identify details in the text that support their answers.

  Why did Gareth's mother make him promise to serve as a kitchen boy? *(She feared for his safety.)*

  What does Gareth ask of the king? *(He asks to be made a knight in secret and to be allowed to "right the first wrong that we hear of.")*

  What happened to Lady Lyonors? *(She has been imprisoned in Castle Perilous, which is guarded by four knights.)*

English Language Learners

Word Learning Strategy

- **Read to Analyze** Read aloud the Close Reader Habit on p. 166 to set the purpose for the second read. Then have students reread the story with a partner and discuss any questions they might have.

Guided Practice

Read

Genre: Legend

Sir Gawain had a younger brother named Gareth. Gareth also wanted to be a knight, but his mother, fearing for his safety, made him promise to serve only as a kitchen-boy in Arthur's palace.

From

The Story of Sir Gareth & Lynette

by Maude L. Radford

1 Gareth served in the kitchen of the king only one month, for his mother became sorry for the promise she had asked of him, and sent armor for him to Arthur's Court, with a letter to the king telling who the youth was. With great joy Gareth then went to Arthur and said, "My lord, I can fight as well as my brother Gawain. At home we have proved it. Then make me a knight, in secret, for I do not want the other knights to know my name. Make me a knight, and give me permission to right the first wrong that we hear of."

2 The king said gravely, "You know all that my knights must promise?"

3 "Yes, my lord Arthur. I am willing to promise all."

4 "I will make you my knight in secret, since you wish it," Arthur said. . . . Then Gareth was secretly made a knight.

5 That same day a beautiful young damsel came into Arthur's hall. She had cheeks as pink as apple blossoms, and very sharp eyes.

6 "Who are you, damsel?" asked the king, "and what do you need?"

7 "My name is Lynette," she said, "and I am of noble blood. I need a knight to fight for my sister Lyonors, a lady, also noble, rich, and most beautiful."

8 "Why must she have a knight?" questioned Arthur.

9 "My Lord King, she lives in Castle Perilous. Around this castle a river circles three times, and there are three passing-places, one over each circle of the river. Three knights, who are brothers, keep a constant guard over these passing-places. A fourth knight, also a brother, clad in black armor, stands guard in front of my sister's castle. We have never seen this knight's face or heard his voice, but his brothers tell us he is the most powerful and daring knight in the world. All these four keep my sister a prisoner."

Close Reader Habits

What inference can you make about what will happen later in the story? Reread the story. **Underline** details that support your inference.

166

English Language Learners

Build Meaning

Archaic Language Explain that because legends are very old stories, they often use older forms of English that do not sound like modern English.

- Point out the first sentence of paragraph 1. Explain that *for* in this instance means "because." Model substituting it into the sentence, and reread it in both ways. Guide students to find another instance of *for* used to mean "because." *(Paragraph 1, Sentence 4)*
- Read aloud the text and put special emphasis or formality in your tone of voice. After you read small sections of text, invite students to share an interpretation of what you are saying. You may wish to give them a moment to write their thoughts before sharing.

Word Learning Strategy

Use Context Clues

- Read aloud paragraph 7.

  What clues in the story can help you figure out what *noble* means? *(Noble and rich are used together. The text also says that Lyonors lives in a castle.)*

  What does the phrase *of noble blood* mean in this paragraph? *(Lynette belongs to a family of nobles, or members of the upper class.)*

- Review that *noble* can also mean "brave and honorable." Ask students to identify a character to whom this meaning of *noble* applies. *(Sir Gareth)* **L.5.4a**

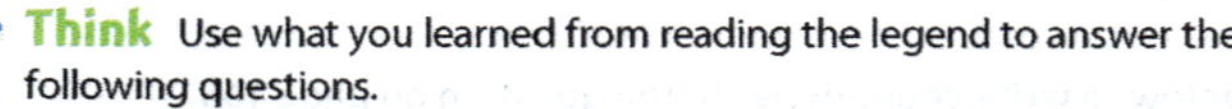

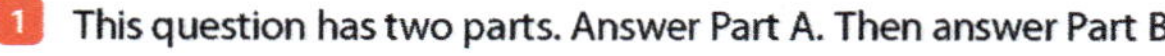

Think Use what you learned from reading the legend to answer the following questions.

Read carefully to figure out why Gareth acts as he does. Why does he want to be a knight? What does he say he will do if he becomes one?

1 This question has two parts. Answer Part A. Then answer Part B.

Part A
Which inference about Gareth is **best** supported by the text?

A Gareth likes working in the kitchen.
(B) Gareth is eager to prove himself to the king.
C Gareth is angry about the promise he made to his mother.
D Gareth wants to prove that he is a better knight than his brother.

Part B
What evidence **best** supports your answer in Part A? Select **two** options.

(A) "'Make me a knight, and give me permission to right the first wrong that we hear of.'" (paragraph 1)
B "'Then make me a knight, in secret, for I do not want the other knights to know my name.'" (paragraph 1)
(C) "'Yes, my lord Arthur. I am willing to promise all.'" (paragraph 3)
D "'I will make you my knight in secret, since you wish it,' Arthur said." (paragraph 4)
E "'Who are you, damsel?' asked the king, 'and what do you need?'" (paragraph 6)
F "'I need a knight to fight for my sister Lyonors, a lady, also noble, rich, and most beautiful.'" (paragraph 7)

Talk

2 The passage is part of a longer story. What do you think Gareth will do later in the story? Why do you think this? Use the organizer on page 169 to collect evidence from the story and record your ideas.

Write

3 **Short Response** Gareth will fight one or more of the brothers near Castle Perilous. Use evidence from the text and your organizer to support this inference. Use the space provided on page 169 to write your answer.

HINT After writing, ask yourself: How well does my evidence support the inference?

167

Lesson 10

Think

- Have students work with a partner to complete item 1. Draw attention to the boldface words **best** and **two**.

TIP Have students turn each option in Part A into a question, such as "Does Gareth like working in the kitchen?" then return to the text for evidence to answer each question.

Answer Analysis

When students have finished, discuss correct and incorrect responses.

1 **Part A**

The correct choice is B. Gareth is eager to prove that he is worthy to be a knight.

- **A, C,** and **D** might make some sense, but they are not the best inferences about Gareth's motivations or supported by any text evidence.

Part B

The correct choices are A and **C.** Both choices show that Gareth is eager to prove himself.

- **B** only expresses that Gareth wishes to become a knight. **D** is Arthur's response to Gareth's request. **E** and **F** happen after Arthur says he will make Gareth a knight.

DOK 3

● **Integrating Standards**

Talk

- Have partners discuss the prompt. Emphasize that students should support their ideas with text details.
- Circulate to clarify misunderstandings.

● **Monitor Understanding**

Write

- See p. 169 for instructional guidance.

Wrap Up

- Ask students to recall the Learning Target. Have them explain how supporting inferences with direct quotes helped them understand what has happened and what will happen in the story.

● Integrating Standards

Use the following questions to further students' understanding of the story.

- **How does Sir Gareth respond to the challenge of having a famous older brother?** *(He wants to become a knight in secret so no one will think he's trying to take advantage of his brother's name and fame.)*
DOK 2 **RL.5.2**
- **What theme do the stories on pp. 164 and 166 have in common?** *(Both stories show that knights do the right thing, even when they are afraid or in danger. To protect the king, Sir Gawain allows the Green Knight to try to cut off his head. Sir Gareth will go off alone to fight the brothers at Castle Perilous.)*
DOK 3 **RL.5.9**

● Monitor Understanding

If... students have difficulty finding text evidence to answer item 2,

then... guide them to use the details they underlined as part of the Close Reader Habit. Then ask:

What does Arthur promise Gareth? *(that he will make Gareth a knight in secret)*

What does Lynette ask of Arthur? *(a knight to fight for her imprisoned sister)*

Discuss with students why the author might have included these events in this order. Help them see that Gareth will be the knight that Arthur sends to fight for Lynette's sister.

Modeled and Guided Instruction

Write

- Remember to use the Response-Writing Routine on pp. A54–A55.

Review Responses

After students complete the writing activity, help them evaluate their responses.

3 Responses may vary but should include quotes from the story about what Sir Gawain does and says. See the sample response on the student book page.
DOK 3

Write Use the space below to write your answer to the question on page 165.

Sir Gawain and the Green Knight

HINT Start by stating at least one of Gawain's traits. Then quote parts of the story that show those traits.

3 **Short Response** What inferences can you make about the kind of person Sir Gawain is? Support your answer with quotes and details from the story and your organizer.

Sample response: It appears that Sir Gawain is a noble, trustworthy, and brave person. When King Arthur tried to volunteer for the Green Knight's challenge, Gawain "offered to take his king's place." When Gawain kept his promise to the Green Knight, he proved himself trustworthy. And although he was scared, as shown by the fact that he "flinched," he bravely chose to keep his promise. Gawain is a noble, trustworthy, and brave person.

Don't forget to check your writing.

Check Your Writing

- ☐ Did you read the prompt carefully?
- ☐ Did you put the prompt in your own words?
- ☐ Did you use the best evidence from the text to support your ideas?
- ☐ Are your ideas clearly organized?
- ☐ Did you write in clear and complete sentences?
- ☐ Did you check your spelling and punctuation?

Scaffolding Support for Reluctant Writers

If students are having a difficult time getting started, use the strategies below. Work individually with struggling students, or have students work with partners.

- Circle the verbs in the prompt that tell you what to do, such as *describe*, *explain*, or *compare*.
- Underline words and phrases in the prompt that show what information you need to provide in your response, such as *causes*, *reasons*, or *character traits*.
- Talk about the details from the text that you will include in your response.
- Explain aloud how you will respond to the prompt.

The Story of Sir Gareth & Lynette

2 **Use the organizer below to gather your ideas and evidence.**

What's in the Text (Evidence)	What I Know (Experience)	My Inference

Write Use the space below to write your answer to the question on page 167.

HINT After writing, ask yourself: How well does my evidence support the inference?

3 **Short Response** Gareth will fight one or more of the brothers near Castle Perilous. Use evidence from the text and your organizer to support this inference.

Sample response: There is a lot of evidence that Gareth will end up fighting one or more of the brothers. For example, Gareth wants so much to be a knight that he asks for the chance "to right the first wrong that we hear of." Right after Gareth is made a knight, "the first wrong" shows up at King Arthur's Court. Lynette comes to ask the king for his help in saving her sister Lyonors. The castle where Lyonors is held prisoner is circled three times by a river and guarded by four brothers, so a rescue will be difficult. But because Gareth is a knight and made a promise to King Arthur, he will probably fight one or more of the four brothers.

Teacher Notes

Talk

2 Students should use the organizer to collect their thoughts and evidence.

Write

- Ask a volunteer to read aloud the Write prompt.
- Invite students to tell what the prompt is asking them to do. Make sure they understand that they must support the inference that is stated in the prompt, rather than one of their own.
- Call attention to the HINT.
- Remember to use the Response-Writing Routine on pp. A54–A55.

Review Responses

After students complete the writing activity, help them evaluate their responses.

3 Responses may vary but should include quotes about what Sir Gareth does and says, as well as the conversation between King Arthur and Lynette. See the sample response on the student book page.
DOK 3

Independent Practice

Get Started

Today you are going to read another legend. You will use what you've learned to make inferences and support them with text evidence and your experience.

- Ask a volunteer to explain why it is important to make inferences that are based on text evidence. Encourage students to use the Academic Talk words and phrases in their response.

English Language Learners

Read

You are going to read the legend independently and use what you have learned to think and write about the text. As you read, pay attention to the inferences you are making about the story and the characters. Make sure your inferences are based on text evidence.

- Read aloud the title of the legend and then encourage students to preview the text, paying close attention to the illustrations.
- Call attention to the Words to Know in the upper left of p. 170.
- If students need support in reading the passage, you may wish to use the Monitor Understanding suggestions.
- When students have finished, have them complete the Think and Write sections.

Monitor Understanding

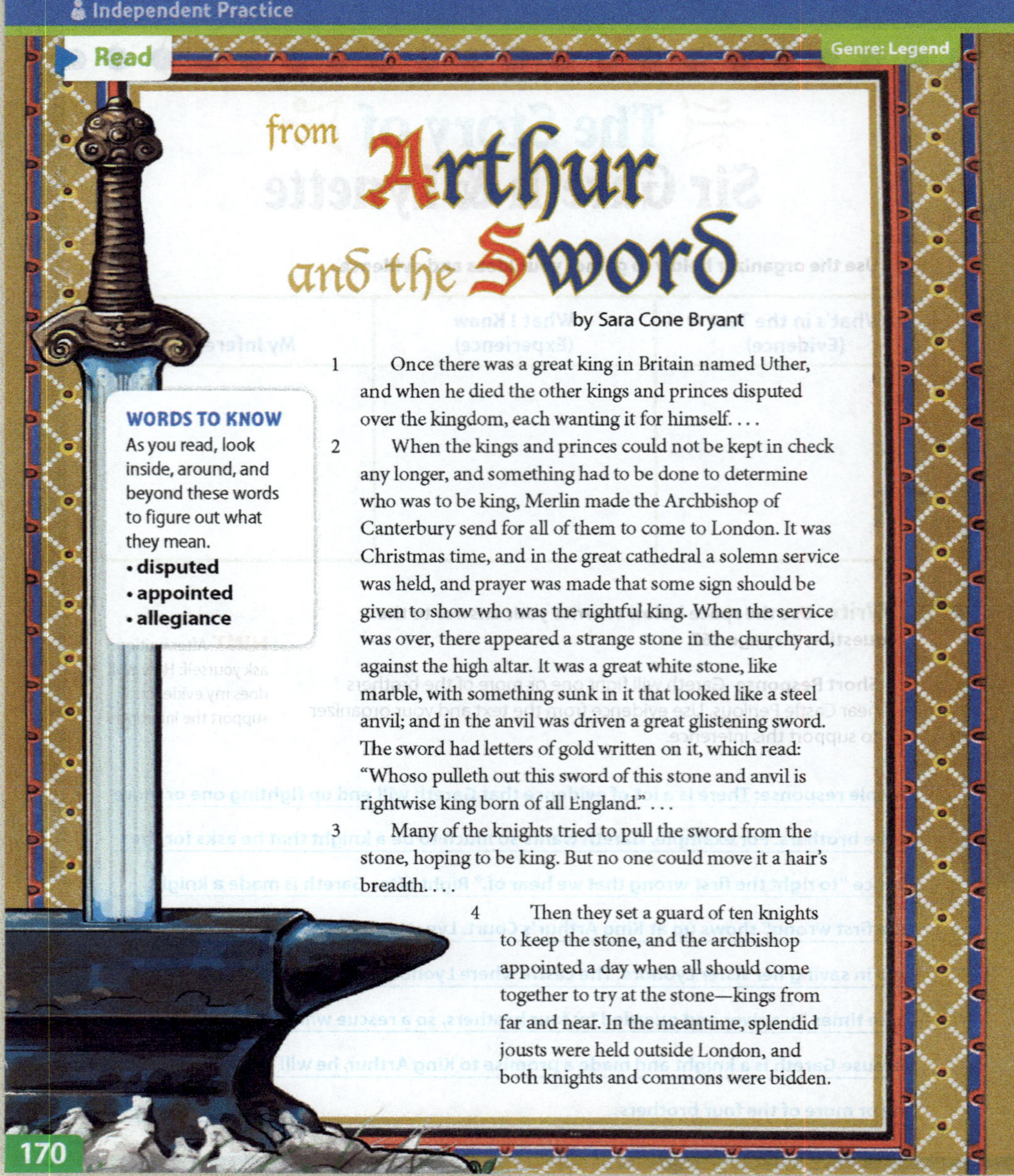

Independent Practice

Read

Genre: Legend

from Arthur and the Sword

by Sara Cone Bryant

WORDS TO KNOW
As you read, look inside, around, and beyond these words to figure out what they mean.
- disputed
- appointed
- allegiance

1 Once there was a great king in Britain named Uther, and when he died the other kings and princes disputed over the kingdom, each wanting it for himself. . . .

2 When the kings and princes could not be kept in check any longer, and something had to be done to determine who was to be king, Merlin made the Archbishop of Canterbury send for all of them to come to London. It was Christmas time, and in the great cathedral a solemn service was held, and prayer was made that some sign should be given to show who was the rightful king. When the service was over, there appeared a strange stone in the churchyard, against the high altar. It was a great white stone, like marble, with something sunk in it that looked like a steel anvil; and in the anvil was driven a great glistening sword. The sword had letters of gold written on it, which read: "Whoso pulleth out this sword of this stone and anvil is rightwise king born of all England." . . .

3 Many of the knights tried to pull the sword from the stone, hoping to be king. But no one could move it a hair's breadth. . . .

4 Then they set a guard of ten knights to keep the stone, and the archbishop appointed a day when all should come together to try at the stone—kings from far and near. In the meantime, splendid jousts were held outside London, and both knights and commons were bidden.

170

English Language Learners

Build Meaning

Archaic Language Remind students that legends are often written in an older style of English than we use today. Write the following sentence on chart paper: "Whoso pulleth out this sword of this stone and anvil is rightwise king born of all England."

- Invite students to identify any words they recognize. Briefly discuss and confirm their meanings, and place a check mark above them. Use the images on p. 171 to help students identify and define *sword* and *anvil*.
- Next guide students to unpack more challenging words and phrases such as *whoso, pulleth, rightwise,* and *born of all England*. Have them look for words they recognize within each word, and update each term on the chart paper with more familiar language as you determine its meaning.
- Reread the revised sentence together, and discuss with students what important information the sword contains. Revisit the title of the legend, and have students make predictions about what might happen.

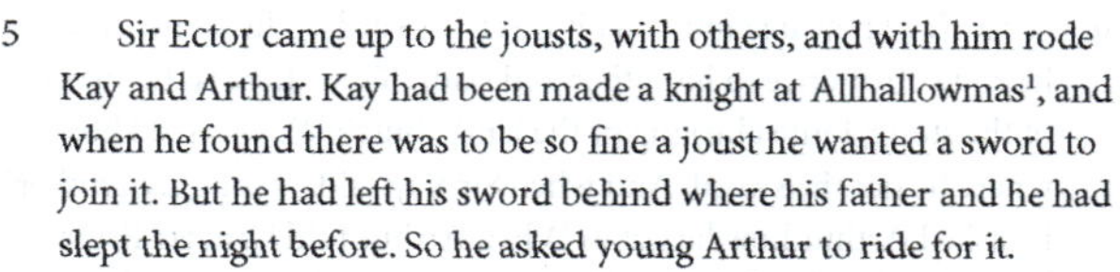

5 Sir Ector came up to the jousts, with others, and with him rode Kay and Arthur. Kay had been made a knight at Allhallowmas[1], and when he found there was to be so fine a joust he wanted a sword to join it. But he had left his sword behind where his father and he had slept the night before. So he asked young Arthur to ride for it.

6 "I will well," said Arthur, and rode back for it. But when he came to the castle, the lady and all her household were at the jousting, and there was none to let him in.

7 Arthur said to himself, "My brother Sir Kay shall not be without a sword this day." And he remembered the sword he had seen in the churchyard. "I will ride to the churchyard," he said, "and take that sword with me." So he rode into the churchyard, tied his horse to the stile, and went up to the stone. The guards were away to the tourney, and the sword was there, alone.

8 Going up to the stone, young Arthur took the great sword by the hilt, and lightly and fiercely he drew it out of the anvil.

9 Then he rode straight to Sir Kay and gave it to him.

[1] **Allhallowmas:** All Saints Day, November 1

Monitor Understanding

If... students struggle to read and understand the passage,

then... use these scaffolding suggestions:

Question the Text Preview the text by asking the following questions:

- **Based on the title and illustrations, what do you predict the legend will be about?**
- **What questions do you have about the text?**

Vocabulary Support Define words that may interfere with comprehension, such as *archbishop, cathedral, anvil, tourney,* and *hilt.*

Read Aloud Read aloud the text with students. You could also have students chorally read the text in a small group.

Check Understanding Use the questions below to check understanding. Encourage students to cite details in the text that support their answers.

- **What happened after King Uther's death?** *(Other kings and princes fought over his kingdom.)*
- **When Kay forgot his sword, what did Arthur have to do?** *(Arthur had to find a sword for Kay and ended up pulling the sword from the stone.)*
- **What happened after everyone realized what Arthur had done?** *(Arthur became king of Britain.)*

Integrating Standards

After students have read the legend, use these questions to discuss the legend with them.

- **How are Arthur and Sir Kay different? Use their character traits and interactions to support your answer.**
  (Arthur is honorable while Sir Kay is dishonorable. Arthur does whatever he can to find a sword for Kay, since Kay was not responsible enough to remember to bring one. Later, Kay takes credit for pulling the sword from the stone instead of telling his father the truth, that Arthur actually did it.)
  DOK 3 **RL.5.3**
- **How would the story change if it were narrated by Sir Kay?**
  (Sir Kay would likely boast about being recently knighted and tell his enthusiasm for the jousts. He would probably make an excuse for forgetting his sword. He would recognize the sword from the stone and make the decision to claim it as his own. Finally, he would reflect on telling the truth and acknowledging Arthur as king.)
  DOK 3 **RL.5.6**
- **According to the legend, "Many knights tried to pull the sword from the stone, hoping to be king. But no one could move it a hair's breadth." What does the phrase *a hair's breadth* mean?**
  (The phrase means that no one could move it even the width of one hair—in other words, not at all. The phrase "but neither could stir it" in paragraph 14 supports this definition.)
  DOK 2 **RL.5.4**
- **Compare and contrast "Sir Gawain and the Green Knight," "The Story of Sir Gareth and Lynette," and "Arthur and the Sword."**
  (All three stories tell about King Arthur and his knights. However, "Sir Gawain" and "Sir Gareth" are about Knights of the Round Table who serve Arthur, while "Arthur and the Sword" is about how Arthur became king.)
  DOK 3 **RL.5.9**

● Theme Connection

10 Sir Kay knew instantly that it was the sword of the stone, and he rode off at once to his father and said, "Sir, lo, here is the sword of the stone; I must be king of the land." But Sir Ector asked him where he got the sword. And when Sir Kay said, "From my brother," he asked Arthur how he got it. When Arthur told him, Sir Ector bowed his head before him. "Now I understand ye must be king of this land," he said to Arthur.

11 "Why me?" said Arthur.

12 "For God will have it so," said Ector. "Never man should have drawn out this sword but he that shall be rightwise king of this land. Now let me see whether ye can put the sword as it was in the stone, and pull it out again."

13 Straightway Arthur put the sword back.

14 Then Sir Ector tried to pull it out, and after him Sir Kay; but neither could stir it. Then Arthur pulled it out. Thereupon, Sir Ector and Sir Kay kneeled upon the ground before him. . . .

15 So Arthur became king of Britain, and all gave him allegiance.

● Theme Connection

- Remind students that the theme of this lesson is Round Table Legends.
- Ask students to identify the head of the Round Table *(King Arthur)* and to name the Knights of the Round Table about whom they have read *(Sir Gawain and Sir Gareth)*.
- Have students locate quotes from each story about what each knight said and did. Discuss the qualities shared by the heroes of each story, as well as why these qualities are important for leaders to have.

Think Use what you learned from reading the legend to answer the following questions.

1 This question has two parts. First, answer Part A. Then answer Part B.

Part A
Which inference about Arthur is supported by the text?

A Arthur believes himself to be rightful king from an early age.
B Arthur is one of ten chosen to guard the stone.
(C) Arthur is a loyal and resourceful person.
D Arthur will face problems because others want to be king.

Part B
Underline **two** sentences in this paragraph that support the answer to Part A.

Arthur said to himself, "My brother Sir Kay shall not be without a sword this day." And he remembered the sword he had seen in the churchyard. "I will ride to the churchyard," he said, "and take that sword with me." So he rode into the churchyard, tied his horse to the stile, and went up to the stone. The guards were away to the tourney, and the sword was there, alone.

2 Read this sentence from paragraph 4.

In the meantime, splendid jousts were held outside London, and both knights and commons were bidden.

Which dictionary entry **best** defines jousts?

A contests in which knights fight common people
B parties held at the palace to celebrate the dead king
C events during which new kings are crowned
(D) competitions in which knights fight each other on horses

173

● **Monitor Understanding**

If... students struggle to complete the items,

then... you may wish to use the following suggestions:

Read Aloud Activities

- As you read, have students note any unfamiliar words or phrases. Clarify any misunderstandings.
- Discuss each item with students to make certain they understand the expectation.

Reread the Text

- Have students complete three-column graphic organizers as they reread. Use the graphic organizer on p. 165 as a model.
- Have students summarize the story.

Think

- Use the Monitor Understanding suggestions to support students in completing items 1–4.

● **Monitor Understanding**

Answer Analysis

When students have finished, discuss correct and incorrect responses.

1 **Part A**

The correct choice is C. Arthur wants to help his brother Kay. When he can't get to Kay's sword, Arthur decides he will take the one he has seen in the stone out of loyalty to his brother.

- **A, B,** and **D** are not supported by details in the passage.

DOK 2 RL.5.1

Part B

See the student book page. Students should underline the first sentence and the third sentence as evidence to support the inference that Arthur is loyal and resourceful.

DOK 3 RL.5.1

2 **The correct choice is D.** The rest of the passage makes it clear that jousts are for knights to compete in.

- **A** is incorrect because, although common people are invited, there is no evidence to suggest that these tournaments are between knights and common people.
- **B** is incorrect because there is no evidence to suggest that jousts are parties to celebrate a dead king.
- **C** is incorrect because there is no evidence to support the conclusion that new kings are typically crowned during jousts.

DOK 2 L.5.4a, RL.5.4

Independent Practice

3 **The correct choices are A and B.** King Uther has died, and the princes and other kings in the area are fighting with each other over the throne. It was during a church service that the new, peaceful method for choosing a king was revealed.

- **C** does not suggest that the kingdom needs a new ruler.
- **D, E,** and **F** are events surrounding the choice of a king, but they do not explain why the kingdom needed a peaceful method of naming a new king.

DOK 3 **RL.5.1**

4 **The correct choice is C.** Arthur did not know that the person who took the sword from the stone would be the rightful king. Sir Ector had to explain this to Arthur.

- **A** is incorrect because many knights did know the message on the stone, but this choice does not explain why Arthur did not know it.
- **B** explains only why Arthur was looking for a sword.
- **D** is the conclusion of the story, telling that Arthur did become king; it does not explain why he was confused about the purpose of the sword in the anvil.

DOK 2 **RL.5.1**

3 Which sentences from the text **best** support the inference that Britain needed a peaceful way of finding a new king to replace Uther? Select **two** options.

(A) "Once there was a great king in Britain named Uther, and when he died the other kings and princes disputed over the kingdom, each wanting it for himself. . . ." (paragraph 1)

(B) "It was Christmas time, and in the great cathedral a solemn service was held, and prayer was made that some sign should be given to show who was the rightful king." (paragraph 2)

C "When the service was over, there appeared a strange stone in the churchyard, against the high altar." (paragraph 2)

D "It was a great white stone, like marble, with something sunk in it that looked like a steel anvil; and in the anvil was driven a great glistening sword." (paragraph 2)

E "In the meantime, splendid jousts were held outside London, and both knights and commons were bidden." (paragraph 4)

F "So he rode into the churchyard, tied his horse to the stile, and went up to the stone." (paragraph 7)

4 Read this sentence and the directions that follow.

When Arthur decides to take the sword from the stone, he has not yet heard about the message that was written on it.

Which sentence from the text **best** supports this inference?

A "Many of the knights tried to pull the sword from the stone, hoping to be king." (paragraph 3)

B "Arthur said to himself, 'My brother Sir Kay shall not be without a sword this day.'" (paragraph 7)

(C) "'Why me?' said Arthur." (paragraph 11)

D "So Arthur became king of Britain, and all gave him allegiance." (paragraph 15)

Monitor Understanding

If... students don't understand the writing task,

then... read aloud the writing prompt. Use the following questions to help students get started.

- **What is the prompt asking you to write about?**
- **Do you need to reread the text to find more information?**
- **How will you identify the information you need to include?**
- Have partners talk about how they will organize their responses.
- Provide a graphic organizer to assist students, if needed.

Write

5 **Short Response** In this story, Sir Kay can be described as a young knight with little experience. Write a paragraph supporting this statement. Use at least **two** details from the story to support your answer.

Sample response: Readers can infer that Sir Kay is a knight with little experience because of his actions and words in the text. First, Kay had only recently been made a knight. This suggests he was young. Second, Kay "left his sword behind where he and his father had slept the night before." An experienced knight would probably not forget his sword. Kay also shows his father the sword and says, "I must be king of the land." Knights are supposed to be honorable, and it is not honorable to take credit for something his brother did, so Kay must not have a lot of experience as a knight.

In this lesson, you used quotes to support inferences about literary texts. Explain how this activity will help you better understand other literary texts you read.

Responses will vary, but students should identify ways that making inferences and supporting them with quotes can help them understand the words and actions of characters, as well as events that happen in the story.

5 2-Point Writing Rubric

Points	Focus	Evidence	Organization
2	My answer does exactly what the prompt asked me to do.	My answer is supported with plenty of details from the text.	My ideas are clear and in a logical order.
1	Some of my answer does not relate to the prompt.	My answer is missing some important details from the text.	Some of my ideas are unclear and out of order.
0	My answer does not make sense.	My answer does not have any details from the text.	My ideas are unclear and not in any order.

Write

- Tell students that using what they read, they will plan and compose a short response to the writing prompt.

Monitor Understanding

Review Responses

After students have completed each part of the writing activity, help them evaluate their responses.

5 Display or pass out copies of the reproducible **2-Point Writing Rubric** on p. TR10. Have students use the rubric to individually assess their writing and revise as needed.

When students have finished their revisions, evaluate their responses. Answers will vary but should include evidence that supports the inference that Sir Kay is a young knight with little experience. See the sample response on the student book page.

DOK 3 RL.5.1

Wrap Up

Learning Target

- Have each student respond in writing to the Learning Target prompt.
- When students have finished, have them share their responses. This may be done with a partner, in small groups, or as a whole class.

Assessment

Get Started

Today you are going to read two passages. The first passage is a poem, and the second is a historical fiction story. You will use what you have learned in this unit to understand what you are reading.

- Ask students to recall what they have learned, such as comparing characters, settings, and events, finding the theme, and summarizing literary texts.
- Encourage students to use the Academic Talk words and phrases from the unit's lessons in their response.

Read

You are going to read the passages independently and use what you have learned to think and write about the text.

- Ask a student to read aloud the titles of the passages. Make certain that students understand they are to read both selections.
- Encourage students to preview the text, paying close attention to the illustrations and text structure.
- Remind students to look inside, around, and beyond when they encounter unfamiliar words. Use the Word Learning Routine on pp. A50–A51.
- When students have finished, have them complete the Think and Write sections.

Read

Genre: Poem

Read the poem. Then answer the questions that follow.

Going Down Hill on a Bicycle, A Boy's Song

by Henry Charles Beeching

With lifted feet, hands still,
I am poised, and down the hill
Dart, with heedful mind;
The air goes by in a wind.

Swifter and yet more swift,
Till the heart with a mighty lift
Makes the lungs laugh, the throat cry:—
"O bird, see; see, bird, I fly.

"Is this, is this your joy?
O bird, then I, though a boy
For a golden moment share
Your feathery life in air!"

Say, heart, is there aught like this
In a world that is full of bliss?
'Tis more than skating, bound
Steel-shod to the level ground.

Speed slackens now, I float
Awhile in my airy boat;
Till, when the wheels scarce crawl,
My feet to the treadles fall.

Alas, that the longest hill
Must end in a vale; but still,
Who climbs with toil, wheresoe'er,
Shall find wings waiting there.

Think

1 Underline the line that tells the reader that the speaker of the poem knows his joyful experience is temporary.

"Is this, is this your joy?
O bird, then I, though a boy
For a golden moment share
Your feathery life in air!"

2 This question has two parts. First, answer Part A. Then answer Part B.

Part A
Which sentence **best** states an important theme in "Going Down Hill on a Bicycle, A Boy's Song"?

A True happiness lasts a lifetime.
(B) Joy is sweeter because it is short-lived.
C Hard work is its own reward.
D If you climb up, you must climb down.

Part B
Choose **three** pieces of evidence from the poem that **best** support the answer to Part A.

- [ ] "With lifted feet, hands still, / I am poised, and down the hill / Dart, with heedful mind" (lines 1–3)
- [ ] "Swifter and yet more swift, / Till the heart with a mighty lift / Makes the lungs laugh, the throat cry" (lines 5–7)
- [x] "Is this, is this your joy? / O bird, then I, though a boy / For a golden moment share / Your feathery life in air!" (lines 9–12)
- [ ] "Say, heart, is there aught like this / In a world that is full of bliss?" (lines 13–14)
- [ ] "'Tis more than skating, bound / Steel-shod to the level ground." (lines 15–16)
- [x] "Speed slackens now, I float / Awhile in my airy boat;" (lines 17–18)
- [x] "Alas, that the longest hill / Must end in a vale . . ." (lines 21–22)
- [x] "Who climbs with toil, wheresoe'er, / Shall find wings waiting there." (lines 23–24)

177

Teacher Notes

Answer Analysis

When students have completed the Interim Assessment, discuss correct and incorrect responses.

1 **Students should underline line 11,** "For a golden moment share." The word *golden* refers to the joyfulness and the word *moment* indicates that the joy only lasts for a limited time.

DOK 1 **RL.5.1**

2 **Part A**

The correct choice is B. The poet describes the fleeting pleasure of riding a bike down a hill. It lasts only for "a golden moment" until the boy reaches the bottom of the hill.

- **A** is incorrect because his happiness comes to an end.
- **C** is incorrect because the boy does not enjoy the effort of climbing the hill.
- **D** is incorrect because he rides or "flies" down, not climbs.

Part B

Students should check choices 3, 7, and 8 (lines 9–12, 17–18, and 21–22, respectively), which support the idea that joy is short-lived. Lines 9–12 describe the "golden moment" that the boy feels joy. Lines 17–18 show the gradual end of joy. Lines 21–22 show that every source of joy comes to an end.

DOK 2 **RL.5.2**

Assessment

3 **The correct choice is D.** The first two stanzas of the poem describe the speed of the downhill ride, using phrases such as "air goes by in a wind" and "Swifter and yet more swift." The speaker feels that the thrilling ride is like flying, and he calls out to a bird to share his joyous feeling.

- **A** is incorrect because the boy doesn't stop to think during the downhill ride.
- **B** is incorrect because Stanza 2 describes the speed and excitement of the ride.
- **C** does not mention the boy going down the hill.

***DOK 2* RL.5.2**

4 After students have completed the Interim Assessment, evaluate their responses to the short-response item using the **2-Point Writing Rubric** below.

Answers will vary but should correctly summarize the important details of the poem. See the sample response on the student book page.

You may wish to display or pass out copies of the reproducible **2-Point Writing Rubric** on page TR10. Have students use the rubric to individually assess their writing and revise as needed.

***DOK 2* RL.5.2**

3 Which sentence provides the **best** summary of the first and second stanzas of the poem?

- **A** A boy darts down a hill, stops to think, and talks to a bird along the way.
- **B** A boy looks down a steep hill, and his heart starts to race with excitement.
- **C** A boy lifts his feet and hands off his bicycle and feels the air whizzing by him.
- **(D)** A boy speeds so fast down a hill that he cries out to a bird that he, too, is flying.

4 **Short Response** Write a one-paragraph summary of the poem "Going Down Hill on a Bicycle, A Boy's Song." Use at least **three** details from the poem in your summary.

Sample Response: In this poem, the speaker describes the joy of a downhill bike ride, and compares the feelings invoked by the ride to the feeling of flying. The speaker feels as if, at least for a moment, he can fly like a bird, and he tells a bird about these feelings. The speaker describes how the feeling ends as the ride slows at the bottom of the hill, but then tells the reader that the feeling can be regained by climbing up the hill again.

2-Point Writing Rubric

All three criteria must be satisfied in order for a response to gain full points.

Points	Focus	Evidence	Organization
2	The response demonstrates comprehension and provides accurate analysis.	The response supports the analysis with adequate textual evidence.	Ideas are clear and follow a logical order.
1	The response demonstrates some comprehension and provides minimally accurate analysis.	The response supports the analysis with limited textual evidence.	Some ideas are unclear or out of order.
0	The response demonstrates no comprehension and provides inaccurate or no analysis.	The response provides little or no textual evidence.	Ideas are unclear or incomplete.

Read

Genre: Historical Fiction

Read the story. Then answer the questions that follow.

Throwing Fire

by Skyler Tegland, *Highlights*

1 *Who will throw his fire the farthest?* Nou wonders as he sits on the beach a short distance from the warrior circle. He watches the other warriors carve their names on their firebrands—dried sticks that they will set alight and throw from the mountain.

2 Nou keeps to himself, for he knows that the others laugh at him. *'Ukiki,* they call him—*little runt*—because they think that he is too small to be a warrior.

3 It is ancient times on the island of Kaua'i, when each river valley is a kingdom and every young man is a warrior. Tonight is the most important night of the year: it is the night of the fire-throwing ceremony.

4 When the sun sets, the warriors will climb swiftly to the top of Mount Makana, and from the highest point, they will hurl their firebrands out over the sea.

5 Far below, the king of Kaua'i will observe from his great canoe, watching the firebrands fly through the air and fall into the sea. He will judge which one has flown the farthest, then he will retrieve it from the water. At the feast, he will read the name from that stick and honor the winner.

6 A sudden gust of warm air sweeps across the beach, silencing the warriors' talk. The wind is rising, making the warriors anxious, for it is difficult to throw well in the wind.

Teacher Notes

7 Nou considers his own branch. It is smaller than most, and much lighter—almost weightless. He made it from papala, a very light wood, carving out the pith center to make it hollow. Now, he carves his name on it and waits for the ceremony to begin.

8 As the sun dips into the sea, the warriors leap to their feet and race to the sacred mountaintop as the villagers cheer. Nou tries to keep up, but the climb is steep and difficult in the growing darkness.

9 One by one, the warriors reach the summit, light their firebrands, and take a place in line. From the beach, the villagers can see a great line of fire along the top of Mount Makana. None of the warriors notice that Nou is missing.

10 The king watches from his canoe as the first firebrand is thrown. Up, up, into the air it soars, and a cheer rises from the beach. Then, slowly, the firebrand begins to fall, streaking a trail of smoke and sparks across the evening sky.

11 One by one, the flaming torches fly up in a tremendous arc, then fall hissing into the sea.

12 Soon there is no more fire on the mountain. The last of the firebrands has been thrown, and the warriors are descending.

13 Suddenly there is an outcry from the beach. Another spark of fire is seen on the mountain. Another firebrand floats slowly, magically upward. Up and up it climbs, much higher than the others. The villagers cheer, for they have never seen anything like it.

14 The firebrand floats up, then outward, far out over the sea, much farther than any warrior has ever thrown a firebrand. It seems to float in the air, and the villagers are amazed.

15 In his canoe, the king watches as this last firebrand soars overhead, buoyed by the wind. When it finally touches gently to the sea, he directs his men to paddle.

16 Once there, the king fishes the smoldering branch from the water. He notices its curious hollowness, and he smiles.

17 That night, as the warriors and villagers sit down to the feast, everyone wonders who threw the last firebrand.

18 The king stands up, holding the stick that he rescued from the water. Finally the king reads the name aloud: "Nou."

19 There is a pause at first, then laughter. The people think that the king is joking. "Nou?" some say. "The 'little runt'?" "How could he possibly throw so far?"

20 The king brings them to silence again with a wave of his hand.

21 "O my people," he begins, "strength is a wonderful quality for a warrior. Strength is very useful, but it is not the only thing he needs. Cleverness and intelligence guide strength. Tonight we honor one who was clever enough to make a friend of the wind instead of fighting it. Come forward, Nou, and sit by me."

22 As Nou rises to take his place beside the king, he notices that no one is laughing.

23 On that night, Nou earns a new nickname from the warriors. *Keakamai*, they call him—*the Clever One*.

Teacher Notes

Assessment

5 **Part A**

The correct choice is B. In the beginning of the story, Nou stays away from the other warriors because he fears they will tease him about his size.

- **A, C,** and **D** do not accurately reflect the events of the story.

Part B

The correct choice is B. This sentence, which tells Nou's nickname, shows that he is smaller than the other warriors.

- **A, C,** and **D** do not support the correct answer to Part A.

DOK 1 RL.5.3

6 After students have completed the Interim Assessment, evaluate their responses to the short-response item using the **2-Point Writing Rubric** below.

Answers will vary but should show that students understand the connection between Nou hollowing out his firebrand and the king finding a hollow firebrand. See the sample response on the student book page.

You may wish to display or pass out copies of the reproducible **2-Point Writing Rubric** on page TR10. Have students use the rubric to individually assess their writing and revise as needed.

DOK 2 RL.5.1

Think

5 This question has two parts. First, answer Part A. Then answer Part B.

Part A
How do the other warriors compare to Nou?

A The other warriors are sneakier than Nou.
(B) The other warriors are bigger than Nou.
C The other warriors are weaker than Nou.
D The other warriors are older than Nou.

Part B
Which sentence from the story **best** supports the answer to Part A?

A "He watches the other warriors carve their names on their firebrands—dried sticks that they will set alight and throw from the mountain."
(B) "*Ukiki*, they call him—*little runt*—because they think that he is too small to be a warrior."
C "The firebrand floats up, then outward, far out over the sea, much farther than any warrior has ever thrown a firebrand."
D "On that night, Nou earns a new nickname from the warriors. *Keakamai*, they call him—*the Clever One*."

6 **Short Response** What text evidence can readers use to infer that the last firebrand belongs to Nou, even before his name is called? Use at least **two** details from the story in your response.

Sample response: At the beginning of the story, Nou has carved out the center of his firebrand, making it hollow. Later, the king notices that the last firebrand is hollow. Readers can infer that Nou's firebrand was the only hollow one.

2-Point Writing Rubric

All three criteria must be satisfied in order for a response to gain full points.

Points	Focus	Evidence	Organization
2	The response demonstrates comprehension and provides accurate analysis.	The response supports the analysis with adequate textual evidence.	Ideas are clear and follow a logical order.
1	The response demonstrates some comprehension and provides minimally accurate analysis.	The response supports the analysis with limited textual evidence.	Some ideas are unclear or out of order.
0	The response demonstrates no comprehension and provides inaccurate or no analysis.	The response provides little or no textual evidence.	Ideas are unclear or incomplete.

7 Compare and contrast Nou with the other warriors. Select **one** word that describes Nou and **one** word that describes the other warriors. Write those words in the columns labeled "Description of Nou" and "Description of Other Warriors." Then complete the chart by writing **one** detail that provides evidence for **each** description.

Possible Descriptions	**Possible Supporting Details**
funny	The other warriors laugh at Nou.
kind	Nou makes his firebrand hollow.
proud	The other warriors throw before Nou.
smart	Nou does not sit with the other warriors.

Description of Nou	Supporting Evidence for Description of Nou	Description of Other Warriors	Supporting Evidence for Description of Other Warriors
smart	Nou makes his firebrand hollow.	proud	The other warriors laugh at Nou.

8 Read these sentences from "Throwing Fire."

> In his canoe, the king watches as this last firebrand soars overhead, <u>buoyed</u> by the wind. When it finally touches gently to the sea, he directs his men to paddle.

What does the word <u>buoyed</u> mean as it is used in the sentence?

A slowed

B touched

(C) carried

D marked

7 See the answers on the student book page.

***DOK 2* RL.5.3**

8 The correct choice is C. <u>Buoyed</u> means "carried" or "kept afloat."

- **A, B,** and **D** do not accurately reflect the word's meaning.

***DOK 2* RL.5.4**

Assessment

Write

Review Responses

9 After students have completed the Interim Assessment, evaluate their responses to the Extended Response using the **4-Point Writing Rubric** below.

Answers will vary but should show that students understand the warriors' and villagers' initial opinion was that Nou was too small to be a warrior, but after he wins the firebrand contest by hollowing out his firebrand, they come to respect his cleverness. See the sample response on the student book page.

DOK 3 **RL.5.3**

 **Write**

9 **Extended Response** The warriors and villagers change their opinion of Nou from the beginning of the story to the end of the story. What was their first opinion of him? What was their opinion at the end of the story? What happened to change their opinion?

In your answer, be sure to
- tell how the warriors and villagers felt about Nou at the beginning of the story
- explain what Nou did that changed their opinions of him
- tell how the warriors and villagers felt about him at the end of the story
- use details from the story in your answer

Check your writing for correct spelling, grammar, capitalization, and punctuation.

Sample Response: In the beginning of the story, the villagers do not respect Nou because he is small. They call him *Ukiki*, or "little runt," which indicates their disregard for him and their belief that he is too small to be a warrior. Nou does not agree with their view, and he works to prove them wrong. He knows that the winner of the firebrand competition will achieve honor, so he cleverly figures out a way to make his firebrand the lightest so that it would fly farther than all the others. Nou's firebrand outsoars all the others, and the king reads Nou's name from his firebrand aloud at the feast. The villagers are at first surprised that little Nou could possibly be the winner, and they think the king is joking when he reads Nou's name aloud. However, the king points out that Nou's cleverness outweighed the strength of the warriors. The villagers recognize Nou's cleverness, and they give him a new name. They now call him *Keakamai* or "the clever one," which indicates that they now respect him.

4-Point Writing Rubric

All three criteria must be satisfied in order for a response to gain full points.

Points	Focus	Evidence	Organization
4	The response demonstrates a full understanding of the prompt and provides accurate analysis.	The response supports the analysis with generous textual evidence.	Ideas are consistently presented in a purposeful and logical order.
3	The response demonstrates a good understanding of the prompt and provides mostly accurate analysis.	The response supports the analysis with adequate textual evidence.	Ideas are generally presented in a purposeful and logical order, although some ideas may be unclear or out of order.
2	The response demonstrates a general understanding of the prompt and provides some accurate analysis but includes inaccurate descriptions or explanations.	The response supports the analysis with limited textual evidence but does not reference the text explicitly.	Some ideas are presented in a purposeful and logical order, but others are unclear or out of order.
1	The response demonstrates a limited understanding of the prompt and provides limited analysis with significant inaccuracies.	The response may use textual evidence, but it does not support the analysis and does not reference the text explicitly.	Most ideas are not presented in a purposeful and logical order.
0	The response does not demonstrate understanding of the prompt.	Ideas are not supported with reference to textual evidence.	The response does not present ideas in a purposeful or logical order.

Review Unit Opener Self-Check

Ask students to complete the unit self-check on page 90 of the student book. Then have them discuss the items in the self-check with a partner. Encourage students to give each other examples from the lessons that show where they really began to understand the skill.

Finally, bring students together for a whole-class discussion. Ask them how knowing these skills have helped make them better readers. Remind them to use their Academic Talk words.

Unit 3
Craft and Structure in Informational Text

UNIT 3

Craft and Structure in Informational Text

Think about how you might arrange boards and bricks to build a model of a skyscraper. Now think about how you might arrange the boards and bricks differently to construct a model of a bridge. You likely pictured different **structures.** One is tall and narrow, and the other is short and wide. The two structures are different because they have different purposes.

Like builders, writers use building materials. Instead of using bricks and boards, authors of informational texts use details to **craft** what they want to say. And, like builders, they put these materials together in different ways for different reasons. A good reader can spot these different structures and explain why an author chose to use a given structure.

That's what you'll learn to do in this unit. You'll also learn to use context clues to determine the meanings of unfamiliar words and to analyze different points of view written about the same topic.

Self Check

Before starting this unit, check off the skills you know below. As you complete each lesson, see how many more skills you can check off!

I can:	Before this unit	After this unit
find the meanings of unfamiliar words and phrases in an informational text.	☐	☐
find similarities and differences between chronological text structures and problem-solution text structures.	☐	☐
find similarities and differences between cause-effect text structures and compare-contrast text structures.	☐	☐
compare and contrast multiple author accounts and points of view regarding the same topic.	☐	☐

186

page 192

page 198

page 202

page 206

page 218

page 238

page 245

At a Glance

- These two pages introduce students to the skills and strategies they will learn in this unit.
- The checklist allows them to see what skills they will be learning and take ownership of their progress.
- The visual table of contents gives a graphic preview of the passages in the unit.

Step by Step

- Explain to students that they are going to begin a new unit of lessons. Tell them that in all the lessons in this unit they will be learning about craft and structure in informational text.
- Have the class read together the introduction to the unit in their books. Invite and respond to comments and questions, if any.
- Then take a few minutes to have each student independently read through the list of skills.
- Ask students to consider each skill and check the box if it is a skill they think they already have. Tell students that they may have worked on similar skills in the past, but these skills go deeper than before.
- Engage students in a brief discussion about the skills. Invite students to comment on which ones they would most like to learn, or which ones seem similar or related to something they already know. Remind them that the goal is to be able to check off one skill at a time until they have them all checked.
- Invite students to look at the graphics and predict what the passages will be about.

Lesson 11
Unfamiliar Words

Standards Focus

Determine the meaning of general academic and domain-specific words and phrases in a text relevant to a Grade 5 topic or subject area. RI.5.4

Lesson Objectives

Reading

- Use context clues to help determine the meanings of unfamiliar words. RI.5.4
- Use domain-specific knowledge to determine the meanings of content- or subject-area words and phrases. RI.5.4

Writing

- Draw evidence from informational texts to support analysis and reflection. W.5.9b

Speaking and Listening

- Pose and respond to specific questions and contribute to discussions. SL.5.1c
- Review the key ideas expressed and draw conclusions. SL.5.1d

Language

- Use context as a clue to the meaning of a word or phrase. L.5.4a
- Acquire and use academic and domain-specific words and phrases. L.5.6

Additional Practice: **RI.5.1, RI.5.2, RI.5.3, RI.5.8**

Academic Talk

See **Glossary of Terms**, pp. TR2–TR9

- academic vocabulary
- topic
- context clues
- domain-specific vocabulary
- subject area

Learning Progression

Grade 4	Grade 5	Grade 6
Students use context clues and/or background knowledge to determine the meaning of general academic and domain-specific words or phrases in a text relevant to Grade 4 subjects.	Building on Grade 4, students determine the meaning of general academic and domain-specific words or phrases in a text relevant to Grade 5 subjects. The complexity of the text students are reading increases from the previous grade.	Grade 6 increases in complexity by requiring students to determine figurative and connotative meanings in addition to denotative meanings based on the context.

Lesson Text Selections

Modeled and Guided Instruction

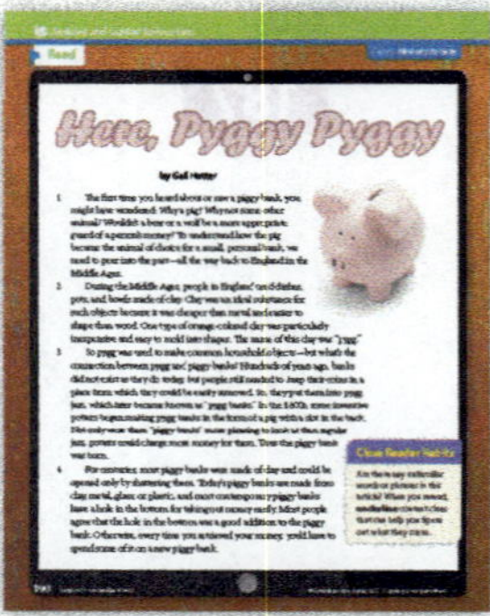
Here, Pyggy Pyggy

Here Pyggy, Pyggy
by Gail Hutter
Genre: History Article

Guided Practice

From Furs to Five-Dollar Bills

From Furs to Five-Dollar Bills
by Jason Liu
Genre: History Article

Independent Practice

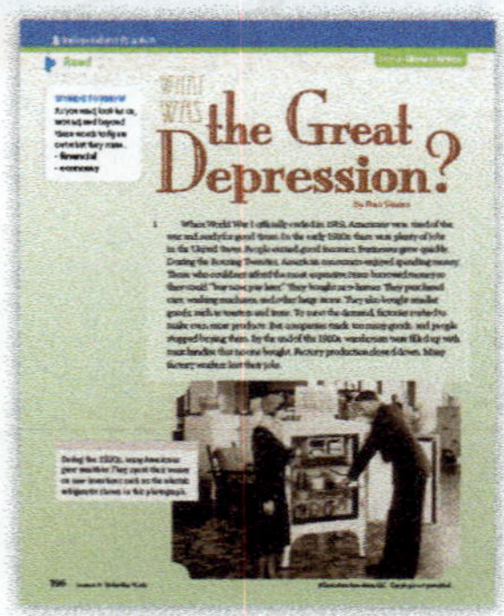
What Was the Great Depression?

What Was the Great Depression?
by Fran Severs
Genre: History Article

Lesson Pacing Guide

Whole Class Instruction *30–45 minutes per day*

Day 1

Teacher-Toolbox.com **Interactive Tutorial**
Determine Word Meanings Using Context Clues—Level E
20 min (optional)

Introduction pp. 188–189
- **Read** **Unfamiliar Words** *10 min*
- **Think** *10 min*
  Graphic Organizer: Four-Column Chart
- **Talk** *5 min*
  Quick Write (TRB) *5 min*

Day 2

Modeled and Guided Instruction pp. 190–191, 194
- **Read** **Here, Pyggy Pyggy** *10 min*
- **Think** *10 min*
  Graphic Organizer: Four-Column Chart
- **Talk** *5 min*
- **Write** Short Response *10 min*

Day 3

Guided Practice pp. 192–193, 195
- **Read** **From Furs to Five-Dollar Bills** *10 min*
- **Think** *10 min*
- **Talk** *5 min*
- **Write** Short Response *10 min*

Day 4

Independent Practice pp. 196–201
- **Read** **What Was the Great Depression?** *15 min*
- **Think** *10 min*
- **Write** Short Response *10 min*

Day 5

Independent Practice pp. 196–201
- *Review* Answer Analysis (TRB) *10 min*
- *Review* Response Analysis (TRB) *10 min*
- *Assign and Discuss* Learning Target *10 min*

Language Handbook
Lesson 4 Perfect Verb Tenses, pp. 444–445
20 min (optional)

Ready Writing Connection

During *Ready Reading* Days 1–5, use:
Lesson 3 Writing a Narrative: Legend

- **Step 1 Study a Mentor Text**
- **Step 2 Unpack Your Assignment**
- **Review the Research Path**
- **Read Source Text**
- **Step 3 Find Text Evidence**
- **Reread Source Text**

See *Ready Writing TRB*, p. 62a for complete lesson plan.

Small Group Differentiation
Teacher-Toolbox.com

Reteach

***Ready Reading* Prerequisite Lesson**
- **Grade 4** Lesson 13 Unfamiliar Words

Teacher-led Activities

Tools for Instruction
- Teach New Word Meanings
- Use Context to Find Word Meaning

Personalized Learning
i-Ready.com

Independent

i-Ready Close Reading Lessons
- **Grade 4** Unfamiliar Words
- **Grade 5** Unfamiliar Words

Introduction

Get Started

- Explain to students that in this lesson they will read several history articles about money and use strategies to figure out the meanings of words they don't know.
- Ask students to explain what they do when they come across an unfamiliar word in an informational text, such as an online article or a science textbook.
- Remind students that they can look at other words in the sentence or surrounding sentences for clues. Explain:

  Suppose you read this sentence: Mike's dad gave him a *loan* to buy the video game, so Mike agreed to do extra chores until it was paid off. The phrases "to buy" and "paid off" are clues that *loan* means "borrowed money." To confirm what I think the definition is, I'll look it up in a dictionary.
- Focus students' attention on the Learning Target. Read it aloud to set the purpose for the lesson.
- Display the Academic Talk words and phrases. Tell students to listen for these terms and their meanings as you work through the lesson together. Use the Academic Talk Routine on pp. A48–A49.

English Language Learners

Genre Focus

Read

- Read aloud the Read section as students follow along. Restate to reinforce:

  As you continue to read and learn about new topics in different subject areas, you will come across unfamiliar words. Some of these are general words called academic vocabulary. You will also come across domain-specific vocabulary, or words used in particular subjects, such as history or science.
- Direct students' attention to the poster. Have them read the text and underline any words they might not know.

Introduction

RI.5.4 Determine the meaning of general academic and domain-specific words and phrases in a text relevant to a grade 5 topic or subject area.

Lesson 11
Unfamiliar Words

Figuring out the meanings of unfamiliar words will help you better understand the texts you read and discuss in school.

Read When you read, you probably come across words you do not know. Some of these unfamiliar words may be **academic vocabulary**, or general words that are found in a variety of subjects you study in school. Others may be **domain-specific vocabulary**, or words used in a particular **subject area**, or field of study. For example, economics is a subject area, and money is one **topic** in this subject area.

Read the poster below. Underline any words you might not know.

The Westfield Animal Shelter Needs Your Help!

We have outgrown our space here. Can you help us build a new shelter to protect our pets?

Please make a donation to the Westfield Animal Shelter today. Even a small amount of money will help. Once we raise $10,000, we'll be able to begin construction.

We at the shelter will be grateful for your generosity in giving. The animals will thank you for your kindness. Remember that each act of benevolence counts!

188

English Language Learners

Develop Language

- **Concept Vocabulary** Point out that students study many subject areas each day. Say: "Every morning, we begin with science. Next we do math." Have students name the rest of the schedule, and write each subject on the board. Label the group *subject area* and *domain.*Explain that these words are synonyms.
- Draw a line from one subject and ask: "What did we learn about in math today?" Record students' answers, and label this group *topic.* Explain that a *topic* is one small part of a whole subject area. Brainstorm examples with students to clarify the meaning.

Genre Focus

History Article

Articles provide information about a topic. History articles offer information and insight into people, places, or events from the past.

An article is structured around a particular topic. The opening usually engages the reader's attention, and the body gives facts, examples, reasons, or descriptions that answer some or all of the questions *who, what, when, where, why,* and *how.*

History articles often include photographs and captions, as well as headings and subheadings, that tell the reader what is coming next.

Think Use the chart below to help determine the meanings of unfamiliar words. The word's context has been provided for you. In the "Possible Meaning" column, write what you think the word means. Then go back to the text, find **context clues** that tell you about the word's meaning, and write them in the "Clues" column.

Unknown Word	Context	Possible Meaning	Clues
Shelter	". . . build a new shelter to protect our pets?"	a place that gives protection	"outgrown our space," "protect our pets"
Donation	"Please make a donation . . ."	something you give to help	"Even a small amount of money will help."
Benevolence	". . . each act of benevolence counts!"	generosity	"generosity in giving," "thank you for your kindness."

Talk Share your chart with a partner.

- Did you come up with similar meanings?
- Did you find the same clues to the words' meanings?
- Are there any school subjects for which figuring out words is especially important? If so, which subjects?

Academic Talk

Use these words and phrases to talk about the text.

- academic vocabulary
- domain-specific vocabulary
- topic
- subject area
- context clues

189

Monitor Understanding

If... students struggle to identify context clues for unknown words, **then...** write the following example on the board: Jimmy told his friend Nasim that she *resembles* her mother because they have the same color eyes and hair.

- **What clues come before *resembles*?** *(none)*
- **What part of speech is *resembles*?** *(verb)*
- **What clues come after *resembles*?** *(Nasim and her mother have the same color eyes and hair.)*
- **What does *resembles* mean?** *("looks like")*

Remind students that looking before, at, and after the word is a helpful system for identifying context clues.

Think

- Have students read aloud the Think section. Explain that the chart will help them organize their thinking.
- Have partners complete the chart. Remind students to think about how each word is used in the sentence, including its part of speech.
- As students work, circulate and provide assistance as needed.
- Ask volunteers to share what they wrote in their charts.
- Make certain students understand that clues to a word's meaning might be in a nearby word or perhaps even in a different sentence.

Talk

- Read aloud the Talk prompts.
- Have partners discuss the possible meanings of the unfamiliar words along with the clues they used to determine each word's meaning.
- Ask volunteers to share their ideas.

Quick Write Have students write a response to the following prompt:

Think about a new or unusual word you read recently on a poster, advertisement, or website. Identify the word and explain what it means. Describe how you figured out the meaning.

Ask students to share their responses.

Wrap Up

- Invite students to share what they've learned so far. Encourage them to use the Academic Talk words and phrases in their explanations.
- Explain to students that when they read historical texts, they can use context clues to learn new vocabulary that will help them better understand the topics they are reading about.

In the next section, we'll read a history article and use context clues to understand the meanings of words and phrases. Finding the meaning of words and phrases will help you expand your vocabulary and better understand what you read.

Monitor Understanding

Get Started

Today you will read a history article related to money. First, you'll read to understand what the text is about. Then you'll read to analyze, using context clues to figure out the meanings of words you don't know.

Read

- Read aloud the title of the article and point out the unexpected spelling of *piggy.* Guide students to predict the topic of the article.
- Have students read the article independently. Tell them to place a check mark above any confusing words and phrases as they read. Remind students that they can look for nearby definitions or examples of the word, words that mean something similar to the unknown word, or words that mean the opposite of the unknown word. Use the Word Learning Routine on pp. A50–A51.
- When students have finished reading, use the questions below to check understanding. Encourage students to identify details in the text that support their answers.

  What is a piggy bank? *(a small container in the shape of a pig that holds coins)*

  How did piggy banks get their name? *(The first ones were made from a kind of clay called "pygg.")*

  Why was the hole in the bottom of a piggy bank a popular idea? *(People could get their money out without breaking the piggy bank.)*

 **English Language Learners**

● **Word Learning Strategy**

Explore

- Read aloud the Explore question at the top of p. 191 to set the purpose for the second read.
- Have students read aloud the Close Reader Habit on p. 190.

> **TIP** Tell students that some context clues use descriptive words to tell what something is like, and others clarify a word's meaning by telling what it is not.

Modeled and Guided Instruction

Read

Genre: History Article

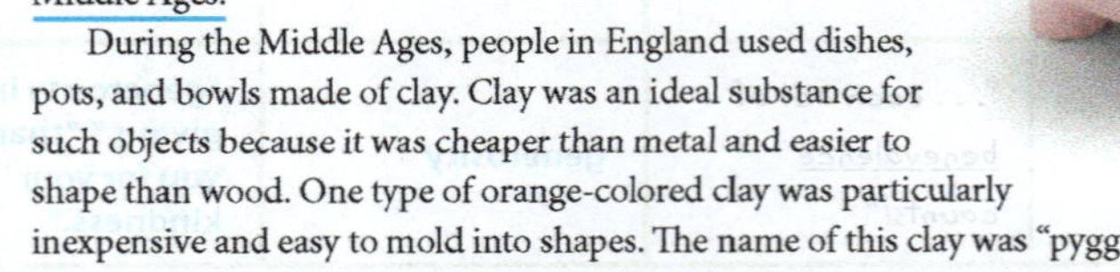

Here, Pyggy Pyggy

by Gail Hutter

1 The first time you heard about or saw a piggy bank, you might have wondered: Why a pig? Why not some other animal? Wouldn't a bear or a wolf be a more appropriate guard of a person's money? To understand how the pig became the animal of choice for a small, personal bank, we need to peer into the past—all the way back to England in the Middle Ages.

2 During the Middle Ages, people in England used dishes, pots, and bowls made of clay. Clay was an ideal substance for such objects because it was cheaper than metal and easier to shape than wood. One type of orange-colored clay was particularly inexpensive and easy to mold into shapes. The name of this clay was "pygg."

3 So pygg was used to make common household objects—but what's the connection between pygg and piggy banks? Hundreds of years ago, banks did not exist as they do today, but people still needed to keep their coins in a place from which they could be easily removed. So, they put them into pygg jars, which later became known as "pygg banks." In the 1800s, some inventive potters began making pygg banks in the form of a pig with a slot in the back. Not only were these "piggy banks" more pleasing to look at than regular jars, potters could charge more money for them. Thus the piggy bank was born.

4 For centuries, most piggy banks were made of clay and could be opened only by shattering them. Today's piggy banks are made from clay, metal, glass, or plastic, and most contemporary piggy banks have a hole in the bottom for taking out money easily. Most people agree that the hole in the bottom was a good addition to the piggy bank. Otherwise, every time you retrieved your money, you'd have to spend some of it on a new piggy bank.

Close Reader Habits

Are there any unfamiliar words or phrases in this article? When you reread, **underline** context clues that can help you figure out what they mean.

190

English Language Learners

Develop Language

- **Homophones** Write *pig* and *pygg* on a white board. Read the words aloud and have students repeat after you. Ask students to tell how the words are alike. *(They have the same sound.)* Explain that the words are homophones, or words that have the same sound but are spelled differently and have different meanings.
- Bring in a real example or provide images of a piggy bank. Have students describe what they see. Where are the coins deposited? How can the saver get the coins out?
- If possible, hold up a ball of modeling clay. Explain that *pygg* is the name of a kind of clay used in the Middle Ages to make dishes, bowls, and jars.

● Word Learning Strategy

Use Context Clues

- Reread paragraph 4. Point to the word *shattering* in the first sentence.
  - **What does *shattering* mean? What clues help you figure out its meaning?**
- Help students identify the word *only* in the same sentence, and have them think about the only way to open something made of clay. Then reread the rest of the paragraph, with details including "the hole . . . was a good addition" and "Otherwise . . . you'd have to spend [money] on a new piggy bank."
- Together determine that *shattering* means "destroying."

L.5.4a

Explore **What context clues can help you understand unfamiliar words and phrases in the text?**

Think

1 Complete the chart below by telling the context of each unfamiliar word or phrase, its possible meaning, and the clues that led you to that definition.

Look for context clues in the same sentence or nearby sentences.

Unfamiliar Word or Phrase	Context	Possible Meaning	Clues
Peer into the past (paragraph 1)	"... we need to peer into the past...."	look at what happened before	"all the way back to England in the Middle Ages."
Inventive potters (paragraph 3)	"... some inventive potters began making pygg banks...."	creative workers who made pots	"began making pygg banks in the form of a pig with a slot," "pleasing to look at"
Contemporary (paragraph 4)	"... most contemporary piggy banks...."	modern, or happening now	"Today's piggy banks"
Retrieved (paragraph 4)	"... every time you retrieved your money...."	took out	"taking out money"

Talk

2 Use context clues to determine why clay was an "ideal substance" for making certain objects.

Write

3 **Short Response** Define the phrase ideal substance. Support your definition with context clues from the passage. Use the space provided on page 194 to write your answer.

HINT First, define *ideal substance*. Then explain how clay fit that definition.

Think Aloud

- The first unfamiliar phrase is "Peer into the past." I'm going to find the phrase in the article and use context clues to figure out what it means.
- I will scan until I find the phrase. I see it in the last sentence of paragraph 1. I'll write under *Context* the words in the text around *peer:* "... we need to peer into the past...."
- Next, I need to figure out what the phrase might mean. I'm going to try replacing the word *peer* with a synonym that makes sense. When I think about the past, I am looking back at what happened. I think *peer* might mean "look." In the *Possible Meaning* column, I'll write "look at what happened before."
- Now I need to look for clues to the meaning. I see "all the way back to England in the Middle Ages." This supports my possible meaning, that *peer into the past* means "look closely at what happened in the past." I'll add "all the way back to England in the Middle Ages" in the column under *Clues*.

Think

- Read aloud the Think section. Explain to students that you will model how to find text evidence to fill in part of the chart. Use the **Think Aloud** below to guide your modeling.
- Revisit the Explore question. Guide students to see that they need to look for more details, using the Close Reader Habit.
- Encourage students to work with a partner to continue rereading the passage and complete the chart. Remind them that the Buddy Tip will help them look for context clues.
- Ask volunteers to share their completed charts.
- Guide students to see that there are many kinds of context clues, and students must be active readers to figure out a word's meaning.

Talk

- Read aloud the Talk prompt.
- Have partners respond to the prompt. Use the Talk Routine on pp. A52–A53.
- Circulate to check that students are discussing and writing about clues that tell what makes clay an ideal substance.

Write

- Ask a volunteer to read aloud the Write prompt.
- Invite a few students to tell what the prompt is asking them to do.
- Make sure students understand that "ideal substance" is a phrase, and they should define both words together as one term.
- Have students turn to p. 194 to write their response.
- Use Review Responses on p. 194 to assess students' writing.

Wrap Up

- Ask students to recall the Learning Target. Have them explain how figuring out the meanings of unfamiliar words and phrases helped them better understand the history article.

Guided Practice

Get Started

Today you will read another history article about money. First you will read to understand what the article is about. Then you will reread with a partner to analyze, using word learning strategies to determine the meanings of unfamiliar words.

Read

- Read aloud the title of the passage. Have students look closely at the images and read the captions. Encourage them to predict what the article is about.
- **Read to Understand** Have students read the article independently. Tell them to place a check mark above any confusing words and phrases. Challenge them to use context clues to figure out the meanings of these words. Use the Word Learning Routine on pp. A50–A51.
- When students have finished reading, use the questions below to check understanding. Encourage students to identify details in the text that support their answers.

  What is commodity money? *(a product or raw material used as payment)*

  Who were the first people to use coins and paper money? *(the Chinese)*

  Why did the Chinese stop using paper money for a long time? *(They printed too much and it lost its value.)*

  What is the article mostly about? *(It is about how goods were traded as payment before coins and paper money were used.)*

ELL English Language Learners

● Word Learning Strategy

- **Read to Analyze** Read aloud the Close Reader Habit on p. 192 to set the purpose for the second read. Then have students reread the article with a partner and discuss any questions they might have.

Guided Practice

Read

Genre: History Article

From Furs to Five-Dollar Bills

by Jason Liu

1 Imagine paying for new sneakers with a handful of shells. In ancient times, people around the world paid for goods with commodity money. A commodity is a product or raw material offered as payment for another thing. Cows, sheep, or other kinds of animals were bartered for what a person wanted. Furs, beads, grain, giant stones, or salt were also exchanged.

2 Gradually, ancient peoples stopped using cattle and crops as money. Around 1000 B.C.E., the Chinese began to exchange metal tools for what they needed. They also used copper and bronze coins. By 700 B.C.E., the first silver and gold coins were produced in Lydia (what is now Turkey). These coins were stamped with images of different gods or important rulers.

3 Paper money developed in China around 800 C.E. Paper was light and easy to carry. But the Chinese printed too much paper money, and it lost its value. In 1455, the Chinese stopped using paper money for several hundred years. Meanwhile, Europeans only began using paper money in the 1600s.

4 After the American Revolution, the Continental Congress established a national currency based on the dollar in 1785. The first American coins were minted in 1793. These copper cents were produced by hand. Nearly seventy years later, the U.S. government began to issue paper money for the first time in 1861. Since then, the appearance of American coins and bills has changed. For example, today's paper money in the United States has a new design every seven to ten years.

In China, knife money was used from 600 to 200 B.C.E.

This is one of the earliest American silver dollars ever minted.

Close Reader Habits

How can you determine the meaning of *minted* in paragraph 4? Reread the text. **Underline** the sentence that gives a context clue.

192

ELL English Language Learners

Develop Language

- **Word Parts** Point to the word *handful* in paragraph 1. Have students say the word aloud. Then break the word into parts: *hand* | *ful*.
- Have students identify the familiar word *hand*. Explain that the suffix *-ful* means "full of."

  How does the suffix *-ful* change the meaning of *hand*? *(It becomes a word that means something that "fills a hand.")*

  How much do you think a *handful* is? *(as many as you can hold in your hand)*

- Have students reread the sentence with this meaning in mind and ask themselves: "Does this make sense?"

● Word Learning Strategy

Use Context Clues

- Point to the words *exchanged / exchange* in paragraphs 1 and 2. Explain that in addition to looking at words and phrases around an unfamiliar word, students should also evaluate the main idea of a paragraph to figure out the context for the word's meaning.
- Reread paragraph 1 aloud. Ask: "What is the main idea of this paragraph? *(how people traded animals or materials, instead of money, to pay for things)* Then look closely at the way *exchanged* is used in the paragraph. Guide students to see that *exchanged* and *bartered* are synonyms, and both describe trading goods as currency.
- Work with students to define *exchange* as "giving and receiving something of equal value."

L.5.4a

Think Use what you learned from reading the text to answer the following questions.

1 This question has two parts. Answer Part A. Then answer Part B.

Part A
What is the meaning of the word currency as it is used in paragraph 4?

A goods used in trade
B an idea accepted by many people
C something that is up-to-date
(D) the money used in a country

Part B
Which phrase from the passage helps the reader understand the meaning of currency?

(A) "based on the dollar"
B "produced by hand"
C "lost its value"
D "a new design"

A context clue may give a definition, an explanation, or an example. Sometimes an author will include a word with a similar meaning. Other times, the clue may be a word with an opposite meaning.

2 Underline the word in the paragraph below that means "traded or exchanged one thing for another."

A commodity is a product or raw material offered as payment for another thing. Cows, sheep, or other kinds of animals were bartered for what a person wanted. Furs, beads, grain, giant stones, or salt were also exchanged.

Talk

3 Discuss the meaning of minted as it is used in paragraph 4 of the text.

Write

4 **Short Response** Define the word minted. Then describe what words or phrases helped you figure out the meaning of minted. Use the space provided on page 195 to write your answer.

HINT Use quotes from the passage to show what words or phrases help you define *minted*.

193

Integrating Standards

Use the following question to further students' understanding of the article.

- **What might have inspired Americans to put the faces of presidents and statesmen on U.S. currency?** *(In 700 B.C.E., silver and gold coins in Lydia were stamped with images of gods and rulers.)*
  DOK 2 RI.5.3
- **Compare the text structure of "Here, Pyggy Pyggy" with "From Furs to Five-Dollar Bills."** *(Both texts are structured in chronological order because, as history articles, they explain the origin and development of something we use today.)*
  DOK 2 RI.5.1

Monitor Understanding

If... students have difficulty finding context clues to answer item 1,

then... use a four-column chart like the one on p. 189. Work with students to fill in the columns. Together, find the sentence with *currency* in paragraph 4 and write the context in the second column. Then have students explain what they think *currency* means, prompting as necessary with such questions as, "What was the currency based on in 1785?" Then have them quote the exact words and phrases that give clues.

Think

- Have students work with a partner to complete items 1 and 2.

TIP Guide students to look for phrases that indicate a definition, synonym, or antonym for an unfamiliar word.

Answer Analysis

When students have finished, discuss correct and incorrect responses.

1 **Part A**
The correct choice is D. In the sentence, *national* is used to describe "currency," and choice D refers to "in a country."

- **A** is not the meaning intended in paragraph 4. **B** and **C** relate to other meanings of the word, but neither meaning is supported by evidence in the text.

Part B
The correct choice is A. Here *currency* means "the money used in a country."

- **B, C,** and **D** are not context clues that help with the meaning of *currency*.

DOK 2

2 **Check that students underlined *bartered*.**
DOK 1

Monitor Understanding

Integrating Standards

Talk

- Have partners discuss the prompt. Emphasize that students should support their ideas with text details.

Write

- See p. 195 for instructional guidance.

Wrap Up

- Ask students to recall the Learning Target. Have them explain how using context clues to figure out the meaning of unfamiliar words helped them better understand this history article.

Modeled and Guided Instruction

Write

- Remember to use the Response–Writing Routine on pp. A54–A55.

Review Responses

After students complete the writing activity, help them evaluate their responses.

3 Responses may vary but should define "ideal substance" as a perfect material for that purpose. Students should support their definition with at least one context clue. See the sample response on the student book page. ***DOK 2***

Write **Use the space below to write your answer to the question on page 191.**

Here, Pyggy Pyggy

HINT First, define *ideal substance*. Then explain how clay fit that definition.

3 **Short Response** Define the phrase ideal substance. Support your definition with context clues from the passage.

Sample response: An "ideal substance" is a material that is perfect for a particular purpose. For example, in the Middle Ages, clay was an "ideal substance" for making dishes, pots, and bowls because it was "cheaper than metal and easier to shape than wood." In other words, clay was an "ideal substance" because it was the best material available for a specific purpose.

Scaffolding Support for Reluctant Writers

If students are having a difficult time getting started, use the strategies below. Work individually with struggling students, or have students work with partners.

- Circle the verbs in the prompt that tell you what to do, such as *describe, explain,* or *compare.*
- Underline words and phrases in the prompt that show what information you need to provide in your response, such as *causes, reasons,* or *character traits.*
- Talk about the details from the text that you will include in your response.
- Explain aloud how you will respond to the prompt.

Write Use the space below to write your answer to the question on page 193.

From Furs to Five-Dollar Bills

HINT Use quotes from the passage to show what words or phrases help you define *minted*.

4 **Short Response** Define the word minted. Then describe what words or phrases helped you figure out the meaning of minted.

Sample response: The word "minted" means "made into coins." The word "coins" is one clue to the meaning of "minted." Another clue is the phrase "copper cents were produced by hand."

Check Your Writing

- ☐ Did you read the prompt carefully?
- ☐ Did you put the prompt in your own words?
- ☐ Did you use the best evidence from the text to support your ideas?
- ☐ Are your ideas clearly organized?
- ☐ Did you write in clear and complete sentences?
- ☐ Did you check your spelling and punctuation?

Teacher Notes

Write

- Ask a volunteer to read aloud the Write prompt.
- Invite students to tell what the prompt is asking them to do. Make sure they understand that their responses must include a definition *and* the words or phrases that helped them figure it out.
- Call attention to the HINT.
- Remember to use the Response–Writing Routine on pp. A54–A55.

Review Responses

After students complete the writing activity, help them evaluate their responses.

4 Responses may vary but should define *minted* and identify clues to its meaning, such as "made into coins" and "copper cents produced by hand." See the sample response on the student book page.
DOK 2

Independent Practice

Get Started

Today you are going to read a history article about a time called the Great Depression. You will use word learning strategies to figure out the meanings of words and phrases you do not know.

- Ask a volunteer to explain how using word learning strategies can help readers better understand what they are reading. Encourage students to use the Academic Talk words and phrases in their response.

 **English Language Learners**

Read

You are going to read the history article independently and use what you have learned to think and write about the text. As you read, remember to use context clues to figure out the meanings of unfamiliar words.

- Read aloud the title of the article and then encourage students to preview the text, paying close attention to the photographs and captions.
- Call attention to the Words to Know in the upper left of p. 196.
- If students need support in reading the passage, you may wish to use the Monitor Understanding suggestions.
- When students have finished, have them complete the Think and Write sections.

● **Monitor Understanding**

Read

Genre: History Article

WORDS TO KNOW
As you read, look inside, around, and beyond these words to figure out what they mean.
- **financial**
- **economy**

What Was the Great Depression?

by Fran Severs

1 When World War I officially ended in 1919, Americans were tired of the war and ready for good times. In the early 1920s, there were plenty of jobs in the United States. People earned good incomes. Businesses grew quickly. During the Roaring Twenties, American consumers enjoyed spending money. Those who could not afford the most expensive items borrowed money so they could "buy now, pay later." They bought new homes. They purchased cars, washing machines, and other large items. They also bought smaller goods, such as toasters and irons. To meet the demand, factories rushed to make even more products. But companies made too many goods, and people stopped buying them. By the end of the 1920s, warehouses were filled up with merchandise that no one bought. Factory production slowed down. Many factory workers lost their jobs.

During the 1920s, many Americans grew wealthier. They spent their money on new inventions such as the electric refrigerator shown in this photograph.

 **English Language Learners**

Build Meaning

Concept Vocabulary Use word webs to help students grasp the volume of concept vocabulary in this article.

- Create a cluster of the words *items, goods, merchandise,* and *products.* Explain that these words are synonyms that are used to talk about making, buying, and selling things.
- Create another cluster of the words *income, jobs, employment,* and *economy.* Explain that these words are not synonyms, but they are related. For example, when the economy is strong, there are more chances for employment, or jobs; therefore, more citizens have income.
- Continue creating additional clusters such as *rent, mortgage, home, borrow, loan.* As you create each cluster, encourage students to demonstrate understanding by restating ideas in their own words.

2 At the same time, many Americans decided to invest money in the stock market. They hoped to get rich quickly. The stock market is a place where shares of stock in different companies are bought and sold. People hope to make a high return by buying stock at a low price and selling it at a higher price. From June through September 1929, the prices of stocks soared. Then prices began to dip slightly. Nervous investors began selling millions of stock shares for less than the purchase price, losing billions of dollars. On October 31, 1929, the stock market crashed when stock prices dropped sharply. The crash caused panic. People took their money out of banks, and banks were forced to close. More than 600 banks failed in 1929.

3 The stock market crash led to a financial crisis called the Great Depression. A depression is a serious slowdown in the economy that causes people to lose their jobs and businesses to fail. At the start of the Great Depression, about 1.5 million Americans were out of work. By 1933, about 13 million Americans had lost their jobs. To earn money, jobless people sold apples, pencils, and other items on the streets. They shined shoes or washed and mended clothing for others. They sold their personal belongings. Some were forced to beg for money.

4 Without an income, thousands of jobless Americans lost their homes because they did not have the money to pay rent. If they had borrowed money to buy a house, they could not pay their loans, so the bank took their homes. People were forced to live with friends or family members. If necessary, they stayed in churches or rooming houses. Sometimes, the homeless built shacks from old crates and scrap metal. These temporary homes lacked electricity or running water.

During the Great Depression, many Americans lost not just their jobs but also their homes. For shelter, these men and women built shacks on the outskirts of cities.

Monitor Understanding

If... students struggle to read and understand the passage,
then... use these scaffolding suggestions:

Question the Text Preview the text by asking the following questions:

- **Based on the title and photographs, what do you predict the article will be about?**
- **What questions do you have about the text?**

Vocabulary Support Define words that may interfere with comprehension, such as *income*, *stock*, *economy*, and *consumers*.

Read Aloud Read aloud the text with students. You could also have students chorally read the text in a small group.

Check Understanding Use the questions below to check understanding. Encourage students to cite details in the text that support their answers.

- **Why did people stop buying things in the late 1920s?** *(Companies had made too many products.)*
- **How did World War II help the U.S. economy?** *(War supplies were needed and businesses hired more people.)*
- **What is the article mostly about?** *(the Great Depression and how it affected the lives of many people)*

Independent Practice

Integrating Standards

After students have read the article, use these questions to discuss the article with them.

- **Explain the cause-and-effect relationship between factory production in the late 1920s and the Great Depression.**

  (Because factories had produced too many goods, people didn't need any more things. Factories stopped producing, and as a result, factory workers lost their jobs. When people lost jobs, they often lost their homes. This chain of events was one reason for the Great Depression.)

  DOK 2 **RI.5.3**

- **What evidence does the author provide to support the idea that the Great Depression was a hard time for people?**

  (The author wrote that millions of people drifted around to find work, food, and shelter. They stood in lines for free food provided by charity.)

  DOK 3 **RI.5.8**

- **Cite evidence to demonstrate how President Franklin D. Roosevelt helped to improve the struggling economy.**

  (President Roosevelt came up with a plan called the New Deal. It helped fix the nation's money problems through government laws that "changed banking systems, provided the needy with aid, and created new jobs.")

  DOK 3 **RI.5.1**

- **What are two main ideas of this article? How is each main idea supported by details?**

  (Students may identify one main idea as the causes of the Great Depression. Details include factories making more goods than people bought, workers losing jobs, and the stock market crash. Students may also talk about the main idea of how Roosevelt's New Deal helped the country's economy recover. Details include changing banking systems, providing aid, and creating new jobs.)

  DOK 2 **RI.5.2**

● **Theme Connection**

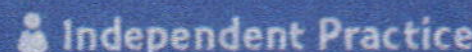

In some cities, long lines of people waiting for food were a common sight during the Great Depression. Charities gave bread and soup to people who could not pay to feed themselves.

5 About two million homeless men, women, and children drifted around the country. They broke the law by hitching free rides on trains. They rode from place to place looking for work, food, and shelter. Millions stood in lines for free bread or soup that charity groups provided. In 1931, charity groups in New York City served about 85,000 free meals every day.

6 Under President Franklin D. Roosevelt, America's economy slowly improved. Roosevelt's plan to fix the nation's money problems was called the New Deal. To improve the situation, the government passed laws that changed banking systems, provided the needy with aid, and created new jobs. In 1933, about 25 percent of Americans were jobless. By 1937, the unemployment rate had fallen to about 14 percent. Unfortunately, nearly 8 million Americans still did not have jobs.

7 The Great Depression lasted for more than ten years. In 1941, the United States entered World War II. Factories started making war supplies, such as airplanes, tanks, and ships. As the need for war supplies increased, businesses hired more and more people. America's hard times finally came to an end.

198

● Theme Connection

- Remind students that the theme of this lesson is Money.
- Display a three-column chart on the board. Label each column with a passage title.
- Ask students to recall important facts and ideas they learned from each passage. List their responses in the appropriate column.
- Ask students to determine how all of the passages relate to the theme of money.

Think Use what you learned from reading the article to answer the following questions.

1 This question has two parts. First, answer Part A. Then answer Part B.

Part A
Read this sentence from paragraph 1.

By the end of the 1920s, warehouses were filled up with merchandise that no one bought.

What does the word merchandise mean as it is used in this sentence?

- (A) goods
- B large items
- C shares of stock
- D jobs

Part B
Which detail from paragraph 1 **best** supports the answer to Part A?

- A "... that no one bought ..."
- (B) "... even more products ..."
- C "... factory production slowed ..."
- D "... lost their jobs ..."

2 The author uses a word that means "a time of intense difficulty, trouble, or danger." Underline a word in the paragraph below that **best** represents that idea.

The stock market crash led to a financial crisis called the Great Depression. A depression is a serious slowdown in the economy that causes people to lose their jobs and businesses to fail. At the start of the Great Depression, about 1.5 million Americans were out of work. By 1933, about 13 million Americans had lost their jobs. To earn money, jobless people sold apples, pencils, and other items on the streets. They shined shoes or washed and mended clothing for others. They sold their personal belongings. Some were forced to beg for money.

● **Monitor Understanding**

If... students struggle to complete the items,

then... you may wish to use the following suggestions:

Read Aloud Activities

- As you read, have students note any unfamiliar words or phrases. Clarify any misunderstandings.
- Discuss each item with students to make certain they understand the expectation.

Reread the Text

- Have students complete a four-column chart with the following headings: *Unfamiliar Word or Phrase, Context, Possible Meaning*, and *Clues*.
- Have partners summarize the text.

Think

- Use the Monitor Understanding suggestions to support students in completing items 1–4.

● **Monitor Understanding**

Answer Analysis

When students have finished, discuss correct and incorrect responses.

1 **Part A**

The correct choice is A. The phrases "warehouses were filled up" and "production slowed" are clues that the word *merchandise* means "goods."

- **B** makes sense in the context, but nothing suggests the items had to be large.
- **C** and **D** do not make sense in the context of the paragraph.

Part B

The correct choice is B. It is the best answer because "goods" and "products" are similar in meaning.

- **A, C,** and **D** do not provide any context supporting the idea that *merchandise* means "goods."

DOK 2 RI.5.4

2 **Check that students underlined the word *crisis*.**
DOK 2 RI.5.4

Independent Practice

3 **Part A**

The correct choice is A. *Hard times* refers to "a period of difficulty."

- **B** and **C** are too specific. The "hard times" affected more people than just farmers and wage earners.
- **D** is not the actual meaning of the phrase, even though "hard times" can cause sadness.

Part B

The correct choice is C. Times were very difficult, indeed, if two million people were without homes.

- **A** is about good times before the Great Depression.
- **B** signals good times when the "prices of stocks soared" and people's wealth increased.
- **D** is about the plan to make things better, not the hard times of the Great Depression.

DOK 2 RI.5.4

4 **The correct choice is C.** The word *rushed* suggests a "strong need" for more products.

- **A** and **B** are meanings of *demand*, but they do not make sense in the context.
- **D** is not a meaning for the word, although students might have heard the word *demand* in the context of the phrase "demand an answer to the question."

DOK 1 RI.5.4, L.5.4c

3 This question has two parts. First, answer Part A. Then answer Part B.

Part A

What is the **best** meaning of the phrase hard times in paragraph 7 of "What Was the Great Depression?"

- **(A)** a period of great difficulty
- **B** a time when farmers couldn't grow crops
- **C** a time when jobs paid low wages
- **D** a period of mild sadness

Part B

Which sentence from the article helps the reader determine the meaning of the phrase hard times as it is used in paragraph 7?

- **A** "When World War I officially ended in 1919, Americans were tired of the war and ready for good times." (paragraph 1)
- **B** "From June through September 1929, the prices of stocks soared." (paragraph 2)
- **(C)** "About two million homeless men, women, and children drifted around the country." (paragraph 5)
- **D** "Roosevelt's plan to fix the nation's money problems was called the New Deal." (paragraph 6)

4 Read the sentence from paragraph 1.

To meet the demand, factories rushed to make even more products.

Which dictionary entry **best** defines demand?

- **A** "forceful statement"
- **B** "wish"
- **(C)** "strong need"
- **D** "question"

Monitor Understanding

If... students don't understand the writing task,

then... read aloud the writing prompt. Use the following questions to help students get started.

- **What is the prompt asking you to write about?**
- **Do you need to reread the text to find more information?**
- **How will you identify the information you need to include?**

- Have partners talk about how they will organize their responses.
- Provide a graphic organizer to assist students, if needed.

Write

5 **Short Response** Paragraph 6 of the passage states, "By 1937, the unemployment rate had fallen to about 14 percent." Define the phrase unemployment rate. Support your definition with at least **one** context clue from the passage.

Sample response: The phrase "unemployment rate" refers to the percentage of the workers who are not employed. One clue to the meaning is: "about 25 percent of Americans were jobless." Another clue is: "had fallen to about 14 percent." "Jobless" refers to people who are not working, or are unemployed. The word "rate" refers to a percent of the total. The percent of total workers who did not have jobs dropped from 25 percent to 14 percent between 1933 and 1937. The sentences show that the percent, or rate, of people who did not have jobs was less, so the "unemployment rate" went down.

Learning Target

In this lesson, you figured out the meanings of academic words and domain-specific vocabulary. Explain how you can use these skills to help you better understand the texts you read in school.

Responses will vary, but students should explain that determining the meaning of academic and domain-specific vocabulary helps them understand texts in most subject areas.

201

5 2-Point Writing Rubric

Points	Focus	Evidence	Organization
2	My answer does exactly what the prompt asked me to do.	My answer is supported with plenty of details from the text.	My ideas are clear and in a logical order.
1	Some of my answer does not relate to the prompt.	My answer is missing some important details from the text.	Some of my ideas are unclear and out of order.
0	My answer does not make sense.	My answer does not have any details from the text.	My ideas are unclear and not in any order.

Write

- Tell students that using what they read, they will plan and compose a short response to the writing prompt.

Monitor Understanding

Review Responses

After students have completed each part of the writing activity, help them evaluate their responses.

5 Display or pass out copies of the reproducible **2-Point Writing Rubric** on p. TR10. Have students use the rubric to individually assess their writing and revise as needed.

When students have finished their revisions, evaluate their responses. Responses will vary but should show that "unemployment rate" refers to the percentage, or number, of workers not employed compared to the total number of workers. Students should support their definition with at least one context clue from the article. See the sample response on the student book page.

DOK 2 **RI.5.4, W.5.9b**

Wrap Up

Learning Target

- Have each student respond in writing to the Learning Target prompt.
- When students have finished, have them share their responses. This may be done with a partner, in small groups, or as a whole class.

LESSON OVERVIEW

Lesson 12 Comparing Text Structures, Part 1: Chronology, Problem–Solution

Standards Focus

Compare and contrast the overall structure (e.g., chronology, problem/solution . . .) of events, ideas, concepts, or information in two or more texts. **RI.5.5**

Lesson Objectives

Reading

- Compare and contrast chronology and problem–solution text structures. **RI.5.5**
- Recognize words that signal particular structures. **RI.5.5**

Writing

- Draw evidence from informational texts to support analysis and reflection. **W.5.9b**

Speaking and Listening

- Pose and respond to specific questions and contribute to discussions. **SL.5.1c**
- Review the key ideas expressed and draw conclusions. **SL.5.1d**

Language

- Determine the meaning of multiple-meaning words and phrases. **L.5.4a**
- Acquire and use academic and domain-specific words and phrases. **L.5.6**

Additional Practice: **RI.5.1, RI.5.2, RI.5.3, RI.5.8**

Academic Talk

See **Glossary of Terms**, pp. TR2–TR9

- text structure
- problem–solution text structure
- chronological text structure

Learning Progression

Grade 4	Grade 5	Grade 6
Students identify different text structures.	Building on Grade 4, students identify and compare the text structure of multiple texts. This helps to prepare students for the analysis required at Grade 6.	Grade 6 increases in complexity by requiring students to analyze specific sections of the text and place the sections in the context of the text's overall structure and ideas.

Lesson Text Selections

Modeled and Guided Instruction

The First Victory of the Space Race

The Hazards of Space Junk

The First Victory of the Space Race
by Anna Kane
Genre: Science Article

The Hazards of Space Junk
by Juan Lima
Genre: Science Article

Guided Practice

Eating in Space

SPACE

Eating in Space
by Amal Kapoor
Genre: Science Article

Farming in Space
by Amy Hansen
Genre: Science Article

Independent Practice

EXPLORING MARS

Exploring Mars
by Hannon Nassir
Genre: Science Article

Living on Mars
by Kevin Charles
Genre: Science Article

Lesson Pacing Guide

Whole Class Instruction *30–45 minutes per day*

Day 1

Introduction pp. 202–203

- **Read** **Comparing Text Structures, Part 1: Chronology, Problem–Solution** *10 min*
- **Think** *10 min*
  Graphic Organizer: Four-Column Chart
- **Talk** *5 min*
  Quick Write (TRB) *5 min*

Day 2

Modeled and Guided Instruction pp. 204–205, 210

- **Read** **The First Victory of the Space Race** and **The Hazards of Space Junk** *10 min*
- **Think** *10 min*
  Graphic Organizer: Four-Column Chart
- **Talk** *5 min*
- **Write** Short Response *10 min*

Day 3

Guided Practice pp. 206–209, 211

- **Read** **Eating in Space** and **Farming in Space** *20 min*
- **Think** *10 min*
- **Talk** *5 min*
- **Write** Short Response *10 min*

Day 4

Independent Practice pp. 212–217

- **Read** **Exploring Mars** and **Living on Mars** *20 min*
- **Think** *10 min*
- **Write** Short Response *10 min*

Day 5

Independent Practice pp. 212–217

- *Review* Answer Analysis (TRB) *10 min*
- *Review* Response Analysis (TRB) *10 min*
- *Assign and Discuss* Learning Target *10 min*

Language Handbook
Lesson 5 Using Verb Tenses, pp. 446–447
20 min (optional)

Ready Writing Connection

During *Ready Reading* Days 1–5, use:
Lesson 3 Writing a Narrative: Legend

- **Think It Through**
- **Step 4 Organize Your Details**
- **Step 5 Draft**

See *Ready Writing TRB*, p. 62a for complete lesson plan.

Small Group Differentiation

Teacher-Toolbox.com

Reteach

***Ready Reading* Prerequisite Lesson**

- **Grade 4** Lesson 15 Text Structures, Part 2: Chronology and Problem–Solution

Teacher-led Activities

Tools for Instruction

- Text Structure

Personalized Learning

i-Ready.com

Independent

i-Ready Close Reading Lessons

- **Grade 4** Text Structures: Chronology and Problem–Solution
- **Grade 5** Text Structures: Chronology and Problem–Solution

Get Started

- Explain to students that in this lesson they will read science articles about space and compare and contrast the text structures of those articles.
- Review with students that *text structure* refers to the way an author organizes ideas and information. The proper organization can highlight key concepts and relationships that are important for readers to understand. Explain:

  Imagine that you are writing a report on clean energy. If you want to highlight the development of clean energy sources over time, you might provide dates and descriptions for each discovery in time order. However, if you want to emphasize clean energy as a solution, you might begin by describing the damage done by harmful pollutants from other energy sources.
- Guide students to understand that an author chooses a text structure based on his or her purpose for writing.
- Focus students' attention on the Learning Target. Read it aloud to set the purpose for the lesson.
- Display the Academic Talk phrases. Tell students to listen for these terms and their meanings as you work through the lesson together. Use the Academic Talk Routine on pp. A48–A49.

English Language Learners

● Genre Focus

Read

- Read aloud the Read section as students follow along. Restate to reinforce:

  When you read science articles, it's helpful to stop and ask yourself how the author connects ideas, events, and people. For example, you might determine that events follow a time order, or you might find that the author examines a related series of problems and solutions. Understanding text structure will help you develop a deeper understanding of the author's purpose.
- Have students read each passage and think about whether the ideas are organized by chronology or problem–solution.

Introduction

RI.5.5 Compare and contrast the overall structure (e.g., chronology, problem-solution . . .) of events, ideas, concepts, or information in two or more texts.

Lesson 12
Comparing Text Structures, Part 1: Chronology, Problem-Solution

When you compare and contrast how the information in texts is structured, you will better understand the purpose of each text.

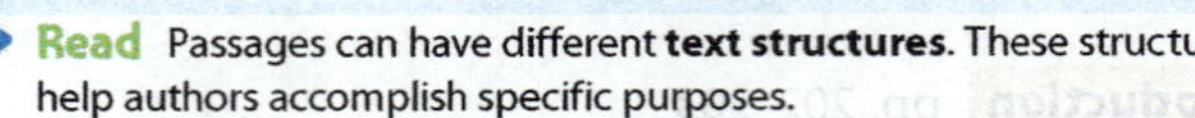

Read Passages can have different **text structures**. These structures help authors accomplish specific purposes.

- A **chronological text structure** tells events in the order they happen. This structure can include dates, times, and words such as *first*, *next*, and *later*.
- A **problem-solution text structure** describes problems and solutions. This structure can include words such as *challenge*, *problem*, and *solution*.

Comparing texts can help you understand their structures and purposes.

Read the passages below. Look for evidence of the structure and the purpose of each one.

Passage 1: The space shuttle *Discovery* made its first flight in 1984. In 1990, *Discovery* launched the Hubble Space Telescope. In 2011, after 30 missions, *Discovery* was taken out of service. *Discovery* then became a display at the National Air and Space Museum.

Passage 2: Like us, astronauts use ordinary toothpaste, a toothbrush, and a little bit of water. The challenge, however, is that they don't have a sink for rinsing out their mouths. Their solution? They spit toothpaste into a washcloth.

202

English Language Learners
Develop Language

Concept Vocabulary To talk about problem–solution structures, students should recognize signal words and phrases.

- Draw a two-column chart and label the columns *Problem* and *Solution*. Under *Problem*, write *challenge*, *concern*, and *hazard*. Explain that a *hazard* is a danger, and discuss how this is synonymous with *problem*. Work with students to brainstorm other words that signal problems, and write them in the chart.
- Under *Solution*, write *solve*, *answer*, and *address*. Discuss each word's meaning. Then ask what other words might signal solutions. Brainstorm several possibilities, such as *fix*, *escape*, *one way*, and *one solution*.

● Genre Focus
Science Articles

Science articles tell about events, discoveries, and ideas in science. They might be about ideas and events from the past, things happening now, or ideas for the future.

A science article may use a chronological text structure when telling the history of an idea or event. It may use a problem–solution text structure when describing some challenges in the science world, and how advances in science or changes in human behavior can address those challenges.

Ask students to name science articles they've read. Discuss which text structure the articles used.

Think What do you know about text structures? Use the chart below to help you compare and contrast the text structures and purposes of the passages.

Passage	Author's Purpose	Text Structure	Evidence of Structure
1	to tell about the shuttle *Discovery* over time	chronological	• "made its first flight in 1984" • "in 1990" • "In 2011, after 30 missions" • "*Discovery* then became"
2	to explain how astronauts solve the problem of not having a sink	problem–solution	• "The challenge, however," • "Their solution?"

Talk Share your chart with a partner.

- Which text structure did the author of Passage 1 use?
- Which text structure did the author of Passage 2 use?
- For each passage, how did the text structure help you understand the author's purpose?

Academic Talk
Use these phrases to talk about the text.

- text structure
- chronological text structure
- problem–solution text structure

Monitor Understanding

If... students struggle to identify text structures,
then... make a chart of signal words to post in the classroom.

- **What words or phrases do you use to tell about events in order?** *(first, next, last, another, then, finally, before, after, following, additionally)*
- **What words or phrases do you use to describe problems and their solutions?** *(the problem is, the difficulty is, it is possible to, if-then, one challenge is, therefore)*

Post the chart in a central location, and encourage students to make a copy in their own notebooks.

Think

- Have students read aloud the Think section. Explain that the chart will help them organize their thinking.
- Have partners complete the chart. Remind students to look for signal words in the passages to identify evidence of each text structure.
- As students work, circulate and provide assistance as needed.
- Ask volunteers to share what they wrote in their charts.
- Make certain students understand that some events can be in time order even though there is no date given. For example, the word *then*, and not a date, tells us when *Discovery* became a display at the museum.

Talk

- Read aloud the Talk prompts.
- Have partners compare their charts and then discuss how each structure supported the author's purpose for writing.
- Ask volunteers to share their ideas.

Quick Write Have students write a response to the following prompt:

Write about a challenge you faced recently. Decide whether you want to tell the events in order or organize your ideas with a problem–solution structure.

Ask students to share their responses.

Wrap Up

- Invite students to share what they've learned so far. Encourage them to use the Academic Talk phrases in their explanations.
- Explain to students that when they read science articles, they need to identify connections between events, ideas, and people. Understanding text structures will help them find such connections.

In the next section, we'll read two science articles and identify their text structures. Then we'll think about how those text structures support each author's purpose for writing.

Monitor Understanding

Modeled and Guided Instruction

Get Started

Today you will read two science articles. First, you'll read to understand what each article is about. Then you'll read to compare and contrast the text structures of the articles.

Read

- Read aloud the title of each article and call attention to the photographs. Invite students to predict what each article will be about.
- Have students read the articles independently. Tell them to place a check mark above any confusing words and phrases as they read. Remind students to look inside, around, and beyond each unknown word to help them figure out its meaning. Use the Word Learning Routine on pp. A50–A51.
- When students have finished reading, clarify the meanings of words and phrases they still find confusing. Then use the questions below to check understanding.

  What was the *space race*? *(a time when the United States and the Soviet Union competed to be the first to go to space)*

  What is space junk? *(debris that humans leave behind from trips into orbit around Earth)*

  What are two possible solutions to the problem of space junk? *(stronger hulls and less space junk)*

English Language Learners

Word Learning Strategy

Explore

- Read aloud the Explore question at the top of p. 205 to set the purpose for the second read. Tell students they will need to examine how each passage presents ideas in order to answer this question.
- Have students read aloud the Close Reader Habit on p. 204.

TIP Tell students that signal words alone might not indicate the main text structure. Students should think about the relationship between ideas in a paragraph and between paragraphs.

Modeled and Guided Instruction

Read

Genre: Science Articles

The First Victory of the Space Race

by Anna Kane

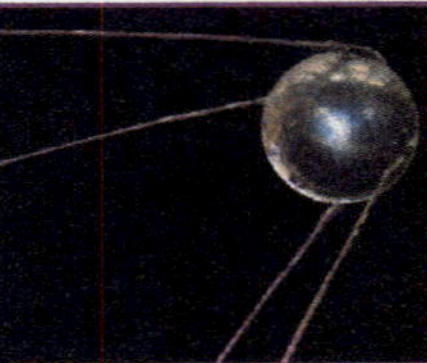
a model of *Sputnik*

1 The space race refers to a time when the United States and the former Soviet Union competed for superiority in space exploration. It began in 1954, when scientists called on the world's governments to put the first satellites into orbit around the Earth. The United States answered the call first, declaring in July 1955 that it would launch satellites by 1958. The Soviet Union quickly promised to launch its own satellites. Engineers in both nations raced to build satellites and the rockets to carry them.

2 The Soviet Union won the first round of the space race, putting a 185-pound satellite called *Sputnik* into orbit on October 4, 1957. As *Sputnik* orbited the planet, Americans could only look up and wonder: Might their nation lose the space race?

The Hazards of **Space Junk**

by Juan Lima

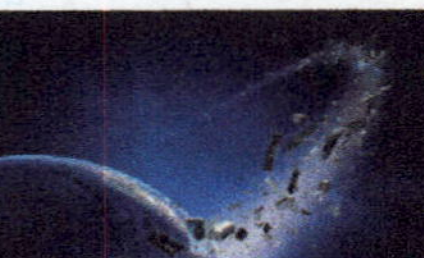

1 Space junk is what humans leave behind from trips into orbit around the Earth. Some junk, such as old satellites and rocket parts, is large. But most junk is less than a centimeter long—pebbles of ice, flecks of paint, and bits of metal.

2 Just as junk on a road threatens cars, space junk is a problem for spaceships. You might think the large pieces are more dangerous than the small ones, but the opposite is true. Scientists can track the large objects and steer spaceships away from them. They cannot track the small objects, and they can't avoid what they can't track. You might think that small objects wouldn't be a challenge, but they zip along at several miles per second. At this speed, something less than a centimeter long might be able to punch through a spaceship's hull.

3 One way to protect spaceships against junk is to give them strong hulls. But the best solution is to have less junk in orbit. Engineers are working on ways to leave less junk behind. They are also designing machines to remove junk from orbit. Hopefully, the coming years will see less junk around our planet.

Close Reader Habits

When you reread the articles, **underline** one sentence in each that tells what the passage is about, and **circle** words or phrases that show the text structure.

204

English Language Learners

Develop Language

- **Concept Vocabulary** Have students look closely at the picture in "The Hazards of Space Junk." Then draw a picture of an oval orbit around Earth. Review that space travelers leave junk—trash or garbage—in space. Then explain that space junk goes into orbit, or begins to travel around Earth. Trace the oval with your finger as you say *orbit*.
- Prompt students to list examples of space junk from the passage. Clarify any words that students identify but do not understand, pointing out context clues in the passage whenever possible. Discuss why this space junk can be dangerous.

Word Learning Strategy

Use Context Clues

- Point to the word *zip* in paragraph 2 of "The Hazards of Space Junk."

  What does *zip* mean in this sentence? *(to move very fast)*

  What other meanings do you know for *zip*? *(to close something with a zipper; shorthand for zip code; compressing a computer file)*

- Emphasize that context clues can help students determine the meaning of a multiple-meaning word. Guide students to identify "several miles per second" as the best context clue in this instance. **L.5.4a**

Explore **What text structure do the authors mainly use to present information in each passage?**

Think

1 Complete the chart below. Identify each passage's purpose and text structure. Identify the evidence of that structure in the passage.

Look for words or phrases that suggest the structure of each passage.

Passage	Author's Purpose	Text Structure	Evidence of Structure
"The First Victory of the Space Race"	to tell about the events in the history of the space race	chronological	• "It began in 1954" • "it would launch satellites by 1958" • "On October 4, 1957"
"The Hazards of Space Junk"	to tell how scientists are dealing with the problem of space junk	problem–solution	• "space junk is a problem for" • "You might think that small objects wouldn't be a challenge" • "One way to protect" • "But the best solution is"

Talk

2 Share your charts. Look at the evidence you each found of the text structures. How does each text structure support the author's purpose? If your partner has any good evidence that you do not, add it to your chart.

Write

3 **Short Response** Explain how the text structure of each passage supports each author's purpose for writing. Use evidence to support your response. Use the space provided on page 210 to write your answer.

HINT Refer to each passage by name so it's clear which one you're writing about.

Think Aloud

- First I will look back at "The First Victory of the Space Race" to find clues about the text structure. I will keep in mind that signal words are just one type of clue, and that I need to think about how the ideas are related as well.
- Before I write anything in my chart, I'm going to read through and get some ideas.

The second sentence says "It began in 1954, " which is a clue about a chronological text structure. I'll continue reading to see if the passage describes what happens next, and then what happens after that. If I see these details, I'll confirm that this is a chronological text structure.

Think

- Read aloud the Think section. Explain to students that you will model how to find text evidence to fill in part of the chart. Use the **Think Aloud** below to guide your modeling.
- Revisit the Explore question. Guide students to determine that they need to look for more details, using the Close Reader Habit.
- Encourage students to work with a partner to continue rereading the articles and complete the chart. Remind them to read the Buddy Tip.
- Ask volunteers to share their completed charts.
- Guide students to see that dates provide the order for "The First Victory of the Space Race." In contrast, "The Hazards of Space Junk" is about a problem and some possible solutions for it. Point out that the titles of the articles give hints about text structure and each author's purpose, as well.

Talk

- Read aloud the Talk prompt.
- Have partners respond to the prompt. Use the Talk Routine on pp. A52–A53.
- Circulate to check that students are comparing their charts and discussing how each text structure supports the author's purpose.

Write

- Ask a volunteer to read aloud the Write prompt.
- Invite a few students to tell what the prompt is asking them to do.
- Make sure students understand that they need to explain both authors' reasons for writing. Point out that details in their charts will provide support for their responses.
- Have students turn to p. 210 to write their response.
- Use Review Responses on p. 210 to assess students' writing.

Wrap Up

- Ask students to recall the Learning Target. Have them explain how comparing the text structures helped them better understand both science articles.

Guided Practice

Get Started

Today you will read two more science articles related to space. First, you will read to understand what the articles are about. Then you will reread with a partner to analyze and contrast the articles' text structures.

Read

- Read aloud the titles of the articles, and ask students to predict what they will be about. Discuss whether the titles give any hints about the text structure each article will have.
- **Read to Understand** Have students read the articles independently. Tell them to place a check mark above any confusing words and phrases as they read. Remind students to look inside, around, and beyond each unknown word or phrase to help them figure out its meaning. Use the Word Learning Routine on pp. A50–A51.
- When students have finished reading, clarify the meanings of words and phrases they still find confusing. Then use the questions below to check understanding. Encourage students to identify details in the text that support their answers.

  How do astronauts plan ahead for eating in space? *(They select everything they are going to eat before they go into space.)*

  How do astronauts prepare food in space? *(They select their food, add water, and heat the meals. Then they attach the food containers to a meal tray and attach the tray to their laps or a wall. Then they open their packages.)*

  Why do we need space gardening? *(Some space voyages will take years or even decades and astronauts cannot bring enough food to survive.)*

  What was one solution to the problem of the confused plants? *(giving plants more light so the stems grew toward light and roots grew downward)*

English Language Learners

- **Word Learning Strategy**

Guided Practice

Read

Genre: Science Article

Eating in Space

by Amal Kapoor

1 Astronauts get hungry—just like the rest of us. Because they are doing hard work in space, they need to eat breakfast, lunch, and dinner. Astronauts can eat everything from fresh fruit to pizza and pudding.

2 Astronauts carry all their food with them into space. Most of their food consists of freeze-dried meals that can be stored at room temperature for a long time. Before a mission, each astronaut chooses what to eat for each meal during the flight. These meals are individually packaged and organized in the order that the astronaut will eat them.

3 At meal times, astronauts go into the galley, a small kitchen area with an oven and a water dispenser. First, the astronauts select their meals, which are stored in locker trays held by a net. Next, they add water to freeze-dried foods. Then they heat the meal in an oven that only reaches a temperature of about 170°F. This process usually takes 20 to 30 minutes.

4 Once food is rehydrated and heated, astronauts attach their food containers to a meal tray using fabric fasteners. Because there's no gravity in space, food containers must be attached to a tray. Otherwise, food would float around the spacecraft! After astronauts attach their trays to the wall or to their laps, they use the trays like a dinner plate. Finally, astronauts open their food packages with scissors and eat their meal with a knife, fork, and spoon. If they want to season the food, they have to add salt and pepper in liquid form.

Close Reader Habits

What is the main text structure used in "Eating in Space"? Reread the article. **Underline** any words or phrases that tell you how the author organized his writing.

206

English Language Learners

Develop Language

- **Word Parts** Write on the board *freeze-dried* + *add water* ⟶ *rehydrated*. Point to *freeze-dried* and use online images or real examples to demonstrate its meaning. Explain that freeze-dried food does not need to go in the refrigerator and it will not spoil for many years.
- Point to *add water* and guide students to explain the meaning of the phrase. Then explain that *rehydrated* means "hydrated again," which means that water has been added. If possible, support comprehension by showing a video from NASA or another source that demonstrates the rehydration of freeze-dried foods.

Genre: Science Article

FROM
FARMING IN SPACE

by Amy Hansen, *Highlights*

1 What will astronauts eat when a space voyage takes years or even decades?

2 Lots of fresh vegetables, says Dr. Mary Musgrave of the University of Massachusetts. She has spent the last 10 years learning how to grow plants in space. And it's a good thing she has already started her work, because extraterrestrial gardening can be tricky.

3 In 1997, while the Mir Space Station spun around Earth, astronaut Mike Foale peered at a sealed growth chamber. The astronaut had planted Dr. Musgrave's quick-growing seedlings in the chamber, but none of the stems were showing.

4 He opened the container and saw the problem. The white stems weren't growing upward. Instead, they threaded downward or sideways. Some of the roots snaked up, while others twisted around. These were confused plants.

5 On Earth, a plant's roots and stems take cues from gravity, using the Earth's pull to find "up" and "down." This process is called gravitropism. On the Mir, there was almost no gravity.

6 Dr. Musgrave suggested a solution: give the plants more light. This idea made sense because plants also use sunlight to find their way—a process called phototropism.

7 And it worked. Once the seedlings had more light, the stems turned up and the roots went down.

8 Now Dr. Musgrave was free to worry about the next problem: Would her baby plants live to flower?

Close Reader Habits

What is the main text structure of "Farming in Space"? Reread the article. **Underline** any words or phrases that tell you how the author organized her writing.

- **Read to Analyze** Read aloud the Close Reader Habits on pp. 206 and 207 to set the purpose for the second read. Then have students reread the articles with a partner and discuss any questions they might have.

TIP Remind students that chronology does not only refer to dates and events in history. It can also mean steps in a process or an order of events in a sequence.

Word Learning Strategy

Use Context Clues

- Reread the final sentence of "Eating in Space." Call attention to the word *season*.

  What does *season* mean in this sentence? *(add flavoring)*

  What other meaning do you know for *season*? *(a time of the year)*

- Emphasize that context clues can help students determine the meaning of a multiple-meaning word. Here the context clue "add salt and pepper" suggests that in this sentence, *season* is a verb that means "to add flavoring."
- Have students reread the final sentence of "Farming in Space." Ask them to explain how the word *flower* is used in the sentence. Guide them to use context clues to determine that it is a verb meaning "to produce flowers." **L.5.4a**

Guided Practice

Think

- Have students work with a partner to complete items 1–3. Draw attention to the boldface words in each item.

TIP If students have trouble answering these questions, have partners write a phrase next to each relevant item to remind them what they are looking for: the best statement, the best evidence, the best reason. Encourage partners to ask, "Is this the best?" as they discuss each answer choice.

Answer Analysis

When students have finished, discuss correct and incorrect responses.

1 Part A

The correct choice is B. The text structure of "Eating in Space" is chronology; the structure of "Farming in Space" is problem–solution.

- **A, C,** and **D** are not supported by a careful reading of the signal words and passage clues.

Part B

The correct choices are B and F. B uses the signal phrase "At meal times" to show the order in which the events happen. **F** presents a solution to a problem discussed by the passage.

- **A** and **C** do not show the text structure of "Eating in Space."
- **D** and **E** do not show the text structure of "Farming in Space." While **D** does mention "10 years" and **E** provides the date 1997, the overall passage structure is problem–solution.

DOK 2

Guided Practice

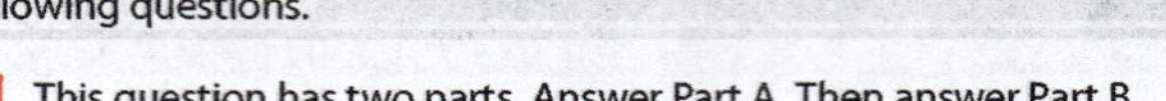

Think Use what you learned from reading the science articles to answer the following questions.

Some science articles focus on the order in which events happen, like the stages of plant growth. Other articles focus on how scientists encountered and solved problems.

1 This question has two parts. Answer Part A. Then answer Part B.

Part A

Which statement **best** describes a major difference between the text structures of the articles "Eating in Space" and "Farming in Space"?

A "Eating in Space" contrasts eating on Earth and in space, while "Farming in Space" contrasts growing plants in space and on Earth.

(B) "Eating in Space" tells the process of eating a meal in space, while "Farming in Space" tells the problems and solutions of growing plants in space.

C "Eating in Space" tells the process of eating a meal in space, while "Farming in Space" tells the process of growing plants in space.

D "Eating in Space" tells about problems and solutions for eating meals in space, while "Farming in Space" tells about the process of growing plants in space.

Part B

Choose **one** sentence from **each** article that supports the answer in Part A.

A "Astronauts can eat everything from fresh fruit to pizza and pudding." ("Eating in Space")

(B) "At meal times, astronauts go into the galley, a small kitchen area with an oven and a water dispenser." ("Eating in Space")

C "Food containers must be attached to a tray." ("Eating in Space")

D "She has spent the last 10 years learning how to grow plants in space." ("Farming in Space")

E "In 1997, while the Mir Space Station spun around Earth, astronaut Mike Foale peered at a sealed growth chamber." ("Farming in Space")

(F) "Dr. Musgrave suggested a solution: give the plants more light." ("Farming in Space")

208

Integrating Standards

Use the following questions to further students' understanding of the articles.

- **In "Eating in Space," what reasons or evidence does the writer give for why meals in space are individually packaged?** *(The author explains that because there is no gravity and things float around, packages make it easier to handle one meal at a time.)*
DOK 2 **RI.5.8**
- **Summarize the main ideas in "Farming in Space" using information from the passage.** *(Without Earth's gravity and sunlight, plants have difficulty growing in space. Scientists today are learning how to add light to make plants grow in space.)*
DOK 2 **RI.5.2**
- **In "Farming in Space," why didn't the plants grow upright at first?** *(There was no light to pull them up and almost no gravity to help pull them down.)*
DOK 3 **RI.5.3**

2 Select **one** sentence from "Eating in Space" and **one** sentence from "Farming in Space" that provide the **best** evidence of each passage's text structure.

- A "Astronauts get hungry—just like the rest of us." ("Eating in Space")
- B "These meals are individually packaged and organized in the order that the astronaut will eat them." ("Eating in Space")
- (C) "Next, they add water to freeze-dried foods." ("Eating in Space")
- D "And it's a good thing she has already started her work, because extraterrestrial gardening can be tricky." ("Farming in Space")
- E "On the Mir, there was almost no gravity." ("Farming in Space")
- (F) "Now Dr. Musgrave was free to worry about the next problem: Would her baby plants live to flower?" ("Farming in Space")

3 Read this sentence from "Farming in Space."

> What will astronauts eat when a space voyage takes years or even decades?

What is the **best** reason the author chose to begin the article with a question?

- (A) to present a puzzle in need of a solution
- B to show that astronauts are curious people
- C to describe how space voyages are a cause of worry
- D to explain why space voyages are so difficult to plan

 Talk

4 Discuss the text structures of both articles. How does each structure help the author organize his or her ideas? Use the chart on page 211 to organize your ideas and evidence.

 Write

5 **Short Response** How and why are the text structures of "Eating in Space" and "Farming in Space" different? Use details from each passage to support your response. Use the space provided on page 211 to write your answer.

HINT Quote words or phrases that are evidence of each text structure.

209

● Monitor Understanding

If... students have difficulty discussing how authors use text structure in item 4,

then... remind them that authors organize texts to serve a purpose. Encourage them to discuss each author's purpose before they begin to fill out their charts. Have them answer the question, "What did the author want me to learn from reading this article?"

2 **The correct choices are C and F. C** uses the signal word *next* to indicate the chronological structure of "Eating in Space." **F** uses the signal word *problem* to indicate the problem–solution structure of "Farming."

- **A, B, D,** and **E** do not give evidence of each passage's structure.

DOK 3

3 **The correct choice is A.** Starting the passage with a question is a way of presenting the puzzle, or problem, that astronauts are solving.

- **B, C,** and **D** are incorrect because they do not reflect the author's purpose for writing.

DOK 2

● Integrating Standards

Talk

- Have partners discuss the prompt. Emphasize that students should support their ideas with text details.
- Circulate to clarify misunderstandings.

● Monitor Understanding

Write

- Ask a volunteer to read aloud the Write prompt.
- Invite students to tell what the prompt is asking them to do. Make sure they understand that they need to explain both how and why the text structures are different.
- Call attention to the HINT.
- Have students turn to p. 211 to write their response.
- Use Review Responses on p. 211 to assess students' writing.

Wrap Up

- Ask students to recall the Learning Target. Have them explain how comparing and contrasting text structures helped them better understand these science articles.

Modeled and Guided Instruction

Write

- Remember to use the Response-Writing Routine on pp. A54–A55.

Review Responses

After students complete the writing activity, help them evaluate their responses.

3 Responses may vary but should identify and give evidence of each text structure. See the sample response on the student book page. ***DOK 3***

Write Use the space below to write your answer to the question on page 205.

The First Victory of the Space Race

The Hazards of **Space Junk**

3 **Short Response** Explain how the text structure of each passage supports each author's purpose for writing. Use evidence to support your response.

HINT Refer to each passage by name so it's clear which one you're writing about.

Sample response: In "The First Victory of the Space Race," the author describes events within a chronological structure. She uses words such as "time," "when," and "first." She also includes dates such as "1954," "July 1955," and "1958." This structure supports the author's purpose, which is to tell about the events of the space race in the order they happened. The author of "The Hazards of Space Junk" organizes his information differently. He uses a problem–solution structure. He first describes the problem that space junk poses to spaceships. After doing so, he describes possible solutions using words such as "problem," "challenge," "one way," and "solution." This text structure supports the author's purpose of wanting to inform the reader of a problem and present possible solutions.

Don't forget to check your writing.

Check Your Writing

- ☐ Did you read the prompt carefully?
- ☐ Did you put the prompt in your own words?
- ☐ Did you use the best evidence from the text to support your ideas?
- ☐ Are your ideas clearly organized?
- ☐ Did you write in clear and complete sentences?
- ☐ Did you check your spelling and punctuation?

Scaffolding Support for Reluctant Writers

If students are having a difficult time getting started, use the strategies below. Work individually with struggling students, or have students work with partners.

- Circle the verbs in the prompt that tell you what to do, such as *describe*, *explain*, or *compare*.
- Underline words and phrases in the prompt that show what information you need to provide in your response, such as *causes*, *reasons*, or *character traits*.
- Talk about the details from the text that you will include in your response.
- Explain aloud how you will respond to the prompt.

Eating in Space

FARMING IN SPACE

4 Use the chart below to organize your ideas and evidence.

Passage	Author's Purpose	Text Structure	Evidence of Structure

Write Use the space below to write your answer to the question on page 209.

5 **Short Response** How and why are the text structures of "Eating in Space" and "Farming in Space" different? Use details from each passage to support your response.

HINT Quote words or phrases that are evidence of each text structure.

Sample response: "Eating in Space" has a chronological text structure. This structure helps the passage describe what steps astronauts follow to eat a meal in space. The passage tells what happens "before a mission" and "at meal times." "Farming in Space," on the other hand, has a problem-solution text structure. The passage explains how scientists are solving the problem of growing plants in space. It tells that scientists like Dr. Musgrave have "suggested a solution" to the problems of growing plants in space.

Teacher Notes

Talk

4 Students should use the chart to organize their thoughts and evidence.

Write

- Remember to use the Response-Writing Routine on pp. A54–A55.

Review Responses

After students complete the writing activity, help them evaluate their responses.

5 Responses may vary but should identify the differences between the text structures and explain how each structure suits the author's purpose for writing. See the sample response on the student book page.
DOK 3

Independent Practice

Get Started

Today you are going to read two science articles and use what you have learned about text structures to compare and contrast the way the articles are organized.

- Ask a volunteer to explain how comparing and contrasting text structures can help readers understand science articles. Encourage students to use the Academic Talk phrases in their response.

English Language Learners

Read

You are going to read the articles independently and use what you have learned to think and write about the texts. As you read, remember to look closely at signal words and phrases in each text to identify the text structure.

- Read aloud the titles of the articles and then encourage students to preview the texts, paying close attention to the photographs.
- Call attention to the Words to Know in the upper left of p. 212 and p. 214.
- If students need support in reading the articles, you may wish to use the Monitor Understanding suggestions.
- When students have finished, have them complete the Think and Write sections.

● **Monitor Understanding**

Read

Genre: Science Article

WORDS TO KNOW
As you read, look inside, around, and beyond these words to figure out what they mean.
- **aeronautics**
- **administration**
- **conducted**

by Hannon Nassir

1 Have you ever thought about exploring Mars? Even if you haven't, other people certainly have. Mars was first explored by telescope in the 1700s. Early astronomers observed ice caps, dust clouds, and dark streaks. They wondered if there could be life on Mars.

2 In modern times, the United States, the former Soviet Union, and other countries have sent spacecraft to gather more information about the "red planet." The first missions to Mars flew near the planet. In November 1964, the U.S. National Aeronautics and Space Administration (NASA) launched *Mariner 4*. This spacecraft flew past Mars in July 1965 and took the first close-up photographs. The pictures were blurry, but they helped scientists learn what Mars looked like.

3 Then new technology allowed the United States to get even closer. In 1975, NASA launched *Viking 1* and *Viking 2*. *Viking 1* landed on the surface of Mars on July 19, 1976. *Viking 2* followed on September 3, 1976. Both *Viking 1* and *Viking 2* explored different parts of the planet. Each took pictures and conducted experiments.

The *Viking 2* spacecraft took this photograph of the Martian surface in 1976. Mars is red because its surface is covered with a dust made of iron oxide, also known as rust.

English Language Learners

Develop Language

Cognates Work with Spanish speakers and speakers of other Latin-based languages to recognize cognates. First, write *amartizaje* ("landing on Mars" or "Mars landing") on the board. Underline *mar* and explain that it is a cognate for *Mars*. Review that *cognates* are words in two languages that share a similar spelling, meaning, and sometimes, pronunciation. Explain that *amartizaje* is a major topic of this article.

Next, explain that many science and technology terms are cognates. Ask students to skim the first three paragraphs of "Exploring Mars" for words they recognize. Work together to generate a list that might include the following: *explore/explorar, telescope/telescopio, astronomers/astronomos, observe/observar, information/información, planet/planeta, mission/misión, launch/lanzamiento, photographs/fotografías, surface/superficie, different parts/partes diferentes*, and *experiments/experimentos*.

Invite students to share prior knowledge for any of these terms, and provide clarification as needed.

4 NASA also built space rovers that could roam the surface of a planet. A rover is a solar-powered vehicle that is operated from Earth by a computer. Several NASA spacecraft have carried rovers to Mars. For example, *Mars Pathfinder* landed the first Mars rover, *Sojourner*, in 1997. *Sojourner* sent more than 500 photographs back to Earth and collected soil samples.

5 Two more rovers were launched in 2003. After landing in 2004, the twin rovers *Spirit* and *Opportunity* discovered evidence of past water on Mars. NASA lost contact with *Spirit* in 2010. But, as of April 2015, *Opportunity* was still collecting data.

6 Finally, on November 26, 2011, NASA launched a large, six-wheeled rover named *Curiosity*. Since landing in 2012, this Mars rover has studied whether the planet has ever been able to support life. *Curiosity* is gathering evidence from rocks and soil.

7 Over the past 50 years, scientists have learned a great deal about Mars. For example, they have a better understanding of its climate, its features, and its atmosphere. With future missions, they hope to learn even more about the red planet.

In this photo, two engineers pose with three Martian rovers at the "Mars Yard" testing site. Here, rovers are tested before being sent to Mars. The smallest rover is identical to *Sojourner*. The one at the left resembles *Spirit* and *Opportunity*. The largest rover is the size of *Curiosity*.

● Monitor Understanding

If... students struggle to read and understand the passages,

then... use these scaffolding suggestions:

Question the Text Preview the texts by asking the following questions:

- **Based on the titles and text features, what do you predict the articles will be about?**
- **What questions do you have about the texts?**

Vocabulary Support Define words that may interfere with comprehension, such as *rover, roam, atmosphere,* and *conditions*.

Read Aloud Read aloud the text with students. You could also have students chorally read the text in a small group.

Check Understanding Use the questions below to check understanding. Encourage students to cite details in the texts that support their answers.

- **What do missions to Mars do now?** *(They land on the surface and gather information.)*
- **What is "Living on Mars" mostly about?** *(the many problems and challenges to overcome if humans ever try to settle on Mars)*
- **Why can't people live on Mars yet?** *(Humans would need to bring air, water, food, and special clothes to survive.)*

Independent Practice

Integrating Standards

After students have read the articles, use these questions to discuss the articles with them.

- **Which sentence from "Exploring Mars" best states the passage's main idea?**

  ("Over the past 50 years, scientists have learned a great deal about Mars." The entire passage shared some of the important things scientists have learned about Mars in the past 50 years or so.)

  DOK 2 **RI.5.1, RI.5.2**

- **According to "Exploring Mars," how did advances in technology lead to learning more about Mars?**

  (New technology allowed spacecraft to get closer to the planet and then to land on it. Rovers increased exploration of the surface and collection of samples. Better technology has led to a better understanding of the planet's climate, features, and atmosphere.)

  DOK 2 **RI.5.3**

- **What evidence does the author of "Living on Mars" provide to show that the cold is a problem? To show that food is a problem?**

  (The author gives the average temperature of –81°F and says you would have to wear a spacesuit there. The author also says that Mars has no plants or animals, and that it would take six months to reach Earth for more supplies.)

  DOK 2 **RI.5.8**

- **How does the information in "Living on Mars" confirm the statements made in paragraph 7 of "Exploring Mars"?**

  ("Exploring Mars" states that scientists now have a better understanding of the climate, atmosphere, and features of Mars. "Living on Mars" gives specific details about this information to support the claim that humans cannot live there yet.)

  DOK 4 **RI.5.9**

● **Theme Connection**

Independent Practice

Genre: Science Article

Living on Mars

WORDS TO KNOW
As you read, look inside, around, and beyond these words to figure out what they mean.
- **conditions**
- **permanent**
- **opportunity**

by Kevin Charles

1 Do you think it is possible to live on Mars? Humans need certain things to live, such as air and water. Mars has frozen water underground and at its polar caps, and it has an atmosphere. Of all the planets in our solar system, Mars has the best conditions to support human life. Yet, if you wanted to settle on Mars, you would have to overcome challenges.

2 One difficulty is the poor atmosphere on Mars. It is much thinner than Earth's atmosphere, and it is mostly made of carbon dioxide. As a result, there is not enough oxygen in the air for humans to breathe. To solve this problem, you could take air with you from Earth or make your own air on Mars.

3 Another problem is that Mars is very cold, windy, and dusty. The average temperature is about –81°F. In order to live on Mars, you would need to wear a spacesuit to keep warm. The spacesuit would have to be light and flexible enough so you could move about freely.

4 The lack of liquid water on the surface of Mars is also an issue. You would have to take ice from deep below the surface and melt it. Melted ice could be used for drinking. Some scientists have suggested using large mirrors to reflect the sun and melt the polar caps on Mars.

5 Having enough food to eat is another challenge that you would face on Mars. At the present time, there are no data showing that Mars has animals or plants on its surface. Therefore, you would have to bring your own food to a settlement, and you would have to learn how to grow food in greenhouses.

6 If you lived in a Mars colony, you would also have to deal with the problem of distance. It takes more than six months to reach Mars. That's a long trip if you need to return to Earth for supplies!

7 Despite all of these problems, some humans are eager to build permanent colonies on Mars. They believe creating a settlement is an important opportunity. Who knows? Maybe one day you'll be making the trip.

Mars has no plants, so people moving there would have to bring their own. The scientists shown above are studying how plants could be used to produce oxygen for humans to breathe during long space flights.

214

● **Theme Connection**

- Remind students that the theme of this lesson is Space.
- Discuss how all the passages in this lesson relate to the theme.
- Have students reflect on the two smaller themes running throughout the passages: the history of exploring space and the problems of exploring or living in space. Make a two-column chart and invite students to name some details that support each topic. Encourage them to use domain-specific vocabulary from the passages in their responses.

Think Use what you learned from reading the science articles to answer the following questions.

1 This question has two parts. First, answer Part A. Then answer Part B.

Part A
Which statement **best** describes a major difference between "Exploring Mars" and "Living on Mars"?

A "Exploring Mars" describes inspiring reasons for human exploration of Mars, while "Living on Mars" argues that it would be too difficult for humans to live there.

B "Exploring Mars" tells about problems NASA has faced in sending spacecraft to Mars and solutions to these problems, while "Living on Mars" presents problems and possible solutions to living on Mars.

(C) "Exploring Mars" tells about events in the history of the exploration of Mars, while "Living on Mars" presents problems and possible solutions to living on Mars.

D "Exploring Mars" describes causes and effects of space exploration, while "Living on Mars" presents expert opinions about why humans should try to build a settlement on Mars.

Part B
Choose **one** sentence from **each** article that supports the answer in Part A.

A "Have you ever thought about exploring Mars?" ("Exploring Mars")

(B) "In November 1964, the U.S. National Aeronautics and Space Administration (NASA) launched *Mariner 4*." ("Exploring Mars")

C "*Curiosity* is gathering evidence from rocks and soil." ("Exploring Mars")

D "Do you think it is possible to live on Mars?" ("Living on Mars")

(E) "Another problem is that Mars is very cold, windy, and dusty." ("Living on Mars")

F "Maybe one day you'll be making the trip." ("Living on Mars")

215

Think

- Use the Monitor Understanding suggestions to support students in completing items 1–3.

● Monitor Understanding

Answer Analysis

When students have finished, discuss correct and incorrect responses.

1 Part A

The correct choice is C. "Exploring Mars" is mainly a chronological history. "Living on Mars" is a problem–solution passage about the main challenges of living on Mars.

- **A, B,** and **D** are not supported by a careful reading of the content in each passage.

Part B

The correct choices are B and E. B uses the phrase "In November 1964" to show when an event happened. **E** tells a problem that must be solved before living on Mars.

- **A, C, D,** and **F** are not supported by a careful reading of the signal words and phrases in each passage.

***DOK 3* RI.5.5**

● Monitor Understanding

If... students struggle to complete the items,

then... you may wish to use the following suggestions:

Read Aloud Activities

- As you read, have students note any unfamiliar words or phrases. Clarify any misunderstandings.
- Discuss each item with students to make certain they understand the expectation.

Reread the Text

- Have students make a list of signal words and phrases as they reread.
- Have partners use their lists to determine text structures and text purposes.

Independent Practice

2 Part A

The correct choice is B. The purpose of "Exploring Mars" is to list the missions to Mars and their purposes. The purpose of "Living on Mars" is to list problems with living on Mars and ways to overcome them.

- **A, C, and D** are not supported by a careful reading of either the content or the signal words in each passage.

Part B

The correct choices are C and F. "Exploring Mars" shares what scientists have learned in the past 50 years, and "Living on Mars" tells how people want to overcome the challenges of living on Mars.

- **A** and **B** do not indicate the purpose of "Exploring Mars." **D** and **E** do not indicate the purpose of "Living on Mars."

***DOK 2* RI.5.5**

3 The correct choice is B. The affix *-ible* means "able to be."

- **A, C** and **D** would require the affixes *–ization, -ful* or *–ious*, and *–est,* respectively.

***DOK 2* L.5.4b**

2 This question has two parts. First, answer Part A. Then answer Part B.

Part A

Which statement **best** describes the difference between the purposes of the articles "Exploring Mars" and "Living on Mars"?

A "Exploring Mars" argues that NASA should continue sending spacecraft to Mars, while "Living on Mars" argues that it is too costly.

(B) "Exploring Mars" describes the purposes of each mission to Mars, while "Living on Mars" describes ways to overcome challenges to living there.

C "Exploring Mars" focuses on the problems each spacecraft faced, while "Living on Mars" is an emotional account of what it is like to live there.

D "Exploring Mars" tells the steps needed to survive a mission to Mars, while "Living on Mars" tells facts about Mars's climate.

Part B

Choose **one** sentence from **each** article that supports the answer in Part A.

A "Then new technology allowed the United States to get even closer." ("Exploring Mars")

B "NASA lost contact with *Spirit* in 2010." ("Exploring Mars")

(C) "Over the past 50 years, scientists have learned a great deal about Mars." ("Exploring Mars")

D "Of all the planets in our solar system, Mars has the best conditions to support human life." ("Living on Mars")

E "That's a long trip if you need to return to Earth for supplies!" ("Living on Mars")

(F) "Despite all of these problems, some humans are eager to build permanent colonies on Mars." ("Living on Mars")

3 Read the sentence from paragraph 3 of "Living on Mars."

The spacesuit would have to be light and flexible enough so you could move about freely.

What does the affix *-ible* in the word flexible mean?

A process of making

(B) able to be

C full of

D most

Monitor Understanding

If... students don't understand the writing task,

then... read aloud the writing prompt. Use the following questions to help students get started.

- **What is the prompt asking you to write about?**
- **Do you need to reread the text to find more information?**
- **How will you identify the information you need to include?**

- Have partners talk about how they will organize their responses.
- Provide a graphic organizer to assist students, if needed.

Write

4 **Short Response** Identify the text structures of "Exploring Mars" and "Living on Mars." Explain why each author chose to use that text structure for his writing. Use details from each text in your response.

Sample response: In "Exploring Mars," the author uses a chronological text structure to describe the history of the exploration of Mars. This structure lets the author describe what exploration has accomplished and how it has changed over time. In "Living on Mars," the author uses a problem–solution text structure to identify the problems people must overcome to live on Mars. The text structure lets the author present challenges to living on Mars and ways of meeting those challenges.

Learning Target

In this lesson, you compared and contrasted how the information in texts is structured. Explain how these skills can help you better understand the purposes of other informational texts you read.

Responses will vary, but students should note how comparing and contrasting the text structures of two or more passages can help them better understand the purpose of each passage. It might also give them strategies for structuring their own writing.

4 **2-Point Writing Rubric**

Points	Focus	Evidence	Organization
2	My answer does exactly what the prompt asked me to do.	My answer is supported with plenty of details from the text.	My ideas are clear and in a logical order.
1	Some of my answer does not relate to the prompt.	My answer is missing some important details from the text.	Some of my ideas are unclear and out of order.
0	My answer does not make sense.	My answer does not have any details from the text.	My ideas are unclear and not in any order.

Write

- Tell students that using what they read, they will plan and compose a short response to the writing prompt.

Monitor Understanding

Review Responses

After students have completed the writing activity, help them evaluate their responses.

4 Display or pass out copies of the reproducible **2-Point Writing Rubric** on p. TR10. Have students use the rubric to individually assess their writing and revise as needed.

When students have finished their revisions, evaluate their responses. Answers will vary but should show that in "Exploring Mars," the author uses a chronological text structure to help readers understand how exploration has changed over time. In "Living on Mars," the author uses a problem–solution text structure to help readers understand why it is difficult but perhaps not impossible for people to settle on Mars.
DOK 3 **RI.5.5, W.5.9b**

Wrap Up

Learning Target

- Have each student respond in writing to the Learning Target prompt.
- When students have finished, have them share their responses. This may be done with a partner, in small groups, or as a whole class.

LESSON OVERVIEW

Lesson 13 Comparing Text Structures, Part 2: Cause-Effect, Compare-Contrast

Standards Focus

Compare and contrast the overall structure (. . . cause/effect, comparison) of events, ideas, concepts, or information in two or more texts. RI.5.5

Lesson Objectives

Reading

- Compare cause-effect and compare-contrast text structures. RI.5.5
- Recognize words that signal particular structures. RI.5.5

Writing

- Draw evidence from informational texts to support analysis and reflection. W.5.9b

Speaking and Listening

- Pose and respond to specific questions and contribute to discussions. SL.5.1c
- Review the key ideas expressed and draw conclusions. SL.5.1d

Language

- Use Greek and Latin affixes and roots as clues to the meaning of a word. L.5.4b
- Acquire and use academic and domain-specific words and phrases. L.5.6

Additional Practice: **RI.5.3, RI.5.4, RI.5.6, RI.5.8, RI.5.9, L.5.4a**

Academic Talk

See **Glossary of Terms**, pp. TR2–TR9

- text structure
- cause-effect text structure
- compare-contrast text structure

Learning Progression

Grade 4	Grade 5	Grade 6
Students identify different text structures.	Building on Grade 4, students identify and compare the text structure of multiple texts. This helps to prepare students for the analysis required at Grade 6.	Grade 6 increases in complexity by requiring students to analyze specific sections of the text and place the sections in the context of the text's overall structure and ideas.

Lesson Text Selections

Modeled and Guided Instruction	Guided Practice	Independent Practice
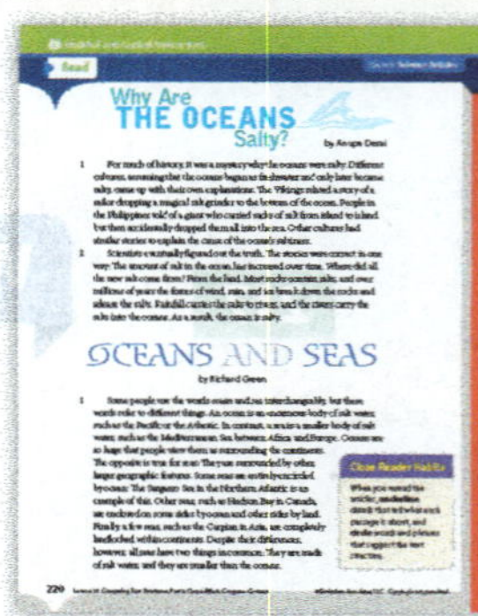	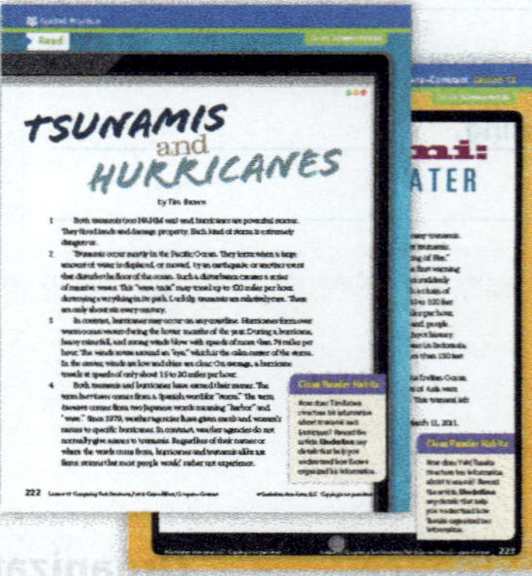	
Why Are the Oceans Salty? by Anupa Desai **Genre:** Science Article	**Tsunamis and Hurricanes** by Tim Brown **Genre:** Science Article	**Florida Keys** by Darrell Otis **Genre:** Journal Entry
Oceans and Seas by Richard Green **Genre:** Science Article	**Tsunami: A Wall of Water** by Yuki Tanaka **Genre:** Science Article	**Keep Coral Reefs Healthy** by Mary Wilford **Genre:** Editorial

Lesson Pacing Guide

Whole Class Instruction *30–45 minutes per day*

Day 1

Introduction pp. 218–219

- **Read** **Comparing Text Structures, Part 2: Cause–Effect, Compare–Contrast** *10 min*
- **Think** *10 min*
  Graphic Organizer: Four-Column Chart
- **Talk** *5 min*
  Quick Write (TRB) *5 min*

Day 2

Modeled and Guided Instruction pp. 220–221, 226

- **Read** **Why Are the Oceans Salty?** and **Oceans and Seas** *10 min*
- **Think** *10 min*
- **Talk** *5 min*
- **Write** Short Response *10 min*

Day 3

Guided Practice pp. 222–225, 227

- **Read** **Tsunamis and Hurricanes** and **Tsunami: A Wall of Water** *20 min*
- **Think** *10 min*
- **Talk** *5 min*
- **Write** Short Response *10 min*

Day 4

Independent Practice pp. 228–233

- **Read** **Florida Keys** and **Keep Coral Reefs Healthy** *20 min*
- **Think** *10 min*
- **Write** Short Response *10 min*

Day 5

Independent Practice pp. 228–233

- *Review* Answer Analysis (TRB) *10 min*
- *Review* Response Analysis (TRB) *10 min*
- *Assign and Discuss* Learning Target *10 min*

Language Handbook
Lesson 6 Shifts in Verb Tense, pp. 448–449
20 min (optional)

Ready Writing Connection

During *Ready Reading* Days 1–5, use:
Lesson 3 Writing a Narrative: Legend

- **Steps 6 and 7** **Revise**
- **Step 8** **Edit**
- **Prepare to Publish**
- **Collaborate**
- **Present**

See *Ready Writing TRB*, p. 62a for complete lesson plan.

Small Group Differentiation

Teacher-Toolbox.com

Reteach

***Ready Reading* Prerequisite Lesson**

- **Grade 4** Lesson 14 Text Structures, Part 1: Cause–Effect and Compare–Contrast

Teacher-led Activities

Tools for Instruction

- Text Structure

Personalized Learning

i-Ready.com

Independent

***i-Ready* Close Reading Lessons**

- **Grade 4** Text Structures: Cause–Effect and Compare–Contrast
- **Grade 5** Text Structures: Cause–Effect and Compare–Contrast

Introduction

Get Started

- Explain to students that in this lesson they will read informational texts about the sea and compare two ways of organizing text: cause–effect and compare–contrast.
- Remind students that the way a text is organized is called *text structure*. Tap into what students already know about text structure. Name the last informational text students read together and ask how the author mainly organized this text.
- Review the elements of cause–effect and compare–contrast text structures:

  A passage that tells how whales and dolphins are alike and different has a compare–contrast text structure. A passage that explains how the moon's gravity causes high and low tides on Earth has a cause–effect text structure. Authors choose a certain text structure in order to highlight key concepts and relationships that are important for readers to understand.
- Focus students' attention on the Learning Target. Read it aloud to set the purpose for the lesson.
- Display the Academic Talk phrases. Tell students to listen for these terms and their meanings as you work through the lesson together. Use the Academic Talk Routine on pp. A48–A49.

English Language Learners

Genre Focus

Read

- Read aloud the Read section as students follow along. Restate to reinforce:

  A passage with a compare–contrast text structure tells how two or more things are alike and different. One with a cause–effect text structure tells how events cause other events to happen. Cause–effect passages typically answer questions that begin with *how* or *why*.
- Have students read each passage and think about whether the ideas are organized by compare–contrast or cause–effect.

Introduction

RI.5.5 Compare and contrast the overall structure (e.g., ... cause/effect, comparison) of events, ideas, concepts, or information in two or more texts.

Lesson 13
Comparing Text Structures, Part 2: Cause–Effect, Compare–Contrast

When you compare and contrast how the information in texts is structured, you will better understand the purpose of each text.

Read How is a house different from a skyscraper? They each have a different structure and purpose. Authors use different **text structures** for specific purposes, too.

- The purpose of a **cause–effect text structure** is to tell about events and explain why they happen. Words and phrases like *cause, effect, because,* and *as a result* are sometimes used in a cause–effect structure.
- The purpose of a **compare–contrast text structure** is to describe how two or more things are similar and different. A compare–contrast text structure will frequently use words like *both, unlike, similarly,* and *in contrast.*

Comparing texts can help you see their structures and purposes.

Read the passages below. Look for evidence of the structure and the purpose of each one.

Passage 1: Octopuses and squids have ink sacks. When threatened, they defend themselves by shooting a thick cloud of dark ink into the water. Because the ink is thick and dark, it hides octopuses and squids from their attackers. As a result, octopuses and squids have time to escape.

Passage 2: Octopuses and squids live in salt water. Both have blue blood, hard beaks, and eight arms lined with suckers. Octopuses live in dens on the sea floor where they hunt for clams, lobsters, and crabs. In contrast, squids live in the open ocean and eat fish and shrimp.

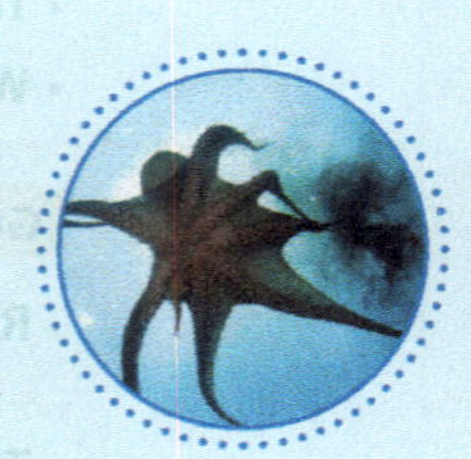

218

English Language Learners
Develop Language

Concept Vocabulary To compare and contrast two or more things, students must be able to correctly use words and phrases such as *both, alike, unlike, similar, in contrast,* and *in common.*

- Demonstrate with some simple examples, such as apples and oranges. Model the words and phrases needed to compare and contrast them: *Both* apples and oranges are fruits. *Unlike* orange peel, an apple's skin is very thin.
- Work with students to complete sentence frames, such as *Both fruits are/have* ________. *Apples are* ________. *In contrast, oranges are* ________. *One thing these fruits have in common is that they are both* ________.

Genre Focus
Journal

Tell students that during Independent Practice, they will read a journal entry called "Florida Keys." Explain that a writer's journal is a record of events and personal thoughts about things that happen in the writer's life.

A journal entry usually includes the date when the entry was written. The writer uses conversational language to tell what happened that day, what he or she observed, and how he or she felt about the day's events.

Point out that diary entries are similar to journal entries. Both *diary* and *journal* mean "a daily record." Ask if students have read or heard of any famous diaries or journals.

Think What have you learned about text structures? Use the chart below to help you compare and contrast the purposes and text structures of the passages. Include evidence of the structure of each passage.

Passage	Author's Purpose	Text Structure	Evidence of Structure
1	to tell how octopuses and squids defend themselves	cause–effect	• "Because the ink is thick and dark" • "As a result, octopuses and squids have time to escape."
2	to describe how octopuses and squids are alike and different	compare–contrast	• "Both have blue blood, hard beaks, and eight arms lined with suckers." • "In contrast, squids live in the open ocean and eat fish and shrimp."

Talk Share your chart with a partner.

- Which text structure did the author of Passage 1 use?
- Which text structure did the author of Passage 2 use?
- How did each text structure support the author's purpose for writing the passage?

Academic Talk

Use these words and phrases to talk about the text.

- text structure
- compare–contrast text structure
- cause–effect text structure

Think

- Have students read aloud the Think section. Explain that the chart will help them organize their thinking.
- Have partners complete the chart. Remind students to use clue words and phrases from each passage to identify its purpose and text structure.
- As students work, circulate and provide assistance.
- Ask volunteers to share what they wrote in their charts.
- Make certain students understand that words and phrases such as *both* and *in contrast* signal compare–contrast relationships, while *because* and *as a result* signal cause–effect relationships.

Talk

- Read aloud the Talk prompts.
- Have partners discuss the purpose and text structure of each passage.
- Ask volunteers to share their ideas.

Quick Write Have students write a response to the following prompt:

Choose two foods you like or dislike. Compare and contrast the foods, using sensory words (sight, smell, sound, taste, touch) to explain how the foods are alike and different. Then describe what happens when you eat the food.

Ask students to share their responses.

Monitor Understanding

If... students struggle to identify text structures,

then... make a chart of signal words to post in the classroom.

- **What words or phrases do you use to compare and contrast?** *(like, similar to, unlike, in contrast, whereas, while, although, different from, as opposed to, instead of, however, as well as, either/or)*
- **What words or phrases do you use to show cause and effect?** *(therefore, as a result, lead(s) to, because of, in order to, for these reasons, if-then, due to)*

Post the chart in a central location, and encourage students to make a copy in their own notebooks.

Wrap Up

- Explain to students that when they compare texts with similar topics, identifying the text structure will help them understand the author's purpose for writing each text. This process will also help them better understand the content of each passage.

  In the next section, we'll read two scientific texts about oceans and seas. Identifying the passages' purposes and text structures will help you understand and remember the information.

Monitor Understanding

Modeled and Guided Instruction

Get Started

Today you will read science articles about the ocean and the sea. First, you'll read to understand the information in each text. Then you'll read to compare and contrast the structure and purpose of the texts.

Read

- Read aloud the title of each article. Invite students to share what they know about oceans and seas.
- Have students read the texts independently. Tell them to place a check mark above any confusing words and phrases as they read. Remind students to look inside, around, and beyond each unknown word to help them figure out its meaning. Use the Word Learning Routine on pp. A50–A51.
- When students have finished reading, clarify the meanings of words and phrases they still find confusing. Then use the questions below to check understanding. Encourage students to identify details in the text that support their answers.

  What question does the first text answer? *(Why are the oceans salty?)*

  Where does the salt in the oceans and seas come from? *(rocks on land)*

  Name the main difference and the main similarity between oceans and seas. *(Main difference: oceans are larger; Main similarity: both oceans and seas are salty.)*

English Language Learners

- **Word Learning Strategy**

Explore

- Read aloud the Explore question at the top of p. 221 to set the purpose for the second read. Tell students they will need to take a closer look at the connection between ideas in each passage.
- Have students read aloud the Close Reader Habit on p. 220.

TIP Remind students that the title of a passage can often give a clue about the text structure.

Read

Genre: Science Articles

Why Are THE OCEANS Salty?

by Anupa Desai

1 For much of history, it was a mystery why the oceans were salty. Different cultures, assuming that the oceans began as freshwater and only later became salty, came up with their own explanations. The Vikings related a story of a sailor dropping a magical salt grinder to the bottom of the ocean. People in the Philippines told of a giant who carried sacks of salt from island to island but then accidentally dropped them all into the sea. Other cultures had similar stories to explain the cause of the ocean's saltiness.

2 Scientists eventually figured out the truth. The stories were correct in one way: The amount of salt in the ocean has increased over time. Where did all the new salt come from? From the land. Most rocks contain salts, and over millions of years the forces of wind, rain, and ice break down the rocks and release the salts. Rainfall carries the salts to rivers, and the rivers carry the salts into the oceans. As a result, the ocean is salty.

OCEANS AND SEAS

by Richard Green

1 Some people use the words *ocean* and *sea* interchangeably, but these words refer to different things. An ocean is an enormous body of salt water, such as the Pacific or the Atlantic. In contrast, a sea is a smaller body of salt water, such as the Mediterranean Sea between Africa and Europe. Oceans are so large that people view them as surrounding the continents. The opposite is true for seas: They are surrounded by other, larger geographic features. Some seas are entirely encircled by ocean: The Sargasso Sea in the Northern Atlantic is an example of this. Other seas, such as Hudson Bay in Canada, are enclosed on some sides by ocean and other sides by land. Finally, a few seas, such as the Caspian in Asia, are completely landlocked within continents. Despite their differences, however, all seas have two things in common: They are made of salt water, and they are smaller than the oceans.

Close Reader Habits

When you reread the articles, **underline** details that tell what each passage is about, and **circle** words and phrases that suggest the text structure.

220

English Language Learners

Build Meaning

Academic Vocabulary To help students understand the differences between oceans and seas as described in the second passage, identify and define some key geography vocabulary.

- Write the following terms on the board: *body of water, continents, geographic features, landlocked.* Work with students to identify these words within the passage. Look for context clues that convey the meaning of each word.
- Use a map featuring an ocean and a sea to illustrate some of the terms. Point out, for example, that *landlocked* is a compound word meaning "surrounded on all sides, or locked in, by land." Encourage students to practice using the terms by identifying features on the map.

Word Learning Strategy

Analyze Word Parts

- Reread the first sentence in "Oceans and Seas." Direct students' attention to the word *interchangeably.*

  What word parts do you see in this word? *(inter-, change, -able, -ly)*

  How do the word parts' meanings help you figure out what *interchangeably* means?

- Guide students to determine the meanings of *inter- ("between; back and forth"); change ("switching one for another"); -able ("able to be");* and *-ly (a suffix that changes an adjective into an adverb).*
- Help students put the meanings together to define *interchangeably* in context.

L.5.4b

Explore What text structure does the author of each passage mainly use to present information?

Look for words that show cause and effect or comparison and contrast.

Think

1 Identify the purpose and text structure of each passage. Then tell what evidence helped you figure out the structure.

Passage	Author's Purpose	Text Structure	Evidence of Structure
"Why Are the Oceans Salty?"	to tell why the oceans are salty	cause and effect	• "mystery why" • "explanations" • "to explain the cause" • "As a result, the ocean is salty."
"Oceans and Seas"	to describe similarities and differences between oceans and seas and between types of seas	compare and contrast	• "but these words refer to different things." • "In contrast, a sea is a smaller body" • "The opposite is true for seas" • "two things in common"

Talk

2 Share your charts. Look at the evidence you found for each text structure. How does each text structure support the author's purpose? If your partner has good evidence that you do not, add it to your chart.

Write

3 **Short Response** Explain how the text structure of each passage supports each author's purpose for writing. Use text evidence to support your response. Use the space provided on page 226 to write your answer.

HINT Be sure to quote words and phrases from each passage as evidence of its text structure.

Think Aloud

- What is the author's purpose for writing "Why Are the Oceans Salty?" Actually, the title basically tells me the author's purpose. Desai wants to answer this question, or find the cause for the oceans' salty water. I'll write this in the *Author's Purpose* column.
- If a passage's main purpose is to explain why something happens, its text structure is most likely cause–effect. I'll look for evidence that "Why Are the Oceans Salty?" is mainly organized to show causes and effects. I'll write my evidence in the *Evidence of Structure* column.

Think

- Read aloud the Think section. Explain to students that you will model how to find text evidence to fill in part of the chart. Use the **Think Aloud** below to guide your modeling.
- Revisit the Explore question. Guide students to determine that they need to look for more details, using the Close Reader Habit.
- Encourage students to work with a partner to continue rereading the passage and complete the chart. Remind them that the Buddy Tip will help them determine the text structure.
- Ask volunteers to share their completed charts.
- Guide students to see that a passage's purpose and text structure are closely related—authors choose a text structure to reinforce their purpose for writing.

Talk

- Read aloud the Talk prompt.
- Have partners respond to the prompt. Use the Talk Routine on pp. A52–A53.
- Circulate to check that students are using their partners' completed charts to improve upon what they wrote in their *Evidence of Structure* columns.

Write

- Ask a volunteer to read aloud the Write prompt.
- Invite a few students to tell what the prompt is asking them to do.
- Make sure students understand that they need to explain how each author chose a particular text structure in order to accomplish his or her purpose for writing.
- Have students turn to p. 226 to write their response.
- Use Review Responses on p. 226 to assess students' writing.

Wrap Up

- Ask students to recall the Learning Target. Have them explain how comparing and contrasting "Why Are the Oceans Salty?" and "Oceans and Seas" helped them understand and remember the information in both passages.

Guided Practice

Get Started

Today you will read two more articles related to oceans and seas. First you will read to understand what each article is about. Then you will reread with a partner to compare and contrast the articles and figure out how the authors organized their texts.

Read

- Read aloud the title of each article and invite students to share any prior knowledge about tsunamis and hurricanes.
- **Read to Understand** Have students read the articles independently. Tell them to place a check mark above any confusing words and phrases as they read. Remind students to look inside, around, and beyond each unknown word or phrase to help them figure out its meaning. Use the Word Learning Routine on pp. A50–A51.
- When students have finished reading, clarify the meanings of words and phrases they still find confusing. Then use the questions below to check understanding. Encourage students to identify details in the text that support their answers.

  What is one similarity between hurricanes and tsunamis? *(Both are dangerous storms that start at sea.)*

  What are some differences between the two? *(A tsunami is a series of tall, destructive waves. A hurricane is a storm made up of strong winds and heavy rain; its winds rotate around a calm point called the "eye.")*

  Name two kinds of events that cause tsunamis. *(earthquakes and landslides under the Pacific Ocean)*

  What mainly causes hurricanes? *(warm water in oceans)*

English Language Learners

- **Word Learning Strategy**

Guided Practice

Read

Genre: Science Article

TSUNAMIS and HURRICANES

by Tim Brown

1 Both tsunamis (soo NAHM eez) and hurricanes are powerful storms. They flood lands and damage property. Each kind of storm is extremely dangerous.

2 Tsunamis occur mostly in the Pacific Ocean. They form when a large amount of water is displaced, or moved, by an earthquake or another event that disturbs the floor of the ocean. Such a disturbance creates a series of massive waves. This "wave train" may travel up to 500 miles per hour, destroying everything in its path. Luckily, tsunamis are relatively rare. There are only about six every century.

3 In contrast, hurricanes may occur on any coastline. Hurricanes form over warm ocean waters during the hotter months of the year. During a hurricane, heavy rains fall, and strong winds blow with speeds of more than 74 miles per hour. The winds rotate around an "eye," which is the calm center of the storm. In the center, winds are low and skies are clear. On average, a hurricane travels at speeds of only about 15 to 20 miles per hour.

4 Both tsunamis and hurricanes have earned their names. The term *hurricane* comes from a Spanish word for "storm." The term *tsunami* comes from two Japanese words meaning "harbor" and "wave." Since 1979, weather agencies have given men's and women's names to specific hurricanes. In contrast, weather agencies do not normally give names to tsunamis. Regardless of their names or where the words come from, hurricanes and tsunamis alike are fierce storms that most people would rather not experience.

Close Reader Habits

How does Tim Brown structure his information about tsunamis and hurricanes? Reread the article. **Underline** any details that help you understand how Brown organized his information.

222

English Language Learners

Build Meaning

Visual Aids Have students work in pairs to reread "Tsunamis and Hurricanes." Tell them to make a list of details related to each storm as they read. Provide a Venn diagram on p. TR24 if necessary.

- When students have finished their lists, have them create a picture of a tsunami and a picture of a hurricane, based on the details in their lists. Students should label the pictures with words from the passage.
- Invite students to share their pictures and describe the details. Encourage the class to notice what is similar and different about the drawings.

Genre: Science Article

Tsunami: A WALL OF WATER

by Yuki Tanaka

1 A tsunami is a series of huge waves. Earthquakes cause many tsunamis. Erupting volcanoes or underwater landslides may also trigger tsunamis. Nearly all tsunamis occur in the Pacific Ocean within the "Ring of Fire."

2 Warning signs tell us when a tsunami is approaching. The first warning sign of an approaching tsunami is called *drawback*. The ocean suddenly recedes, or draws back, and then roars forward violently with a chain of extremely high waves. These surging waves can reach from 30 to 100 feet above sea level. They can crash onto land at speeds of 500 miles per hour, causing damage to buildings and injuring or killing animals and people.

3 There have been many record-breaking tsunamis throughout history. One of the largest tsunamis happened after Krakatoa, a volcano in Indonesia, erupted in 1883. The eruption caused some waves to rise more than 130 feet above sea level. As a result, about 36,000 people drowned.

4 The most deadly tsunami in modern times occurred in the Indian Ocean in 2004. People in India, Thailand, Indonesia, and other parts of Asia were taken by surprise when the tsunami slammed into the coast. This tsunami left millions homeless and killed more than 300,000 people.

5 More recently, a powerful earthquake rocked Japan on March 11, 2011. The earthquake caused 60-foot tsunami waves. This resulted in more than 15,000 deaths and more than 25,000 injuries. It destroyed buildings and damaged a nuclear power station. Although Japan has a good warning system, many Japanese could not escape from the dark wall of surging water.

Close Reader Habits

How does Yuki Tanaka structure her information about tsunamis? Reread the article. **Underline** any details that help you understand how Tanaka organized her information.

223

Lesson 13

- **Read to Analyze** Read aloud the Close Reader Habits on pp. 222 and 223 to set the purpose for the second read. Then have students reread the articles with a partner and discuss any questions they might have.

TIP Remind students that, while signal words are usually good signs of a particular text structure, authors do not always use them. Readers should always consider the author's purpose while they read, asking themselves, "Why is the author telling me this?" and "Why is this detail or idea important?"

Word Learning Strategy

Analyze Word Parts

- Identify the following words from each passage:
  "Tsunamis and Hurricanes"–*powerful* (paragraph 1); *displaced, disturbs* (paragraph 2); *Regardless* (paragraph 4)
  "Tsunami: A Wall of Water"–*recedes* (paragraph 2)
  Read aloud the sentence in which each word appears and write the words on the board.

  What prefixes and suffixes can you find in these words? *(-ful, dis-, -less, and re-)*

  How can you use the affixes' meanings to help you figure out the whole words' meanings? *(Example:* -ful *means "full of";* powerful *means "full of power.")*
- Encourage students to use dictionaries to define any roots or affixes they do not know. Then help them use the affix meanings, base-word meanings, and sentence context to define each of the whole words.
  L.5.4b

Guided Practice

Think

- Have students work with a partner to complete items 1–3. Draw attention to the boldface words in each item.

TIP For item 1, remind students that one article is about both tsunamis and hurricanes, while the other is only about tsunamis. Have them move through the Details list once to eliminate any details that cannot appear in both places. For the remaining details, encourage them to skim each article to look for key words in the bulleted detail.

Answer Analysis

When students have finished, discuss correct and incorrect responses.

1 **See the answers on the student book page.** Explain that this item simulates a drag-and-drop item students may encounter on a computer-based assessment.
DOK 3

Think Use what you learned from reading the science articles to answer the following questions.

Some science articles tell what happened and why it happened. Others compare and contrast events, ideas, or concepts.

1 The box below gives details on how the articles by Tim Brown and Yuki Tanaka present information.

Details
• Describes how tsunamis and hurricanes are different
• Explains what causes tsunamis
• Explains what causes hurricanes
• Gives examples of what happens when storms reach land
• Explains what caused several tsunamis in the past
• Gives reasons why tsunamis are deadly

Write details from the list to complete the chart below. Use **each** detail **one** time.

Article by Tim Brown	Article by Yuki Tanaka	Both Articles
Describes how tsunamis and hurricanes are different	Explains what caused several tsunamis in the past	Explains what causes tsunamis
Explains what causes hurricanes	Gives reasons why tsunamis are deadly	Gives examples of what happens when storms reach land

Integrating Standards

Use the following questions to further students' understanding of the articles.

- **In what way are Tim Brown's and Yuki Tanaka's points of view (feelings, opinions, and attitudes) about tsunamis similar? Give text evidence to support your answer.** *(Both authors think that tsunamis are very dangerous. Brown writes that both tsunamis and hurricanes are "extremely dangerous." Tanaka explains that tsunamis can damage buildings and injure or kill animals and people.)*
DOK 3 **RI.5.6, RI.5.9**
- **Explain the relationship between geographic features of the earth and powerful storms like hurricanes and tsunamis. Give text evidence from both articles to support your answer.** *(Tsunamis are formed when an earthquake, an erupting volcano, an underwater landslide, or any other movement disturbs the ocean floor. A hurricane forms over very warm ocean waters, usually during the hotter months of the year.)*
DOK 3 **RI.5.3, RI.5.9**

2 Select **one** sentence from **each** article that provides the **best** evidence of each article's text structure.

A "Such a disturbance creates a series of massive waves." ("Tsunamis and Hurricanes")

B "In the center, winds are low and skies are clear." ("Tsunamis and Hurricanes")

(C) "In contrast, weather agencies do not normally give names to tsunamis." ("Tsunamis and Hurricanes")

D "A tsunami is a series of huge waves." ("Tsunami: A Wall of Water")

E "There have been many record-breaking tsunamis throughout history." ("Tsunami: A Wall of Water")

(F) "This resulted in more than 15,000 deaths and more than 25,000 injuries." ("Tsunami: A Wall of Water")

3 In "Tsunami: A Wall of Water," how is paragraph 3 **different** from the ones that come before and after it?

(A) It is the first paragraph that describes a specific tsunami.

B It is the last paragraph that explains the causes of tsunamis.

C It is the last paragraph that describes famous tsunamis in history.

D It is the first paragraph that explains how tsunamis damage buildings.

Talk

4 State the purpose of each passage. Then compare how each author presents information about tsunamis. Use the chart on page 227 to organize your ideas and evidence.

Write

5 **Short Response** Compare and contrast the purpose and text structure of "Tsunamis and Hurricanes" with that of "Tsunami: A Wall of Water." Use details from **each** passage in your response. Use the space provided on page 227 to write your answer.

HINT Briefly state how the passages are alike. Then discuss how their purposes and structures differ.

Monitor Understanding

If... students have difficulty completing item 4,

then... have them return to their answers for items 1–3. Remind them that the text structure an author chooses to use directly supports his or her purpose for writing. For example, if an author chooses a cause–effect structure, he or she wants to explain why something happens, or what happens as a result of something else.

2 **Choices C and F are correct. C** uses the phrase "in contrast," which indicates the compare–contrast text structure of "Tsunamis and Hurricanes." **F** uses the phrase "resulted in," which indicates the cause–effect text structure of "Tsunami: A Wall of Water."

- **A** and **B** do not provide clear evidence of the compare–contrast text structure of "Tsunamis and Hurricanes." **D** and **E** do not provide clear evidence of the cause–effect text structure of "Tsunami: A Wall of Water."

DOK 3

3 **The correct choice is A.** Paragraph 3 describes the tsunami in 1883 caused by the explosion of Krakatoa.

- **B** is incorrect because paragraphs 4 and 5 also describe the causes of tsunamis. **C** is incorrect because paragraph 3 is the first paragraph to describe famous tsunamis. **D** is incorrect because paragraph 2 describes how tsunamis damage buildings.

DOK 2

Integrating Standards

Talk

- Have partners discuss the prompt. Emphasize that students should support their ideas with text details.
- Circulate to clarify misunderstandings.

Monitor Understanding

Write

- See p. 227 for instructional guidance.

Wrap Up

- Ask students to recall the Learning Target. Have them explain how comparing and contrasting the two articles and identifying the text structure helped them better understand each article.

Modeled and Guided Instruction

Write

- Remember to use the Response-Writing Routine on pp. A54–A55.

Review Responses

After students complete the writing activity, help them evaluate their responses.

3 Responses may vary but should explain how the text structure of each passage supports the author's purpose for writing, giving examples to support their ideas. See the sample response on the student book page.
DOK 3

Write Use the space below to write your answer to the question on page 221.

Why Are THE OCEANS Salty? OCEANS AND SEAS

HINT Be sure to quote words and phrases from each passage as evidence of its text structure.

3 **Short Response** Explain how the text structure of each passage supports each author's purpose for writing. Use text evidence to support your response.

Sample Response: In "Why Are the Oceans Salty?" the author uses a cause-effect structure to explain why the oceans are salty. She uses words and phrases such as "why," "explanations," and "as a result." She also poses questions and answers them. In "Oceans and Seas," the author uses a compare-contrast structure to make clear the similarities and differences between the oceans and seas. He uses words and phrases such as "but," "different," "opposite," and "in contrast" to compare oceans to seas. He also compares the different types of seas by using the words and phrases "some," "other," "a few," and "two things in common."

Check Your Writing

- ☐ Did you read the prompt carefully?
- ☐ Did you put the prompt in your own words?
- ☐ Did you use the best evidence from the text to support your ideas?
- ☐ Are your ideas clearly organized?
- ☐ Did you write in clear and complete sentences?
- ☐ Did you check your spelling and punctuation?

226

Scaffolding Support for Reluctant Writers

If students are having a difficult time getting started, use the strategies below. Work individually with struggling students, or have students work with partners.

- Circle the verbs in the prompt that tell you what to do, such as *describe*, *explain*, or *compare*.
- Underline words and phrases in the prompt that show what information you need to provide in your response, such as *causes*, *reasons*, or *character traits*.
- Talk about the details from the text that you will include in your response.
- Explain aloud how you will respond to the prompt.

TSUNAMIS and HURRICANES

Tsunami: A WALL OF WATER

4 Use the chart below to organize your ideas and evidence.

Passage	Author's Purpose	Text Structure	Evidence of Structure

Write Use the space below to write your answer to the question on page 225.

5 **Short Response** Compare and contrast the purpose and text structure of "Tsunamis and Hurricanes" with that of "Tsunami: A Wall of Water." Use details from **each** passage in your response.

HINT Briefly state how the passages are alike. Then discuss how their purposes and structures differ.

Sample response: Both "Tsunamis and Hurricanes" and "Tsunami: A Wall of Water" discuss tsunamis, but each has a different purpose and text structure. "Tsunamis and Hurricanes" tells about the similarities and differences between tsunamis and hurricanes. It uses a compare–contrast structure, as shown by words and phrases such as "both," "alike," and "in contrast." "Tsunami: A Wall of Water" explains the causes and effects of tsunamis. It uses a cause–effect structure, as shown by words and phrases such as "cause," "as a result," and "this resulted in."

227

Teacher Notes

Talk

4 Students should use the chart to record and organize their thoughts and evidence.

Write

- Ask a volunteer to read aloud the Write prompt.
- Invite students to tell what the prompt is asking them to do. Make sure they understand that they need to identify each article's text structure and give one example from each article to support their responses.
- Call attention to the HINT.
- Remember to use the Response-Writing Routine on pp. A54–A55.

Review Responses

After students complete the writing activity, help them evaluate their responses.

5 Responses may vary but should compare and contrast the text structure of each passage as well as the author's purpose for writing, giving examples to support those ideas. See the sample response on the student book page.
DOK 3

Get Started

Today you are going to read a journal entry and an editorial. You will use what you have learned to identify the author's purpose and the text structure of each passage.

- Ask a volunteer to explain how identifying the text structure of a passage can help readers understand and remember the information in the passage. Encourage students to use the Academic Talk phrases in their response.

 **English Language Learners**

Read

You are going to read the journal entry and the editorial independently and use what you have learned to think and write about the texts. As you read the passages, remember to compare and contrast them. Figure out each author's purpose for writing and identify the text structure that each author uses to support that purpose.

- Read aloud the titles of the passages and then encourage students to preview the texts, paying close attention to the photographs and captions.
- Call attention to the Words to Know boxes at the upper left of pp. 228 and 230.
- If students need support in reading the passages, you may wish to use the Monitor Understanding suggestions.
- When students have finished, have them complete the Think and Write sections.

Monitor Understanding

Read

Genre: Journal Entry

WORDS TO KNOW

As you read, look inside, around, and beyond these words to figure out what they mean.

- **colonies**
- **structure**
- **habitats**

by Darrell Otis

1 *July 12.* So far, our summer vacation in Key Largo has been great. We went to Pennekamp Coral Reef State Park yesterday, took a tour on a glass-bottom boat, and saw some amazing coral reefs. Did you know that the Florida Keys have the only living coral barrier reef in North America?

2 Our guide told us that the reef is made of coral polyps. These tiny sea animals have soft bodies and live in warm, shallow waters. They form large colonies and are connected to one another. When coral polyps die, they leave behind a hard limestone skeleton. Over time, layers of skeletons build up to form a structure called a reef. A coral reef grows slowly upward from the ocean floor, and it may only grow one inch every year.

3 On top of the reef, there are thousands of living coral polyps. Because coral polyps are animals, they need to eat food. At night, they reach out their tentacles, or long feelers, to catch food that floats by. They also get their food from tiny algae that live inside them. The algae use the sun's energy to produce food.

Check out this close-up photo of a coral polyp! It clearly shows the tentacles (the long feelers) that they use to catch food.

English Language Learners

Build Meaning

Preview the Text Have students preview both passages. Work with them to point out text features that can provide additional information, such as the photographs and their captions. Read aloud the caption text and then prompt discussion with the following questions:

- **Based on the photos and captions, what do you predict each text will be about?**
- **What questions do you have about the texts?**

List students' questions. Encourage them to seek answers to these questions as they read the text, and to confirm or correct their predictions.

I took this photo while scuba diving in a kelp forest off the coast of California. The bass at the upper left looks pretty cozy—this is his natural habitat, after all.

4 Many types of animals live in the coral reefs in Key Largo. They swim and hide among forty kinds of soft and hard corals. I saw colorful tropical fish, spiny lobsters, and sea urchins. Shrimps and crabs also live on coral reefs.

5 Last year, our family took a trip to California. There, I had a chance to look at kelp forests up close. Both kelp forests and coral reefs are underwater habitats.

6 Kelp is long, brown algae, that lives in cool, shallow waters. Similar to coral polyps, kelp needs sunlight and a hard surface in order to grow. Kelp has three parts: the holdfast, the stipe, and the blade. The holdfast is the part that attaches to the ocean floor; the stipe connects the holdfast to the blade; and the blade is the leafy part that takes in sunlight and converts it to food.

7 Kelp forests form when kelp grows closely in crowded groups. Like coral reefs, kelp forests provide homes for many kinds of sea life, including fish, jellyfish, sea urchins, and otters. These animals can hide in the long, swaying kelp.

8 Kelp can grow two feet a day! At Monterey Bay Aquarium, I saw kelp that grew 28 feet high, but some giant kelp reaches a height of 200 feet. I like going to places where I can learn while having fun.

Monitor Understanding

If... students struggle to read and understand the passages,

then... use these scaffolding suggestions:

Question the Text Preview the texts by asking the following questions:

- **Based on the title and text features, what do you predict each passage will be about?**
- **What questions do you have about the texts?**

Vocabulary Support Define terms that may interfere with comprehension, such as *key* ("small island"), *barrier reef*, and *algae* in the journal entry; and *support* ("nurture"), *therefore*, and *acid rain* in the editorial.

Read Aloud Read aloud the text with students. You could also have students chorally read the text in a small group.

Check Understanding Use the questions below to check understanding. Encourage students to cite details in the texts that support their answers.

- **What are the journal writer's two main subjects?** *(coral reefs and kelp forests)*
- **What is the editorial writer trying to convince readers to do?** *(help protect coral reefs)*
- **What is the main similarity between the two texts?** *(Both provide information about coral reefs.)*

Independent Practice

Integrating Standards

After students have read the passages, use these questions to discuss the texts with them.

- **Use information from "Florida Keys" to define the word *reef*.**
  (A reef is an underwater mound made up of layers of limestone coral skeletons.)
  DOK 2 RI.5.4, L.5.4a
- **In "Keep Coral Reefs Healthy," what examples does the author give to support the idea that people can help preserve coral reefs?**
  (The author states that people can "walk or ride a bike instead of using a car" to reduce air and water pollution. She also writes that people can "stop littering and dumping harmful chemicals into the ocean" to help reduce pollution that harms coral reefs.)
  DOK 3 RI.5.8
- **Use both texts to explain the relationship between coral polyps and algae. Include information on the effects that rising water temperatures and pollution have on coral polyps and algae.**
  (Algae live inside coral polyps. Algae use sunlight to create food for coral polyps. When ocean water temperatures rise, polyps become stressed and expel the algae inside them. Since algae give polyps their color, the polyps become "chalky white" without algae inside them. Without the food that algae provide, the polyps die. Water pollution clouds the ocean water and blocks out sunlight that algae need to create food for polyps. This, too, causes polyps to die.)
  DOK 4 RI.5.3, RI.5.9

Theme Connection

Independent Practice

Genre: Editorial

WORDS TO KNOW
As you read, look inside, around, and beyond these words to figure out what they mean.

- **benefit**
- **fragile**
- **substances**

Keep Coral Reefs Healthy

by Mary Wilford

1 Coral reefs are extremely important. Known as the "rainforests of the sea," they provide homes to millions of different plants and animals. Coral reefs support roughly 25 percent of all the ocean's creatures. Furthermore, they benefit the economy by encouraging tourism and the fishing industry. Also, they provide ingredients to make new medicines. We must try to protect our fragile coral reefs.

2 Coral reefs are made of small animals called coral polyps (PAH lips). Coral polyps are sensitive. They often react to changes in their environment. For example, one change that causes harm to coral reefs is a rise in the water temperature. Usually, corals live in water that is 70°F to 85°F. If the temperature rises by only one or two degrees, coral polyps become stressed. As a result, they will expel, or push out, the tiny plants called algae that live inside their bodies. However, coral polyps need these algae to survive. The algae provide oxygen and food. Without algae, coral polyps cannot get enough food. Therefore, they may starve and die.

3 If algae are expelled, coral polyps change color. They turn chalky white because their brilliant colors came from the algae in their tissues. This process is known as coral bleaching. Bleached coral reefs can sometimes recover. However, a large number of coral polyps may die as a result of bleaching. One of the worst examples of coral bleaching happened in 1998. About 16 percent of the coral reefs around the world were damaged or died.

4 Another threat to coral reefs is pollution. Acid rain, oil spills, and chemical fertilizers cause water pollution. These substances poison coral polyps and other animals that live in coral reefs. Coral polyps can only grow in very clear, clean water with plenty of sunlight. The algae that live in coral polyps use sunlight to make food. But water pollution makes the water cloudy. There is less sunlight, so algae cannot make food for the coral polyps.

5 We can help preserve and protect our precious coral reefs. First, we need to reduce air and water pollution. One way to do this is walk or ride a bike instead of using a car. Another way is to stop littering and dumping harmful chemicals into the ocean. You don't have to live near the ocean to help the coral reefs. Let's start today!

230

Theme Connection

- Remind students that the theme of this lesson is Under the Sea.
- Ask students how each passage's content relates to the theme of oceans and seas. For example, the two short passages on p. 218 tell about two kinds of sea creatures: octopuses and squids.
- Discuss how the text structures of each passage in this lesson helped support the author's purpose for writing. What did each author want readers to know or understand about the sea after reading?

Think

Use what you learned from reading the journal entry and the editorial to answer the following questions.

1 This question has two parts. First, answer Part A. Then answer Part B.

Part A

Which statement **best** describes a major difference between the text structures of "Florida Keys" and "Keep Coral Reefs Healthy"?

- **A** "Florida Keys" tells why it is more important to save the kelp than the coral reefs, while "Keep Coral Reefs Healthy" tells about events in the history of coral reefs.
- **(B)** "Florida Keys" explains the similarities and differences between coral reefs and kelp, while "Keep Coral Reefs Healthy" tells about causes and effects of damage to coral reefs.
- **C** "Florida Keys" is a personal account of seeing life in the ocean, while "Keep Coral Reefs Healthy" compares the different types of damage that pollution does to the coral.
- **D** "Florida Keys" presents inspiring reasons for learning more about ocean life, while "Keep Coral Reefs Healthy" presents inspiring reasons for saving the reefs.

Part B

Choose **one** sentence from **each** passage that supports the answer in Part A.

- **A** "Our guide told us that the reef is made of coral polyps." ("Florida Keys")
- **B** "The algae use the sun's energy to produce food." ("Florida Keys")
- **(C)** "Similar to coral polyps, kelp needs sunlight and a hard surface in order to grow." ("Florida Keys")
- **D** "Coral reefs are extremely important." ("Keep Coral Reefs Healthy")
- **(E)** "For example, one change that causes harm to coral reefs is a rise in the water temperature." ("Keep Coral Reefs Healthy")
- **F** "Let's start today!" ("Keep Coral Reefs Healthy")

● Monitor Understanding

If... students struggle to complete the items,

then... you may wish to use the following suggestions:

Read Aloud Activities

- As you read, have students note any unfamiliar words or phrases. Clarify any misunderstandings.
- Discuss each item with students to make certain they understand the expectation.

Reread the Text

- For "Florida Keys," have students complete a Venn diagram as they reread. For "Keep Coral Reefs Healthy," have them complete a cause-effect chart as they reread.
- Have partners summarize each of the two texts.

Think

- Use the Monitor Understanding suggestions to support students in completing items 1–3.

● **Monitor Understanding**

Answer Analysis

When students have finished, discuss correct and incorrect responses.

1 **Part A**

The correct choice is B. The first passage's text structure is compare–contrast, and the second passage's text structure is cause–effect.

- **A** gives incorrect information about both texts.
- **C** and **D** provide some correct information about both texts but do not identify the texts' structures.

Part B

The correct choices are C and E. Students should identify the signal word *similar* in **C** and the signal word *causes* in **E**.

- **A, B, D** and **F** do not include signal words that indicate the passages' text structures.

DOK 3 RI.5.5

Independent Practice

2 **See the answers on the student book page.** Explain to students that this item simulates a drag-and-drop item they may encounter on a computer-based assessment.
DOK 3 **RI.5.5**

3 **The correct choice is D.** Students should understand that kelp uses sunlight to produce food.

- **A, B,** and **C** are not synonyms for *converts*, and the context does not support these choices.

DOK 1 **L.5.4a**

2 The box below gives details about how the journal entry by Darrell Otis and the editorial by Mary Wilford present information.

Details
• Explains how coral grow
• Explains why it is important to take care of ocean life
• Describes what kelp looks like
• Describes the effects of pollution on ocean life
• Describes the topic with emotional language
• Describes the difference between kelp and coral

Write details from the list to complete the chart below. Use **each** detail **one** time.

Journal Entry by Darrell Otis	Editorial by Mary Wilford	Both Passages
Describes the difference between kelp and coral	Explains why it is important to take care of ocean life	Explains how coral grow
Describes what kelp looks like	Describes the effects of pollution on ocean life	Describes the topic with emotional language

3 In paragraph 6 of "Florida Keys," what is the meaning of converts?

A reaches
B attaches
C digests
(D) changes

232

Monitor Understanding

If... students don't understand the writing task,

then... read aloud the writing prompt. Use the following questions to help students get started.

- **What is the prompt asking you to write about?**
- **Do you need to reread the text to find more information?**
- **How will you identify the information you need to include?**

- Have partners talk about how they will organize their responses.
- Provide a graphic organizer to assist students, if needed.

 Write

4 **Short Response** Identify the text structures of "Florida Keys" and "Keep Coral Reefs Healthy." Describe how each structure helps the author present his or her ideas. Use details from **each** text to support your response.

Sample response: "Florida Keys" uses a compare–contrast text structure. The author chose this text structure because his purpose is to describe the similarities and differences between coral reefs and kelp forests. "Keep Coral Reefs Healthy" uses a cause–effect text structure. The author chose to use this text structure to explain why coral reefs die and what happens when they do.

Learning Target

In this lesson, you compared and contrasted how information in texts is structured. Explain how these skills can help you better understand informational texts you read.

Responses will vary, but students should recognize that comparing and contrasting how information in texts is structured helps them better understand the author's overall purpose in presenting information.

233

4 2-Point Writing Rubric

Points	Focus	Evidence	Organization
2	My answer does exactly what the prompt asked me to do.	My answer is supported with plenty of details from the text.	My ideas are clear and in a logical order.
1	Some of my answer does not relate to the prompt.	My answer is missing some important details from the text.	Some of my ideas are unclear and out of order.
0	My answer does not make sense.	My answer does not have any details from the text.	My ideas are unclear and not in any order.

Lesson 13

Write

- Tell students that using what they read, they will plan and compose a short response to the writing prompt.

● **Monitor Understanding**

Review Responses

After students have completed each part of the writing activity, help them evaluate their responses.

4 Display or pass out copies of the reproducible **2-Point Writing Rubric** on p. TR10. Have students use the rubric to individually assess their writing and revise as needed.

When students have finished their revisions, evaluate their responses. Answers will vary but should identify each passage's text structure and tell why each author might have chosen that structure. See the sample response on the student book page.

DOK 3 **RI.5.5, W.5.9b**

Wrap Up

Learning Target

- Have each student respond in writing to the Learning Target prompt.
- When students have finished, have them share their responses. This may be done with a partner, in small groups, or as a whole class.

Lesson 14
Analyzing Accounts of the Same Topic

Standards Focus

Analyze multiple accounts of the same events or topic, noting important similarities and differences in the point of view they represent. RI.5.6

Lesson Objectives

Reading

- Identify the focus and point of view in several texts about the same event or topic. RI.5.6
- Compare and contrast differences in focus and point of view in several texts about the same event or topic. RI.5.6

Writing

- Draw evidence from informational texts to support analysis and reflection. W.5.9b

Speaking and Listening

- Pose and respond to specific questions and contribute to discussions. SL.5.1c
- Review the key ideas expressed and draw conclusions. SL.5.1d

Language

- Use context as a clue to the meaning of a word or phrase. L.5.4a
- Acquire and use academic and domain-specific words and phrases. L.5.6

Additional Practice: **RI.5.1, RI.5.2, RI.5.3, RI.5.4, RI.5.9, L.5.4c, L.5.5b**

Academic Talk

See **Glossary of Terms**, pp. TR2–TR9

- account
- analyze
- point of view

Learning Progression

Grade 4	Grade 5	Grade 6
Students describe differences in focus and information between a primary and a secondary source about the same topic.	Building on Grade 4, students analyze several accounts of the same topic with a focus on comparing and contrasting the point of view each text represents.	Grade 6 increases in complexity by requiring students to identify an author's point of view and give textual evidence showing how the point of view is illustrated.

Lesson Text Selections

Modeled and Guided Instruction

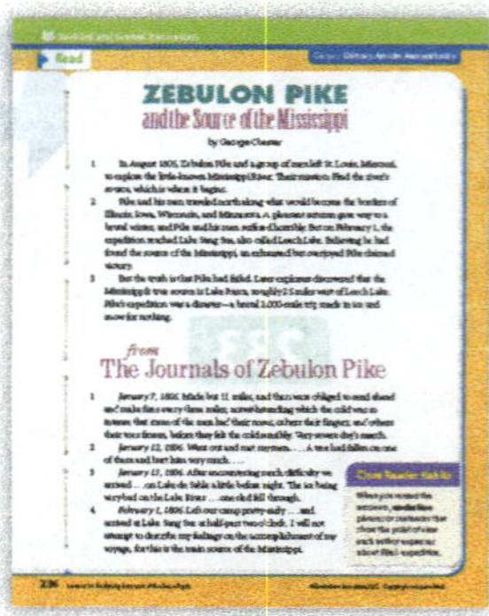

Zebulon Pike and the Source of the Mississippi
by George Chester
Genre: History Article

The Journals of Zebulon Pike
Genre: Journal Entry

Guided Practice

Village Life in America
by Caroline Cowles Richards
Genre: Journal Entry

U.S. Marshal Arrests Anthony
Genre: News Article

Rochester Union and Advertiser
Genre: Editorial

On Women's Right to Vote
by Susan B. Anthony
Genre: Speech

Independent Practice

Speak Softly and Carry a Big Stick
by Ian Dudney
Genre: Biography

Theodore Roosevelt: An Intimate Biography
by William Roscoe Thayer
Genre: Biography

Letters to His Children
by Theodore Roosevelt
Genre: Letter

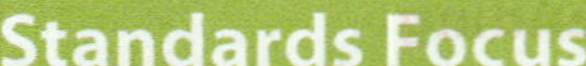

Lesson Pacing Guide

Whole Class Instruction *30–45 minutes per day*

Day 1

Teacher-Toolbox.com **Interactive Tutorial**
Analyzing Accounts of the Same Topic—Level E
20 min (optional)

Introduction pp. 234–235
- **Read** **Analyzing Accounts of the Same Topic** *10 min*
- **Think** *10 min*
  Graphic Organizer: Point-of-View Organizer
- **Talk** *5 min*
  Quick Write (TRB) *5 min*

Day 2

Modeled and Guided Instruction pp. 236–237, 242
- **Read** **Zebulon Pike and the Source of the MIssissippi** and **The Journals of Zebulon Pike** *10 min*
- **Think** *10 min*
  Graphic Organizer: Point-of-View Organizer
- **Talk** *5 min*
- **Write** Short Response *10 min*

Day 3

Guided Practice pp. 238–241, 243
- **Read** **Village Life in America, U.S. Marshal Arrests Anthony, Rochester Union and Advertiser,** and **On Women's Right to Vote** *20 min*
- **Think** *10 min*
- **Talk** *5 min*
- **Write** Short Response *10 min*

Day 4

Independent Practice pp. 244–249
- **Read** **Speak Softly and Carry a Big Stick, Theodore Roosevelt: An Intimate Biography,** and **Letters to His Children** *20 min*
- **Think** *10 min*
- **Write** Extended Response *15 min*

Day 5

Independent Practice pp. 244–249
- *Review* Answer Analysis (TRB) *10 min*
- *Review* Response Analysis (TRB) *10 min*
- *Assign and Discuss* Learning Target *10 min*

Ready Writing Connection

During *Ready Reading* Days 1–5, use:
Lesson 4 Writing to Analyze Literature: Essay

- **Step 1** **Study a Mentor Text**
- **Step 2** **Unpack Your Assignment**
- **Review the Research Path**
- **Read Source Text**
- **Step 3** **Find Text Evidence**
- **Reread Source Text**

See *Ready Writing TRB*, p. 90a for complete lesson plan.

Small Group Differentiation

Teacher-Toolbox.com

Reteach

***Ready Reading* Prerequisite Lesson**
- **Grade 4** Lesson 16 Comparing Accounts of the Same Topic

Personalized Learning

i-Ready.com

Independent

i-Ready Close Reading Lessons

- **Grade 4** Comparing Accounts of the Same Topic
- **Grade 5** Analyzing Accounts of the Same Topic

Get Started

- Explain to students that in this lesson they will read sets of passages about a topic and examine them closely to determine how the authors think or feel about the topic.
- Tap into what students already know about point of view. For example, present a brother's and sister's account of reading the same book. The sister might say: "My brother and I read a great book about whales." The brother might say: "My sister and I read a boring book about whales."
- Guide students to understand that in this example, the topic is the same but each person has a different point of view. Explain:

  Two people may read the same book or observe the same event and have different points of view about it. In the example, the sister thought the book was great but her brother thought it was boring. Both are firsthand accounts using *I* and *my*. Both describe their own feelings and experiences.
- Focus students' attention on the Learning Target. Read it aloud to set the purpose for the lesson.
- Display the Academic Talk words and phrases. Tell students to listen for these terms and their meanings as you work through the lesson together. Use the Academic Talk Routine on pp. A48–A49.

● **Genre Focus**

Read

- Read aloud the Read section as students follow along. Restate to reinforce:

  When you read two or more accounts about the same event or topic, analyze the details to determine how each author thinks and feels about it. To develop a deeper understanding of the topic, look for how the authors' points of view are alike and different.
- Direct students' attention to the illustration. Have them study the details in the picture and the speech bubbles to figure out the man's point of view and the boy's point of view.

RI.5.6 Analyze multiple accounts of the same event or topic, noting important similarities and differences in the point of view they represent.

Lesson 14 Analyzing Accounts of the Same Topic

Analyzing two or more accounts of the same topic will help you better understand different points of view about that topic.

Read An **account** is something written or told about an event or topic. An account is told from the author's **point of view** and shows what he or she thinks and feels about that event or topic.

When you read two or more accounts about the same event or topic, **analyze** (closely study) each author's point of view to tell how the accounts are similar and different.

In the cartoon below, what points of view do the man and the boy have about what is happening? Circle any details that suggest each person's point of view.

234

English Language Learners

Develop Language

Academic Vocabulary Help students unpack the term *point of view.*

- Divide students into two groups and place a multi-sided object between them.
- Have the groups spend three minutes quietly discussing and writing notes to describe what they see.
- Invite each group to share their observations, and record them in a Venn diagram.
- Emphasize that *point of view* means "how you see something." It can be literal, as in the way something looks, or it can be figurative, where *see* means the way you think or feel about it. Point out that students looked at the same object but saw different things.

● Genre Focus

Speech

Explain that during Guided Practice, students will read a speech—written remarks that are spoken and delivered to an audience.

Speakers delivering a speech often want to inform or persuade their audience. The speaker's goal is to share his or her point of view and support it with solid evidence, including facts, details, quotes, and examples. Often the speaker wants the audience to share his or her point of view.

Discuss some examples of well known speeches, such as Dr. Martin Luther King, Jr.'s "I Have a Dream."

Think Consider what you've learned so far about analyzing different accounts of the same topic or event. Complete the *point-of-view organizer* below.

Event

the tree being cut down

Details About Man's Point of View	Details About Boy's Point of View
How he looks: **happy**	How he looks: **sad**
What he says: **"I'm glad to get rid of this ugly tree."**	What he says: **"I loved climbing that tree."**
His point of view about the event: **The man feels happy about the tree being cut down.**	His point of view about the event: **The boy is sad to see the tree being cut down.**

Talk Share your point-of-view organizer with a partner.

- What point of view does each person have about the event?
- Did you list the same details?
- How do the details you listed help you analyze the two points of view?

Academic Talk
Use these words and phrases to talk about the text.
- **account**
- **analyze**
- **point of view**

235

Monitor Understanding

If... students struggle to identify similarities and differences in points of view,

then... demonstrate an example. Have students consider the different points of view people might have about a proposal to raise taxes to build a community swimming pool.

- **Who would probably think this proposal is a good idea?** *(people who like to swim; people who do not have a pool)*
- **Who might oppose it?** *(people who don't swim; people who don't have enough money for the increased taxes)*

Ask students to provide their own examples of topics that people may have similar or different opinions about.

Think

- Have students read aloud the Think section. Explain that the point-of-view organizer will help them capture their thoughts and ideas.
- Have partners complete the organizer. Remind students to use the details in both the picture and the words to identify the event and two points of view about it.
- As students work, circulate and provide assistance as needed.
- Ask volunteers to share what they wrote.
- Make certain students understand that they must make an inference about the little boy's point of view, which is not stated directly.

Talk

- Read aloud the Talk prompts.
- Have partners discuss the details they listed and compare their point-of-view statements.
- Ask volunteers to share their ideas.

Quick Write Have students write a response to the following prompt:

Describe a recent event, book, or movie that you and someone else had different opinions about. How did your point of view differ from the other person's? What do you think caused them to be different?

Ask students to share their responses.

Wrap Up

- Invite students to share what they've learned so far. Encourage them to use the Academic Talk words and phrases in their explanations.
- Explain to students that when they read accounts of historical events, they can examine the details in the text to determine the authors' thoughts and feelings about the topic.

In the next section, we'll read a history article and a journal entry and explore two authors' points of view about the same event. Analyzing their points of view will help you better understand the topic.

● **Monitor Understanding**

Modeled and Guided Instruction

Get Started

Today you will read two accounts about the same event in history. First, you'll read to understand what the authors say. Then you'll read to analyze how the points of view are alike and different.

Read

- Read aloud the title of each passage. Call attention to the name Zebulon Pike in both titles. Guide students to make predictions about the accounts.
- Have students read the passages independently. Tell them to place a check mark above any confusing words and phrases as they read. Remind students to look inside, around, and beyond each unknown word or phrase to help them figure out its meaning. Use the Word Learning Routine on pp. A50–A51.
- When students have finished reading, clarify the meanings of words and phrases they still find confusing. Then use the questions below to check understanding. Encourage students to identify details in the text that support their answers.

  What is the topic of both passages? *(Zebulon Pike's exploration)*

  Why did Pike make the journey? *(to find the source of the Mississippi River)*

  Who wrote the history article? *(George Chester)*

  Who wrote the journal? *(Zebulon Pike)*

 **English Language Learners**

● **Word Learning Strategy**

Explore

- Read aloud the Explore question at the top of p. 237 to set the purpose for the second read. Tell students they will need to take a closer look at each author's thoughts and feelings to answer this question.
- Have students read aloud the Close Reader Habit on p. 236.

> **TIP** Remind students that adjectives often give clues about someone's point of view. Have them look carefully at the words each author uses to describe the situation.

Modeled and Guided Instruction

Read

Genres: History Article/Journal Entry

ZEBULON PIKE
and the Source of the Mississippi

by George Chester

1 In August 1805, Zebulon Pike and a group of men left St. Louis, Missouri, to explore the little-known Mississippi River. Their mission: Find the river's source, which is where it begins.

2 Pike and his men traveled north along what would become the borders of Illinois, Iowa, Wisconsin, and Minnesota. A pleasant autumn gave way to a brutal winter, and Pike and his men suffered horribly. But on February 1, the expedition reached Lake Sang Sue, also called Leech Lake. Believing he had found the source of the Mississippi, an exhausted but overjoyed Pike claimed victory.

3 But the truth is that Pike had failed. Later explorers discovered that the Mississippi's true source is Lake Itasca, roughly 25 miles west of Leech Lake. Pike's expedition was a disaster—a brutal 2,000-mile trip made in ice and snow for nothing.

from The Journals of Zebulon Pike

1 *January 7, 1806.* Made but 11 miles, and then were obliged to send ahead and make fires every three miles; notwithstanding which the cold was so intense that some of the men had their noses, others their fingers, and others their toes frozen, before they felt the cold sensibly. Very severe day's march.

2 *January 12, 1806.* Went out and met my men. . . . A tree had fallen on one of them and hurt him very much. . . .

3 *January 13, 1806.* After encountering much difficulty we arrived . . . on Lake de Sable a little before night. The ice being very bad on the Lake River . . . one sled fell through.

4 *February 1, 1806.* Left our camp pretty early . . . and arrived at Lake Sang Sue at half-past two o'clock. I will not attempt to describe my feelings on the accomplishment of my voyage, for this is the main source of the Mississippi.

Close Reader Habits

When you reread the accounts, **underline** phrases or sentences that show the point of view each author expresses about Pike's expedition.

236

English Language Learners
Build Meaning

Prior Knowledge Help students understand that a *journal* is closely related to a diary. Explain that both are daily records of personal experiences and thoughts.

- Discuss the ways in which diary or journal entries are different from formal writing. Help students recognize that diary or journal entries are more like a conversation, so they usually contain slang and incomplete sentences. To reinforce the discussion, point out examples students will encounter in Pike's journal: "Made but 11 miles, and then were obliged to send ahead. . ." "Very severe day's march."

● Word Learning Strategy
Use Context Clues

- Point out the phrase *gave way to* in paragraph 2 of Chester's account. Explain that some phrases, called *idioms*, can't be understood from the meanings of the individual words. *Gave way to* is an idiom.

  What do you think *gave way to* means? What clues help you figure out the meaning?

- Guide students to find the phrases "pleasant autumn" and "brutal winter." Putting together what they know about winter following autumn, along with the antonyms *pleasant* and *brutal*, students can figure out that *gave way to* means "was replaced by." **L.5.4a, L.5.5b**

Explore What are the similarities and differences in the points of view of the two accounts?

Two authors can reach different conclusions about the same topic.

Think

1 Complete this point-of-view organizer by identifying the topic of the accounts. Then list details that describe the point of view each author expresses. How do the authors' conclusions differ?

Topic

Zebulon Pike's exploration of the Mississippi

Details About George Chester's Point of View	Details About Zebulon Pike's Point of View
• 1805, Pike explored Mississippi to find river's source • brutal winter • reached Lake Sang Sue and thought it was the source • real source is Lake Itasca • expedition failed	• January 7, 1806, traveled 11 miles in intense cold • January 12, 1806, one man hurt when tree fell on him • January 13, 1806, one sled fell through ice on Lake de Sable • February 1, 1806, believed Lake Sang Sue was source of Mississippi • despite difficulties, felt expedition was success

Talk

2 Analyze the point of view each author expresses about Pike's expedition. What information did Chester include that Pike did not? What is similar and different in the accounts? Can you add any information to your chart?

Write

3 **Short Response** Compare and contrast each account's point of view about Zebulon Pike's expedition. Use details from both accounts in your response. Use the space provided on page 242 to write your answer.

HINT Use terms such as "point of view" and "topic" in your response.

237

Think Aloud

- We've read both passages once already, so we know they are both about Zebulon Pike's exploration of the Mississippi River. I will add that to the *Topic* cell of my chart.
- Now I need to look for details about each writer's point of view. I can do this a couple of ways: I can find a detail in Chester's account and then look for a related detail in Pike's account. Or, I can write down all the details from Chester's, and then all the details from Pike's, and compare and contrast them afterward. I think I will do it that way.
- The first paragraph of Chester's account gives important information, but he does not give an opinion about it. This is what we call *neutral*. He does not feel one way or another about what happened. I'll keep reading.
- In the second paragraph, I see descriptive words that show some opinion. "A pleasant autumn gave way to a brutal winter, and Pike and his men suffered horribly." The words *brutal* and *suffered horribly* show that Chester recognized how hard the conditions were for Pike and his men. I'm going to add the term *brutal winter* to my chart under *Details about George Chester's Point of View.*

Think

- Read aloud the Think section. Explain to students that you will model how to find text evidence to fill in part of the organizer. Use the **Think Aloud** below to guide your modeling.
- Revisit the Explore question. Guide students to determine that they need to look for more details, using the Close Reader Habit.
- Encourage students to work with a partner to continue rereading the passage and complete the point-of-view organizer. Point out that the Buddy Tip will help them understand how to figure out point of view.
- Ask volunteers to share their completed organizers.
- Guide students to see that the two authors had opposite points of view on the success of the mission. Pike believed that he succeded, while Chester considered the mission a failure.

Talk

- Read aloud the Talk prompt.
- Have partners respond to the prompt. Use the Talk Routine on pp. A52–A53.
- Circulate to check that students are comparing and contrasting the two accounts. They should understand that Chester included information that Pike did not have at the time of his expedition.

Write

- Ask a volunteer to read aloud the Write prompt.
- Invite a few students to tell what the prompt is asking them to do.
- Make sure students understand that they need to include information from both accounts in their responses.
- Have students turn to p. 242 to write their response.
- Use Review Responses on p. 242 to assess students' writing.

Wrap Up

- Ask students to recall the Learning Target. Have them explain how identifying similarities and differences in the points of view helped them better understand the shared topic of the accounts.

Guided Practice

Get Started

Today you will read four historical accounts. First you will read to understand what each account is about. Then you will reread with a partner to analyze similarities and differences in the authors' points of view.

Read

- Read aloud the title of each passage and identify its genre. Discuss the date at the beginning of Richards' journal entry to help students establish context for the time period.
- Have students predict what the accounts will be about based on the title of each passage.
- **Read to Understand** Have students read the accounts independently. Tell them to place a check mark above any confusing words and phrases as they read. Remind students to look inside, around, and beyond each unknown word or phrase to help them figure out its meaning. Use the Word Learning Routine on pp. A50–A51.
- When students have finished reading, clarify the meanings of words and phrases they still find confusing. Then use the questions below to check understanding. Encourage students to identify details in the text that support their answers.

  What is the topic of all four accounts? *(women's right to vote)*

  Who was Susan B. Anthony? *(a speaker who encouraged women to vote and was arrested for voting illegally)*

  Why did Anthony believe women had a right to vote? *(The preamble of the Constitution granted all citizens the right to vote.)*

English Language Learners

- **Word Learning Strategy**

Guided Practice

Read

Genres: Journal Entry/News Article

from *Village Life in America*

by Caroline Cowles Richards

Susan B. Anthony

1 *December 20, 1855.* Susan B. Anthony is in town and spoke in Bemis Hall this afternoon. . . . She had a large audience and talked very plainly about our rights and how we ought to stand up for them, and said the world would never go right until the women had just as much right to vote and rule as the men. She asked us all to come up and sign our names who would promise to do all in our power to bring about that glad day when equal rights should be the law of the land. A whole lot of us went up and signed the paper. . . . I could not make Grandmother agree with her at all and she said we might better all of us stayed at home.

U.S. Marshal Arrests Anthony

1 **Rochester, New York**—Susan B. Anthony was arrested at her home on Madison Street on November 28. She was charged with the crime of illegal voting.

2 On November 1, Miss Anthony, her three sisters, and eleven other Rochester women registered to vote at a local barbershop. At first, election inspectors refused. Then Miss Anthony threatened to take the inspectors to court and sue them for a large sum of money. Finally the election supervisor agreed to allow the women to register to vote in Rochester's Eighth Ward. Four days later, Anthony and the other women voted in the 1872 presidential election.

3 A poll watcher who observed the election process filed a complaint about Miss Anthony's actions. William Storrs acted on the complaint. He ordered Miss Anthony's arrest on November 14. Mr. Storrs also ordered the arrests of the other women and the election inspectors.

Close Reader Habits

What does Caroline Richards think about Anthony's ideas? Reread her journal. **Underline** one sentence that hints at Richards' point of view.

238

English Language Learners

Develop Language

Multiple-meaning Words Read aloud the second sentence in "Village Life in America" and call attention to the words *rights, right,* and *right*. Explain that *right* is a multiple-meaning word that is used two ways in this sentence.

- Focus on *right* as a noun first. Draw a concept map with the word *right* in the middle. Model filling in the first bubble with *vote*. Then help students identify other rights they have, both at school and at home; for example, the right to be kept safe, to go to school, to speak one's opinion. Guide students to define *right* as "something a person is allowed to have or do." Use context to decide which use or uses of *right* in the sentence this meaning applies to. *(first and third)*
- Then discuss *right* as an adverb. Reread the phrase "the world would never go right" and brainstorm with students what this could mean. Guide them to see that in this instance, it means "be good or correct."
- Remind students that they should use the context of a sentence to determine how a multiple-meaning word is being used.

Genres: Editorial/Speech

from
ROCHESTER UNION AND ADVERTISER
November 3, 1872

1 Citizenship no more carries the right to vote than it carries the power to fly to the moon. If these women in the Eighth Ward offer to vote, they should be . . . prosecuted to the full extent of the law. . . .

from
On Women's Right to Vote

by Susan B. Anthony, June 19, 1873

1 Friends and fellow citizens: I stand before you tonight under indictment[1] for the alleged crime of having voted at the last presidential election, without having a lawful right to vote. It shall be my work this evening to prove to you that in thus voting, I not only committed no crime, but, instead, simply exercised my citizen's rights, guaranteed to me and all United States citizens by the National Constitution, beyond the power of any state to deny.

2 The preamble of the Federal Constitution says:

3 "We, the people of the United States, in order to form a more perfect union, establish justice, insure domestic tranquility, provide for the common defense, promote the general welfare, and secure the blessings of liberty to ourselves and our posterity, do ordain and establish this Constitution for the United States of America."

4 It was we, the people; not we, the white male citizens; nor yet we, the male citizens; but we, the whole people, who formed the Union. And we formed it, not to give the blessings of liberty, but to secure them; not to the half of ourselves and the half of our posterity, but to the whole people—women as well as men.

Close Reader Habits

What do the editorial writer and Anthony think about whether a woman trying to vote is a crime? Reread the editorial and the speech. **Underline** sentences that express their points of view.

[1]**Indictment:** a charge of a serious crime

239

Lesson 14

- **Read to Analyze** Read aloud the Close Reader Habits on pp. 238 and 239 to set the purpose for the second read. Then have students reread each passage with a partner and discuss any questions they might have.

TIP Point out that strong beliefs and opinions about a topic often lead to emotional responses. Suggest that students look for words expressing emotions and feelings in the editorial and speech.

Monitor Understanding

Word Learning Strategy
Use Context Clues

- Reread paragraph 2 of "U.S. Marshal Arrests Anthony." Call attention to the word *registered*.

  How is *registered* used in this sentence? *(They registered to vote. It is an action.)*

  Is registering the same as voting? How do you know? *(No. They registered four days before they voted.)*

- Help students determine that registering is a step taken before voting. When people register, they sign up so their vote is counted. **L.5.4a**

Monitor Understanding

If… students have difficulty with the order of events in the four accounts,

then… have them create a time line of the dates: "Village Life in America" was written on December 20, 1855. "U.S. Marshal Arrests Anthony" reports that Anthony registered on November 1, 1872, and voted four days later. She was arrested on November 28. The editorial from "Rochester Union and Advertiser" was written on November 3, 1872, which would have been after she registered but before she voted. Anthony's speech was given on June 19, 1873.

Guided Practice

Think

- Have students work with a partner to complete items 1 and 2. Draw attention to the boldface words **best** and **one** in item 1.

TIP If students have trouble answering item 1, remind them to examine the type of writing. Journal entries and speeches commonly give an opinion, while news articles are generally more neutral or impartial.

Answer Analysis

When students have finished, discuss correct and incorrect responses.

1 Part A

The correct choice is D. It correctly states both the news article writer's and Anthony's points of view about Anthony's attempt to vote.

- **A** and **B** are incorrect because the news article writer does not say whether Anthony's attempt to vote was right or wrong.
- **C** is not supported by the text because Anthony does not admit that she committed a crime. She is telling her listeners that others have accused her of committing a crime.

Part B

The correct choices are B and D. The news article was impartial in its report, and Anthony denies she committed a crime.

- **A** does not mention voting.
- **C** does not tie the arrest to Anthony's voting.
- **E** and **F** are from Anthony's speech about the right to vote but do not mention her voting in the election or her arrest.

DOK 3

Think Use what you learned from reading the accounts to answer the following questions.

Authors of journals, editorials, and speeches often express clear points of view. Authors of newspaper articles usually do not.

1 This question has two parts. Answer Part A. Then answer Part B.

Part A

Which statement **best** describes the difference in how Anthony's attempt to vote is presented in the article "U.S. Marshal Arrests Anthony" and Anthony's speech "On Women's Right to Vote"?

- **A** The article writer thinks Anthony's attempt to vote was criminal, but Anthony thinks her act was not a crime.
- **B** The article writer thinks Anthony's attempt to vote was brave, but Anthony does not think she acted bravely.
- **C** The article writer reports Anthony's attempt to vote without taking sides, but Anthony reports that she committed a crime.
- **(D)** The article writer does not say whether Anthony's attempt to vote was right or wrong, but Anthony says her act was not a crime.

Part B

Select **one** detail from the article and **one** detail from the speech that support the answer to Part A.

- **A** "Then Miss Anthony threatened to take the inspectors to court and sue them for a large sum of money." ("U.S. Marshal Arrests Anthony")
- **(B)** "On November 1, Miss Anthony, her three sisters, and eleven other Rochester women registered to vote at a local barbershop." ("U.S. Marshal Arrests Anthony")
- **C** "He ordered Miss Anthony's arrest on November 14." ("U.S. Marshal Arrests Anthony")
- **(D)** "It shall be my work this evening to prove to you that in thus voting, I not only committed no crime, but, instead, simply exercised my citizen's rights. . . ." ("On Women's Right to Vote")
- **E** "It was we, the people; not we, the white male citizens; nor yet we, the male citizens; but we, the whole people, who formed the Union." ("On Women's Right to Vote")
- **F** "And we formed it, not to give the blessings of liberty, but to secure them; not to the half of ourselves and the half of our posterity, but to the whole people—women as well as men." ("On Women's Right to Vote")

240

● Monitor Understanding

If... students have difficulty placing the items correctly to answer item 2,

then... first use a point-of-view organizer to help them organize the details for the two selections. Write the headings *Topic, News Article's Point of View,* and *Anthony's Point of View.* Work with students to fill in details for each point of view. They can then look for a detail that is in both accounts.

2 The box below contains two details from "U.S. Marshal Arrests Anthony," two details from "On Women's Right to Vote," and one detail from both texts.

• supports claims with quotes from the Constitution	• describes voting in a presidential election
• addresses fellow citizens	• tells how other women were arrested
• includes information about the poll watcher's complaint	

Write the details from the box into the correct places in the table below.

"U.S. Marshall Arrests Anthony"	Both Accounts	"On Women's Right to Vote"
includes information about the poll watcher's complaint	describes voting in a presidential election	supports claims with quotes from the Constitution
tells how other women were arrested		addresses fellow citizens

Talk

3 What points of view do the journal entry, the editorial, and the speech express about the topic of women voting? Use the point-of-view organizer on page 243 to capture details from all three accounts that show their points of view.

Write

4 **Short Response** Compare the points of view expressed in the journal entry, the editorial, and the speech on the topic of women voting. Use details from your point-of-view organizer to develop your response. Use the space provided on page 243 to write your answer.

HINT First compare the journal entry and the speech, which have similar points of view.

241

● Integrating Standards

Use the following questions to further students' understanding of the passages.

- **What caused Susan B. Anthony to give a speech on June 19, 1873, and what events led up to the speech?** *(Susan B. Anthony spoke to present her case for her innocence. Earlier she had registered to vote, voted in the presidential election of 1872, been noticed by a poll watcher, and then arrested and charged with voting illegally. But Anthony does not feel that what she did was illegal, so she gave the speech.)*
  DOK 2 RI.5.3
- **In "Village Life in America," why do you think the speaker's grandmother refused to sign the paper? What details from other passages help you make this inference?** *(Richards's grandmother likely refused to sign the paper because she was afraid of getting into legal trouble. In the "Rochester Union and Advertiser" editorial, the writer expresses the opinion that women who offer to vote should be "prosecuted to the full extent of the law. . . ." The grandmother probably was afraid of being prosecuted if she signed the paper.)*
  DOK 2 RI.5.1, RI.5.9

2 **See the answers on the student book page.** Discuss students' responses to make sure they understand which details came from the passages. Remind students that this item simulates drag-and-drop items they may see on computer-based assessments.
DOK 2

● Monitor Understanding

● Integrating Standards

Talk

- Have partners discuss the prompt. Emphasize that students should support their ideas with text details.
- Circulate to clarify misunderstandings.

Write

- Ask a volunteer to read aloud the Write prompt.
- Invite students to tell what the prompt is asking them to do. Make sure they understand that they need to consider the point of view in each of the passages, not just some of them.
- Call attention to the HINT.
- Have students turn to p. 243 to write their response.
- Use Review Responses on p. 243 to assess students' writing.

Wrap Up

- Ask students to recall the Learning Target. Have them explain how finding similarities and differences in points of view helped them better understand these accounts and the broader topic of women voting.

Modeled and Guided Instruction

Write

- Remember to use the Response-Writing Routine on pp. A54–A55.

Review Responses

After students complete the writing activity, help them evaluate their responses.

3 Responses may vary but should show that Chester and Pike have contrasting points of view about the success of Pike's expedition. See the sample response on the student book page.
DOK 3

Write Use the space below to write your answer to the question on page 237.

ZEBULON PIKE and the Source of the Mississippi

The Journals of Zebulon Pike

3 **Short Response** Compare and contrast each account's point of view about Zebulon Pike's expedition. Use details from both accounts in your response.

HINT Use terms such as "point of view" and "topic" in your response.

Sample response: The point of view of George Chester, the author of the historical article, is that Zebulon Pike's expedition was a "disaster" because he did not find the real source of the Mississippi River. The entries from Zebulon Pike's journals are on the same topic of the search for the source of the Mississippi River, but Pike's conclusion about his efforts was different. He believed his expedition, which he calls an "accomplishment," was successful.

Check Your Writing

- ☐ Did you read the prompt carefully?
- ☐ Did you put the prompt in your own words?
- ☐ Did you use the best evidence from the text to support your ideas?
- ☐ Are your ideas clearly organized?
- ☐ Did you write in clear and complete sentences?
- ☐ Did you check your spelling and punctuation?

Scaffolding Support for Reluctant Writers

If students are having a difficult time getting started, use the strategies below. Work individually with struggling students, or have students work with partners.

- Circle the verbs in the prompt that tell you what to do, such as *describe*, *explain*, or *compare*.
- Underline words and phrases in the prompt that show what information you need to provide in your response, such as *causes*, *reasons*, or *character traits*.
- Talk about the details from the text that you will include in your response.
- Explain aloud how you will respond to the prompt.

Village Life in America

ROCHESTER UNION AND ADVERTISER

"On Women's Right to Vote"

3 **Use the point-of-view organizer below to organize your ideas.**

Topic		
Village Life in America	*Rochester Union and Advertiser*	"On Women's Right to Vote"

Write **Use the space below to write your answer to the question on page 241.**

4 **Short Response** Compare the points of view expressed in the journal entry, the editorial, and the speech on the topic of women voting. Use details from your point-of-view organizer to develop your response.

HINT First compare the journal entry and the speech, which have similar points of view.

Sample response: The journal entry and the speech express similar points of view, but the editorial expresses a different one. In the journal, Richards says she "could not make Grandmother agree" with Anthony's ideas about women voting, suggesting that Richards (unlike her grandmother) agrees with those ideas. Anthony believes women should vote, stating that she exercised rights that no state could take away. The editorial, in contrast to both the journal entry and speech, states that women who vote should be "prosecuted to the full extent of the law."

243

Teacher Notes

Guided Practice

Talk

3 Students should use the point-of-view organizer to collect their thoughts and evidence.

Write

- Remember to use the Response-Writing Routine on pp. A54–A55.

Review Responses

After students complete the writing activity, help them evaluate their responses.

4 Responses may vary but should compare and contrast the different points of view, recognizing that the journal entry and speech express similar points of view while the editorial view differs and suggests women should be prosecuted for voting. See the sample response on the student book page.
DOK 3

Independent Practice

Get Started

Today you are going to read two biographies about Theodore Roosevelt and a letter that Roosevelt wrote to his children. You will use what you've learned about analyzing the points of view in accounts about the same topic.

- Ask a volunteer to explain why analyzing different accounts about the same topic will help readers better understand each text as well as the topic. Encourage students to use the Academic Talk words and phrases in their response.

 **English Language Learners**

Read

You are going to read the biographies and letter independently and use what you have learned to think and write about the texts. As you read, remember to look closely at the accounts to analyze the points of view expressed.

- Read aloud the title of each passage and then encourage students to preview the texts, paying close attention to the photographs and captions.
- Call attention to the Words to Know on pp. 244, 245, and 246.
- If students need support in reading the passages, you may wish to use the Monitor Understanding suggestions.
- When students have finished, have them complete the Think and Write sections.

● **Monitor Understanding**

Read

Genre: Biography

WORDS TO KNOW
As you read, look inside, around, and beyond these words to figure out what they mean.
- **commanding**
- **doctrine**
- **commerce**

Speak Softly and Carry a Big Stick

by Ian Dudney

1 Theodore "Teddy" Roosevelt was one of the most powerful presidents of the United States. From his active lifestyle to his commanding leadership, Roosevelt was a strong man. It is surprising that this energetic man was a sickly child. As a boy, he suffered from asthma, a condition that makes breathing difficult, especially during exercise. Yet, Roosevelt overcame this challenge. He went on to pursue a vigorous lifestyle.

2 Before becoming president, Roosevelt demonstrated his physical strength and courage during the Spanish–American War. He led the "Rough Riders," cowboy-like soldiers who rode horses into battle. As president, Roosevelt used his war experience to build up the U.S. military so America could play a more active role in world politics. He described the United States as needing to "speak softly and carry a big stick" when relating to other nations. Under the Monroe Doctrine, Roosevelt gave the United States power to control Latin America and protect it from Europe. He oversaw the construction of the Panama Canal, improving commerce between the Atlantic and the Pacific. Roosevelt led the United States into its position as a world leader.

3 In contrast to his public life, Roosevelt's home life was relaxed and fun-loving. He and his wife, Ethel, had six children: Alice, Theodore, Kermit, Edith, Archibald, and Quentin. He was an adoring and playful father. He and his children would romp all over the White House, even having pillow fights in the halls! He drew silly pictures and wrote letters to his family when they were separated. He shared his thoughts, delights, and dreams with them. He cared deeply about the environment and taught his children to do the same. Together they enjoyed taking hikes, riding horses, and collecting animals.

4 Theodore Roosevelt spoke softly at home, lovingly devoted to his family, and he carried a big stick in the world, vigorously devoted to his country.

 **English Language Learners**

Develop Language

Figurative Language Reread the title of the biography on p. 244. Ask students to explain or act out the literal meaning of this expression.

- Explain that when Roosevelt used this expression, he meant it as a metaphor. Invite a student to review the meaning of *metaphor* ("a comparison between two things").
  - **How do you feel when someone speaks softly to you? Are you afraid?** *(No, I feel comfortable and safe.)*
  - **How would you feel if you saw someone carrying a big stick, or other type of weapon?** *(I might feel scared, intimidated, or threatened.)*
- Discuss the opposing ideas of speaking softly but also appearing to threaten. Guide them to see that Roosevelt's plan was to talk peacefully with other nations as much as possible, but to be powerful and ready to fight if needed.

Genre: Biography

In this excerpt from a biography of Roosevelt, Ambassador Jusserand of France describes a typical "hike" with the President.

FROM Theodore Roosevelt
AN INTIMATE BIOGRAPHY

by William Roscoe Thayer

WORDS TO KNOW
As you read, look inside, around, and beyond these words to figure out what they mean.
- **promenade**
- **punctually**

1 Yesterday President Roosevelt invited me to take a promenade with him this afternoon at three.

2 I arrived at the White House punctually, in afternoon dress and silk hat. . . . To my surprise, the President soon joined me in a tramping suit, with knickerbockers and thick boots, and soft felt hat, much worn. Two or three other gentlemen came. We started off at what seemed to me a breakneck pace. We were soon out of the city. On reaching the country, the President went pell-mell over the fields. He did not follow a road or path, always on, on, straight ahead! I was much winded, but I would not give in, nor ask him to slow down.

3 At last we came to the bank of a stream. It was rather wide and too deep to be forded. I sighed relief, because I thought that now we had reached our goal and would rest a moment and catch our breath, before turning homeward. But judge of my horror when I saw the President unbutton his clothes! I heard him say, "We had better strip, so as not to wet our things in the creek." Then I, too, for the honor of France, removed my clothing, everything except my lavender kid gloves. The President looked at these as if they, too, must come off. I quickly said, "With your permission, Mr. President, I will keep these on, otherwise it would be embarrassing if we should meet ladies." And so we jumped into the water and swam across.

3

Monitor Understanding

If... students struggle to read and understand the passages,

then... use these scaffolding suggestions:

Question the Text Preview the texts by asking the following questions:

- **Based on the titles and photographs, what do you predict the passages will be about?**
- **What questions do you have about the texts?**

Vocabulary Support Define words that may interfere with comprehension, such as *energetic, vigorous, breakneck,* and *cunningest*.

Read Aloud Read aloud the text with students. You could also have students chorally read the text in a small group.

Check Understanding Use the questions below to check understanding. Encourage students to cite details in the texts that support their answers.

- **Who was Theodore Roosevelt?** *(a United States President)*
- **Why was his energy as an adult surprising?** *(He had asthma as a boy and exercise was difficult.)*
- **What are the three texts mostly about?** *(Roosevelt's leadership, his energy, and his enjoyment of family life)*

Independent Practice

Integrating Standards

After students have read the passages, use these questions to discuss the passages with them.

- **After reading "Speak Softly and Carry a Big Stick" and "Theodore Roosevelt: An Intimate Biography," why might you infer that Roosevelt had courage and strength? Provide at least two examples to support your answer.**

  (Roosevelt overcame childhood illness to have an active lifestyle. He led the "Rough Riders" into battle and made the United States a powerful nation. The ambassador of France reported that Roosevelt walked at a fast pace into the country, took off across the fields, and then swam across a stream.)

  DOK 3 RI.5.1

- **Roosevelt said the United States needed to "speak softly and carry a big stick." What evidence does Dudney give to show how Roosevelt followed these words?**

  (As president, Roosevelt built up the military to give America muscle, or "a big stick," to deal with other countries. He worked to construct the Panama Canal, which improved trade and communication with other nations. This was the "speak softly" part of Roosevelt's approach.)

  DOK 2 RI.5.2

- **Explain the relationship between Roosevelt and Jusserand.**

  (Jusserand was an ambassador, and in this role he and Roosevelt worked together formally, but the account of the afternoon walk shows the two had a friendly relationship as well.)

  DOK 2 RI.5.3

- **In "Letters to His Children," what context clues help you know the meaning of *melancholy*?**

  (According to Roosevelt, "the house seemed empty and lonely." The words empty *and* lonely *are clues that* melancholy *means "sad.")*

  DOK 2 RI.5.4

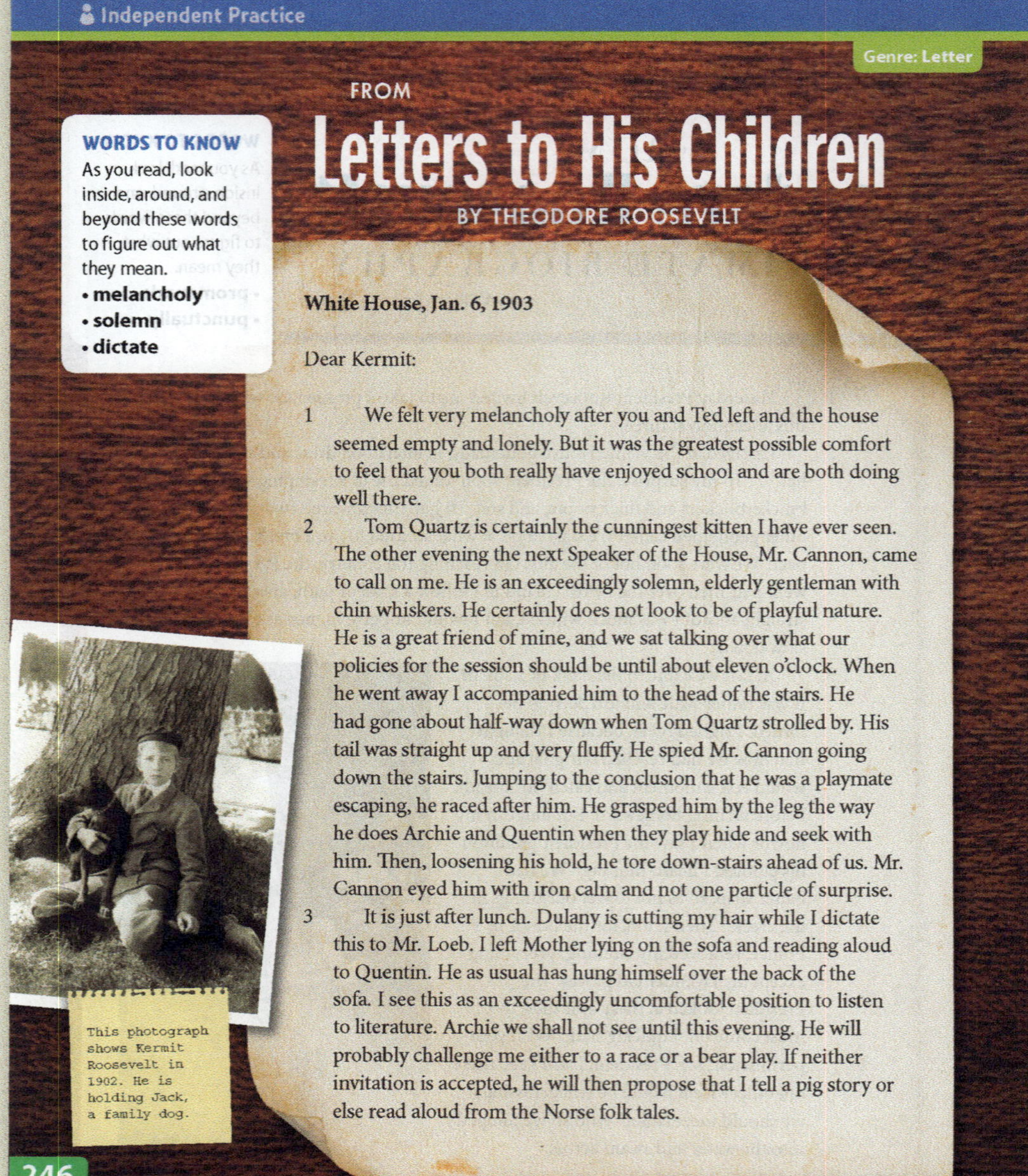

Independent Practice

Genre: Letter

FROM

Letters to His Children

BY THEODORE ROOSEVELT

WORDS TO KNOW
As you read, look inside, around, and beyond these words to figure out what they mean.
- **melancholy**
- **solemn**
- **dictate**

White House, Jan. 6, 1903

Dear Kermit:

1 We felt very melancholy after you and Ted left and the house seemed empty and lonely. But it was the greatest possible comfort to feel that you both really have enjoyed school and are both doing well there.

2 Tom Quartz is certainly the cunningest kitten I have ever seen. The other evening the next Speaker of the House, Mr. Cannon, came to call on me. He is an exceedingly solemn, elderly gentleman with chin whiskers. He certainly does not look to be of playful nature. He is a great friend of mine, and we sat talking over what our policies for the session should be until about eleven o'clock. When he went away I accompanied him to the head of the stairs. He had gone about half-way down when Tom Quartz strolled by. His tail was straight up and very fluffy. He spied Mr. Cannon going down the stairs. Jumping to the conclusion that he was a playmate escaping, he raced after him. He grasped him by the leg the way he does Archie and Quentin when they play hide and seek with him. Then, loosening his hold, he tore down-stairs ahead of us. Mr. Cannon eyed him with iron calm and not one particle of surprise.

3 It is just after lunch. Dulany is cutting my hair while I dictate this to Mr. Loeb. I left Mother lying on the sofa and reading aloud to Quentin. He as usual has hung himself over the back of the sofa. I see this as an exceedingly uncomfortable position to listen to literature. Archie we shall not see until this evening. He will probably challenge me either to a race or a bear play. If neither invitation is accepted, he will then propose that I tell a pig story or else read aloud from the Norse folk tales.

This photograph shows Kermit Roosevelt in 1902. He is holding Jack, a family dog.

246

Theme Connection

- Remind students that the theme of this lesson is Eyewitness to History. Through discussion, guide students to an understanding that an eyewitness is someone who has observed what happened firsthand and can report on it. Point out that most of the accounts in the lesson are from people who actually participated in or observed the historical events.
- Display a three-column chart on the board. Label each column with the name of a person discussed in the lesson: *Zebulon Pike, Susan B. Anthony,* and *Theodore Roosevelt.*
- Ask students to recall facts and ideas they learned about each person from the accounts about that person. List their responses in the appropriate column.
- Discuss how being an eyewitness affects someone's account of an event. Emphasize that two people who witness the same event may give different accounts of it.

Think Use what you learned from reading the accounts to answer the following questions.

1 The box below contains five details. Two are from "Speak Softly and Carry a Big Stick," two are from *Letters to His Children*, and one is from both accounts.

• tells how he misses his children when they are away	• describes how his family behaves
• shows that he loved to play with his children	• speaks respectfully about his military experiences
• tells about letters he wrote to his family	

Write the details from the box into the correct places in the table below.

"Speak Softly and Carry a Big Stick"	Both Accounts	*Letters to His Children*
speaks respectfully about his military experiences	shows that he loved to play with his children	tells how he misses his children when they are away
tells about letters he wrote to his family		describes how his family behaves

2 Read the sentences from *Letters to His Children*.

He is an exceedingly solemn, elderly gentleman with chin whiskers. He certainly does not look to be of playful nature.

Which dictionary entry **best** defines nature as used in the sentence?

A the physical world
B forces that control objects
C how a person behaves (circled)
D a landscape of plants and animals

Monitor Understanding

If... students struggle to complete the items,

then... you may wish to use the following suggestions:

Read Aloud Activities

- As you read, have students note any unfamiliar words or phrases. Clarify any misunderstandings.
- Discuss each item with students to make certain they understand the expectation.

Reread the Text

- Have students complete a point-of-view organizer as they reread.
- Have partners summarize the texts.

Think

- Use the Monitor Understanding suggestions to support students in completing items 1–3.

Monitor Understanding

Answer Analysis

When students have finished, discuss correct and incorrect responses.

1 **See the answers on the student book page.** Discuss students' responses to make sure they understand which details came from the passages. Remind students that this item simulates drag-and-drop items students may see on computer-based assessments.
DOK 2 RI.5.6

2 **The correct choice is C.** The gentleman described is "solemn" and not "playful." *Nature* here must mean "temperament" or "behavior."

- **A, B,** and **D** are dictionary definitions of *nature* but do not clarify the word's use in the text.

DOK 2 L.5.4c

Independent Practice

3 **The correct choice is C.** Both the author and ambassador are impressed by Roosevelt's physical energy.

- **A** describes only the author's point of view, not the ambassador's.
- **B** is about being impressed by Roosevelt's sense of fashion. Dudney doesn't mention Roosevelt's style of dress, and the ambassador is surprised but not impressed by Roosevelt's sense of fashion.
- **D** is addressed in "Speak Softly and Carry a Big Stick" but not mentioned in *Theodore Roosevelt: An Intimate Biography.*

DOK 2 RI.5.6

Write

- Tell students that using what they read, they will plan and compose an extended response to the writing prompt. Provide copies of the chart on p. TR12.

Monitor Understanding

Review Responses

After students have completed each part of the writing activity, help them evaluate their responses.

4 Display the **Sample Response** for the planning chart on the next page. Have students compare their chart with the sample. Are they missing any information?
DOK 3 RI.5.6

5 Display or pass out copies of the reproducible **2-Point Writing Rubric** on p. TR10. Have students use the rubric to individually assess their writing and revise as needed.

When students have finished their revisions, evaluate their responses. Answers will vary but should analyze each account, noting the similarities and differences in the points of view in the accounts.
DOK 4 RI.5.6, W.5.9b

3 How is the author's point of view in "Speak Softly and Carry a Big Stick" similar to the French ambassador's point of view in *Theodore Roosevelt: An Intimate Biography?*

A Both admire Roosevelt's love for his family.
B Both are impressed by Roosevelt's sense of fashion.
(C) Both think highly of Roosevelt's physical energy.
D Both respect Roosevelt's political skill.

Write

You've read three accounts related to Theodore Roosevelt. Each account has a point of view on the man and his life. What does each account tell you about Roosevelt's personality? Underline text details that provide clear evidence of Roosevelt's personality. Then complete numbers 4 and 5.

4 **Plan Your Response** Before you write, use a graphic organizer to gather evidence from each account. Be sure to capture any similarities and differences in details the accounts provide about Roosevelt's personality.

5 **Write an Extended Response** Describe what the accounts tell you about Roosevelt's personality. Support your response with details from all three accounts.

Responses will vary. A top-scoring response will analyze each account, noting the similarities and differences in each account about Roosevelt's personality.

Monitor Understanding

If... students don't understand the writing task,

then... read aloud the writing prompt. Use the following questions to help students get started.

- **What is the prompt asking you to write about?**
- **Do you need to reread the text to find more information?**
- **How will you identify the information you need to include?**
- Have partners talk about how they will organize their responses.

Learning Target

In this lesson, you analyzed the points of view of different accounts about the same topic or event. Explain how this kind of analysis will help you better understand other accounts you read.

Responses will vary, but students should explain how analyzing points of view on the same event or topic helps them understand that people can have different points of view and use different evidence to support those viewpoints.

Wrap Up

Learning Target

- Have each student respond in writing to the Learning Target prompt.
- When students have finished, have them share their responses. This may be done with a partner, in small groups, or as a whole class.

4 Sample Response

Topic: Roosevelt's Personality

Dudney Wrote About	Ambassador Wrote About	Roosevelt Showed
• vigorous lifestyle • powerful president and world leader • playful and relaxed at home	• hiking outfit • "breakneck speed" • swam without clothes • liked physical challenges	• missed family when apart • observant • enjoyment of animals • liked to read to his children

5 2-Point Writing Rubric

Points	Focus	Evidence	Organization
2	My answer does exactly what the prompt asked me to do.	My answer is supported with plenty of details from the text.	My ideas are clear and in a logical order.
1	Some of my answer does not relate to the prompt.	My answer is missing some important details from the text.	Some of my ideas are unclear and out of order.
0	My answer does not make sense.	My answer does not have any details from the text.	My ideas are unclear and not in any order.

Assessment

Get Started

Today you are going to read three articles. The first two passages are historic eyewitness accounts, and the third is a historic newspaper article. You will use what you have learned in this unit to understand what you are reading.

- Ask students to recall what they have learned, such as using context clues, comparing text structures, and analyzing accounts of the same topic.
- Encourage students to use the Academic Talk words and phrases from the unit's lessons in their response.

Read

You are going to read the articles independently and use what you have learned to think and write about the text.

- Ask a student to read aloud the titles of the passages. Make certain that students understand they are to read all three selections.
- Encourage students to preview the text, paying close attention to the photographs, captions, and text structure.
- Remind students to look inside, around, and beyond when they encounter unfamiliar words. Use the Word Learning Routine on pp. A50–A51.
- When students have finished, have them complete the Think and Write sections.

Read

Genre: Eyewitness Account

Read the eyewitness account. Then answer the questions that follow.

Joshua Wyeth was only 16 years old when he was a participant in the Boston Tea Party. He reported the details of his adventurous night to a local pastor. This first-hand account was found and published in a book edited by Francis S. Drake. The full title of the book is *Tea Leaves: Being a Collection of Letters and Documents Relating to the Shipment of Tea to the American Colonies in the year 1773, by the East India Tea Company.*

Boston Tea Party Eyewitness Account: Joshua Wyeth

from *Tea Leaves*

1 Our numbers were between twenty-eight and thirty. . . . I had but a few hours warning of what was intended to be done. We first talked of [setting fire to] the ships, but feared the fire would [spread] to the town. We then proposed sinking them, but dropped that [idea] through fear that we should alarm the town before we could [finish.]

2 We had [noticed] that very few persons remained on board the ships. So, we finally concluded that we could take possession of them, and discharge the tea into the harbor without danger or opposition. To prevent discovery, we agreed to [dress] to resemble Indians as much as possible. [We smeared] our faces with grease and lamp black or soot, and should not have known each other except by our voices. Our most intimate friends among the spectators had not the least knowledge of us.

3 At the appointed time, we met in an old building at the head of the wharf. We fell in one after another, as if by accident, so as not to excite suspicion. We placed a sentry at the head of the wharf, another in the

middle, and one on the bow of each ship as we took possession. We boarded the ship moored by the wharf[1]. Our leader, in a very stern and resolute[2] manner, ordered the captain and crew to open the hatchways. [He ordered them to] hand us the hoisting tackle and ropes, assuring them that no harm was intended them. The captain asked what we intended to do. Our leader told him that we were going to unload the tea, and ordered him and the crew below. They instantly obeyed.

4 Some of our number then jumped into the hold, and passed the chests to the tackle. As they were hauled on deck, others knocked them open with axes. Others raised them to the railing and discharged their contents overboard. All who were not needed for discharging this ship went on board the others, [tied] them to the wharf, where the same ceremonies were repeated. We were merry, in an undertone, at the idea of making so large a cup of tea for the fishes. [But we] were as still as the nature of the case would admit, using no more words than were absolutely necessary. We [moved quickly] from the moment we left our dressing-room. I never worked harder in my life.

[1] **Moored by the wharf:** anchored to a structure, such as a pier, in the harbor

[2] **Resolute:** determined or set in purpose

Teacher Notes

Answer Analysis

When students have completed the Interim Assessment, discuss correct and incorrect responses.

1 **The correct choice is B.** The context of the sentence, including the word *overboard*, indicates that *discharged* means "emptied."

- **A** does not make sense in the context of the sentence.
- **C** implies that the contents are going back into the sea.
- **D** would suggest that they "opened their contents overboard," which doesn't make sense.

DOK 2 RI.5.4

2 **Students should underline sentry.**

DOK 2 RI.5.4

Think

1 Read this sentence from "Boston Tea Party Eyewitness Account: Joshua Wyeth."

Others raised them to the railing and discharged their contents overboard.

What is the meaning of the word discharged as it is used in this sentence?

A rearranged
B emptied
C returned
D opened

2 Joshua Wyeth uses a word that describes someone whose job is to stand guard, like a watchman or lookout. Underline that word in the paragraph below.

At the appointed time, we met in an old building at the head of the wharf. We fell in one after another, as if by accident, so as not to excite suspicion. We placed a sentry at the head of the wharf, another in the middle, and one on the bow of each ship as we took possession. We boarded the ship moored by the wharf. Our leader, in a very stern and resolute manner, ordered the captain and crew to open the hatchways. [He ordered them to] hand us the hoisting tackle and ropes, assuring them that no harm was intended them. The captain asked what we intended to do. Our leader told him that we were going to unload the tea, and ordered him and the crew below. They instantly obeyed.

Read

Genre: Letter

Read the eyewitness account. Then answer the questions that follow.

John Andrews was an eyewitness to the Boston Tea Party. In a letter to a friend written just after the incident, he describes what he witnessed.

Boston Tea Party Eyewitness Account: John Andrews

from *Tea Leaves*

1 The [meeting] house was so crowded that I could get no further than the porch. The moderator was just declaring the meeting to be [over]. That caused another general shout outdoors and in, and three cheers. What with that and the consequent noise of breaking up the meeting, you'd [have] thought the inhabitants[1] of the infernal[2] regions had broke loose. For my part, I went contentedly home and finished my tea. [I] was soon informed what was going forward. Not [believing it without seeing it for myself], I went and was satisfied.

2 They gathered, I'm told, upon Fort Hill, to the number of about two hundred. They then proceeded, two by two, to Griffin's wharf, where [the ships captained by Hall, Bruce, and Coffin] lay. [Captain Coffin's ship] was freighted with a large quantity of other goods. They took the greatest care not to injure [those] in the least. Before nine o'clock in the evening, every chest on board the three vessels was knocked to pieces and flung over the sides.

[1] **Inhabitants:** people who live in a certain area

[2] **Infernal:** awful; related to the mythical world of the dead

Teacher Notes

3 They say the actors were Indians from Narragansett. To [an] observer they appeared as such, being clothed in blankets, with their heads [covered], and copper-colored [faces]. They were each armed with a hatchet or axe, or pair of pistols, [and] their jargon[3] was unintelligible to all but themselves. Not the least insult was offered to any person save one Captain Connor. [He] had [ripped] up the lining of his coat and waistcoat under the arms, and . . . had nearly filled them with tea. [When discovered, he] was handled pretty roughly. They not only stripped him of his clothes, but gave him a coat of mud, with a severe bruising into the bargain. Nothing but their utter aversion[4] to making any disturbance prevented his being tarred and feathered.[5]

[3] **Jargon:** subject-area language that is not understood by most others

[4] **Aversion:** a strong feeling of dislike

[5] **Tarred and feathered:** historical punishment that involved coating the person's midsection in a layer of pine tar followed by a layer of feathers

Teacher Notes

Think

3 This question has two parts. First, answer Part A. Then answer Part B.

Part A
What is the meaning of the word freighted as it is used in paragraph 2 of John Andrews's account?

A sent
B intended
(C) filled
D delivered

Part B
Which phrase helps the reader understand the meaning of freighted?

A "then proceeded, two by two"
(B) "a large quantity of other goods"
C "took the greatest care not to injure"
D "knocked to pieces and flung over"

Teacher Notes

3 **Part A**

The correct choice is C. The word describes the way the ship was loaded with cargo.

- **A** is incorrect because the ship had not been sent anywhere; it was lying in the wharf.
- **B** and **D** do not fit the context because they apply to the ship, rather than the goods.

Part B

The correct choice is B. The words *quantity* and *goods* indicate cargo, which implies that *freighted* means "carried."

- **A** and **D** refer to the protesters' actions, not to the ship and its cargo.
- **C** refers to how the protesters treated the cargo and does not reference the meaning of *freighted*.

DOK 2 **RI.5.4**

Assessment

4 Part A

The correct choice is A. Students who do not correctly analyze the points of view the accounts represent may choose one of the distractors.

Part B

The correct choices are B and D. They support the firsthand point of view in both accounts.

- **A, C,** and **E** describe an event from the point of view of someone other than the person giving the account.

***DOK 3* RI.5.6**

4 This question has two parts. First, answer Part A. Then answer Part B.

Part A

What is an important similarity in the points of view the two accounts represent?

- **(A)** Both are firsthand accounts.
- **B** Both are secondhand accounts.
- **C** Both men witnessed the protest from afar.
- **D** Both men enjoyed taking part in the protest.

Part B

Select **one** sentence from Joshua Wyeth's account and **one** sentence from John Andrews' account that **best** support the answer to Part A.

- **A** "They instantly obeyed." (Joshua Wyeth)
- **(B)** "Some of our number then jumped into the hold, and passed the chests to the tackle." (Joshua Wyeth)
- **C** "As they were hauled on deck, others knocked them open with axes." (Joshua Wyeth)
- **(D)** "I went and was satisfied." (John Andrews)
- **E** "They gathered, I'm told, upon Fort Hill, to the number of about two hundred." (John Andrews)
- **F** "They say the actors were Indians from Narragansett." (John Andrews)

256

5 The box below gives details about how the accounts by Joshua Wyeth and John Andrews tell about the same event.

Details
- Describes the crowd at the meeting house.
- Describes what the participants looked like.
- Describes what happened to the chests of tea.
- Explains why Captain Connor was treated roughly.
- Explains that the men disguised themselves as Indians.
- Describes what it was like to participate in the Boston Tea Party.

Write details from the list to complete the chart below. Use **each** detail **one** time.

Account by Joshua Wyeth	Account by John Andrews	Both Accounts
Explains that the men disguised themselves as Indians.	Describes the crowd at the meeting house.	Describes what happened to the chests of tea.
Describes what it was like to participate in the Boston Tea Party.	Explains why Captain Connor was treated roughly.	Describes what the participants looked like.

Teacher Notes

5 **See the answers on the student book page.**

***DOK 3* RI.5.5**

Assessment

6 After students have completed the Interim Assessment, evaluate their responses to the short-response item using the **2-Point Writing Rubric** below.

Answers will vary but should show that students understand the structures follow chronological order. See the sample response on the student book page.

You may wish to display or pass out copies of the reproducible **2-Point Writing Rubric** on page TR10. Have students use the rubric to individually assess their writing and revise as needed.

DOK 3 **RI.5.5, RI.5.6**

6 **Short Response** The overall structures of the accounts by Joshua Wyeth and John Andrews are similar. Identify the text structure in both texts and tell why this overall structure is necessary to develop each of the accounts. Include details from the passage in your response.

The accounts by Joshua Wyeth and John Andrews each use a chronological text structure, telling about the events of the Tea Party in the order they occurred. Wyeth describes the events of the Tea Party using words and phrases such as first, then, at the appointed time, and finally. Describing events in order helps Wyeth produce a clear picture of the protest's events. Andrews also tells about the events in the order that he witnessed them. He tells what happened first, at the organizers meeting, then what happened next, on the ships, and finally tells about the appearance of the participants and how they treated the British shipmates. Both accounts are ordered sequentially.

2-Point Writing Rubric

All three criteria must be satisfied in order for a response to gain full points.

Points	Focus	Evidence	Organization
2	The response demonstrates comprehension and provides accurate analysis.	The response supports the analysis with adequate textual evidence.	Ideas are clear and follow a logical order.
1	The response demonstrates some comprehension and provides minimally accurate analysis.	The response supports the analysis with limited textual evidence.	Some ideas are unclear or out of order.
0	The response demonstrates no comprehension and provides inaccurate or no analysis.	The response provides little or no textual evidence.	Ideas are unclear or incomplete.

Read

Genre: Newspaper Article

Read the newspaper article. Then answer the question that follows.

The Massachusetts Gazette published this account on December 23, 1773, just days after the famous Boston Tea Party occurred.

from The Massachusetts Gazette

1 Just before the [end] of the meeting, a number of brave and resolute men, dressed in the Indian manner, approached near the door of the Assembly. [They] gave the war whoop. [It] rang through the house and was answered by some in the galleries. Silence [was] commanded, [and it was quiet until the end of the meeting.] The Indians, as they were then called, [went] to the wharf where the ships lay. [They] were followed by hundreds of people [who wanted] to see [what] those who made so grotesque an appearance [were going to do].

2 They, the Indians, immediately [went] on board Captain Hall's ship. They hoisted out the chests of tea, and when upon deck [broke] the chests and emptied the tea overboard. Having cleared this ship they proceeded to Captain Bruce's and then to Captain Coffin's brig. They applied themselves so [seriously] to the destruction of [the tea] that in the space of three hours they broke up 342 chests. [That] was the whole number in those vessels. [They] discharged the contents into the dock. . . . There was the greatest care taken to prevent the tea from being [stolen] by the populace. One or two, being detected in [trying] to pocket a small quantity, were stripped of their acquisitions and very roughly handled.

Assessment

7 **The correct choices are A and C.** The article is a secondhand account, and the last sentence of the article says that the masters and owners of the ships were "well pleased" whereas the firsthand accounts do not include this information.

- **B, E** and **F** do not address details in the passage.
- **D** is incorrect because all the texts explain events in chronological order.

DOK 3 **RI.5.6**

3 It is worthy of remark that . . . no injury was sustained. . . . [Even when] a small padlock belonging to the captain of one of the ships [was broken], another was sent to him. The town was very quiet during the whole evening and night following. Those persons who were from the country returned with a merry heart. The next day joy appeared in almost every [face], some on occasion of the destruction of the tea, others on account of the quietness with which it was effected. One of Monday's papers says that the masters and owners are well pleased that their ships are thus cleared.

THE DESTRUCTION OF TEA AT BOSTON HARBOR.

Think

7 What are **two** important differences between the newspaper article from the *Massachusetts Gazette* and the accounts by Joshua Wyeth and John Andrews?

(A) The article describes the ship owners' feelings.
B The article compares colonists and ship captains.
(C) The article is based on what others said and saw.
D The article explains key events in the correct order.
E The article tells how the British reacted to the event.
F The article provides details about tools used by colonists.

260

8 **Short Response** Explain how the first sentence of the article from the *Massachusetts Gazette* establishes the writer's point of view. Then describe how this point of view is similar to or different from the points of view in the accounts by Joshua Wyeth and John Andrews.

The first sentence of the article describes the colonists who dressed like Indians as "brave and resolute men." This suggests that the reporter who wrote the article admires the colonists who participated in the Boston Tea Party. The accounts by Joshua Wyeth and John Andrews do not include opinions or judgments like this one about the participants' courage.

8 After students have completed the Interim Assessment, evaluate their responses to the short-response item using the **2-Point Writing Rubric** below.

Answers will vary but should explain that the first sentence suggests the colonists were admirable for their actions. See the sample response on the student book page.

You may wish to display or pass out copies of the reproducible **2-Point Writing Rubric** on page TR10. Have students use the rubric to individually assess their writing and revise as needed.

***DOK 3* RI.5.6**

2-Point Writing Rubric

All three criteria must be satisfied in order for a response to gain full points.

Points	Focus	Evidence	Organization
2	The response demonstrates comprehension and provides accurate analysis.	The response supports the analysis with adequate textual evidence.	Ideas are clear and follow a logical order.
1	The response demonstrates some comprehension and provides minimally accurate analysis.	The response supports the analysis with limited textual evidence.	Some ideas are unclear or out of order.
0	The response demonstrates no comprehension and provides inaccurate or no analysis.	The response provides little or no textual evidence.	Ideas are unclear or incomplete.

Write

Review Responses

9 After students have completed the Interim Assessment, evaluate their responses to the Extended Response using the **4-Point Writing Rubric** below.

Answers will vary but should show that students understand the passages are similar because they all describe the Boston Tea Party, but where two are firsthand accounts, the third is secondhand. The firsthand accounts are different from each other because one is told by a participant, the other by a witness. See the sample response on the student book page.

DOK 4 **RI.5.5, RI.5.6**

Write

9 **Extended Response** How are the three accounts of the Boston Tea Party similar and different? Write your answer to the question. In your answer, be sure to

- identify the overall structure of each text.
- explain how the three writers' points of view are alike and different.
- use key details from the three accounts in your answer.

Check your writing for correct spelling, grammar, capitalization, and punctuation.

The accounts are similar because they all tell about the events of the Boston Tea Party in the order in which the events happened. Joshua Wyeth's account of the Tea Party was a firsthand account. He was a participant in the protest, and he describes the events as he personally experienced them. He provides details about what he and the others used to disguise themselves, such as grease and soot, which only a participant would be able to describe. He also provides details about his feelings of merriment after the protest was complete.

John Andrews's account is also a firsthand account, but he describes the event from the point of view of an observer rather than a participant. He describes the actions of the protesters by telling about his observations. His account is similar to Wyeth's account in that they are both firsthand accounts of the protest. The accounts are different, however, because Andrews was an observer while Wyeth was a participant.

The reporter's account is a secondhand account. The reporter described the events as they had been reported to him. The reporter was not at the event, like Andrews and Wyeth were, so his account provides historical facts that he gathered from different sources. For example, he tells about how a broken padlock was replaced, which was not something that either Wyeth or Andrews personally experienced.

4-Point Writing Rubric

All three criteria must be satisfied in order for a response to gain full points.

Points	Focus	Evidence	Organization
4	The response demonstrates a full understanding of the prompt and provides accurate analysis.	The response supports the analysis with generous textual evidence.	Ideas are consistently presented in a purposeful and logical order.
3	The response demonstrates a good understanding of the prompt and provides mostly accurate analysis.	The response supports the analysis with adequate textual evidence.	Ideas are generally presented in a purposeful and logical order, although some ideas may be unclear or out of order.
2	The response demonstrates a general understanding of the prompt and provides some accurate analysis but includes inaccurate descriptions or explanations.	The response supports the analysis with limited textual evidence but does not reference the text explicitly.	Some ideas are presented in a purposeful and logical order, but others are unclear or out of order.
1	The response demonstrates a limited understanding of the prompt and provides limited analysis with significant inaccuracies.	The response may use textual evidence, but it does not support the analysis and does not reference the text explicitly.	Most ideas are not presented in a purposeful and logical order.
0	The response does not demonstrate understanding of the prompt.	Ideas are not supported with reference to textual evidence.	The response does not present ideas in a purposeful or logical order.

Review Unit Opener Self-Check

Ask students to complete the unit self-check on page 186 of the student book. Then have them discuss the items in the self-check with a partner. Encourage students to give each other examples from the lessons that show where they really began to understand the skill.

Finally, bring students together for a whole-class discussion. Ask them how knowing these skills have helped make them better readers. Remind them to use their Academic Talk words.

Unit 4

Craft and Structure in Literature

Craft and Structure in Literature

You probably know the story of the Three Little Pigs. But have you read a book called *The True Story of the Three Little Pigs*, by Jon Scieszka? The basic story is the same. However, this time the story is told from the point of view of the wolf. He claims he really did nothing wrong. In fact, he blames the pigs for building flimsy houses. Because the point of view changes, our feelings as readers change. In this unit, you'll learn about how the point of view in a story changes depending on who is telling it.

In this unit, you'll also study how similes and metaphors can describe people, things, and ideas. You'll develop a better understanding of how authors, poets, and playwrights **craft** and **structure** literature. You will do this by learning about how stanzas in poems and scenes in plays build on each other.

✓ Self Check

Before starting this unit, check off the skills you know below. As you complete each lesson, see how many more skills you can check off!

I can:	Before this unit	After this unit
find the meanings of figurative language, including similes and metaphors.	☐	☐
explain how scenes build on each other within a play.	☐	☐
describe the ways stanzas fit together to provide structure and meaning.	☐	☐
determine the point of view within a literary text.	☐	☐
describe how a narrator's or speaker's point of view influences the description of events.	☐	☐

264

page 270

page 276

page 282

page 290

page 304

265

At a Glance

- These two pages introduce students to the skills and strategies they will learn in this unit.
- The checklist allows them to see what skills they will be learning and take ownership of their progress.
- The visual table of contents gives a graphic preview of the passages in the unit.

Step by Step

- Explain to students that they are going to begin a new unit of lessons. Tell them that in all the lessons in this unit they will be learning about craft and structure in literature.
- Have the class read together the introduction to the unit in their books. Invite and respond to comments and questions, if any.
- Then take a few minutes to have each student independently read through the list of skills.
- Ask students to consider each skill and check the box if it is a skill they think they already have. Tell students that they may have worked on similar skills in the past, but these skills go deeper than before.
- Engage students in a brief discussion about the skills. Invite students to comment on which ones they would most like to learn, or which ones seem similar or related to something they already know. Remind them that the goal is to be able to check off one skill at a time until they have them all checked.
- Invite students to look at the graphics and predict what the passages will be about.

Lesson 15
Language and Meaning

Standards Focus

Determine the meaning of words and phrases as they are used in a text, including figurative language such as metaphors and similes. RL.5.4

Lesson Objectives

Reading

- Use context to determine the meaning of figurative language phrases. RL.5.4
- Recognize the use and meaning of metaphors and similes in a text. RL.5.4

Writing

- Draw evidence from literary texts to support analysis and reflection. W.5.9a

Speaking and Listening

- Pose and respond to specific questions and contribute to discussions. SL.5.1c
- Review the key ideas expressed and draw conclusions. SL.5.1d

Language

- Use context as a clue to the meaning of a word or phrase. L.5.4a
- Acquire and use academic and domain-specific words and phrases. L.5.6

Additional Practice: **RL.5.1, RL.5.2, RL.5.3, RL.5.6**

Academic Talk

See **Glossary of Terms**, pp. TR2–TR9

- figurative language
- personification
- metaphor
- mood
- simile

Learning Progression

Grade 4	Grade 5	Grade 6
Students find the meaning of a word, including the meanings of words that refer to characters in mythology.	At Grade 5, for the first time students determine the figurative meaning of words and phrases. The standard emphasizes that students need to understand denotative and figurative meanings of words and phrases in context.	Grade 6 increases in complexity by requiring students to examine the connotative meaning of words in addition to identifying the denotative and figurative meanings.

Lesson Text Selections

Modeled and Guided Instruction

Rain in Summer
by Henry Wadsworth Longfellow
Genre: Lyric Poem

Guided Practice

Wildlife Worries
by Annika Pederson
Genre: Realistic Fiction

Independent Practice

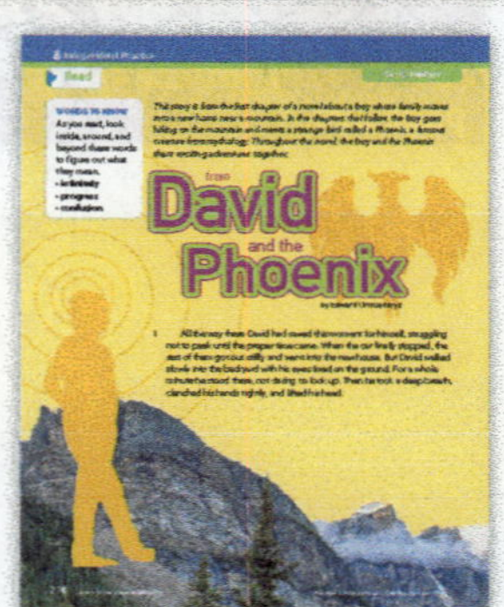

David and the Phoenix
by Edward Ormondroyd
Genre: Fantasy

Lesson Pacing Guide

Whole Class Instruction *30–45 minutes per day*

Day 1

Teacher-Toolbox.com **Interactive Tutorial**
Understanding Figurative Language—Level E
20 min (optional)

Introduction pp. 266–267

- **Read** **Language and Meaning** *10 min*
- **Think** *10 min*
  Graphic Organizer: Three-Column Chart
- **Talk** *5 min*
  Quick Write (TRB) *5 min*

Day 2

Modeled and Guided Instruction pp. 268–269, 272

- **Read** **Rain in Summer** *10 min*
- **Think** *10 min*
  Graphic Organizer: Three-Column Chart
- **Talk** *5 min*
- **Write** Short Response *10 min*

Day 3

Guided Practice pp. 270–271, 273

- **Read** **Wildlife Worries** *10 min*
- **Think** *10 min*
- **Talk** *5 min*
- **Write** Short Response *10 min*

Day 4

Independent Practice pp. 274–279

- **Read** **David and the Phoenix** *15 min*
- **Think** *10 min*
- **Write** Short Response *10 min*

Day 5

Independent Practice pp. 274–279

- *Review* Answer Analysis (TRB) *10 min*
- *Review* Response Analysis (TRB) *20 min*
- *Assign and Discuss* Learning Target *10 min*

Language Handbook
Lesson 8 Punctuating Items in a Series, pp. 452–453
20 min (optional)

Ready Writing Connection

During *Ready Reading* Days 1–5, use:
Lesson 4 Writing to Analyze Literature: Essay

- **Think It Through**
- **Step 4 Organize Your Evidence**
- **Step 5 Draft**

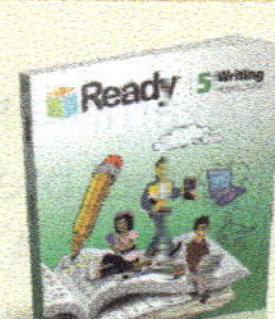

See *Ready Writing TRB*, p. 90a for complete lesson plan.

Small Group Differentiation

Teacher-Toolbox.com

Reteach

***Ready Reading* Prerequisite Lesson**

- **Grade 4** Lesson 17 Understanding Vocabulary in Literary Texts

Teacher-led Activities

Tools for Instruction

- Interpret Figurative Language: Metaphor and Simile

Personalized Learning

i-Ready.com

Independent

i-Ready Close Reading Lessons

- **Grade 4** Understanding Vocabulary in Literary Texts
- **Grade 5** Language and Meaning

Get Started

- Explain to students that in this lesson they will read to analyze and understand figurative language in poems and stories.
- Review the meanings of the terms *literal* and *figurative*. Guide students to understand that the terms are opposites: *literal* means "exact" and *figurative* means "not literal" or "representing an idea."
- Provide an example to demonstrate the difference, such as "The cool breeze kissed my cheeks as I stepped outside." Ask:

  Is this literal or figurative? The literal meaning doesn't make sense because a breeze doesn't have lips to kiss with, so it is figurative. But why phrase it this way? Well, a kiss is a nice thing. This language hints that the cool breeze feels nice on my face. Plus, you know what a kiss on your cheek feels like, so you can picture just how the wind feels.
- Focus students' attention on the Learning Target. Read it aloud to set the purpose for the lesson.
- Display the Academic Talk words and phrases. Tell students to listen for these terms and their meanings as you work through the lesson together. Use the Academic Talk Routine on pp. A48–A49.

 **English Language Learners**

● **Genre Focus**

Read

- Read aloud the Read section as students follow along. Restate to reinforce:

  Figurative language can make a text more interesting by engaging your senses or making you think about things in new or unusual ways. It also conveys the mood of a story or poem, such as joyful, fearful, anxious, or silly.
- Have students read "The Tree Bats." Encourage them to use the photo to tell why the poet compares the bats to fruit.

RL.5.4 Determine the meaning of words and phrases as they are used in a text, including figurative language such as metaphors and similes.

Lesson 15
Language and Meaning

Figuring out the meanings of figurative language in literary texts will help you better understand and enjoy such texts.

Read Writers often use **figurative language** to help us imagine familiar things and events in new and sometimes strange ways.

- A **simile** uses the words *like* or *as* to compare two things that are not alike.
- A **metaphor** also compares unlike things, but does not use *like* or *as*.
- **Personification** gives human qualities to nonliving things.

Writers often use figurative language to produce a **mood**, or feeling.

As you read this poem, think about how its figurative language helps you imagine familiar things and events in new ways. Also think about how the poem might be making you feel.

The Tree Bats

The tree bats sway like fruit with wings,
From the branches of a tall old tree,
Prisoners of light throughout the day,
Till nightfall comes to set them free.

The sun goes down, the sleepers stir,
To the gentle voice of mother night.
Then the tree lets go its fluttering fruit—
A dark whirlwind of sudden flight!

266

English Language Learners
Develop Language

Concept Vocabulary To help students understand figurative language, provide a creative comparison. Display the sentence "He was a shining light in the darkness."

- Ask if it is possible for a person to shine. Explain that because the comparison is not possible, it is a type of figurative language called a *metaphor*.
- Change it to a simile ("He is *like* a shining light in the darkness."). Ask students to identify the difference. Label the second version as a *simile*.
- Discuss what kind of mood, or feeling, you are creating about the person with the simile and metaphor *(positive, inspiring)*.

● Genre Focus
Poetry

Explain that during Modeled and Guided Instruction, students will read a poem. Poetry often uses language in unusual ways to express emotions, ideas, or experiences. One type of poetry is a lyric poem, which often has the following characteristics:

- rhyme—the repeated use of sounds at the end of words
- rhythm—the pattern of beats, or stressed syllables
- figurative language—similes, metaphors, and personification

Review some well-known lyric poets, including Robert Burns, Robert Frost, and Langston Hughes.

Think Consider what you know about figurative language. Use the chart below to help you think about the figurative language in "The Tree Bats."

What I Read	Type of Figurative Language	What It Means
"The tree bats sway like fruit with wings,"	Simile: compares the bats to fruit	The tree bats are hanging upside down.
"Prisoners of light throughout the day,"	Personification: the light is a jailer, the bats are prisoners	Bats only come out at night.
"the gentle voice of mother night."	Personification: the sounds of night are like a mother talking	The sounds of the night wake up the bats.
"A dark whirlwind of sudden flight!"	Metaphor: the bats' flight is like a whirlwind	The bats take off quickly and fly away.

Talk Share your chart with a partner.

- What types of figurative language did you identify?
- Did you come up with similar meanings for each example?
- Pick **one** example from the "What I Read" column. What mood is the poet trying to make with that example?

Academic Talk
Use these words and phrases to talk about the text.

- **figurative language**
- **metaphor**
- **simile**
- **personification**
- **mood**

Think

- Have students read aloud the Think section. Explain that the figurative language chart will help them organize their thinking.
- Have partners complete the chart. Remind students that the details in the poem work together to create a mood, or overall feeling.
- As students work, circulate and provide assistance as needed.
- Ask volunteers to share what they wrote in their charts.
- Make certain students understand that the literal language in much of the poem does not make sense. Students should picture what the words suggest instead.

Talk

- Read aloud the Talk prompts.
- Have partners compare their charts and then decide on the mood of one example. Encourage them to think about how the words make them feel.
- Ask volunteers to share their ideas.

Quick Write Have students write a response to the following prompt:

> **Think about an animal you know well, such as a dog or a cat. Describe how this animal eats, sleeps, makes sounds, or moves, using figurative language.**

Ask students to share their responses.

Wrap Up

- Invite students to share what they've learned so far. Encourage them to use the Academic Talk words and phrases in their explanations.
- Explain to students that when they read poems and stories, they discover more about the people, animals, things, and events when they analyze figurative language.

  In the next section, we'll read another poem that uses figurative language. Thinking about the comparisons in the poem and the mood they create will help you understand the poem.

Monitor Understanding

Monitor Understanding

If… students struggle to identify figurative language,

then… emphasize how figurative language makes nonliteral comparisons. Ask students about what really happens and what doesn't really happen:

- **Can tree bats really hang from a tree?** *(Yes.)* **Then that is *not* figurative language.**
- **Are the tree bats really prisoners?** *(No.)* **Then that *is* figurative language.**

Reread the first stanza. Explain that the poet is emphasizing that bats are nocturnal, or nighttime creatures, by using figurative language.

- **How does the speaker describe the bats during the daytime?** *(The speaker compares the bats to fruit and prisoners of light.)*

Reread the second stanza.

- **How does the night seem like a person?** *(It is a mother; it has a gentle voice.)* Review that giving the night human qualities is an example of personification.

Modeled and Guided Instruction

Get Started

Today you will read from a poem called "Rain in Summer." First, you'll read to understand what the poem is about. Then you'll read to analyze the figurative language.

Read

- Read aloud the title and the name of the poet. Ask students to explain what rain is like in summer. Guide them to make predictions, based on the title, about what mood the poet will create.
- Have students read the poem independently. Tell them to place a check mark above any confusing words and phrases as they read. Remind students to look inside, around, and beyond each unknown word to help them figure out its meaning. Use the Word Learning Routine on pp. A50–A51.
- When students have finished reading, clarify the meanings of words and phrases they still find confusing. Then use the questions below to check understanding. Encourage students to identify details in the text that support their answers.

Where is the rain falling? *(It is falling in the streets of a town or city.)*

How is the rain falling? *(heavily; It is pouring.)*

Who is watching the rain? *(a man sick with a fever)*

English Language Learners

Word Learning Strategy

Explore

- Read aloud the Explore question at the top of p. 269 to set the purpose for the second read. Tell students they will need to look closely for nonliteral language as they read.
- Have students read aloud the Close Reader Habit on p. 268.

TIP Figurative language often uses aural or visual imagery to make its comparison more effective. If students don't understand the comparison being made, provide images or audio to help them make the association.

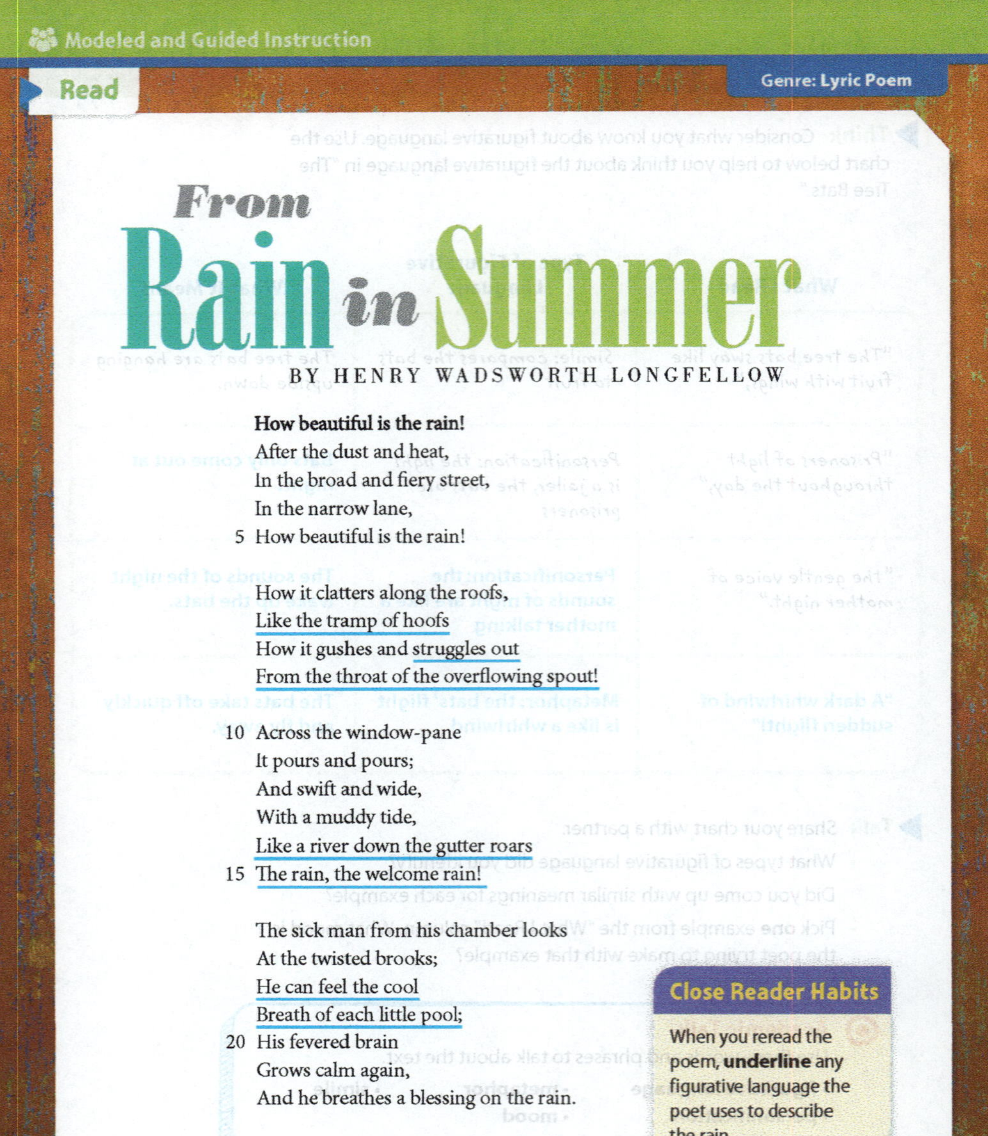

Modeled and Guided Instruction

Read

Genre: Lyric Poem

From

Rain in Summer

BY HENRY WADSWORTH LONGFELLOW

How beautiful is the rain!
After the dust and heat,
In the broad and fiery street,
In the narrow lane,
How beautiful is the rain!

How it clatters along the roofs,
Like the tramp of hoofs
How it gushes and struggles out
From the throat of the overflowing spout!

Across the window-pane
It pours and pours;
And swift and wide,
With a muddy tide,
Like a river down the gutter roars
The rain, the welcome rain!

The sick man from his chamber looks
At the twisted brooks;
He can feel the cool
Breath of each little pool;
His fevered brain
Grows calm again,
And he breathes a blessing on the rain.

Close Reader Habits

When you reread the poem, **underline** any figurative language the poet uses to describe the rain.

268

English Language Learners

Develop Language

Figurative Language Guide students to acquire a basic understanding of the events and experiences described in the poem.

What is happening in the first two stanzas? *(The speaker is watching and listening to a rainstorm.)*

What does the speaker hear? *(the "clatter" and "tramp" of the rain on the roof)*

- Ask students to name animals that have hooves. Have one student describe what running hooves sound like and another describe what rain on the roof sounds like.
- Have students share what the simile helps them to understand about the poem.

Word Learning Strategy

Use Context Clues

- Reread the second stanza. Point out the word *gushes*.

What does *gushes* describe? *(the movement of the water)*

What nearby words help you figure out the meaning of *gushes*? *(struggles, overflowing, pours)*

- Guide students to determine that *gush* means "to flow out with force." Also point out that it is an example of onomatopoeia.
- Invite students to use *gush* in sentences.

L.5.4a

Explore What figurative language does the poet use to describe the rain?

A poet chooses words to help you imagine things and events in special ways.

Think

1 Use the chart below to identify and explain the poem's figurative language.

What I Read	Type of Figurative Language	What It Means
"How it clatters along the roofs, / Like the tramp of hoofs"	Simile: Compares the sound of the rain to "hoofs."	The rain is very loud when it falls on the roof.
"How it gushes and struggles out / From the throat of the overflowing spout!"	Metaphor: Compares water to a creature escaping another creature's throat.	The rainwater is moving powerfully through the spout.
"He can feel the cool / Breath of each little pool;"	Personification: The pools of rainwater breathe.	Rainwater settles in small, cool, calm pools.

Talk

2 Suppose you want to draw a picture to show the motion and energy of the rain. First, talk about how the poet describes the rain. Then draw your picture on a separate piece of paper.

Write

3 **Short Response** Explain how the figurative language shows the change in the rain over time. Use examples to support your response. Use the space provided on page 272 to write your answer.

HINT Use the phrase "figurative language" and the words "metaphor," "simile," and "personification" in your response.

Think Aloud

- Part of the chart has already been filled in for me. It is a simile that says, "How it clatters along the roofs, / like the tramp of hoofs." The word *it* refers to the rain. The rain clatters like the tramp of hoofs. Yes, this is a simile because it compares the rain to the sound of hoofs using the word *like*.
- Let me think about what the simile means. A horse is one type of animal with hooves. When horses tramp, or move with heavy steps, it makes a clip/clap noise (Drum to demonstrate.) I can see how heavy rain overhead would create this same clatter, or rattling sound. I'll write "The rain is very loud when it falls on the roof" in the *What It Means* section of my chart.

Think

- Read aloud the Think section. Explain to students that you will model how to find text evidence to fill in part of the chart. Use the **Think Aloud** below to guide your modeling.
- Revisit the Explore question. Guide students to determine that they need to look for more details, using the Close Reader Habit.
- Encourage students to work with a partner to continue rereading the poem and complete the chart. Remind them to read the Buddy Tip.
- Ask volunteers to share their completed charts.
- Guide students to see that the figurative language helps them hear and see how hard the rain falls in stanzas 2 and 3. Then, in stanza 4, the figurative language helps them feel what the sick man feels as he watches the rain.

Talk

- Read aloud the Talk prompt.
- Have partners respond to the prompt. Use the Talk Routine on pp. A52–A53.
- Circulate to check that students are sketching hard rain for stanzas 2 and 3 and puddles for stanza 4.

Write

- Ask a volunteer to read aloud the Write prompt.
- Invite a few students to tell what the prompt is asking them to do.
- Make sure students understand that they need to think about how hard the rain is falling at the beginning of the poem and then tell what the rain is like at the end. Remind them to use the evidence in their charts to support their writing.
- Have students turn to p. 272 to write their responses.
- Use Review Responses on p. 272 to assess students' writing.

Wrap Up

- Ask students to recall the Learning Target. Have them explain how analyzing the figurative language helped them understand and enjoy the poem.

Guided Practice

Get Started

Today you will read a story about nature. First, you will read to understand what happens. Then you will reread with a partner to analyze the figurative language.

Read

- Read aloud the title of the story. Ask students to give examples of wildlife. Identify the moose in the photograph as an example of wildlife that lives in forest areas.
- Have students predict what the story will be about based on the title and the photograph.
- **Read to Understand** Have students read the story independently. Tell them to place a check mark above any confusing words and phrases as they read. Remind students to look inside, around, and beyond each unknown word to help them figure out its meaning. Use the Word Learning Routine on pp. A50–A51.
- When students have finished reading, clarify the meanings of words and phrases they still find confusing. Then use the questions below to check understanding. Encourage students to identify details in the text that support their answers.

  Where are the characters, and what are they doing? *(They are hiking on a trail in the woods.)*

  What wildlife do they see? *(a moose)*

  What surprises the narrator? *(She assumed a moose would not be dangerous. Aunt Sheryl explains that a moose is one of the most dangerous wild animals in North America.)*

 **English Language Learners**

● **Word Learning Strategy**

- **Read to Analyze** Read aloud the Close Reader Habit on p. 270 to set the purpose for the second read. Then have students reread the story with a partner and discuss any questions they might have.

Guided Practice

Read

Genre: Realistic Fiction

WILDLIFE WORRIES

by Annika Pederson

1 When my Aunt Sheryl and Uncle Don invited Mom and me to go hiking with them along the North Shore of Lake Superior, we couldn't wait to go. It wasn't until we got there that I found out that the woods are home to some serious wildlife—wolves, bobcats, coyotes, and bears! Although I was excited, I was also terrified of dangerous animals.

2 An amazing waterfall near the park entrance swept away my fears at first. Next, we hiked a trail that snaked upriver, through a gold mine of maple, birch, pine, and spruce. As we walked on, though, I felt myself sinking back into a black bog of dread. And just then, in a shallow glassy bend of the river up ahead, I saw an animal I *wanted* to see. "Look!" I said. "A moose! I'm going to go feed it!"

3 Aunt Sheryl grabbed my shoulder with an iron hand. "Nikki, stop, now," she said quietly. We all climbed to some rocks high above the river, with an eagle's nest view of the moose. Aunt Sheryl explained to me that a bull moose topped the list as one of the most dangerous wild animals in North America, and that it was more likely for a human to be hurt by a moose in these parts than a wolf or bear.

4 It felt strange, after all my misplaced fears, to discover that this beautiful animal that looked as tame as a cow back home had to be treated with caution. I decided that before our next trip, I was going to do a little homework about the animals here and trade my wildlife worries for . . . what should I call it? *Wildlife wonder.*

Close Reader Habits

How does the author describe the characters? Reread the story. **Underline** any figurative language that describes the characters, including the moose.

270

English Language Learners

Develop Language

Words and Word Phrases Review with students the meaning of the word *until*. Together, recall that it means "up to a specific time." Challenge students to use it in a sentence.

- Reread the second sentence, and point out the phrase *not until*. Explain that together, these words mean "not before a specific time."
- Discuss what the narrator did not know before they got to the woods. Invite students to practice using the phrase *not until* in a sentence.

● Word Learning Strategy

Use Context Clues

- Reread the last paragraph. Guide students to find the meaning of *caution*.

  What has to be "treated with caution"? *("this beautiful animal," or the moose)*

  What might happen if the animal isn't "treated with caution"? *(A human might be hurt by the moose.)*

  What does this tell you about what *caution* means? *(being careful to avoid getting hurt)*

- Invite students to suggest other examples of times when they must use caution.

L.5.4a

Think Use what you learned from reading the story to respond to the following questions.

Figurative language describes familiar events in interesting ways. For example, in paragraph 3 the narrator says she has "an eagle's nest view of the moose." This is an interesting way of saying, "I looked at the moose from above."

1 Read this sentence from the story.

> Next, we hiked a trail that snaked upriver, through a gold mine of maple, birch, pine, and spruce.

What does the comparison of "maple, birch, pine, and spruce" to a "gold mine" suggest?

- (A) The park is a valuable natural resource.
- B The park is near a gold mine in which trees grow.
- C The trees make the trail seem dark, like being in a mine.
- D The park has several kinds of trees with yellow leaves.

2 Read the sentence from the text. Then answer the question that follows.

> As we walked on, though, I felt myself sinking back into a <u>black bog of dread</u>.

What feelings is the author trying to create by using the metaphor <u>black bog of dread</u>? Select **two** options.

- A a sense of adventure
- (B) a feeling of fear
- C a sense of happiness
- (D) a sense of being stuck
- E a feeling of regret
- F a sense of awe

Talk

3 In paragraph 4, the narrator uses the phrase <u>tame as a cow back home</u>. What does this tell you about both the narrator and the moose? Use the figurative language chart on page 273 to capture your thoughts and evidence.

HINT The narrator refers to "a cow back home." What can you infer about the kind of setting she knows best?

Write

4 **Short Response** Use the information from your chart to explain what the narrator's use of the phrase <u>tame as a cow back home</u> tells you about both the moose and the narrator. Use the space provided on page 273 to write your answer.

Integrating Standards

Use these questions to further students' understanding of the story.

- **What can you infer from the last paragraph?** *(The narrator learned a lesson on this trip and wants to go hiking again.)* ***DOK 2*** **RL.5.1**
- **What is one theme of this story? Support your response with evidence from the story.** *("Things are not always what they seem." The moose looks calm and peaceful, but the narrator learns that it is actually quite dangerous.)* ***DOK 3*** **RL.5.2**

Monitor Understanding

If... students have difficulty finding text evidence to answer item 3,

then... guide students to describe what cows look like and do. Students should identify that cows are calm, grazing animals who stand still and do not harm people. Have students compare these details to the description of the moose in the story.

Think

- Have students work with a partner to complete items 1–2. Point out the word **two** in item 2.

TIP If students have trouble with item 1, guide them to see that a gold mine is a positive thing, so they can eliminate answers that suggest negative feelings.

Answer Analysis

When students have finished, discuss correct and incorrect responses.

1 **The correct choice is A.** The phrase "gold mine" suggests wealth and value.

- **B, C,** and **D** are not supported by text evidence.

DOK 2

2 **The correct choices are B and D.** The "black bog of dread" is meant to create a mood of fear and of being stuck.

- **A, C,** and **F** describe emotions the narrator feels, but none is connected to the phrase "black bog of dread."
- **E** is incorrect because the narrator never expresses regret.

DOK 2

Integrating Standards

Talk

- Have partners discuss the prompt. Emphasize that students should support their ideas with text details.
- Circulate to clarify misunderstandings.

Monitor Understanding

Write

- See p. 273 for instructional guidance.

Wrap Up

- Ask students to recall the Learning Target. Have them explain how identifying and analyzing figurative language helped them understand the story.

 Modeled and Guided Instruction

Write

- Remember to use the Response-Writing Routine on pp. A54–A55.

Review Responses

After students complete the writing activity, help them evaluate their responses.

3 Responses may vary but should show and support the idea of heavy rain in stanzas 2 and 3, where the water "gushes" and "pours and pours," and standing rain in "each little pool" in stanza 4. See the sample response on the student book page.

DOK 3

Modeled and Guided Instruction

 **Write** Use the space below to write your answer to the question on page 269.

Rain in Summer

3 **Short Response** Explain how the figurative language shows the change in the rain over time. Use examples to support your response.

HINT Use the phrase "figurative language" and the words "metaphor," "simile," and "personification" in your response.

Sample response: The poet uses figurative language to show us that the rain first moves powerfully but then slows and stops. First, he says the sound of the falling rain is "like the tramp of hoofs" on the roofs. This simile tells us how hard the falling rain strikes the roofs. He then says the rainwater "struggles out / From the throat of the overflowing spout!" This metaphor, which compares the water's movement to one animal fighting to escape the throat of another animal, shows the water's energy. But by the last stanza, the rainwater has stopped moving. It is in little pools, each producing a gentle, calming "cool breath"—an example of personification.

Check Your Writing

- ☐ Did you read the prompt carefully?
- ☐ Did you put the prompt in your own words?
- ☐ Did you use the best evidence from the text to support your ideas?
- ☐ Are your ideas clearly organized?
- ☐ Did you write in clear and complete sentences?
- ☐ Did you check your spelling and punctuation?

Don't forget to check your writing.

272

Scaffolding Support for Reluctant Writers

If students are having a difficult time getting started, use the strategies below. Work individually with struggling students, or have students work with partners.

- Circle the verbs in the prompt that tell you what to do, such as *describe*, *explain*, or *compare*.
- Underline words and phrases in the prompt that show what information you need to provide in your response, such as *causes*, *reasons*, or *character traits*.
- Talk about the details from the text that you will include in your response.
- Explain aloud how you will respond to the prompt.

WILDLIFE WORRIES

3 Use the chart below to organize your ideas and details.

What I Read	Type of Figurative Language	What It Means

Write Use the space below to write your answer to the question on page 271.

4 **Short Response** Use the information from your chart to explain what the narrator's use of the phrase tame as a cow back home tells you about both the moose and the narrator.

The simile "tame as a cow back home" suggests the narrator is from a place with cows, such as a farm or small town. This suggests she is not used to being near wild animals, although she might be more comfortable in nature than a city dweller is. The simile also expresses how calm and gentle the moose looks, even though Aunt Sheryl points out how dangerous it can be.

Teacher Notes

Guided Practice

Talk

3 Students should use the chart to organize their thoughts and evidence.

Write

- Ask a volunteer to read aloud the Write prompt.
- Invite students to tell what the prompt is asking them to do. Make sure they understand that they need to explain not only the comparison, but what it tells about the narrator.
- Call attention to the HINT.
- Remember to use the Response-Writing Routine on pp. A54–A55.

Review Responses

After students complete the writing activity, help them evaluate their responses.

4 Responses may vary but should include the idea that the comparison "tame as a cow back home" suggests the narrator is from a place with cows, such as a farm or small town. The simile suggests how calm and gentle the moose looks, even though it can be dangerous. See the sample response on the student book page.
DOK 3

Independent Practice

Get Started

Today you are going to read the first chapter from a novel called *David and the Phoenix*. You will use what you have learned about figurative language to analyze the characters, the events, and the mood of the story.

- Ask a volunteer to explain how identifying and analyzing figurative language will help readers better understand the story. Encourage students to use the Academic Talk words and phrases in their response.

 **English Language Learners**

Read

You are going to read the story independently and use what you have learned to think and write about the text. As you read, remember to look closely at the figurative language in order to get a sense of the characters' feelings and the mood of the story.

- Read aloud the title of the novel and then encourage students to preview the text, paying close attention to the illustrations.
- Call attention to the Words to Know in the upper left of p. 274
- If students need support in reading the passage, you may wish to use the Monitor Understanding suggestions.
- When students have finished, have them complete the Think and Write sections.

● **Monitor Understanding**

Independent Practice

Read

Genre: Fantasy

WORDS TO KNOW
As you read, look inside, around, and beyond these words to figure out what they mean.
- **infinitely**
- **progress**
- **confusion**

This story is from the first chapter of a novel about a boy whose family moves into a new home near a mountain. In the chapters that follow, the boy goes hiking on the mountain and meets a strange bird called a Phoenix, a famous creature from mythology. Throughout the novel, the boy and the Phoenix share exciting adventures together.

from **David and the Phoenix**

by Edward Ormondroyd

1 All the way there David had saved this moment for himself, struggling not to peek until the proper time came. When the car finally stopped, the rest of them got out stiffly and went into the new house. But David walked slowly into the backyard with his eyes fixed on the ground. For a whole minute he stood there, not daring to look up. Then he took a deep breath, clenched his hands tightly, and lifted his head.

274

English Language Learners
Build Meaning

Prior Knowledge Have students read the note preceding the title. Ask:

- **What is the novel about?** *(a boy whose family moves into a new home near a mountain)*

Call attention to the two key ideas—*moving* and *mountain*. Then preview the illustrations. Have students describe what they see.

Discuss the concepts of moving and mountains. Invite students to share their experiences with each topic. Help students find the related vocabulary to fit their descriptions, such as *pack, unpack, relocate, hike, peak,* and *summit*.

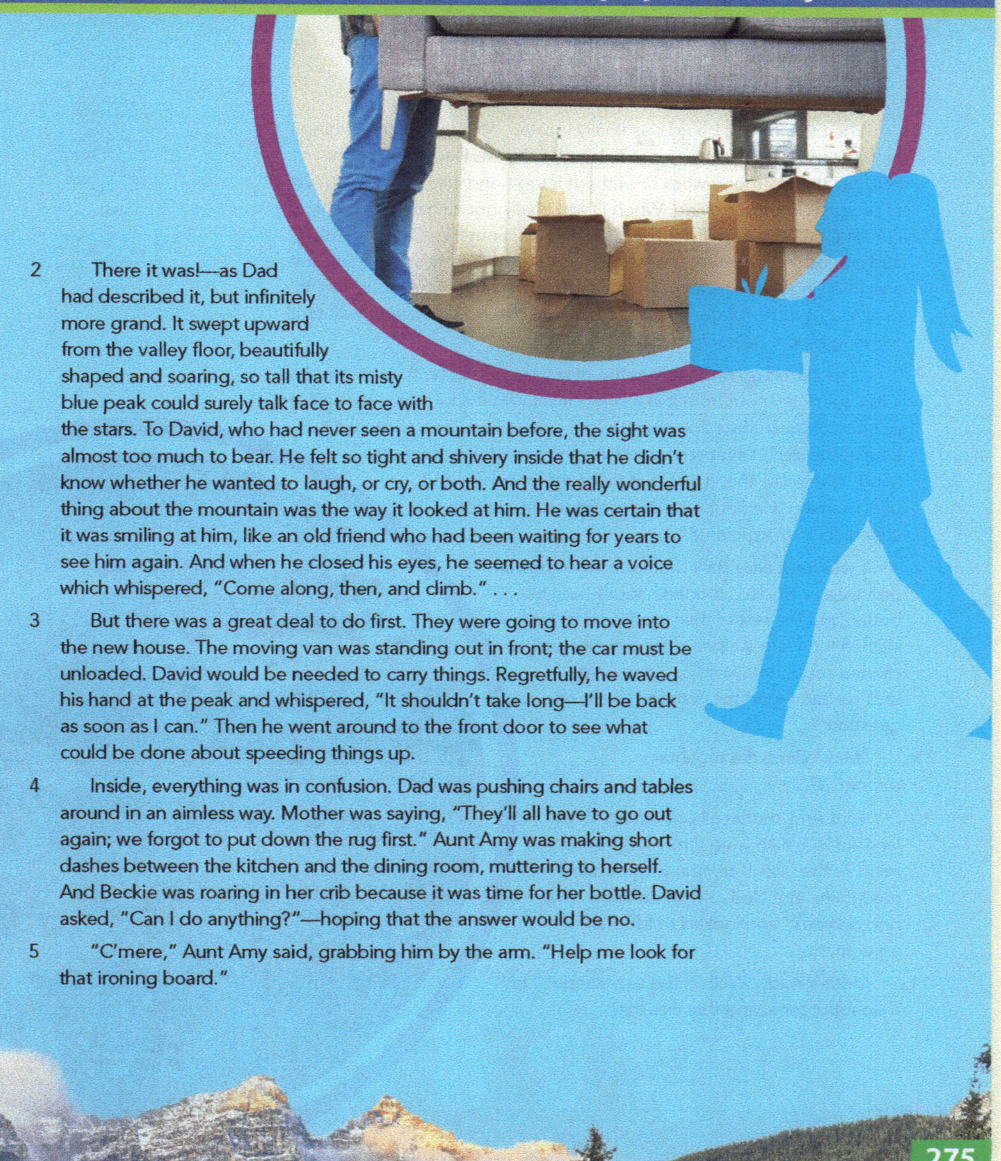

Language and Meaning Lesson 15

2 There it was!—as Dad had described it, but infinitely more grand. It swept upward from the valley floor, beautifully shaped and soaring, so tall that its misty blue peak could surely talk face to face with the stars. To David, who had never seen a mountain before, the sight was almost too much to bear. He felt so tight and shivery inside that he didn't know whether he wanted to laugh, or cry, or both. And the really wonderful thing about the mountain was the way it looked at him. He was certain that it was smiling at him, like an old friend who had been waiting for years to see him again. And when he closed his eyes, he seemed to hear a voice which whispered, "Come along, then, and climb." . . .

3 But there was a great deal to do first. They were going to move into the new house. The moving van was standing out in front; the car must be unloaded. David would be needed to carry things. Regretfully, he waved his hand at the peak and whispered, "It shouldn't take long—I'll be back as soon as I can." Then he went around to the front door to see what could be done about speeding things up.

4 Inside, everything was in confusion. Dad was pushing chairs and tables around in an aimless way. Mother was saying, "They'll all have to go out again; we forgot to put down the rug first." Aunt Amy was making short dashes between the kitchen and the dining room, muttering to herself. And Beckie was roaring in her crib because it was time for her bottle. David asked, "Can I do anything?"—hoping that the answer would be no.

5 "C'mere," Aunt Amy said, grabbing him by the arm. "Help me look for that ironing board."

275

Monitor Understanding

If... students struggle to read and understand the passage,

then... use these scaffolding suggestions:

Question the Text Preview the text by asking the following questions:

- **Based on the title and illustrations, what do you predict the story will be about?**
- **What questions do you have about the text?**

Vocabulary Support Define words that may interfere with comprehension, such as *summit* and *landslides*.

Read Aloud Read aloud the text with students. You could also have students chorally read the text in a small group.

Check Understanding Use the questions below to check understanding. Encourage students to cite details in the text that support their answers.

- **Where are David and his family?** *(They have just arrived at their new house, which is in the mountains.)*
- **What is the rest of the family doing?** *(David's father, mother, and aunt are moving into the house, carrying boxes from the moving van and car. His sister Beckie is in her crib.)*
- **What does David want?** *(to climb the mountain)*

Independent Practice

Integrating Standards

After students have read the story, use these questions to discuss it with them.

- **In paragraph 1, make an inference about why David didn't want to "peek until the proper time came." Use specific examples from the story to support your response.**

  (He doesn't want to peek because he is excited about seeing the mountain. The text says that "[he] walked slowly into the backyard with his eyes fixed on the ground." This also shows his excitement about seeing the mountain. He wants to delay the moment until he finally sees it.)

  DOK 3 RL.5.1

- **What is one theme of this story? Use specific examples from the story to support your response.**

  (Nature or the mountains are a calming force during the confusion of moving day. David uses words such as grand, swept, and soaring to describe the mountain, and conversely describes the "confusion" of the move with people moving in all directions and Beckie "roaring in her crib.")

  DOK 3 RL.5.2

- **How does the setting of the story change?**

  (The setting changes from the tranquil outdoors, where David first sees the majestic mountain, to the bustling unpacking happening indoors. It also changes from daytime to evening.)

  DOK 2 RL.5.3

- **David sees the mountain and is immediately awestruck. How might the story be different if it were told from David's dad's point of view?**

  (Dad has seen a mountain before, and so he might describe its beauty but more briefly, and seeming less awestruck by it. His description of events would likely be about the chaos of the day and his feelings about moving to a new place.)

  DOK 3 RL.5.6

● **Theme Connection**

6 When the ironing board was finally located, Mother had something for him to do. And when he was finished with that, Dad called for his help. So the afternoon wore on without letup—and also without any signs of progress in their moving. When David finally got a chance to sneak out for a breathing spell, he felt his heart sink. Somehow, in all the rush and confusion, the afternoon had disappeared. Already the evening sun was throwing shadows across the side of the mountain and touching its peak with a ruddy blaze. It was too late now. He would have to wait until morning before he could climb.

7 As he gazed up miserably at the glowing summit, he thought he saw a tiny speck soar out from it in a brief circle. Was it a bird of some sort, or just one of those dots that swim before your eyes when you stare too long at the sky? It almost seemed like the mountain waving its hand, as if to say that it was quite all right for him to wait until morning. He felt better then, and returned more cheerfully to the moving.

8 It was long after dark before the moving van drove away. Beckie crooned happily over her bottle, and the rest of them gathered in the kitchen for a late supper of sandwiches and canned soup. But David could not eat until he had found the courage to ask one question:

9 "May I climb the mountain tomorrow?"

10 Aunt Amy muttered something about landslides, which were firmly fixed in her mind as the fate of people who climbed mountains. But Dad said, "I don't see why not, do you?" and looked to Mother for agreement.

11 Mother said, "Well . . . be very careful," in a doubtful tone, and that was that.

● **Theme Connection**

- Remind students that the theme of this lesson is Nature.
- Explain that nature is a common topic for authors and poets because people tend to have strong feelings about it.
- Display a four-column chart on the board, and title each column with the name of a passage from this lesson (including "The Tree Bats"). Briefly review the details of each passage, specifically how the author or speaker describes nature. Together, determine a mood for each passage. Point out that a mood can change within a text.
- Discuss how nature is used in other stories, poems, and movies to create a certain mood.

Think Use what you learned from reading the story to respond to the following questions.

1 This question has two parts. First, answer Part A. Then answer Part B.

Part A
What does David think about the mountain?

- (A) It is kind.
- B It is alive.
- C It is haunted.
- D It is dangerous.

Part B
Which example of figurative language from the story **best** supports the answer to Part A?

- A "And the really wonderful thing about the mountain was the way it looked at him."
- (B) "He was certain that it was smiling at him, like an old friend who had been waiting for years to see him again."
- C "And when he closed his eyes, he seemed to hear a voice, which whispered, 'Come along, then, and climb.'"
- D "Already the evening sun was throwing shadows across the side of the mountain and touching its peak with a ruddy blaze."

2 Read the sentence. Then answer the question.

> It swept upward from the valley floor, beautifully shaped and soaring, so tall that its misty blue peak could surely talk face to face with the stars.

What mood is the author trying to create by using the personification talk face to face with the stars? Select **two** options.

- (A) awe
- B coldness
- C fear
- (D) wonder
- E loneliness
- F suspense

Monitor Understanding

If... students struggle to complete the items,

then... you may wish to use the following suggestions:

Read Aloud Activities

- As you read, have students note any unfamiliar words or phrases. Clarify any misunderstandings.
- Discuss each item with students to make certain they understand the expectation.

Reread the Text

- Have students record descriptive and figurative language about the mountain and about David's interactions with it as they reread.
- Have partners summarize the text.

Think

- Use the Monitor Understanding suggestions to support students in completing items 1–4.

Monitor Understanding

Answer Analysis

- When students have finished, discuss correct and incorrect responses.

1 **Part A**
The correct choice is A. David feels as if the mountain is kind, or friendly.

- **B** is incorrect; feeling that the mountain is friendly is not the same as believing it is alive.
- **C** is incorrect; the mountain seems to be whispering, but it is not haunted.
- **D** is incorrect; nothing states or suggests that David thinks the mountain is dangerous.

Part B
The correct choice is B. An old friend is kind.

- **A** does not give enough information about the mountain.
- **C** is incorrect; the mountain seems to be whispering, but that does not suggest that it is kind.
- **D** is incorrect; it is more about the evening shadows than the mountain.

DOK 2 **RL.5.4**

2 **The correct choices are A and D.** A mountain large enough to "talk face to face with the stars" is a sight that would inspire awe and wonder.

- **B, C, E,** and **F** are incorrect; although the peak of a mountain might be cold or inspire fear, loneliness, or suspense, none of these correlate to the mood the author wants to create with the phrase "talk face to face with the stars."

DOK 2 **RL.5.4**

Independent Practice

3 **Part A**

The correct choice is D. The word *fixed* has multiple meanings, but the one that makes sense in this sentence is "focused."

- **A, B,** and **C** are incorrect; although "tied," "installed," and "repaired" are meanings of the word *fixed,* none of these words fits within the context of the sentence.

Part B

The correct choice is B. "For a whole minute he stood there, not daring to look up."

- **A** does not have to do with David's eyes.
- **C** refers to David's hands, not his eyes.
- **D** refers to David's head, once he raises his gaze from where it was "fixed on the ground."

***DOK 2* RL.5.4**

4 Students should underline "So the afternoon wore on without letup—and also without any signs of progress in their moving." These details provide evidence about what *sneak out for a breathing spell* means.

***DOK 2* RL.5.4**

3 This question has two parts. First, answer Part A. Then answer Part B.

Part A

Read the sentence from paragraph 1.

But David walked slowly into the backyard with his eyes fixed on the ground.

What does the word fixed mean as it is used in the sentence?

A tied
B installed
C repaired
D focused

Part B

Which detail from the story provides the **best** clue for the meaning of the word fixed?

A ". . . David had saved this moment for himself, . . ."
B ". . . not daring to look up."
C ". . . clenched his hands tightly, . . ."
D ". . . and lifted his head."

4 Read the sentence and the directions that follow.

When David finally got a chance to sneak out for a breathing spell, he felt his heart sink.

Underline the sentence in the paragraph below that **best** helps you understand the meaning of the phrase sneak out for a breathing spell.

When the ironing board was finally located, Mother had something for him to do. And when he was finished with that, Dad called for his help. So the afternoon wore on without letup—and also without any signs of progress in their moving. When David finally got a chance to sneak out for a breathing spell, he felt his heart sink. Somehow, in all the rush and confusion, the afternoon had disappeared. Already the evening sun was throwing shadows across the side of the mountain and touching its peak with a ruddy blaze. It was too late now. He would have to wait until morning before he could climb.

Monitor Understanding

If . . . students don't understand the writing task,

then . . . read aloud the writing prompt. Use the following questions to help students get started.

- **What is the prompt asking you to write about?**
- **Do you need to reread the text to find more information?**
- **How will you identify the information you need to include?**

- Have partners talk about how they will organize their responses.
- Provide a graphic organizer to assist students, if needed.

Write

5 **Short Response** Read the following sentence from the story.

It almost seemed like the mountain waving its hand, as if to say that it was quite all right for him to wait until morning.

What does the phrase like the mountain waving its hand tell the reader about the mountain? Use details from the story to support your answer.

Sample response: The phrase "like the mountain waving its hand" is an example of the author comparing the mountain to a friendly person. When David first sees the mountain, he is sure it smiles at him, as a person would do. The mountain seems to whisper an invitation to climb, and only a person can whisper an invitation. When David realizes it is too dark to climb the mountain, he thinks the mountain waves at him, as if to say he can climb in the morning.

Learning Target

In this lesson, you looked at how texts use figurative language. Explain how figuring out the meanings of figurative language can help you better understand and enjoy such texts.

Responses will vary, but students should understand that interpreting figurative language can increase both the understanding and enjoyment of a text.

279

5 **2-Point Writing Rubric**

Points	Focus	Evidence	Organization
2	My answer does exactly what the prompt asked me to do.	My answer is supported with plenty of details from the text.	My ideas are clear and in a logical order.
1	Some of my answer does not relate to the prompt.	My answer is missing some important details from the text.	Some of my ideas are unclear and out of order.
0	My answer does not make sense.	My answer does not have any details from the text.	My ideas are unclear and not in any order.

Write

- Tell students that using what they read, they will plan and compose a short response to the writing prompt.

Monitor Understanding

Review Responses

After students have completed each part of the writing activity, help them evaluate their responses.

5 Display or pass out copies of the reproducible **2-Point Writing Rubric** on p. TR10. Have students use the rubric to individually assess their writing and revise as needed.

When students have finished their revisions, evaluate their responses. Answers will vary but should reflect an understanding that the mountain is not actually waving, but rather, according to David's point of view, seeming to welcome him, greet him, or draw him toward it. See the sample response.

DOK 3 RL.5.4, W.5.9a

Wrap Up

Learning Target

- Have each student respond in writing to the Learning Target prompt.
- When students have finished, have them share their responses. This may be done with a partner, in small groups, or as a whole class.

LESSON OVERVIEW

Lesson 16
Understanding Literary Structure

Standards Focus

Explain how a series of . . . scenes, or stanzas fits together to provide the overall structure of a particular . . . drama, or poem. RL.5.5

Lesson Objectives

Reading

- Explain how a series of scenes or stanzas create the structure of a play or poem. RL.5.5
- Draw meaning from the structure of a play or poem. RL.5.5

Writing

- Draw evidence from literary texts to support analysis and reflection. W.5.9a

Speaking and Listening

- Pose and respond to specific questions and contribute to discussions. SL.5.1c
- Review the key ideas expressed and draw conclusions. SL.5.1d

Language

- Use context as a clue to the meaning of a word or phrase. L.5.4a
- Acquire and use academic and domain-specific words and phrases. L.5.6

Additional Practice: **RL.5.1, RL.5.2, RL.5.3, RL.5.4, RL.5.6**

Academic Talk

See **Glossary of Terms**, pp. TR2–TR9

- acts
- stanzas
- scenes
- structures
- dramas

Learning Progression

Grade 4	Grade 5	Grade 6
Students compare poems, drama, and prose, and expand their understanding of structural elements of poems (e.g., verse, rhythm, meter) and drama (e.g., casts of characters, settings, descriptions, dialogue, stage directions) and refer to those elements when writing or speaking about a text.	Building on Grade 4, students explain how scenes in a drama and stanzas in a poem fit together, emphasizing the connection between structure and meaning.	Grade 6 increases in complexity by emphasizing analysis of a text's structure and by requiring students to consider not only how part of the text fits into the structure but how it contributes to the theme, setting, or plot.

Lesson Text Selections

Modeled and Guided Instruction

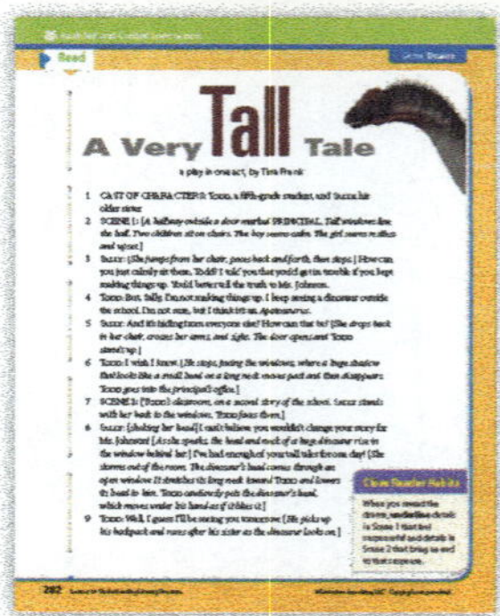

A Very Tall Tale
a play in one act, by Tina Frank
Genre: Drama

Guided Practice

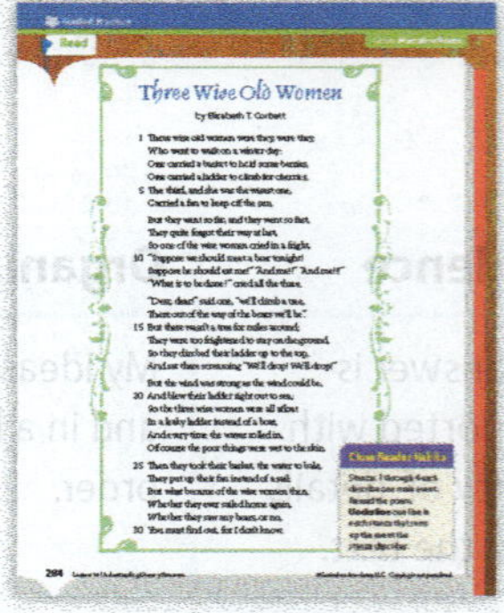

Three Wise Old Women
by Elizabeth T. Corbett
Genre: Narrative Poem

Independent Practice

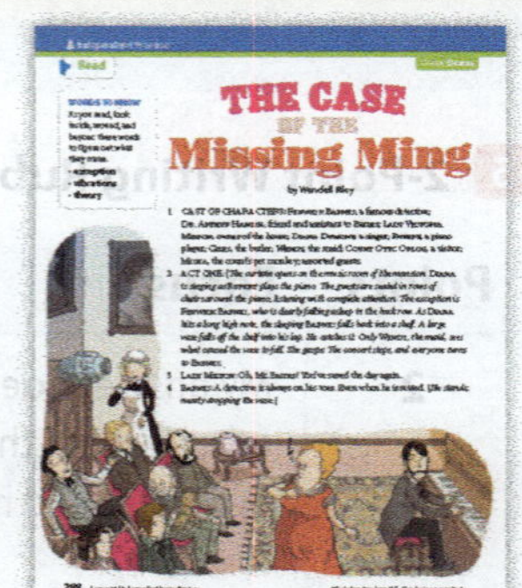

The Case of the Missing Ming
by Wendell Riley
Genre: Drama

Lesson Pacing Guide

Whole Class Instruction *30–45 minutes per day*

Day 1

Teacher-Toolbox.com Interactive Tutorial
Explaining the Structure of a Poem—Level E
20 min (optional)

Introduction pp. 280–281
- **Read** **Understanding Literary Structure** *10 min*
- **Think** *10 min*
  Graphic Organizer: Venn Diagram
- **Talk** *5 min*
  Quick Write (TRB) *5 min*

Day 2

Modeled and Guided Instruction pp. 282–283, 286
- **Read** **A Very Tall Tale** *10 min*
- **Think** *10 min*
  Graphic Organizer: Two-Column Chart
- **Talk** *5 min*
- **Write** Short Response *10 min*

Day 3

Guided Practice pp. 284–285, 287
- **Read** **Three Wise Old Women** *10 min*
- **Think** *10 min*
- **Talk** *5 min*
- **Write** Short Response *10 min*

Day 4

Independent Practice pp. 288–293
- **Read** **The Case of the Missing Ming** *15 min*
- **Think** *10 min*
- **Write** Extended Response *15 min*

Day 5

Independent Practice pp. 288–293
- *Review* Answer Analysis (TRB) *10 min*
- *Review* Response Analysis (TRB) *10 min*
- *Assign and Discuss* Learning Target *10 min*

Language Handbook
Lesson 9 Commas After Introductory Elements, pp. 454–455
20 min (optional)

Ready Writing Connection

During *Ready Reading* Days 1–5, use:
Lesson 4 Writing to Analyze Literature: Essay

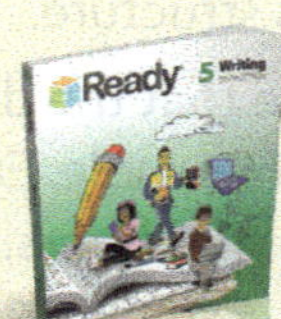

- **Steps 6 and 7 Revise**
- **Step 8 Edit**
- **Prepare to Publish**
- **Collaborate**
- **Present**

See *Ready Writing TRB*, p. 90a for complete lesson plan.

Small Group Differentiation

Teacher-Toolbox.com

Reteach

***Ready Reading* Prerequisite Lessons**
Grade 4
- Lesson 19 Elements of Poetry
- Lesson 20 Elements of Plays

Teacher-led Activities

Tools for Instruction
- Analyze Story Elements

Personalized Learning

i-Ready.com

Independent

i-Ready Close Reading Lessons

- **Grade 5** Understanding Structure in Poetry
- **Grade 5** Understanding Structure in Stories
- **Grade 5** Understanding Structure in Drama

Introduction

Get Started

- Explain to students that in this lesson they will read funny plays and poems and explore the parts that each piece is made up of.
- Review the concept of structure. Draw a house or apartment building with a basement, several stories, and a roof. Have students identify each part and discuss how together they make up the building's structure.
- Emphasize that the different parts work together to make the whole. Each part is important and related to the others. The same is true in poems and plays. Explain:

  Different scenes and, sometimes, acts fit together to make up a drama. Each one is related to the others and helps tell the meaning of the drama. Different stanzas fit together to make up a poem. Each one is related to the others and helps tell the meaning of the poem.
- Focus students' attention on the Learning Target. Read it aloud to set the purpose for the lesson.
- Display the Academic Talk words. Tell students to listen for these words and their meanings as you work through the lesson together. Use the Academic Talk Routine on pp. A48–A49.

English Language Learners

- **Genre Focus**

Read

- Read aloud the Read section as students follow along. Restate to reinforce:

  When you read poems and dramas, it's helpful to stop and ask yourself about how each section is alike and different. Figuring out why the author structured the poem or play in a particular way can help you understand the author's purpose for writing.
- Have students read the brief poem on p. 280. Challenge them to think about what each pair of lines has in common and how all the pairs work together.

Introduction

RL.5.5 Explain how a series of . . . scenes, or stanzas fits together to provide the overall structure of a particular . . . drama, or poem.

Lesson 16 Understanding Literary Structure

Learning Target **Knowing how dramas and poems are structured will help you better understand what they mean.**

Read Dramas and poems have **structures** that organize what they say and help the reader understand what they mean.

- **Dramas** are divided into **acts**. Each act tells a main part of the drama. Acts are often divided into **scenes**, which show different times and places.
- Poems are often organized in **stanzas**, or groups of lines that have something in common.

Examining how such features work together can help you understand not just how a text is structured but why it is structured that way.

Read this poem. Notice how the lines are organized into stanzas. Why do you think the poet organized the lines this way?

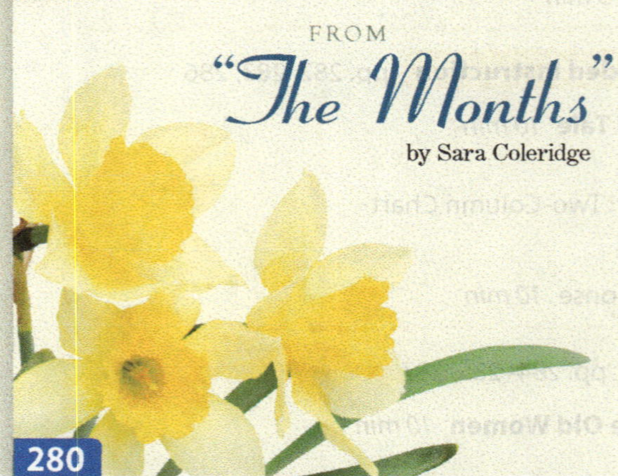

FROM

"The Months"

by Sara Coleridge

January brings the snow,
Makes our feet and fingers glow.

February brings the rain,
Thaws the frozen lake again.

March brings breezes loud and shrill,
Stirs the dancing daffodil.

280

English Language Learners

Build Meaning

Text Features Display examples of dramas and poems so students can annotate them with a marker.

- First, show a poem with several stanzas. Circle the first stanza. Then have volunteers circle subsequent stanzas so students grasp that the stanzas break the poem into pieces. Ask students to count the stanzas.
- Repeat the activity with one or more dramas. Point out that acts may be labeled with Roman numerals and that one-act plays only have scenes.
- Display new examples of each text type, and have students point to the stanzas, acts, and scenes, using the vocabulary to describe what they're pointing to.

Genre Focus

Drama

Explain that a drama, or play, is a story that is usually acted out on a stage. Plays are organized into scenes that present a certain time and place. Longer plays have acts, which are groups of related scenes.

Ask students to share examples of plays they have read, heard, or seen.

Note that students will read a play called "A Very Tale Tall" in the Guided Practice section of this lesson. Then they will read another play called "The Case of the Missing Ming" during Independent Practice.

Think Consider what you know about the features of dramas and poems. What are their main features? What purposes do those features share? Use the *Venn diagram* to organize your thoughts.

Drama Only

Features and Their Purposes

Acts: to tell a main part of a drama

Scenes: to divide acts into specific times and places

Both

The features organize what the text says. The features help the reader understand what the text means.

Poem Only

Feature and Its Purpose

Stanzas: to organize groups of lines that have some kind of similarity

Use the words *lines* and *stanzas* to describe the structure of "The Months." Explain why the poet chose the structure she did.

Sample response: Each stanza uses two lines to describe a month of the year. The structure helps the reader know that each stanza is about a different month.

Talk Discuss the poem "The Months" with a partner.

- What features of poetry did you see in the excerpt from "The Months"?
- How did those features help you understand what the poem is about?

Academic Talk

Use these words to talk about the text.

- **acts**
- **scenes**
- **dramas**
- **stanzas**
- **structures**

Monitor Understanding

If... students struggle to understand the concept of structure,

then... relate it to the organization of the school day. Have students name the different parts of your school day, such as the time for different subjects; lunchtime; times for art, music, and physical education; and dismissal.

Have students put the events in order. Explain that sometimes, structure is time order, just like in the poem "The Months." Each stanza in the poem is about a month. The poem moves in order throughout the months of the year, in the same way the parts of the school day move from beginning to end.

Think

- Have students read aloud the Think section. Explain that the Venn diagram will help them organize their thinking.
- Have partners complete the Venn diagram and the brief activity below it, using what they have learned about the parts of poems and dramas.
- As students work, circulate and provide assistance as needed.
- Ask volunteers to share their diagrams and responses.
- Make certain students understand that the features of a poem or drama help to organize ideas and help readers understand its meaning.

Talk

- Read aloud the Talk prompts.
- Have partners discuss the structure of the poem. Guide them to see how the stanzas separate parts of the poem while building related ideas—each stanza is about one month of the year.

Quick Write Have students write a response to the following prompt:

Think of something you use or play with that is made up of different pieces. Tell what the pieces are, and explain why the object would not work as well without one or more of the pieces.

Ask students to share their responses.

Wrap Up

- Invite students to share what they've learned so far. Encourage them to use the Academic Talk words in their explanations.
- Explain to students that when they read poems and plays, they can think about how the parts fit together to create meaning.

In the next section, we'll read a play and think about how its scenes work together. Thinking about the structure of the play will help you better understand what happens.

Monitor Understanding

Modeled and Guided Instruction

Get Started

Today you will read a funny play called "A Very Tall Tale." First, you'll read to understand what happens. Then you'll read to analyze how the scenes fit together to create the action of the play.

Read

- Read aloud the title of the play. Ask students to suggest what a *tall tale* might be.
- Have students read the play independently. Tell them to place a check mark above any confusing words and phrases as they read. Remind students to look inside, around, and beyond each unknown word to help them figure out its meaning. Use the Word Learning Routine on pp. A50–A51.
- When students have finished reading, clarify the meanings of words and phrases they still find confusing. Then use the questions below to check understanding. Encourage students to identify details in the text that support their answers.

 In Scene 1, why is Sally upset with Todd? *(She thinks that he is about to lie to the principal about having seen a dinosaur.)*

 What happens in the principal's office? *(Todd says that he has seen a dinosaur.)*

 What happens to Todd at the end of Scene 2? *(A dinosaur's head comes through the school window; Todd pets it.)*

 **English Language Learners**

● **Word Learning Strategy**

Explore

- Read aloud the Explore question at the top of p. 283 to set the purpose for the second read. Tell students they will need to take a closer look at what happens in each scene to answer this question.
- Have students read aloud the Close Reader Habit on p. 282.

> **TIP** Explain that authors usually create suspense by making readers want to know more. Have students look for details that make them curious about what is happening.

Modeled and Guided Instruction

Read | Genre: Drama

A Very Tall Tale

a play in one act, by Tina Frank

1 **CAST OF CHARACTERS:** TODD, a fifth-grade student, and SALLY, his older sister

2 **SCENE 1:** [*A hallway outside a door marked* PRINCIPAL. *Tall windows line the hall. Two children sit on chairs. The boy seems calm. The girl seems restless and upset.*]

3 SALLY: [*She jumps from her chair, paces back and forth, then stops.*] How can you just calmly sit there, Todd? I told you that you'd get in trouble if you kept making things up. You'd better tell the truth to Ms. Johnson.

4 TODD: But, Sally, I'm not making things up. I keep seeing a dinosaur outside the school. I'm not sure, but I think it's an *Apatosaurus*.

5 SALLY: And it's hiding from everyone else? How can that be? [*She drops back in her chair, crosses her arms, and sighs. The door opens and* TODD *stands up.*]

6 TODD: I wish I knew. [*He stops, facing the windows, where a huge shadow that looks like a small head on a long neck moves past and then disappears.* TODD *goes into the principal's office.*]

7 **SCENE 2:** [TODD*'s classroom, on a second story of the school.* SALLY *stands with her back to the windows.* TODD *faces them.*]

8 SALLY: [*shaking her head*] I can't believe you wouldn't change your story for Ms. Johnson! [*As she speaks, the head and neck of a huge dinosaur rise in the window behind her.*] I've had enough of your tall tales for one day! [*She storms out of the room. The dinosaur's head comes through an open window. It stretches its long neck toward* TODD *and lowers its head to him.* TODD *cautiously pets the dinosaur's head, which moves under his hand as if it likes it.*]

9 TODD: Well, I guess I'll be seeing you tomorrow. [*He picks up his backpack and races after his sister as the dinosaur looks on.*]

Close Reader Habits

When you reread the drama, **underline** details in Scene 1 that feel suspenseful and details in Scene 2 that bring an end to that suspense.

282

English Language Learners

Develop Language

- **Idioms** Ask a volunteer to reread lines 3–4 aloud. Point out the term *making things up* in each line.
- Explain that *making things up* is an idiom. The phrase has a meaning that is different from the individual meanings of each word.
- Guide students to look for clues about the phrase's meaning. Help them see "get in trouble" and "You'd better tell the truth" as clues that *making things up* is a bad thing. Together, determine that the phrase means "lying."
- Invite students to practice using *making things up* and *made it up* in sentences until they are comfortable with its meaning.

● Word Learning Strategy

Use Context Clues

- Reread lines 7–8. Point out the word *story* in each line. Explain that *story* is a multiple-meaning word.
- Have students look for clues to determine the meaning of *story* in line 7. Guide them to see that Todd and Sally are inside the room of a school. In this instance, *story* means "the level of a building."
- Repeat the exercise with *story* in line 8. Help students identify "tall tales" as a clue that in this instance, *story* means "a tale or narrative."
- Remind students that when they encounter a multiple-meaning word, they can use the dictionary to confirm the correct meaning once they have inferred it from context clues.

L.5.4a

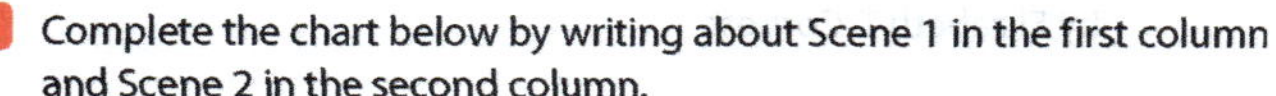

Explore How do Scenes 1 and 2 work together to tell a complete story?

Think

1 Complete the chart below by writing about Scene 1 in the first column and Scene 2 in the second column.

In a drama, each scene has a purpose. Use details from each scene to support your ideas about their purposes.

Scene 1	Scene 2
Setting: hallway lined with windows, outside the principal's office	**Setting:** Todd's classroom on second story of school
What happens: • Sally accuses Todd of making things up, but he insists he keeps seeing a dinosaur. A dinosaur-shaped shadow slides past the window.	**What happens:** • Sally is upset and leaves. The dinosaur puts its head through the window, and Todd pets it. He tells the dinosaur he'll see it tomorrow.

Talk

2 Use the questions below to discuss how Scenes 1 and 2 work together to produce a complete story.

- In Scene 1, whom do you believe at first: Todd or Sally?
- At the end of Scene 1, do you know for certain what the "huge shadow" is?
- What happens in Scene 2 that brings the suspense to an end?

If needed, use your answers to these questions to improve your charts.

Write

3 **Short Response** Explain how Scenes 1 and 2 work together to produce a complete story about Todd, Sally, and the dinosaur. Use details from both scenes and your chart to support your response. Use the space provided on page 286 to write your answer.

HINT Consider how your understanding of the drama would differ if you had read only Scene 1.

283

Think Aloud

- To answer the Explore question, I need to look at how the scenes work together to tell the whole story. First, I'll look for the setting in Scene 1.
- The stage directions in line 2 describe the setting—it's a hallway lined with windows. The characters are sitting in this hallway, just outside of the principal's office. I'll add this information to my chart.
- Next, I need to write what happens. I'll start by rereading the dialogue. Sally warns Todd to tell the truth; she is accusing him of making things up. Since the title of the play is about tall tales, or made-up events, I think this detail might be important. I'll write it under *What Happens* in my chart.

Lesson 16

Think

- Read aloud the Think section. Explain to students that you will model how to find text evidence to fill in part of the chart. Use the **Think Aloud** below to guide your modeling.
- Revisit the Explore question. Guide students to determine that they need to look for more details, using the Close Reader Habit.
- Encourage students to work with a partner to continue rereading the passage and complete the chart. Point out that the Buddy Tip will help them focus on how the scenes fit together to tell a story.
- Ask volunteers to share their completed charts.
- Guide students to see how the events in each scene are related to the setting. Help them see how the setting and events work together to create suspense.

Talk

- Read aloud the Talk prompt.
- Have partners respond to the prompt. Use the Talk Routine on pp. A52–A53.
- Circulate to check that students are discussing details that come from the play only.

Write

- Ask a volunteer to read aloud the Write prompt.
- Invite a few students to tell what the prompt is asking them to do.
- Make sure students understand that they need to connect Scene 1 to Scene 2 by thinking about where the conflict is introduced and where and how the events come to a close.
- Have students turn to p. 286 to write their response.
- Use Review Responses on p. 286 to assess students' writing.

Wrap Up

- Ask students to recall the Learning Target. Have them explain why thinking about how the scenes fit together helped them better understand the play.

Get Started

Today you will read a funny poem. First, you will read to understand what the poem is about. Then you will reread with a partner to analyze how the stanzas fit together to create the structure of the poem.

Read

- Read aloud the title of the poem. Ask students to think about what *wise* means and give examples of what they think the old women will do and say.
- **Read to Understand** Have students read the poem independently. Tell them to place a check mark above any confusing words and phrases as they read. Remind students to look inside, around, and beyond each unknown word or phrase to help them figure out its meaning. Use the Word Learning Routine on pp. A50–A51.
- When students have finished reading, clarify the meanings of words and phrases they still find confusing. Then use the questions below to check understanding. Encourage students to identify details in the text that support their answers.

  Why did the women get lost? *(They went so far and so fast that they forgot their way.)*

  Why were the women afraid? *(They thought they would meet a bear and it would eat them.)*

  What happened to the women after they set sail on the ladder? *(Even the speaker of the poem does not know.)*

 **English Language Learners**

● **Word Learning Strategy**

- **Read to Analyze** Read aloud the Close Reader Habit on p. 284 to set the purpose for the second read. Then have students reread the poem with a partner and discuss any questions they might have.

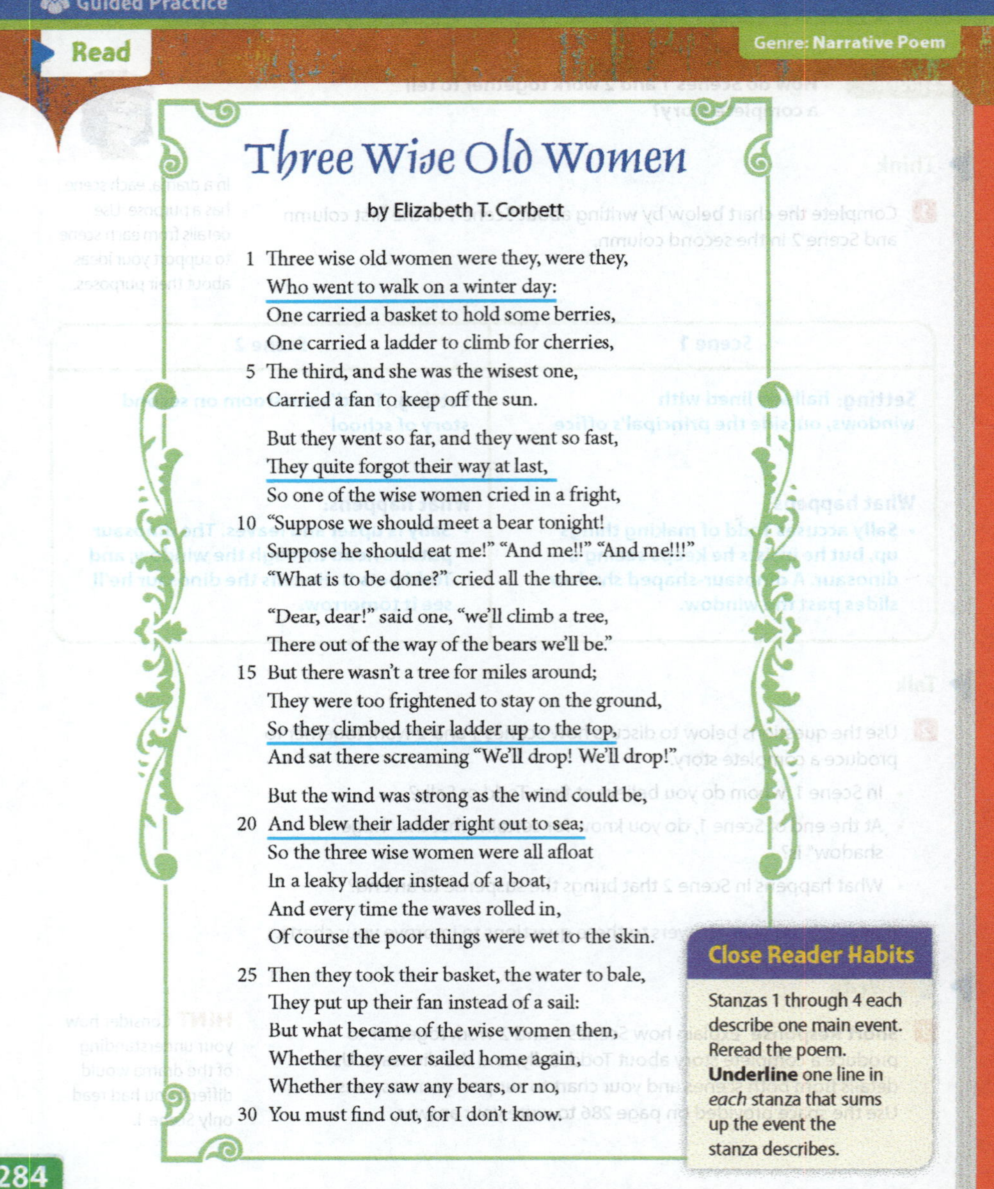

Guided Practice

Read

Genre: Narrative Poem

Three Wise Old Women

by Elizabeth T. Corbett

Three wise old women were they, were they,
Who went to walk on a winter day:
One carried a basket to hold some berries,
One carried a ladder to climb for cherries,
The third, and she was the wisest one,
Carried a fan to keep off the sun.

But they went so far, and they went so fast,
They quite forgot their way at last,
So one of the wise women cried in a fright,
"Suppose we should meet a bear tonight!
Suppose he should eat me!" "And me!!" "And me!!!"
"What is to be done?" cried all the three.

"Dear, dear!" said one, "we'll climb a tree,
There out of the way of the bears we'll be."
But there wasn't a tree for miles around;
They were too frightened to stay on the ground,
So they climbed their ladder up to the top,
And sat there screaming "We'll drop! We'll drop!"

But the wind was strong as the wind could be,
And blew their ladder right out to sea;
So the three wise women were all afloat
In a leaky ladder instead of a boat,
And every time the waves rolled in,
Of course the poor things were wet to the skin.

Then they took their basket, the water to bale,
They put up their fan instead of a sail:
But what became of the wise women then,
Whether they ever sailed home again,
Whether they saw any bears, or no,
You must find out, for I don't know.

Close Reader Habits

Stanzas 1 through 4 each describe one main event. Reread the poem. **Underline** one line in *each* stanza that sums up the event the stanza describes.

284

English Language Learners

Build Meaning

- **Visual Aids** Display pictures of the three objects in the poem: a ladder, a basket, and a fan. As you identify each object, have students locate the word in the poem. Invite students to share what they may already know about these objects.
- Review that the three "wise" women in the poem try to use the ladder as a boat. Discuss why this might be problematic, including the idea that the women try to bale water with the basket. As needed, mime or show a brief video of baling water, and ask volunteers to tell what is funny about trying to bale water from a ladder.

● Word Learning Strategy

Use Context Clues

- Point out the word *cried* in line 9. Have students share the meaning they are most familiar with. *("to weep")*
- Discuss whether there is any evidence in the poem that the women are weeping. Then guide students to look for clues to an alternate meaning of *cried*. Help them see that each time the women *cried*, they were speaking.
- Work with students to identify the exclamation points as well as the phrase "in a fright." Guide them to determine that another meaning of *cried* is "shouted in alarm."
- Remind students that when they encounter a multiple-meaning word, they should use context to determine the word's meaning. **L.5.4a**

Think Use what you learned from reading the narrative poem to answer the following questions.

Like the early paragraphs of a story, the early stanzas of a narrative poem may introduce the characters, a setting, and a problem.

1 This question has two parts. Answer Part A. Then answer Part B.

Part A
What purpose do stanzas 1 and 2 serve in "Three Wise Old Women"?

A They show the women's fear of meeting a bear.
(B) They introduce all three women and a problem they face.
C They show that the third woman was the wisest of the three.
D They describe the adventures the three women have after they get lost.

Part B
Choose **one** detail from **each** stanza to support your answer to Part A.

(A) "Three wise old women were they, were they" (stanza 1)
B "One carried a basket to hold some berries," (stanza 1)
C "The third, and she was the wisest one" (stanza 1)
D "But they went so far, and they went so fast" (stanza 2)
(E) "They quite forgot their way at last" (stanza 2)
F "So one of the wise women cried in a fright" (stanza 2)

Talk

2 Describe what stanzas 3 and 4 add to the narrative in terms of settings and events. Use the chart on page 287 to organize your ideas and record details from the stanzas.

Write

3 **Short Response** Explain how stanzas 3 and 4 help to develop the narrative. Using your chart, support your answer with **two** details from the text. Use the space provided on page 287 to write your answer.

HINT First describe what happens in stanzas 3 and 4. Then explain how they connect the beginning to the end of the poem.

Think

- Have students work with a partner to complete item 1. Draw attention to the boldface words **one** and **each** in Part B.

TIP Remind students that the Buddy Tip can help them think about the types of jobs that stanzas might do.

Answer Analysis

When students have finished, discuss correct and incorrect responses.

1 **Part A**

The correct choice is B. Stanza 1 introduces the characters. Stanza 2 tells how they get lost.

- **A** is only about stanza 2. **C** does not tell either stanza's purpose. **D** is incorrect because stanza 1 is not about what happens after they get lost.

Part B

The correct choices are A and E. Stanza 1 introduces the women. Stanza 2 introduces the problem.

- **B** and **C** are unrelated to the main purpose of stanza 1. **D** and **F** are unrelated to the main purpose of stanza 2.

DOK 3

● **Monitor Understanding**

● **Integrating Standards**

Talk

- Have partners discuss the prompt. Emphasize that students should support their ideas with text details.
- Circulate to clarify misunderstandings.

Write

- See p. 287 for instructional guidance.

Wrap Up

- Ask students to recall the Learning Target. Have them explain why figuring out how the stanzas work together helped them better understand the poem.

● Integrating Standards

Use the following questions to further students' understanding of the poem.

- **Why did the author use *wise* in the poem's title?** *(Wise is used as a joke. Everything the women do is unwise, including trying to climb a ladder to escape a bear and using a ladder as a boat.)*
DOK 2 RL.5.4
- **After the women became lost, one of the women "cried in a fright." How did her point of view influence how the remaining events were described?** *(The one who cried out frightened the others. The rest of the poem is about their reaction to their fear.)*
DOK 3 RL.5.6

● Monitor Understanding

If... students have difficulty answering Part B,

then... explain that they are reading a narrative poem, or a poem that tells a story. Make a story map with the headings *Characters, Setting,* and *Problem.* Work with students to identify each story part. For characters, reread the first line, noting that sometimes poems use unexpected word order. Then guide students to identify the evidence for being lost and afraid. *("They quite forgot their way at last" and "'Suppose he [a bear] should eat me!'")*

 **Modeled and Guided Instruction**

Write

- Remember to use the Response-Writing Routine on pp. A54–A55.

Review Responses

After students complete the writing activity, help them evaluate their responses.

3 Responses may vary but should reflect an understanding of the events that occur in each scene. See the sample response on the student book page.
DOK 3

Write Use the space below to write your answer to the question on page 283.

A Very Tall Tale

3 Short Response Explain how Scenes 1 and 2 work together to produce a complete story about Todd, Sally, and the dinosaur. Use details from both scenes and your chart to support your response.

HINT Consider how your understanding of the drama would differ if you had read only Scene 1.

Sample response: Scene 1 introduces Todd and his sister, Sally. She thinks he is making up stories, but he insists he sees an *Apatosaurus*. At the end of Scene 1, a shadow moves past the windows. Although it is the shape of a dinosaur, the audience is not sure of this, producing some suspense. In Scene 2, Sally leaves, but the dinosaur reappears. This time the audience learns that it is a real *Apatosaurus*, as it puts its head through a second-story window and Todd pets it. This resolves the suspense, bringing the story to a definite conclusion.

Don't forget to check your writing.

Check Your Writing

- ☐ Did you read the prompt carefully?
- ☐ Did you put the prompt in your own words?
- ☐ Did you use the best evidence from the text to support your ideas?
- ☐ Are your ideas clearly organized?
- ☐ Did you write in clear and complete sentences?
- ☐ Did you check your spelling and punctuation?

Scaffolding Support for Reluctant Writers

If students are having a difficult time getting started, use the strategies below. Work individually with struggling students, or have students work with partners.

- Circle the verbs in the prompt that tell you what to do, such as *describe*, *explain*, or *compare*.
- Underline words and phrases in the prompt that show what information you need to provide in your response, such as *causes*, *reasons*, or *character traits*.
- Talk about the details from the text that you will include in your response.
- Explain aloud how you will respond to the prompt.

Three Wise Old Women

2 Use the chart below to organize your ideas.

Stanza 3	Stanza 4

Write Use the space below to write your answer to the question on page 285.

> **HINT** First describe what happens in stanzas 3 and 4. Then explain how they connect the beginning to the end of the poem.

3 **Short Response** Explain how stanzas 3 and 4 help to develop the narrative. Using your chart, support your answer with **two** details from the text.

Sample response: In stanza 3, the women want to climb a tree to get away from bears. This is foolish: not only are there no bears around, there are also no trees to climb. Instead, they climb their ladder. Stanza 4 describes how the women and their ladder are blown out to sea. Here their ladder becomes a "leaky boat," and they get soaked. Stanzas three and four connect the first two main events of the poem (the women go for a walk and then get lost) with the last event of the poem (the women deal with being at sea).

287

Teacher Notes

Talk

2 Students should use the chart to organize their thoughts.

Write

- Ask a volunteer to read aloud the Write prompt.
- Invite students to tell what the prompt is asking them to do. Make sure they understand that they must explain how stanzas 3 and 4 build on details from stanzas 1 and 2 to continue telling the story of the three women.
- Call attention to the HINT.
- Remember to use the Response-Writing Routine on pp. A54–A55.

Review Responses

After students complete the writing activity, help them evaluate their responses.

3 Responses may vary but should accurately reflect the events that occur in stanza 3: the women want to climb a tree to get away from bears they only imagine; and in stanza 4: the women are blown out to sea, use their ladder as a "boat," and get soaked by the waves. See the sample response on the student book page. *DOK 3*

Independent Practice

Get Started

Today you are going to read a play called "The Case of the Missing Ming" and use what you have learned to explain how the acts of the play work together to create the story.

- Ask a volunteer to explain how analyzing the play's structure can help readers better understand the play. Encourage students to use the Academic Talk words in their response.

ELL English Language Learners

Read

You are going to read the play independently and use what you have learned to think and write about the text. As you read, remember to look closely at what happens in each of the three acts.

- Read aloud the title of the play and then encourage students to preview the text, paying close attention to the setting, the stage directions, and the illustrations.
- Call attention to the Words to Know in the upper left of p. 288.
- If students need support in reading the play, you may wish to use the Monitor Understanding suggestions.
- When students have finished, have them complete the Think and Write sections.

● **Monitor Understanding**

Independent Practice

Read

Genre: Drama

WORDS TO KNOW
As you read, look inside, around, and beyond these words to figure out what they mean.
- **exception**
- **vibrations**
- **theory**

THE CASE OF THE Missing Ming

by Wendell Riley

1 CAST OF CHARACTERS: Fenwick Barnes, a famous detective; Dr. Arthur Hamish, friend and assistant to Barnes; Lady Victoria Milton, owner of the house; Diana Dumont, a singer; Rupert, a piano player; Giles, the butler; Wendy, the maid; Count Otto Orlog, a visitor; Misha, the count's pet monkey; assorted guests.

2 ACT ONE: [*The curtain opens on the music room of the mansion.* Diana *is singing as* Rupert *plays the piano. The guests are seated in rows of chairs around the piano, listening with complete attention. The exception is* Fenwick Barnes, *who is clearly falling asleep in the back row. As* Diana *hits a long high note, the sleeping* Barnes *falls back into a shelf. A large vase falls off the shelf into his lap. He catches it. Only* Wendy, *the maid, sees what caused the vase to fall. She gasps. The concert stops, and everyone turns to* Barnes.]

3 Lady Milton: Oh, Mr. Barnes! You've saved the day again.

4 Barnes: A detective is always on his toes. Even when he is seated. [*He stands, nearly dropping the vase.*]

288

ELL English Language Learners

Build Meaning

Preview Illustrations Have students preview the illustrations prior to reading the play.

- Organize students in pairs or small groups, and have them label every part of the illustrations that they recognize, including the people, objects, and even facial expressions that reveal emotion.
- Once students have finished their labels, project the illustrations and call on volunteers to share. Provide substitutions for words as needed that will help with comprehending the story (e.g., substituting *vase* if students label the falling object a *jar*).
- Once you have labeled the images, read the Act One stage directions aloud and work with students to identify in the illustration each detail you describe.

5 LADY MILTON: [*taking the large blue and white vase from his hands*] This vase is priceless to me! It is a rare moonflask from the Ming Dynasty in China. It's worth millions! Whatever could have made it fall?

6 DR. HAMISH: Perhaps the vibrations from the piano and Miss Dumont's extraordinary voice shook it from its place.

7 BARNES: Yes, Doctor! Good work! Let's go with that theory.

8 COUNT ORLOG: May I see this beautiful moonflask? [*He sets his monkey on the piano and takes the vase.*] Oh, what I wouldn't do to have a piece like this!

9 DIANA: Wouldn't we all, Count, wouldn't we all! [*The guests all nod in agreement.*]

10 ACT TWO: [*The next morning.* LADY MILTON *walks into the music room, looks around, then screams. All her guests, including* BARNES, *in a long nightshirt and nightcap, come running into the room.*]

11 LADY MILTON: My Ming! It's gone! It's been stolen!

12 DR. HAMISH: But surely none of your honored guests would do such a thing!

13 BARNES: [*looking from face to face*] And yet, last night, every single person in the room expressed the wish that he or she might possess such a piece of priceless beauty! [*The guests all mutter amongst themselves, offended.*] Someone is missing. Where is Wendy, the maid?

14 LADY MILTON: Why, she left at dawn for her mother's in the village. It's her day off.

15 BARNES: Everyone else stays until we get to the bottom of this. [*He turns to* DR. HAMISH.] A private word with you, Doctor. [*He leads him away from the other guests.*] There's one thing you must do for me.

16 DR. HAMISH: Anything, Fenwick! You know that!

17 BARNES: Don't let me sleep past noon. I've got a case to solve! [*He leaves the room.*]

289

Monitor Understanding

If... students struggle to read and understand the play, **then...** use these scaffolding suggestions:

Question the Text Preview the text by asking the following questions:

- **Based on the title and illustrations, what do you predict the play will be about?**
- **What questions do you have about the text?**

Vocabulary Support Define words that may interfere with comprehension, such as *assistant, dynasty,* and *extraordinary.*

Read Aloud Read aloud the text with students. You could also have students chorally read the text in a small group.

Check Understanding Use the questions below to check understanding. Encourage students to cite details in the text that support their answers.

- **What happens to Detective Barnes in Act One?** *(A Ming vase falls in his lap while he is sleeping during the concert.)*
- **What does Lady Milton discover in Act Two?** *(The Ming vase has disappeared.)*
- **Where does Detective Barnes find the Ming vase?** *(in a fish barrel)*

Independent Practice

Integrating Standards

After students have read the play, use these questions to discuss the play with them.

- **What does Barnes mean by the phrase "always on his toes" as it is used in Act One?**

  (Barnes says, "A detective is always on his toes," referring to himself. The phrase means he is always alert or aware. The phrase adds humor to the play as Barnes was actually asleep.)

  DOK 2 RL.5.4

- **Why is Wendy the maid just as important to the plot as Detective Barnes?**

  (In Act One, Detective Barnes causes the vase to fall, which is the main problem of the whole play. Wendy the maid actually knew what caused the vase to fall, so later she took steps to protect it. In Act Two, Wendy adds a bit of suspense because she is the only suspect who is missing. In Act Three, Detective Barnes reveals that Wendy hid the vase in the fish barrel.)

  DOK 3 RL.5.3

- **Summarize the last act of the play.**

  (Barnes enters the living room with a big barrel. He opens it and takes the vase out, explaining it was in the barrel for protection. Wendy enters the room and says she is sorry Barnes found it, showing that she was the one who hid it. As the play ends, Barnes trips and almost breaks the vase again, but Wendy catches it.)

  DOK 2 RL.5.2

- **What inference can you make about why the guests are looking "anxious" in Act Three?**

  (In Act Two, Detective Barnes says that no one can leave the house until the vase is found, which shows that he suspects all of them of having stolen it. The guests must be worried that they will be accused at the beginning of Act Three.)

  DOK 3 RL.5.1

Theme Connection

18 **ACT THREE:** [*Evening of the same day. The guests, looking anxious, are all gathered in the music room.*]

19 DR. HAMISH: Thank you all for coming. Mr. Barnes will be here shortly to solve the mystery. [*At that moment,* BARNES *enters the room rolling a large barrel, which he stands upright.*] Good heavens. Barnes! What are you doing with a barrel of herring?

20 LADY MILTON: And have you solved the case?

21 BARNES: I think I know where the vase is, and why. But I'm not so sure about who put it there. [*He pries the lid from the barrel and starts throwing fish over his shoulder.* GILES, *the butler, runs back and forth, catching them.*] Where is the last place you would look for a priceless vase?

22 DR. HAMISH: Why, in a fish barrel, I suppose.

23 BARNES: Exactly! But the purpose was not just to hide the vase; it was to protect it. The herring provide a perfectly safe cushion around such a fragile object. Ah, I have it! [*Just as he pulls the vase from the barrel,* WENDY *enters wearing her hat and coat.*]

24 WENDY: Oh, no! You've found it!

25 BARNES: Safe and sound, just as you intended. [*He turns to the guests.*] You see, the vase never actually was stolen. After the events of last night, Wendy meant only to protect it.

26 WENDY: What you say is true, sir. I know how much the Ming means to Lady Milton. And you sir, more than anyone, know how accidents can happen.

27 BARNES: And that's why you'd best look after this. [*As he walks toward* WENDY, *he trips. The vase flies high into the air but* WENDY *catches it.*] Case solved!

Theme Connection

- Remind students that the theme of this lesson is Laughter.
- Display a three-column chart on the board. Label each column with the passage titles.
- Ask students to tell what is funny in each poem or play. Discuss how the author purposely structured each play or poem in a certain way in order to create humor.
- Invite students to share examples of other humorous texts, and discuss whether the structure of those texts contributes to their humor.

Think Use what you learned from reading the drama to answer the following questions.

1 Why did the playwright **most likely** include stage directions in line 2?

A to give details about who the characters are
B to let the audience know who stole the Ming vase
C to explain that the play is set in the music room of a wealthy woman's mansion
(D) to describe the setting and events that happen before the first actor's line

2 The playwright used the event of the concert in Act One to set up events for Act Two and Act Three. Why did the playwright **most likely** do this?

A to explain to the audience why Fenwick Barnes fell asleep
(B) to describe the value of, and interest in, the Ming moonflask
C to explain why Lady Milton thinks Fenwick Barnes is a great detective
D to describe a theory about how sound vibrations can make things fall

3 Read line 13 from Act Two of the drama.

> BARNES: [*looking from face to face*] And yet, last night, every single person in the room expressed the wish that he or she might possess such a piece of priceless beauty! [*The guests all mutter amongst themselves, offended.*] Someone is missing. Where is Wendy, the maid?

Select **three** choices that **best** describe why the playwright included line 13.

A to show Lady Milton's distress over the loss
(B) to show that every person is a suspect
(C) to show the value of the Ming vase
(D) to show the characters' suspicion of Wendy
E to show the guests do not like Barnes
F to show that no guest caused the vase's disappearance

● **Monitor Understanding**

If... students struggle to complete the items,

then... you may wish to use the following suggestions:

Read Aloud Activities

- As you read, have students note any unfamiliar words or phrases. Clarify any misunderstandings.
- Discuss each item with students to make certain they understand the expectation.

Reread the Text

- Have students complete a three-column chart with a summary of the main events in each act.
- Have partners summarize the text.

Think

- Use the Monitor Understanding suggestions to support students in completing items 1–4.

● **Monitor Understanding**

Answer Analysis

When students have finished, discuss correct and incorrect responses.

1 **The correct choice is D.** The playwright uses the lengthy stage direction in line 2 to explain everything from the setting to the action that leads to the first line of dialogue.

- **A** is incorrect because the characters are introduced in line 1, not line 2.
- **B** isn't revealed until the end of Act Three.
- **C** is only a small part of the purpose of the lengthy stage direction, not the reason why the playwright included it.

***DOK 2* RL.5.5**

2 **The correct choice is B.** The concert provides an opportunity for the playwright to introduce the Ming vase, describe its great value, and show that all the guests are interested in it. Lady Milton, for example, says that the vase is "worth millions." Count Orlog says, "Oh, what I wouldn't do to have a piece like this!"

- **A** is incorrect because, while Barnes's falling asleep does happen in Act One, it is not mentioned again in Acts Two and Three.
- **C** describes Lady Milton's high opinion of Barnes, but that doesn't move the story forward.
- **D** simply describes Dr. Hamish's plausible but mistaken theory about why the vase fell.

***DOK 3* RL.5.5**

3 **The correct choices are B, C, and D.** It is important to build suspense by suggesting all guests are suspects, the vase is valuable, and one person is missing who might be responsible.

- **A** is incorrect because Line 13 does not mention Lady Milton.
- **E** and **F** are not supported by line 13 of the drama.

***DOK 3* RL.5.5**

Independent Practice

4 **The correct choice is A.** Barnes prevents the disaster of a broken Ming vase.

- **B** is incorrect because Barnes does not keep the sun from setting.
- **C** is not a strong enough definition for a phrase like "save the day."
- **D** is not supported by the text.

***DOK 2* RL.5.4, L.5.4a**

Write

- Tell students that using what they read, they will plan and compose an extended response to the writing prompt. Provide copies of the three-column chart on p. TR12.

Monitor Understanding

Review Responses

After students have completed each part of the writing activity, help them evaluate their responses.

5 Display the **Sample Response** for the planning chart on the next page. Have students compare their chart with the sample. Are they missing any information?

***DOK 3* RL.5.5**

6 Display or pass out copies of the reproducible **2-Point Writing Rubric** on p. TR10. Have students use the rubric to individually assess their writing and revise as needed.

When students have finished their revisions, evaluate their responses. Answers will vary but students should identify what happens in each act of the play and explain how the acts work together to create the overall structure of the drama.

***DOK 3* RL.5.5, W.5.9a**

4 What is the meaning of the phrase saved the day as it is used in line 3?

- **A** stopped a disaster
- **B** kept the sun from setting
- **C** gave a solution to a problem
- **D** set aside time for planning

Write

How do the three acts work together to provide the structure for the events of "The Case of the Missing Ming"? Reread the play. Underline the key events in each act. Then complete numbers 5 and 6.

5 **Plan Your Response** Think about the following details in the play: How the characters are introduced, when the main problem occurs, and when the problem is solved. Use a three-column chart to organize details about Acts One, Two, and Three.

6 **Write an Extended Response** Describe how the three-act structure of the play develops the narrative. Be sure to discuss how the structure relates to the characters, the problem, and the solution of the problem.

Responses will vary. A top-scoring response will identify what happens in each act of the play and explain how the acts work together to support the overall narrative structure. Students may identify that the characters and the vase are introduced in Act One, the problem is introduced in Act Two, and the problem is resolved in Act Three.

292

Monitor Understanding

If... students don't understand the writing task,

then... read aloud the writing prompt. Use the following questions to help students get started.

- **What is the prompt asking you to write about?**
- **Do you need to reread the text to find more information?**
- **How will you identify the information you need to include?**

- Have partners talk about how they will organize their responses.

Learning Target

In this lesson, you explained how acts, scenes, and stanzas work together to provide structure and meaning in a drama or poem. Explain how you can apply what you've learned to other dramas and poems you read.

Responses will vary, but students should explain how understanding the ways scenes, acts, or stanzas fit together will help them better understand not just the structure but also the meaning of dramas and poems they read.

Wrap Up

Learning Target

- Have each student respond in writing to the Learning Target prompt.
- When students have finished, have them share their responses. This may be done with a partner, in small groups, or as a whole class.

5 Sample Response

Act One	Act Two	Act Three
Setting: the music room **What happens:** • guests are listening to concert • Barnes falls asleep and backs into a shelf • vase falls in his lap • Lady Milton thankful • vase is valuable • all guests would like to have it	**Setting:** next morning in music room **What happens:** • Ming is gone • all guests are suspected • Wendy is missing • Barnes says he has a case to solve	**Setting:** the music room on evening of same day **What happens:** • Barnes brings in a barrel of herring • discloses where the Ming is hiding • vase put there to keep it safe • Wendy did it to protect vase from accidents

6 2-Point Writing Rubric

Points	Focus	Evidence	Organization
2	My answer does exactly what the prompt asked me to do.	My answer is supported with plenty of details from the text.	My ideas are clear and in a logical order.
1	Some of my answer does not relate to the prompt.	My answer is missing some important details from the text.	Some of my ideas are unclear and out of order.
0	My answer does not make sense.	My answer does not have any details from the text.	My ideas are unclear and not in any order.

Lesson 17 Point of View

Standards Focus

Describe how a narrator's or speaker's point of view influences how events are described. **RL.5.6**

Lesson Objectives

Reading

- Identify the narrator's or speaker's point of view. **RL.5.6**
- Describe how a narrator's or speaker's point of view influences the description of events. **RL.5.6**

Writing

- Draw evidence from literary texts to support analysis and reflection. **W.5.9a**

Speaking and Listening

- Pose and respond to specific questions and contribute to discussions. **SL.5.1c**
- Review the key ideas expressed and draw conclusions. **SL.5.1d**

Language

- Use context as a clue to the meaning of a word or phrase. **L.5.4a**
- Acquire and use academic and domain-specific words and phrases. **L.5.6**

Additional Practice: **RL.5.1, RL.5.2, RL.5.3, RL.5.4, RL.5.5**

Academic Talk

See **Glossary of Terms**, pp. TR2–TR9

- narrators
- point of view
- speakers
- influence

Learning Progression

Grade 4	Grade 5	Grade 6
Students compare and contrast the point of view of two stories and identify whether the narrators are first- or third-person narrators.	Building on Grade 4, students describe the way that point of view influences how events are described. This standard emphasizes that students need to understand the different kinds of narrative point of view in a text and how the different points of view affect how a story is told.	Grade 6 builds in complexity by requiring students to be aware of the ways in which the author reveals the narrator's point of view and how the narrator's attitude develops and changes throughout a text.

Lesson Text Selections

Modeled and Guided Instruction

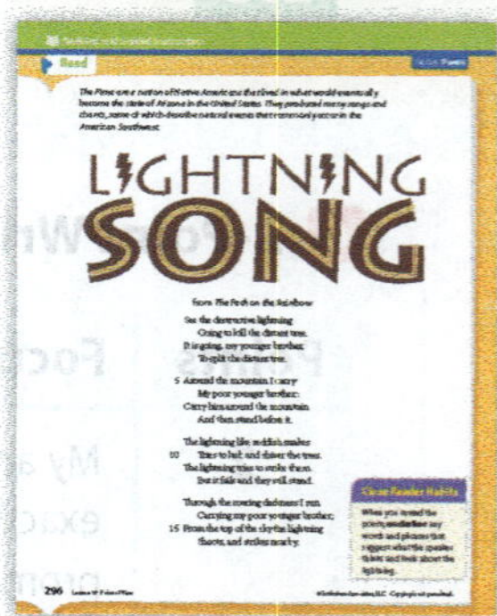

Lightning Song
Genre: Poem

Guided Practice

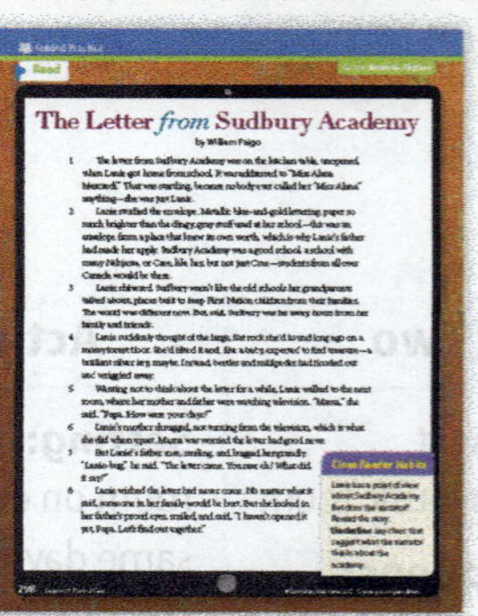

The Letter from Sudbury Academy
by William Paigo
Genre: Realistic Fiction

Independent Practice

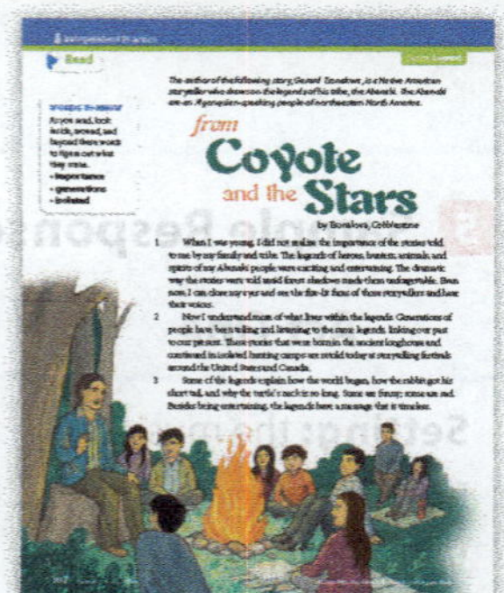

Coyote and the Stars
by Tsonakwa
Genre: Legend

Lesson Pacing Guide

Whole Class Instruction *30–45 minutes per day*

Day 1

Teacher-Toolbox.com **Interactive Tutorial**
Exploring Points of View in Literature—Level E
20 min (optional)

Introduction pp. 294–295

- **Read** **Point of View** *10 min*
- **Think** *10 min*
  Graphic Organizer: Three-Column Chart
- **Talk** *5 min*
  Quick Write (TRB) *5 min*

Day 2

Modeled and Guided Instruction pp. 296–297, 300

- **Read** **Lightning Song** *10 min*
- **Think** *10 min*
  Graphic Organizer: Three-Column Chart
- **Talk** *5 min*
- **Write** Short Response *10 min*

Day 3

Guided Practice pp. 298–299, 301

- **Read** **The Letter from Sudbury Academy** *10 min*
- **Think** *10 min*
- **Talk** *5 min*
- **Write** Short Response *10 min*

Day 4

Independent Practice pp. 302–307

- **Read** **Coyote and the Stars** *15 min*
- **Think** *10 min*
- **Write** Short Response *10 min*

Day 5

Independent Practice pp. 302–307

- *Review* Answer Analysis (TRB) *10 min*
- *Review* Response Analysis (TRB) *10 min*
- *Assign and Discuss* Learning Target *10 min*

Language Handbook
Lesson 10 More Uses for Commas, pp. 456–457
20 min (optional)

Small Group Differentiation

Teacher-Toolbox.com

Reteach

Ready Reading **Prerequisite Lesson**

- **Grade 4** Lesson 18 Comparing Points of View

Teacher-led Activities

Tools for Instruction

- Interpret Narrator's Point of View

Personalized Learning

i-Ready.com

Independent

i-Ready Close Reading Lessons

- **Grade 4** Comparing Points of View
- **Grade 5** Point of View in Literature

Introduction

Get Started

- Explain to students that in this lesson they will read different types of literature and explore the narrator's or speaker's point of view in each text.
- Review what students already know about point of view. For example, have them think about when a parent asks them to do chores. The parent's point of view is that chores teach responsibility; the students' point of view is that chores are boring and tedious. Each person looks at the same task differently, based on their own interests and experiences.
- Guide students to recall that the narrator of a story or the speaker of a poem also has a point of view. Explain:

  In *Diary of a Wimpy Kid,* Greg describes life through his eyes. He shares his point of view, or thoughts and feelings, about events and other characters. When we read this book, we should think about what causes Greg to describe people and events a certain way. What is it about his feelings, interests, or experiences that shapes his telling of events?

- Focus students' attention on the Learning Target. Read it aloud to set the purpose for the lesson.
- Display the Academic Talk words and phrases. Tell students to listen for these terms and their meanings as you work through the lesson together. Use the Academic Talk Routine on pp. A48–A49.

English Language Learners

● Genre Focus

Read

- Read aloud the Read section as students follow along. Restate to reinforce:

  When you read literature, it's helpful to identify the narrator's or speaker's point of view, or perspective. Knowing how a point of view influences writing will help you better understand the story or poem.

- Direct students' attention to the comic strip. Have them study the details in the pictures and read the speech bubbles to identify each character's point of view.

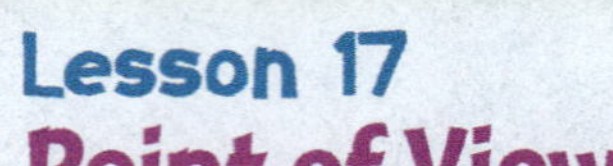
Introduction

RL.5.6 Describe how a narrator's or speaker's point of view influences how events are described.

Lesson 17
Point of View

Learning Target

Knowing that a narrator's or speaker's point of view influences their descriptions will improve your understanding of stories and poems.

▶ **Read** **Point of view** is how a person thinks or feels about something. Both **narrators** in stories and **speakers** in poems have points of view. The background and culture of an author can **influence**, or affect, that author's point of view.

In the comic strip below, look for evidence of each character's point of view.

English Language Learners

Develop Language

Concept Vocabulary Help students understand the difference between the first-person and third-person points of view.

- Say: "On Friday, I called my friend Pat." Explain that the pronouns *I* and *my* are clues to the first-person point of view. When a character in the story tells what happens, the story has a first-person narrator.
- Then say: "On Friday, Mauricio called his friend Pat." The person's name and the pronoun *his* are clues to the third-person point of view. The narrator is telling about, but is not part of, the action.

● Genre Focus

Realistic Fiction

Explain that during Guided Practice, students will read a realistic fiction story. Unlike myths or legends, realistic fiction stories feature ordinary characters that mirror the types of people readers might encounter in real life. These characters speak and act in a familiar, relatable way, and the themes of realistic fiction stories usually reflect the types of challenges and lessons that everyday people face.

Invite students to share examples of realistic fiction they've read, such as *Lemonade Wars* and *Winners Take All*. Have them share examples of the characters or events in these books that seem relatable to everyday life.

Think Consider what you've learned so far about point of view. Use this chart to describe each character's point of view about the grouse. Then provide evidence of the points of view based on what the characters say and do.

Character	Character's Point of View About Grouse	Evidence of Character's Point of View
City cousin	Thinks grouse are amazing.	• "Whoa! What's that thing?" • "How are you not amazed? That's so cool."
Country cousin	Thinks grouse are ordinary.	• "They're everywhere." • "I'm just used to it."

Talk Share your chart with a partner.

- Why do the cousins have different points of view about grouse?
- What evidence did you give for each cousin's point of view?
- Suppose each cousin narrated a story about meeting the grouse. How would the stories differ?

Academic Talk
Use these words and phrases to talk about the text.
- narrator
- point of view
- speaker
- influence

295

Monitor Understanding

If... students struggle to understand point of view,
then... provide an example. Say:

I would rather read a story about a real adventure than one about creatures from outer space, but my friend prefers science fiction.

- **What is my point of view about stories?** *(Real adventures are more interesting to read than science fiction.)*
- **What is my friend's point of view about stories?** *(Science fiction stories are better than real adventures.)*

Ask students to provide their own point-of-view examples about stories they like to read.

Think

- Have students read aloud the Think section. Explain that the chart will help them organize their thinking.
- Have partners complete the chart. Remind students to use the details in the pictures and the speech bubbles to determine each character's point of view about the grouse.
- As students work, circulate and provide assistance as needed.
- Ask volunteers to share what they wrote in their charts.
- Make certain students understand that the city cousin is amazed because he has never seen a grouse. The country cousin thinks grouse are ordinary because she has seen them many times.

Talk

- Read aloud the Talk prompts.
- Have partners discuss the evidence they wrote to support each character's point of view. Encourage students to discuss how the cousins' backgrounds influenced their different points of view.
- Ask volunteers to share their ideas.

Quick Write Have students write a response to the following prompt:

Think of something you enjoy doing but your sibling or friend does not. Describe the activity and each of your feelings about it. Then explain why you feel differently. What causes each of you to have your point of view?

Ask students to share their responses.

Wrap Up

- Invite students to share what they've learned so far. Encourage them to use the Academic Talk words and phrases in their explanations.
- Explain to students that when they read literature, they can analyze the narrator's or the speaker's point of view to better understand what they read.

In the next section, we'll read a poem and explore the speaker's point of view. We will also think about how background and culture can influence a poet's point of view and word choices.

Monitor Understanding

Modeled and Guided Instruction

Get Started

Today you will read a poem written by a member of the Pima (pee-mah) Native American nation. First, you'll read to understand the poem. Then you'll read to analyze the speaker's point of view about the events.

Read

- Read aloud the title of the poem and call attention to the note above the title. As needed, help students locate Arizona on a United States map.
- Have students read the poem independently. Tell them to place a check mark above any confusing words and phrases as they read. Remind students to look inside, around, and beyond each unknown word to help them figure out its meaning. Use the Word Learning Routine on pp. A50–A51.
- When students have finished reading, clarify the meanings of words and phrases they still find confusing. Then use the questions below to check understanding. Encourage students to identify details in the text that support their answers.

  What is this poem mostly about? *(a lightning storm)*

  Where does the poem take place? *(near or on a mountain)*

  What is the speaker doing? *(carrying his or her younger brother somewhere during a lightning storm)*

 **English Language Learners**

● **Word Learning Strategy**

Explore

- Read aloud the Explore question at the top of p. 297 to set the purpose for the second read. Tell students they will need to take a closer look at evidence in the poem to answer this question.
- Have students read aloud the Close Reader Habit on p. 296.

TIP Remind students that a speaker's point of view can often be determined by the descriptive language he or she uses. Have them look closely at the verbs and adjectives used to describe the lightning storm.

Modeled and Guided Instruction

Read Genre: Poem

The Pima are a nation of Native Americans that lived in what would eventually become the state of Arizona in the United States. They produced many songs and chants, some of which describe natural events that commonly occur in the American Southwest.

LIGHTNING SONG

from *The Path on the Rainbow*

See the destructive lightning
  Going to kill the distant tree.
It is going, my younger brother,
  To split the distant tree.

Around the mountain I carry
  My poor younger brother:
Carry him around the mountain
  And then stand before it.

The lightning like reddish snakes
  Tries to lash and shiver the trees.
The lightning tries to strike them.
  But it fails and they still stand.

Through the roaring darkness I run,
  Carrying my poor younger brother;
From the top of the sky the lightning
  Shoots, and strikes nearby.

Close Reader Habits

When you reread the poem, **underline** any words and phrases that suggest what the speaker thinks and feels about the lightning.

296

English Language Learners

Build Meaning

Figurative Language Ask a volunteer to reread lines 9 and 10 of the poem. Call attention to the phrase *like reddish snakes*.

- Explain that this phrase is a *simile*, a type of figurative language. Poets often use figurative language to help readers imagine something clearly.
- Review the characteristics of snakes, including their shape and behavior. Be sure to note the way snakes *lash*, as described in line 10.
- Discuss why the poet used this simile. Guide students to understand that snakes are long and thin, and they dart quickly, just like a lightning bolt. People often fear both lightning and snakes because of their ability to strike quickly and do harm.

● Word Learning Strategy

Use Context Clues

- Point out the phrase *the destructive lightning* in line 1.

  What do you think *destructive* means? What clues help you figure out the meaning?

- Guide students to find the words "kill the distant tree" in line 2 and "split the distant tree" in line 4. Discuss the meanings of *kill* and *split*. Together, determine that *destructive* means "having the power to end or defeat."
- Remind students that when they come to an unknown word or phrase, they can look at the surrounding words for a clue to the meaning. **L.5.4a**

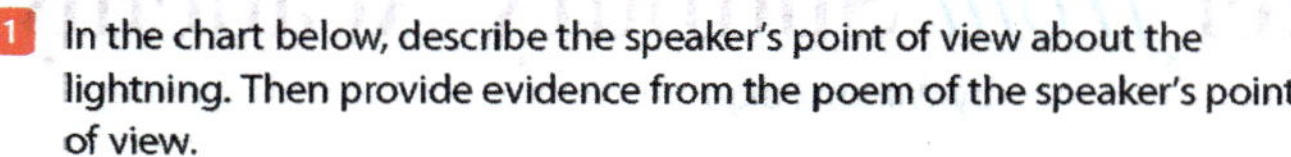

Explore What is the speaker's point of view about the lightning?

Think

1 In the chart below, describe the speaker's point of view about the lightning. Then provide evidence from the poem of the speaker's point of view.

Imagine you could ask the speaker what he or she thinks of the lightning. What would the speaker tell you?

Speaker	Speaker's Point of View	Evidence of Point of View
an older brother or sister	The lightning is scary and powerful, but not all-powerful.	• "the destructive lightning" • "Going to kill the distant tree" • "lightning like reddish snakes / Tries to lash and shiver the trees." • "it fails and they still stand"

Talk

2 Take turns reading "Lightning Song" aloud. Does reading the poem aloud affect your understanding of it? Does the speaker express a point of view without stating it directly? Make changes to your chart, if necessary.

Write

3 **Short Response** What is the speaker's point of view about the lightning? How does it affect the way the speaker describes what the lightning does? Use details from the poem in your response. Use the space provided on page 300 to write your answer.

HINT One main event of the poem occurs when the lightning tries to strike the trees.

Think Aloud

- To answer the Explore question, I need to determine the speaker's point of view about the lightning. To do this, I will go back to the poem and look closely at the speaker's word choices that describe the lightning.
- In the first stanza, the speaker uses very strong language to describe the lightning. "See the destructive lightning / Going to kill the distant tree." The tone of the words *destructive* and *kill* is very dark and threatening. It's interesting that the speaker says the lightning is "[g]oing to kill"—that detail suggests that the speaker sees the lightning as something that has force and power.
- I'll write the details from the first two lines in my chart, but I'm not going to make up my mind about the speaker's point of view just yet. I'll keep reading to see if it changes at all.

Think

- Read aloud the Think section. Explain to students that you will model how to find text evidence to fill in part of the chart. Use the **Think Aloud** below to guide your modeling.
- Revisit the Explore question. Guide students to determine that they need to look for more details, using the Close Reader Habit.
- Encourage students to work with a partner to continue rereading the poem and complete the chart. Remind them that the Buddy Tip will help them find the speaker's point of view.
- Ask volunteers to share their completed charts.
- Guide students to see that they should consider the entire poem, and not just one part of it, to determine the speaker's point of view.

Talk

- Read aloud the Talk prompt.
- Have partners respond to the prompt. Use the Talk Routine on pp. A52–A53.
- Circulate to check that students are reading the poem aloud and discussing whether the tone of the words used by the speaker indicate his or her point of view.

Write

- Ask a volunteer to read aloud the Write prompt.
- Invite a few students to tell what the prompt is asking them to do.
- Make sure students understand that they need to answer both questions in the prompt, supporting their ideas with text evidence.
- Have students turn to p. 300 to write their response.
- Use Review Responses on p. 300 to assess students' writing.

Wrap Up

- Ask students to recall the Learning Target. Have them explain how considering the way a speaker's point of view influences the way events are described improved their understanding of this poem.

Guided Practice

Get Started

Today you will read a realistic fiction story. First you will read to understand what the story is about. Then you will reread with a partner to analyze the narrator's point of view.

Read

- Read aloud the title of the story. Ask if anyone knows what *academy* means. Establish that an academy is a school, often a private school.
- Have students predict what the story will be about based on the title.
- **Read to Understand** Have students read the story independently. Tell them to place a check mark above any confusing words and phrases as they read. Remind students to look inside, around, and beyond each unknown word or phrase to help them figure out its meaning. Use the Word Learning Routine on pp. A50–A51.
- When students have finished reading, clarify the meanings of words and phrases they still find confusing. Then use the questions below to check understanding. Encourage students to identify details in the text that support their answers.

  What does Lanie notice about the envelope addressed to her? *(The lettering and paper are of high quality.)*

  How does Lanie feel about Sudbury Academy? *(She has mixed feelings because it is a good school but far away from her family and friends.)*

  Why is the letter important? *(It will tell whether or not Lanie has been accepted at Sudbury Academy.)*

English Language Learners

Word Learning Strategy

- **Read to Analyze** Read aloud the Close Reader Habit on p. 298 to set the purpose for the second read. Then have students reread the story with a partner and discuss any questions they might have.

> **TIP** If students struggle to make inferences about the narrator's point of view, have them think about the school described in the opposite way. The non-example can help to clarify the narrator's word choices.

Guided Practice

Read

Genre: Realistic Fiction

The Letter *from* Sudbury Academy

by William Paigo

1 The letter from Sudbury Academy was on the kitchen table, unopened, when Lanie got home from school. It was addressed to "Miss Alana Mercredi." That was startling, because nobody ever called her "Miss Alana" anything—she was just Lanie.

2 Lanie studied the envelope. Metallic blue-and-gold lettering, paper so much brighter than the dingy, gray stuff used at her school—this was an envelope from a place that knew its own worth, which is why Lanie's father had made her apply. Sudbury Academy was a good school, a school with many *Nehiyaw*, or Cree, like her, but not just Cree—students from all over Canada would be there.

3 Lanie shivered. Sudbury wasn't like the old schools her grandparents talked about, places built to keep First Nation children from their families. The world was different now. But, still, Sudbury was far away, hours from her family and friends.

4 Lanie suddenly thought of the large, flat rock she'd found long ago on a mossy forest floor. She'd lifted it and, like a baby, expected to find treasure—a brilliant silver key, maybe. Instead, beetles and millipedes had flooded out and wriggled away.

5 Wanting not to think about the letter for a while, Lanie walked to the next room, where her mother and father were watching television. "Mama," she said. "Papa. How were your days?"

6 Lanie's mother shrugged, not turning from the television, which is what she did when upset. Mama was worried the letter had good news.

7 But Lanie's father rose, smiling, and hugged her grandly. "Lanie-bug," he said. "The letter came. You saw, eh? What did it say?"

8 Lanie wished the letter had never come. No matter what it said, someone in her family would be hurt. But she looked in her father's proud eyes, smiled, and said, "I haven't opened it yet, Papa. Let's find out together."

Close Reader Habits

Lanie has a point of view about Sudbury Academy. But does the narrator? Reread the story. **Underline** any clues that suggest what the narrator thinks about the academy.

298

English Language Learners

Build Meaning

Background Knowledge Guide students to understand that the setting for "The Letter from Sudbury Academy" is Canada, and the main character, Lanie, is descended from the Cree people.

- Write the phrase *First Nation* on the board. Explain that *First Nation* people were the indigenous people of the Americas. *Indigenous* people are native to an area, which means they were the first to live there. In North America, the Cree people were one of the largest groups of Native Canadians, or Native Americans.

Word Learning Strategy

Use Context Clues

- Reread the first two sentences in paragraph 2, and point out the word *worth*.

  What does the word *worth* mean as it is used in this sentence? *(value)*

  What words in the sentence help you figure out the meaning?
- Remind students that some context clues are antonyms. In this case, the bright paper from Sudbury Academy was contrasted with the dingy, gray paper used at Lanie's school, to emphasize the idea that the school knew its own worth.
- Have students practice using the word in other sentences to demonstrate understanding.

L.5.4a

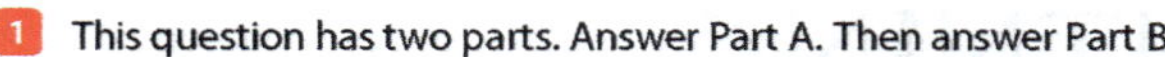

Think Use what you learned from reading the story to answer the following questions.

1 This question has two parts. Answer Part A. Then answer Part B.

Part A
How does the narrator's point of view influence how the events are described?

A By including only Lanie's actions, words, and thoughts, the narrator can't reveal how her parents feel.

B By giving the detail about the rock with bugs under it, the narrator shows Lanie doesn't want to face her parents.

(C) By showing Lanie's thoughts about the letter, the narrator reveals that she is worried about each parent's feelings.

D By focusing on the letter from the school, the narrator shows how much Lanie hopes she will be accepted there.

Part B
Which detail from the passage supports the answer in Part A?

A ". . . from a place that knew its own worth. . . ." (paragraph 2)

B "But, still, Sudbury was far away, . . ." (paragraph 3)

C ". . . places built to keep First Nation children from their families." (paragraph 3)

(D) ". . . someone in her family would be hurt." (paragraph 8)

This story has a third-person narrator, or someone standing outside the story. Look for clues that show the narrator's thoughts and feelings.

Talk

2 Reread paragraphs 2 and 3. What is the narrator's point of view about Sudbury Academy? Use the chart on page 301 to write your ideas and evidence.

HINT Look at the words and phrases the narrator uses to describe both the letter and the academy.

Write

3 **Short Response** What inference can you make about the narrator's point of view toward Sudbury Academy? Use the details from your chart to support your response. Use the space provided on page 301 to write your answer.

Integrating Standards

Use the following questions to further students' understanding of the story.

- **What is the meaning of *apply* as it is used in paragraph 2?** *(Lanie's father made her apply to Sudbury Academy. Lanie is going to find out whether she was accepted. Apply means "to ask to go to the school.")* ***DOK 2*** **RL.5.4**
- **How does paragraph 4 connect to the events in the story?** *(Lanie thought the rock hid treasure, but to her surprise, bugs crawled out when she lifted it. Similarly, the school seems to be a "treasure" of opportunity, but she worries the school won't be all she expects.)* ***DOK 3*** **RL.5.3**

Monitor Understanding

If... students have difficulty answering item 2,

then... help them understand what a neutral tone would sound like. Say:

> **Lanie studied the envelope. It had metallic blue-and-gold lettering. As she held it, she shivered.**

Discuss with students which details are missing from the "just the facts" version. Guide them to understand that the narrator provided the additional details to let readers know how prestigious the school is, and why the decision is so important to Lanie.

Think

- Have students work with a partner to complete item 1.

TIP Remind students that a character's point of view may not be the same as the point of view of an outside narrator.

Answer Analysis

When students have finished, discuss correct and incorrect responses.

1 **Part A**
The correct choice is C. The narrator knows Lanie's thoughts as well as her words and actions.

- **A** is incorrect because the narrator does show how Lanie's parents feel. **B** is incorrect because the details about the bugs don't explain the influence of the narrator's point of view.
  D is incorrect because Lanie is uncertain about going to the academy.

Part B
The correct choice is D. It shows Lanie is worried about hurting one of her parents.

- **A** and **B** are incorrect because they only give information about the school, not Lanie's thoughts about her parents' feelings.
  C is incorrect because it is about the older schools of her grandparents' time.

DOK 3

- **Integrating Standards**

Talk

- Have partners discuss the prompt. Emphasize that students should support their ideas with text details.
- Circulate to clarify misunderstandings.

- **Monitor Understanding**

Write

- See p. 301 for instructional guidance.

Wrap Up

- Ask students to recall the Learning Target. Have them explain how the narrator's point of view influenced the description of the events in the story.

Modeled and Guided Instruction

Write

- Remember to use the Response-Writing Routine on pp. A54–A55.

Review Responses

After students complete the writing activity, help them evaluate their responses.

3 Responses may vary but should show an understanding that the speaker finds lightning to be incredibly powerful. See the sample response on the student book page. ***DOK 3***

Write Use the space below to write your answer to the question on page 297.

LIGHTNING SONG

3 **Short Response** What is the speaker's point of view about the lightning? How does it affect the way the speaker describes what the lightning does? Use details from the poem in your response.

HINT One main event of the poem occurs when the lightning tries to strike the trees.

Sample response: The speaker's point of view about the lightning is that it is powerful and possibly frightening. He says that the lightning is "destructive" and wants to "kill the distant tree." The speaker describes the lightning as acting like "reddish snakes" lashing the trees, which seems like a scary way to describe what the lightning is doing at that moment. Even though the lightning fails to destroy any trees, it "shoots, and strikes nearby," suggesting the speaker feels the lightning is still dangerous.

Check Your Writing

- ☐ Did you read the prompt carefully?
- ☐ Did you put the prompt in your own words?
- ☐ Did you use the best evidence from the text to support your ideas?
- ☐ Are your ideas clearly organized?
- ☐ Did you write in clear and complete sentences?
- ☐ Did you check your spelling and punctuation?

Scaffolding Support for Reluctant Writers

If students are having a difficult time getting started, use the strategies below. Work individually with struggling students, or have students work with partners.

- Circle the verbs in the prompt that tell you what to do, such as *describe*, *explain*, or *compare*.
- Underline words and phrases in the prompt that show what information you need to provide in your response, such as *causes*, *reasons*, or *character traits*.
- Talk about the details from the text that you will include in your response.
- Explain aloud how you will respond to the prompt.

The Letter *from* Sudbury Academy

2 **Use the chart below to organize your ideas and evidence.**

Narrator	Narrator's Point of View	Evidence of Narrator's Point of View

Write **Use the space below to write your answer to the question on page 299.**

3 **Short Response** What inference can you make about the narrator's point of view toward Sudbury Academy? Use the details from your chart to support your response.

Sample response: The narrator describes Sudbury Academy positively. The paper's envelope is " brighter than the dingy, gray stuff" used at Lanie's school. This comparison suggests that Lanie's current school is not as good as Sudbury Academy. The narrator also says that the envelope is "from a place that knew its own worth," indicating that the academy is a worthwhile place to go. The narrator thinks the academy is a good one.

Teacher Notes

Talk

2 Students should use the chart to organize their thoughts and evidence.

Write

- Ask a volunteer to read aloud the Write prompt.
- Invite students to tell what the prompt is asking them to do. Make sure they understand that they need to make an inference about the narrator's point of view.
- Call attention to the HINT.
- Remember to use the Response-Writing Routine on pp. A54–A55.

Review Responses

After students complete the writing activity, help them evaluate their responses.

3 Responses may vary but should demonstrate that the positive descriptions of Sudbury Academy suggest that the narrator has a favorable point of view about the academy. See the sample response on the student book page. ***DOK 3***

Independent Practice

Get Started

Today you are going to read a legend and use what you have learned about a narrator's point of view to explain how it influences the descriptions in the text.

- Ask a volunteer to explain how a narrator's point of view can influence the telling of events, and how understanding this can help readers better understand literature. Encourage students to use the Academic Talk words and phrases in their response.

 **English Language Learners**

Read

You are going to read the legend independently and use what you have learned to think and write about the text. As you read, remember to look closely at the descriptions in the text to identify the narrator's point of view.

- Read aloud the title of the legend and then encourage students to preview the text, paying close attention to the illustrations.
- Call attention to the Words to Know in the upper left of p. 302.
- If students need support in reading the legend, you may wish to use the Monitor Understanding suggestions.
- When students have finished, have them complete the Think and Write sections.

● **Monitor Understanding**

Read

Genre: Legend

The author of the following story, Gerard Tsonakwa, is a Native American storyteller who draws on the legends of his tribe, the Abenaki. The Abenaki are an Algonquian-speaking people of northeastern North America.

WORDS TO KNOW
As you read, look inside, around, and beyond these words to figure out what they mean.
- **importance**
- **generations**
- **isolated**

from Coyote and the Stars

by Tsonakwa, *Cobblestone*

1 When I was young, I did not realize the importance of the stories told to me by my family and tribe. The legends of heroes, hunters, animals, and spirits of my Abenaki people were exciting and entertaining. The dramatic way the stories were told amid forest shadows made them unforgettable. Even now, I can close my eyes and see the fire-lit faces of those storytellers and hear their voices.

2 Now I understand more of what lives within the legends. Generations of people have been telling and listening to the same legends, linking our past to our present. These stories that were born in the ancient longhouse and continued in isolated hunting camps are retold today at storytelling festivals around the United States and Canada.

3 Some of the legends explain how the world began, how the rabbit got his short tail, and why the turtle's neck is so long. Some are funny; some are sad. Besides being entertaining, the legends have a message that is timeless.

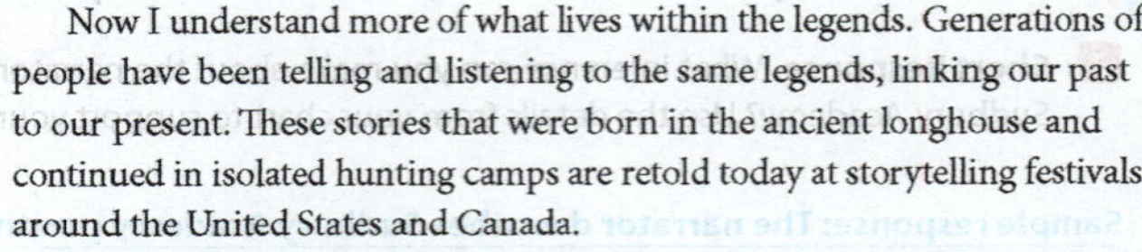

English Language Learners

Build Meaning

Preview Illustrations Have students work in pairs to preview the illustrations in the text. Direct them to label as many elements in each picture as they are able.

- When students have finished, invite them to share their labels. Provide vocabulary as needed to support the discussion. Then challenge students to summarize what is happening in each picture.
- Tell students that as they read, they should look for the words in the text that match the words they used to label each illustration.

4 Now I will tell you a story told to my father when he was young, then told to me when I was a child at my father's knee. I speak his words and voice so that he lives while the story is told. It is a story of Coyote and of stars. Perhaps you have heard coyotes crying pitifully in the night. I will tell you why that is and why the stars are scattered in a great mess all across the sky!

5 On the second morning of creation time, the Great Father set about the great task of filling the nighttime sky with beauty. He took a bag and went out on the muskeg [swamp], and there he picked the little flowers we call Morning Stars. He filled the bag with the star flowers, and then he cut a long stick so that he could put the flowers on the end of the stick and place them in the sky just so, in a fine pattern, like beadwork. Then he found the highest hill in the land, so that from that high place he could set the little flowers in the sky, just so. But when he had climbed the mountain, it was still light, so the Great Father decided to take a nap.

Monitor Understanding

If... students struggle to read and understand the selection,
then... use these scaffolding suggestions:

Question the Text Preview the text by asking the following questions:

- **Based on the title and illustrations, what do you predict the story will be about?**
- **What questions do you have about the text?**

Vocabulary Support Define words that may interfere with comprehension, such as *generations, longhouse,* and *pitifully.*

Read Aloud Read aloud the text with students. You could also have students chorally read the text in a small group.

Check Understanding Use the questions below to check understanding. Encourage students to cite details in the text that support their answers.

- **Who is Tsonakwa?** *(the storyteller, a native American of the Abenaki people)*
- **Why did Coyote grab the bag?** *(He thought it was filled with food.)*
- **What does the legend explain?** *(why the stars are scattered randomly across the sky)*

Independent Practice

Integrating Standards

After students have read the legend, use these questions to discuss the legend with them.

- **How does the author's culture or background affect his perspective about the way the story links the past to the present?**
  (The author has been hearing these stories since childhood. He says they are a way to "link our past to our present." He tells readers that the stories teach the modern Abenakis lessons that were important in the past and are important today.)
  DOK 2 **RL.5.6**
- **What is the theme of the legend about Coyote?**
  (The theme is "One should think about the consequences of actions before making a choice." The legend illustrates that some mistakes are too big to fix and can have lasting effects.)
  DOK 3 **RL.5.2**
- **What does the reader learn about the Abenaki culture from the legend? Support your response with specific details from the text.**
  (The reader learns that the Abenaki people value storytelling as a way to preserve their past. The author writes, "Generations of people have been telling and listening to the same legends . . ." The Abenaki told stories to explain the world as they observed it. They still tell stories "at storytelling festivals around the United States and Canada.")
  DOK 3 **RL.5.1**
- **Paragraphs 1–4 and 5–7 have different purposes. How does the structure of the story help you better understand what the author is telling you?**
  (Paragraphs 1–4 give the author's background. They tell about Abenaki storytelling and legends, as well as why these stories are important to the author. Paragraphs 5–7 tell the story of one particular legend, that of Coyote and the Stars. The first part of the story gives meaning to the second part by providing background.)
  DOK 3 **RL.5.5**

● **Theme Connection**

6 So he laid the bag down in the shade of a tree. And while he was sleeping, Coyote came along. Coyote is like all dogs—he's always thinking of food. He saw the Creator sleeping, and right nearby a great bag filled with something. Coyote said to himself, "I bet there's food in that bag. I'm going to look inside and see." So Coyote grabbed the bag and ran off. But as he ran, he tripped and fell, and the bag ripped open and the stars spilled out and flashed across the sky, every which-way. Then the Great Creator woke up from his nap, and the first thing he saw were his stars flashing all across the sky. And he looked down, and he saw Coyote standing there with the bag in his teeth, ripped open. And the Great Father said to Coyote, "Look what you've done! I wished to put those stars in the sky in a fine pattern, like beads, and look at the mess you've made!"

7 Poor Coyote. He looked up and tears filled his eyes as shame filled his heart to see what he had done to the night sky. And Coyote began to howl. This is why today the stars are scattered all across the sky every which-way, and this is why coyotes, when they see the night sky and the mess their great-grandfather made, fill up with shame and howl.

● Theme Connection

- Remind students that the theme of this lesson is Native Voices.
- Display a three-column chart. Label each column with the passage titles: "Lightning Song," "The Letter from Sudbury Academy," and "Coyote and the Stars."
- Have students recall the narrator or speaker's point of view in each passage. For "Lightning Song" and "Coyote and the Stars," discuss how the Native American narrator's background influenced the way the events were described. Guide them to understand that Native Americans have a great respect for nature.

Think Use what you learned from reading the legend to answer the following questions.

1 This question has two parts. First, answer Part A. Then answer Part B.

Part A
How does the narrator's point of view influence how events are described in paragraph 6?

A By including the Great Father's reaction to Coyote's actions, the narrator shows how cruel the Great Father is.

(B) By focusing on why Coyote took the bag, the narrator shows that Coyote is greedy but not evil.

C By including a description of the Great Father's nap, it shows how little the Great Father cares about his work.

D By focusing on how clumsy Coyote is, the narrator provides information on how Coyote got that way.

Part B
Which sentence from paragraph 6 supports the answer in Part A?

A "And while he was sleeping, Coyote came along."

(B) "Coyote is like all dogs—he's always thinking of food."

C "But as he ran, he tripped and fell, and the bag ripped open and the stars spilled out and flashed across the sky, every which-way."

D "'I wished to put those stars in the sky in a fine pattern, like beads, and look at the mess you've made!'"

2 What does the word pattern mean as it is used in paragraphs 5 and 6 of the story?

A a model or good example

B an obvious personality trait

C a flight path for an airplane

(D) a decorative or artistic design

● Monitor Understanding

If… students struggle to complete the items,

then… you may wish to use the following suggestions:

Read Aloud Activities

- As you read, have students note any unfamiliar words or phrases. Clarify any misunderstandings.
- Discuss each item with students to make certain they understand the expectation.

Reread the Text

- Have students complete a chart as they reread.
- Have partners summarize the text.

Think

- Use the Monitor Understanding suggestions to support students in completing items 1–4.

● Monitor Understanding

Answer Analysis

When students have finished, discuss correct and incorrect responses.

1 **Part A**

The correct choice is B. The author presents Coyote as being greedy, not evil.

- **A** is incorrect. The Great Father gets angry at Coyote but is not cruel to him.
- **C** is incorrect. Although the Great Father rests and leaves the bag unguarded, this does not mean that he is uncaring about the work he does.
- **D** is incorrect. The author shows Coyote being clumsy but does not explain why Coyote is clumsy.

Part B

The correct choice is B. By saying that Coyote "is like all dogs—he's always thinking of food," the author shows that Coyote is simply greedy, not necessarily evil.

- **A, C,** and **D** are details in the story, but they are not related to Coyote's greed.

DOK 3 RL.5.6

2 **The correct choice is D.** The Great Father wanted to create "a fine pattern, like beadwork," suggesting the stars would be arranged artistically in a design.

- **A, B,** and **C** are definitions of *pattern* but not as the word is used in the text.

DOK 2 RL.5.4, L.5.4a

Independent Practice

3 Part A

The correct choice is D. The narrator states, "Generations of people have been telling and listening to the same legends, linking our past to our present." He wants to carry on that tradition.

- **A** is incorrect. Although some readers might find being in a forest at night scary, there is no evidence the author feels this way.
- **B** is incorrect. The stories did not lead the author to dislike his cultural traditions—in fact, they led to just the opposite.
- **C** is incorrect. The author only refers to longhouses and hunting camps. He does not say he learned how to build them.

Part B

The correct choice is C. It supports the idea that the narrator respects how long his culture has been around.

- **A** and **B** describe the setting in which the stories were told.
- **D** presents no evidence of how the author feels about his culture.

DOK 3 **RL.5.6**

4 The correct choice is D. Coyote would likely explain why he felt shame for his actions if the story were told from his point of view.

- **A** is incorrect. There is no evidence in the original story to support this version of the retelling.
- **B** is incorrect. The question asks about how a retelling of the story would be different from Coyote's point of view, so it would still have to be about Coyote's responsibility in the events.
- **C** is incorrect. In this story, Coyote is described as "clumsy" but not devious.

DOK 3 **RL.5.6**

3 This question has two parts. First, answer Part A. Then answer Part B.

Part A
How was the author's point of view influenced by events from his childhood?

- **A** Those events made him fearful of being in the forest at night.
- **B** Those events caused him to dislike the traditions of his culture.
- **C** Those events taught him how to build longhouses and hunting camps.
- **(D)** Those events led him to respect how long his culture has been around.

Part B
Which detail from the passage **best** supports the answer to Part A?

- **A** "The dramatic way the stories were told amid forest shadows made them unforgettable." (paragraph 1)
- **B** "Even now, I can close my eyes and see the fire-lit faces of those storytellers and hear their voices." (paragraph 1)
- **(C)** "Generations of people have been telling and listening to the same legends, linking our past to our present." (paragraph 2)
- **D** "I will tell you why that is and why the stars are scattered in a great mess all across the sky!" (paragraph 4)

4 How might the story be different if it were told from Coyote's point of view?

- **A** It would explain that Coyote and the Great Father are enemies.
- **B** It would give a different reason why the stars look as they do.
- **C** It would show that Coyote is a clever and sneaky trickster.
- **(D)** It would tell why Coyote feels shame for scattering the stars.

306

Monitor Understanding

If... students don't understand the writing task,

then... read aloud the writing prompt. Use the following questions to help students get started.

- **What is the prompt asking you to write about?**
- **Do you need to reread the text to find more information?**
- **How will you identify the information you need to include?**

- Have partners talk about how they will organize their responses.
- Provide a graphic organizer to assist students, if needed.

Write

5 **Short Response** The narrator feels sympathy toward Coyote. Support this conclusion with details from the text.

Sample Response: The narrator feels sympathy toward Coyote. When the narrator says that Coyote, like all dogs, is "always thinking of food," he suggests that Coyote, while greedy, cannot help his actions. When the narrator says "Poor Coyote" and describes Coyote's tear-filled shame about what he did to the night sky, the narrator wants the reader to feel sympathy toward Coyote.

Learning Target

In this lesson, you explored how the point of view of narrators or speakers can influence how they describe events. Explain how knowing this will help you better understand any stories or poems you read.

Responses may vary, but students should identify that describing how a narrator's or speaker's point of view affects their description of events gives them a deeper understanding of what the story or poem is about.

5 **2-Point Writing Rubric**

Points	Focus	Evidence	Organization
2	My answer does exactly what the prompt asked me to do.	My answer is supported with plenty of details from the text.	My ideas are clear and in a logical order.
1	Some of my answer does not relate to the prompt.	My answer is missing some important details from the text.	Some of my ideas are unclear and out of order.
0	My answer does not make sense.	My answer does not have any details from the text.	My ideas are unclear and not in any order.

Write

- Tell students that using what they read, they will plan and compose a short response to the writing prompt.

● Monitor Understanding

Review Responses

After students have completed each part of the writing activity, help them evaluate their responses.

5 Display or pass out copies of the reproducible **2-Point Writing Rubric** on p. TR10. Have students use the rubric to individually assess their writing and revise as needed.

When students have finished their revisions, evaluate their responses. Answers will vary but should show how the narrator's point of view influences the descriptions of Coyote. See the sample response on the student page. *DOK 3* **RL.5.6, W.5.9a**

Wrap Up

Learning Target

- Have each student respond in writing to the Learning Target prompt.
- When students have finished, have them share their responses. This may be done with a partner, in small groups, or as a whole class.

Assessment

Get Started

Today you are going to read two passages. The first passage is a poem and the second is a historical fiction story. You will use what you have learned in this unit to understand what you are reading.

- Ask students to recall what they have learned, such as understanding figurative language, recognizing the structure of poems, and identifying how the point of view influences the description of events.
- Encourage students to use the Academic Talk words and phrases from the unit's lessons in their response.

Read

You are going to read the articles independently and use what you have learned to think and write about the text.

- Ask a student to read aloud the titles of the passages. Make certain that students understand they are to read both selections.
- Encourage students to preview the text, paying close attention to the illustrations and text structure.
- Remind students to look inside, around, and beyond when they encounter unfamiliar words. Use the Word Learning Routine on pp. A50–A51.
- When students have finished, have them complete the Think and Write sections.

Interim Assessment

Read Genre: Poem

Read the poem. Then answer the questions that follow.

The Spider and the Fly

A Fable
by Mary Howitt

"Will you walk into my parlor?" said the spider to the fly;
"'Tis the prettiest little parlor that ever you did spy.
The way into my parlor is up a winding stair,
And I have many pretty things to show when you are there."
"O no, no," said the little fly, "To ask me is in vain,
For who goes up your winding stair can ne'er come down again."

"I'm sure you must be weary, dear, with soaring up so high;
Will you rest upon my little bed?" said the spider to the fly.
"There are pretty curtains drawn around, the sheets are fine and thin,
And if you like to rest awhile, I'll snugly tuck you in."
"O no, no," said the little fly, "for I've often heard it said,
They never, never wake again, who sleep upon your bed."

Said the cunning spider to the fly, "Dear friend, what shall I do,
To prove the warm affection I've always felt for you?
I have within my pantry good store of all that's nice;
I'm sure you're very welcome; will you please to take a slice?"
"O no, no," said the little fly, "kind sir, that cannot be;
I've heard what's in your pantry, and I do not wish to see."

"Sweet creature!" said the spider, "you're witty and you're wise,
How handsome are your gauzy wings, how brilliant are your eyes!
I have a little looking-glass upon my parlor shelf,
If you'll step in one moment dear, you shall behold yourself."
"I thank you, gentle sir," she said, "for what you're pleased to say,
And bidding you good-morning now, I'll call another day."

308

The spider turned him round about, and went into his den,
For well he knew the silly fly would soon be back again:
So he wove a subtle web, in a little corner sly,
And set his table ready to dine upon the fly.
Then he came out to his door again, and merrily did sing,
"Come hither, hither, pretty fly, with the pearl and silver wing:
Your robes are green and purple; there's a crest upon your head;
Your eyes are like the diamond bright, but mine are dull as lead."

Alas, alas! how very soon this silly little fly,
Hearing his wily flattering words, came slowly flitting by.
With buzzing wings she hung aloft, then near and nearer drew,
Thinking only of her crested head—poor foolish thing! At last,
Up jumped the cunning spider, and fiercely held her fast.
He dragged her up his winding stair, into his dismal den,
Within his little parlor; but she ne'er came out again!

And now, dear little children, who may this story read,
To idle, silly, flattering words, I pray you ne'er give heed;
Unto an evil counselor close heart, and ear, and eye,
And take a lesson from this tale of the Spider and the Fly.

Teacher Notes

Assessment

Answer Analysis

When students have completed the Interim Assessment, discuss correct and incorrect responses.

1 **The correct choice is D.** The spider compares his web to a beautiful old house with a "winding stair" and "parlor," and he later mentions a bed and a well-stocked pantry.

- **A, B,** and **C** don't accurately describe the comparison being made by the metaphor in this line.

DOK 3 **RL.5.4**

2 **The correct choice is B.** In the first stanza of the poem, the spider invites the fly to the "prettiest little parlor." In the second stanza, the spider describes his comfortable bed, and in the third stanza, the spider describes a pantry full of "all that's nice." The spider wants to draw the fly into the spider's "home," or web.

- **A** supports an incorrect inference that the spider that the spider has real concern for the fly.
- **C** is not supported by the plot of the poem and does not support the real reason the spider is making his home sound appealing, which is to catch the fly to eat.
- **D** does not support the real reason the spider is making his home sound appealing, which is to catch the fly to eat.

DOK 3 **RL.5.6**

3 **Students should underline the first 2 lines in each stanza.** These lines describe the way the spider addresses the fly. The middle two lines of each stanza describe the spider's home. The last two lines of each stanza are written from the fly's point of view.

DOK 2 **RL.5.6**

Interim Assessment

Think

1 Read this line from the poem.

The way into my parlor is up a winding stair,

Which sentence below **best** describes the meaning of the metaphor in this line from the poem?

A The poet is comparing the spider's legs to steps on a winding stair.
B The spider is comparing the way the fly moves to a winding staircase.
C The poet is describing the spider as a friendly next-door neighbor to the fly.
(D) The spider is describing his web to the fly as if it were a beautiful old house.

2 How does the spider's point of view influence how he describes his "home" to the fly in the first three stanzas?

A He sees the fly could use some food and rest and tells her what he can offer.
(B) He wants to make his home sound as appealing as possible to attract the fly.
C He doesn't get many visitors so he makes his place sound better than it really is.
D He can't help boasting about his home to the fly because he's really proud of it.

3 Underline the lines in **each** stanza that reflect the spider's point of view of the fly.

Said the cunning spider to the fly, "Dear friend, what shall I do,
To prove the warm affection I've always felt for you?
I have within my pantry good store of all that's nice;
I'm sure you're very welcome; will you please to take a slice?"
"O no, no," said the little fly, "kind sir, that cannot be;
I've heard what's in your pantry, and I do not wish to see."

"Sweet creature!" said the spider, "you're witty and you're wise,
How handsome are your gauzy wings, how brilliant are your eyes!
I have a little looking-glass upon my parlor shelf,
If you'll step in one moment dear, you shall behold yourself."
"I thank you, gentle sir," she said, "for what you're pleased to say,
And bidding you good-morning now, I'll call another day."

310

4 What is the meaning of the word <u>subtle</u>, as it is used in stanza 5 to describe the spider's web?

A very colorful
(B) hard to see
C large enough to catch the fly
D extremely sticky

5 **Short Response** How does the last stanza of the poem connect to what happens in the stanzas that come before it? Explain your answer using details from the poem.

The last stanza of the poem is about the lesson to be learned from the story. This line builds on previous stanzas by telling why the fly gets caught by the spider. The fly made the mistake of listening to the spider's "idle, silly, flattering words" and believing they were true. The spider says, "you're witty and you're wise" in stanza 4 and "your eyes are like the diamond bright" in stanza 5. When the fly hears the spider's "wily flattering words," she draws "nearer and nearer" to his web and is caught. The lesson of the poem is to be aware of false flattery.

4 **The correct choice is B.** The word <u>subtle</u> describes something that is faint or hard to see.

- **A** means the opposite of <u>subtle</u> since a colorful object would be easy to see.
- **C** does not have the same meaning as the word <u>subtle</u>.
- **D** does not relate to whether or not the web is difficult to see.

***DOK 2* RL.5.4**

5 After students have completed the Interim Assessment, evaluate their responses to the short-response item using the **2-Point Writing Rubric** below.

Answers will vary but should show that students understand the last stanza reveals the theme of the poem, that flattery may be misleading. See the sample response on the student book page.

You may wish to display or pass out copies of the reproducible **2-Point Writing Rubric** on page TR10. Have students use the rubric to individually assess their writing and revise as needed.

***DOK 3* RL.5.5**

2-Point Writing Rubric

All three criteria must be satisfied in order for a response to gain full points.

Points	Focus	Evidence	Organization
2	The response demonstrates comprehension and provides accurate analysis.	The response supports the analysis with adequate textual evidence.	Ideas are clear and follow a logical order.
1	The response demonstrates some comprehension and provides minimally accurate analysis.	The response supports the analysis with limited textual evidence.	Some ideas are unclear or out of order.
0	The response demonstrates no comprehension and provides inaccurate or no analysis.	The response provides little or no textual evidence.	Ideas are unclear or incomplete.

Read

Genre: Historical Fiction

Read the story. Then answer the questions that follow.

Kate's Vigil*

by Thomas R. Levine

1 Kate Alden was worried about her father, Captain Joshua Alden. Captain Alden commanded a whaler. He was a month late returning home from his latest whaling voyage. Whaling was an important industry in Nantucket in the early 1800s. Whale oil lit the lamps in many homes. Whalebone, which is actually the stiff plates hanging from the roof of the mouth of a baleen whale, was used to make everything from umbrella ribs to springs. To Kate, the money that whaling brought to her island home paled next to the safety of her father—for whaling was a dangerous business indeed.

2 Kate awoke with a start and listened intently to the sounds of the household stirring. Was that her father's tread in the hall? Had he come home in the middle of the night and no one had awoken her? No, it was just her older brother, Daniel, leaving for work at the ships' store down by the docks. Kate flung off the covers and threw a warm shawl over her shoulders. She slipped into her boots, grabbed the spyglass her father had given her, and raced up the long, narrow flight of stairs to the rooftop. Here on a high porch called a widow's walk, Kate could gaze out into the ocean for her father's ship. Her eyes frantically scanned the waters, as they did every day. Today, as on every day this past month, Kate spotted many ships, but she saw no evidence of her father's ship sailing into the harbor.

3 That night at dinner, Daniel talked of the ships that had arrived in port that day, of his work at the chandlery, and of the rumors of coming bad weather. Daniel tried to keep the conversation going, but no one was much in the mood for talking. Although Daniel spoke not a word about his father, Kate could see Daniel's anxiety in the deep lines that creased his forehead. Before long, Kate begged to be excused from the table. She drifted aimlessly from room to room, unable to settle down in any one place.

* **Vigil:** staying awake and being watchful during the night or normal hours for sleeping

4 Without being conscious of going there, Kate found herself again on the widow's walk. Fast-moving clouds blanked out the stars, further dimming her hopes. As the night wore on, Kate's mother joined her daughter. She wrapped a blanket around the girl and tried to calm her fears with soothing words and warm embraces. Kate wanted to be reassured, but at the same time she needed the truth. Instead of allowing her worries to be whisked away, Kate accepted the worry that her mother barely hid behind her own eyes. They hugged each other, and together they wept. Were they just another Nantucket family watching in vain from a rooftop porch for a father, husband, brother, or son who would never return?

5 Before long, Kate's mother headed back down the stairs into the house while Kate remained on the porch. At dawn, Kate woke up cold and uncomfortable. Somehow she'd fallen asleep on the small porch. Kate pulled herself up and leaned her elbows on the rail. Her eyes were a sunless sea, watching and waiting for signs of hope. She knew she should get on with the duties of the day. But not being there, watching and waiting, seemed out of the question.

6 Kate's eyes automatically scoured the waters for her father's ship. One by one, she eliminated each of the ships that she spotted. Some ships were clearly too big, others too small. Some ships carried too many or too few sails and masts. The rigging on others had the wrong kind or arrangement of sails and masts. Having grown up around ships, Kate could easily tell the difference among ships of various kinds.

7 Then one odd-looking ship caught Kate's eye like a bit of precious gold in the gray rock slab of the sea. It looked somewhat similar to her father's ship except that its main mast was far too short. The more Kate looked at that mast, she realized that it was far shorter than it should have been on any ship of any kind. With a shout that woke her family and half the neighborhood, Kate realized that it truly was her father's ship. The main mast had obviously broken halfway down, and only the lower sails were flying. Her father was home at long last.

Teacher Notes

Assessment

6 **The correct choices are A and C.** Paragraphs 3 and 4 build suspense by showing the anxiety the characters' thoughts and feelings about whether Kate's father will return home.

- **B** is incorrect because the paragraphs do not provide foreshadowing.
- **D** is incorrect because the problem in the story is established in paragraphs 1 and 2, not in paragraphs 3 and 4.
- **E** is incorrect because paragraph 1 explains why whaling is important in Nantucket, not paragraphs 3 and 4.

DOK 2 **RL.5.5**

7 **Part A**

The correct choice is C. For Kate, the money that her father earned from whaling "paled next to" his safety, meaning that the money was far less important to her than Captain Alden's well being.

- **A, B,** and **D** do not have meanings that make sense in the context of the story.

Part B

The correct choice is A. The danger of whaling is what worries Kate and her family, and the word *indeed* emphasizes the danger and shows that it outweighs the money her father makes.

- **B, C,** and **D** do not apply either to money or to danger.

DOK 2 **RL.5.4**

Interim Assessment

Think

6 Which **two** statements explain how paragraphs 3 and 4 contribute to the overall structure of the story?

(A) They build suspense.
B They foreshadow the ending.
(C) They develop the main characters.
D They establish the problem in the story.
E They explain why whaling is important in Nantucket.

7 This question has two parts. First, answer Part A. Then answer Part B.

Part A
Read the following sentence from the passage.

To Kate, the money that whaling brought to her island home paled next to the safety of her father—for whaling was a dangerous business indeed.

Which words have about the same meaning as paled next to?

A more than made up for
B was worth the risk
(C) was far less important than
D lessened concerns about

Part B
Which of the phrases from the passage **best** helps the reader understand the meaning of paled next to?

(A) "a dangerous business indeed"
B "was used to make everything"
C "lit the lamps in many homes"
D "an important industry in Nantucket"

314

8 **Short Response** How does paragraph 7 contribute to the overall structure of the story? Use details from the story in your response.

Paragraph 7 provides the resolution for the story. It describes how the problem in the story—the fear that Kate's father may never return—is resolved when he gets home safely to the relief of his family.

8 After students have completed the Interim Assessment, evaluate their responses to the short-response item using the **2-Point Writing Rubric** below.

Answers will vary but should show that students understand that paragraph 7 depicts the resolution of the conflict when Kate's father safely returns, putting her fears to rest. See the sample response on the student book page.

You may wish to display or pass out copies of the reproducible **2-Point Writing Rubric** on page TR10. Have students use the rubric to individually assess their writing and revise as needed.

DOK 3 **RL.5.5**

2-Point Writing Rubric

All three criteria must be satisfied in order for a response to gain full points.

Points	Focus	Evidence	Organization
2	The response demonstrates comprehension and provides accurate analysis.	The response supports the analysis with adequate textual evidence.	Ideas are clear and follow a logical order.
1	The response demonstrates some comprehension and provides minimally accurate analysis.	The response supports the analysis with limited textual evidence.	Some ideas are unclear or out of order.
0	The response demonstrates no comprehension and provides inaccurate or no analysis.	The response provides little or no textual evidence.	Ideas are unclear or incomplete.

Write

Review Responses

9 After students have completed the Interim Assessment, evaluate their responses to the Extended Response using the **4-Point Writing Rubric** below.

Answers will vary but should show that students understand how Kate's point of view is like her family's because they are all worried about Captain Alden. They are different in the ways they express their concern. See the sample response on the student book page.

DOK 3 **RL.5.6**

Write

9 **Extended Response** "Kate's Vigil" is told in the third person from Kate's point of view, which includes her descriptions of her brother and mother. Does Kate's point of view differ from her mother's and her brother's points of view? In your answer, be sure to

- describe Kate's point of view about what is happening
- describe and quote details that tell about Kate's mother's point of view about what is happening
- describe and quote details that tell about Kate's brother's point of view about what is happening
- explain how the three points of view compare

Check your writing for correct spelling, grammar, punctuation, and capitalization.

"Kate's Vigil" opens with the sentence "Kate Alden was worried about her father, Captain Joshua Alden." The rest of the story describes how that worry shapes all of Kate's thoughts, feelings, and actions. Everything she thinks and does reflects her fear that her father has been lost at sea on a whaling trip because his return home has been delayed. Kate spends most of her time at the top of her house on a "widow's walk," watching for her father's ship.

Kate's mother is also deeply concerned about her husband. In the story, Mrs. Alden joins Kate on the widow's walk at night. Mrs. Alden "tried to calm her fears with soothing words and warm embraces," but Kate can see "the worry that her mother barely hid behind her own eyes." When they hug each other and weep, they are letting each other know that they both fear the worst has happened. Both mother and daughter believe that Captain Alden may never come home.

Like Kate, Daniel is also worried about his father. He continues to go to work and doesn't talk openly about his father, but Kate can see that he is worried by the look on his face. She "could see Daniel's anxiety in the deep lines that creased his forehead."

316

4-Point Writing Rubric

All three criteria must be satisfied in order for a response to gain full points.

Points	Focus	Evidence	Organization
4	The response demonstrates a full understanding of the prompt and provides accurate analysis.	The response supports the analysis with generous textual evidence.	Ideas are consistently presented in a purposeful and logical order.
3	The response demonstrates a good understanding of the prompt and provides mostly accurate analysis.	The response supports the analysis with adequate textual evidence.	Ideas are generally presented in a purposeful and logical order, although some ideas may be unclear or out of order.
2	The response demonstrates a general understanding of the prompt and provides some accurate analysis but includes inaccurate descriptions or explanations.	The response supports the analysis with limited textual evidence but does not reference the text explicitly.	Some ideas are presented in a purposeful and logical order, but others are unclear or out of order.
1	The response demonstrates a limited understanding of the prompt and provides limited analysis with significant inaccuracies.	The response may use textual evidence, but it does not support the analysis and does not reference the text explicitly.	Most ideas are not presented in a purposeful and logical order.
0	The response does not demonstrate understanding of the prompt.	Ideas are not supported with reference to textual evidence.	The response does not present ideas in a purposeful or logical order.

All three members of the Alden family share a similar point of view about Captain Alden. They all understand the risks and dangers of whaling, but they are worried when Captain Alden's ship is a month late in returning to Nantucket. Kate, Daniel, and Mrs. Alden can't help but wonder if they are waiting in vain "for a father, husband, brother, or son who would never return."

Review Unit Opener Self-Check

Ask students to complete the unit self-check on page 264 of the student book. Then have them discuss the items in the self-check with a partner. Encourage students to give each other examples from the lessons that show where they really began to understand the skill.

Finally, bring students together for a whole-class discussion. Ask them how knowing these skills have helped make them better readers. Remind them to use their Academic Talk words.

Unit 5

Integration of Knowledge and Ideas in Informational Text

Integration of Knowledge and Ideas in Informational Text

Imagine you are shopping for a new bicycle. You might want to do some research first. You might look at different types of bikes, read about bicycles on the Internet, and even try riding a few models. In this way, you are making smart choices about what to purchase.

Reading a text can be a little like buying something. You could say that a reader "purchases" **knowledge** and **ideas**. Effective readers examine more than one source of information about a topic. They evaluate an author's opinion, looking for evidence to support it. Finally, effective readers **integrate information** from several sources to become truly informed.

In this unit, you'll use several sources about a topic to find the answer to a question. You'll explain how authors use reasons and evidence to support specific points. And, you'll pull together information from more than one source in order to get as much information as possible. In doing so, you'll become an effective consumer of information!

✓ Self Check

Before starting this unit, check off the skills you know below. As you complete each lesson, see how many more skills you can check off!

I can:	Before this unit	After this unit
locate information from multiple sources, including diagrams.	☐	☐
find answers to questions or problems within multiple sources.	☐	☐
explain how authors use reasons and evidence to support their points.	☐	☐
identify supporting reasons and evidence in texts with multiple points.	☐	☐
combine information from multiple sources about the same topic.	☐	☐

318

page 324

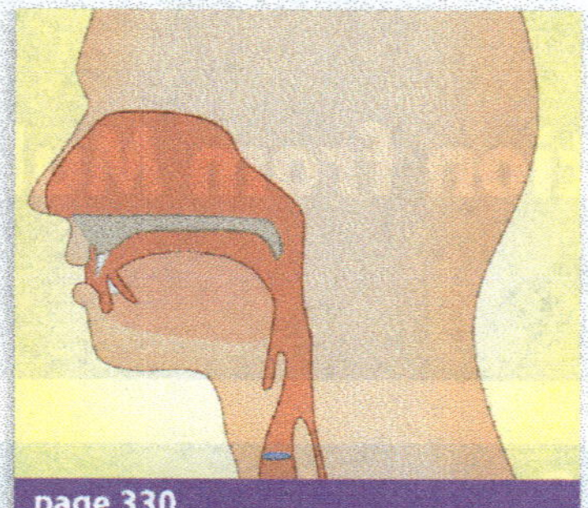
page 330

page 345

page 362

page 372

page 373

319

At a Glance

- These two pages introduce students to the skills and strategies they will learn in this unit.
- The checklist allows them to see what skills they will be learning and take ownership of their progress.
- The visual table of contents gives a graphic preview of the passages in the unit.

Step by Step

- Explain to students that they are going to begin a new unit of lessons. Tell them that in all the lessons in this unit they will be learning about the integration of knowledge and ideas in informational text.
- Have the class read together the introduction to the unit in their books. Invite and respond to comments and questions, if any.
- Then take a few minutes to have each student independently read through the list of skills.
- Ask students to consider each skill and check the box if it is a skill they think they already have. Tell students that they may have worked on similar skills in the past, but these skills go deeper than before.
- Engage students in a brief discussion about the skills. Invite students to comment on which ones they would most like to learn, or which ones seem similar or related to something they already know. Remind them that the goal is to be able to check off one skill at a time until they have them all checked.
- Invite students to look at the graphics and predict what the passages will be about.

Lesson 18
Finding Information from Multiple Sources

Standards Focus

Draw on information from multiple print or digital sources, demonstrating the ability to locate an answer to a question quickly or to solve a problem efficiently. RI.5.7

Lesson Objectives

Reading

- Bring together information from more than one source. RI.5.7
- Quickly locate information or solve a problem using multiple sources. RI.5.7

Writing

- Draw evidence from informational texts to support analysis and reflection. W.5.9b

Speaking and Listening

- Pose and respond to specific questions and contribute to discussions. SL.5.1c
- Review the key ideas expressed and draw conclusions. SL.5.1d

Language

- Use context as a clue to the meaning of a word or phrase. L.5.4a
- Acquire and use academic and domain-specific words and phrases. L.5.6

Additional Practice: **RI.5.1, RI.5.2, RI.5.3, RI.5.4, RI.5.8, RI.5.9, L.5.5a**

Academic Talk

See **Glossary of Terms**, pp. TR2–TR9

- digital source
- source
- print source

Learning Progression

Grade 4	Grade 5	Grade 6
Students explain how visual information (charts, graphs, interactive elements, etc.) contributes to the information presented in a text.	Departing from the visual focus of Grade 4, students must use reading strategies (skimming, scanning), print text features (subheads, footnotes), and digital text features to synthesize information from multiple texts.	Grade 6 is similar to the standard in Grade 5; however, this standard emphasizes integrating information from different media or formats to fully understand a topic.

Lesson Text Selections

Modeled and Guided Instruction

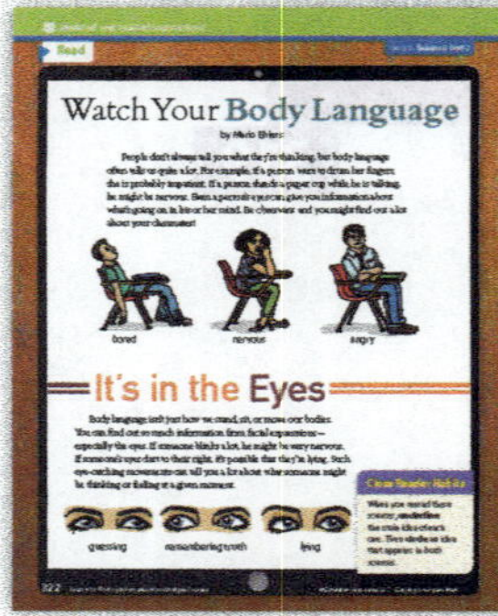

Watch Your Body Language
by Mario Ehlers
Genre: Science Text

It's in the Eyes
Genre: Science Text

Guided Practice

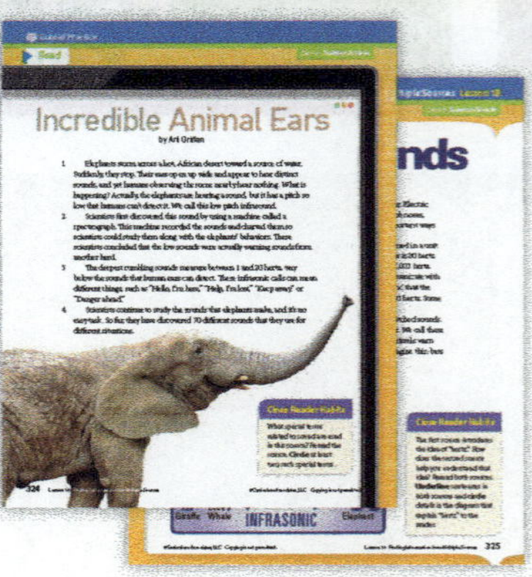

Incredible Animal Ears
by Ari Griffen
Genre: Science Article

Animal Sounds
by Philipe Gelinas
Genre: Science Article

Independent Practice

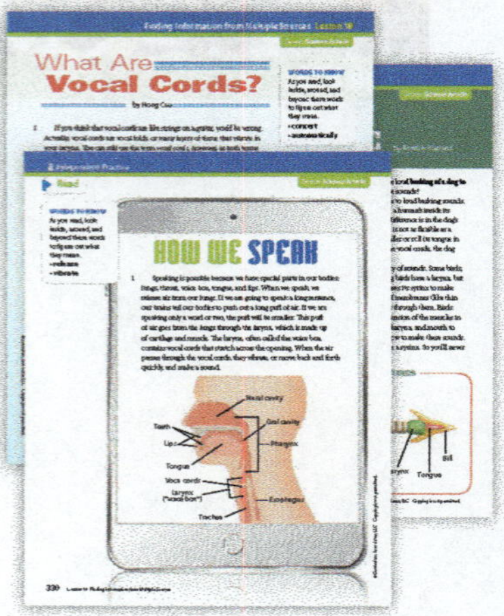

How We Speak
Genre: Science Article

What Are Vocal Cords?
by Hong Cao
Genre: Science Article

Dogs and Birds: Making Noise
by Anatoly Kuznets
Genre: Science Article

Lesson Pacing Guide

Whole Class Instruction *30–45 minutes per day*

Day 1

Teacher-Toolbox.com **Interactive Tutorial**
Using Information from Different Media Sources to Investigate a Topic—Level F
20 min (optional)

Introduction pp. 320–321

- **Read** **Finding Information from Multiple Sources** *10 min*
- **Think** *10 min*
  Graphic Organizer: Four-Column Chart
- **Talk** *5 min*
  Quick Write (TRB) *5 min*

Day 2

Modeled and Guided Instruction pp. 322–323, 328

- **Read** **Watch Your Body Language** and **It's in the Eyes** *10 min*
- **Think** *10 min*
  Graphic Organizer: Two-Column Chart
- **Talk** *5 min*
- **Write** Short Response *10 min*

Day 3

Guided Practice pp. 324–327, 329

- **Read** **Incredible Animal Ears** and **Animal Sounds** *20 min*
- **Think** *10 min*
- **Talk** *5 min*
- **Write** Short Response *10 min*

Day 4

Independent Practice pp. 330–335

- **Read** **How We Speak, What Are Vocal Cords,** and **Dogs and Birds: Making Noise** *20 min*
- **Think** *10 min*
- **Write** Extended Response *15 min*

Day 5

Independent Practice pp. 330–335

- *Review* Answer Analysis (TRB) *10 min*
- *Review* Response Analysis (TRB) *10 min*
- *Assign and Discuss* Learning Target *10 min*

Language Handbook
Lesson 11 Punctuating Titles of Works, pp. 458–459
20 min (optional)

Small Group Differentiation

Teacher-Toolbox.com

Reteach

***Ready Reading* Prerequisite Lesson**

- **Grade 4** Lesson 22 Interpreting Visual Information

Personalized Learning

i-Ready.com

Independent

i-Ready Close Reading Lessons

- **Grade 4** Interpreting Visual Information
- **Grade 5** Finding Information from Multiple Sources

Introduction

Get Started

- Explain to students that in this lesson they will read about ways that people and animals communicate. They will also explore ways to use multiple sources to quickly and efficiently answer questions or solve problems.
- Review what students already know about *sources*, or places to find information. Invite students to share places where they find information when doing a research project or when they're curious about something. Guide them to list examples such as the Internet, books, newspapers, maps, magazines, and pictures.
- Emphasize that students often need multiple sources for information. Explain:

  When you wrote a report about Dr. Martin Luther King, Jr., you found information online and in books. Some sources were only about his childhood, while others were only about the "I Have a Dream" speech. To get the whole story of his life, you had to take information from several different sources.
- Explain that when readers use more than one source, they compare and contrast the information they get from each source.
- Focus students' attention on the Learning Target. Read it aloud to set the purpose for the lesson.
- Display the Academic Talk words and phrases. Tell students to listen for these terms and their meanings as you work through the lesson together. Use the Academic Talk Routine on pp. A48–A49.

English Language Learners

Genre Focus

Read

- Read aloud the Read section as students follow along. Restate to reinforce:

  Sources that use computer technology are called *digital sources*, while sources like books and magazines are called *print sources*. Using multiple sources can help you find the most information on your topic.
- Direct students' attention to the cartoon. Tell them to study the details closely to identify the source of information that each family member is using.

Introduction

RI.5.7 Draw on information from multiple print or digital sources, demonstrating the ability to locate an answer to a question quickly or to solve a problem efficiently.

Lesson 18 Finding Information from Multiple Sources

Learning Target

Knowing how to get information from many sources can help you answer questions, solve problems, and gather information quickly.

Read When looking for information or the answer to a question, you must often read several **sources.** Sometimes you can find that information in a **print source** such as a book or magazine. Other times you can find the information in a **digital source** such as a website.

Use text features such as tables of contents, website menus, headings, picture captions, and keywords to help you locate information quickly and efficiently.

In the cartoon below, a family wants to get to a theme park. Circle the sources of information they are using to get there.

320

English Language Learners

Develop Language

Concept Vocabulary Guide students to an understanding of the terms for different sources of information. Provide pictures or examples of the following objects with labels: newspaper, magazine, book, map, photograph/painting, smartphone, computer, tablet.

- Use the computer as an example. Visit a student-friendly news website. If possible, hold up a smartphone and tablet to show the same website. Explain that because these resources are available *online*, they are *digital*.
- Ask students to group the pictures or objects into two categories: print and digital. Have student pairs discuss which types of information are available both in print and online.

Genre Focus

Science Article

Explain to students that in this lesson they will read science articles—informational texts that inform or explain about topics in science. Writers of science articles often include images and graphics to help make information clear to readers, such as a chart showing the distance between planets or a diagram of an engine.

Ask students to discuss how they gather information from charts, diagrams, images, and captions. Guide them to understand that the information in these visual aids supports and sometimes adds to the information given in the text.

Think Consider what you know about print and digital sources. You can use a chart to keep track of the information you find in multiple sources.

Complete the chart below to describe the information they probably got from each of the four sources.

Sign	Map	Computer	Smartphone
Shows that either road leads to the theme park	Shows a picture that tells them which way to go	Gives them step-by-step directions using an online map	Provides a way to call the theme park to ask for directions or gives them directions through a map app

Talk Share your chart with a partner.

- Which sources in the cartoon are print sources?
- Which sources are digital sources?
- How will using multiple sources help the family decide which road to take to the theme park?

Academic Talk
Use these words and phrases to talk about the text.
- **digital source**
- **print source**
- **source**

Monitor Understanding

If... students struggle to distinguish between print and digital sources,
then... reinforce that the same content might be available in both places.

- Display a copy of a national newspaper. Then project the website for this newspaper. Demonstrate how you can find some of the same articles in both places.
- Use this opportunity to point out some differences, as well. For example, the website will have links to related information, a search tool, or possibly even some additional visual aids. Explain that the print newspaper has a limited amount of space to fit information, but the website does not have that same restriction.
- Discuss with students some of the advantages and disadvantages of using just one source or one type of source for information.

Think

- Have students read aloud the Think section. Explain that the chart will help them organize their ideas.
- Have partners complete the chart. Remind students to use the details in the cartoon to identify the type of source each person is using. Have them use their own knowlege and experiences to imagine how each source might help solve the family's problem.
- As students work, circulate and provide assistance as needed.
- Ask volunteers to share what they wrote in their charts.
- Lead students to understand that the family can solve their problem with several sources. Each source gives a slightly different kind of information or presents it a little differently.

Talk

- Read aloud the Talk prompts.
- Have partners discuss how each resource might help the family make a decision about which way to go.
- Ask volunteers to share their ideas.

Quick Write Have students write a response to the following prompt:

When you have a question you want to answer, describe the way you go about finding information. What sources do you use? When do you decide that you have found all the information you need?

Ask students to share their responses.

Wrap Up

- Invite students to share what they've learned so far. Encourage them to use the Academic Talk words and phrases in their explanations.
- Explain to students that when they use more than one informational text to answer a question or solve a problem, they have a better chance of finding accurate information.

In the next section, we'll read two sources about ways that people show their feelings without speaking. Both sources are on the same topic, but we'll learn unique facts and details from each source.

Monitor Understanding

Modeled and Guided Instruction

Get Started

Today you will read two short texts about body language. First, you'll read to understand what each author says. Then you'll read to compare and contrast the facts provided in each text.

Read

- Read aloud the titles of the texts and call attention to the illustrations and captions. Guide students to understand that both passages tell about how people communicate with their bodies.
- Have students read the texts independently. Tell them to place a check mark above any confusing words and phrases as they read. Remind students to look inside, around, and beyond each unknown word to help them figure out its meaning. Use the Word Learning Routine on pp. A50–A51.
- When students have finished reading, clarify the meanings of words and phrases they still find confusing. Then use the questions below to check understanding. Encourage students to identify details in the text that support their answers.

  What is body language? *(ways that people show their feelings with their bodies, including their eyes)*

  What might a person who is slumped back in his or her chair be feeling? *(boredom)*

  What are the passages mostly about? *(understanding emotions and thoughts through body language and expressions)*

English Language Learners

● **Word Learning Strategy**

Explore

- Read aloud the Explore question at the top of p. 323 to set the purpose for the second read. Tell students they will need to take a closer look at the content of each text to compare and contrast the passages and answer this question.
- Have students read aloud the Close Reader Habit on p. 322.

TIP Point out that comparing and contrasting the illustrations and captions provides a quick way to identify the focus of each article.

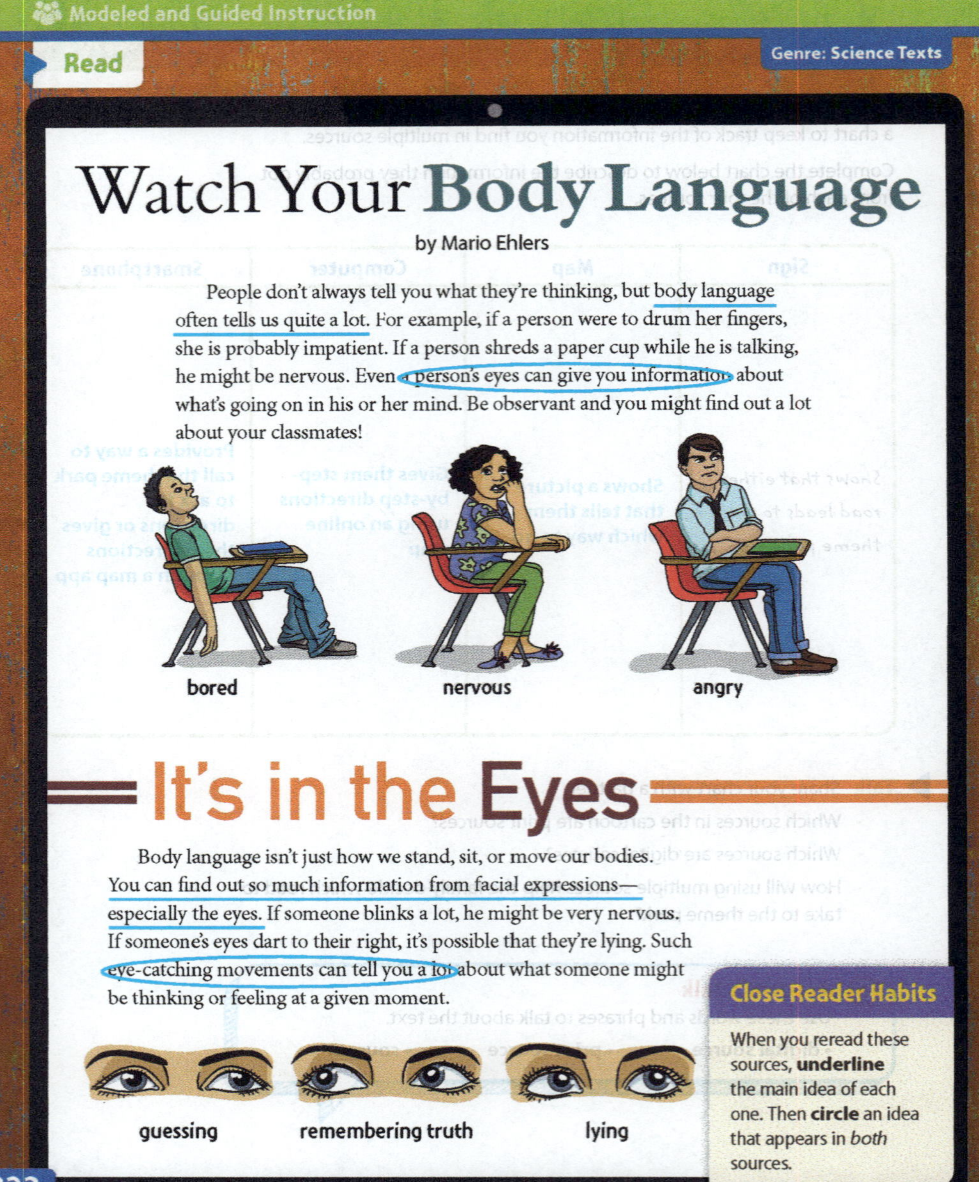

Modeled and Guided Instruction

Read

Genre: Science Texts

Watch Your Body Language

by Mario Ehlers

People don't always tell you what they're thinking, but body language often tells us quite a lot. For example, if a person were to drum her fingers, she is probably impatient. If a person shreds a paper cup while he is talking, he might be nervous. Even a person's eyes can give you information about what's going on in his or her mind. Be observant and you might find out a lot about your classmates!

bored

nervous

angry

It's in the Eyes

Body language isn't just how we stand, sit, or move our bodies. You can find out so much information from facial expressions—especially the eyes. If someone blinks a lot, he might be very nervous. If someone's eyes dart to their right, it's possible that they're lying. Such eye-catching movements can tell you a lot about what someone might be thinking or feeling at a given moment.

guessing

remembering truth

lying

Close Reader Habits

When you reread these sources, **underline** the main idea of each one. Then **circle** an idea that appears in *both* sources.

322

English Language Learners

Build Meaning

Act It Out Use total physical response to reinforce understanding. Have students imitate the body positions and eye movements shown in the illustrations. Ask them to follow directions such as these:

Show how you sit when you are bored. Show how your eyes might move if you were lying.

Have partners mimic the body language and eye movements shown in the texts and state each emotion aloud, using the captions for guidance. Then guide students to mime the body movements that are named in the text only. Demonstrate and then have students repeat your motions.

● Word Learning Strategy

Use Context Clues

- Reread "Watch Your Body Language." Point out the word *observant* in the last sentence.

  What do you think *observant* means? What clues help you figure out the meaning?

- Encourage students to look again at the whole text, including the title. Help them notice the word *watch*, the clue "people don't always tell you," and the statement "you might find out a lot." They should determine that to be *observant* means "to pay close attention to visual details."
- Invite students to share other times when they are or should be observant, such as when receiving instructions or crossing a street.

L.5.4a

Explore How does reading two sources give you a deeper understanding of body language than if you had read just one source?

Look for similar information in both sources. This is a clue the information is important.

Think

1 Complete the chart below with information from each source.

"Watch Your Body Language"	"It's in the Eyes"
Drumming fingers could show impatience.	Blinking the eyes a lot can show nervousness.
Shredding a paper cup could show nervousness.	Eyes darting to the right might mean a person is lying.
Eyes can show what someone is thinking.	Eye movements can also show guessing or remembering the truth.

Talk

2 What important ideas are found in "Watch Your Body Language" and "It's in the Eyes"? If necessary, revise your charts to add more information.

HINT Always study pictures and captions. They can provide as much useful information as the text itself.

Write

3 **Short Response** The topic of each source is body language. But what specific idea appears in **both** sources? Use details from both sources to support your response. Use the space provided on page 328 to write your answer.

323

Think Aloud

- To answer the Explore question, I need to go back to the texts and identify what information each one tells me about body language. I'll start by rereading the first passage. One detail, the one about an impatient person drumming his or her fingers, has already been filled in for me.
- Another detail I see in the third sentence is that a nervous person might shred a paper cup. That's another example of body language, so I'll add it to my chart.
- I'll keep reading to find one more detail from the first passage, then I'll do the same thing to fill in details about the second passage. I'll keep in mind the details provided in the images, too.

Think

- Read aloud the Think section. Explain to students that you will model how to find text evidence to fill in part of the chart. Use the **Think Aloud** below to guide your modeling.
- Revisit the Explore question. Guide students to determine that they need to look for more details, using the Close Reader Habit.
- Encourage students to work with a partner to continue rereading the passage and complete the chart. Point out that the Buddy Tip will help them find the information they need.
- Ask volunteers to share their completed charts.
- Guide students to identify the ideas that are common to both texts. *(Body language is a good indicator of what people are thinking and feeling, and looking at someone's eyes can help you understand what that person is feeling.)*

Talk

- Read aloud the Talk prompt.
- Have partners respond to the prompt. Use the Talk Routine on pp. A52–A53.
- Circulate to check that students are talking about the similarities between the two texts. Encourage students to use information in their partner's chart to revise their own chart, if necessary.

Write

- Ask a volunteer to read aloud the Write prompt.
- Invite a few students to tell what the prompt is asking them to do.
- Make sure students understand that they need to identify the information that appears in both texts. Remind students that the information that appears in the images and captions is also important.
- Have students turn to p. 328 to write their response.
- Use Review Responses on p. 328 to assess students' writing.

Wrap Up

- Ask students to recall the Learning Target. Have them explain how reading two sources about body language helped them better understand the topic.

Guided Practice

Get Started

Today you will read two articles on ways that people and animals use sound to communicate. First you will read to understand what the articles are about. Then you will reread with a partner to analyze how the information in both articles helps you better understand the topic.

Read

- Read aloud the titles of the articles. Ask what students already know about sounds that animals can hear but people can't.
- Have students predict what the articles will be about based on the titles and the illustrations.
- **Read to Understand** Have students read the articles independently. Tell them to place a check mark above any confusing words and phrases as they read. Remind students to look inside, around, and beyond each unknown word or phrase to help them figure out its meaning. Use the Word Learning Routine on pp. A50–A51.
- When students have finished reading, clarify the meanings of words and phrases they still find confusing. Then use the questions below to check understanding. Encourage students to identify details in the texts that support their answers.

  Why can't humans hear some of the sounds that elephants hear? *(because the sounds are too low for people to hear)*

  What messages do elephants send using low sounds? *(They say, "Hello, I'm here," "Help, I'm lost," "Keep away," or "Danger ahead.")*

  What is the first passage mostly about? *(infrasonic sounds, messages sent and received by elephants)*

  Which animals can hear infrasound? *(elephants, giraffes, whales)*

  Which animals can hear ultrasound? *(dolphins, rats, squirrels, bats, butterflies, snakes, frogs)*

  What is the second passage mostly about? *(the frequencies heard by different animals compared to frequencies heard by humans)*

English Language Learners

- **Word Learning Strategy**

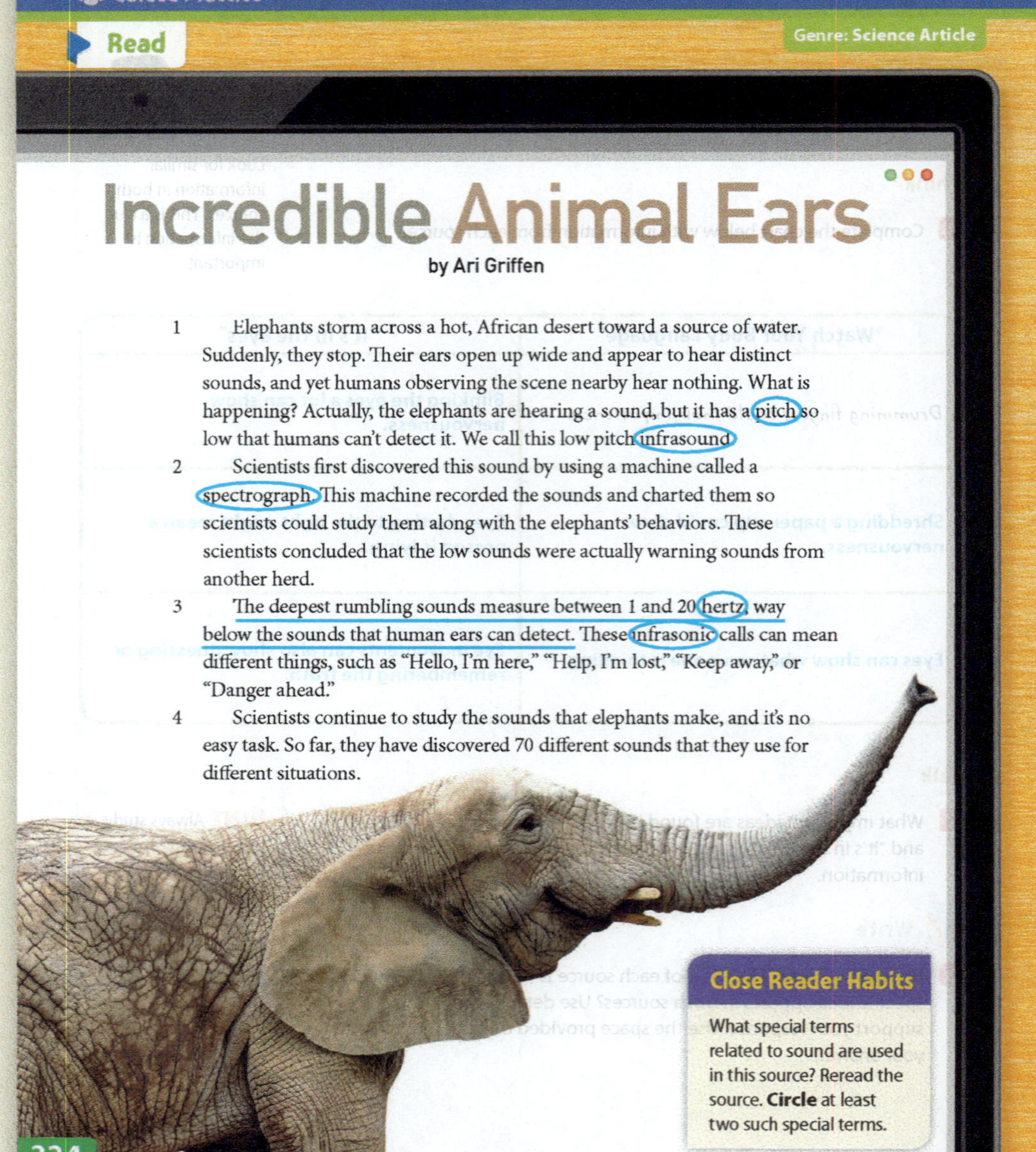

Guided Practice

Read

Genre: Science Article

Incredible Animal Ears

by Ari Griffen

1 Elephants storm across a hot, African desert toward a source of water. Suddenly, they stop. Their ears open up wide and appear to hear distinct sounds, and yet humans observing the scene nearby hear nothing. What is happening? Actually, the elephants are hearing a sound, but it has a pitch so low that humans can't detect it. We call this low pitch infrasound.

2 Scientists first discovered this sound by using a machine called a spectrograph. This machine recorded the sounds and charted them so scientists could study them along with the elephants' behaviors. These scientists concluded that the low sounds were actually warning sounds from another herd.

3 The deepest rumbling sounds measure between 1 and 20 hertz, way below the sounds that human ears can detect. These infrasonic calls can mean different things, such as "Hello, I'm here," "Help, I'm lost," "Keep away," or "Danger ahead."

4 Scientists continue to study the sounds that elephants make, and it's no easy task. So far, they have discovered 70 different sounds that they use for different situations.

Close Reader Habits

What special terms related to sound are used in this source? Reread the source. **Circle** at least two such special terms.

324

English Language Learners

Develop Language

Concept Vocabulary Explain to students that much of what they will learn in these selections deals with sound. Draw a concept map to help introduce and organize sound-related words.

- In the center bubble write *sound*. Invite students to suggest related words they may know, including *hear, ears,* and *noise*. Add those to the map in appropriate clusters.
- Work with students to find sound-related words in the passage, including *pitch, infrasound, hertz, infrasonic, ultrasound,* and *frequency*. Point out that *pitch* is a multiple-meaning word. Students may be familiar with the verb meaning "to throw," but here the word relates to sound.
- Guide students to return to the text and look for clues about the meaning of each word. Together determine meanings to the best of your ability, and then have students use a dictionary to clarify or confirm the meanings.

Genre: Science Article

Animal Sounds

by Philipe Gelinas

1 Bees dance or emit smells to communicate with one another. Electric eels use electricity to communicate with one another. Horses rub noses, and giraffes press their necks together. Yet, one of the most important ways animals communicate is by sound.

2 Sound travels in waves, and its pitch, or frequency, is measured in a unit that scientists call *hertz*. The lowest frequency a person can hear is 20 hertz (20 cycles per second). The highest frequency we can hear is 20,000 hertz.

3 Some animals have incredible hearing. Elephants can communicate with other elephants up to ten miles away using a very low infrasound that the human ear cannot hear. Giraffes can pick up sounds less than 20 hertz. Some whales can hear sounds as low as 10 hertz.

4 Other types of whales, such as dolphins, mainly use high-pitched sounds. Most of these sounds are also out of the range of the human ear. We call these sounds *ultrasound*. Rats giggle at the ultrasound levels, and squirrels warn one another of danger by making high-pitched noises. And imagine this: bats can hear sounds that can measure as high as 100,000 hertz!

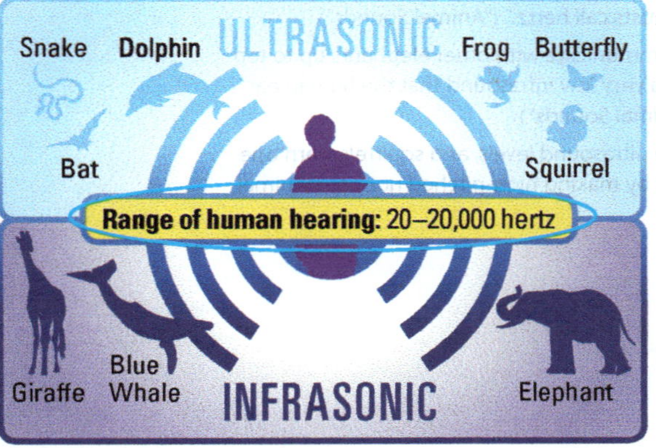

Close Reader Habits

The first source introduces the idea of "hertz." How does the second source help you understand that idea? Reread both sources. **Underline** sentences in both sources and **circle** details in the diagram that explain "hertz" to the reader.

Lesson 18

- **Read to Analyze** Read aloud the Close Reader Habits on pp. 324 and 325 to set the purpose for the second read. Then have students reread the articles with a partner and discuss any questions they might have.

TIP If students have trouble figuring out the meaning of *hertz*, remind them to look at how it is used in both passages. Ask them which passage gives more information about *hertz* and prompt them to look in that passage for a working definition based on the context.

• Word Learning Strategy

Use Context Clues

- Draw students' attention to the word *distinct* in paragraph 1 of "Incredible Animal Ears."

  What does *distinct* mean as it is used in this sentence? What clues help you figure out the meaning?

- Guide students to see that *distinct* is an adjective that describes *sounds*. In the clues around the sentence, the elephants' ears open up wide and the humans nearby can't hear anything at all. Together determine that hearing a *distinct*, or "clear," sound is the opposite of hearing nothing.
- Discuss why this contrast is important to the main idea of the text. **L.5.4a**

Guided Practice

Think

- Have students work with a partner to complete items 1–2. Draw attention to the boldface words.

TIP If students have trouble answering Part A of item 1, encourage them to skim each passage looking for key words related to each answer choice. For example, to check choice A, students should skim for the words *ultrasound* and *infrasound* in both passages.

Answer Analysis

When students have finished, discuss correct and incorrect responses.

1 Part A

The correct choice is B. Both sources describe how animals use sound to warn each other of possible threats.

- **A** is untrue in that neither source says that all animals use ultrasound and infrasound.
- **C** might be true, but neither source discusses scientists making new discoveries.
- **D** might be true, but neither source develops this idea.

Part B

The correct choices are B and F.

- **A** is an example of humans being unable to hear some sounds made by elephants.
- **C** tells the number of sounds elephants use to communicate.
- **D** explains what a *hertz* is.
- **E** describes how humans cannot hear some sounds made by elephants.

DOK 3

Think Use what you learned from reading the sources to answer the following questions.

When you read different sources on the same topic, look for information in one source that clarifies what you read in the others.

1 This question has two parts. Answer Part A. Then answer Part B.

Part A
What conclusion can you base on evidence found in **both** sources?

A All animals can use ultrasound and infrasound to communicate.
(B) Some animals use sounds to tell each other about possible threats.
C Scientists continue to discover new ways that animals communicate.
D Body language is as important to elephant communication as sound is.

Part B
Choose **one** detail from **each** source to support the answer in Part A.

A "Their ears open up wide and appear to hear distinct sounds, and yet the humans observing the scene nearby hear nothing." ("Incredible Animal Ears")
(B) "These scientists concluded that the low sounds were actually warning sounds from another herd." ("Incredible Animal Ears")
C "So far, they have discovered 70 different sounds that they use for different situations." ("Incredible Animal Ears")
D "Sound travels in waves, and its pitch, or frequency, is measured in a unit that scientists call hertz." ("Animal Sounds")
E "Elephants can communicate with other elephants up to ten miles away using a very low infrasound that the human ear cannot hear." ("Animal Sounds")
(F) "Rats giggle at the ultrasound levels, and squirrels warn one another of danger by making high-pitched noises." ("Animal Sounds")

326

Integrating Standards

Use the following questions to further students' understanding of the texts.

- **What is the main idea of each article?** *(The main idea of "Incredible Animal Ears" is that elephants make a range of different sounds to communicate with one another. The main idea of "Animal Sounds" is a common way that many types of animals use to communicate, from very low-pitched sounds to very high-pitched sounds.)*
  DOK 2 **RI.5.2**
- **In "Incredible Animal Ears," what causes the elephants to stop suddenly? Why wouldn't the reason for stopping have been immediately clear to humans observing nearby?** *(They hear warning sounds from another herd. The sounds are made at a lower pitch than humans can hear without technology.)*
  DOK 2 **RI.5.3**

2 This question has two parts. Answer Part A. Then answer Part B.

Part A
What main idea do **both** sources share?

A Humans can hear sounds that are between 20 and 20,000 hertz.
(B) Animals communicate with each other using sounds, many of which people cannot hear.
C Some animals communicate with high-pitched sounds called ultrasound; other animals use low-pitched sounds.
D Elephants use different sounds for different situations, such as signaling their location or a need for help.

Part B
Choose **one** detail from **each** source to support the answer in Part A.

(A) "Actually, the elephants are hearing a sound, but it has a pitch so low that humans can't detect it." ("Incredible Animal Ears")
B "Scientists continue to study the sounds that elephants make, and it's no easy task." ("Incredible Animal Ears")
C "So far, they have discovered 70 different sounds that they use for different situations." ("Incredible Animal Ears")
D "Bees dance or emit smells to communicate with one another." ("Animal Sounds")
(E) "Yet, one of the most important ways animals communicate is by sound." ("Animal Sounds")
F "The lowest frequency a person can hear is 20 hertz (20 cycles per second)." ("Animal Sounds")

Talk

3 Look for details in both sources that describe what "hertz" is. Use the chart on page 329 to collect evidence from the sources.

HINT Some sources only briefly describe an idea. Other sources can describe the idea in much more depth.

Write

4 **Short Response** Explain how the description of "hertz" in "Animal Sounds" develops an idea introduced in "Incredible Animal Ears." Include details from each source to support your response. Use the space provided on page 329 to write your answer.

327

Monitor Understanding

If... students struggle to answer Part A of item 2,
then... demonstrate how to turn each choice into a question that students can answer by going back into each passage.

- **What is Part A asking you to do?** *(find a main idea that both sources share)*
- **Write each answer option as a question that begins with "Do both passages..."** *(Example: Option A: Do both passages state that humans can hear sounds between 20 and 20,000 hertz?)*
- **Go back to the passages to answer the questions you've written. Remember that both passages must provide details to answer your question.** *(Option A: No; I only read about that in "Animal Sounds.")*

2 **Part A**
The correct choice is B. The main idea that animals communicate using sounds that people cannot hear appears in both passages.

- **A** and **C** describe details, not main ideas. Also, these details are found only in "Animal Sounds," not in "Incredible Animal Ears."
- **D** describes a detail, not a main idea. Also, this detail appears in "Incredible Animal Ears" only, not in "Animal Sounds."

Part B
The correct choices are A and E. Both support the idea that animals communicate with each other by sound which humans often can't hear.

- **B** does not support the idea that humans can't hear some sounds that elephants make.
- **C, D,** and **F** are not directly related to the main idea that the two articles share.

DOK 3

Monitor Understanding

Integrating Standards

Talk

- Have partners discuss the prompt. Emphasize that students should support their ideas with text details.
- Call attention to the HINT.
- Circulate to clarify misunderstandings.

Write

- Ask a volunteer to read aloud the Write prompt.
- Invite students to tell what the prompt is asking them to do. Make sure they understand that they need to explain how the definition of *hertz* in "Animal Sounds" helps readers understand the information about elephants' sounds that is presented in "Incredible Animal Ears."
- Have students turn to p. 329 to write their response.
- Use Review Responses on p. 329 to assess students' writing.

Wrap Up

- Ask students to recall the Learning Target. Have them explain how reading two sources helped them better understand how humans and animals communicate.

Write

- Remember to use the Response-Writing Routine on pp. A54–A55.

Review Responses

After students complete the writing activity, help them evaluate their responses.

3 Responses may vary but should include information from both passages about what people can learn from looking at someone's eyes. See the sample response on the student book page. *DOK 3*

Modeled and Guided Instruction

Write Use the space below to write your answer to the question on page 323.

Watch Your Body Language
It's in the Eyes

3 **Short Response** The topic of each source is body language. But what specific idea appears in **both** sources? Use details from both sources to support your response.

Sample response: The idea found in both sources is that we can learn about people by studying what their eyes do. In "Watch Your Body Language," we read the sentence, "Even a person's eyes can give you information about what's going on in his or her mind." In "It's in the Eyes," we read the sentence, "Such eye-catching movements can tell you a lot about what someone might be thinking or feeling at a given moment." The illustrations in both sources provide examples of eyes that show thoughts or feelings, although this information is developed in greater detail in "It's in the Eyes."

Don't forget to check your writing.

Check Your Writing

- ☐ Did you read the prompt carefully?
- ☐ Did you put the prompt in your own words?
- ☐ Did you use the best evidence from the text to support your ideas?
- ☐ Are your ideas clearly organized?
- ☐ Did you write in clear and complete sentences?
- ☐ Did you check your spelling and punctuation?

328

Scaffolding Support for Reluctant Writers

If students are having a difficult time getting started, use the strategies below. Work individually with struggling students, or have students work with partners.

- Circle the verbs in the prompt that tell you what to do, such as *describe*, *explain*, or *compare*.
- Underline words and phrases in the prompt that show what information you need to provide in your response, such as *causes*, *reasons*, or *character traits*.
- Talk about the details from the text that you will include in your response.
- Explain aloud how you will respond to the prompt.

Incredible Animal Ears
Animal Sounds

3 **Use the chart below to organize your ideas.**

Information About the Concept of "Hertz"

"Incredible Animal Ears"	"Animal Sounds"

Write **Use the space below to write your answer to the question on page 327.**

4 **Short Response** Explain how the description of "hertz" in "Animal Sounds" develops an idea introduced in "Incredible Animal Ears." Include details from each source to support your response.

Sample response: "Incredible Animal Ears" introduces the idea of "hertz," but the article "Animal Sounds" develops that idea more fully. "Incredible Animal Ears" states that elephants can hear sounds that "measure between 1 and 20 hertz, way below the sounds that human ears can detect." This statement tells us only that "hertz" is somehow related to sound. But paragraph 2 of "Animal Sounds" states, "Sound travels in waves, and its pitch, or frequency, is measured in a unit that scientists call hertz." This sentence makes clear what "Incredible Animal Ears" did not—that "hertz" is a unit scientists use to measure the frequency of sound waves.

329

Teacher Notes

Talk

3 Students should use the chart to collect their evidence and ideas.

Write

Remember to use the Response-Writing Routine on pp. A54–A55.

Review Responses

After students complete the writing activity, help them evaluate their responses.

4 Responses may vary but should include details from both articles about the concept of *hertz*. See the sample response on the student book page.
DOK 3

Independent Practice

Get Started

Today you are going to read three related science articles and consider what you have learned about using multiple sources to answer questions and solve problems.

- Ask a volunteer to explain how using multiple sources helps readers answer questions and better understand a topic. Encourage students to use the Academic Talk words and phrases in their response.

 **English Language Learners**

Read

You are going to read the articles independently and use what you have learned to think and write about the texts. As you read, remember to look closely at the details in each text to help you understand complicated information in the other two texts.

- Read aloud the titles of the articles and then encourage students to preview the texts, paying close attention to the diagrams and their labels.
- Call attention to the Words to Know boxes on pp. 330, 331, and 332.
- If students need support in reading the passages, you may wish to use the Monitor Understanding suggestions.
- When students have finished, have them complete the Think and Write sections.

● **Monitor Understanding**

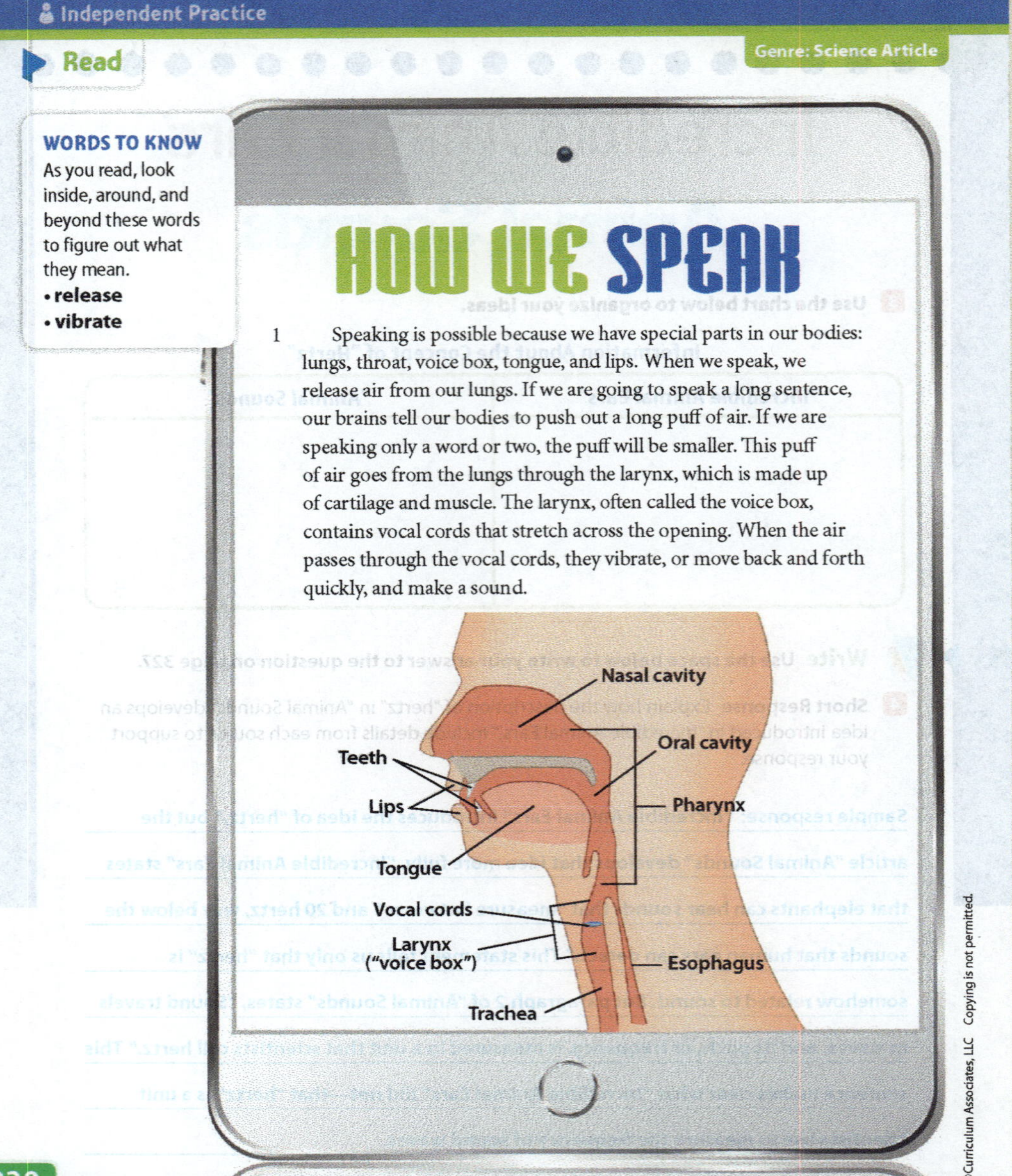
Independent Practice

Read

Genre: Science Article

WORDS TO KNOW
As you read, look inside, around, and beyond these words to figure out what they mean.
- **release**
- **vibrate**

HOW WE SPEAK

1 Speaking is possible because we have special parts in our bodies: lungs, throat, voice box, tongue, and lips. When we speak, we release air from our lungs. If we are going to speak a long sentence, our brains tell our bodies to push out a long puff of air. If we are speaking only a word or two, the puff will be smaller. This puff of air goes from the lungs through the larynx, which is made up of cartilage and muscle. The larynx, often called the voice box, contains vocal cords that stretch across the opening. When the air passes through the vocal cords, they vibrate, or move back and forth quickly, and make a sound.

330

 **English Language Learners**

Build Meaning

Preview Illustrations Help students preview the three diagrams. For the first diagram, read aloud the labels and have students echo you. Explain that the second diagram shows straight inside of a human mouth, back into the throat. For the third diagram, explain that students are looking sideways at a bird's anatomy. As needed, draw a bird outline around the diagram to help students gain perspective. Then prompt discussion with the following questions:

- **Based on the first two diagrams, what do you predict the first two articles will be about?** *(ways people use their mouths and throats to speak)*
- **What does the third diagram show? How is it similar to and different from the first two diagrams?** *(It shows the inside of a bird's mouth, throat, and chest. It probably explains how a bird makes different sounds and how it sings.)*

Encourage students to look for details that confirm or challenge their predictions as they read.

Genre: Science Article

What Are Vocal Cords?

by Hong Cao

WORDS TO KNOW
As you read, look inside, around, and beyond these words to figure out what they mean.
- **concert**
- **automatically**

1 If you think that vocal cords are like strings on a guitar, you'd be wrong. Actually, vocal cords are vocal folds, or many layers of tissue that vibrate in your larynx. You can still use the term *vocal cords*, however, as both terms mean the same thing. The vocal cords have a V-shape.

2 How do we use the vocal cords? To make a high sound, we tighten the vocal cords. To make a low sound, we relax the cords. And most people do all this without even thinking!

3 So now the sound is coming through the vocal cords, but the sound isn't a word yet. What happens next is that we use our throat, tongue, mouth, and lips to shape the sound into vowels and consonants.

4 For example, say a word like *football* or *window*. Notice how you open your mouth and move it around when you change vowels and consonants. Notice how you move your tongue and change its shape as you speak. You're making a fancy concert of sounds inside your mouth!

5 Speaking seems like the most natural thing in the world, and when we do speak, we rarely, if ever, think about how we create words and sentences. Even so, we aren't born knowing how to make words automatically.

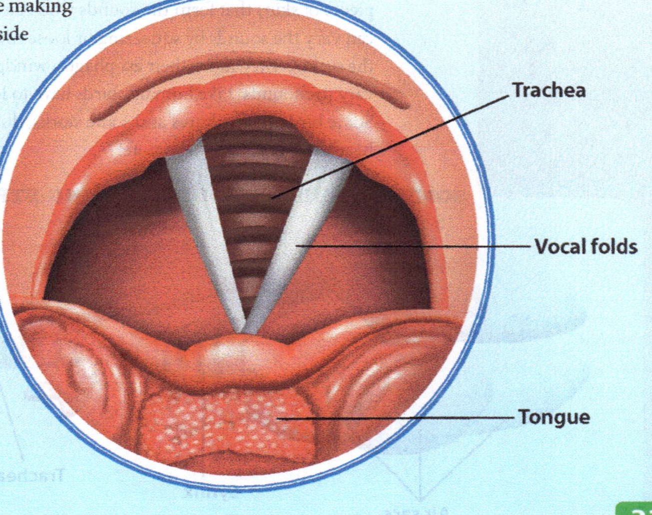

● Monitor Understanding

If... students struggle to read and understand the passages, **then...** use these scaffolding suggestions:

Question the Text Preview the texts by asking the following questions:

- **Based on the titles and the diagrams, what do you predict each article will be about?**
- **What questions do you have about each text?**

Vocabulary Support Define terms that may interfere with comprehension, such as *lungs*, *air sacs*, and *cords*.

Read Aloud Read aloud the text with students. You could also have students chorally read the text in a small group.

Check Understanding Use the questions below to check understanding. Encourage students to cite details in the texts that support their answers.

- **How are the first two passages alike and different?** *(They both explain how people use special body parts to speak. The second article goes into more detail about ways that people form words.)*
- **Why can't a dog form as many sounds as a person or a bird?** *(A dog's mouth is not as flexible as a person's or a bird's. Also, humans and birds have more special body parts in their throats and mouths that allow them to form many different sounds.)*

Independent Practice

Integrating Standards

After students have read the articles, use these questions to discuss the articles with them.

- **What body parts work together to help humans speak? Which details helped you come to this conclusion?**

  ("How We Speak" explains that people puff air from their lungs through their larynx, where vocal cords or folds vibrate to create different kinds of sound. "What Are Vocal Cords?" explains how people use their tongue, mouth, and lips to form consonant and vowel sounds in words.)

  DOK 3 RI.5.9

- **The author of "What Are Vocal Cords?" says in paragraph 4 that a speaker makes "a fancy concert of sounds" with his or her mouth when he or she speaks. What does this phrase mean?**

  (The author uses this metaphor to compare the variety of sounds a person's mouth can make with the variety of sounds that orchestra instruments can make. This metaphor calls attention to the many different vowel and consonant sounds a speaker must make in order to form words.)

  DOK 3 L.5.5a

- **In "Dogs and Birds: Making Noise," what clue words help you figure out what *membranes* means in paragraph 3?**

  *(*Membranes *is followed by an explanation in parentheses. This is a type of context clue that tells what membranes are like: "thin pieces of skin.")*

  DOK 2 RI.5.4, L.5.4a

- **In "Dogs and Birds: Making Noise," what evidence does the author provide to support his claim that vultures and some storks will never be heard singing?**

  (The text says "vultures and some storks don't have a syrinx." The syrinx works similarly to the vocal cords in humans. Readers can infer that without a syrinx, a bird would not be able to make a variety of sounds, including singing.)

  DOK 3 RI.5.1, RI.5.8

Theme Connection

- Remind students that the theme of this lesson is Human and Animal Communication.
- Display a three-column chart on the board. Label each column with the passage topics, including "body language," "animal hearing," and "human speech and animal noises."
- Ask students to recall facts and ideas they learned from each of the passages. List their responses in the appropriate column.
- Ask students to determine how all of the passages relate to the theme of human and animal communication.

Independent Practice

Genre: Science Article

Dogs and Birds: MAKING NOISE

by Anatoly Kuznets

WORDS TO KNOW
As you read, look inside, around, and beyond these words to figure out what they mean.
- **variety**
- **anatomy**
- **imitate**

1 Animals can make a variety of sounds—from the loud barking of a dog to the sweet song of a bird. How do animals make these sounds?

2 A dog can make quite a few sounds, from whines to loud barking sounds. Scientists say that the dog has vocal cords much like a human's inside its thorax, or chest. So why can't a dog speak? The big difference is in the dog's anatomy, or the structure of its body. A dog's mouth is not as flexible as a human's. A dog can't move its mouth to make it smaller or roll its tongue in different positions. So after the air passes through the vocal cords, the dog can't change the sound very much.

3 Birds, on the other hand, can make a wide variety of sounds. Some birds, like parrots, can even imitate human speech. Singing birds have a larynx, but they don't have vocal cords. Instead, a singing bird uses its syrinx to make sounds. The syrinx is in the throat and is made up of membranes (like thin pieces of skin) that form the sounds when air passes through them. Birds can vary the sounds by squeezing or loosening the tension of the muscles in the syrinx. They move their esophagus, windpipe, pharynx, and mouth to vary the sounds. Like humans, birds have to learn how to make these sounds. Some birds, like vultures and some storks, don't have a syrinx. So you'll never hear these birds singing a note!

SOME OF A BIRD'S SOUND-MAKING STRUCTURES

332

Think Use what you learned from reading the sources to answer the following questions.

1 This question has two parts. First, answer Part A. Then answer Part B.

Part A
What idea do "How We Speak" and "What Are Vocal Cords?" share?

- (A) Several parts of our bodies work together to let us speak.
- B We can make sounds because we have vocal folds.
- C Your mouth and tongue help you form vowels.
- D Air travels from the lungs to the voice box.

Part B
Choose **one** detail from **each** source to support the answer in Part A.

- (A) "Speaking is possible because we have special parts in our bodies: lungs, throat, voice box, tongue, and lips." ("How We Speak")
- B "When we speak, we release air from our lungs." ("How We Speak")
- C "The larynx, often called the voice box, contains vocal cords that stretch across the opening." ("How We Speak")
- D "Actually, vocal cords are vocal folds, or many layers of tissue that vibrate in your larynx." ("What Are Vocal Cords?")
- E "To make a high sound, we tighten the vocal cords." ("What Are Vocal Cords?")
- (F) "What happens next is that we use our throat, tongue, mouth, and lips to shape the sound into vowels and consonants." ("What Are Vocal Cords?")

2 Circle the word in the paragraph below that means "capable of bending easily without breaking."

So why can't a dog speak? The big difference is in the dog's anatomy, or the structure of its body. A dog's mouth is not as (flexible) as a human's. A dog can't move its mouth to make it smaller or roll its tongue in different positions. So after the air passes through the vocal cords, the dog can't change the sound very much.

● Monitor Understanding

If... students struggle to complete the items,

then... you may wish to use the following suggestions:

Read Aloud Activities

- As you read, have students note any unfamiliar words or phrases. Clarify any misunderstandings.
- Discuss each item with students to make certain they understand the expectation.

Reread the Text

- Have students complete a three-column chart as they reread each passage.
- Have partners summarize the text.

Think

- Use the Monitor Understanding suggestions to support students in completing items 1–3.

● Monitor Understanding

Answer Analysis

When students have finished, discuss correct and incorrect responses.

1 **Part A**

The correct choice is A. Both passages say that people can speak because we have the following body parts: vocal cords, a throat, a tongue, a mouth, and lips.

- **B** and **C** apply only to the second passage, "What Are Vocal Cords?"
- **D** gives a detail that appears in "How We Speak" only.

Part B

The correct choices are A and F. Both support the idea that vocal cords alone will not help us speak.

- **B** mentions only the role that our lungs play in forming sounds.
- **C** is about the larynx and vocal cords only; it does not explain how various body parts work together to create speech.
- **D** is about the larynx and vocal cords only.
- **E** is about our ability to form sounds, not our ability to speak.

DOK 3 RI.5.7

2 **Students should circle the word *flexible*.** The following sentence addresses the dog's inability to move its mouth into different positions.

DOK 2 L.5.4a

Independent Practice

3 **The correct choice is C.** It supports the idea that dogs can't speak because they can't move their mouths to form words, as people can.

- **A** is about forming sounds, not forming words.
- **B** does not relate to the reason why dogs can't form words.
- **D** doesn't show a difference between humans and dogs. Like humans, dogs have vocal cords.

DOK 2 RI.5.7

Write

- Tell students that using what they read, they will plan and compose an extended response to the writing prompt. Provide copies of the three-column chart on p. TR12.

● **Monitor Understanding**

Review Responses

After students have completed each part of the writing activity, help them evaluate their responses.

4 Display the **Sample Response** for the planning chart on the next page. Have students compare their chart with the sample. Are they missing any information?

DOK 3 RI.5.7

5 Display or pass out copies of the reproducible **2-Point Writing Rubric** on p. TR10. Have students use the rubric to individually assess their writing and revise as needed.

When students have finished their revisions, evaluate their responses. Answers will vary but should explain how humans, dogs, and birds make sounds. Students should compare and contrast the information in each article. Students should also synthesize what they learned about the topic in general.

DOK 3 RI.5.7, W.5.9b

3 What information in "What Are Vocal Cords?" helps the reader understand why dogs can't speak, as stated in "Dogs and Birds: Making Noise"?

- **A** People can make higher sounds by tightening the vocal cords and lower sounds by relaxing the cords.
- **B** Even though we don't often think about how we say words and sentences, we don't learn to speak automatically.
- **(C)** People move their mouths to form words from the sounds made by the vocal cords.
- **D** The vocal cords of humans are not like the strings on a guitar because they have a V-shape.

Write

Using information from all three sources, explain how humans and animals make sounds. What similarities and differences are pointed out in the three sources? Reread each source and underline details that will help you explain how humans and animals make sounds. Then complete numbers 4 and 5.

4 **Plan Your Response** Use a three-column chart to make notes about the specific information in each source. You will use these notes to provide examples for the points in your essay.

5 **Write an Extended Response** Using evidence from the sources and information from your chart, explain how people and animals make sounds.

Responses will vary. A top-scoring response will include information from each of the three sources. The student will use that information to explain how humans and animals make sounds. Students should compare and contrast the information in each source, while synthesizing what they learned about the topic in general.

● **Monitor Understanding**

If... students don't understand the writing task,

then... read aloud the writing prompt. Use the following questions to help students get started.

- **What is the prompt asking you to write about?**
- **Do you need to reread the text to find more information?**
- **How will you identify the information you need to include?**

- Have partners talk about how they will organize their responses.

Learning Target

In this lesson, you used several sources to find information and answer questions. Explain how using multiple print and digital sources will help you find complete and accurate information.

Responses will vary, but students should identify ways that using multiple print and digital sources will help them find information quickly and answer questions, which will be useful when completing research for school projects.

335

Wrap Up

Learning Target

- Have each student respond in writing to the Learning Target prompt.
- When students have finished, have them share their responses. This may be done with a partner, in small groups, or as a whole class.

4 Sample Response

"How We Speak"	"What Are Vocal Cords?"	"Dogs and Birds: Making Noise"
Speaking is possible because we have these body parts: lungs, throat, voice box, tongue, and lips.	Vocal cords are layers of tissue that vibrate in the larynx.	Dogs can make many sounds.
The larynx contains vocal cords that vibrate to make a sound.	Vocal cords are the same as vocal folds.	Scientists believe dogs have vocal cords inside their chests.
	We use the throat, tongue, mouth, and lips to shape sound into words.	Dogs can't speak because their mouths aren't flexible.
	Humans must learn to create words from sounds.	Birds can make a variety of sounds because they have a syrinx in the throat.
		Like humans, birds have to learn to make different sounds.

5 2-Point Writing Rubric

Points	Focus	Evidence	Organization
2	My answer does exactly what the prompt asked me to do.	My answer is supported with plenty of details from the text.	My ideas are clear and in a logical order.
1	Some of my answer does not relate to the prompt.	My answer is missing some important details from the text.	Some of my ideas are unclear and out of order.
0	My answer does not make sense.	My answer does not have any details from the text.	My ideas are unclear and not in any order.

Lesson 19
Understanding Supporting Evidence

Standards Focus

Explain how an author uses reasons and evidence to support particular points in a text, identifying which reasons and evidence support which point(s). RI.5.8

Lesson Objectives

Reading

- Identify an author's points and supporting evidence in a text. RI.5.8
- Explain how the evidence supports particular points in a text. RI.5.8

Writing

- Draw evidence from informational texts to support analysis and reflection. W.5.9b

Speaking and Listening

- Pose and respond to specific questions and contribute to discussions. SL.5.1c
- Review the key ideas expressed and draw conclusions. SL.5.1d

Language

- Use Greek and Latin affixes and roots as clues to the meaning of a word. L.5.4b
- Acquire and use academic and domain-specific words and phrases. L.5.6

Additional Practice: **RI.5.1, RI.5.2, RI.5.3, RI.5.4, L.5.5b**

Academic Talk

See **Glossary of Terms**, pp. TR2–TR9

- points
- reason
- evidence

Learning Progression

Grade 4	Grade 5	Grade 6
Students identify an author's points and supporting evidence for those points.	Building on Grade 4, students not only identify an author's points and supporting evidence, but also explain how the evidence supports particular points, which requires them to judge and evaluate the text.	Grade 6 increases in complexity by requiring students to evaluate the argument and claims in a text.

Lesson Text Selections

Modeled and Guided Instruction

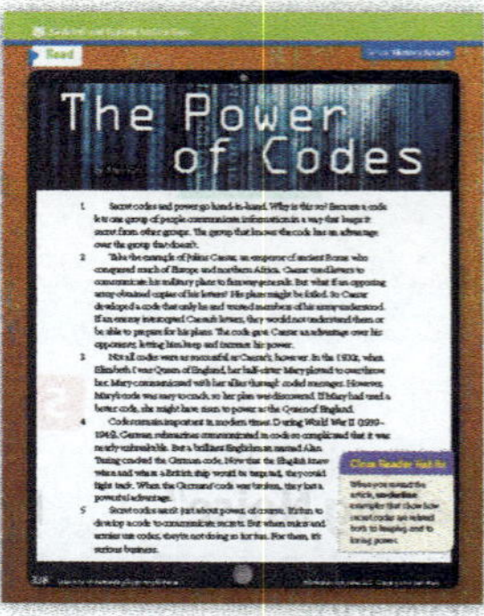

The Power of Codes
by Alan Kim
Genre: History Article

Guided Practice

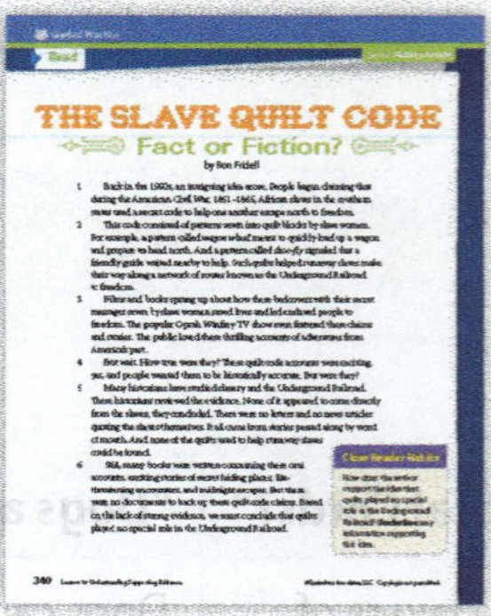

The Slave Quilt Code: Fact or Fiction?
by Ron Fridell
Genre: History Article

Independent Practice

Human Code Machines
by Bruce Watson
Genre: History Article

Lesson Pacing Guide

Whole Class Instruction *30–45 minutes per day*

Day 1

Teacher-Toolbox.com **Interactive Tutorial**
Understanding Supporting Evidence—Level E
20 min (optional)

Introduction pp. 336–337

- **Read** **Understanding Supporting Evidence** *10 min*
- **Think** *10 min*
  Graphic Organizer: Three-Column Chart
- **Talk** *5 min*
  Quick Write (TRB) *5 min*

Day 2

Modeled and Guided Instruction pp. 338–339, 342

- **Read** **The Power of Codes** *10 min*
- **Think** *10 min*
  Graphic Organizer: Three-Column Chart
- **Talk** *5 min*
- **Write** Short Response *10 min*

Day 3

Guided Practice pp. 340–341, 343

- **Read** **The Slave Quilt Code: Fact or Fiction?** *10 min*
- **Think** *10 min*
- **Talk** *5 min*
- **Write** Short Response *10 min*

Day 4

Independent Practice pp. 344–349

- **Read** **Human Code Machines** *15 min*
- **Think** *10 min*
- **Write** Short Response *15 min*

Day 5

Independent Practice pp. 344–349

- *Review* Answer Analysis (TRB) *10 min*
- *Review* Response Analysis (TRB) *10 min*
- *Assign and Discuss* Learning Target *10 min*

Language Handbook
Lesson 12 Revising Sentences, pp. 460–461
20 min (optional)

Ready Writing Connection

During *Ready Reading* Days 1–5, use:
Lesson 5 Writing to Inform: Book Chapter

- **Step 1** **Study a Mentor Text**
- **Step 2** **Unpack Your Assignment**
- **Review the Research Path**
- **Read Source Text**
- **Step 3** **Find Text Evidence**
- **Reread Source Text**

See *Ready Writing TRB*, p. 120a for complete lesson plan.

Small Group Differentiation

Teacher-Toolbox.com

Reteach

***Ready Reading* Prerequisite Lesson**

- **Grade 4** Lesson 23 Explaining an Author's Reasons and Evidence

Teacher-led Activities

Tools for Instruction

- Evaluate Arguments

Personalized Learning

i-Ready.com

Independent

i-Ready Close Reading Lessons

- **Grade 4** Explaining an Author's Reasons and Evidence
- **Grade 5** Understand Supporting Evidence

Introduction

Get Started

- Explain to students that in this lesson they will read about code communication and analyze how authors use reasons and evidence to support their points.
- Review the concepts of points, reasons, and evidence. Remind students that when they do opinion writing, they use each of these elements to create a strong product. Explain:

  Let's say you wanted to write an essay about why video games are good for students. That is the point you must support. To do this, you would give reasons: video games are educational and entertaining. Then you would support each reason with specific facts, or evidence. Some video games help improve students' memory and problem-solving skills.
- Remind students that a *reason* is an explanation for why the point is true. *Evidence* is a fact or example that supports the reason.
- Focus students' attention on the Learning Target. Read it aloud to set the purpose for the lesson.
- Display the Academic Talk words. Tell students to listen for these words and their meanings as you work through the lesson together. Use the Academic Talk Routine on pp. A48–A49.

English Language Learners

- **Genre Focus**

Read

- Read aloud the Read section as students follow along. Restate to reinforce:

  When you read informational texts that make points or try to persuade you, it's helpful to stop and ask yourself what the author's reasons are and what evidence supports them. This will help you decide whether the author's point is strong or weak.
- Direct students' attention to the comic strip. Have them look for the girl's point, reason, and evidence.

Introduction

RI.5.8 Explain how an author uses reasons and evidence to support particular points in a text, identifying which reasons and evidence support which point(s).

Lesson 19 Understanding Supporting Evidence

Understanding the reasons and evidence an author uses to support points will help you better understand a text.

Read When reading informational texts, look for the **points** the author presents to convince you an idea is true. To figure out whether an author's points are supported, look for any reasons and evidence he or she supplies for each point. A **reason** is an explanation for why the idea might be true. A piece of **evidence** is a fact that can be proven true.

In the comic strip below, identify the reasons and evidence the girl gives for needing a secret code.

336

English Language Learners

Develop Language

Multiple-meaning Words To talk about reasons and evidence during this lesson, students will need to use the related words *support, supporting,* and *supported.*

- Write *support* on the board and explain that it can be used as a noun or a verb. Provide sentence frames, such as *The author ______ her claim with evidence. (supports; supported) The ______ for her claim is made up of three examples. (support)* Have students explain how they know whether the word is being used as a noun or a verb.
- Repeat the same procedure with *supporting* as a verb and an adjective.

Genre Focus

History Article

Articles are texts that provide information about a topic. History articles offer information and insight into people, places, or events from the past.

An article is structured around a particular topic. The opening usually engages the reader's attention and the body gives facts, examples, reasons, or descriptions that answer some or all of the questions *who, what, when, where, why,* and *how.*

History articles often include photographs and captions as well as headings and subheadings that tell the reader what is coming next.

Think What have you learned about points, reasons, and evidence? Complete the chart below for the comic strip on the previous page.

What Does the Girl Think?	Why Does She Think This?	What Evidence Supports Her Thinking?
		Her diary keeps moving around her room.
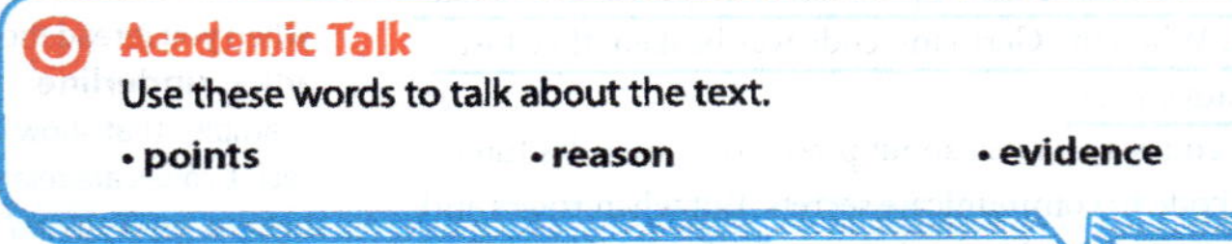 She needs a code.	Her little brother keeps reading her diary.	She keeps finding it open.
		Her brother tells her to write more neatly.

Talk Share your chart with a partner.

- What does the girl think?
- Why does she think what she thinks?
- What evidence supports her thinking?

Academic Talk
Use these words to talk about the text.
- points
- reason
- evidence

337

Think

- Have students read aloud the Think section. Explain that the chart will help them organize their thinking.
- Have partners complete the chart. Remind students to use the girl's words in the comic strip to identify her reason and her evidence.
- As students work, circulate and provide assistance as needed.
- Ask volunteers to share what they wrote in their charts.
- Make certain students understand that a point is explained by one or more reasons and supported by evidence.

Talk

- Read aloud the Talk prompts.
- Review that evidence often consists of facts and examples. Have partners discuss whether each piece of evidence in their charts is a fact, an example, or both.
- Ask volunteers to share their ideas.

Quick Write Have students write a response to the following prompt:

> **Should students be allowed to use their music or gaming devices at school? Give your opinion and tell why you feel this way. Then support your reasons with evidence.**

Ask students to share their responses.

Monitor Understanding

If... students struggle to distinguish points, reasons, and evidence, **then...** use a graphic organizer to illustrate. Ask a question such as, "Should our school cafeteria sell candy?" Gather the popular opinion and write it on the board. For example: *Our school cafeteria should not sell candy.*

- Draw two lines down from the statement and ask students to provide two reasons that explain the point. For example: *Candy is not good for us; We will spend too much money.* Record their reasons.
- Ask students to support each of their reasons with facts or examples. Draw a line down from each reason and record the evidence below. For example: *Sugar causes cavities; Candy bars cost $2.*
- Review the organizer with students and have them identify the point, reasons, and evidence and use their own words to explain how they work together.

Wrap Up

- Invite students to share what they've learned so far. Encourage them to use the Academic Talk words in their explanations.
- Explain to students that when they read nonfiction, they should look for reasons and evidence that support the author's point, or main idea.

In the next section, we'll read a history article, identify the author's main point, and explore the reasons and evidence for that point. Thinking about how the author supports his point will help you better understand the information in the text.

Monitor Understanding

Modeled and Guided Instruction

Get Started

Today you will read a history article about secret codes. First, you'll read to understand what the article is about. Then you'll read to analyze the main point and the reasons and evidence that support the point.

Read

- Read aloud the title of the article and have students infer what it might be about.
- Have students read the article independently. Tell them to place a check mark above any confusing words and phrases as they read. Remind students to look inside, around, and beyond each unknown word to help them figure out its meaning. Use the Word Learning Routine on pp. A50–A51.
- When students have finished reading, clarify the meanings of words and phrases they still find confusing. Then use the questions below to check understanding. Encourage students to identify details in the text that support their answers.

How did Julius Caesar use a code? *(He wrote letters to his generals in code.)*

Why didn't Mary's code work? *(It was too easy to "crack," or figure out.)*

What happened when the Germans used a code in World War II? *(An Englishman broke the code and took away the Germans' advantage.)*

 **English Language Learners**

● **Word Learning Strategy**

Explore

- Read aloud the Explore question at the top of p. 339 to set the purpose for the second read. Tell students they will need to take a closer look at the examples of codes described in the article.
- Have students read aloud the Close Reader Habit on p. 338.

TIP Tell students that authors will often, though not always, devote a paragraph to each reason and/or piece of evidence that supports the main point.

Read

Genre: History Article

The Power of Codes

by Alan Kim

1 Secret codes and power go hand-in-hand. Why is this so? Because a code lets one group of people communicate information in a way that keeps it secret from other groups. The group that knows the code has an advantage over the group that doesn't.

2 Take the example of Julius Caesar, an emperor of ancient Rome who conquered much of Europe and northern Africa. Caesar used letters to communicate his military plans to faraway generals. But what if an opposing army obtained copies of his letters? His plans might be foiled. So Caesar developed a code that only he and trusted members of his army understood. If an enemy intercepted Caesar's letters, they would not understand them or be able to prepare for his plans. The code gave Caesar an advantage over his opponents, letting him keep and increase his power.

3 Not all codes were as successful as Caesar's, however. In the 1500s, when Elizabeth I was Queen of England, her half-sister Mary plotted to overthrow her. Mary communicated with her allies through coded messages. However, Mary's code was easy to crack, so her plan was discovered. If Mary had used a better code, she might have risen to power as the Queen of England.

4 Codes remain important in modern times. During World War II (1939–1945), German submarines communicated in code so complicated that it was nearly unbreakable. But a brilliant Englishman named Alan Turing cracked the German code. Now that the English knew when and where a British ship would be targeted, they could fight back. When the Germans' code was broken, they lost a powerful advantage.

5 Secret codes aren't just about power, of course. It's fun to develop a code to communicate secrets. But when rulers and armies use codes, they're not doing so for fun. For them, it's serious business.

Close Reader Habits

When you reread the article, **underline** examples that show how secret codes are related both to keeping *and* to losing power.

338

English Language Learners

Build Meaning

- **Concept Map** Work with students to develop a *who-what-why* concept map around the idea of secret codes.
- Review the article with students, and guide them to add *emperor, queen, submarines* under *who*; *letters, messages* under *what*; and *communication, power, advantage* under *why*. Encourage students to use text clues to define each word, and clarify as needed.
- Invite volunteers to sum up the concept map.

● Word Learning Strategy

Analyze Word Parts

- Point out the word *intercepted* in paragraph 2. Break the word into its parts, and explain that the prefix *inter-* means "between" or "among" and the Latin root *cept* means "take" or "catch."

What other words or phrases could take the place of *intercepted* in this sentence? *(took; seized; got between the letter writer and the receiver)*

- Ask what other words students know with the prefix *inter- (interview, interchange, interstate, international)*. Ask how the meaning of "between" or "among" is related to the meaning of each word.

L.5.4b

Explore What reasons and evidence does the author use to support his idea about codes?

Think

1 The author states, "Secret codes and power go hand-in-hand." Complete the chart to explain why the author thinks this and describe three pieces of evidence supporting his thinking.

The author has an idea about the relationship between codes and power. He has to support this idea.

What Does the Author Think?	Why Does He Think This?	What Evidence Supports His Thinking?
"Secret codes and power go hand-in-hand."	Historically, a group has had an advantage if it has a code that can keep information secret from another group. Groups that have their codes broken no longer have an advantage.	Julius Caesar used a secret code in letters to his generals.
		Elizabeth I held on to her power because Mary's coded letters were too easy to figure out.
		After Alan Turing cracked the German code, the British knew when their ships were targeted.

Talk

2 How does the author support his idea about secret codes? If necessary, revise the second and third columns of your chart.

Write

3 **Short Response** The author states that a group with a secret code has an advantage over groups that do not. Explain how the author supports this idea. Use details from the passage in your response. Use the space provided on page 342 to write your answer.

HINT Use phrases such as "one example" and "a second example" to organize your response.

Think Aloud

- The Explore question asks me to identify the reasons and evidence the author uses to support his point about codes. The point is written out in the first column of the chart: "Secret codes and power go hand-in-hand."
- The first paragraph introduces the author's point. I'll keep reading until I come to a reason that explains his point about codes and power.
- In paragraph 2, the first sentence says that one "example" is Julius Caesar. The paragraph states that he used coded letters to his generals. I know that examples are a type of evidence. I'm going to write "Julius Caesar used a secret code in letters to his generals" in the last column.
- So now I need to figure out why Caesar used the code. I see the reason at the end of the paragraph: "The code gave Caesar an advantage over his opponents." That might be what I write in the *Why Does He Think This* column. But I'll wait to see what the other two body paragraphs say first.

Think

- Read aloud the Think section. Explain to students that you will model how to find text evidence to fill in part of the chart. Use the **Think Aloud** below to guide your modeling.
- Revisit the Explore question. Guide students to determine that they need to look for more details, using the Close Reader Habit.
- Encourage students to work with a partner to continue rereading the passage and complete the chart. Remind them that the Buddy Tip will help them find the reasons and evidence.
- Ask volunteers to share their completed charts.
- Guide students to see that each paragraph shows evidence (in the form of examples) that show how codes and power go hand-in-hand.

Talk

- Read aloud the Talk prompt.
- Have partners respond to the prompt. Use the Talk Routine on pp. A52–A53.
- Circulate to check that students are finding examples of times when people in history gained or lost power because they used or broke a secret code.

Write

- Ask a volunteer to read aloud the Write prompt.
- Invite a few students to tell what the prompt is asking them to do.
- Make sure students understand that they must explain how using codes led to an advantage. Remind them to use details in their charts to support their responses.
- Have students turn to p. 342 to write their response.
- Use Review Responses on p. 342 to assess students' writing.

Wrap Up

- Ask students to recall the Learning Target. Have them explain how identifying the author's reasons and supporting evidence helped them better understand this history article.

Guided Practice

Get Started

Today you will read another history article about secret codes. First, you will read to understand what the article is about. Then you will reread with a partner to analyze the author's main point, the reasons, and the evidence.

Read

- Read aloud the title of the article. Establish that a *quilt* is a blanket pieced together—usually in a pattern—from many different fabrics.
- Have students predict what the article will be about based on the title.
- **Read to Understand** Have students read the article independently. Tell them to place a check mark above any confusing words and phrases as they read. Remind students to look inside, around, and beyond each unknown word or phrase to help them figure out its meaning. Use the Word Learning Routine on pp. A50–A51.
- When students have finished reading, clarify the meanings of words and phrases they still find confusing. Then use the questions below to check understanding. Encourage students to identify details in the text that support their answers.

  What are some examples of messages that people thought the quilts contained? *(load up a wagon and prepare to head north; a friendly guide is nearby)*

  What happened to show that the ideas about slave quilts were likely untrue? *(Historians found no evidence quoting the slaves themselves. They did not find any quilts, either.)*

  What is the article mostly about? *(what slave quilts may have been, how they became a recent topic of discussion, and why the theories about them are probably unlikely)*

English Language Learners

Word Learning Strategy

- **Read to Analyze** Read aloud the Close Reader Habit on p. 340 to set the purpose for the second read. Then have students reread the article with a partner and discuss any questions they might have.

Guided Practice

Read

Genre: History Article

THE SLAVE QUILT CODE
Fact or Fiction?

by Ron Fridell

1 Back in the 1990s, an intriguing idea arose. People began claiming that during the American Civil War, 1861–1865, African slaves in the southern states used a secret code to help one another escape north to freedom.

2 This code consisted of patterns sewn into quilt blocks by slave women. For example, a pattern called *wagon wheel* meant to quickly load up a wagon and prepare to head north. And a pattern called *shoo-fly* signaled that a friendly guide waited nearby to help. Such quilts helped runaway slaves make their way along a network of routes known as the Underground Railroad to freedom.

3 Films and books sprang up about how these bedcovers with their secret messages sewn by slave women saved lives and led enslaved people to freedom. The popular Oprah Winfrey TV show even featured these claims and stories. The public loved these thrilling accounts of adventures from America's past.

4 But wait. How true were they? These quilt code accounts were exciting, yes, and people wanted them to be historically accurate. But were they?

5 Many historians have studied slavery and the Underground Railroad. These historians reviewed the evidence. None of it appeared to come directly from the slaves, they concluded. There were no letters and no news articles quoting the slaves themselves. It all came from stories passed along by word of mouth. And none of the quilts used to help runaway slaves could be found.

6 Still, many books were written concerning these oral accounts, exciting stories of secret hiding places, life-threatening encounters, and midnight escapes. But there were no documents to back up these quilt code claims. Based on the lack of strong evidence, we must conclude that quilts played no special role in the Underground Railroad.

Close Reader Habits

How does the author support the idea that quilts played no special role in the Underground Railroad? **Underline** any information supporting this idea.

340

English Language Learners

Develop Language

Cognates Reread the first sentence, and point out the words *intriguing, idea,* and *public.* Ask Spanish-speaking students (or speakers of other Latin-based languages) if they know the Spanish word for *intriguing* (*intrigante*). Do the same for *idea* and *public* (*idea; pública*).

- Explain that these words are *cognates,* or words in two languages that share a similar spelling, meaning, and sometimes, pronunciation. Ask students how recognizing cognates can help them when they read in English.
- Have students look for other cognates throughout the passage, such as *secret/secreto, code/código, slave/esclavo,* and *routes/rutas.*

Word Learning Strategy

Analyze Word Parts

- Point to the word *enslaved* in paragraph 3. Have students identify its parts *(en-, slave, -ed).* Explain that the suffix *-ed* can form adjectives, or describing words, such as *enslaved,* as well as verbs and verb forms.

  What does the prefix *en-* mean as it is used in *enslaved*? *("in"; "into"' "to put in or into")*

  What does enslaved mean? *("put into slavery"; "in a state of slavery")*

- Ask students to name other words with the prefix *en-*, such as *entomb, encircle, enrich, encode.* Guide students to explain how the meaning of each word relates to the meaning of *en-*.

L.5.4b

Think Use what you learned from reading the article to answer the following questions.

History articles can state ideas that readers find surprising. The author must give good reasons and evidence to support such ideas.

1 This question has two parts. Answer Part A. Then answer Part B.

Part A
How does the author support the idea that people wanted to believe African slaves in the South used a secret code?

A by showing that the history of the quilt code wasn't known before the 1990s, and then it became a popular topic
B by showing that experts believe the quilts' patterns had different meanings and gave signals to escaping slaves
C by showing that the slave quilt codes were related to the Underground Railroad, which is an interesting topic
(D) by showing that the stories about the quilt codes were the subjects of popular books, films, and shows

Part B
Which detail from the article supports the answer in Part A?

(A) "The popular Oprah Winfrey TV show even featured these claims. . . ."
B "Many historians have studied slavery and the Underground Railroad."
C "It all came from stories passed along by word of mouth. . . ."
D ". . . there was nothing to back up these quilt code claims."

Talk

2 The author states that quilts with secret messages played no part in helping enslaved people escape to the North. How does the author support this idea? Use the chart on page 343 to record your ideas and the evidence.

Write

3 **Short Response** How does the author support the idea about quilts not having secret messages? Provide **two** examples of the evidence the author uses to support the idea. Use the space provided on page 343 to write your answer.

HINT Start by restating the author's conclusion. Then tell how he supports it.

● Integrating Standards

Use the following questions to further students' understanding of the article.

- **How did media help to spread misinformation about the slave quilts?** *(They presented the idea that messages about escaping to freedom were sewn into slave quilts.)*
  DOK 2 RI.5.3
- **Summarize the article's main idea and key details.** *(In the 1990s, the public believed that secret messages about escaping to freedom had been sewn into slave quilts. Media endorsed this idea, but historians could not find evidence to support it. The author concludes that quilts did not play a role in helping slaves escape to freedom.)*
  DOK 2 RI.5.2

● Monitor Understanding

If... students have difficulty answering Part A,

then... model looking back at the text to find the answer. Work with students to annotate the main purpose of each paragraph, beginning with paragraph 1 (introduces the idea of slave quilts as codes). After you finish, discuss which paragraph answers the question. *(paragraph 3)*

Think

- Have students work with a partner to complete item 1.

TIP Remind students that *idea* is a synonym for *point*. Have them reframe the question: *What evidence supports the author's point that people wanted to believe African slaves in the South used a secret code?*

Answer Analysis

When students have finished, discuss correct and incorrect responses.

1 **Part A**
The correct choice is D. The popularity of media stories about slave quilts is evidence that the stories became well known among the public. **A** and **C** do not explain why the stories became well known in the 1990s. **B** is not supported by text details.

Part B
The correct choice is A. It connects the idea of the secret codes in quilts to the mass popularity of the idea. **B, C,** and **D** are not about how quilt codes became the subject of books, films, and television shows.
DOK 3

● **Monitor Understanding**

● **Integrating Standards**

Talk

- Have partners discuss the prompt. Emphasize that students should support their ideas with text details.
- Circulate to clarify misunderstandings.

Write

- See p. 343 for instructional guidance.

Wrap Up

- Ask students to recall the Learning Target and explain how identifying the author's point, reasons, and evidence helped them better understand the article.

Modeled and Guided Instruction

Write

- Remember to use the Response-Writing Routine on pp. A54–A55.

Review Responses

After students complete the writing activity, help them evaluate their responses.

3 Responses may vary but should include specific examples of advantages such as Caesar's advantage over his opponents and the British advantage over the Germans. Students may also use the example of how a bad code, such as the code used by Mary, proved to be a disadvantage. See the sample response on the student book page.
DOK 3

Write Use the space below to write your answer to the question on page 339.

The Power of Codes

HINT Use phrases such as "one example" and "a second example" to organize your response.

3 **Short Response** The author states that a group with a secret code has an advantage over groups that do not. Explain how the author supports this idea. Use details from the passage in your response.

Sample response: Alan Kim uses examples from history to support his idea that a group with a secret code has an advantage over groups that do not. One example is Julius Caesar, who used a code to describe his plans to members of his army. It would not matter if Caesar's enemies intercepted his letters, because they would not be able to understand what they said. This gave Caesar an advantage over his enemies. A second example is the work of Alan Turing, who cracked a German code that conveyed messages about submarine warfare. Because Turing cracked that code, the Germans lost a big advantage over the British in World War II.

Don't forget to check your writing.

Check Your Writing

- ☐ Did you read the prompt carefully?
- ☐ Did you put the prompt in your own words?
- ☐ Did you use the best evidence from the text to support your ideas?
- ☐ Are your ideas clearly organized?
- ☐ Did you write in clear and complete sentences?
- ☐ Did you check your spelling and punctuation?

Scaffolding Support for Reluctant Writers

If students are having a difficult time getting started, use the strategies below. Work individually with struggling students, or have students work with partners.

- Circle the verbs in the prompt that tell you what to do, such as *describe*, *explain*, or *compare*.
- Underline words and phrases in the prompt that show what information you need to provide in your response, such as *causes*, *reasons*, or *character traits*.
- Talk about the details from the text that you will include in your response.
- Explain aloud how you will respond to the prompt.

THE SLAVE QUILT CODE

Fact or Fiction?

2 Use the chart below to organize your ideas and evidence.

What Does the Author Think?	Why Does He Think This?	What Evidence Supports His Thinking?

Write Use the space below to write your answer to the question on page 341.

HINT Start by restating the author's conclusion. Then tell how he supports it.

3 **Short Response** How does the author support the idea about quilts not having secret messages? Provide **two** examples of the evidence the author uses to support the idea.

Sample response: Ron Fridell concludes, "quilts played no special role in the Underground Railroad." To support his conclusion, Fridell states that historians who studied the Underground Railroad have found no concrete evidence, such as the quilts themselves. Fridell also states that historians found no letters or news articles including quotes from enslaved or escaped people about such quilts. Lacking evidence in the form of either quilts or documents, the author believes that we cannot assume that quilts with secret codes played a role in the Underground Railroad.

343

Teacher Notes

Talk

2 Students should use the chart to organize their thoughts and evidence.

Write

- Ask a volunteer to read aloud the Write prompt.
- Invite students to tell what the prompt is asking them to do. Make sure they understand that they need to state the evidence for the author's point about the quilts not being codes.
- Call attention to the HINT.
- Remember to use the Response-Writing Routine on pp. A54–A55.

Review Responses

After students complete the writing activity, help them evaluate their responses.

3 Responses may vary but should include at least two of these three examples given in the article: Letters to and from slaves did not show evidence; articles of the time did not show evidence; no such slave quilts were actually found. See the sample response on the student book page.
DOK 3

Independent Practice

Get Started

Today you are going to read a history article and use what you have learned about reasons and evidence to analyze how the author supports his main points.

- Ask a volunteer to explain why making connections between points, reasons, and evidence will help readers better understand informational texts. Encourage students to use the Academic Talk words in their response.

English Language Learners

Read

You are going to read the history article independently and use what you have learned to think and write about the text. As you read, remember to look closely at the details in the text to identify the author's main point, reasons, and supporting evidence.

- Read aloud the title of the article and then encourage students to preview the text, paying close attention to the photographs and captions.
- Call attention to the Words to Know in the upper left of p. 344.
- If students need support in reading the passage, you may wish to use the Monitor Understanding suggestions.
- When students have finished, have them complete the Think and Write sections.

● **Monitor Understanding**

Read

Genre: History Article

WORDS TO KNOW
As you read, look inside, around, and beyond these words to figure out what they mean.
- **intercepting**
- **dialects**
- **barren**

FROM

by Bruce Watson, *Odyssey*

1 On the sands of Iwo Jima island, any other World War II code machine would have been too slow to use in the heat of battle. But the Marines had highly mobile crytographs[1], each with two arms, two legs, and an unbreakable code. . . .

2 *Naastosi Thanzie Dibeh Shida Dahnestsa Tkin Shush Wollachee Moasi Lin Achi.*

3 Ordinary Marines listening to this babble were as baffled as Japanese soldiers intercepting the messages. Had they spoken Navajo, they would have recognized the words —"Mouse Turkey Sheep Uncle Ram Ice Bear Ant Cat Horse Intestines."

4 But what could such nonsense mean? To the Navajo Code Talkers, the first letter of each word spelled out Mt. Suribachi. Other code filled in the announcement: Iwo Jima was under American control.

5 The Navajo Code Talkers were unique in cryptographic history. From 1942 to 1945, more than 400 Code Talkers stormed the beaches of Pacific islands. Instantly encoding and decoding messages, they helped Marines win the war in the Pacific. Even today, their code remains one of the few in history that was never broken.

The Navajo Code Talkers played an important role during World War II. Shown below are two Code Talkers in a jungle close to the front lines.

[1]cryptographs: code-makers

English Language Learners

Develop Language

Metaphor Read aloud the title "Human Code Machines." Invite students to use cognates if possible to connect words from the title to words in their first languages.

- Explain that the title is a metaphor, or a comparison between two things. Ask:

  What does a code machine do? *(creates codes quickly and repeatedly)*

  What do you think a *human code machine* is? *(a person who makes codes quickly and repeatedly)*

- Preview the text with students. Have them describe what they see in the pictures, and invite volunteers to read the captions aloud. Have them predict what the text will be about, based on the pictures, captions, and title.

When World War II broke out, hundreds of Navajo men volunteered to fight for the United States. This photo shows two Navajo Code Talkers being trained at an army base in Australia.

6 When World War II began, hundreds of Navajo men volunteered to fight. Most had never been off their reservation, a high, barren plain stretching across Arizona, Utah, and New Mexico. There they lived as a separate nation, as many still do today. The reservation had no electricity or indoor plumbing, and only a few schools. Most Navaho herded sheep and bought from government trading posts what little they needed and could not make. They spoke some English, but the business of their daily lives was conducted in their own language.

7 Among languages that were spoken by only tens of thousands of Americans, Navajo was the language least likely to be known to foreigners. The language was entirely oral. Not a single book had ever been written in Navajo. . . .

8 The Navajo code was proposed by a non-Navajo, Philip Johnston, the son of missionaries on the reservation. Marine officers were skeptical at first. American armies had used other Indian languages to send messages during World War I. Yet because the ancient dialects had no words for machine gun or tank, the experiment failed. Johnston had a better idea—a language combined with a code. . . .

Monitor Understanding

If... students struggle to read and understand the passage,

then... use these scaffolding suggestions:

Question the Text Preview the text by asking the following questions:

- **Based on the title and photographs, what do you predict the article will be about?**
- **What questions do you have about the text?**

Vocabulary Support Define words that may interfere with comprehension, such as the idiom *heat of battle,* as well as *encoding and decoding.*

Read Aloud Read aloud the text with students. You could also have students chorally read the text in a small group.

Check Understanding Use the questions below to check understanding. Encourage students to cite details in the text that support their answers.

- **Where did the Navajo Code Talkers do their work?** *(They worked to develop the code before they went to battle; then they worked on the battlefield.)*
- **Why was the Navajo language a good choice for a secret code?** *(Foreigners were unlikely to know it. It had never been recorded in a book.)*
- **How did the Code Talkers deal with the problem of words that were not in their language?** *(They used terms from nature.)*

Independent Practice

Integrating Standards

After students have read the article, use these questions to discuss the article with them.

- **What evidence from the text helps you understand what the author means in the phrase "encoded a Navajo zoo" in paragraph 10?**

  (To create an alphabet, the Navajo used their words for different animals, such as "Wollachee" for ant, "Shush" for bear, and so on. The phrase "encoded a Navajo zoo" means their code was based on animal names.)

  DOK 2 **RI.5.1, RI.5.4**

- **The author says, "With just 400 words encoded, the Navajo put their cryptology to the acid test." What do you think the idiom "acid test" means?**

  (The context suggests that an acid test makes it clear whether the code works or doesn't work. So the idiom "put to the acid test" means to prove something is good or effective beyond doubt.)

  DOK 2 **L.5.5b**

- **How did Philip Johnston play a role in creating the Navajo code?**

  (Because he was the son of missionaries and had grown up on the Navajo reservation, he knew about the Navajo language. He suggested the idea of using the Navajo language to make an unbreakable code.)

  DOK 2 RI.5.3

- **What are the main ideas of "Human Code Machines"?**

  (One main idea is that the Navajo Code Talkers helped win the war. Another main idea is that the code they developed was unbreakable. A third main idea is that the code arose from things the Code Talkers knew already from their own language and culture, such as names for animals.)

  DOK 3 **RI.5.2**

Theme Connection

Making a Code

9 The Navajo language contained no words for the horrors of war. Bomber, battleship, grenade—all were terms foreign to the Navajo. But in making their code, the Navajo soldiers rooted it, like their lives, in nature. They named military planes after birds. *Gini*, Navajo for "chicken hawk," became "dive bomber." *Neasjah*, meaning "owl," meant "observation plane." They named ships after fish. *Lotso*, meaning "whale," was the code word for "battleship," and *beshlo*—"iron fish"—meant "submarine."

10 To spell out proper names, the Code Talkers encoded a Navajo zoo. Marines spell out abbreviations with their own alphabet, which begins Able, Baker, Charlie . . . The Navajo version began *Wollachee, Shush, Moasi*, meaning Ant, Bear, Cat.

11 Finally, Code Talkers created clever terms for friends and enemies. Lieutenant was translated as "One Silver Bar." Mussolini, Italy's fascist dictator, was *Adee-yaats-iin-Tsoh*—"Big Gourd Chin." Hitler became *Daghailchiih*—"Moustache Smeller."

In 2001, the United States awarded four Navajo Code Talkers the Congressional Medal of Honor—the highest award a soldier who has been in battle can receive.

Test Time

12 With just 400 words encoded, the Navajo put their cryptology to the acid test. They handed a message to Navy intelligence officers, who spent three weeks trying and failing to decipher it. Then, armed with a code and M-1 rifles, a few dozen Code Talkers shipped out to the Pacific. Two more remained behind to teach the code to other Navajo recruits. . . .

13 Between invasions, the Code Talkers convened[2] to encode new battle terms. Before the war ended, several were killed in action. Yet they transmitted thousands of messages without error. In a language that needs no decoding, Marine major Howard Conner assessed their contribution. "Without the Navajos," Conner said, "the Marines would never have taken Iwo Jima."

onvened: gathered

Theme Connection

- Remind students that the theme of this lesson is Code Communication.
- Ask discussion questions such as, *How do good codes work? Why are codes needed? How have codes helped Julius Caesar, the British, and the Americans?*
- Review the title of each article in this lesson. Ask: *Overall, did the authors convince you that codes are a good thing or a bad thing? Use evidence from the articles to support your point.*

Think Use what you learned from reading the history article to answer the following questions.

1 This question has two parts. First, answer Part A. Then answer Part B.

Part A
How does the author support the idea that the Navajo men who volunteered to fight in World War II had been living isolated lives?

A by stating that their messages were impossible to understand
(B) by stating that most had never been off their reservation
C by stating that they communicated orally and not in writing
D by stating that they named planes and boats after animals

Part B
Which paragraph in the text **best** supports the answer to Part A?

A paragraph 3
B paragraph 5
(C) paragraph 6
D paragraph 9

2 The author uses a word that means "doubtful" in the text. Circle a word in the paragraph that **best** represents that idea.

The Navajo code was proposed by a non-Navajo, Philip Johnston, the son of missionaries on the reservation. Marine officers were (skeptical) at first. American armies had used other Indian languages to send messages during World War I. Yet because the ancient dialects had no words for machine gun or tank, the experiment failed. Johnston had a better idea—a language combined with a code. . . .

Monitor Understanding

If... students struggle to complete the items,
then... you may wish to use the following suggestions:

Read Aloud Activities

- As you read, have students note any unfamiliar words or phrases. Clarify any misunderstandings.
- Discuss each item with students to make certain they understand the expectation.

Reread the Text

- Have students complete a chart as they reread.
- Have partners summarize the text.

Think

- Use the Monitor Understanding suggestions to support students in completing items 1–4.

Monitor Understanding

Answer Analysis

When students have finished, discuss correct and incorrect responses.

1 **Part A**
The correct choice is B. Having never been off the reservation suggests that these men had lived isolated lives.

- **A** is a claim about their messages, not about the men's lives.
- **C** does not support the idea that the men had lived isolated lives.
- **D** is a detail about their code, not support for the idea about the men's isolation before the war.

Part B
The correct choice is C. Paragraph 6 tells about the Navajo men's lives before they volunteered to fight.

- **A, B,** and **D** are paragraphs that tell about events after the men volunteered to fight.

DOK 2 **RI.5.8**

2 **See the student book page.** Students should circle the word *skeptical* as a synonym for *doubtful.*
DOK 2 **L.5.5c, RI.5.4**

Independent Practice

3 **Part A**

The correct choice is A. The author shows through examples that the Navajo Code Talkers were successful because they developed a code that combined their language and elements of their culture.

- **B, C,** and **D** are not related to how the Navajo soldiers were able to make a code related to war even though their language lacked words for it.

Part B

The correct choices are C and D. The Code Talkers' success came from combining what they knew best—nature and their own language—to produce a code that could express ideas related to war.

- **A** doesn't explain how the Navajo were able to make a code from their language.
- **B** doesn't give enough detail to show how the Navajo soldiers were able to make a good code.
- **E** is about the Marines' use of abbreviations, not the Navajo code.
- **F** is not about the code but how it was put to use.

DOK 3 RI.5.8

4 **The correct choice is C.** The fact that the code was one of the few unbroken codes in history supports the author's idea that the Navajo code was difficult to crack.

- **A** and **D** only state facts about the Navajo language and code. They do not support the author's idea that the code was hard to crack.
- **B** states an opinion, but it does not support the author's idea about the Navajo code being hard to crack.

DOK 2 RI.5.8

3 This question has two parts. First, answer Part A. Then answer Part B.

Part A

How does the author support the idea that the Navajo soldiers were able to make a code related to war even though their language lacked words for it?

- **(A)** by showing how they mixed language and culture in the code
- **B** by showing that they started by encoding 400 words
- **C** by showing how they proved the Navy couldn't break the code
- **D** by showing that they met several times to encode new terms

Part B

Which **two** details from the article support the answer in Part A?

- **A** ". . . the business of their daily lives was conducted in their own language."
- **B** ". . . Navajo was the language least likely to be known to foreigners."
- **(C)** ". . . the Navajo soldiers rooted it, like their lives, in nature."
- **(D)** "*Lotso*, meaning 'whale,' was the code word for "battleship'. . . ."
- **E** "Marines spell out abbreviations with their own alphabet. . . ."
- **F** ". . . remained behind to teach the code. . . ."

4 Which of the following **best** supports the idea that the Navajo code was hard to crack?

- **A** ". . . the first letter of each word spelled out Mt. Suribachi."
- **B** "The Navajo Code Talkers were unique in cryptographic history."
- **(C)** "Even today, their code remains one of the few in history that was never broken."
- **D** "The Navajo language contained no words for the horrors of war."

348

Monitor Understanding

If... students don't understand the writing task,

then... read aloud the writing prompt. Use the following questions to help students get started.

- **What is the prompt asking you to write about?**
- **Do you need to reread the text to find more information?**
- **How will you identify the information you need to include?**

- Have partners talk about how they will organize their responses.
- Provide a graphic organizer to assist students, if needed.

Write

5 **Short Response** The author states that the Navajo Code Talkers helped win the war in the Pacific. Explain how the author supports this idea. Use at least **two** details in your answer.

Sample response: The author states that the Code Talkers helped win the war in the Pacific because they combined the Navajo language with a code they developed from their knowledge of nature. He points out that the Code Talkers named planes after birds and spelled out proper names using Navajo names for animals. The author also states that they were successful because they quickly coded and decoded messages on the ground during battles and "transmitted thousands of messages without error."

In this lesson, you explained how an author uses reasons and evidence to support points. Explain how this work will help you better understand other informational texts that you read.

Responses may vary, but students should identify that identifying and explaining an author's reasons and evidence in an informational text will help them better understand how he or she supports those ideas.

5 2-Point Writing Rubric

Points	Focus	Evidence	Organization
2	My answer does exactly what the prompt asked me to do.	My answer is supported with plenty of details from the text.	My ideas are clear and in a logical order.
1	Some of my answer does not relate to the prompt.	My answer is missing some important details from the text.	Some of my ideas are unclear and out of order.
0	My answer does not make sense.	My answer does not have any details from the text.	My ideas are unclear and not in any order.

Write

- Tell students that using what they read, they will plan and compose a short response to the writing prompt.

Monitor Understanding

Review Responses

After students have completed each part of the writing activity, help them evaluate their responses.

5 Display or pass out copies of the reproducible **2-Point Writing Rubric** on p. TR10. Have students use the rubric to individually assess their writing and revise as needed.

When students have finished their revisions, evaluate their responses. Answers will vary but should show that the code worked because it was unbreakable. Answers may also include reasons why it was unbreakable, such as the language never having been recorded and being unfamiliar to others. See the sample response on the student book page.

DOK 3 RI.5.8, W.5.9b

Wrap Up

Learning Target

- Have each student respond in writing to the Learning Target prompt.
- When students have finished, have them share their responses. This may be done with a partner, in small groups, or as a whole class.

Lesson 20
Using Multiple Sources for Writing and Speaking

Standards Focus

Integrate information from several texts on the same topic in order to write or speak about the subject knowledgeably. RI.5.9

Lesson Objectives

Reading

- Combine information from several texts on the same topic. RI.5.9
- Use the integrated information to write or speak about the topic. RI.5.9

Writing

- Draw evidence from informational texts to support analysis and reflection. W.5.9b

Speaking and Listening

- Pose and respond to specific questions and contribute to discussions. SL.5.1c
- Review the key ideas expressed and draw conclusions. SL.5.1d

Language

- Use Greek and Latin affixes and roots as clues to the meaning of a word. L.5.4b
- Acquire and use academic and domain-specific words and phrases. L.5.6

Additional Practice: **RI.5.1, RI.5.2, RI.5.3, RI.5.4, RI.5.5**

Academic Talk

See **Glossary of Terms**, pp. TR2–TR9

- integrate
- source
- topic

Learning Progression

Grade 4	Grade 5	Grade 6
Students synthesize information from two texts to write or speak about a subject knowledgeably.	At Grade 5, the repetition of the Grade 4 standard emphasizes the importance of integrating information from multiple texts as students work toward gaining an understanding of a subject.	Grade 6 uses the strong base of the Grades 4 and 5 standards to introduce the concept of analyzing the way multiple texts work together.

Lesson Text Selections

Modeled and Guided Instruction	Guided Practice	Independent Practice
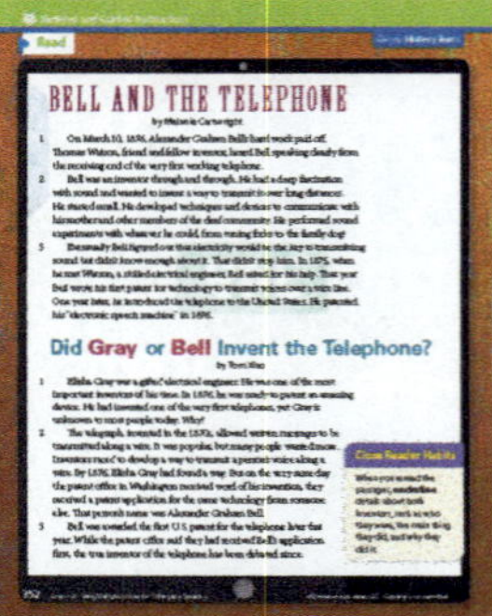	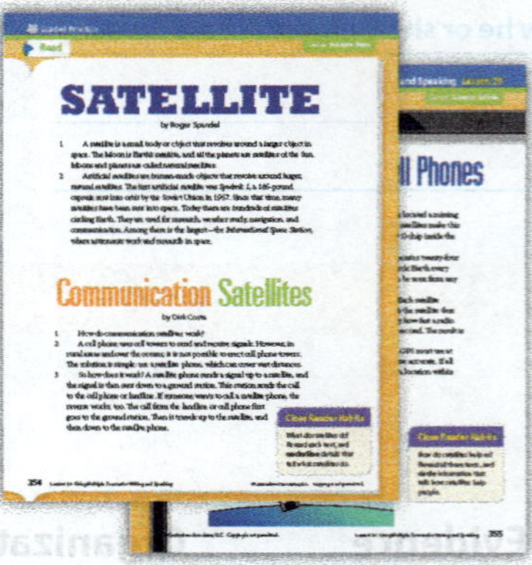	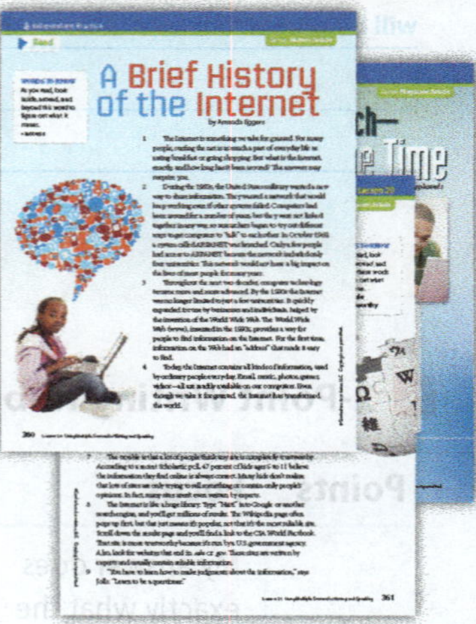
Bell and the Telephone by Melanie Cartwright **Genre:** History Text	**Satellite** by Roger Spandel **Genre:** Science Text	**A Brief History of the Internet** by Amanda Eggers **Genre:** History Article
Did Gray or Bell Invent the Telephone? by Tom Xiao **Genre:** History Text	**Communication Satellites** by Dirk Costa **Genre:** Science Text	**Get Wiki Wise** by Laura Modigliani **Genre:** Magazine Article
	How Satellites Track Cell Phones by Jane Woo **Genre:** Science Article	**Staying in Touch—All the Time** by Laurie Shinbaum **Genre:** Magazine Article

Lesson Pacing Guide

Whole Class Instruction *30–45 minutes per day*

Day 1 **Introduction** pp. 350–351
- **Read** **Using Multiple Sources for Writing and Speaking** *10 min*
- **Think** *10 min*
  Graphic Organizer: Four-Column Chart
- **Talk** *5 min*
  Quick Write (TRB) *5 min*

Day 2 **Modeled and Guided Instruction** pp. 352–353, 358
- **Read** **Bell and the Telephone** and **Did Gray or Bell Invent the Telephone?** *10 min*
- **Think** *10 min*
  Graphic Organizer: Three-Column Chart
- **Talk** *5 min*
- **Write** Short Response *10 min*

Day 3 **Guided Practice** pp. 354–357, 359
- **Read** **Satellite, Communication Satellites,** and **How Satellites Track Cell Phones** *20 min*
- **Think** *10 min*
- **Talk** *5 min*
- **Write** Short Response *10 min*

Day 4 **Independent Practice** pp. 360–367
- **Read** **A Brief History of the Internet, Get Wiki Wise,** and **Staying in Touch—All the Time** *20 min*
- **Think** *10 min*
- **Write** Extended Response *15 min*

Day 5 **Independent Practice** pp. 360–367
- *Review* Answer Analysis (TRB) *10 min*
- *Review* Response Analysis (TRB) *10 min*
- *Assign and Discuss* Learning Target *10 min*

Language Handbook
Lesson 13 Combining Sentences, pp. 462–463
20 min (optional)

Ready Writing Connection

During *Ready Reading* Days 1–5, use:
Lesson 5 Writing to Inform: Book Chapter

- **Think It Through**
- **Step 4 Organize Your Evidence**
- **Step 5 Draft**

See *Ready Writing TRB*, p. 120a for complete lesson plan.

Small Group Differentiation
Teacher-Toolbox.com

Reteach

***Ready Reading* Prerequisite Lesson**
- **Grade 4** Lesson 24 Integrating Information from Two Sources

Personalized Learning
i-Ready.com

Independent

i-Ready Close Reading Lessons

- **Grade 4** Integrating Information from Two Sources
- **Grade 5** Using Multiple Sources for Writing and Speaking

Get Started

- Explain to students that in this lesson they will read science and history texts and explore how to combine information from several sources in order to speak or write about a topic.
- Review the concept of combining things to get a more complete picture. For example, have students think about a jigsaw puzzle.
- Guide them to understand that it's not until they put all the pieces of a puzzle together that they can see the whole picture. Explain:

  When you read about a subject—such as dogs—you learn information. One text might describe different breeds of dog. Another might give information about the types of jobs certain dogs do. A third text might explain ways that you can rescue a dog. After reading all of these texts, you have a more complete understanding of the topic.
- Focus students' attention on the Learning Target. Read it aloud to set the purpose for the lesson.
- Display the Academic Talk words. Tell students to listen for these words and their meanings as you work through the lesson together. Use the Academic Talk Routine on pp. A48–A49.

- Genre Focus

Read

- Read aloud the Read section as students follow along. Restate to reinforce:

  To speak or write knowledgeably about a topic, it helps to integrate, or combine, the information from more than one source. Gathering information from multiple sources gives you a more complete understanding of the topic.
- Direct students' attention to the comic strip. Challenge them to figure out the whole message by integrating the pieces of information each character gets.

RI.5.9 Integrate information from several texts on the same topic in order to write or speak about the subject knowledgeably.

Lesson 20 Using Multiple Sources for Writing and Speaking

Putting together information from several texts on one topic will make you knowledgeable about that topic.

Read When you read, you learn information about a **topic**, or what a text is about. You can **integrate**, or put together, information on a topic from more than one **source**. As a result, you will be able to speak and write more knowledgeably about the topic.

Read this comic strip. Think about why the characters must put together information from multiple sources.

350

English Language Learners

Build Meaning

Visual Aids Remind students that *integrate* means "combine."

- Display three different images of a single topic, such as a park with trees, a park with a bench, and a park with a playground. Label each image "Park."
- Have students label what they see in each picture.
- Write the following sentence frame on the board: *You can find* ______, ______*, and* ______ *at a park.* Have students choose words from the images to fill in the blanks.
- Emphasize that students integrated information from multiple sources to make one statement about parks.

Genre Focus

Science Article

Explain that during Guided Practice, students will read three science articles about communication satellites.

Science articles usually include objective writing, or writing that is free from judgment or opinion. The topics of science articles are often related to nature, space, and technology. Writers use facts and evidence to inform or explain about these topics.

Share examples of magazine or newspaper articles on science topics, and encourage students to discuss science articles they have read.

Think Consider what you've learned so far about putting together information from different sources to get a complete picture of a topic. In the comic strip, what information about the party does each character get? Complete the chart to identify each piece of information.

Question	Answers		
	First Message	Second Message	Third Message
Where and when is the mystery party?	First Street, Palace	Tenth, The Pizza	April, at 7 P.M.

On the lines below, describe everything you know about the party after combining the information in the three messages. Use any details you can see in the comic strip as well as the information in your chart.

By combining the information in the messages, the three people can figure out they are invited to a mystery party that will take place on April 10th at 7 P.M. at The Pizza Palace on First Street.

Talk Share your chart and description with a partner.

- Did you include the same information about the second and third messages?
- How were your descriptions of the party similar and different?
- What did this activity teach you about the importance of getting information from more than one source?

Academic Talk

Use these words to talk about the text.

- integrate
- topic
- source

351

Monitor Understanding

If... students struggle to integrate information from several sources, **then...** provide an example from their everyday lives. Ask:

- **What information do you use when trying to decide which movie to see?** *(friends' opinions; movie descriptions; movie reviews)*
- **Why do you consider all of these before deciding?** *(Each source only gives me partial information. Thinking about all of the information together helps me decide whether I will like the movie.)*

Have students provide additional examples, such as what they think about before planning a party or choosing a recipe to cook.

Think

- Have students read aloud the Think section. Explain that the chart will help them organize their thinking.
- Have partners complete the chart along with the brief written response beneath it. Remind students to use the information each character received to solve the mystery of where and when the party will take place.
- As students work, circulate and provide assistance as needed.
- Ask volunteers to share what they wrote for each part of the activity.
- Make certain students understand that each message includes only part of the information about the party. The three people must combine the pieces of information in their messages to figure out the invitation.

Talk

- Read aloud the Talk prompts.
- Have partners discuss the information they included in their charts. Encourage students to compare their descriptions of the party.
- Ask volunteers to share their ideas.

Quick Write Have students write a response to the following prompt:

Think about a mystery story or movie you've read or seen. Explain how putting together clues, or different pieces of information, helped you or a character solve the mystery.

Ask students to share their responses.

Wrap Up

- Invite students to share what they've learned so far. Encourage them to use the Academic Talk words in their explanations.
- Explain to students that when they read more than one text about the same topic, they can combine information from the texts for a more complete understanding of the topic.

In the next section, we'll read two history texts about the invention of the telephone and explore how using more than one source gives us a better understanding of the topic.

Monitor Understanding

Modeled and Guided Instruction

Get Started

Today you will read two history texts about the invention of the telephone. First, you'll read to understand what the texts are about. Then you'll read to analyze and combine information from both sources.

Read

- Read aloud the title of each passage and invite students to predict the topic.
- Have students read the texts independently. Tell them to place a check mark above any confusing words and phrases as they read. Remind students to look inside, around, and beyond each unknown word to help them figure out its meaning. Use the Word Learning Routine on pp. A50–A51.
- When students have finished reading, clarify the meanings of words and phrases they still find confusing. Then use the questions below to check understanding. Encourage students to identify details in the text that support their answers.

  Who were Bell and Gray? *(inventors who created some of the first telephones)*

  Why did Bell and Gray invent the telephone at the same time? *(The telegraph had been invented to send written messages and many inventors were working to find a way to send voices over a wire.)*

  Why do most people credit Bell with inventing the telephone? *(The patent office said they received his application first.)*

English Language Learners

● Word Learning Strategy

Explore

- Read aloud the Explore question at the top of p. 353 to set the purpose for the second read. Tell students they will need to take a closer look at both sources to answer this question.
- Have students read aloud the Close Reader Habit on p. 352.

TIP Remind students to ask themselves the following question as they read: *Who invented the telephone?* They should think about how each source answers this question.

Modeled and Guided Instruction

Read

Genre: History Texts

BELL AND THE TELEPHONE

by Melanie Cartwright

1 On March 10, 1876, Alexander Graham Bell's hard work paid off. Thomas Watson, friend and fellow inventor, heard Bell speaking clearly from the receiving end of the very first working telephone.

2 Bell was an inventor through and through. He had a deep fascination with sound and wanted to invent a way to transmit it over long distances. He started small. He developed techniques and devices to communicate with his mother and other members of the deaf community. He performed sound experiments with whatever he could, from tuning forks to the family dog!

3 Eventually Bell figured out that electricity would be the key to transmitting sound but didn't know enough about it. That didn't stop him. In 1875, when he met Watson, a skilled electrical engineer, Bell asked for his help. That year Bell wrote his first patent for technology to transmit voices over a wire line. One year later, he introduced the telephone to the United States. He patented his "electronic speech machine" in 1876.

Did Gray or Bell Invent the Telephone?

by Tom Xiao

1 Elisha Gray was a gifted electrical engineer. He was one of the most important inventors of his time. In 1876, he was ready to patent an amazing device. He had invented one of the very first telephones, yet Gray is unknown to most people today. Why?

2 The telegraph, invented in the 1870s, allowed written messages to be transmitted along a wire. It was popular, but many people wanted more. Inventors raced to develop a way to transmit a person's voice along a wire. By 1876, Elisha Gray had found a way. But on the very same day the patent office in Washington received word of his invention, they received a patent application for the same technology from someone else. That person's name was Alexander Graham Bell.

3 Bell was awarded the first U.S. patent for the telephone later that year. While the patent office said they had received Bell's application first, the true inventor of the telephone has been debated since.

Close Reader Habits

When you reread the passages, **underline** details about both inventors, such as who they were, the main thing they did, and why they did it.

352

English Language Learners

Develop Language

Concept Vocabulary To help students comprehend these passages, make sure they understand what *patent* means.

- Explain that *patent* can be both a noun and a verb. Write the following sentence frames on the board:

  Bell got a _________ *for the telephone.*

  Gray tried to _________ *the telephone at the same time.*

- Guide students to complete each sentence and identify the part of speech for each use of *patent.*
- Discuss the meaning of *patent* based on the information in each passage. Help students determine that it is "the right to build, use, or sell an invention" (noun) or "to establish as one's own" (verb).

● Word Learning Strategy

Analyze Word Parts

- Point out the word *transmit* in paragraph 2 of the first passage. Write the word on the board and break it apart into *trans-* and *mit.*
- Explain that *trans-* is a prefix meaning "across, or through," and *mit* is a Latin root meaning "send." Help students determine that in this sentence, *transmit* means "sending sound through a wire."
- Follow the same procedure with the word *telegraph. Tele-* means "far off" or "at a distance" and *graph* means "write."
- Invite students to share examples of words containing *trans-, tele-, mit,* and *graph.*

L.5.4b

Explore How does integrating information from both passages help you understand Alexander Graham Bell's and Elisha Gray's work?

Figure out the topic of the texts. What does each text add to your knowledge of it?

Think

1 Complete the chart below by using information from both passages.

Questions	Answers: "Bell and the Telephone"	Answers: "Did Gray or Bell Invent the Telephone?"
Who were Bell and Gray?	Bell was an inventor.	Gray was an electrical engineer and inventor.
What work did they do?	Bell patented his "electronic speech machine" in 1876.	Gray invented one of the first telephones in 1876.
Why did they do it?	Bell wanted to send sound over distances.	Gray wanted to find a way to send a person's voice over a wire, improving on the concept of the telegraph.

Talk

2 Compare the details you used to fill out the charts. Do the details you chose truly answer those questions? Are there more details you should add? Revise your chart if you need to.

Write

3 **Short Response** Explain who Bell and Gray were, the main thing each man did, and why they did it. Use details from both passages in your response. Use the space provided on page 358 to write your answer.

HINT The prompt shows a way to organize your response.

353

Think Aloud

- The Explore question is asking me to figure out how integrating information from both passages helps me understand these scientists' work.
- I need to find answers to the questions in the first column of the chart. I'll start by rereading the first paragraph of "Bell and the Telephone." I learn that on March 10, 1876, Bell and his friend, "a fellow inventor," spoke to each other over "the very first working telephone." The first sentence in paragraph 2 confirms this. I'll write "Bell was an inventor" in the chart under *"Bell and the Telephone."*
- Now I'll keep reading to find examples of Bell's work that are provided in this passage.

Think

- Read aloud the Think section. Explain to students that you will model how to find text evidence to fill in part of the chart. Use the **Think Aloud** below to guide your modeling.
- Revisit the Explore question. Guide students to determine that they need to look for more details, using the Close Reader Habit.
- Encourage students to work with a partner to continue rereading the texts and complete the chart. Remind them that the Buddy Tip will help them integrate, or combine, the information in the two texts.
- Ask volunteers to share their completed charts.
- Guide students to see that using two sources gives them a more complete understanding of the history of the telephone because they learned that Elisha Gray may have invented the telephone before Alexander Graham Bell.

Talk

- Read aloud the Talk prompt.
- Have partners respond to the prompt. Use the Talk Routine on pp. A52–A53.
- Circulate to check that students are discussing and writing about the details in their charts. Point out that they may want to add details based on their discussions.

Write

- Ask a volunteer to read aloud the Write prompt.
- Invite a few students to tell what the prompt is asking them to do.
- Make sure students understand that they need to respond to each part of the prompt, using details from both passages.
- Have students turn to p. 358 to write their response.
- Use Review Responses on p. 358 to assess students' writing.

Wrap Up

- Ask students to recall the Learning Target. Have them explain how integrating information from two sources helped them better understand the topic.

Guided Practice

Get Started

Today you will read three science texts about communication. First, you will read to understand what the texts are about. Then you will reread with a partner to combine information from the sources.

Read

- Read aloud the title of each text. Invite students to share whether they know the meaning of *satellite* or have heard the word used in a certain way. Students may suggest *satellite dish* or *satellite radio* as familiar terms.
- **Read to Understand** Have students read the texts independently. Tell them to place a check mark above any confusing words and phrases as they read. Remind students to look inside, around, and beyond each unknown word or phrase to help them figure out its meaning. Use the Word Learning Routine on pp. A50–A51.
- When students have finished reading, clarify the meanings of words and phrases they still find confusing. Then use the questions below to check understanding. Encourage students to identify details in the text that support their answers.

  What is a *satellite?* *(a small body or object that revolves around a larger object in space)*

  What is an artificial satellite? *(a satellite made by humans and sent into orbit in space)*

  Why are communication satellites needed? *(It is not possible to erect cell towers in rural areas or over oceans; They can help find missing persons using the GPS chip in the phone.)*

  How is a GPS chip used to track a cell phone? *(Satellites send radio signals that can be picked up by a chip in a GPS on Earth. The satellite can calculate the distance using a formula based on the speed of a radio wave.)*

  What is the shared topic of all three passages? *(satellites and their uses)*

English Language Learners

• Word Learning Strategy

Guided Practice

Read

Genre: Science Texts

SATELLITE

by Roger Spandel

1 A satellite is a small body or object that revolves around a larger object in space. The Moon is Earth's satellite, and all the planets are satellites of the Sun. Moons and planets are called natural satellites.

2 Artificial satellites are human-made objects that revolve around larger, natural satellites. The first artificial satellite was *Sputnik 1*, a 185-pound capsule sent into orbit by the Soviet Union in 1957. Since that time, many satellites have been sent into space. Today there are hundreds of satellites circling Earth. They are used for research, weather study, navigation, and communication. Among these is the largest—the *International Space Station*, where astronauts work and research in space.

Communication Satellites

by Dirk Costa

1 How do communication satellites work?

2 A cell phone uses cell towers to send and receive signals. However, in rural areas and over the oceans, it is not possible to erect cell phone towers. The solution is simple: use a satellite phone, which can cover vast distances.

3 So how does it work? A satellite phone sends a signal up to a satellite, and the signal is then sent down to a ground station. This station sends the call to the cell phone or landline. If someone wants to call a satellite phone, the reverse works, too. The call from the landline or cell phone first goes to the ground station. Then it travels up to the satellite, and then down to the satellite phone.

Close Reader Habits

What do satellites do? Reread each text, and **underline** details that tell what satellites do.

354

English Language Learners

Build Meaning

- **Visual Aids** Display pictures of key terms from these passages, including *artificial satellite, cell tower,* and *rural.* As you display each image, have students describe what they notice.
- Encourage partners to draw and label a diagram or picture of what each passage describes. For example, to represent "Satellite," students might draw a smaller object revolving around a larger object. Have them write notes or short sentences explaining their pictures.
- Invite partners to share their pictures with the class. Encourage classmates to support one another by supplying missing vocabulary or correcting any misunderstanding about the content of the passage.

• Word Learning Strategy

Analyze Word Parts

- Point out the word *revolves* in paragraph 1 of "Satellite." Write it on the board, and break it into its parts.
- Explain that *re-* is a prefix and ask if anyone knows its meaning. *("back" or "again")* Then explain that *volv* is a Latin root that means "roll." Ask students to define *revolve. ("to move or turn around.")*
- Follow the same procedure for *television* in paragraph 1 of "How Satellites Track Cell Phones." *Tele-* means "far, over a distance," and *vision* comes from the Latin *vid* that means "see."

L.5.4b

Genre: Science Article

How Satellites Track Cell Phones

by Jane Woo

1 You might have seen television shows where the police located a missing person by locating his or her cell phone. Communication satellites make this possible if the phone has a Global Positioning System (GPS) chip inside the phone.

2 Some 22,000 miles high above us, the United States operates twenty-four communication satellites that orbit Earth. The satellites circle Earth every twelve hours. They are positioned so that five satellites can be seen from any point on Earth at any time of the day.

3 These satellites transmit radio signals down to Earth. Each satellite measures the time it takes for a signal from a chip to reach the satellite (less than one-tenth of a second). Then it multiplies the time by how fast a radio wave moves—some 186,000 miles (300,000 kilometers) a second. The result is the distance between the GPS chip and the satellite.

4 To determine an accurate location of a cell phone, the GPS must use at least three satellites. Four satellites make the data even more accurate. If all this sounds unbelievable, imagine this: GPS can pinpoint a location within 35 feet!

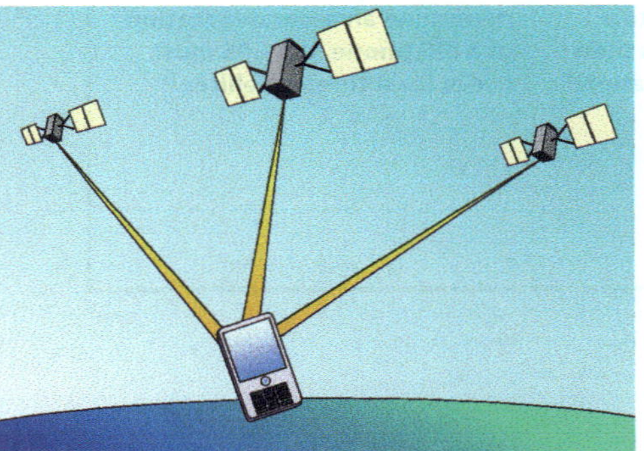

Close Reader Habits

How do satellites help us? Reread all three texts, and **circle** information that tells how satellites help people.

Monitor Understanding

If... students have difficulty combining information,

then... make a three-column chart, and write the title of each passage in the columns. For each column, ask:

- **What is this text about?**

Jot notes in the appropriate column for each passage. Then ask:

- **What does every passage tell about?**

Guide students to identify that together, the passages inform them about satellites and communication. Separately, each passage explains what a satellite is or a specific way in which it communicates.

- **Read to Analyze** Read aloud the Close Reader Habits on pp. 354 and 355 to set the purpose for the second read. Then have students reread the texts with a partner and discuss any questions they might have.

TIP If students have trouble deciding which details to underline and circle, suggest that they reword the questions in the Close Reader Habits. For example, *What do satellites do?* might be reworded as, *How do satellites work?* The second question, *How do satellites help us?* might be reworded as, *What do we use satellites for?*

Guided Practice

Think

- Have students work with a partner to complete items 1–3. Draw attention to the boldface words in each item.

TIP Make certain students understand that each item names one or more specific passages. Students must look for evidence in those passages only in order to find the correct answer.

Answer Analysis

When students have finished, discuss correct and incorrect responses.

1 Part A

The correct choice is D. Both passages explain how cell phones can use satellites to relay data.

- **A** and **C** show information only found in "How Satellites Track Cell Phones."
- **B** shows information only found in "Communication Satellites."

Part B

See the answers on the student book page. Discuss students' responses to make sure they understand which details came from each passage. Remind students that this item simulates drag-and-drop items they may see on computer-based assessments.

DOK 4

● **Monitor Understanding**

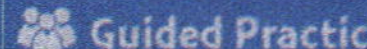

Guided Practice

Think Use what you learned from reading the passages to answer the following questions.

1 This question has two parts. Answer Part A. Then answer Part B.

Part A
Which idea is in both "Communication Satellites" and "How Satellites Track Cell Phones"?

A Satellites orbit the Earth every 12 hours.
B In rural areas, it is not always possible to build cell towers.
C Some cell phones have a Global Positioning System.
(D) Phones can use satellites to send and receive data.

Part B
Choose **one** sentence from "Communication Satellites" and **one** sentence from "How Satellites Track Cell Phones" that support the answer to Part A. Write each sentence in the appropriate "Supporting Detail" box below.

Supporting Detail from "Communication Satellites"	Supporting Detail from "How Satellites Track Cell Phones"
Possible response: "A satellite phone sends a signal up to a satellite, and the signal is then sent down to a ground station."	Possible response: "To determine an accurate location of a cell phone, the GPS must use at least three satellites."

356

● **Monitor Understanding**

If... students have difficulty finding supporting details for item 1, Part B,

then... make sure they understand that the correct answer to Part A is "Cell phones can use satellites to send and receive data." Then have students review the two selections to find a detail from each that is about signals between satellites and phones on the ground.

2 Based on information found in both “Satellite” and “Communication Satellites,” which idea is **true**?

- A The first satellite was put in orbit around Earth in 1957.
- B A cell phone relies on cell towers.
- (C) There are special satellites that are used for communication.
- D Satellite phones allow communication over long distances.

Science texts often cover topics that are very broad. Authors can choose to focus on one part of the topic to make the text more useful to the reader.

3 Satellites help us to communicate with each other. Choose **one** detail from “Satellite” and **one** detail from “How Satellites Track Cell Phones” that **best** support this idea.

- A “. . . object that revolves around a larger object. . . . ” (“Satellite”)
- (B) “. . . used for research, weather, study, navigation, and communication.” (“Satellite”)
- C “. . . astronauts work and research in space.” (“Satellite”)
- (D) “. . . satellites transmit radio signals down to Earth.” (“How Satellites Track Cell Phones”)
- E “. . . less than one-tenth of a second. . . .” (“How Satellites Track Cell Phones”)
- F “. . . GPS can pinpoint a location within 35 feet.” (“How Satellites Track Cell Phones”)

Talk

4 How do satellites help us? Consider the information you read in all three sources. Use the chart on page 359 to organize information from each source to answer the question.

HINT Think about what satellites do, then think about how that can help us.

Write

5 **Short Response** Using information from all three sources, explain how satellites help us. Use the space provided on page 359 to write your answer.

2 **The correct choice is C.** It is the only choice with information found in both texts.

- **A** has information only found in “Satellite.”
- **B** and **D** have information only found in “Communication Satellites.”

DOK 4

3 **The correct choices are B and D.** “Satellite” states that satellites are used for communication, among other things. The fact that satellites transmit radio signals to Earth supports the idea that satellites help make communication possible.

- **A, C, E,** and **F** do not support the idea that satellites make communication possible.

DOK 4

● **Integrating Standards**

Talk

- Have partners discuss the prompt. Emphasize that students should support their ideas with text details.
- Circulate to clarify misunderstandings.

Write

- Ask a volunteer to read aloud the Write prompt.
- Invite students to tell what the prompt is asking them to do. Make sure they understand that they need to use all three sources.
- Call attention to the HINT.
- Have students turn to p. 359 to write their response.
- Use Review Responses on p. 359 to assess students’ writing.

Wrap Up

- Ask students to recall the Learning Target. Have them explain how integrating information from three sources helped them understand the topic.

● Integrating Standards

Use the following questions to further students’ understanding of the articles.

- **How does the word *pinpoint* in paragraph 4 of “How Satellites Track Cell Phones” help to explain the ability of satellites and GPS chips to track a cell phone?** (Pinpoint *has two smaller words,* pin *and* point. *The point of a pin is a very small area. GPS has the ability to find an exact location if it uses at least three satellites. The author says “GPS can pinpoint a location within 35 feet!” That’s very accurate from about ”22,000 miles high.”)*
  DOK 2 RI.5.1, L.5.4b
- **Explain the relationship between communication satellites and cell phones.** *(People communicate by means of communication satellites and satellite phones where cell phones don’t work, such as in rural areas and over the oceans. Also, communication satellites help people locate a cell phone if the phone has a GPS chip.)*
  DOK 3 RI.5.3

Modeled and Guided Instruction

Write

- Remember to use the Response-Writing Routine on pp. A54–A55.

Review Responses

After students complete the writing activity, help them evaluate their responses.

3 Responses may vary but should show that Bell and Gray were inventors who separately invented telephones in 1876 and applied for patents on the same day. See the sample response on the student book page. *DOK 4*

Write Use the space below to write your answer to the question on page 353.

BELL AND THE TELEPHONE

Did Gray or Bell Invent the Telephone?

3 **Short Response** Explain who Bell and Gray were, the main thing each man did, and why they did it. Use details from both passages in your response.

HINT The prompt shows a way to organize your response.

Sample response: Alexander Graham Bell and Elisha Gray were inventors. Both wanted to invent a machine that would let people speak over distances along a wire. Bell figured out that electricity was the key and asked an electrical engineer to help him. Both men eventually figured out how to send sound along a wire, and did so at about the same time. In 1876, Bell got a patent for his "electronic speech machine." On the same day, Gray applied for a patent.

Don't forget to check your writing.

Check Your Writing

- ☐ Did you read the prompt carefully?
- ☐ Did you put the prompt in your own words?
- ☐ Did you use the best evidence from the text to support your ideas?
- ☐ Are your ideas clearly organized?
- ☐ Did you write in clear and complete sentences?
- ☐ Did you check your spelling and punctuation?

358

Scaffolding Support for Reluctant Writers

If students are having a difficult time getting started, use the strategies below. Work individually with struggling students, or have students work with partners.

- Circle the verbs in the prompt that tell you what to do, such as *describe*, *explain*, or *compare*.
- Underline words and phrases in the prompt that show what information you need to provide in your response, such as *causes*, *reasons*, or *character traits*.
- Talk about the details from the text that you will include in your response.
- Explain aloud how you will respond to the prompt.

SATELLITE

Communication Satellites

How Satellites Track Cell Phones

4 Use the chart below to organize your ideas.

Question	Answers		
	"Satellite"	"Communication Satellites"	"How Satellites Track Cell Phones"
How do satellites help us?			

Write Use the space below to write your answer to the question on page 357.

5 **Short Response** Using information from all three sources, explain how satellites help us.

Sample response: Satellites help us because they are used for research, studying weather, and communicating with others over long distances. Where cell towers can't be constructed, such as over oceans, a satellite phone sends a signal to a satellite. That signal is then sent down to ground, and the ground station sends the call to the cell phone. Finally, because satellites transmit radio signals to Earth, they make it possible to locate a cell phone on Earth using the Global Positioning System.

Teacher Notes

Talk

4 Students should use the chart to organize their thoughts and evidence.

Write

- Remember to use the Response-Writing Routine on pp. A54–A55.

Review Responses

After students complete the writing activity, help them evaluate their responses.

5 Responses may vary but should explain that satellites help us do research, study weather, and communicate over long distances. Responses should include the ideas that satellites transmit radio signals to Earth, making it possible to use cell phones in places where cell towers can't be built and to locate a cell phone that has a Global Positioning System. See the sample response on the student book page.
DOK 4

Independent Practice

Get Started

Today you are going to read a history article and two magazine articles and use what you have learned about integrating information from multiple sources to better understand the topic.

- Ask a volunteer to explain why integrating information from multiple sources will help readers better understand a topic. Encourage students to use the Academic Talk words in their response.

 **English Language Learners**

Read

Begin by reading the first two articles. As you read independently, remember to think about the information given in each text and how the texts work together to inform you about a topic. Then you will read a third article and use what you have learned to think and write about all three texts.

- Read aloud the titles of the first two articles and then encourage students to preview the texts, thinking about how the titles can help them anticipate what they will learn.
- Call attention to the Words to Know on p. 360 and p. 361.
- If students need support in reading the texts, you may wish to use the Monitor Understanding suggestions.
- Explain that students will complete the Think and Write sections after they read a third article on the same topic.

● **Monitor Understanding**

Independent Practice

Read

Genre: History Article

WORDS TO KNOW
As you read, look inside, around, and beyond this word to figure out what it means.
- **access**

A Brief History of the Internet

by Amanda Eggers

1 The Internet is something we take for granted. For many people, surfing the net is as much a part of everyday life as eating breakfast or going shopping. But what is the Internet, exactly, and how long has it been around? The answers may surprise you.

2 During the 1960s, the United States military wanted a new way to share information. They wanted a network that would keep working even if other systems failed. Computers had been around for a number of years, but they were not linked together in any way, so researchers began to try out different ways to get computers to "talk" to each other. In October 1969, a system called ARPANET was launched. Only a few people had access to ARPANET because the network included only four universities. This network would not have a big impact on the lives of most people for many years.

3 Throughout the next two decades, computer technology became more and more advanced. By the 1990s the Internet was no longer limited to just a few universities. It quickly expanded for use by businesses and individuals, helped by the invention of the World Wide Web. The World Wide Web (www), invented in the 1990s, provides a way for people to find information on the Internet. For the first time, information on the Web had an "address" that made it easy to find.

4 Today, the Internet contains all kinds of information, used by ordinary people every day. Email, music, photos, games, videos—all are readily available on our computers. Even though we take it for granted, the Internet has transformed the world.

360

English Language Learners

Build Meaning

Prior Knowledge Prior to reading, have a discussion with students about what they already know and understand about the Internet.

- Draw a concept map on the board, and invite students to share the reasons why they use the Internet. Add their reasons to the map.
- Dig deeper into each reason and have students share, for example, how they go about searching for information. Introduce terms such as *reliable* during this discussion.
- Tell students to refer to this map as they read the next three articles. Encourage them to add terms to the map and make new connections between ideas when they have finished reading.

Genre: Magazine Article

Get Wiki Wise

by Laura Modigliani, *Scholastic News*

WORDS TO KNOW
As you read, look inside, around, and beyond these words to figure out what they mean.
- **reliable**
- **trustworthy**

1 If you've ever searched for information online, you've probably come across Wikipedia. The online encyclopedia was launched in January 2001. Today, the site includes 3.5 million articles in English alone. Wikipedia is the biggest online encyclopedia.

2 It's easy to see why people like it. The site has detailed articles on just about any topic you can think of—from Iraq and the human eye to *iCarly*.

3 But even though it's popular, does that mean you can trust it?

A Group Effort

4 Wikipedia is not like other encyclopedias. The *wiki* in its name means that anyone—even you—can write or change an entry. Because experts don't check it, the information may not always be correct.

5 Wikipedia can, however, be a helpful research tool—if you know how to use it. "It's been attacked because kids often go to Wikipedia and cite that as their only source," says Tessa Jolls. She's the president of the Center for Media Literacy in Malibu, California.

6 Jolls says Wikipedia can be a great starting point for finding more reliable sources of information. Wikipedia articles often have links to other sources.

What's Reliable?

7 The trouble is that a lot of people think any site is completely trustworthy. According to a recent Scholastic poll, 47 percent of kids ages 9 to 11 believe the information they find online is always correct. Many kids don't realize that lots of sites are only trying to sell something or contain only people's opinions. In fact, many sites aren't even written by experts.

8 The Internet is like a huge library. Type "Haiti" into Google or another search engine, and you'll get millions of results. The Wikipedia page often pops up first, but that just means it's popular, not that it's the most reliable site. Scroll down the results page and you'll find a link to the CIA World Factbook. That site is more trustworthy because it's run by a U.S. government agency. Also, look for websites that end in *.edu* or *.gov*. These sites are written by experts and usually contain reliable information.

9 "You have to learn how to make judgments about the information," says Jolls. "Learn to be a questioner."

Monitor Understanding

If... students struggle to read and understand the articles, **then...** use these scaffolding suggestions:

Question the Text Preview the texts by asking the following questions:

- **Based on the titles and illustrations, what do you predict the articles will be about?**
- **What questions do you have about the texts?**

Vocabulary Support Define words that may interfere with comprehension, such as *launched*, *network*, and *impact*.

Read Aloud Read aloud the texts with students. You could also have students chorally read the texts in small groups.

Check Understanding Use the questions below to check understanding. Encourage students to cite details in the texts that support their answers.

- **Who wanted a way to share information in the 1960s?** *(the U.S. military)*
- **Why do people use the Internet today?** *(to find information, exchange email, listen to music, share photos and videos, or play games)*
- **What makes Wikipedia a useful tool?** *(It's the biggest online encyclopedia and a good starting point for doing research because it has links to reliable sources.)*

Independent Practice

 **English Language Learners**

Read

Now you are going to read a magazine article about the Internet. As you read, think about what you read in the first two articles and what new information you discover in this article. After reading, you will combine the information from all three articles to think and write about the topic.

- Read aloud the title of the article and then encourage students to preview the text.
- Call attention to the Words to Know in the upper left of p. 362.
- If students need support in reading the passage, you may wish to use the Monitor Understanding suggestions.
- When students have finished, have them complete the Think and Write sections.

● **Monitor Understanding**

Genre: Magazine Article

WORDS TO KNOW
As you read, look inside, around, and beyond these words to figure out what they mean.
- **media**
- **virtual**
- **network**

by Laurie Shinbaum, *Appleseeds*

1 Do you like being poked?

2 Most people don't—unless it's on Facebook, a popular Internet site. Facebook members can poke a friend, which is a message that loosely means, "Hey, I'm still here!"

3 Not that long ago, Facebook did not exist. Today, social networking sites like Facebook make staying in touch easier than ever.

4 You know what a network is—a set of links or ties between one place, person, or thing and another. What about social? Social means having to do with groups of people, or society. So a social network is a set of links among people. Sometimes these sites are also called "social media."

5 Social networking sites like Facebook, Twitter, Ning, and MySpace are websites that connect people on the Internet. Through them, people are able to meet, speak, and share information with each other. These sites create virtual communities for adults—and sometimes teenagers. Today, we use the word *virtual* to mean something that exists but not in actual form. For example, Facebook creates a real community, but it is not a physical community like your town.

362

 **English Language Learners**

Build Language

Concept Vocabulary Explain to students that the popularity of the Internet has created a new vocabulary. Work together to review and discuss some common terms.

- Ask whether students know what a bird's tweet sounds like. Note that the sound is short, and explain that we now use *tweet* on the social networking site Twitter to mean "a very short message." Point out that *tweet* can be both a noun and a verb. Demonstrate with a sentence for each: *I posted a tweet about my new hobby; I tweeted about my new hobby.*
- Repeat with terms such as *blog, network,* and *app.*

6 Facebook is one of the most popular social networking sites. It was created on a college campus in 2004. At first, it was open only to college students. Now you can join Facebook if you are over 13. (Between 13 and 18, you must be a high school or college student.) More than 500 million people around the world have joined.

7 Twitter is another hugely successful network. On Twitter people send short messages called "tweets" to and from cell phones and computers. A tweet can be no longer than 140 characters.

8 Schools use social networking, too. In some schools, teachers use special online networks to communicate with their students. They can give quizzes, assign homework, and send reminders about upcoming classwork. The social networks are improving every day. Who knows what social networks will exist for you in the future? You might even invent one of your own.

Social Media Update

Since this article was first published in 2011, the social media landscape has shifted. Some teens have found new virtual hangouts, including the following:

Instagram Users post photos or short videos with captions, which their followers may "like" or comment on. A single post can get hundreds of responses.

Snapchat This app lets friends exchange photos or videos, and then the post disappears. But anyone can take a screenshot, so it's not really gone forever!

Tumblr On this site, users combine short messages with photos and videos to make super-short blogs.

Google+ Users can watch their circles of friends grow on this networking site. A bonus is the chance to video-chat in Google Hangouts.

Kik This app is like texting, but it allows users to socialize as they send messages to each other.

Monitor Understanding

If... students struggle to read and understand the article,

then... use these scaffolding suggestions:

Question the Text Preview the text by asking the following questions:

- **What do you predict the article will be about?**
- **What questions do you have about the text?**

Vocabulary Support Define words that may interfere with comprehension, such as *site*, *community*, and *landscape*.

Read Aloud Read aloud the text with students. You could also have students chorally read the text in a small group.

Check Understanding Use the questions below to check understanding. Encourage students to cite details in the text that support their answers.

- **Why do people belong to social networks?** *(It keeps them in touch and lets them share experiences and interests with others.)*
- **What are some popular social networking sites?** *(Facebook, Instagram, Snapchat, MySpace, Tumblr, Google+, Kik)*

Integrating Standards

After students have read the articles, use these questions to discuss the articles with them.

- **Use context clues to explain the two meanings of *community* as it is used in this sentence: "For example, Facebook creates a real *community*, but is it not a physical *community* like your town."**

  (In the first example, community *means "a group of people who have similar interests." In the second example,* community *means "a group of people who live in the same area.")*

  DOK 2 RI.5.4

- **Reread "Social Media Update" on p. 363. Explain why someone would choose one of the sites over the others. Use details in the descriptions to support your response.**

  (Responses will vary but should provide specific reasons for using one of the sites. For example, someone who is looking for comments on short videos would choose Instagram over Snapchat where posts disappear, and someone who wants to send a photo or video with a message longer than a caption would choose Tumblr over Instagram.)

  DOK 4 RI.5.1

- **What are the similarities and differences in the ways the ideas are presented in "A Brief History of the Internet" and "Staying In Touch—All the Time"? How does the structure of each passage help the author deliver her information?**

  ("A Brief History of the Internet" is organized using mainly chronological order, which helps explain how the Internet came to be a part of our daily lives. In "Staying in Touch—All the Time," the author uses mainly a compare-contrast structure, which helps the reader understand the purpose of each social networking site the author mentions.)

  DOK 3 RI.5.5

- **How could you use information from all three articles to summarize the development of the Internet from the 1960s to today?**

  (To find information about the beginnings of the Internet, "A Brief History of the Internet" is a good source. It explains that the U.S. military wanted to link computers in the 1960s and that the World Wide Web was started in the 1990s. "Get Wiki Wise" shows how much information is available and the fact that an online encyclopedia is a popular resource. "Staying in Touch—All the Time" shows that the number of social media sites is growing rapidly.)

  DOK 2 RI.5.2

Independent Practice

Think

- Use the Monitor Understanding suggestions to support students in completing items 1–3.

● **Monitor Understanding**

Answer Analysis

When students have finished, discuss correct and incorrect responses.

1 Part A

The correct choice is B. Both articles show that the Internet has a wealth of information on many topics.

- **A** has information only in "A Brief History of the Internet."
- **C** and **D** have information only in "Get Wiki Wise."

Part B

See the answers on the student book page. Discuss students' responses to make sure they understand which details came from each passage. Remind students that this item simulates drag-and-drop items they may see on computer-based assessments.

DOK 4 **RI.5.9**

2 **The correct choice is C.** The root *form* means "shape." Figuratively speaking, the Internet changed the shape of the world.

- **A, B,** and **D** do not support the meaning of the root *form*.

DOK 2 **L.5.4b**

Think Use what you learned from reading the articles to answer the following questions.

1 This question has two parts. First, answer Part A. Then answer Part B.

Part A

Which idea is found in **both** "A Brief History of the Internet" and "Get Wiki Wise"?

A The Internet expanded quickly in the 1990s.

(B) The Internet has information that people can find.

C Not all information on the Internet is accurate.

D It is important to use Internet sites written by experts.

Part B

Choose **one** sentence from "A Brief History of the Internet" and **one** sentence from "Get Wiki Wise" that support the answer to Part A. Write **each** sentence in the appropriate "Supporting Details" box below.

Supporting Details from "A Brief History of the Internet"	Supporting Details from "Get Wiki Wise"
Possible response: "The World Wide Web (www), invented in the 1990s, provides a way for people to find information on the Internet."	**Possible response: "The Internet is like a huge library."**

2 Read the following sentence from "A Brief History of the Internet."

Even though we take it for granted, the Internet has <u>transformed</u> the world.

What does the root *form* mean in the word <u>transformed</u>?

A rule

B know

(C) shape

D organize

● **Monitor Understanding**

If... students struggle to complete the items,

then... you may wish to use one or more of the following suggestions:

- Read the questions aloud and ask students to identify any words or phrases they don't understand.
- Discuss each item with students to make certain they understand the expectation.
- Have students review the texts and write notes about the important idea or ideas in each one.
- Have partners summarize the topics.

3 This question has two parts. First, answer Part A. Then answer Part B.

Part A

How does the information in "A Brief History of the Internet" help the reader understand the topic of "Staying in Touch—All the Time"?

- **(A)** "A Brief History of the Internet" explains how computers were eventually taught to talk to each other, which is how the social networks discussed in "Staying in Touch—All the Time" work.
- **B** "A Brief History of the Internet" explains how the Internet got started in the 1960s, and the Internet is a main topic discussed in "Staying in Touch—All the Time."
- **C** "A Brief History of the Internet" explains how videos and images are sent using the Internet, and those are popular in social networking, which is the topic of "Staying in Touch—All the Time."
- **D** "A Brief History of the Internet" explains how each website has an address that makes it easy to find, which also helps people create a social network, as described in "Staying in Touch—All the Time."

Part B

Choose **two** pieces of evidence, one from **each** article, that support the answer to Part A.

- **(A)** "Computers had been around for a number of years, but they were not linked together in any way, so researchers began to try out different ways to get computers to 'talk' to each other." ("A Brief History of the Internet")
- **B** "In October 1969, a system called ARPANET was launched." ("A Brief History of the Internet")
- **C** "Email, music, photos, games, videos—all are readily available on our computers." ("A Brief History of the Internet")
- **D** "Today, social networking sites like Facebook make staying in touch easier than ever." ("Staying in Touch—All the Time")
- **(E)** "You know what a network is—a set of links or ties between one place, person, or thing and another." ("Staying in Touch—All the Time")
- **F** "Who knows what social networks will exist for you in the future?" ("Staying in Touch—All the Time")

365

Theme Connection

- Remind students that the theme of this lesson is Electronic Communication.
- Display a three-column chart. Label the columns with these headings: *Phones, Satellites, Internet*.
- Ask students to recall facts and ideas they learned from each passage about inventions that help people communicate over large distances. List their responses in the appropriate column.
- Ask students to determine how all of the passages relate to the theme of electronic communication.

3 Part A

The correct choice is A.

- **B** The fact that the Internet got started in the 1960s is true, but the Internet in general is not the topic of the passage "Staying In Touch—All the Time."
- **C** While it is true that videos and images are popular forms of social media (referenced in the sidebar in "Staying in Touch—All the Time"), "A Brief History of the Internet" does not explain how videos and images can be sent over the Internet, just that it is possible.
- **D** There is no evidence in either passage to support the idea that it is easier to build a social network because things are easy to find online.

Part B

The correct choices are A and E. Each choice supports the idea that because the Internet allows computers to "talk" to each other, people can use the Internet to create social networks.

- **B** and **C** are unimportant details from the article "A Brief History of the Internet."
- **D** and **F** are unimportant details from the article "Staying in Touch —All the Time."

***DOK 4* RI.5.9**

Theme Connection

Independent Practice

Write

- Tell students that using what they read, they will plan and compose an extended response to the writing prompt. Provide copies of the chart on p. TR11.

● **Monitor Understanding**

Review Responses

After students have completed each part of the writing activity, help them evaluate their responses.

4 Display the **Sample Response** for the planning chart on the next page. Have students compare their chart with the sample. Are they missing any information?
DOK 2 **RI.5.9**

5 Display or pass out copies of the reproducible **2-Point Writing Rubric** on p. TR10. Have students use the rubric to individually assess their writing and revise as needed.

When students have finished their revisions, evaluate their responses. Answers will vary but should integrate information about the Internet, Wikipedia, and social networks from the three articles. Students should identify the sources and explain how the Internet helps people find information.
DOK 4 **RI.5.9, W.5.9b**

Write

What is the Internet, and how do people use it to find information and connect with each other? Reread all three articles. Underline key ideas about the Internet. Then complete numbers 4 and 5.

4 **Plan Your Response** What important ideas did you learn from each article? How can you put together that information to explain what the Internet is and how it can be used? Use a chart to organize your thoughts and evidence from the articles before you write.

5 **Write an Extended Response** Explain what the Internet is and how people use it to find information and connect with each other. Use evidence from each article and your chart in your response.

Responses will vary. A top-scoring response will integrate information about the Internet, Wikipedia, and social networks from each article. Students will clearly state where each piece of information came from, and they will come to a clear conclusion about what the Internet is and how it helps people find information and connect with each other.

366

● **Monitor Understanding**

If… students don't understand the writing task,

then… read aloud the writing prompt. Use the following questions to help students get started.

- **What is the prompt asking you to write about?**
- **Do you need to reread the text to find more information?**
- **How will you identify the information you need to include?**

- Have partners talk about how they will organize their responses.

Learning Target

In this lesson, you practiced integrating information from several texts on the same topic. Explain how this skill will help you when you have to do research on other topics.

Responses will vary, but students should identify ways that integrating information from several texts on the same topic helped them develop a deeper understanding of a topic in order to write or speak about it.

Wrap Up

Learning Target

- Have each student respond in writing to the Learning Target prompt.
- When students have finished, have them share their responses. This may be done with a partner, in small groups, or as a whole class.

4 Sample Response

"A Brief History. . ."	"Get Wiki Wise"	"Staying in Touch— . . ."
• 1960s: U.S. military wanted to share information • 1990s: WWW invented • Today many use Internet: email, music, photos, games	• Wikipedia is biggest online encyclopedia • Information may not be correct • Links to sources • Questioning Internet information	• Social networking allows people to meet, share information • Popular sites: Facebook, Twitter, MySpace • New social media added recently

5 2-Point Writing Rubric

Points	Focus	Evidence	Organization
2	My answer does exactly what the prompt asked me to do.	My answer is supported with plenty of details from the text.	My ideas are clear and in a logical order.
1	Some of my answer does not relate to the prompt.	My answer is missing some important details from the text.	Some of my ideas are unclear and out of order.
0	My answer does not make sense.	My answer does not have any details from the text.	My ideas are unclear and not in any order.

Get Started

Today you are going to read three science articles. You will use what you have learned in this unit to understand what you are reading.

- Ask students to recall what they have learned, such as finding information in multiple sources, using them for writing, and understanding an author's points and supporting evidence.
- Encourage students to use the Academic Talk words and phrases from the unit's lessons in their response.

Read

You are going to read the articles independently and use what you have learned to think and write about the text.

- Ask a student to read aloud the titles of the passages. Make certain that students understand they are to read all three selections.

  Answers will vary but should show that the author supports this point with details about the people who are clearing the rain forests. See the sample response on the student book page.
- Encourage students to preview the text, paying close attention to the photographs, captions, and chart.
- Remind students to look inside, around, and beyond when they encounter unfamiliar words. Use the Word Learning Routine on pp. A50–A51.
- When students have finished, have them complete the Think and Write sections.

Read

Genre: Science Article

Read the science article. Then answer the questions that follow.

The Rain Forest—Worth Saving

by Julia Webster

1 Picture a forest with amazingly tall trees, brilliantly colored flowers, and twisting vines. Then add unusual butterflies, birds, and animals to the picture. The forest you imagine is a tropical rain forest. Tropical rain forests are the places that have the greatest biodiversity[1] in the world. They cover less than 6 percent of the world's land area, yet they contain more than half of the world's plant and animal species.

2 Today, rain forests are in danger of disappearing. Loggers and ranchers cut down valuable trees, and large companies cut down forests to make space for coffee and banana plantations. Poachers[2] capture rare rain forest animals and sell the animals for great profits. And miners clear large, open pits to dig for gold, oil, and iron. The mining process causes pollution of rivers and other water supplies.

3 It is critical that we save the rain forests. Trees and plants of the rain forests release gases that provide much of the world's oxygen supply. Also, the world's climate is affected by rain forests. When trees are cut down, the remaining parts release carbon dioxide into the air, causing global warming.

[1] **Biodiversity:** many different kinds of plants and animals in an environment

[2] **Poachers:** people who kill or steal wild animals

4 Many products come from the rain forest. Various medicines used worldwide have been developed from rain forest plants. Rubber, bamboo, and many spices come from rain forest plants. Are you a chocolate or vanilla fan? Both of these flavors come from the rain forest.

5 Efforts are being made to preserve our rain forests. Some have been selected to be national parks where logging and mining aren't allowed. Farmers and ranchers are learning methods that don't harm the soil and cause pollution. Tourists are encouraged to visit and learn about rain forests. Once they experience the beauty and value of the rain forest, many tourists volunteer to help. We all depend on rain forests, so they are certainly worth saving.

Teacher Notes

Assessment

Answer Analysis

When students have completed the Interim Assessment, discuss correct and incorrect responses.

1 Part A

The correct choice is C. If humans do not save the rain forests, then according to the passage, the world's climate and oxygen supply will be threatened.

- **A** describes the rain forest but not why people should save it.
- **B** is an example of what the rain forest must be saved from.
- **D** provides further information about the value of the rain forest but is not the reason the author gives for saving it.

Part B

The correct choice is D. In the third paragraph, the author explains that rain forest plants are crucial to Earth's environment.

- **A** doesn't give a clear reason for preserving rain forests.
- **B** doesn't provide a reason rain forests should be preserved.
- **C** doesn't support the author's point about the importance of saving the rain forests.

DOK 2 **RI.5.8**

2 After students have completed the Interim Assessment, evaluate their responses to the short-response item using the **2-Point Writing Rubric** below.

Answers will vary but should show that the author supports this point with details about the people who are clearing the rain forests. See the sample response on the student book page.

You may wish to display or pass out copies of the reproducible **2-Point Writing Rubric** on page TR10. Have students use the rubric to individually assess their writing and revise as needed.

DOK 2 **RI.5.8**

Interim Assessment

Think

1 This question has two parts. First, answer Part A, then answer Part B.

Part A
Why does the author make the point that "It is critical that we save the rain forests"?

A Rain forests are filled with tall trees, beautiful flowers, and rare animals.
B Companies are destroying rain forests for logging, farming, and mining.
(C) Destroying rain forests would be harmful for the rest of the world.
D Many kinds of plants and animals can be found only in the rain forest.

Part B
Which detail from the article provides evidence for the answer in Part A?

A "Tropical rain forests are the places that have the greatest biodiversity in the world."
B "The mining process causes pollution of rivers and other water supplies."
C "Poachers capture rare rain forest animals and sell the animals for great profits."
(D) "When trees are cut down, the remaining parts release carbon dioxide into the air, causing global warming."

2 Explain how the author of "The Rain Forest—Worth Saving" supports the following point: "Today, rain forests are in danger of disappearing." Include at least **one** sentence from the text that provides a reason the author holds this point of view.

Sample response: The author supports that point with details about how loggers, ranchers, and large companies are all cutting down rain forest trees.

370

2-Point Writing Rubric

All three criteria must be satisfied in order for a response to gain full points.

Points	Focus	Evidence	Organization
2	The response demonstrates comprehension and provides accurate analysis.	The response supports the analysis with adequate textual evidence.	Ideas are clear and follow a logical order.
1	The response demonstrates some comprehension and provides minimally accurate analysis.	The response supports the analysis with limited textual evidence.	Some ideas are unclear or out of order.
0	The response demonstrates no comprehension and provides inaccurate or no analysis.	The response provides little or no textual evidence.	Ideas are unclear or incomplete.

3 This question has two parts. First, answer Part A. Then answer Part B.

Part A

Choose the statement that best describes a conclusion that can be drawn about the author's line of reasoning in paragraph 5.

- **(A)** When people learn about the rain forest, they often decide to protect it.
- **B** People are working to protect rain forests, but it is too late to save them.
- **C** Only people who do not profit from harming rain forests want to save them.
- **D** The best way to save the rain forests is to turn them into national parks.

Part B

Underline the sentence from the text that **best** supports your answer in Part A.

Efforts are being made to preserve our rain forests. Some have been selected to be national parks where logging and mining aren't allowed. Farmers and ranchers are learning methods that don't harm the soil and cause pollution. Tourists are encouraged to visit and learn about rain forests. Once they experience the beauty and value of the rain forest, many tourists volunteer to help. We all depend on rain forests, so they are certainly worth saving.

3 Part A

The correct choice is A. The author reasons that educating tourists persuades them to support rain forest conservation.

- **B** goes further than the author in stating "it is too late to save" the rain forests.
- **C** is untrue; the author states that farmers and ranchers are helping save the rain forests.
- **D** is an opinion about "the best way" to save rain forests, but the author lists three different ways without ranking them.

Part B

Students should underline the fifth sentence of the paragraph, "Once they experience the beauty and value of the rain forest, many tourists volunteer to help."

DOK 2 **RI.5.8**

Assessment

Read

Genre: Science Article

Read the science article. Then answer the questions that follow.

Animals of the Rain Forest

by Shawn Parcell

1 Most animals that live in the emergent layer of the rain forest can jump, fly, or glide. One example is the pygmy glider. This squirrel-like animal has a flap of skin that extends between its front and back legs. When its legs are stretched out, the pygmy glider can swoop from treetop to treetop in search of insects to eat.

2 About half of the world's species of animals inhabit the canopy layer. One species includes the extremely slow-moving sloth. Sloths hang upside down in trees and rarely leave the canopy layer. Some don't come down for decades! Although scientists estimate that fifty percent of the world's species of animals currently live in this layer, they also suspect that as rain forests have been cleared for farming and development, some species may have become extinct before they were even discovered.

3 The poison dart frog is a surprising inhabitant of the understory layer. Unlike most understory inhabitants, this thumbnail-size frog doesn't depend on camouflage for protection. Its brilliant colors warn predators to stay away. These tiny frogs possess a powerful poison. An amount smaller than a grain of salt can kill a person!

4 The largest and the smallest animals of the rain forest live on the forest floor. Elephants, tigers, and jaguars live there along with millions of tiny insects. Some insects, such as beetles, keep the forest floor clean by eating decayed matter. Army ants also live on the floor. Colonies of up to 700,000 army ants roam the forest floor in search of food. They will attack and kill anything that moves. Army ants can eat a horse in only a few hours!

Emergent Layer	• Few trees, some as tall as 200 feet • Most trees are hardwood broadleaved evergreens • Trees get much sunlight; also high heat and strong winds
Canopy Layer	• Trees can be between 50 and 130 feet tall • Branches spread out and form a canopy, or roof, over the lower layers • Gets much sunlight and rainfall • About 90% of the plants and animals live in this layer
Understory Layer	• Up to 60-foot trees, vines, and shrubs packed in tightly • Receives little sunlight • Tangle of plants provides great camouflage for animals living there
Forest Floor	• Moss, ferns, and a few types of plants live here • Little to no sunlight gets through; shaded, unless a large tree falls and opens a gap in the canopy • Branches, leaves, seeds, and fruits decay on the forest floor

Teacher Notes

Assessment

4 Part A

The correct choice is D. This topic is addressed in the texts of both passages and could provide a topic for a report.

- **A** is only supported by "The Rain Forest—Worth Saving."
- **B** is only supported by "Animals of the Rain Forest."
- **C** is only supported by the diagram in "Animals of the Rain Forest."

Part B

The correct choices are A and C. These paragraphs both include details about the harmful effects of disappearing rain forests. For example, Paragraph 3 of "The Rain Forest—Worth Saving" says, "When trees are cut down, the remaining parts release carbon dioxide into the air, causing global warming." Paragraph 2 of "Animals of the Rain Forest" states, "as rain forests have been cleared for farming and development, some species [of animals] may have become extinct before they were even discovered."

- **B** discusses products that are made from materials found in the rain forest.
- **D** gives details about the poison dart frog.
- **E** shows information about the different layers of the rain forest.

DOK 3 RI.5.7

Think

4 This question has two parts. First, answer Part A. Then answer Part B.

Part A
Which of the following topics could you write a report about based on information in both "The Rain Forest—Worth Saving" and "Animals of the Rain Forest"?

- **A** common products that come from rain forests
- **B** dangerous animals that live in the rain forest
- **C** how tall some trees grow in the rain forest
- **(D)** harmful effects of disappearing rain forests

Part B
What information would **best** help you develop the topic you chose in Part A? Identify **one** section from "The Rain Forest—Worth Saving" and **one** section from "Animals of the Rain Forest."

- **(A)** paragraph 3 of "The Rain Forest—Worth Saving"
- **B** paragraph 4 of "The Rain Forest—Worth Saving"
- **(C)** paragraph 2 of "Animals of the Rain Forest"
- **D** paragraph 3 of "Animals of the Rain Forest"
- **E** the diagram from "Animals of the Rain Forest"

5 This question has two parts. First, answer Part A. Then answer Part B.

Part A
Which idea is found in both the article "Animals of the Rain Forest" and the diagram?

- (A) More animals and plants of the rain forest live in the canopy than in any other layer.
- B The forest floor is mostly shaded unless a large tree falls and opens a gap in the canopy.
- C Species of the canopy layer may have already become extinct before they were discovered.
- D The largest and the smallest of the rain forest animals live on the forest floor.

Part B
Choose **one** detail from the article and **one** detail from the sidebar that support the answer to Part A. Write each of the details into the box labeled "Supporting Details."

Details from Article	Details from Diagram
Most animals that live in the emergent layer of the rain forest can jump, fly, or glide. About half of the world's species of animals inhabit the canopy layer. As rain forests have been cleared for farming and development, some species may have become extinct before they were even discovered. The largest and the smallest animals of the rain forest live on the forest floor.	Emergent Layer: Most trees are hardwood broadleaved evergreens Canopy Layer: About 90% of the plants and animals live in this layer Understory Layer: Tangle of plants provides great camouflage for animals living there Forest Floor: Moss, ferns, and a few types of plants live here

Supporting Detail from Article	Supporting Detail from Diagram
About half of the world's species of animals inhabit the canopy layer.	**About 90% of the plants and animals live in this layer**

Teacher Notes

5 **Part A**

The correct choice is A. Both sources describe the large number of species that live in the canopy.

- **B** appears only in the diagram.
- **C** appears only in the article.
- **D** appears only in the article.

Part B

See the answers on the student book page.

DOK 2 **RI.5.8**

Read

Genre: Science Article

Read the science article. Then answer the questions that follow.

Medicinal Plants of the Rain Forest

by Lea Rossi

1 People who live in rain forests have used their trees and plants to treat illnesses for thousands of years. Yet, modern-day scientists have only recently begun to discover the benefits of these plants. The rain forest has been called "Nature's Medicine Cabinet." About 7,000 medicines come from plants found in rain forests around the world.

2 These medicines are used to treat a wide variety of conditions, from toothaches and colds to cancer and AIDS. One example is quinine. This chemical comes from the bark of the cinchona tree that grows to a height of about 65 feet. Quinine is used to treat malaria.

3 Another example is a fast-acting poison called curare [kyoo RAHR ee]. It comes from a vine that climbs trees from the floor of the rain forest to the canopy. Native people use curare to poison the tips of darts and arrows. Surprisingly, scientists discovered that curare could also be used to save lives. They discovered that it could be used to relax patients' muscles during surgery.

Cinchona blossoms

Cocoa tree

4 About 150 different chemicals come from the cocoa tree. These trees thrive in the understory layer of the rain forest. Chemicals from this tree are used in medicines that treat fevers, coughs, and cuts.

5 More than two-thirds of all cancer-fighting medicines come from rain forests. Cat's claw is one example of a cancer-fighting plant. It is a vine that grows in the canopy layer of the rain forest.

6 Scientists have only just begun to tap the resources of rain forest plants. Today, less than one percent of plants found in rainforests have been tested to discover medicinal benefits. As rain forests are cleared for farming, ranching, and logging, scientists estimate that about 137 plants and animals become extinct every day. As rain forests disappear, so do the possibilities of finding cures and life-saving drugs.

Teacher Notes

6 **The correct choice is C.** The diagram shows where different kinds of rain forest plants grow, and the text of "Medicinal Plants in the Rain Forest" describes the helpful effects of some of these plants.

- **A** is incorrect because the diagram does not help readers visualize how plants and animals could be destroyed; instead, the diagram shows the layers that make up the rain forest as well as the kinds of plants that grow in each layer.
- **B** is incorrect because the diagram does not help readers visualize how and why plants can help people; rather, the diagram shows the various layers of the rain forest and the kinds of plants that grow in each layer.
- **D** is incorrect because the diagram does not help readers understand why poisonous plants may help people but instead shows that vines are found in the understory layer.

DOK 2 RI.5.7

7 After students have completed the Interim Assessment, evaluate their responses to the short-response item using the **2-Point Writing Rubric** below.

Answers will vary but should include poison dart frogs and curare vines, which both create deadly poisons. See the sample response on the student book page.

You may wish to display or pass out copies of the reproducible **2-Point Writing Rubric** on page TR10. Have students use the rubric to individually assess their writing and revise as needed.

DOK 3 RI.5.9

Think

6 How does the diagram on page 373 help the reader better understand "Medicinal Plants of the Rain Forest"?

A It helps the reader visualize how plants and animals could be destroyed in the rain forest.

B It helps the reader visualize how and why different plants can help people.

(C) It helps the reader understand where different plants grow and thrive.

D It helps the reader understand why different plants can sometimes help people.

7 **Short Response** Write a paragraph about poisons based on what you read in "Medicinal Plants of the Rain Forest" and "Animals of the Rain Forest." Use at least **one** detail from **each** passage in your response.

Sample response: Some rain forest plants and animals produce poisons that can kill people. "Animals of the Rain Forest" says that just a tiny amount of poison from the poison dart frog can kill a person. "Medicinal Plants of the Rain Forest" mentions curare, which people have used to make poison arrows. But even though it is a poison, curare can also be used as a medicine to help people who are having surgery.

2-Point Writing Rubric

All three criteria must be satisfied in order for a response to gain full points.

Points	Focus	Evidence	Organization
2	The response demonstrates comprehension and provides accurate analysis.	The response supports the analysis with adequate textual evidence.	Ideas are clear and follow a logical order.
1	The response demonstrates some comprehension and provides minimally accurate analysis.	The response supports the analysis with limited textual evidence.	Some ideas are unclear or out of order.
0	The response demonstrates no comprehension and provides inaccurate or no analysis.	The response provides little or no textual evidence.	Ideas are unclear or incomplete.

8 This question has two parts. First, answer Part A. Then answer Part B.

Part A

Which main idea in "Medicinal Plants of the Rain Forest" is **best** supported by information in "The Rain Forest—Worth Saving"?

- **A** Native people made poison arrows from rain forest plants.
- **B** Rain forest plants can provide treatments for AIDS and cancer.
- **(C)** Medicines we use today come from rain forest plants.
- **D** Scientists have already tested most rain forest plants.

Part B

Complete the chart below by writing **one** sentence from "Medicinal Plants of the Rain Forest" that states the main idea in Part A, and **one** sentence from "The Rain Forest—Worth Saving" that supports that main idea.

Main idea statement from "Medicinal Plants of the Rain Forest"	Supporting Detail from "The Rain Forest—Worth Saving"
The rain forest has been called "Nature's Medicine Cabinet." About 7,000 medicines come from plants found in rain forests around the world.	Various medicines used worldwide have been developed from rain forest plants.

8 **Part A**

The correct choice is C. This is a main idea in "Medicinal Plants of the Rain Forest," and it is also supported by paragraph 4 of "The Rain Forest—Worth Saving."

- **A** discusses poisons, not medicines.
- **B** is a supporting detail, not a main idea, of "Medicinal Plants of the Rain Forest."
- **D** does not accurately reflect information from "Medicinal Plants of the Rain Forest."

Part B

See the answers on the student book page.

DOK 2 RI.5.7

Assessment

Write

Review Responses

9 After students have completed the Interim Assessment, evaluate their responses to the Extended Response using the **4-Point Writing Rubric** below.

Answers will vary but should argue that rain forests must be saved because of the unique plants and animals that live there, the medical discoveries that are made there, and the environmental harm their destruction creates. See the sample response on the student book page.

DOK 4 **RI.5.9**

Write

9 **Extended Response** Imagine you are a tour guide in a protected rain forest. Write a presentation for visitors in which you explain why it is important to save the rain forests. Use details from all three passages and the diagram to tell about the value of the rain forests.

In your answer, be sure to
- explain the reasons rain forests are unique and important
- describe what kinds of plants and animals are found in the rain forests
- tell how rain forests contribute to the field of medicine
- use details from all three passages and the diagram in your answer

Check your writing for correct spelling, grammar, capitalization, and punctuation.

Sample Response

Welcome to the rain forest. The rain forest is home to many plants and animals. Many of the world's animal species live in the different layers of the rain forest. For example, the pygmy glider lives in the emergent layer, the sloth lives in the canopy, and the poison dart frog inhabits the understory. It is important to save the rain forest so animals like these will always have a home.

The rain forest has many kinds of plants, including those that provide important medicines. The cocoa tree from the understory, for instance, provides chemicals that are used in medicines to treat cuts, fevers, and coughs. It is important to save the rain forest so that people can continue to get these necessary medicines and so that new medicines may be discovered.

Rain forests play an important role in Earth's environment. For example, rain forest trees give off oxygen. If these trees are cut down, there is less oxygen, and what's left of the trees gives off carbon dioxide. Too much carbon dioxide in the air can cause global warming. It is important to save the rain forest so that humans have oxygen to breath and Earth is protected from global warming.

4-Point Writing Rubric

All three criteria must be satisfied in order for a response to gain full points.

Points	Focus	Evidence	Organization
4	The response demonstrates a full understanding of the prompt and provides accurate analysis.	The response supports the analysis with generous textual evidence.	Ideas are consistently presented in a purposeful and logical order.
3	The response demonstrates a good understanding of the prompt and provides mostly accurate analysis.	The response supports the analysis with adequate textual evidence.	Ideas are generally presented in a purposeful and logical order, although some ideas may be unclear or out of order.
2	The response demonstrates a general understanding of the prompt and provides some accurate analysis but includes inaccurate descriptions or explanations.	The response supports the analysis with limited textual evidence but does not reference the text explicitly.	Some ideas are presented in a purposeful and logical order, but others are unclear or out of order.
1	The response demonstrates a limited understanding of the prompt and provides limited analysis with significant inaccuracies.	The response may use textual evidence, but it does not support the analysis and does not reference the text explicitly.	Most ideas are not presented in a purposeful and logical order.
0	The response does not demonstrate understanding of the prompt.	Ideas are not supported with reference to textual evidence.	The response does not present ideas in a purposeful or logical order.

Unit 6
Integration of Knowledge and Ideas in Literature

Integration of Knowledge and Ideas in Literature

What is your favorite kind of story to read? Some people like science fiction, some like mystery, and some like adventure. There are various kinds of stories within the same genre (type of writing). Not suprisingly, stories in the same genre have similar themes and topics. Think about mysteries, for example. Stories about detectives such as Sherlock Holmes, Encyclopedia Brown, and Nancy Drew all include the topics of crimes and clues. They tell messages about truth and not giving up. The stories would not be complete if the mystery was not solved at the end. However, mystery stories have different twists and turns. In this unit, you'll learn to compare and contrast topics and themes of stories within genres such as mystery and adventure.

You'll also learn to use visuals to gain a better understanding of stories and poems you read. Have you heard the saying, "A picture is worth a thousand words"? That might be an exaggeration, but illustrations and photographs often add many details that are not described with words. In addition, you'll learn how these visuals contribute to the understanding of the tone and your appreciation of stories and poems.

✓ Self Check

Before starting this unit, check off the skills you know below. As you complete each lesson, see how many more skills you can check off!

I can:	Before this unit	After this unit
notice how visual elements help to develop a deeper meaning of a text.	☐	☐
analyze how visual elements may add to the tone of a text.	☐	☐
compare and contrast approaches to themes of stories in similar genres.	☐	☐
compare and contrast different author approaches to the same topic in similar genres.	☐	☐

382

page 384

page 386

page 388

page 394

page 409

page 410

page 417

383

At a Glance

- These two pages introduce students to the skills and strategies they will learn in this unit.
- The checklist allows them to see what skills they will be learning and take ownership of their progress.
- The visual table of contents gives a graphic preview of the passages in the unit.

Step by Step

- Explain to students that they are going to begin a new unit of lessons. Tell them that in all the lessons in this unit they will be learning about the integration of knowledge and ideas in literature.
- Have the class read together the introduction to the unit in their books. Invite and respond to comments and questions, if any.
- Then take a few minutes to have each student independently read through the list of skills.
- Ask students to consider each skill and check the box if it is a skill they think they already have. Tell students that they may have worked on similar skills in the past, but these skills go deeper than before.
- Engage students in a brief discussion about the skills. Invite students to comment on which ones they would most like to learn, or which ones seem similar or related to something they already know. Remind them that the goal is to be able to check off one skill at a time until they have them all checked.
- Invite students to look at the graphics and predict what the passages will be about.

Lesson 21
Analyzing Visual Elements in Literary Texts

Standards Focus

Analyze how visual . . . elements contribute to the meaning, tone, or beauty of a text (e.g., graphic novel, multimedia presentation of fiction, folktale, myth, poem). **RL.5.7**

Lesson Objectives

Reading

- Analyze ways in which visual elements add meaning or tone to a text. **RL.5.7**
- View visual presentations to analyze the contribution of visual elements to understanding the text. **RL.5.7**

Writing

- Draw evidence from literary texts to support analysis and reflection. **W.5.9a**

Speaking and Listening

- Pose and respond to specific questions and contribute to discussions. **SL.5.1c**
- Review the key ideas expressed and draw conclusions. **SL.5.1d**

Language

- Use context as a clue to the meaning of a word or phrase. **L.5.4a**
- Acquire and use academic and domain-specific words and phrases. **L.5.6**

Additional Practice: **RL.5.1, RL.5.2, RL.5.4, RL.5.6**

Academic Talk

See **Glossary of Terms**, pp. TR2–TR9

- analyze
- tone
- visual elements
- beauty
- meaning

Learning Progression

Grade 4	Grade 5	Grade 6
Students make connections between a text and a visual or oral presentation of the text.	Building on Grade 4, students focus on what visual and multimedia elements bring to the text. Specifically, students analyze how these elements work with the text, and, in some cases, provide information beyond the text to create meaning and tone.	Grade 6 increases in complexity by requiring students to bring together what they learned in Grades 4 and 5 to compare the experience of reading a text to listening to or watching a live version of the text.

Lesson Text Selections

Modeled and Guided Instruction

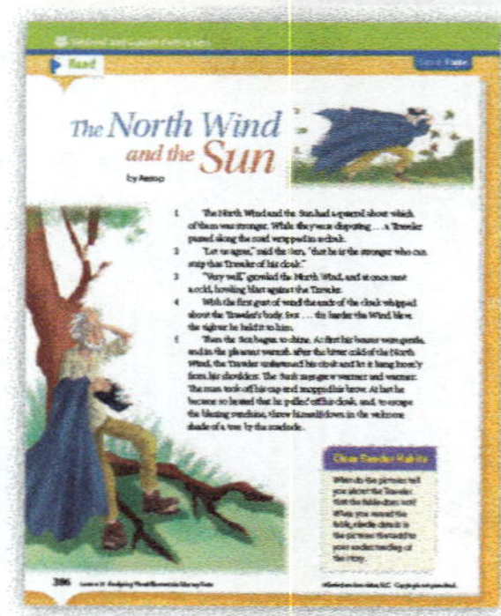

The North Wind and the Sun
by Aesop
Genre: Fable

Guided Practice

Windy Nights
by Robert Louis Stevenson
Genre: Lyric Poem

Independent Practice

Phaethon
by Flora J. Cooke
Genre: Myth

Lesson Pacing Guide

Whole Class Instruction *30–45 minutes per day*

Day 1

Teacher-Toolbox.com **Interactive Tutorial**
Comparing and Contrasting Literature in Print to Multimedia Versions—Level F
20 min (optional)

Introduction pp. 384–385

- **Read** **Analyzing Visual Elements in Literary Texts** *10 min*
- **Think** *10 min*
  Graphic Organizer: Three-Column Chart
- **Talk** *5 min*
  Quick Write (TRB) *5 min*

Day 2

Modeled and Guided Instruction pp. 386–387, 390

- **Read** **The North Wind and the Sun** *10 min*
- **Think** *10 min*
  Graphic Organizer: Three-Column Chart
- **Talk** *5 min*
- **Write** Short Response *10 min*

Day 3

Guided Practice pp. 388–389, 391

- **Read** **Windy Nights** *10 min*
- **Think** *10 min*
- **Talk** *5 min*
- **Write** Short Response *10 min*

Day 4

Independent Practice pp. 392–397

- **Read** **Phaethon** *15 min*
- **Think** *10 min*
- **Write** Extended Response *15 min*

Day 5

Independent Practice pp. 392–397

- *Review* Answer Analysis (TRB) *10 min*
- *Review* Response Analysis (TRB) *10 min*
- *Assign and Discuss* Learning Target *10 min*

Language Handbook
Lesson 14 Varieties of English: Dialect and Register, pp. 464–465
20 min (optional)

Ready Writing Connection

During *Ready Reading* Days 1–5, use:
Lesson 5 Writing to Inform: Book Chapter

- **Steps 6 and 7** **Revise**
- **Step 8** **Edit**
- **Prepare to Publish**
- **Collaborate**
- **Present**

See *Ready Writing TRB*, p. 120a for complete lesson plan.

Small Group Differentiation
Teacher-Toolbox.com

Reteach

***Ready Reading* Prerequisite Lesson**

- **Grade 4** Media Feature Connecting Presentations of a Text

Personalized Learning
i-Ready.com

Independent

i-Ready Close Reading Lessons

- **Grade 4** Connecting Presentations of a Text
- **Grade 5** Analyzing Visual Elements in Literary Texts

Introduction

Get Started

- Explain to students that in this lesson they will read several types of literature and analyze the pictures that go along with each text.
- Tap into what students already know about visuals. Brainstorm forms of stories that have visual elements, such as picture books, comic strips, magazines, and graphic novels.
- Discuss with students how many of these formats rely on the details in the pictures to help convey meaning. Display a magazine advertisement, for example, and say:

  There aren't many words on this page. Here we just see the brand name and a short message. But look at the picture—we see a group of kids laughing on a sunny afternoon. They seem to be having a great time. The picture helps me understand that this product makes people happy, and that kids especially enjoy it. I couldn't have gotten that by reading the words alone. I needed to analyze the picture, as well.
- Focus students' attention on the Learning Target. Read it aloud to set the purpose for the lesson.
- Display the Academic Talk words and phrases. Tell students to listen for these terms and their meanings as you work through the lesson together. Use the Academic Talk Routine on pp. A48–A49.

English Language Learners

● **Genre Focus**

Read

- Read aloud the Read section as students follow along. Restate to reinforce:

  When you read a text, you should also examine any visual elements the author included, such as photographs and illustrations. These elements add beauty to the story but they can also help you understand things about the story that you wouldn't understand from reading the words alone.
- Direct students' attention to the passage and the illustration. Have them read the passage and then look for details in the illustration that support and expand upon the words.

Introduction

RL.5.7 Analyze how visual . . . elements contribute to the meaning, tone, or beauty of a text (e.g., graphic novel, multimedia presentation of fiction, folktale, myth, poem).

Lesson 21
Analyzing Visual Elements in Literary Texts

Figuring out how pictures add to the meaning, tone, or beauty of texts will help you better understand both the texts and the pictures.

Read When you read literature, you **analyze**, or examine carefully, the entire work, including any **visual elements** such as pictures that appear with the text. Pictures can add **meaning** and **beauty** to the text. Visual elements also help contribute to the **tone**, or the general feeling, of the text.

Read the fable below and analyze the picture. What can you learn from the picture that isn't in the text?

The Two Travelers and the Purse

by Aesop

Two men were traveling in company along the road when one of them picked up a well-filled purse.

"How lucky I am!" he said. "I have found a purse. Judging by its weight it must be full of gold."

"Do not say 'I have found a purse,'" said his companion. "Say rather 'we have found a purse' and 'how lucky we are.' . . . Travelers ought to share alike the fortunes or misfortunes of the road."

384

English Language Learners

Develop Language

Concept Vocabulary Help students understand that visual elements include features that help them "see" the text and the story better.

- Draw a concept map on the board with *visual element* in the center. On one side, work with students to brainstorm common associated words, such as *picture, illustration, photograph, image*. On the other side, map out the things readers look for in visual elements, including *beauty, meaning, tone*. Help students understand these words, using examples as needed.
- Invite volunteers to describe what the map shows.

● **Genre Focus**

Myths

Explain that during Independent Practice, students will read a myth. Myths are made-up stories written long ago. They commonly have one or more of the following characteristics:

- They try to explain events in nature, such as thunder and lightning.
- They tell about the adventures of superhuman beings, such as Hercules, and about the actions of gods, such as Zeus.
- They tell about the interactions between humans and gods.

Ask students to name examples of myths they have read or viewed.

Think Consider what you've learned so far about analyzing the relationship between visual elements and a text. Complete the chart below for the fable about the two travelers.

Quote from the Text	What Does the Picture Show About Each Man?	What Does the Picture Show About the Purse?
"Two men were traveling in company along the road when one of them picked up a well-filled purse."	• Both men are looking down at the purse. • The man on the left is wearing fine clothes and a nice hat and boots. The man on the right is wearing worn clothes and flimsy footwear. • The man on the left looks richer and healthier than the man holding the purse.	• The purse has many decorations on it. • It looks like a wealthy person's purse.

Talk Share your chart with a partner.

- Did you see the same details about each man? How about the purse?
- What did the picture add to your understanding of the fable?
- Would you have a different understanding of the men and the fable if you hadn't seen the picture? If so, what?

Academic Talk
Use these words and phrases to talk about the text.
- analyze
- visual elements
- meaning
- tone
- beauty

Monitor Understanding

If... students struggle to determine how details in pictures add meaning to a story,

then... demonstrate with a live example. Write a short statement on the board: *The girl sat by herself before soccer try-outs.*

- **What might the girl be feeling?** *(Sample response: She could be feeling loneliness, excitement, nervousness, confidence, impatience.)*

Ask one volunteer to help you. Whisper to the student that she should stand up at the front of the class and put on a worried or nervous face.

- **Now there is a visual aid. The girl sat by herself before soccer try-outs. How do you think she is feeling?** *(worried or nervous)*

Explain that visual aids can clarify details in a story.

Think

- Have students read aloud the Think section. Explain that the chart will help them organize their thinking.
- Have partners complete the chart. Remind students to pay close attention to the characters, including what they are wearing and what inferences you might make about them.
- As students work, circulate and provide assistance as needed.
- Ask volunteers to share what they wrote in their charts.
- Make certain students understand that the details they list on the chart must be supported with details from the story or the illustration.

Talk

- Read aloud the Talk prompts.
- Have partners discuss various possible interpretations of the picture and the fable. Encourage students to imagine how the story would change if the picture changed—for example, if the characters were dressed similarly.
- Ask volunteers to share their ideas.

Quick Write Have students write a response to the following prompt:

What is your favorite illustrated story? Briefly tell what happens in the story and explain how the illustrations add to the story's meaning.

Ask students to share their responses.

Wrap Up

- Invite students to share what they've learned so far. Encourage them to use the Academic Talk words and phrases in their explanations.
- Explain to students that when they combine information from words and pictures, they broaden their understanding of the literature.

In the next section, we'll read a fable and analyze how visual elements create beauty and meaning in the story and how they help us better understand the text.

Monitor Understanding

Modeled and Guided Instruction

Get Started

Today you will read another fable—an old folk story. First, you'll read to understand the story. Then you'll read to analyze how the illustrations add meaning to the text.

Read

- Read aloud the title of the story and call attention to both illustrations. Remind students that in some stories, non-living things can be characters that behave just like humans.
- Have students read the fable independently. Tell them to place a check mark above any confusing words and phrases as they read. Remind students to look inside, around, and beyond each unknown word to help them figure out its meaning. Use the Word Learning Routine on pp. A50–A51.
- When students have finished reading, clarify the meanings of words and phrases they still find confusing. Then use the questions below to check understanding. Encourage students to identify details in the text that support their answers.

  What are the Sun and the North Wind quarreling about? *(which of them is stronger)*

  How do they settle the argument? *(They both try to remove the Traveler's cloak.)*

  Which is stronger, the North Wind or the Sun, and why? *(The Sun is stronger because he gets the Traveler to remove his cloak.)*

 **English Language Learners**

● **Word Learning Strategy**

Explore

- Read aloud the Explore question at the top of p. 387 to set the purpose for the second read. Tell students they will need to take a closer look at what the illustrations tell them about the Traveler.
- Have students read aloud the Close Reader Habit on p. 386.

TIP Remind students to look for details that show how the characters are feeling or reacting to events.

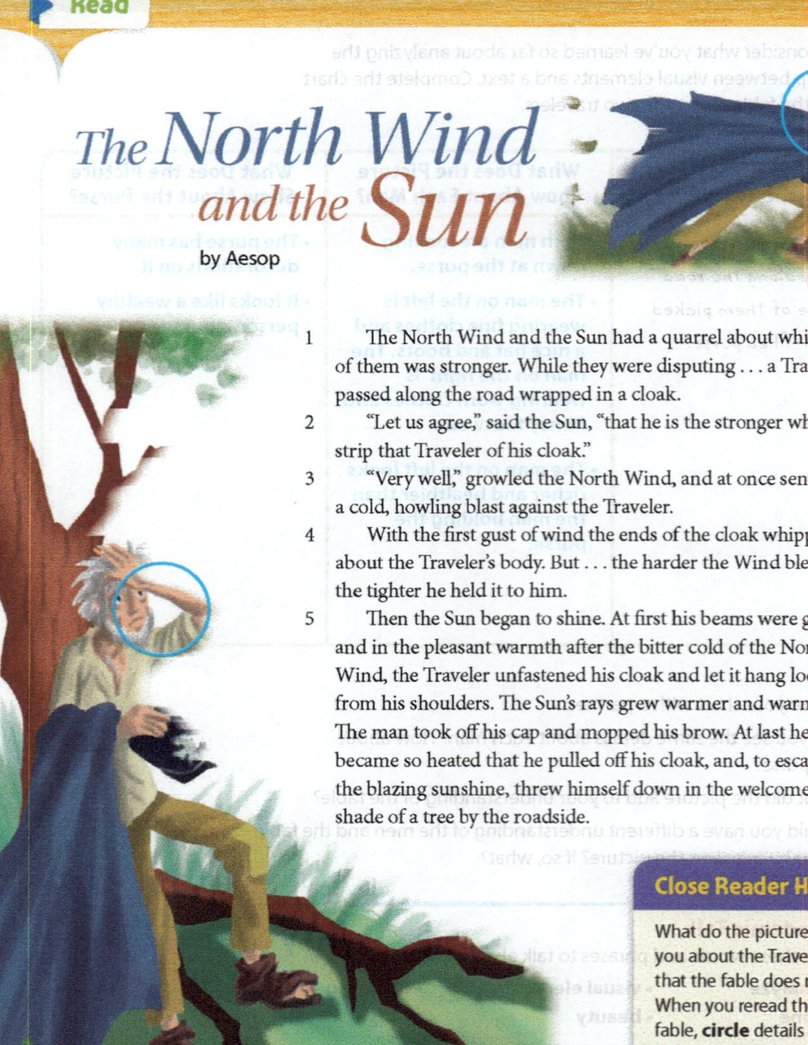

Modeled and Guided Instruction

Read

Genre: Fable

The North Wind and the Sun

by Aesop

1 The North Wind and the Sun had a quarrel about which of them was stronger. While they were disputing . . . a Traveler passed along the road wrapped in a cloak.

2 "Let us agree," said the Sun, "that he is the stronger who can strip that Traveler of his cloak."

3 "Very well," growled the North Wind, and at once sent a cold, howling blast against the Traveler.

4 With the first gust of wind the ends of the cloak whipped about the Traveler's body. But . . . the harder the Wind blew, the tighter he held it to him.

5 Then the Sun began to shine. At first his beams were gentle, and in the pleasant warmth after the bitter cold of the North Wind, the Traveler unfastened his cloak and let it hang loosely from his shoulders. The Sun's rays grew warmer and warmer. The man took off his cap and mopped his brow. At last he became so heated that he pulled off his cloak, and, to escape the blazing sunshine, threw himself down in the welcome shade of a tree by the roadside.

Close Reader Habits

What do the pictures tell you about the Traveler that the fable does not? When you reread the fable, **circle** details in the pictures that add to your understanding of the story.

386

English Language Learners

Develop Language

- **Act It Out** Work with students to identify some descriptive action verbs from the text, such as *disputing, growled, whipped, unfastened, mopped, pulled,* and *threw.*
- Together determine the definition of each word. Encourage students to use context clues from the story as well as a dictionary as needed. Then model the action that each verb describes. Have students repeat after you.
- Have teams take turns acting out the story without using words. Stop the action at random places and ask other students to identify the verb or phrase that has just been acted out, using direct quotes from the text.

● Word Learning Strategy

Use Context Clues

- Draw students' attention to synonyms and antonyms that help establish meaning. Start with the word *quarrel* in the first sentence.

  What other word in the first paragraph has the same meaning as *quarrel*? *(disputing)*

  What word in the second paragraph has an opposite meaning? *(agree)*

  What is the definition of *quarrel*? *(an argument or disagreement)*
- Repeat this process to help students define *bitter.* Help them find the words *cold, howling, blast, gust,* and *blew* and the antonyms *warmth, gentle, pleasant, heated,* and *blazing.*
- As students discover each word, ask them to use the word in a sentence. **L.5.4a**

Explore **What do the pictures contribute to the fable's meaning?**

Think

1 Complete the chart below. Look for details in the text about how the Traveler feels. Then explain what the pictures add to the story.

Study the pictures closely. Small details in a picture can add a lot to a text.

Quotes from the Text	Based on the Text, How Does the Traveler Feel?	What Do the Pictures Add to the Meaning?
"With the first gust of wind the ends of the cloak whipped about the Traveler's body. But . . . the harder the Wind blew, the tighter he held it to him."	The Traveler must feel **very cold to pull the cloak around him for warmth.**	The Traveler's face shows **pain and discomfort.** It looks like it's hard to walk forward because **the wind is blowing in his face and he is traveling on foot.**
"At last he became so heated that he pulled off his cloak, and, to escape the blazing sunshine, threw himself down in the welcome shade of a tree by the roadside."	**The Traveler feels warmer and warmer until he has take off his cloak and get out of the Sun's rays.**	**The Traveler wipes sweat from his forehead, showing he is very warm. He is slumped under the tree because the heat has made him too tired to keep walking.**

Talk

2 Talk about what the pictures contribute to your understanding of the fable. Add details to your chart if necessary.

HINT The pictures add details about the Traveler and how he reacts to the cold and heat.

Write

3 **Short Response** Analyze what the pictures add to the meaning of the fable. Use details from the text **and** the pictures to support your answer. Use the space provided on page 390 to write your answer.

387

Think Aloud

- The first question in the chart asks me to look for details about how the Traveler feels. I'll go back to the fable and reread to find details.
- The quote in the first column comes from paragraph 4. In this paragraph, I see that the cold North Wind "whipped" the Traveler's cloak around. That made him hold it tighter around himself. That's a clue to how he must be feeling—cold and miserable!
- Now I'll look for details in the picture that support this. The chart prompts me to look at the Traveler's face. His brow is furrowed and he seems to be straining. He looks very uncomfortable. I will complete the first sentence in column 3 by writing "pain and discomfort."

Think

- Read aloud the Think section. Explain to students that you will model how to find text evidence to fill in part of the chart. Use the **Think Aloud** below to guide your modeling.
- Revisit the Explore question. Guide students to determine that they need to lock for more details, using the Close Reader Habit.
- Encourage students to work with a partner to continue rereading the passage and complete the chart. Remind them that the Buddy Tip will help them find the information they need.
- Ask volunteers to share their completed charts.
- Guide students to find details in the pictures that go with direct quotes from the text, as well as details in the pictures that are not found in the text.

Talk

- Read aloud the Talk prompt.
- Have partners respond to the prompt. Use the Talk Routine on pp. A52–A53.
- Circulate to check that students are discussing and writing about how the images add to their understand of the details and events in the fable.

Write

- Ask a volunteer to read aloud the Write prompt.
- Invite a few students to tell what the prompt is asking them to do.
- Make sure students understand that they need to explain both how the pictures support the words in the story and offer details that are not included in the story.
- Have students turn to p. 390 to write their response.
- Use Review Responses on p. 390 to assess students' writing.

Wrap Up

- Ask students to recall the Learning Target. Have them explain how analyzing the pictures helped them better understand the fable.

Get Started

Today you will read a lyric poem—a poem that has musical qualities. First, you will read to understand the poem. Then you will reread with a partner to analyze how the illustrations add to the meaning of the poem.

Read

- Read aloud the title of the poem and the name of the poet.
- Have students predict what the poem will be about, based on the title and the illustration.
- **Read to Understand** Have students read the poem independently. Tell them to place a check mark above any confusing words and phrases as they read. Remind students to look inside, around, and beyond each unknown word or phrase to help them figure out its meaning. Use the Word Learning Routine on pp. A50–A51.
- When students have finished reading, clarify the meanings of words and phrases they still find confusing. Then use the questions below to check understanding. Encourage students to identify details in the text that support their answers.

  When does the rider go out riding? *(at night when it's windy and stormy)*

  What does the phrase "whenever the wind is high" mean? *(whenever it is very windy out)*

  What question is the speaker trying to answer? *("Why does he gallop and gallop about?")*

● **Word Learning Strategy**

- **Read to Analyze** Read aloud the Close Reader Habit on p. 388 to set the purpose for the second read. Then have students reread the poem with a partner and discuss any questions they might have.

Guided Practice

Read

Genre: Lyric Poem

Windy Nights

by Robert Louis Stevenson

Whenever the moon and stars are set,
Whenever the wind is high,
All night long in the dark and wet,
A man goes riding by.
Late in the night when the fires are out,
Why does he gallop and gallop about?

Whenever the trees are crying aloud,
And ships are tossed at sea,
By, on the highway, low and loud,
By at the gallop goes he.
By at the gallop he goes, and then
By he comes back at the gallop again.

Close Reader Habits

How do the poem and the picture work together to produce a tone of mystery? Reread the poem and study the picture. **Underline** the lines in the poem that suggest that the rider is mysterious. **Circle** details in the picture that add to the feeling of mystery.

388

English Language Learners

Develop Language

- **Visual Aids** Work with students to match details in the illustration to words in the poem. First, choose simple examples such as *moon, man,* and *trees.* Direct students to label the picture in their own books.
- Then point to phrases and figurative language in the poem and ask students to identify visual elements that illustrate them. For example, have students match visual elements to the phrases "in the dark and wet," "Late in the night," and "riding by."

● Word Learning Strategy

Use Context Clues

- Draw students' attention to line 8. Guide them to explain the phrase *tossed at sea.*

  What does *tossed* mean? *(thrown)*

  What tosses a ship? *(winds and waves)*

  What is happening or about to happen when ships are *tossed at sea?* *(a storm)*

  What details in the picture add to your understanding of the phrase *tossed at sea?* *(The picture shows waves and branches of trees being tossed in the wind.)*
- Ask students to use this process to explain the phrase *by at the gallop* in lines 10–12.

L.5.4a

Think Use what you learned from reading the lyric poem to answer the following questions.

The poem and picture create a tone of mystery because they give so little information about the rider.

1 This question has two parts. Answer Part A. Then answer Part B.

Part A
Which statement **best** describes what the picture adds to the poem?

A The picture shows that the rider is angry.
(B) The picture shows that the rider is determined.
C The picture shows that the rider is calm and relaxed.
D The picture shows that the rider is brave.

Part B
Which line from the poem **best** supports the answer to Part A?

A "Whenever the moon and stars are set, . . ."
B "Whenever the wind is high, . . ."
(C) "All night long in the dark and wet, . . ."
D "And ships are tossed at sea, . . ."

Talk

2 The picture adds to the mysterious tone of the poem "Windy Nights." What details can you see in the picture to support the statement that the poem creates a feeling of mystery? Use the three-column chart on page 391 to organize your ideas and the details you see.

HINT Think about the time of day, the weather, and what the reader knows or doesn't know about the rider.

Write

3 **Short Response** Explain how the picture supports the mysterious tone of the poem. Include **two** details you find in the picture that suggest there is something mysterious about the rider and his actions. Use the space provided on page 391 to write your answer.

389

Integrating Standards

Use the following questions to further students' understanding of the poem.

- **What is the speaker's point of view? How does it affect the meaning of the poem?** *(The speaker tells about the story from the outside, never sharing the rider's thoughts or feelings. This adds to the mystery of the poem.)*
  DOK 2 RL.5.6
- **What is the meaning of "crying aloud" as it is used in line 7?** *(It means the wind is whistling through the branches, creating a moaning sound that seems as though the trees are crying.)*
  DOK 2 RL.5.4

Monitor Understanding

If... students have difficulty completing the chart as they answer item 2,

then... use non-examples to clarify. Say:

Imagine that it is daytime and sunny. Imagine that the poem describes birds chirping. How would this poem be different?

Guide students to understand that certain elements naturally create mystery. For example, in the darkness of night, it is hard to see what's up ahead. Discuss how students feel during stormy weather. Have them add these ideas to their charts.

Think

- Have students work with a partner to complete item 1. Draw attention to the boldface words **best** in Parts A and B.

TIP Have students match each option in Part A to the illustration. Guide them to eliminate any options that don't appear in the image.

Answer Analysis

When students have finished, discuss correct and incorrect responses.

1 **Part A**
The correct choice is B. The rider is galloping hard and leaning into the wind, suggesting that he is determined not to stop his actions.
- **A** and **D** are not supported by details in the picture.
- **C** does not describe the rider. The scene suggests he is energetic and engaged, not calm and relaxed.

Part B
The correct choice is C. The phrase "all night long" suggests determination and purpose.
- **A, B,** and **D** describe the setting and the weather, not the rider.

DOK 2

Integrating Standards

Talk

- Have partners discuss the prompt. Emphasize that students should support their ideas with text details.
- Circulate to clarify misunderstandings.

Monitor Understanding

Write

- See p. 391 for instructional guidance.

Wrap Up

- Ask students to recall the Learning Target. Have them explain how analyzing illustrations helps them develop a deeper understanding of a text.

Modeled and Guided Instruction

Write

- Remember to use the Response-Writing Routine on pp. A54–A55.

Review Responses

After students complete the writing activity, help them evaluate their responses.

3 Responses may vary but should show an understanding of both the words and illustrations. See the sample response on the student book page.
DOK 3

Write **Use the space below to write your answer to the question on page 387.**

The North Wind and the Sun

3 **Short Response** Analyze what the pictures add to the meaning of the fable. Use details from the text **and** the pictures to support your answer.

Sample response: The details in the first picture show the Traveler must feel very cold as he pulls the cloak around him. With the Wind blowing in his face, the Traveler holds his hat tightly, and his face clearly shows discomfort. It looks as if it is hard to walk forward into the wind. After the Sun warms the Traveler, he becomes too hot for his cloak. A detail in the second picture shows sweat running down his face. That he is slumped under a tree suggests the heat has made him tired.

Check Your Writing

- ☐ Did you read the prompt carefully?
- ☐ Did you put the prompt in your own words?
- ☐ Did you use the best evidence from the text to support your ideas?
- ☐ Are your ideas clearly organized?
- ☐ Did you write in clear and complete sentences?
- ☐ Did you check your spelling and punctuation?

390

Scaffolding Support for Reluctant Writers

If students are having a difficult time getting started, use the strategies below. Work individually with struggling students, or have students work with partners.

- Circle the verbs in the prompt that tell you what to do, such as *describe*, *explain*, or *compare*.
- Underline words and phrases in the prompt that show what information you need to provide in your response, such as *causes*, *reasons*, or *character traits*.
- Talk about the details from the text that you will include in your response.
- Explain aloud how you will respond to the prompt.

Windy Nights

2 Use the chart below to organize your ideas.

Quotes from the Poem	How Do the Quotes Produce the Tone?	What Do the Pictures Add to the Tone?

Write Use the space below to write your answer to the question on page 389.

3 **Short Response** Explain how the picture supports the mysterious tone of the poem. Include **two** details you find in the picture that suggest there is something mysterious about the rider and his actions.

Sample response: The picture adds to the mysterious tone of the poem by showing the dark night with the only light coming from the crescent moon. In the picture, the artist has shown the "high wind" blowing the trees about. The rider and horse are headed into the wind, and the artist didn't show the man's face, making the man mysterious. With the line, "Why does he gallop and gallop about?," the speaker suggests that nobody knows why the rider is doing what he does. The picture emphasizes and enhances the mystery of these lines in the poem.

Teacher Notes

Talk

2 Students should use the chart to organize their thoughts and evidence.

Write

- Ask a volunteer to read aloud the Write prompt.
- Invite students to tell what the prompt is asking them to do. Make sure they understand that they need to use details from the visual elements to support their ideas about tone.
- Call attention to the HINT.
- Remember to use the Response-Writing Routine on pp. A54–A55.

Review Responses

After students complete the writing activity, help them evaluate their responses.

3 Responses may vary but should explain how the illustration adds to the poem's mysterious tone, using specific examples from the poem and the illustration. See the sample response on the student book page.
DOK 3

Independent Practice

Get Started

Today you are going to read a myth and use what you have learned about analyzing visual elements to develop a better understanding of the text.

- Ask a volunteer to explain why analyzing the visual elements that go with stories and poems will help readers better understand literary texts. Encourage students to use the Academic Talk words and phrases in their response.

 **English Language Learners**

Read

You are going to read the myth independently and use what you have learned to think and write about the words and pictures. As you read, remember to look closely at the details in the pictures and think about how they support the text and offer additional information.

- Read aloud the title of the myth and then encourage students to preview the text, paying close attention to the illustrations.
- Call attention to the Words to Know on p. 392.
- If students need support in reading the passage, you may wish to use the Monitor Understanding suggestions.
- When students have finished, have them complete the Think and Write sections.

● **Monitor Understanding**

Read

Genre: Myth

from PHAETHON

by Flora J. Cooke

WORDS TO KNOW

As you read, look inside, around, and beyond these words to figure out what they mean.

- **companions**
- **persist**
- **harnessing**

1 Phaethon was the son of Helios, who drove the chariot of the sun . . . One day when Phaethon was telling his companions about his father, the sky king, they laughed and said, "How do you know that he is your father? You have never seen him. If, as you say, he cannot safely come nearer to the earth, why do you not go to his land?"

2 Phaethon answered, "My father's throne is far away from this valley. My mother has promised that when I am stronger, I shall go to my father's palace. I often watch his golden chariot roll by in its path and think perhaps some day I shall drive the glorious horses of the sun." . . .

3 When Phaethon told his mother what his companions had said, she answered, "Go, my child, ask great Helios if you are his son. If you are worthy to be the son of Helios you will be given strength and courage for the journey."

 **English Language Learners**

Build Meaning

Preview Vocabulary Explain that this myth contains some words that might be confusing because they are not commonly used. Have students use dictionaries for support in answering questions such as the following:

- **What does the word *chariot* mean, in paragraph 1?** *(a very fast vehicle drawn by horses)*
- **What visual element in the story shows a chariot?** *(the picture on p. 394)*
- **What word in paragraph 13 means the same as *chariot*?** *(car)*

Repeat this process with the word *palace*.

4 Phaethon gladly and bravely climbed the unused path to the palace of the sun . . . Helios saw the brave youth and knew that it was his son. . . . "You are indeed my son," he said. "I will put an end to your doubts. Ask any gift you will, and it shall be yours."

5 Phaethon had always had one wish in his heart and said, "O, my father, let me drive the wonderful golden chariot of the sun for just one day."

6 Helios shook his head sadly and said, "That is the one thing which you must not ask to do. You are my son, and I love you. For your own sake, I cannot let you do this. You have neither the strength nor the wisdom for the great work."

7 Phaethon would not listen, but threw his arms around his father's neck and begged to go. Helios said at last, "If you persist, foolish boy, you shall have your wish, for I cannot break my promise."

8 Dawn had drawn back the purple curtains of the morning and the Hours were harnessing the horses to the chariot . . . Helios said, "O, my son, go not too high or you will scorch the dwelling of heaven, nor too low, lest you set the world on fire. Keep to the middle path; that is best."

Monitor Understanding

If... students struggle to read and understand the myth,

then... use these scaffolding suggestions:

Question the Text Preview the text by asking the following questions:

- **Based on the title and illustrations, what do you predict the myth will be about?**
- **What questions do you have about the text?**

Vocabulary Support Define words that may interfere with comprehension, such as *glorious*, *youth*, *scorch*, and *plunged*.

Read Aloud Read aloud the text with students. You could also have students chorally read the text in a small group.

Check Understanding Use the questions below to check understanding. Encourage students to cite details in the illustrations that support their answers.

- **Who is the main character?** *(Phaethon, the son of the sky king, Helios)*
- **Where does Phaethon travel?** *(to his father's palace in the sky)*
- **What happens to Phaethon?** *(He asks his father if he can drive the chariot of the sun, but he's not strong enough to manage it and he causes destruction.)*

Independent Practice

Integrating Standards

After students have read the myth, use these questions to discuss the text with them.

- **A metaphor is a figure of speech that creatively compares one thing to another. What things are being compared in the metaphors "the Eastern gates of day" and "the purple curtains of the morning"?**

  (Both are comparisons to dawn or daybreak. The first metaphor compares dawn to a gateway, and the second compares dawn to a curtain that can be drawn back.)

  ***DOK 2* RL.5.4**

- **Why does the author say that Poseidon "cried out in terror from the sea"?**

  (The author wants readers to realize how devastating Phaethon's actions are. Poseidon, god of the sea, is afraid that his home will dry up from the fire.)

  ***DOK 3* RL.5.1**

- **How would the story be different if Helios told it?**

  (As a narrator, Helios would likely describe his hesitation at letting Phaethon drive the chariot and the tension he feels about putting trust in his son. He would also show his dismay in the aftermath of Phaethon's destruction.)

  ***DOK 3* RL.5.6**

- **What natural features of Earth does this myth explain? What paragraph contains details that support this answer?**

  (Phaethon's actions explain why the tops of mountains don't have any trees and why there are deserts. Paragraph 13 states, "The deserts and barren mountaintops still tell the story of the day Phaethon tried to drive the chariot of the sun.")

  ***DOK 3* RL.5.1**

- **What is a theme of the myth? What details in the text show the theme?**

  (One theme of the myth is that one should know one's limits. Helios sums up this theme in paragraph 8: "Keep to the middle path; that is best.")

  ***DOK 4* RL.5.2**

● Theme Connection

9 Phaethon leapt into the golden chariot . . . as the fiery horses sprang forth from the eastern gates of Day. They soon missed the strong steady hand of their master. Up, up they went, far into the sky, above the stars, and then plunged downward toward the earth.

10 The clouds smoked, the mountaintops caught fire, many rivers dried up and whole countries became deserts. Great cities burned, and even Poseidon cried out in terror from the sea. Then the people on Earth learned with what great wisdom the path of the sun was planned.

11 Helios saw that the whole world would soon be on fire, and cried to father Zeus to save the earth from the flames. Zeus searched all the heavens for clouds and hurled his thunderbolts from the sky.

12 Phaethon fell from the chariot, down, down into a clear river . . . His sisters came to the banks of the river and wept. That they might be always near Phaethon, Zeus, in pity, changed them into poplar trees, and their tears became clear amber as they fell into the water.

13 At last the tired horses became quiet, and the great car rolled slowly back into its old path. But the deserts and barren mountaintops still tell the story of the day Phaethon tried to drive the chariot of the sun.

● Theme Connection

- Remind students that the theme of this lesson is Picturing Literature. Ask them to explain how all the passages in the lesson relate to this theme.
- Encourage students to share examples of how visual elements added to the beauty, tone, and meaning of each story or poem.

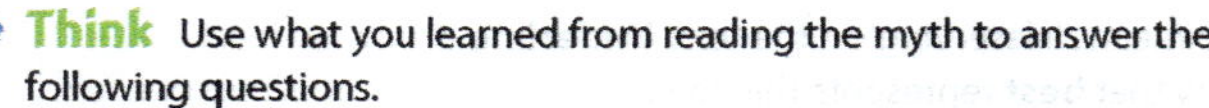

Think Use what you learned from reading the myth to answer the following questions.

1 This question has two parts. First, answer Part A. Then answer Part B.

Part A
Which statement **best** describes what the picture on page 392 adds to the story?

- A The picture suggests that Phaethon is happy with his friends.
- B The picture suggests that Phaethon is a member of the royal family.
- (C) The picture suggests that Phaethon is doubted by his friends.
- D The picture suggests that Phaethon is shy around people.

Part B
Which line from the story **best** supports the answer to Part A?

- A "Phaethon was the son of Helios, who drove the chariot of the sun. . . ."
- (B) "One day when Phaethon was telling his companions about his father, the sky king, they laughed. . . ."
- C "Phaethon had always had one wish in his heart. . . ."
- D "Phaethon leapt into the golden chariot . . . as the fiery horses sprang forth from the eastern gates of Day."

2 How does the picture on page 394 help the reader understand why Helios does not want Phaethon to drive the chariot? Pick the two **best** choices.

- A It shows why Helios does not believe Phaethon is his son.
- B It shows why Helios thinks Phaethon plans to destroy the earth.
- (C) It shows why Helios believes Phaethon is not wise enough to drive the chariot.
- D It shows why Helios will let only Zeus and Poseidon drive the chariot.
- (E) It shows why Helios believes Phaethon isn't strong enough for the task.
- F It shows why Helios thinks Phaethon will drive the chariot into the sun.

395

● **Monitor Understanding**

If... students struggle to complete the items,

then... you may wish to use the following suggestions:

Read Aloud Activities

- As you read, have students note any unfamiliar words or phrases. Clarify any misunderstandings.
- Discuss each item with students to make certain they understand the expectation.

Reread the Text

- Have students complete three-column graphic organizers as they reread.
- Have partners summarize the story or ask teams to act out the scenes.

Think

- Use the Monitor Understanding suggestions to support students in completing items 1–3.

● **Monitor Understanding**

Answer Analysis

When students have finished, discuss correct and incorrect responses.

1 **Part A**

The correct choice is C. The friends' facial expressions suggest that they doubt Phaethon.

- **A** is incorrect because Phaethon looks sincere, rather than happy.
- **B** is incorrect because nothing in the pictures indicates that Phaethon is royal.
- **D** is incorrect because Phaethon is talking actively to his friends, not being shy.

Part B

The correct choice is B. It shows Phaethon talking with young friends who laugh at his bragging about being the son of Helios.

- **A** describes who Phaethon and Helios are.
- **C** tells about Phaethon's wish, which is not In the picture.
- **D** is not correct because Phaethon's leap into the chariot is not pictured.

DOK 2 RL.5.7

2 **The correct choices are C and E.** In paragraph 6, Helios says, "You have neither the strength nor the wisdom for the great work."

- **A** is incorrect because Helios does accept Phaethon as his son.
- **B** is incorrect because Phaethon does not think his son is planning to destroy the earth on purpose.
- **D** is incorrect because Helios does let Phaethon drive the chariot.
- **F** is incorrect because although Helios fears something bad might happen, nothing suggests that he thinks Phaethon will drive right into the sun.

DOK 3 RL.5.7

Independent Practice

3 **Students should underline the word *worthy* as a synonym for "deserving."**
DOK 2 L.5.5c

Write

- Tell students that using what they read, they will plan and compose an extended response to the writing prompt. Provide copies of the chart on p. TR11.

Monitor Understanding

Review Responses

After students have completed each part of the writing activity, help them evaluate their responses.

4 Display the **Sample Response** for the planning chart on the next page. Have students compare their chart with the sample. Are they missing any information?
DOK 3 RL.5.7

5 Display or pass out copies of the reproducible **2-Point Writing Rubric** on p. TR10. Have students use the rubric to individually assess their writing and revise as needed.

When students have finished their revisions, evaluate their responses. Answers will vary but should include explanations and details from all three pictures as well as details from the text.
DOK 3 RL.5.7, W.5.9a

3 The author uses a word that means "deserving" in the text. **Underline** a word in the paragraph below that **best** represents that idea.

> When Phaethon told his mother what his companions had said, she answered, "Go, my child, ask great Helios if you are his son. If you are worthy to be the son of Helios you will be given strength and courage for the journey."

Write

A *myth* is a made-up story written long ago. Myths can explain natural events. They can also describe interactions between humans and gods. "Phaethon" is a myth set in ancient Greece. What do the three pictures contribute to your understanding that "Phaethon" is a Greek myth?

4 **Plan Your Response** Make a three-column chart with these headings: First Picture, Second Picture, Third Picture. For each picture, identify and record at least **one** detail you see in **each** picture that adds to your understanding that Phaethon is a myth set in ancient Greece.

5 **Write an Extended Response** Explain what the pictures add to your understanding that "Phaethon" is a myth set in ancient Greece. Refer to details you see in each picture in your response.

Responses will vary. A top-scoring response will refer to at least one detail from each picture to support the idea that "Phaethon" is a myth set in ancient Greece.

Monitor Understanding

If... students don't understand the writing task,

then... read aloud the writing prompt. Use the following questions to help students get started.

- **What is the prompt asking you to write about?**
- **Do you need to reread the text to find more information?**
- **How will you identify the information you need to include?**

- Have partners talk about how they will organize their responses.

Learning Target

In this lesson, you analyzed relationships between pictures and texts. Explain why it is important to analyze such relationships in what you read.

Responses will vary, but students should identify ways that analyzing pictures helps them understand how the pictures contribute meaning, tone, and beauty to what a text says.

397

Wrap Up

Learning Target

- Have each student respond in writing to the Learning Target prompt.
- When students have finished, have them share their responses. This may be done with a partner, in small groups, or as a whole class.

4 Sample Response

First Picture	Second Picture	Third Picture
• Phaethon and his friends wear clothes that seem like something ancient people wear. • Phaethon and his friends sit in front of a temple and a statue of a goddess.	• Helios' entire palace glows. • Helios's eyes glow. • Phaethon looks small, dirty, and human compared with Helios' size and golden color.	• Phaethon and a chariot of horses are flying and pulling the Sun around Earth. • The horses and the chariot are both blazing. • Earth is burning because the chariot is too close to it.

5 2-Point Writing Rubric

Points	Focus	Evidence	Organization
2	My answer does exactly what the prompt asked me to do.	My answer is supported with plenty of details from the text.	My ideas are clear and in a logical order.
1	Some of my answer does not relate to the prompt.	My answer is missing some important details from the text.	Some of my ideas are unclear and out of order.
0	My answer does not make sense.	My answer does not have any details from the text.	My ideas are unclear and not in any order.

Lesson 22
Comparing and Contrasting Stories in the Same Genre

Standards Focus

Compare and contrast stories in the same genre (e.g., mysteries and adventure stories) on approaches to similar themes and topics. RL.5.9

Lesson Objectives

Reading

- Compare stories in the same genre, such as mysteries and adventures. RL.5.9
- Analyze similarities and differences between the themes and topics of stories in the same genre. RL.5.9

Writing

- Draw evidence from literary texts to support analysis and reflection. W.5.9a

Speaking and Listening

- Pose and respond to specific questions and contribute to discussions. SL.5.1c
- Review the key ideas expressed and draw conclusions. SL.5.1d

Language

- Consult reference materials, both print and digital, to determine or clarify the precise meaning of words and phrases. L.5.4c
- Acquire and use academic and domain-specific words and phrases. L.5.6

Additional Practice: **RL.5.1, RL.5.2, RL.5.3, RL.5.4, RL.5.5, RL.5.6, L.5.5a**

Academic Talk

See **Glossary of Terms**, pp. TR2–TR9

- compare
- contrast
- genre
- topic
- theme

Learning Progression

Grade 4	Grade 5	Grade 6
Students compare the treatment of similar themes and topics and patterns of events (e.g., the quest) in stories, myths, and traditional literature from different cultures.	Building on Grade 4, students note similar qualities within genres. This standard emphasizes comparing and contrasting stories in the same genre (e.g., mysteries and adventure stories) on their approaches to similar themes and topics.	Grade 6 increases in complexity by requiring students to compare and contrast texts in different forms or genres (e.g., stories and poems; historical novels and fantasy stories) in terms of their approaches to similar themes and topics.

Lesson Text Selections

Modeled and Guided Instruction	Guided Practice	Independent Practice
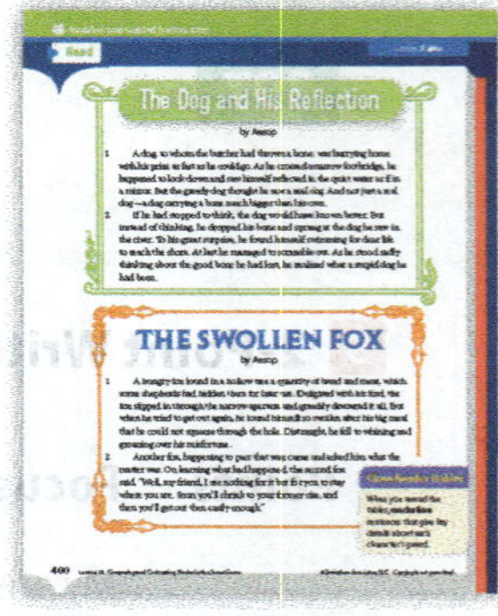	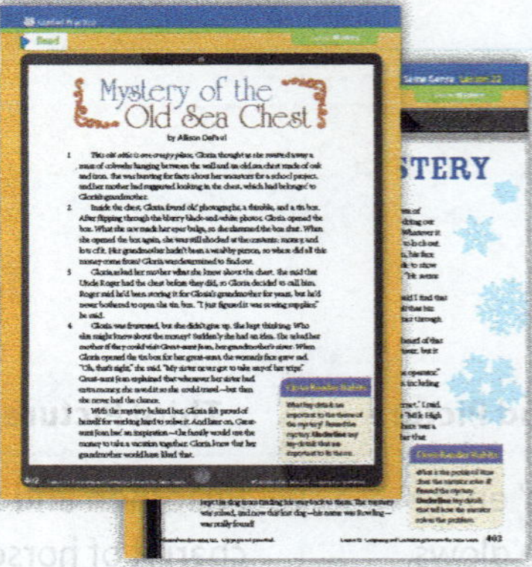	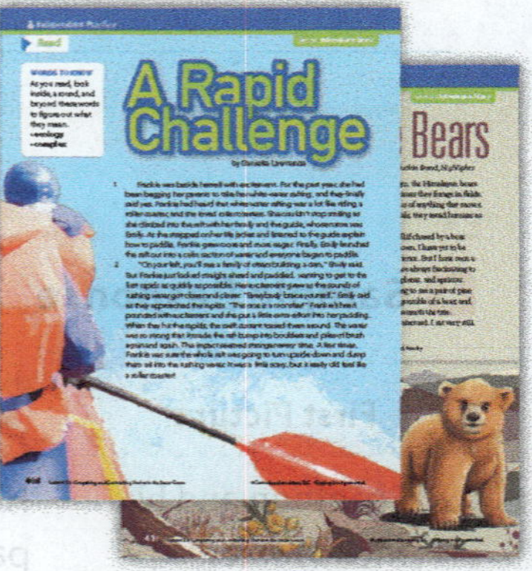
The Dog and His Reflection by Aesop **Genre:** Fable	**Mystery of the Old Sea Chest** by Allison DePaul **Genre:** Mystery	**A Rapid Challenge** by Danielle Lawrence **Genre:** Adventure Story
The Swollen Fox by Aesop **Genre:** Fable	**Mile-High Mystery** by Joanna Banks **Genre:** Mystery	**Those Three Bears** by Ruskin Bond **Genre:** Adventure Story

Lesson Pacing Guide

Whole Class Instruction *30–45 minutes per day*

Day 1

Introduction pp. 398–399

- **Read** **Comparing and Contrasting Stories in the Same Genre** *10 min*
- **Think** *10 min*
  Graphic Organizer: Venn Diagram
- **Talk** *5 min*
  Quick Write (TRB) *5 min*

Day 2

Modeled and Guided Instruction pp. 400–401, 406

- **Read** **The Dog and His Reflection** and **The Swollen Fox** *10 min*
- **Think** *10 min*
  Graphic Organizer: Venn Diagram
- **Talk** *5 min*
- **Write** Short Response *10 min*

Day 3

Guided Practice pp. 402–405, 407

- **Read** **Mystery of the Old Sea Chest** and **Mile-High Mystery** *20 min*
- **Think** *10 min*
- **Talk** *5 min*
- **Write** Short Response *10 min*

Day 4

Independent Practice pp. 408–415

- **Read** **A Rapid Challenge** and **Those Three Bears** *20 min*
- **Think** *10 min*
- **Write** Extended Response *15 min*

Day 5

Independent Practice pp. 408–415

- *Review* Answer Analysis (TRB) *10 min*
- *Review* Response Analysis (TRB) *10 min*
- *Assign and Discuss* Learning Target *10 min*

Ready Writing Connection

Lesson 6 Writing an Opinion: Speech

During *Ready Reading* Days 1–5, use:

- **Step 1** **Study a Mentor Text**
- **Step 2** **Unpacking Your Assignment**
- **Review the Research Path**
- **Read Source Text**
- **Step 3** **Find Text Evidence**

Small Group Differentiation

Teacher-Toolbox.com

Reteach

***Ready Reading* Prerequisite Lesson**

- **Grade 4** Lesson 25 Comparing Topics and Themes in Stories

Personalized Learning

i-Ready.com

Independent

***i-Ready* Close Reading Lesson**

- **Grade 4** Comparing Topics and Themes in Stories
- **Grade 5** Compare and Contrast Stories in the Same Genre

Get Started

- Explain to students that in this lesson they will read pairs of stories in the same genre, or type of text. They will compare and contrast the stories' topics and themes.
- Have students briefly review the meanings of *topic* and *theme*. Invite volunteers to share examples that demonstrate understanding.
- Choose two familiar stories that share a genre, such as "Hansel and Gretel" and "Little Red Riding Hood." Work with students to briefly review the plot of each story. Explain:

  Hansel and Gretel go to a stranger's house and she turns out to be a witch who wants to cook them. Little Red Riding Hood talks to a stranger in the woods and he turns out to be a wolf who wants to eat her. Both fairy tales are about young children's interaction with strangers, and both share the theme that one should be careful around strangers.
- Focus students' attention on the Learning Target. Read it aloud to set the purpose for the lesson.
- Display the Academic Talk words. Tell students to listen for these words and their meanings as you work through the lesson together. Use the Academic Talk Routine on pp. A48–A49.

English Language Learners

- **Genre Focus**

Read

- Read aloud the Read section as students follow along. Restate to reinforce:

  Stories in the same genre usually have similar topics and themes. Sometimes comparing and contrasting similar stories can make the theme clearer or more obvious.
- Have students read "Goodbye, DXL-597" and "The Last Imperfection." Tell them to think about how the passages are alike and different during and after reading.

Introduction

RL.5.9 Compare and contrast stories in the same genre (e.g., mysteries and adventure stories) on their approaches to similar themes and topics.

Lesson 22
Comparing and Contrasting Stories in the Same Genre

Comparing and contrasting how stories in the same genre approach similar themes and topics will deepen your understanding and enjoyment of each story.

Read Stories are grouped by **genre**, such as mystery, adventure, or science fiction. Stories in the same genre often have similar themes and topics. The **theme** is the message of a story, such as "friends are always there for you." The **topic** is the subject of the story, such as horses or time travel. **Comparing** and **contrasting** stories in the same genre can help you see their themes and topics more clearly.

Read the stories below. Compare and contrast their themes and topics.

GOODBYE, DXL-597

"Mom, where's DXL-597? I need that pile of bolts to help me with my homework."

"Narbla, you're always complaining about DXL-597, so I traded it in for a DXL-600. It knows 900 languages and has a faster processor!"

"Will the new robot shoot hoops or go skyboarding with me, just like DXL-597 did?"

"I'm afraid none of the new ones do that. They're for education only."

THE LAST IMPERFECTION

EF2020 stood between two other Zaxons in a line that stretched to the horizon on both sides. Their screens faced the sky, watching the last ship leave Earth. The humans had created the Zaxons, but the Zaxons had driven the humans out.

EF2020 looked down the line of robots to his right, perfect and straight. There were no more imperfections on Earth, he thought. There would be no mistakes or accidents. Then he had another thought: There would be no more music or laughter, either.

EF2020 moved ahead of the Zaxons beside him by an inch. It was a start.

398

English Language Learners
Build Meaning

Background Knowledge Tell students that "Goodbye, DXL-597" and "The Last Imperfection" are science fiction, a type of fantasy literature that combines some elements of science and technology with realistic things about everyday life.

- Have students discuss whether the pictures are realistic. Guide students to determine that in real life, humans do not play sports with robots.
- Explain that in each passage, students should think about DXL-597 and EF2020 as a person with human qualities.

Genre Focus
Mystery

Explain that in Guided Practice, students will read a pair of mysteries, fictional stories with characters who try to solve a crime or an unexplained event.

Characters in mysteries often are or act like detectives who search for clues. These types of stories thrill and excite readers by creating suspense: readers don't know how the story will resolve until the main character figures it out.

Ask students to tell about mysteries they have read or seen. Who were the characters? What were they trying to find out? How did they finally solve the mystery?

Think Consider what you've learned so far about comparing and contrasting stories in the same genre. What happens in each story? Do they share topics or themes? Use the *Venn diagram* below to organize your thinking about the stories.

"Goodbye, DXL-597"	Alike	"The Last Imperfection"
What happens: Narbla gets a new robot because she has been asking for one. However, the new robot doesn't do all the fun things the old robot did.	Genre: Both are science fiction stories. Topic: Both are about robots. Theme: Be careful what you wish for, as you might just get it.	What happens: The robots have driven the humans away from Earth, but EF2020 will miss their music and laughter. He will try to be different from the other robots.

Talk Share your Venn diagram with a partner.

- What is the genre of each story?
- Did you both identify the same similarities and differences?
- How did comparing and contrasting the stories help you better understand each of them?

Academic Talk
Use these words to talk about the text.

- compare
- contrast
- genre
- topic
- theme

399

Monitor Understanding

If... students struggle to compare and contrast,
then... hold up a marker and a pen. Ask students to state how the objects are alike and different.

- **How are they alike?** *(Both are used for writing. They are about the same length.)*
- **How are they different?** *(The marker can be used for coloring. The pen is mainly used for writing. The marker is wider than the pen, which is very thin.)*

Ask students to compare and contrast other objects or concepts, guiding them to use the words *one, both, alike, similar,* and *different* in their descriptions. Explain that a Venn diagram, like the one on p. 399, can help them organize similarities and differences.

Think

- Have students read aloud the Think section. Explain that the Venn diagram will help them organize their thinking.
- Have partners complete the Venn diagram. Remind students to use the details in both passages as they compare and contrast the stories.
- As students work, circulate and provide assistance as needed.
- Ask volunteers to share what they wrote.
- Make certain students understand that while the stories are about different events and characters, they share a genre (science fiction), a topic (robots), and a theme (Be careful what you wish for.)

Talk

- Read aloud the Talk prompts.
- Have partners discuss the characters, events, and the message or lesson in each story. Encourage students to use phrases that tell what story they want to reference. *"Goodbye, DXL-597" was... "The Last Imperfection" was... Both stories were...*
- Ask volunteers to share their ideas.

Quick Write Have students write a response to the following prompt:

How do the events in "Goodbye, DXL-597" and "The Last Imperfection" illustrate the theme "Be careful what you wish for"?

Ask students to share their responses.

Wrap Up

- Invite students to share what they've learned so far. Encourage them to use the Academic Talk words in their explanations.
- Explain to students that when they compare and contrast stories in the same genre, they can better understand each story.

In the next section, we'll read two fables and compare and contrast their themes and topics. Understanding how stories in the same genre approach themes and topics will help you better understand and enjoy the stories.

Monitor Understanding

Modeled and Guided Instruction

Get Started

Today you will read two fables. First, you'll read to understand what happens. Then you'll read to analyze by comparing and contrasting the fables.

Read

- Read aloud the titles of the fables, and have students read the fables independently. Tell them to place a check mark above any confusing words and phrases as they read. Remind students to look inside, around, and beyond each unknown word to help them figure out its meaning. Use the Word Learning Routine on pp. A50–A51.
- When students have finished reading, clarify the meanings of words and phrases they still find confusing. Then use the questions below to check understanding. Encourage students to identify details in the text that support their answers.

  Why does the dog drop his bone? *(He sees a reflection of what he thinks is a bigger bone.)*

  What happens to the dog at the end of the story? *(He loses the bone he had and almost loses his life, too.)*

  How does the fox become swollen? *(He eats too much of the food that he finds.)*

  What is the fox doing at the end of the story? *(He is stuck in the tree waiting to shrink back down.)*

English Language Learners

● Word Learning Strategy

Explore

- Read aloud the Explore question at the top of p. 401 to set the purpose for the second read. Tell students they will need to take a closer look at why the dog and fox act as they do.
- Have students read aloud the Close Reader Habit on p. 400.

> **TIP** One way students can compare and contrast these passages is by asking how the lessons learned by the dog and the fox are the same or different.

Modeled and Guided Instruction

Read — Genre: Fable

The Dog and His Reflection

by Aesop

1 A dog, to whom the butcher had thrown a bone, was hurrying home with his prize as fast as he could go. As he crossed a narrow footbridge, he happened to look down and saw himself reflected in the quiet water as if in a mirror. But the greedy dog thought he saw a real dog. And not just a real dog—a dog carrying a bone much bigger than his own.

2 If he had stopped to think, the dog would have known better. But instead of thinking, he dropped his bone and sprang at the dog he saw in the river. To his great surprise, he found himself swimming for dear life to reach the shore. At last he managed to scramble out. As he stood sadly thinking about the good bone he had lost, he realized what a stupid dog he had been.

THE SWOLLEN FOX

by Aesop

1 A hungry fox found in a hollow tree a quantity of bread and meat, which some shepherds had hidden there for later use. Delighted with his find, the fox slipped in through the narrow aperture and greedily devoured it all. But when he tried to get out again, he found himself so swollen after his big meal that he could not squeeze through the hole. Distraught, he fell to whining and groaning over his misfortune.

2 Another fox, happening to pass that way, came and asked him what the matter was. On learning what had happened, the second fox said, "Well, my friend, I see nothing for it but for you to stay where you are. Soon you'll shrink to your former size, and then you'll get out then easily enough."

Close Reader Habits

When you reread the fables, **underline** sentences that give key details about each character's greed.

400

English Language Learners

Build Meaning

Prior Knowledge Use a mirror to reinforce the concept of a reflection. Point to your image in a mirror and say "reflection." Point out that *reflection* has a cognate in several languages, and invite students to share it in their first language as applicable.

- Discuss whether a reflection is always accurate. Tip the mirror to show how a reflection can distort your image. Have students describe what is happening.
- Note that In "The Dog and His Reflection," a dog looks into water and sees his reflection and also the reflection of a big bone. Invite students to explain why the dog saw a bigger bone.

● Word Learning Strategy

Use a Dictionary

- Reread paragraph 1 of "The Swollen Fox." Direct students' attention to the word *aperture*.

  What do you think *aperture* means?
- Explain that while context clues such as "hollow tree" can sometimes help students get a sense of what a word means, other times they must verify that meaning in a dictionary.
- Ask a volunteer to look up *aperture* and read its part of speech *(noun)* and meaning *(a small hole or opening)*.
- Have students subsitute the meaning into the paragraph to confirm that it makes sense.

L.5.4c

Explore How does each story approach the topic of greed?

Think

1 Complete the Venn diagram below. It will help you identify the similarities and differences between the stories.

In each story, identify key details about characters, events, and so on. You'll use these key details to support your ideas.

"The Dog and His Reflection"	Alike	"The Swollen Fox"
What happens: • The dog's greed for the bone he sees in his reflection causes him to lose the bone he has. • The dog's greed nearly causes him to drown as he swims back to shore.	• Both are fables. • Both use animals to show how greed leads to bad endings. • Both animals regret their actions.	What happens: • The fox's greed for the shepherds' food causes him to get stuck in a tree. • No one can help the fox; he has to wait until he shrinks back down to normal size.

Talk

2 Consider how the stories deal with the topic of greed. What happens to the animals as a result of their greed? If necessary, add or change the details in your Venn diagram.

 **Write**

3 **Short Response** How does each fable develop the topic of greed? Use key details from each story in your response. Use the space provided on page 406 to write your answer.

HINT Start by telling what the fables have in common. Then describe their differences.

Think Aloud

- I need to answer the question, "How does each story approach the topic of greed?" First I'll think about how the characters' actions are greedy.
- I'll start by rereading "The Dog and His Reflection." In this story, the dog has a bone. Then he crosses a footbridge and thinks he sees a bigger bone in the water below him. He jumps in the water to get that bone—which isn't really there—and he loses the bone he has in the process. I'll summarize this beneath the correct title on the Venn diagram.
- Now I'll do the same for "The Swollen Fox." This character finds some food in a hollow tree and eats so much that he can't get out of the tree. I'll add this to the other side of the Venn diagram.

Think

- Read aloud the Think section. Explain to students that you will model how to find text evidence to fill in part of the Venn diagram. Use the **Think Aloud** below to guide your modeling.
- Revisit the Explore question. Guide students to determine that they need to look for more details, using the Close Reader Habit.
- Encourage students to work with a partner to continue rereading the passage and complete the Venn diagram. Remind them to read the Buddy Tip.
- Ask volunteers to share their completed Venn diagrams.
- Guide students to see how the stories are alike. Both fables use animals to show how greed can lead to undesirable consequences.

Talk

- Read aloud the Talk prompt.
- Have partners respond to the prompt. Use the Talk Routine on pp. A52–A53.
- Circulate to check that students are discussing what is similar and different about the stories.

Write

- Ask a volunteer to read aloud the Write prompt.
- Invite a few students to tell what the prompt is asking them to do.
- Make sure students understand that they need to include the text evidence that shows greed, such as abandoning the bone in favor of a bigger one and eating so much that swelling occurs.
- Have students turn to p. 406 to write their response.
- Use Review Responses on p. 406 to assess students' writing.

Wrap Up

- Ask students to recall the Learning Target. Have them explain how comparing and contrasting the characters, events, and themes helped them better understand the fables.

Guided Practice

Get Started

Today you will read two mysteries. First, you will read the mysteries to find out what happens. Then you will reread with a partner to analyze the stories by comparing and contrasting them.

Read

- Read aloud the title of each mystery. Ask students what a *sea chest* is. Draw or display an image of a trunk or pirate treasure chest.
- Have students predict what mystery the sea chest holds. Then ask them to predict what a mile-high mystery might be.
- **Read to Understand** Have students read the stories independently. Tell them to place a check mark above any confusing words and phrases as they read. Remind students to look inside, around, and beyond each unknown word to help them figure out its meaning. Use the Word Learning Routine on pp. A50–A51.
- When students have finished reading, clarify the meanings of words and phrases they still find confusing. Then use the questions below to check understanding. Encourage students to identify details in the text that support their answers.

What mysterious thing does Gloria find in the sea chest? *(lots of money)*

How does Gloria go about solving the mystery? *(She first asks her mother. Then she asks her Uncle Roger. Finally, she asks her Great-aunt Jean, who tells her that Gloria's grandmother was saving the money for trips.)*

What mystery does the narrator of "Mile-High Mystery" solve? *(who owns the dog)*

How does the narrator solve the mystery? *(by following the suggestion to look for an animal clinic and by using the Internet)*

English Language Learners

- **Word Learning Strategy**

Guided Practice

Read

Genre: Mystery

Mystery of the Old Sea Chest

by Allison DePaul

1 *This old attic is one creepy place,* Gloria thought as she swatted away a mass of cobwebs hanging between the wall and an old sea chest made of oak and iron. She was hunting for facts about her ancestors for a school project, and her mother had suggested looking in the chest, which had belonged to Gloria's grandmother.

2 Inside the chest, Gloria found old photographs, a thimble, and a tin box. After flipping through the blurry black-and-white photos, Gloria opened the box. What she saw made her eyes bulge, so she slammed the box shut. When she opened the box again, she was still shocked at the contents: money, and lots of it. Her grandmother hadn't been a wealthy person, so where did all this money come from? Gloria was determined to find out.

3 Gloria asked her mother what she knew about the chest. She said that Uncle Roger had the chest before they did, so Gloria decided to call him. Roger said he'd been storing it for Gloria's grandmother for years, but he'd never bothered to open the tin box. "I just figured it was sewing supplies," he said.

4 Gloria was frustrated, but she didn't give up. She kept thinking: Who else might know about the money? Suddenly she had an idea. She asked her mother if they could visit Great-aunt Jean, her grandmother's sister. When Gloria opened the tin box for her great-aunt, the woman's face grew sad. "Oh, that's right," she said. "My sister never got to take any of her trips." Great-aunt Jean explained that whenever her sister had extra money, she saved it so she could travel—but then she never had the chance.

5 With the mystery behind her, Gloria felt proud of herself for working hard to solve it. And later on, Great-aunt Jean had an inspiration—the family would use the money to take a vacation together. Gloria knew that her grandmother would have liked that.

Close Reader Habits

What key details are important to the theme of the mystery? Reread the mystery. **Underline** any key details that are important to its theme.

402

English Language Learners

Develop Language

Concept Vocabulary Remind students that they are reading mysteries in this part of the lesson. Encourage speakers of Latin-based languages to identify cognates for the word *mystery* and explain what it means in their own words.

- Discuss the traits of a person who solves a mystery. Point to the word *determined* in both stories, and again guide students to recognize and define cognates in their first languages.
- Point to the expression "give up" in each story. Invite students to share ideas about its meaning. Guide them to understand that this expression means "stop trying." Discuss how a good problem solver, like the main character in each story, never gives up.

Genre: Mystery

MILE-HIGH MYSTERY

by Joanna Banks

1 It was a bitterly cold and snowy Tuesday afternoon in my town of Fairbanks, Alaska. My sister Missy and I sat at the kitchen table doing our homework when we heard an eerie wail coming from outside. "Whatever it is, it's on the porch," Missy whispered, and she lifted the curtain to look out.

2 On our porch sat the shaggiest, saddest dog we had ever seen, his face and paws encrusted with ice. We brought the poor creature inside to show our parents, and I rubbed down his back and head with a towel. "He seems healthy," I said, "so he must belong to someone."

3 I was determined to get him back to his owner—but how could I find that person? Just then I heard a muffled jingle of metal from under all that fur. "Hey, he's wearing a collar with a tag! Maybe we can find his owner through this . . . oh. It just says 'Mile High' on the tag. Nothing else."

4 "So maybe it's an animal clinic?" said Mom. "But I've never heard of that one before." In response, I dug a phone book out of a kitchen drawer, but it didn't have a listing for a "Mile High" animal clinic.

5 "Maybe it's a new clinic and isn't listed yet," I said. "I'll call the operator." But the operator told me that Fairbanks didn't have any business, including an animal clinic, with that name.

6 I sighed, but I just couldn't give up. "This is a job for the Internet," I said. A Web search revealed that Denver, Colorado, is nicknamed the "Mile High City." Next I searched for animal clinics in Denver, and bingo! There was a "Mile High Animal Clinic" in Denver, along with a phone number that I called immediately.

7 After getting off the phone, I explained that a family who took their dog to the Mile High Animal Clinic had recently moved to Fairbanks. Their house wasn't far from ours, but the heavy snow and unfamiliar neighborhood must have kept the dog from finding his way back to them. The mystery was solved, and now this lost dog—his name was Rowling—was really found!

Close Reader Habits

What is the problem? How does the narrator solve it? Reread the mystery. **Underline** key details that tell how the narrator solves the problem.

Word Learning Strategy

Use a Dictionary

- Reread paragraph 4 of "Mile-High Mystery." Direct students' attention to the word *clinic*.

  What do you think *clinic* means?

- Explain that while the context clue "animal" gives some information, readers must use a dictionary to find the complete meaning.
- Ask students to find *clinic* in the dictionary and name its part of speech *(noun)* and its meaning *(a place to get health care).* Discuss the meaning in the context of the story.

L.5.4c

- **Read to Analyze** Read aloud the Close Reader Habits on pp. 402 and 403 to set the purpose for the second read. Then have students reread the mysteries with a partner and discuss any questions they might have.

TIP Remind students that what happens at the end of a story is often a clue to the story's theme. Sometimes characters learn a lesson based on mistakes or poor decisions they've made. Other times, readers might learn a lesson based on how the main character chooses to solve his or her problem.

Guided Practice

Think

- Have students work with a partner to complete items 1–3. Draw attention to the boldface words.

TIP Remind students that they need to refer to both stories in order to answer each item.

Answer Analysis

When students have finished, discuss correct and incorrect responses.

1 Part A

The correct choice is B. One character finds money in a sea chest. The other finds a dog from Colorado in Alaska.

- **A** is incorrect because only "Mile-High" mentions homework.
- **C** is incorrect because the weather has no impact on "Sea Chest."
- **D** is incorrect because no character talks to a distant relative in "Mile-High."

Part B

The correct choices are A and D. Both show moments when the unexpected element is discovered.

- **B** and **C** are incorrect because Gloria asks her mother and her great-aunt about the chest after finding the money.
- **E** is incorrect because most dogs wear collars.
- **F** is incorrect because the Internet is a likely place to find information.

DOK 3

2 The correct choice is B. Both stories involve characters working together to solve a mystery.

- **A** is incorrect because neither the money nor the dog is stolen.
- **C** is incorrect because "Mile-High" only leads to the dog being returned.
- **D** is incorrect because only "Sea Chest" leads to a family secret being discovered.

DOK 3

● **Monitor Understanding**

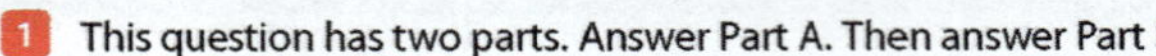

Think Use what you learned from reading the mysteries to respond to the following questions.

In a mystery, the main character or characters set out to solve a problem. How characters respond to a problem can tell you a lot about the theme.

1 This question has two parts. Answer Part A. Then answer Part B.

Part A
Which of the following statements is true about **both** mysteries?

A Each mystery has to do with homework assignments.
(B) Something unexpected is discovered in an unlikely place.
C Weather makes the main character's problem worse.
D Talking to a distant family member finally solves the mystery.

Part B
Choose **two** pieces of evidence, one from **each** story, that support the answer in Part A.

(A) "When she opened the box again, she was still shocked at the contents: money, and lots of it." ("Mystery of the Old Sea Chest")
B "Gloria asked her mother what she knew about the chest." ("Mystery of the Old Sea Chest")
C "'Oh, that's right,' she said. 'My sister never got to take any of her trips.'" ("Mystery of the Old Sea Chest")
(D) "On our porch sat the shaggiest, saddest dog we had ever seen, his face and paws encrusted with ice." ("Mile-High Mystery")
E "Just then I heard a muffled jingle of metal from under all that fur." ("Mile-High Mystery")
F "A Web search revealed that Denver, Colorado, is nicknamed the 'Mile High City.'" ("Mile-High Mystery")

2 Which statement about both mysteries is **true**?

A Both mysteries are about things that are stolen.
(B) Both mysteries involve families working together.
C Both mysteries lead to further adventures.
D Both mysteries lead to family secrets being discovered.

404

● Monitor Understanding

If... students have difficulty finding text evidence to answer item 2, **then...** use a simple story map or sequence chain to show the main events of each mystery. Events for "Mystery of the Old Sea Chest" include *Gloria opens the chest; Gloria finds a lot of money; Gloria asks her mother and Uncle Roger about the money but learns nothing; Gloria asks Great-aunt Jean about the money and solves the mystery.* Repeat with the main events in "Mile-High Mystery."

3 The main characters in each story turn to others for help in solving their mysteries. Choose **two** pieces of evidence, one from each story, that **best** support this statement.

A "What she saw made her eyes bulge, so she slammed the box shut." ("Mystery of the Old Sea Chest")

(B) "Gloria asked her mother what she knew about the chest." ("Mystery of the Old Sea Chest")

C "Gloria was frustrated, but she didn't give up." ("Mystery of the Old Sea Chest")

D "In response, I dug a phone book out of a kitchen drawer, but it didn't have a listing for a 'Mile High' animal clinic." ("Mile-High Mystery")

E "I sighed, but I just couldn't give up. 'This is a job for the Internet,' I said." ("Mile-High Mystery")

(F) "There was a 'Mile High Animal Clinic' in Denver, along with a phone number that I called immediately." ("Mile-High Mystery")

Talk

4 The stories "Mystery of the Old Sea Chest" and "Mile-High Mystery" share a theme: *Determination is key to solving problems.* Use the Venn diagram on page 407 to organize key details from each story that develop this theme.

 **Write**

5 **Short Response** Use the information from your Venn diagram to compare and contrast how each story approaches the theme of determination being key to solving problems. Use **two** details from **each** story in your response. Use the space provided on page 407 to write your answer.

HINT Great words to use in a compare–contrast response include *both, similar to, like, but, different than,* and *unlike.*

405

Integrating Standards

Use these questions to further students' understanding of the mysteries.

- **In "Mystery of the Old Sea Chest," Great-aunt Jean tells Gloria that her grandmother never got to take any of her trips. What can you infer from this?** *(Gloria's grandmother passed away before she was able to use her money. That is why Great-aunt Jean's expression grows sad when she opens the tin box. It also implies why Gloria is not able to ask her grandmother directly where the money in the tin box came from.)*
  DOK 2 RL.5.1
- **Explain how the paragraphs in each story build on each other to create suspense.** *(In "The Mystery of the Old Sea Chest," we learn why Gloria is in the attic. After she makes her discovery, she endeavors to solve the mystery. By the end of paragraph 3, she has hit a dead end. Paragraph 4 states "Suddenly she had an idea." This signals that the mystery will be solved, as shown in paragraph 5. In "Mile-High Mystery, the end of paragraph 2 establishes the mystery, saying "He must belong to someone." In paragraphs 3, 4, and 5, the narrator continues to try despite hitting several obstacles. In paragraph 6, we see the word "Bingo!" which indicates that the mystery is solved.)*
  DOK 2 RL.5.5

3 **The correct choices are B and F.** Both show the main characters turning to others for help solving the mystery.

- **A** shows only Gloria's reaction.
- **C** shows only Gloria's persistence.
- **D** and **E** show the narrator turning to forms of media, not individual people, to solve the mystery.

DOK 3

Integrating Standards

Talk

- Have partners discuss the prompt. Emphasize that students should support their ideas with text details.
- Circulate to clarify misunderstandings.

Write

- Ask a volunteer to read aloud the Write prompt.
- Invite students to tell what the prompt is asking them to do. Make sure they know that they need to focus on how the girls keep going until they have solved the mystery.
- Call attention to the HINT.
- Have students turn to p. 407 to write their response.
- Use Review Responses on p. 407 to assess students' writing.

Wrap Up

- Ask students to recall the Learning Target. Have them explain how comparing and contrasting the characters and events helped them better understand the stories.

 **Modeled and Guided Instruction**

Write

- Remember to use the Response-Writing Routine on pp. A54–A55.

Review Responses

After students complete the writing activity, help them evaluate their responses.

3 Responses may vary but should show that both fables warn readers about the negative outcomes of greed. Students should use details from both stories in their answers. See the sample response on the student book page. ***DOK 3***

Write Use the space below to write your answer to the question on page 401.

The Dog and His Reflection

and

THE SWOLLEN FOX

HINT Start by telling what the fables have in common. Then describe their differences.

3 **Short Response** How does each fable develop the topic of greed? Use key details from each story in your response.

Sample response: Both fables warn readers about the negative outcomes of greed, but they do so with different characters, settings, and events. In "The Dog and His Reflection," a dog nearly drowns because he wants a bigger bone. He also loses the bone he has by dropping it in a river. In "The Swollen Fox," a fox gets stuck in a hole in a tree because he has eaten too much. Even his friend can't help him. Both animals regret their actions and realize too late that they shouldn't have been so greedy.

Don't forget to check your writing.

Check Your Writing

- ☐ Did you read the prompt carefully?
- ☐ Did you put the prompt in your own words?
- ☐ Did you use the best evidence from the text to support your ideas?
- ☐ Are your ideas clearly organized?
- ☐ Did you write in clear and complete sentences?
- ☐ Did you check your spelling and punctuation?

406

Scaffolding Support for Reluctant Writers

If students are having a difficult time getting started, use the strategies below. Work individually with struggling students, or have students work with partners.

- Circle the verbs in the prompt that tell you what to do, such as *describe*, *explain*, or *compare*.
- Underline words and phrases in the prompt that show what information you need to provide in your response, such as *causes*, *reasons*, or *character traits*.
- Talk about the details from the text that you will include in your response.
- Explain aloud how you will respond to the prompt.

Mystery of the Old Sea Chest and MILE-HIGH MYSTERY

4 Use the Venn diagram below to organize your ideas and evidence from the stories.

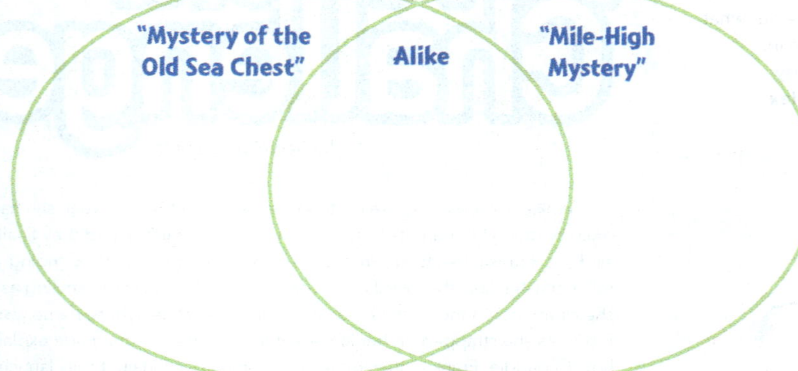

Write Use the space below to write your answer to the question on page 405.

HINT Great words to use in a compare–contrast response include *both, similar to, like, but, different than,* and *unlike.*

5 **Short Response** Use the information from your Venn diagram to compare and contrast how each story approaches the theme of determination being key to solving problems. Use **two** details from **each** story in your response.

Sample response: The mysteries are similar in that both convey the theme that determination is key to solving problems. However, the mysteries are different in how they show this theme. In the first story, Gloria shows determination when she talks to her mother and her uncle. When they can't give her an answer, she talks to her great-aunt and finally gets the answer. The second story is similar in that the narrator works with family members to solve the mystery, but it is different in that the narrator also checks a phone book and the Internet.

407

Teacher Notes

Guided Practice

Talk

4 Students should use the Venn diagram to organize their thoughts and evidence.

Write

- Remember to use the Response-Writing Routine on pp. A54–A55.

Review Responses

After students complete the writing activity, help them evaluate their responses.

5 Responses may vary but should include details about both girls' determination to solve their mysteries. Students should use details from both stories to support their response. See the sample response on the student book page.
DOK 3

Independent Practice

Get Started

Today you are going to read two stories and use what you have learned about comparing and contrasting stories in the same genre.

- Ask a volunteer to explain how comparing and contrasting two stories on the same topic can help them understand both stories better. Encourage students to use the Academic Talk words in their response.

English Language Learners

Read

You are going to read the stories independently and use what you have learned to think and write about their similarities and differences. As you read, remember to look closely at the characters and events to determine how the stories approach the topic and theme.

- Read aloud the titles of the stories and then encourage students to preview the text, paying close attention to the illustrations.
- Call attention to the Words to Know in the upper left of p. 408.
- If students need support in reading "A Rapid Challenge," you may wish to use the Monitor Understanding suggestions.
- When students have finished reading "A Rapid Challenge," have them read "Those Three Bears" before beginning the Think and Write sections.

● **Monitor Understanding**

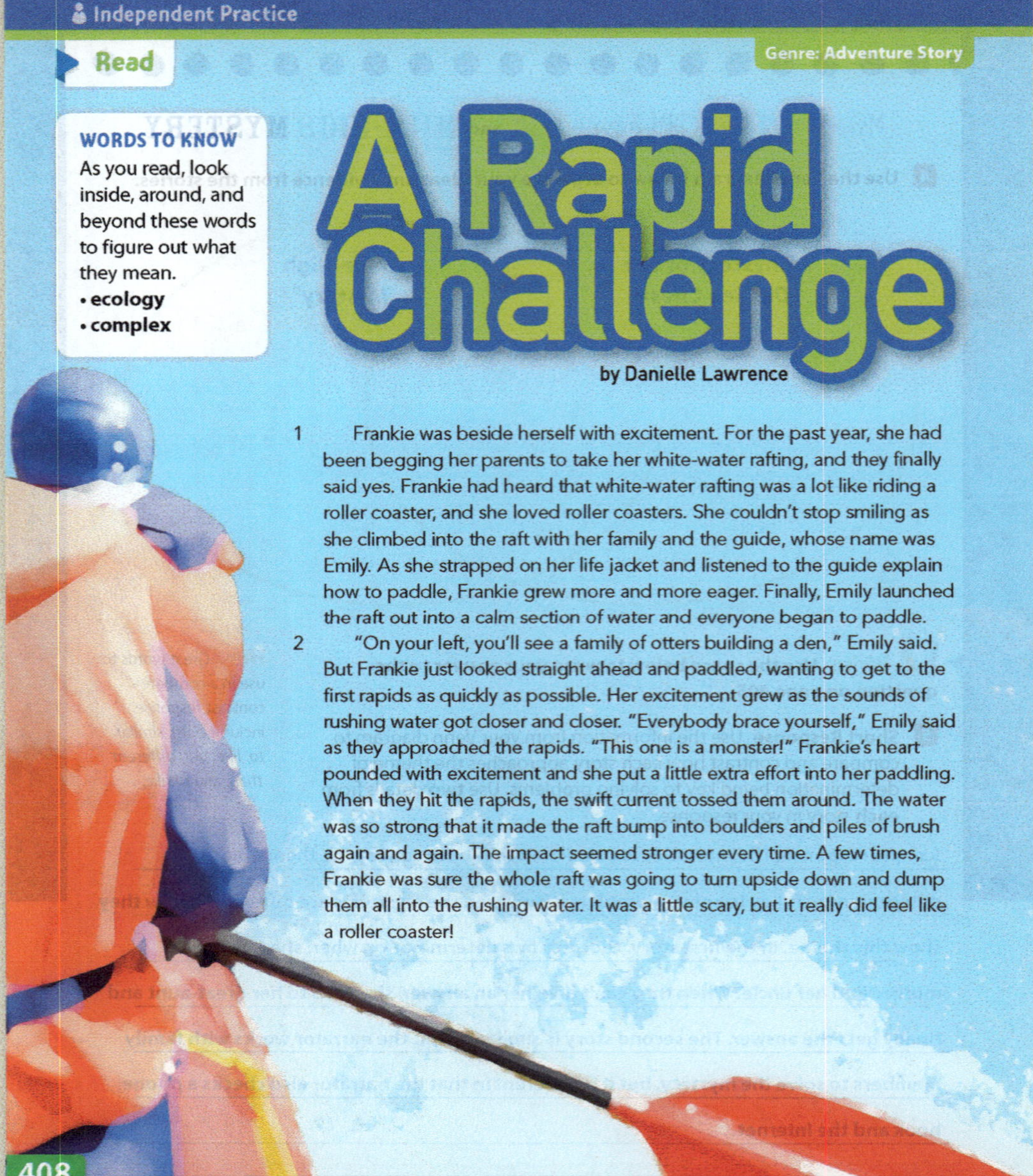

Independent Practice

Read

Genre: Adventure Story

WORDS TO KNOW
As you read, look inside, around, and beyond these words to figure out what they mean.
• **ecology**
• **complex**

A Rapid Challenge

by Danielle Lawrence

1 Frankie was beside herself with excitement. For the past year, she had been begging her parents to take her white-water rafting, and they finally said yes. Frankie had heard that white-water rafting was a lot like riding a roller coaster, and she loved roller coasters. She couldn't stop smiling as she climbed into the raft with her family and the guide, whose name was Emily. As she strapped on her life jacket and listened to the guide explain how to paddle, Frankie grew more and more eager. Finally, Emily launched the raft out into a calm section of water and everyone began to paddle.

2 "On your left, you'll see a family of otters building a den," Emily said. But Frankie just looked straight ahead and paddled, wanting to get to the first rapids as quickly as possible. Her excitement grew as the sounds of rushing water got closer and closer. "Everybody brace yourself," Emily said as they approached the rapids. "This one is a monster!" Frankie's heart pounded with excitement and she put a little extra effort into her paddling. When they hit the rapids, the swift current tossed them around. The water was so strong that it made the raft bump into boulders and piles of brush again and again. The impact seemed stronger every time. A few times, Frankie was sure the whole raft was going to turn upside down and dump them all into the rushing water. It was a little scary, but it really did feel like a roller coaster!

408

English Language Learners

Develop Language

Cognates Explain that *rapid* has two related meanings in English just as it has in Spanish: *rapid* and *rápido* are both adjectives meaning "fast." Similarly, *rapids* and *rápidos* are both nouns meaning "fast moving areas of water in a river." Help speakers of other Latin-based languages link to related cognates for these words.

- **Based on the title and illustrations, where do you predict "A Rapid Challenge" will take place?**
- **What do you predict will happen?**

Provide, or ask students to provide, cognates for the Words to Know on p. 408 *(ecología, complejo).*

Students may also wish to volunteer other cognates they know or recognize such as, at the beginning of "A Rapid Challenge," *guide/guía, finally/finalmente, explain/explicar, calm/calma, section/sección, family/familia.*

3 Finally, the raft slid out of the rushing water and into a calm pool. Everyone was smiling. "That was fun!" Frankie yelled. "Where are the next rapids?"

4 "Not for a while," Emily answered. "The next couple of miles are pretty calm. We have a perfect chance to do some nature watching!"

5 Frankie sighed. The rapids were all she was really interested in. But as long as she had to wait, she thought she might as well enjoy the sights. Frankie took a break from paddling to listen to Emily, who was explaining how the river creatures lived and worked together. "River ecology is very complex," said Emily. "All of the animals—wait!" Emily lowered her voice. "Be very quiet, pick up your paddles, and look at what's behind that tree on the right bank of the river."

6 Frankie squinted as her eyes followed the line formed by Emily's pointing finger. When she finally saw what Emily was showing her, she gasped. It was a mother wolf and two tiny wolf pups. The mother was peering out from behind a tree as the pups batted at each other's faces under the mother's legs. "She has probably been teaching her pups to hunt here by the river," whispered Emily. "Maybe even showing them how to catch fish!" Frankie smiled to herself, imagining those wolf pups splashing around in the water, pawing at fish. Just then, her eyes met the mother wolf's. For at least a minute, they just looked at each other. Frankie wished the whole raft could become invisible so they could just watch the wolf family all day.

7 The mother wolf looked away from Frankie and nudged her pups to run away from the riverbank. In an instant, they were gone. "We were very lucky," Emily said. "Not many people get to see wolves in the wild. They're very good at hiding."

8 Frankie sighed as the sound of approaching rapids began to get closer and closer. They all put their paddles back in the water. "Here we go again!" said Emily. But Frankie's paddling was much slower than it had been before. She was still thinking about those tiny wolf pups, and the long look she had shared with a mother wolf.

Monitor Understanding

If... students struggle to read and understand the passage,
then... use these scaffolding suggestions:

Question the Text Preview the text by asking the following questions:

- **Based on the title and illustrations, what do you predict the story will be about?**
- **What questions do you have about the text?**

Vocabulary Support Define words and phrases that may interfere with comprehension, such as *brace yourself* and *boulders*.

Read Aloud Read aloud the text with students. You could also have students chorally read the text in a small group.

Check Understanding Use the questions below to check understanding. Encourage students to cite details in the text that support their answers.

- **At the beginning of "A Rapid Challenge," what is Frankie's mind focused on?** *(She is thinking only of the rapids.)*
- **How does Frankie change in the story? Why?** *(After viewing the wolves and meeting the mother wolf's eyes, Frankie starts to paddle more slowly and consider the wildlife.)*

Independent Practice

Read

- Remind students that they need to read both selections before they begin the Think and Write activities.

English Language Learners

- Call attention to the Words to Know in the upper left of p. 410.
- If students need support in reading "Those Three Bears," you may wish to use the Monitor Understanding suggestions.
- When students have finished reading, have them complete the Think and Write sections.

Monitor Understanding

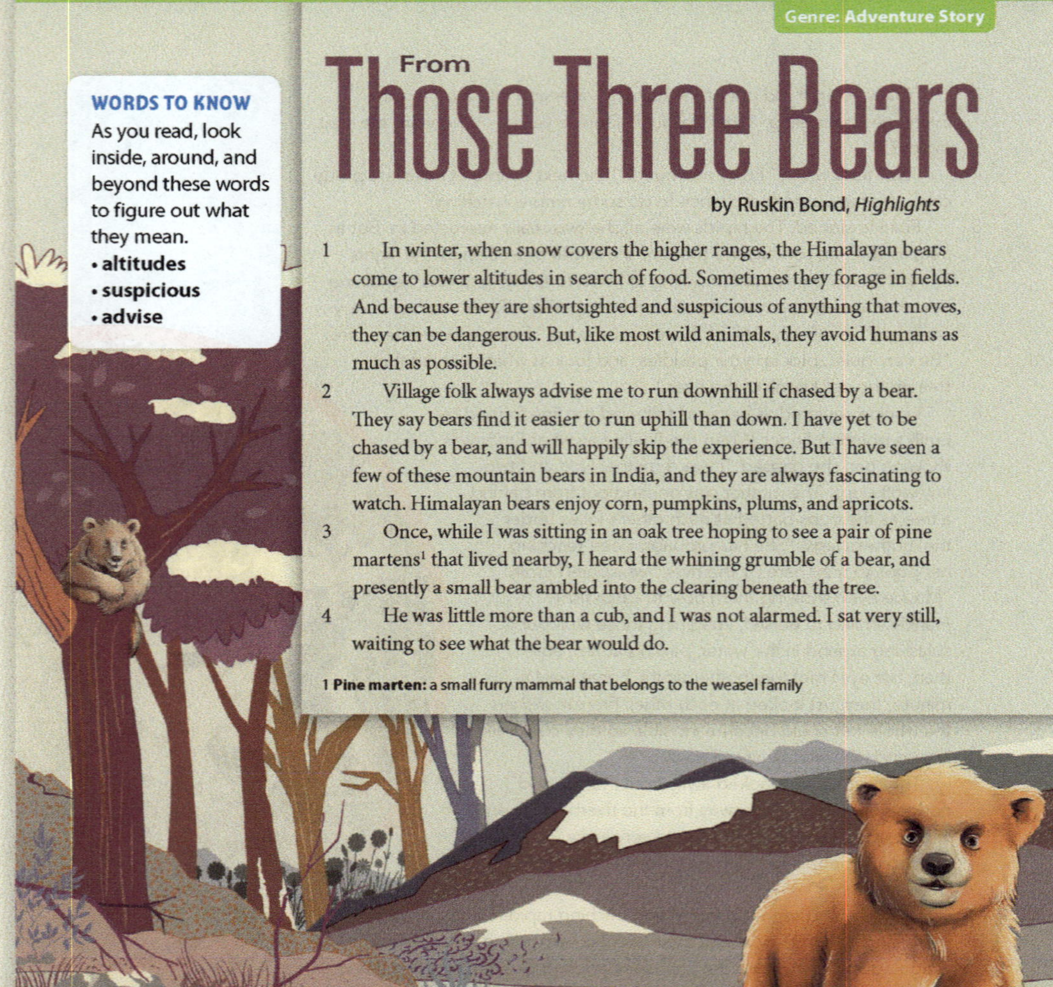

Independent Practice

Genre: Adventure Story

WORDS TO KNOW
As you read, look inside, around, and beyond these words to figure out what they mean.
- **altitudes**
- **suspicious**
- **advise**

From Those Three Bears

by Ruskin Bond, *Highlights*

1 In winter, when snow covers the higher ranges, the Himalayan bears come to lower altitudes in search of food. Sometimes they forage in fields. And because they are shortsighted and suspicious of anything that moves, they can be dangerous. But, like most wild animals, they avoid humans as much as possible.

2 Village folk always advise me to run downhill if chased by a bear. They say bears find it easier to run uphill than down. I have yet to be chased by a bear, and will happily skip the experience. But I have seen a few of these mountain bears in India, and they are always fascinating to watch. Himalayan bears enjoy corn, pumpkins, plums, and apricots.

3 Once, while I was sitting in an oak tree hoping to see a pair of pine martens[1] that lived nearby, I heard the whining grumble of a bear, and presently a small bear ambled into the clearing beneath the tree.

4 He was little more than a cub, and I was not alarmed. I sat very still, waiting to see what the bear would do.

1 **Pine marten:** a small furry mammal that belongs to the weasel family

410

English Language Learners

Develop Language

Synonyms Explain that Ruskin Bond, the author of "Those Three Bears," uses many synonyms to explain the movement of the bears. Invite students to share the cognate for *synonym* and together review that it describes two or more words with similar meanings.

- Point out the word *chased* in paragraph 2, *ambled* in paragraph 3, *made his way* in paragraph 5, *scrambled* in paragraph 6, and *fled* in paragraph 8.
- Review each word in the context of the paragraph, and demonstrate for students what each type of movement looks like. Invite students to repeat after you. Encourage them to describe the movement in their own words.
- Have students take turns directing a partner on how to move, using one of the newly-learned words in a sentence.

5 He put his nose to the ground and sniffed his way along until he came to a large anthill. Here he began huffing and puffing, blowing rapidly in and out of his nostrils so that the dust from the anthill flew in all directions. But the anthill had been deserted, and so, grumbling, the bear made his way up a nearby plum tree. Soon he was perched high in the branches. It was then that he saw me.

6 The bear at once scrambled several feet higher up the tree and lay flat on a branch. Since it wasn't a very big branch, there was a lot of bear showing on either side. He tucked his head behind another branch. He could no longer see me, so he apparently was satisfied that he was hidden, although he couldn't help grumbling.

7 Like all bears, this one was full of curiosity. So, slowly, inch-by-inch, his black snout appeared over the edge of the branch. As soon as he saw me, he drew his head back and hid his face. He did this several times. I waited until he wasn't looking, then moved some way down my tree. When the bear looked over and saw that I was missing, he was so pleased that he stretched right across to another branch and helped himself to a plum. At that, I couldn't help bursting into laughter.

8 The startled young bear tumbled out of the tree, dropped through the branches some fifteen feet, and landed with a thump in a pile of dried leaves. He was unhurt, but fled from the clearing, grunting and squealing all the way.

Integrating Standards

After students have read the passages, use these questions to discuss the passages with them.

- **In "A Rapid Challenge," what does the author mean when she says, "Frankie was beside herself with excitement"?**
  (The phrase beside oneself with excitement *is an idiom that means "overly excited." Frankie is "overly excited" because she can't wait to experience the thrill of the rapids.)*
  DOK 2 RL.5.4, L.5.5a
- **One theme of "A Rapid Challenge" is that we can't always anticipate what will happen to us. What events and story details show this theme?**
  (The main events are the encounter with the wolves and Frankie's changed feelings about the rapids after she sees the animals. In the beginning, all Frankie cares about is the excitement of being on the rapids. At the end, her ideas have been challenged by what she has seen.)
  DOK 2 RL.5.2
- **From what point of view is "Those Three Bears" told? How does this affect how the events are described?**
  (The story is told in the first person. Because of this, readers see the story from the narrator's point of view. They get to share in the narrator's thoughts and feelings and experience the events based on how the narrator experiences them.)
  DOK 2 RL.5.6
- **How do the narrator and the bear interact with each other in "Those Three Bears"?**
  (The bear causes the narrator to shift his attention away from looking for pine martens. But the bear's awareness of the man causes it to hide at first. Then it sneaks a few peeks at the man. Then, thinking the man is gone, it moves around freely. The bear's actions make the man laugh, and his laughter causes the bear to fall and run off.)
  DOK 2 RL.5.3

Monitor Understanding

If… students struggle to read and understand the passage,
then… use these scaffolding suggestions:

Vocabulary Support Define words and phrases that may interfere with comprehension, such as *shortsighted* and *huffing and puffing*.

Read Aloud Read aloud the text with students. You could also have students chorally read the text in a small group.

Check Understanding Use the questions to the right to check understanding. Encourage students to cite details in the text that support their answers.

- **What did the narrator do when he first saw the small Himalayan bear?** *(He sat still and waited to see what the bear would do.)*
- **How did the bear react to the narrator?** *(He seemed worried and hid, but also seemed curious, because he kept peeking out to have a look at the narrator.)*
- **What did the narrator do that startled the bear?** *(He moved down in his tree.)*

Independent Practice

Think

- Use the Monitor Understanding suggestions to support students in completing items 1–4.

● **Monitor Understanding**

Answer Analysis

When students have finished, discuss correct and incorrect responses.

1 Part A

The correct choice is A.

- **B, C,** and **D** are incorrect because "forage" means to search for food, and these definitions are not supported by any textual evidence.

Part B

The correct choice is D. The word "forage" is used in a sentence right after the author has explained that the bears come down the mountain in search of food.

- **A, B,** and **C** do not provide clues for the meaning of "forage" and are not related to why the bears would come down the mountain.

DOK 2 RL.5.4, L.5.4a

2 The correct choices are C and F. A raft turning upside down amid rapids is a dangerous prospect. Bears are dangerous and suspicious of anything that moves, including humans.

- **A** and **B** are incorrect because, while both excerpts suggest that being in nature can be exciting, that is not the same as dangerous.
- **D** and **E** are incorrect because, while both excerpts describe the behaviors of bears, they do not describe the risk that being around them can bring.

DOK 3 RL.5.9

Think Use what you learned from reading the stories to respond to the following questions.

1 This question has two parts. First, answer Part A. Then answer Part B.

Part A

Read the sentence from paragraph 1 of "Those Three Bears."

Sometimes they forage in fields.

What does the word forage mean as it is used in the sentence?

- **(A)** search for food
- **B** look for water
- **C** chase each other
- **D** hide from each other

Part B

Which detail from the story provides the **best** clue for the meaning of the word forage?

- **A** ". . . like most wild animals, they avoid humans as much as possible."
- **B** ". . . folk always advise me to run downhill if chased by a bear."
- **C** ". . . they are shortsighted and suspicious of anything that moves, . . ."
- **(D)** ". . . the Himalayan bears come to lower altitudes in search of food."

2 Select **one** excerpt from **each** story showing that being in nature brings risks.

- **A** "Her excitement grew as the sounds of rushing water got closer. . . ." ("A Rapid Challenge")
- **B** "Frankie's heart pounded with excitement. . . ." ("A Rapid Challenge")
- **(C)** ". . . Frankie was sure the whole raft was going to turn upside down. . . ." ("A Rapid Challenge")
- **D** ". . . the Himalayan bears come to lower altitudes in search of food." ("Those Three Bears")
- **E** ". . . they avoid humans as much as possible." ("Those Three Bears")
- **(F)** ". . . because they are shortsighted and suspicious of anything that moves, they can be dangerous." ("Those Three Bears")

● **Monitor Understanding**

If... students struggle to complete the items,

then... you may wish to use the following suggestions:

Read Aloud Activities

- As you read, have students note any unfamiliar words or phrases. Clarify any misunderstandings.
- Discuss each activity with students to make certain they understand the expectation.

Reread the Text

- Have students complete a simple story map for each selection as they reread.
- Have partners use the story map to summarize each text.

3 "A Rapid Challenge" and "Those Three Bears" develop this theme: *The natural world is a source of surprises.* Underline **one** sentence from **each** passage that shows the source of each surprise.

from "A Rapid Challenge"	from "Those Three Bears"
Frankie squinted as her eyes followed the line formed by Emily's pointing finger. When she finally saw what Emily was showing her, she gasped. It was a mother wolf and two tiny wolf pups. The mother was peering out from behind a tree as the pups batted at each other's faces under the mother's legs. "She has probably been teaching her pups to hunt here by the river," whispered Emily. "Maybe even showing them how to catch fish!" Frankie smiled to herself, imagining those wolf pups splashing around in the water, pawing at fish. Just then, her eyes met the mother wolf's.	Once, while I was sitting in an oak tree hoping to see a pair of pine martens that lived nearby, I heard the whining grumble of a bear, and presently a small bear ambled into the clearing beneath the tree. He was little more than a cub, and I was not alarmed. I sat very still, waiting to see what the bear would do. He put his nose to the ground and sniffed his way along until he came to a large anthill. Here he began huffing and puffing, blowing rapidly in and out of his nostrils so that the dust from the anthill flew in all directions.

4 Read these sentences from "A Rapid Challenge" by Danielle Lawrence.

> Frankie sighed. The rapids were all she was really interested in. But as long as she had to wait, she thought she might as well enjoy the sights.

These sentences show Frankie is more interested in the river than in watching wildlife. Which sentence from "Those Three Bears" shows that the narrator's interests are different than Frankie's?

A "And because they are shortsighted and suspicious of anything that moves, they can be dangerous."

(B) "But I have seen a few of these mountain bears in India, and they are always fascinating to watch."

C "Here he began huffing and puffing, blowing rapidly in and out of his nostrils so that the dust from the anthill flew in all directions."

D "When the bear looked over and saw that I was missing, he was so pleased that he stretched right across to another branch and helped himself to a plum."

3 **See the answers on the student book page.** These sentences show the sources of the surprise experienced by the main characters in the stories.
DOK 3 RL.5.9

4 **The correct choice is B.** Unlike Frankie, the narrator of "Those Three Bears" is interested in seeing wildlife; he set out "hoping to see a pair of pine martens."

- **A, C, and D** describe details involving animal behavior, which doesn't relate to the sentence about Frankie being uninterested in the sights.
DOK 3 RL.5.9

Theme Connection

- Remind students that the theme of this lesson is Similar Stories.
- Make a web showing all four genres students compared in this lesson, and the titles in each genre.
- Ask students to reflect on which genre was easiest to compare and why, as well as which pair of stories appeared to be most similar and why. Students might also reflect on how comparing helped them appreciate differences between each set of stories.

Independent Practice

Write

- Tell students that using what they read, they will plan and compose an extended response to the writing prompt. Provide copies of the Venn diagram on p. TR24.

Monitor Understanding

Review Responses

After students have completed each part of the writing activity, help them evaluate their responses.

5 Display the **Sample Response** for the planning diagram on the next page. Have students compare their diagram with the sample. Are they missing any information?
DOK 3 **RL.5.9**

6 Display or pass out copies of the reproducible **2-Point Writing Rubric** on p. TR10. Have students use the rubric to individually assess their writing and revise as needed.

When students have finished their revisions, evaluate their responses. Answers will vary but should include details that compare and contrast how each story develops the topic of appreciating nature.
DOK 3 **RL.5.9, W.5.9a**

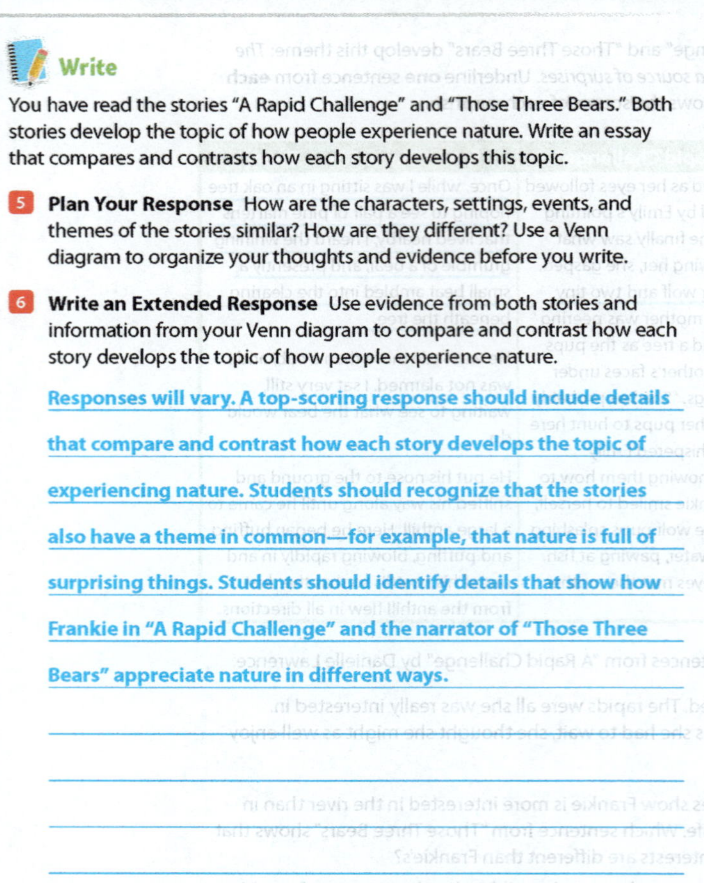

Independent Practice

Write

You have read the stories "A Rapid Challenge" and "Those Three Bears." Both stories develop the topic of how people experience nature. Write an essay that compares and contrasts how each story develops this topic.

5 **Plan Your Response** How are the characters, settings, events, and themes of the stories similar? How are they different? Use a Venn diagram to organize your thoughts and evidence before you write.

6 **Write an Extended Response** Use evidence from both stories and information from your Venn diagram to compare and contrast how each story develops the topic of how people experience nature.

Responses will vary. A top-scoring response should include details that compare and contrast how each story develops the topic of experiencing nature. Students should recognize that the stories also have a theme in common—for example, that nature is full of surprising things. Students should identify details that show how Frankie in "A Rapid Challenge" and the narrator of "Those Three Bears" appreciate nature in different ways.

414

Monitor Understanding

If... students don't understand the writing task,

then... read aloud the writing prompt. Use the following questions to help students get started.

- **What is the prompt asking you to write about?**
- **Do you need to reread the text to find more information?**
- **How will you identify the information you need to include?**

- Have partners talk about how they will organize their responses.

Learning Target

In this lesson, you compared and contrasted how stories in the same genre approach similar themes and topics. Explain how the work you did will deepen your understanding and enjoyment of stories you read later.

Responses will vary, but students should identify that comparing and contrasting the topics and themes of stories in the same genre helps them make connections and develop a deeper understanding of how stories tell their tales.

415

Wrap Up

Learning Target

- Have each student respond in writing to the Learning Target prompt.
- When students have finished, have them share their responses. This may be done with a partner, in small groups, or as a whole class.

5 Sample Response

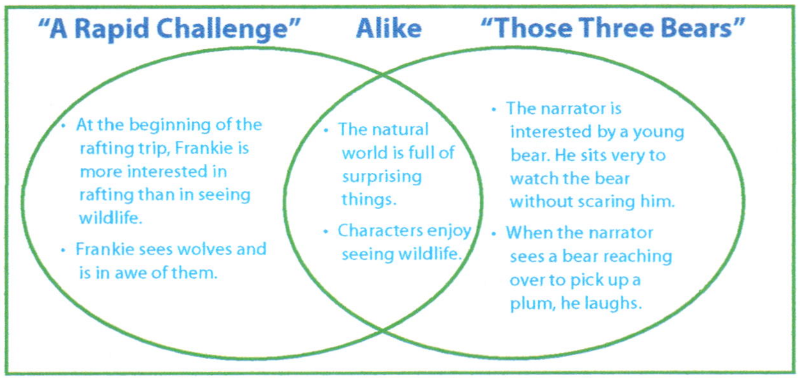

"A Rapid Challenge"	Alike	"Those Three Bears"
• At the beginning of the rafting trip, Frankie is more interested in rafting than in seeing wildlife. • Frankie sees wolves and is in awe of them.	• The natural world is full of surprising things. • Characters enjoy seeing wildlife.	• The narrator is interested by a young bear. He sits very to watch the bear without scaring him. • When the narrator sees a bear reaching over to pick up a plum, he laughs.

6 2-Point Writing Rubric

Points	Focus	Evidence	Organization
2	My answer does exactly what the prompt asked me to do.	My answer is supported with plenty of details from the text.	My ideas are clear and in a logical order.
1	Some of my answer does not relate to the prompt.	My answer is missing some important details from the text.	Some of my ideas are unclear and out of order.
0	My answer does not make sense.	My answer does not have any details from the text.	My ideas are unclear and not in any order.

Assessment

Get Started

Today you are going to read two excerpts from fantasy novels. You will use what you have learned in this unit to understand what you are reading.

- Ask students to recall what they have learned, such as analyzing visual elements and comparing and contrasting stories in the same genre.
- Encourage students to use the Academic Talk words and phrases from the unit's lessons in their response.

Read

You are going to read the articles independently and use what you have learned to think and write about the text.

- Ask a student to read aloud the titles of the passages. Make certain that students understand they are to read both selections.
- Encourage students to preview the text, paying close attention to the photographs, captions, and text structure.
- Remind students to look inside, around, and beyond when they encounter unfamiliar words. Use the Word Learning Routine on pp. A50–A51.
- When students have finished, have them complete the Think and Write sections.

Read

Genre: Novel

Read the story. Then answer the questions that follow.

In his famous fantasy, Peter Pan, *J. M. Barrie tells the story of Peter, a boy who never grows up. Peter discovers the children in the Darling family—Wendy, Michael, and John. He invites them to go with him to Neverland, teaches them to fly, and guides them on a grand adventure.*

by J. M. Barrie

1 "Second to the right, and straight on till morning."

2 That, Peter had told Wendy, was the way to the Neverland; but even birds, carrying maps and consulting them at windy corners, could not have sighted it with these instructions. Peter, you see, just said anything that came into his head.

3 At first his companions trusted him implicitly, and so great were the delights of flying that they wasted time circling round church spires or any other tall objects on the way that took their fancy.

4 John and Michael raced, Michael getting a start.

5 They recalled with contempt that not so long ago they had thought themselves fine fellows for being able to fly round a room.

6 Not so long ago. But how long ago? They were flying over the sea before this thought began to disturb Wendy seriously. John thought it was their second sea and their third night.

7 Sometimes it was dark and sometimes light, and now they were very cold and again too warm. Did they really feel hungry at times, or were

they merely pretending, because Peter had such a jolly new way of feeding them? His way was to pursue birds who had food in their mouths suitable for humans and snatch it from them; then the birds would follow and snatch it back; and they would all go chasing each other gaily for miles, parting at last with mutual expressions of good-will. But Wendy noticed with gentle concern that Peter did not seem to know that this was rather an odd way of getting your bread and butter, nor even that there are other ways.

8 Certainly they did not pretend to be sleepy, they were sleepy; and that was a danger, for the moment they popped off, down they fell. The awful thing was that Peter thought this funny.

9 "There he goes again!" he would cry gleefully, as Michael suddenly dropped like a stone.

Teacher Notes

10 "Save him, save him!" cried Wendy, looking with horror at the cruel sea far below. Eventually Peter would dive through the air, and catch Michael just before he could strike the sea, and it was lovely the way he did it; but he always waited till the last moment, and you felt it was his cleverness that interested him and not the saving of human life. Also he was fond of variety, and the sport that engrossed him one moment would suddenly cease to engage him, so there was always the possibility that the next time you fell he would let you go.

11 He could sleep in the air without falling, by merely lying on his back and floating, but this was, partly at least, because he was so light that if you got behind him and blew he went faster.

12 "Do be more polite to him," Wendy whispered to John, when they were playing "Follow my Leader."

13 "Then tell him to stop showing off," said John.

14 When playing Follow my Leader, Peter would fly close to the water and touch each shark's tail in passing, just as in the street you may run your finger along an iron railing. They could not follow him in this with much success, so perhaps it was rather like showing off, especially as he kept looking behind to see how many tails they missed.

15 "You must be nice to him," Wendy impressed on her brothers. "What could we do if he were to leave us?"

16 "We could go back," Michael said.

17 "How could we ever find our way back without him?"

18 "Well, then, we could go on," said John.

19 "That is the awful thing, John. We should have to go on, for we don't know how to stop."

Teacher Notes

Think

1 Which sentence from *Peter Pan* is **best** supported by the illustration?

- **A** "They recalled with contempt that not so long ago they had thought themselves fine fellows for being able to fly round a room."
- **B** "Sometimes it was dark and sometimes light, and now they were very cold and again too warm."
- **(C)** "His way was to pursue birds who had food in their mouths suitable for humans and snatch it from them."
- **D** "When playing Follow my Leader, Peter would fly close to the water and touch each shark's tail in passing."

2 This question has two parts. First, answer Part A. Then answer Part B.

Part A
Based on both the illustration and descriptions in *Peter Pan*, how do Wendy and her brothers most likely feel about Peter?

- **A** They are angry with Peter for risking their lives.
- **(B)** They are curious about his strange behavior.
- **C** They wish Peter would take them home right away.
- **D** They are worried that Peter makes too much mischief.

Part B
Which sentence from *Peter Pan* **best** supports the answer to Part A?

- **A** "At first his companions trusted him implicitly, and so great were the delights of flying that they wasted time circling round church spires or any other tall objects on the way that took their fancy."
- **B** "Certainly they did not pretend to be sleepy, they were sleepy; and that was a danger, for the moment they popped off, down they fell."
- **(C)** "But Wendy noticed with gentle concern that Peter did not seem to know that this was rather an odd way of getting your bread and butter, nor even that there are other ways."
- **D** "How could we ever find our way back without him?"

Answer Analysis

When students have completed the Interim Assessment, discuss correct and incorrect responses.

1 **The correct choice is C.** The illustration shows the children taking food from the beaks of different kinds of birds, which supports this sentence from the novel.

- **A** is incorrect because in the illustration the children don't have looks of contempt, or scorn.
- **B** is incorrect because there are no clues in the illustration to show that it is dark or that the children are too cold or too hot.
- **D** is incorrect because there are no sharks or water in the illustration.

DOK 2 RL.5.7

2 **Part A**

The correct choice is B. The illustration shows the children flying and taking food from the birds. The children follow Peter's example because they have never done anything like this before.

- **A** is incorrect because nothing in the illustration suggests that they are angry with Peter.
- **C** is incorrect because nothing in the illustration suggests that they want to go home.
- **D** is incorrect because neither the text nor the illustration suggests that they think Peter is a troublemaker.

Part B

The correct choice is C. This sentence shows that, even though Wendy and her brothers are having fun playing with Peter, the Darlings know that this is a strange way to get food.

- **A** shows how well the children follow Peter's example, not that they think his behavior is strange.
- **B** does show how the children struggle to mimic Peter's behavior, but it is not the best response.
- **D** shows that the Darlings have become reliant on Peter, not their feelings about him.

DOK 2 RL.5.7

Assessment

3 After students have completed the Interim Assessment, evaluate their responses to the short-response item using the **2-Point Writing Rubric** below.

Answers may vary but should show that students understand the illustration depicts the enjoyment described in the text, adding to the carefree tone. See the sample response on the student book page.

You may wish to display or pass out copies of the reproducible **2-Point Writing Rubric** on page TR10. Have students use the rubric to individually assess their writing and revise as needed.

DOK 3 RL.5.7

4 **Students should circle the word *recalled*.**

DOK 2 L.5.4c

3 Explain how details in the text of *Peter Pan* and in the illustration work together to contribute to the tone of the story. Include at least **one** detail from the text and **one** visual detail to support your response.

According to the text of the story, the children discover "the delights of flying." From the text, the reader knows that the children enjoy themselves. The illustration shows that the children are smiling and having fun as they follow Peter's lead. These details work together to contribute to the carefree, joyful tone of the story.

4 The following excerpt from *Peter Pan* uses a word that has the following definition: "to remember something that happened in the past." Read the excerpt and circle the word that **best** fits this definition.

John and Michael raced, Michael getting a start.

They recalled with contempt that not so long ago they had thought themselves fine fellows for being able to fly round a room.

Not so long ago. But how long ago? They were flying over the sea before this thought began to disturb Wendy seriously. John thought it was their second sea and their third night

2-Point Writing Rubric

All three criteria must be satisfied in order for a response to gain full points.

Points	Focus	Evidence	Organization
2	The response demonstrates comprehension and provides accurate analysis.	The response supports the analysis with adequate textual evidence.	Ideas are clear and follow a logical order.
1	The response demonstrates some comprehension and provides minimally accurate analysis.	The response supports the analysis with limited textual evidence.	Some ideas are unclear or out of order.
0	The response demonstrates no comprehension and provides inaccurate or no analysis.	The response provides little or no textual evidence.	Ideas are unclear or incomplete.

Read

Genre: Novel

Read the story. Then answer the questions that follow.

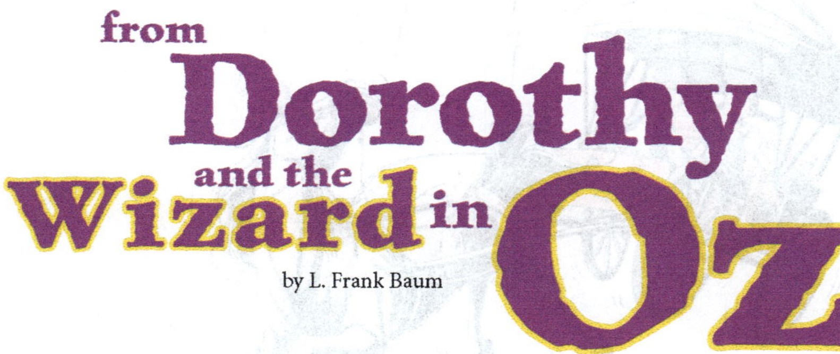

from Dorothy and the Wizard in Oz

by L. Frank Baum

1 When Dorothy recovered her senses they were still falling, but not so fast. The top of the buggy caught the air like a parachute or an umbrella filled with wind, and it held them back so that they floated downward with a gentle motion that was not so very disagreeable to bear.

2 Just then the buggy tipped slowly over upon its side, the body of the horse tipping also. But they continued to fall, all together, and the boy and girl had no difficulty in remaining upon the seat, just as they were before. Then they turned bottom side up, and continued to roll slowly over until they were right side up again. During this time Jim struggled frantically, all his legs kicking the air; but on finding himself in his former position the horse said, in a relieved tone of voice:

3 "Well, that's better!"

4 Dorothy and Zeb looked at one another in wonder. "Can your horse talk?" she asked.

5 "Never knew him to, before," replied the boy.

6 "Those were the first words I ever said," called out the horse, who had overheard them.

7 "And I can't explain why I happened to speak then. This is a nice scrape you've got me into, isn't it?"

8 "As for that, we are in the same scrape ourselves," answered Dorothy, cheerfully. "But never mind; something will happen pretty soon."

Teacher Notes

9 "Of course," growled the horse; "and then we shall be sorry it happened."

10 Zeb gave a shiver. All this was so terrible and unreal that he could not understand it at all, and so had good reason to be afraid. . . .

11 "We've got to come to the bottom some time," remarked Zeb, with a deep sigh. "We can't keep falling forever, you know."

12 "Of course not," said Dorothy. "We are somewhere in the middle of the earth, and the chances are we'll reach the other side of it before long. But it's a big hollow, isn't it?"

13 "Awful big!" answered the boy.

14 "We're coming to something now," announced the horse. . . .

15 They seemed to be falling right into the middle of a big city, which had many tall buildings with glass domes and sharp-pointed spires. These spires were like great spear-points, and if they tumbled upon one of them they were likely to suffer serious injury.

16 Jim the horse had seen these spires, also, and his ears stood straight up with fear, while Dorothy and Zeb held their breaths in suspense. But no; they floated gently down upon a broad, flat roof, and came to a stop at last.

17 When Jim felt something firm under his feet the poor beast's legs trembled so much that he could hardly stand; but Zeb at once leaped out of the buggy to the roof, and he was so awkward and hasty that he kicked over Dorothy's bird-cage, which rolled out upon the roof so that the bottom came off. At once a pink kitten crept out of the upset cage, sat down upon the glass roof, and yawned and blinked its round eyes.

18 "Oh," said Dorothy. "There's Eureka."

19 "First time I ever saw a pink cat," said Zeb.

20 "Eureka isn't pink; she's white. It's this queer light that gives her that color."

21 "Where's my milk?" asked the kitten, looking up into Dorothy's face. "I'm 'most starved to death."

22 "Oh, Eureka! Can you talk?"

23 "Talk! Am I talking? Good gracious, I believe I am. Isn't it funny?" asked the kitten.

24 "It's all wrong," said Zeb, gravely. "Animals ought not to talk. But even old Jim has been saying things since we had our accident."

25 "I can't see that it's wrong," remarked Jim, in his gruff tones. "At least, it isn't as wrong as some other things. What's going to become of us now?"

26 "I don't know," answered the boy, looking around him curiously.

Teacher Notes

Assessment

5 **The correct choice is A.** The children's expressions show fear at plummeting down headfirst.

- **B** is incorrect because the illustration shows events that would likely never happen in real life.
- **C** is incorrect because the illustration does not give more details about the story's setting.
- **D** is incorrect because Dorothy seems fearful, not happy, in the illustration.

DOK 3 **RL.5.7**

6 After students have completed the Interim Assessment, evaluate their responses to the short-response item using the **2-Point Writing Rubric** below.

Answers will vary but should show that students understand the danger of the scene, the horse struggling as they fall through the air. See the sample response on the student book page.

You may wish to display or pass out copies of the reproducible **2-Point Writing Rubric** on page TR10. Have students use the rubric to individually assess their writing and revise as needed.

DOK 3 **RL.5.7**

Think

5 How does the illustration contribute to readers' understanding of what happens in this excerpt of *Dorothy and the Wizard in Oz*?

(A) It shows how thrilling Dorothy's arrival is.
B It proves this could happen in real life.
C It gives details about the setting that are not in the story.
D It shows how happy Dorothy is to hear the horse talk.

6 Explain how details in the text of *Dorothy and the Wizard in Oz* and in the illustration work together to contribute to the tone of the story. Include at least **one** detail from the text and **one** detail from the illustration to support your response.

Sample response: These details work together to show the darker tone of the story. Dorothy and her friends face real danger, and they are scared. According to the text, "Jim struggled frantically" as they fell. The illustration emphasizes how dangerous and scary falling was for the characters.

2-Point Writing Rubric

All three criteria must be satisfied in order for a response to gain full points.

Points	Focus	Evidence	Organization
2	The response demonstrates comprehension and provides accurate analysis.	The response supports the analysis with adequate textual evidence.	Ideas are clear and follow a logical order.
1	The response demonstrates some comprehension and provides minimally accurate analysis.	The response supports the analysis with limited textual evidence.	Some ideas are unclear or out of order.
0	The response demonstrates no comprehension and provides inaccurate or no analysis.	The response provides little or no textual evidence.	Ideas are unclear or incomplete.

7 Both *Peter Pan* and *Dorothy and the Wizard in Oz* develop this theme:

Leaving home can lead to great surprises.

Underline **one** sentence from each passage that develops this theme.

from *Peter Pan*	from *Dorothy and the Wizard In Oz*
"Second to the right, and straight on till morning." That, Peter had told Wendy, was the way to the Neverland; but even birds, carrying maps and consulting them at windy corners, could not have sighted it with these instructions. Peter, you see, just said anything that came into his head. At first his companions trusted him implicitly, and so great were the delights of flying that they wasted time circling round church spires or any other tall objects on the way that took their fancy.	. . . Then they turned bottom side up, and continued to roll slowly over until they were right side up again. During this time, Jim struggled frantically, all his legs kicking the air; but on finding himself in his former position the horse said, in a relieved tone of voice: "Well, that's better!" Dorothy and Zeb looked at one another in wonder. "Can your horse talk?" she asked. "Never knew him to, before," replied the boy.

Teacher Notes

7 **See the answers on the student book page.**

DOK 3 **RL.5.9**

Assessment

8 **Part A**

The correct choice is D. The children in *Peter Pan* face the unknown as they fly in the sky. They don't know what would happen to them if Peter left because they don't know how to stop flying or how to find their way back. The children in *Dorothy and the Wizard in Oz* also face the unknown as they fall into a bottomless pit in the middle of the earth. They don't know when they will land or what will happen when they do.

- **A** is incorrect because the characters don't keep any secrets in either story.
- **B** is incorrect because the characters don't face the challenges of growing up in either story.
- **C** is incorrect because Wendy, John, and Michael are already friends with Peter in this part of *Peter Pan* and because Dorothy and Zeb are already friends in this part of *Dorothy and the Wizard in Oz*.

Part B

The correct choices are C and E. These quotations describe characters feeling afraid.

- **A** is incorrect because it does not illustrate that flying with Peter was both exciting and scary.
- **B** is incorrect because, unlike the Darling children, Peter is not afraid of the unknown.
- **D** shows the horse is surprised, not afraid.
- **F** emphasizes how scary the setting is to readers, but not the characters' fear.

DOK 3 **RL.5.9**

Interim Assessment

8 This question has two parts. First, answer Part A. Then answer Part B.

Part A
What theme is present in both stories?

A It is easy to keep secrets.
B It is difficult to grow up.
(C) Making new friends can be entertaining.
D Facing the unknown can be frightening.

Part B
Choose **one** sentence from *Peter Pan* and **one** sentence from *Dorothy and the Wizard in Oz* that **best** support the answer in Part A.

A "'Second to the right, and straight on till morning.'" (*Peter Pan*)
B "Peter, you see, just said anything that came into his head." (*Peter Pan*)
(C) "'Save him, save him!' cried Wendy, looking with horror at the cruel sea far below." (*Peter Pan*)
D "'Those were the first words I ever said,' called out the horse, who had overheard them." (*Dorothy and the Wizard in Oz*)
(E) "All this was so terrible and unreal that he could not understand it at all, and so had good reason to be afraid." (*Dorothy and the Wizard in Oz*)
F "They seemed to be falling right into the middle of a big city, which had many tall buildings with glass domes and sharp-pointed spires." (*Dorothy and the Wizard in Oz*)

426

9 This question has two parts. First, answer Part A. Then answer Part B.

Part A
Which definition of the word scrape is used in paragraphs 7 and 8 of *Dorothy and the Wizard in Oz?*

A to cut the skin by rubbing against a rough surface
(B) a dangerous or bad situation
C to do something with great difficulty
D an unpleasant sound made by rubbing a hard surface

Part B
Which sentence from the story supports your answer in Part A?

A "'Well, that's better!'"
B "'Those were the first words I ever said,' called out the horse, who had overheard them."
(C) "All this was so terrible and unreal that he could not understand it at all, and so had good reason to be afraid. . . ."
D "But no; they floated gently down upon a broad, flat roof, and came to a stop at last."

10 How does the illustration help you understand the following excerpt from the story?

When Dorothy recovered her senses they were falling, but not so far. The top of the buggy caught the air like a parachute or an umbrella filled with wind, and it held them back so that they floated downward with a gentle motion that was not so very disagreeable to bear.

Just then the buggy tipped slowly over on its side, the body of the horse tipping also. But they continued to fall, all together, and the boy and girl had no difficulty in remaining upon the seat, just as they were before.

(A) It shows what the top of the buggy looked like.
B It shows that Dorothy and Zeb are safe.
C It shows that Jim is an unruly horse.
D It shows that the buggy is about to tip over.

Teacher Notes

9 **Part A**

The correct choice is B. Dorothy, Zeb, and Jim are in a bad situation because they are falling through the sky without knowing when or if they'll land safely.

- **A, C,** and **D** are incorrect because they are not supported by the context of the passage.

Part B

The correct choice is C. This detail is evidence of the bad situation the characters are in.

- **A, B,** and **D** are incorrect because they do not point to the meaning of *scrape* as it is used in the passage.

DOK 2 L.5.4c

10 **The correct choice is A.** The illustration helps explain the phrase "like a parachute or an umbrella filled with wind."

- **B** is incorrect because, while it may be true that the falling buggy isn't "so very disagreeable to bear," the characters are still in a dangerous situation.
- **C** is not supported by the passage or the illustration.
- **D** is true based on the text of the passage, but this event is not part of the illustration.

DOK 3 RL.5.7

Write

Review Responses

11 After students have completed the Interim Assessment, evaluate their responses to the Extended Response using the **4-Point Writing Rubric** below.

Answers will vary but should show that students understand the different approaches the authors take toward adventure, showing the characters in *Peter Pan* enthusiastic about their choice and those in *Dorothy and the Wizard in Oz* more frightened by their accidental exploit. See the sample response on the student book page.

DOK 4 RL.5.9

Write

11 **Extended Response** Although both stories use the topic of adventure, the authors approach the topic in different ways. Explain the difference between the ways that the authors approach the topic of adventure in these stories.

Use this chart to help organize your thoughts for writing.

Story	How did the adventure begin?	What were the characters' reactions to the adventure?
Peter Pan		
Dorothy and the Wizard in Oz		

Now use the information in the chart to write your response. In your answer, be sure to

- tell how each of the adventures began
- tell how characters in each story reacted to the adventure
- explain how each author approached the topic of adventure
- compare and contrast how the authors approached the topic of adventure
- use specific details from each story to support your answer

Check your writing for correct spelling, grammar, capitalization, and punctuation.

In *Peter Pan*, J. M. Barrie approaches the topic of adventure by exploring why it is important to weigh the possible risks. The author makes it clear that Wendy, John, and Michael make the decision to follow Peter Pan on an adventure. At first, they are delighted about being able to fly. They fly over buildings on land, and then over the ocean. After a few days, they begin to question whether the adventure is a good idea. They realize that they are dependent on Peter Pan. "What could we do if he were to leave us?" asks Wendy. This worries them because they recognize that they are lost

4-Point Writing Rubric

All three criteria must be satisfied in order for a response to gain full points.

Points	Focus	Evidence	Organization
4	The response demonstrates a full understanding of the prompt and provides accurate analysis.	The response supports the analysis with generous textual evidence.	Ideas are consistently presented in a purposeful and logical order.
3	The response demonstrates a good understanding of the prompt and provides mostly accurate analysis.	The response supports the analysis with adequate textual evidence.	Ideas are generally presented in a purposeful and logical order, although some ideas may be unclear or out of order.
2	The response demonstrates a general understanding of the prompt and provides some accurate analysis but includes inaccurate descriptions or explanations.	The response supports the analysis with limited textual evidence but does not reference the text explicitly.	Some ideas are presented in a purposeful and logical order, but others are unclear or out of order.
1	The response demonstrates a limited understanding of the prompt and provides limited analysis with significant inaccuracies.	The response may use textual evidence, but it does not support the analysis and does not reference the text explicitly.	Most ideas are not presented in a purposeful and logical order.
0	The response does not demonstrate understanding of the prompt.	Ideas are not supported with reference to textual evidence.	The response does not present ideas in a purposeful or logical order.

without him. They don't know their way back, and they "don't know how to stop." The children think about the consequences of their adventure—but only after they are flying over the sea.

On the other hand, L. Frank Baum approaches the topic of adventure in *Dorothy and the Wizard in Oz* by exploring why it is important to enjoy the experience. The author makes it clear that the adventure of falling into a pit is not the characters' idea. Dorothy and Zeb are out for a buggy ride when the earth opens up, and they suddenly fall into a bottomless pit. Unlike the children in *Peter Pan*, the characters in *Dorothy and the Wizard in Oz* accept that they are on a strange yet possibly dangerous adventure. They don't spend time worrying about it and wishing that they were not on the adventure. Dorothy says, "We are somewhere in the middle of the earth, and the chances are we'll reach the other side of it before long." She feels confident that "something will happen pretty soon." Although Dorothy and Zeb are afraid, they know that they cannot "understand it at all" and remain curious about what will happen next.

Teacher Notes

Glossary

absorb *v.* to take in and make part of a whole: *Our city* ***absorbed*** *the smaller town next to us and made it part of our city.*

access *n.* permission to enter or use: *Only members have* ***access*** *to the pool.*

administration *n.* a government agency or group: *The new* ***administration*** *will monitor education in the state.*

advise *v.* to give information that helps another: *The coach meets with the players to* ***advise*** *them on how to improve for the next game.*

aeronautics *n.* the science of flying: *Nathan is studying* ***aeronautics*** *so he can understand how airplanes work.*

allegiance *n.* loyalty to a country or leader: *The knights gave their* ***allegiance*** *to the queen.*

altitudes *n.* heights, as on the side of a mountain: *The goats went down the mountain to lower* ***altitudes*** *in the winter.*

anatomy *n.* the structure or parts of a living thing: *The* ***anatomy*** *of a bird is very different from that of a snake.*

annex *n.* a small room or area attached to a larger space: *We use our basement* ***annex*** *to store old boxes.*

anticipate *v.* to think something will happen in the future: *Our teacher* ***anticipated*** *our questions and had a list of answers ready.*

appointed *v.* to decide or set officially: *The coach* ***appointed*** *Emma team captain.*

assess *v.* to determine the size of a problem: *When our car broke down, my mom got out to* ***assess*** *the situation.*

assure *v.* to make certain; convince: *Lakshmi* ***assured*** *me that she would not be late this time.*

automatically *adv.* done without thinking: *Your heart beats* ***automatically,*** *whether you think about it or not.*

barren *adj.* not having many plants: *The desert was* ***barren*** *except for a few cacti.*

benefit *v.* to have a good effect on: *Daily exercise can* ***benefit*** *a person's health.*

cite *v.* to mention or give credit to: *Henry was careful to* ***cite*** *all the sources he used to write his report.*

colony *n.* a group of animals or plants living in one place: *Honeybees live in* ***colonies.***

commanding *adj.* having the ability to attract attention: *The speaker's* ***commanding*** *presence kept the entire audience focused on her.*

commerce *n.* the act of buying and selling goods and services: *Our state's* ***commerce*** *improved as people from all over the country bought the products made here.*

companion *n.* a person with whom someone spends time: *I walk to school with my* ***companions*** *every morning.*

complain *v.* to say something that expresses dislike or dissatisfaction: *My brother* ***complained*** *that he was cold until we brought him a sweater.*

complex *adj.* having many parts linked in complicated ways: *A car's engine is a* ***complex*** *machine.*

concert *n.* a public performance of music: *The band puts on a* ***concert*** *at the end of the year.*

conditions *n.* state or situation: *The weather* ***conditions*** *were perfect for a picnic in the park.*

conduct *v.* to take part in an activity: *The group* ***conducted*** *a search for the missing cat.*

confusion *n.* a situation in which many things are happening in a disorganized way: *In all the* ***confusion*** *at the party, Milo lost his phone.*

demand *n.* a strong need for something: *The* ***demand*** *for air conditioning increases in the summer.*

despise *v.* to dislike very much: *Samantha liked the movie, but I* ***despised*** *it.*

determined *adj.* having made a decision to do something without letting anything get in the way: *Hiro is* ***determined*** *to make the soccer team this year.*

dialect *n.* a variety of a language spoken in a particular area: *British English and American English are two* ***dialects*** *of the language.*

dictate *v.* to say something for someone else to write down: *Because Nancy has a broken arm, she will* ***dictate*** *her homework assignment to her brother.*

disorder *n.* a messy state: *My dad told me to clean up the* ***disorder*** *in my room.*

dispute *v.* to argue: *My brother and I always* ***disputed*** *over what to watch on TV.*

doctrine *n.* an official government policy: *The government's* ***doctrine*** *on foreign trade helps to keep our national budget balanced.*

ecology *n.* the science of how living things relate to where they live: *We studied the* ***ecology*** *of the prairie by looking at the plants and animals that live there.*

economy *n.* the structure in which goods and services are bought and sold: *The island country's* ***economy*** *was based on fishing.*

efficient *adj.* causing a desired result without much waste: *An* ***efficient*** *worker does not waste time or energy in completing a task.*

exception *n.* something that is different from everything else: *As a cat owner, Lexi was the* ***exception*** *in a room full of dog owners.*

exchange *n.* the act of giving something to another and getting something in return: *My friends and I have a book* ***exchange*** *in which we trade our favorites.*

expression *n.* the way someone's face shows feelings: *I could tell the team lost by looking at their sad* ***expressions.***

facility *n.* something built for a particular purpose: *The hospital's* ***facilities*** *serve different kinds of patients.*

feeble *adj.* very weak: *The* ***feeble*** *tree branch broke during the thunderstorm.*

financial *adj.* relating to money: *A bank offers* ***financial*** *services.*

fragile *adj.* easily damaged or broken: *I dropped and broke the* ***fragile*** *mirror.*

generation *n.* a group of people born and living during the same time period: *That watch has been in my family for two* ***generations.***

habitat *n.* a place where an animal or plant lives: *Lakes and rivers are two* ***habitats*** *for freshwater fish.*

harness *v.* to attach a horse or other animal to something with a harness: *The boy was* ***harnessing*** *a horse to the cart.*

hover *v.* to float in the air without moving: *The helicopter was* ***hovering*** *over the beach.*

I

imitate *v.* to copy or do the same thing as: *Mockingbirds can* ***imitate*** *other birds' sounds.*

importance *n.* the state of having great value or significance: *Ms. Richardson stressed the* ***importance*** *of studying for the test.*

infinitely *adv.* beyond measure: *In my opinion, the seashore is* ***infinitely*** *better than the mountains.*

inspire *v.* to make someone want to do something: *This book will* ***inspire*** *readers to plant trees.*

intercept *v.* to stop something before it gets where it is supposed to go: *My dog is great at* ***intercepting*** *a treat thrown for another dog.*

inward *adv.* toward the inside: *The ice skater pulled her arms* ***inward*** *to spin faster.*

isolated *adj.* far away from others: *My grandparents live on an* ***isolated*** *farm miles from the nearest town.*

judgment *n.* a decision made after careful thought: *After the presentation, the principal's* ***judgment*** *was to allow us to form a new club.*

justice *n.* the process of applying laws: *The man who had been robbed demanded* ***justice*** *from the court.*

media *n.* ways to communicate that reach a large number of people: *Television, newspapers, and the Internet are types of* ***media****.*

melancholy *adj.* very sad: *I felt* ***melancholy*** *when my best friend moved away.*

migrant *adj.* made up of people who move from place to place looking for work: *The* ***migrant*** *group moved to California to work on a farm.*

network *n.* **1.** a system of connected computers: *The school's computer* ***network*** *has 25 laptops.* **2.** a group of people who work or interact with each other: *When I need advice, I go to my* ***network*** *of friends.*

observe *v.* to watch closely: *We used a telescope to* ***observe*** *the comet.*

opportunity *n.* a chance to do something: *Our ballet teacher showed us the steps and then gave everyone an* ***opportunity*** *to try them.*

permanent *adj.* lasting forever: *The flood did* ***permanent*** *damage to the riverbank.*

persist *v.* to continue to do something even when others tell you to stop: *My brother will* ***persist*** *in bothering me even after I yell at him.*

pressure *n.* the stress of important matters: *Jayden felt* ***pressure*** *to do well on his exams.*

progress *n.* forward movement toward a goal: *The traffic jam stopped us from making* ***progress*** *toward school.*

promenade *n.* a walk in a public place: *Kaitlyn and I took a* ***promenade*** *around the park.*

protest *v.* to speak in a way that shows disagreement: *I didn't want to go to the pool, so I* ***protested****.*

punctually *adv.* on time: *All of the guests arrived* ***punctually*** *at 6 p.m. for dinner.*

reaction *n.* the result of one chemical changing to another: *Nuclear* ***reactions*** *create a tremendous amount of energy.*

rebellion *n.* an effort by a large group to change the government: *The American colonies'* ***rebellion*** *against the British was successful.*

regard *v.* to think of someone in a particular way: *My uncle was* ***regarded*** *as the best mechanic in town.*

release *v.* to let out: *A balloon gets smaller when you* ***release*** *air from it.*

reliable *adj.* able to be trusted or believed: *I'll ask Colin to help me because he's always* ***reliable****.*

S

sensation *n.* a cause of great excitement: *The singer's new album was an instant* ***sensation*** *and sold out quickly.*

solemn *adj.* very serious or formal: *Karen looked very* ***solemn*** *as she gave us the bad news.*

structure *n.* a building or other object made from several parts: *After many years, the rickety old* ***structure*** *was torn down.*

substance *n.* a kind of material or matter: *The school removed harmful* ***substances*** *from the chemistry lab.*

suspicious *adj.* having a feeling that something is wrong: *Mr. Tran was* ***suspicious*** *that Jasmine was lying.*

system *n.* a group of things that work together: *The school* ***system*** *has a joint concert for all the schools at the end of the year.*

theory *n.* an explanation of events: *Grace had a* ***theory*** *that her brother had been reading her diary.*

trustworthy *adj.* deserving of belief: *Jacob never lies, so we know he is* ***trustworthy****.*

variety *n.* a number of different things: *The library offers a* ***variety*** *of different kinds of books.*

vaster *adj.* greater in size: *The desert was* ***vaster*** *than I remembered from our last trip.*

vibrate *v.* to move back and forth with quick movements: *The music was so loud that it made the walls* ***vibrate****.*

vibrations *n.* small, quick movements: *The* ***vibrations*** *from my phone startled me.*

virtual *adj.* existing on the Internet or only on computers; not physical: *I played a* ***virtual*** *hockey game on my computer.*

Language Handbook

Conventions of Standard English

Knowledge of Language

Vocabulary Acquisition and Use

Introduction

- Read aloud the Introduction. As you discuss the charts, explain to students that changing the conjunction can change the meaning of a sentence.

  The meaning of a sentence can change depending on which conjunction is used. Be sure to determine the purpose of the conjunction in the sentence. Try using different conjunctions until the sentence makes sense.

- Write the following sentences on a chart or project them on a whiteboard.

  I have math ____________ science homework. *(and)*

  An apple is a good snack ____________ it's healthy. *(because)*

  We can't cross the river ____________ we use the bridge. *(unless)*

- Model how to choose a conjunction to complete each sentence. Explain that different conjunctions are used in different situations. For example, in the second sentence, *because* explains why the apple is a good snack.

Guided Practice

- Read aloud the sentences.
- Have students complete the activity.
- Remind students to determine which conjunction to use based on the purpose of the sentence.

Scaffolded Instruction

Explore Coordinating Conjunctions

Ask students to explain how the meaning of the following sentences changes based on the conjunction that is used.

1. I save my money, or I make a donation. *(shows a choice between saving and donating)*
2. I save my money, and I make a donation. *(shows two things the writer does: saves and donates)*
3. I save my money, so I make a donation. *(shows a cause, saving money, and the effect, donating)*

Lesson 1

Coordinating and Subordinating Conjunctions

L.5.1a: Explain the function of conjunctions . . . in general and their function in particular sentences.

Introduction A **conjunction** is a word used to connect words, phrases, or clauses.

- **Coordinating conjunctions** connect words, phrases, or clauses of equal importance.

Coordinating	When to Use	Example
and	to add information	Many animals live in places with plenty of food and water.
but	to show a difference	Deer eat many plants but still do not always get enough food.
or	to show a choice	They know that finding food is a matter of life or death.
so	to show cause and effect	They need more food, so they move on in search of it.

- **Subordinating conjunctions** are used to connect a **dependent clause** to another clause. A dependent clause has a subject and a predicate but cannot stand alone.

Subordinating	When to Use	Example
because	to explain why	Raccoons don't mind living in populated areas because they aren't afraid of people.
before, during, when, while	to show time	When deer cannot find food in their natural habitats, they will often go looking for it in people's yards.
although, unless	to show contrast	Although some animals avoid living near humans, other animals are comfortable being near people.

Guided Practice Write a conjunction from the box to complete each sentence.

HINT If you're not certain which conjunction to use in a sentence, try each one.

unless and when although so

1. All animals need food, water, ___and___ shelter to survive.
2. ___When___ these are available, animals can thrive.
3. ___Although___ opossums can live in just about any habitat, elk are very particular about where they live.
4. Cats and dogs have learned to depend on humans, ___so___ they are considered "domesticated" animals.
5. Cougars avoid humans ___unless___ they are in search of food.

438

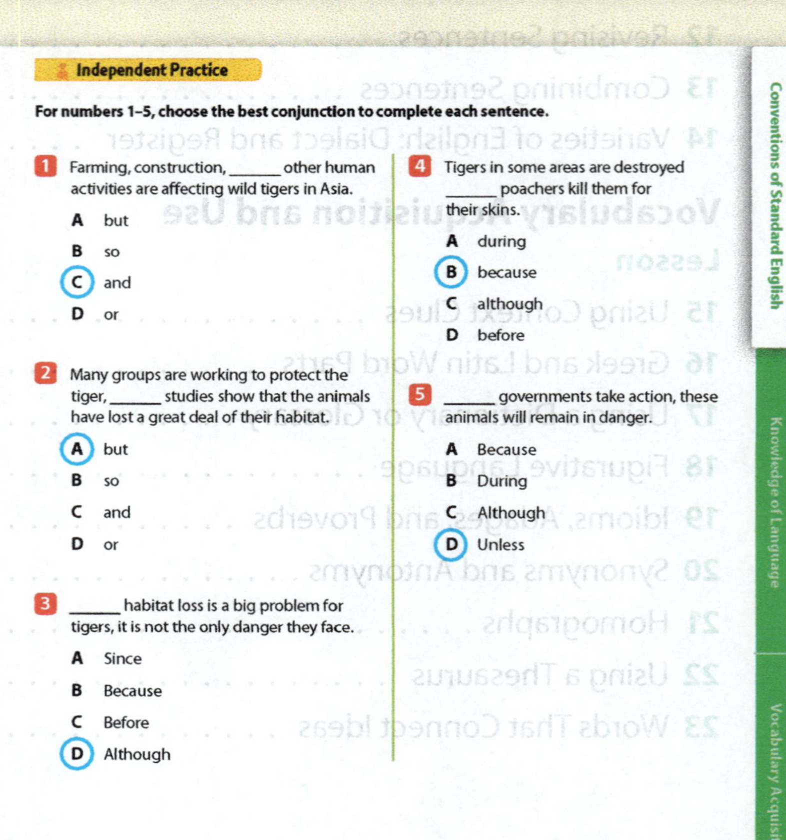

Independent Practice

For numbers 1–5, choose the best conjunction to complete each sentence.

1. Farming, construction, ______ other human activities are affecting wild tigers in Asia.
   - A but
   - B so
   - C and (circled)
   - D or
2. Many groups are working to protect the tiger, ______ studies show that the animals have lost a great deal of their habitat.
   - A but (circled)
   - B so
   - C and
   - D or
3. ______ habitat loss is a big problem for tigers, it is not the only danger they face.
   - A Since
   - B Because
   - C Before
   - D Although (circled)
4. Tigers in some areas are destroyed ______ poachers kill them for their skins.
   - A during
   - B because (circled)
   - C although
   - D before
5. ______ governments take action, these animals will remain in danger.
   - A Because
   - B During
   - C Although
   - D Unless (circled)

Conventions of Standard English | Knowledge of Language | Vocabulary Acquisition and Use

439

Lesson 2

Prepositions and Prepositional Phrases

L.5.1a: Explain the function of prepositions . . . in general and their function in particular sentences.

Introduction A **preposition** is a word that shows how other words in a sentence are related. Words such as *about, by, in, of, on, to,* and *under* are prepositions.

- A **prepositional phrase** begins with a preposition and ends with a noun or a pronoun. The noun or pronoun is called the **object** of the preposition.

The Emperor penguins [of] [**Antarctica**] spend winter [on] the open [**ice.**]
(preposition: of, object: Antarctica; preposition: on, object: ice)

- A preposition tells about the relationship between the object of the preposition and another word in the sentence. Look at these sentences.

Emperor penguins swim **under the** ice when they hunt.

I recently saw a movie **about these amazing** penguins.

- In the first sentence, the preposition *under* tells about the relationship between *ice* and the verb *swim*. In the second sentence, the preposition *about* tells about the relationship between *penguins* and the noun *movie*.
- A prepositional phrase sometimes tells *how, when, where,* or *what kind.* In the sentences you just read, the prepositional phrase *under the ice* tells *where* the penguins swim. The prepositional phrase *about these amazing penguins* tells *what kind* of movie it was.

Guided Practice

Underline the prepositional phrase in each sentence and circle the preposition. Then draw an arrow from the object of the preposition to the word it relates to.

HINT Most prepositional phrases come after the noun or verb they describe.

Example:
I read a book **about Emperor penguins.**

1. Emperor penguins breed in the winter.
2. Female Emperor penguins lay eggs on the ice.
3. Males watch the eggs while the females travel to the sea.
4. The warmth of the males' feathers protects the eggs.
5. The females return and provide food for the little chicks.

Independent Practice

For numbers 1–3, choose the prepositional phrase in each sentence.

1. Emperor penguins can be found on only one continent.
   - A found on only one continent
   - B can be found
   - C only one continent
   - D on only one continent
2. Antarctica's winter begins in late March.
   - A winter begins
   - B begins in
   - C in late March
   - D begins in late March
3. There are 17 types of penguins, and the Emperor penguin is the largest.
   - A of penguins
   - B and the Emperor penguin
   - C is the largest
   - D are 17 types of

For numbers 4 and 5, answer the question.

4. Read this sentence.

   Most animals move to a warmer place each winter, but Emperor penguins do not.

   What is the purpose of the underlined preposition?
   - A to describe when animals move
   - B to connect *warmer* with *animals*
   - C to connect two phrases about winter
   - D to show a relationship between *move* and *place*
5. Read this sentence.

   The feathers of the penguin keep out cold air and water.

   What is the purpose of the underlined preposition?
   - A to connect *feathers* with *cold*
   - B to show a relationship between *feathers* and *penguin*
   - C to tell what a penguin's feathers do
   - D to show a relationship between *penguin* and *cold*

Conventions of Standard English | Knowledge of Language | Vocabulary Acquisition and Use

Introduction

- Read aloud the Introduction and examples. Hold up an object such as a pen. Place it in different locations (*on* your head, *behind* your back, *under* the desk, etc.) and have students tell you the location of the object. Point out the prepositions.

  A preposition clarifies the relationship of an object to another word in a sentence.

  A preposition can tell you where an object is, but it can also reveal how, when, or what kind.
- Write the following riddles on a chart or project them on a whiteboard.

  I live in Australia. I climb up trees. I have gray fur on my body. What am I? *(a koala)*

  I work in a hive. I land on flowers. I can fly through the air. What am I? *(a bee)*
- After students answer each riddle, model how to identify the preposition and prepositional phrase. Then discuss which word in the sentence each object relates to.

Guided Practice

- Read aloud the sentences.
- Have students complete the activity.
- Remind students to first identify the prepositions and then underline the prepositional phrase.

English Language Learners

Understand Prepositional Phrases

Help English language learners understand the meanings of common prepositions, such as the following, by acting them out.

1. Put the pencil on your desk.
2. Bring the book to me.
3. Walk by the door.

Introduction

- Read aloud the Introduction and examples. Explain to students that interjections are a part of speech, just like nouns, pronouns, and adjectives.

  An interjection typically begins a sentence. It expresses an emotion. Interjections are more common when people are speaking. Try to avoid using interjections in formal essays.

- Write the following sentences on a chart or project them on a whiteboard.

  __________ I dropped my pencil. *(Oops,)*

  __________ We made it to the bus stop on time. *(Whew!)*

  __________ Watch where you're going! *(Hey!)*

- Model for students how to choose an interjection to add emotion to each sentence. Explain that interjections expressing strong emotions, such as joy or shock, are followed by an exclamation point.

Guided Practice

- Read aloud the sentences.
- Have students complete the activity.
- Explain to students that some interjections can be used interchangeably. For example, the interjections *Hooray!* and *Yippee!* mean the same as *Yay!* and could be used in place of it in a sentence.

English Language Learners

Support Use of Interjections

Some English interjections may be unfamiliar to students. Act out as many interjections as you can, conveying meaning using facial expressions, inflection, and gestures.

1. Ouch! I hurt my foot!
2. Oops! I dropped my books.
3. Whew! I'm glad I made it on time.

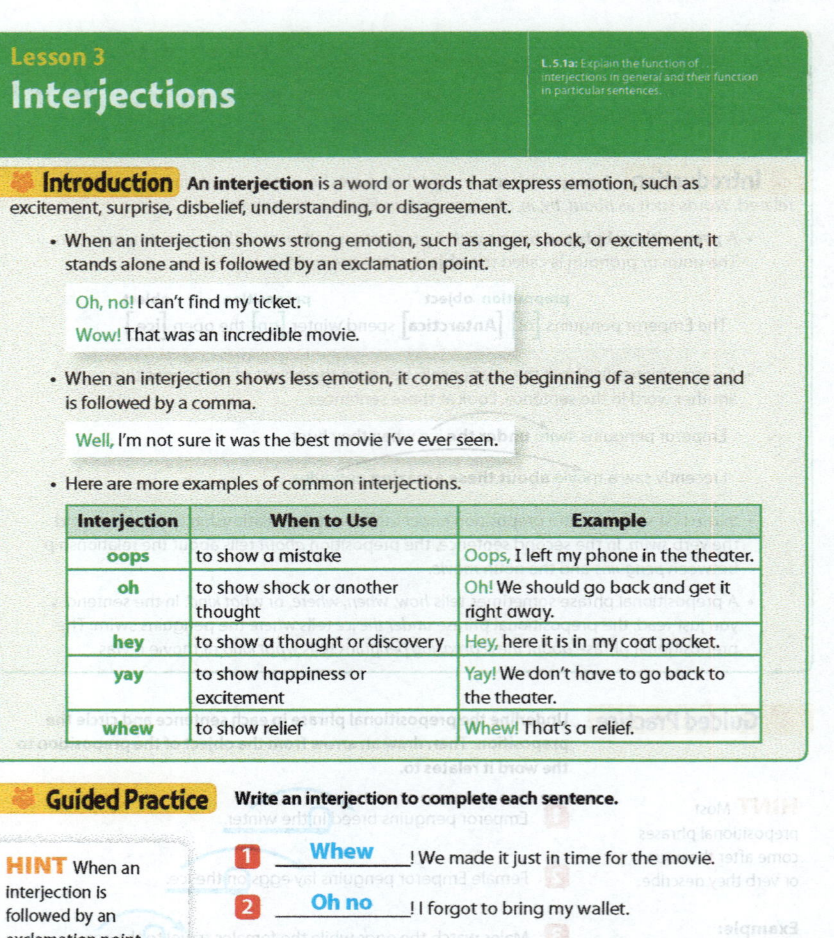

Lesson 3

Interjections

L.5.1a: Explain the function of interjections in general and their function in particular sentences.

Introduction An **interjection** is a word or words that express emotion, such as excitement, surprise, disbelief, understanding, or disagreement.

- When an interjection shows strong emotion, such as anger, shock, or excitement, it stands alone and is followed by an exclamation point.

  Oh, no! I can't find my ticket.
  Wow! That was an incredible movie.

- When an interjection shows less emotion, it comes at the beginning of a sentence and is followed by a comma.

  Well, I'm not sure it was the best movie I've ever seen.

- Here are more examples of common interjections.

Interjection	When to Use	Example
oops	to show a mistake	Oops, I left my phone in the theater.
oh	to show shock or another thought	Oh! We should go back and get it right away.
hey	to show a thought or discovery	Hey, here it is in my coat pocket.
yay	to show happiness or excitement	Yay! We don't have to go back to the theater.
whew	to show relief	Whew! That's a relief.

Guided Practice Write an interjection to complete each sentence.

HINT When an interjection is followed by an exclamation point, it should begin with a capital letter.

1. ___Whew___! We made it just in time for the movie.
2. ___Oh no___! I forgot to bring my wallet.
3. ___Well___, I can loan you money for a ticket.
4. ___Yay___! I just found some money in my pocket.
5. ___Hey___, thanks a lot. That's really nice of you.

442

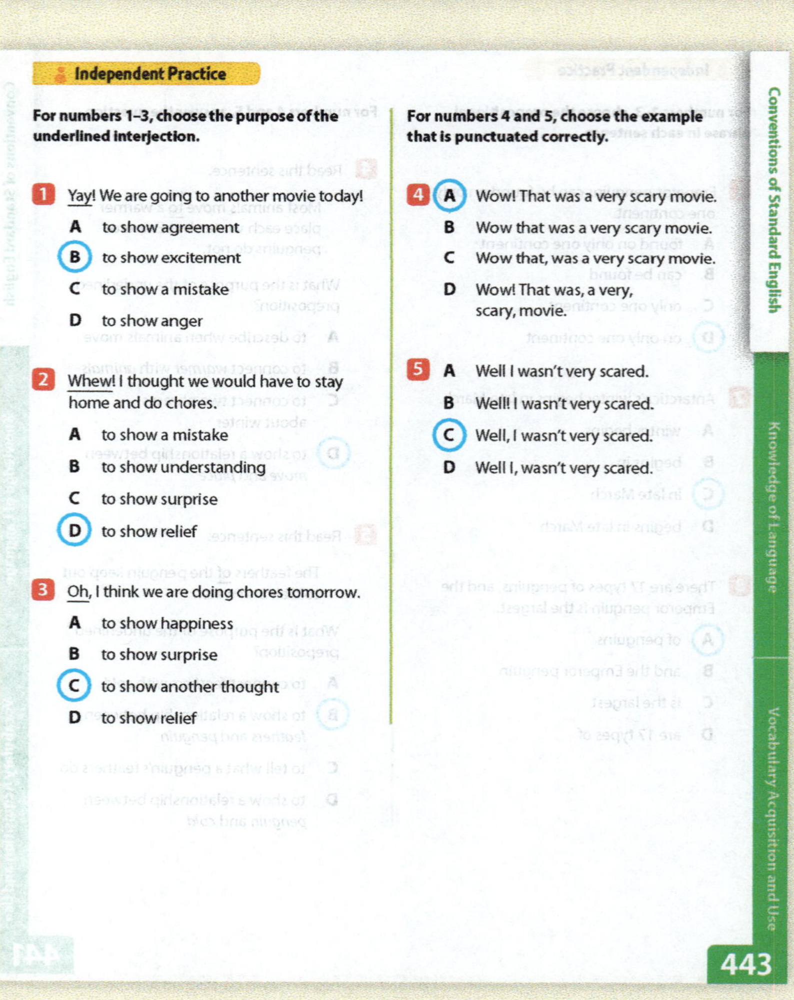

Independent Practice

For numbers 1–3, choose the purpose of the underlined interjection.

1. Yay! We are going to another movie today!
   - A to show agreement
   - **B to show excitement**
   - C to show a mistake
   - D to show anger
2. Whew! I thought we would have to stay home and do chores.
   - A to show a mistake
   - B to show understanding
   - C to show surprise
   - **D to show relief**
3. Oh, I think we are doing chores tomorrow.
   - A to show happiness
   - B to show surprise
   - **C to show another thought**
   - D to show relief

For numbers 4 and 5, choose the example that is punctuated correctly.

4. - **A Wow! That was a very scary movie.**
   - B Wow that was a very scary movie.
   - C Wow that, was a very scary movie.
   - D Wow! That was, a very, scary, movie.
5. - A Well I wasn't very scared.
   - B Well! I wasn't very scared.
   - **C Well, I wasn't very scared.**
   - D Well I, wasn't very scared.

Conventions of Standard English
Knowledge of Language
Vocabulary Acquisition and Use

443

Lesson 4

Perfect Verb Tenses

L.5.1b: Form and use the perfect (e.g., *I had walked; I have walked; I will have walked*) verb tenses.

Introduction The **perfect verb tenses** tell about actions that happened, that will happen, or that may still be happening. They are made by joining a form of the helping verb *have* with the past form of a main verb. Together, the helping verb and the main verb make up a **verb phrase**.

helping verb main verb
Workers [had] [installed] new swings in Grant Park.

- The **present perfect tense** tells about an action that took place in the past and may still be happening. To form this tense, use *has* or *have* with the past form of a main verb.

  Volunteers have turned Grant Park into a beautiful spot.

- The **past perfect tense** tells about an action that was completed before another past action. To form this tense, use *had* with the past form of a main verb.

  Grant Park had become neglected, so people stopped going there.

- The **future perfect tense** tells about an action that will be completed before another future action. To form this tense, use *will have* with the past form of a main verb.

  By next week, we will have cleared the park of trash.

Guided Practice **Write the correct helping verb or verbs to form the perfect tense named in parentheses ( ). The main verbs are underlined.**

HINT To form the present perfect, use *has* when the subject is singular and *have* when the subject is plural.

1. The park opened in 1991 after people ___had___ demanded it.
   past perfect
2. Sadly, they ___have___ forgotten how important the park is.
   present perfect
3. Now the day ___has___ come to rebuild the playground.
   present perfect
4. By next summer, we ___will have___ rebuilt the entire playground.
   future perfect

Independent Practice

In numbers 1–3, which words should replace the underlined verb phrase to make the sentence correct?

1. Our town will have changed by the time the 21st century began.
   - A will had changed
   - B had changed
   - C has changed
   - D have changed
2. Many families have moved away before the cleanup started.
   - A had moved
   - B will had moved
   - C has moved
   - D will have moved
3. Today, many families had returned.
   - A will had returned
   - B have returned
   - C will have returned
   - D has returned

For numbers 4 and 5, choose the sentence in which the underlined verb phrase is correct.

4.
   - A Last year, the mayor has conducted a survey on Grant Park.
   - B Last year, the mayor have conducted a survey on Grant Park.
   - C Last year, the mayor had conducted a survey on Grant Park.
   - D Last year, the mayor will have conducted a survey on Grant Park.
5.
   - A City officials has completed a report by next year.
   - B City officials had completed a report by next year.
   - C City officials have completed a report by next year.
   - D City officials will have completed a report by next year.

Conventions of Standard English

Knowledge of Language

Vocabulary Acquisition and Use

Introduction

- Read aloud the Introduction and examples. Explain that the helping verb *have* takes the form *has* or *have* in the present tense, *had* in the past tense, and *will have* in the future tense.

  Present, past, and future perfect verb tenses all use the past form of the main verb. To determine the tense of a verb phrase, look at the form of the helping verb *have*.

- Write the following sentences on a chart or project them on a whiteboard.

  Our class has collected nine hundred bottle caps so far this year. *(present)*

  By next week, our class will have collected a thousand bottle caps. *(future)*

  In past years, the class had collected around five hundred bottle caps. *(past)*

- Model for students how to determine if each verb phrase is in the present, past, or future tense.

Guided Practice

- Read aloud the sentences and Hint.
- Have students complete the activity.
- Remind students that *has/have* is present tense, *had* is past tense, and *will have* is future tense.

Extend Learning

Practice Perfect Verb Tenses

Ask students to complete each sentence with the past, present, or future perfect verb tense of the verb *walk*.

1. Zach ____________ this trail long before it was paved. *(had walked)*
2. Zach ____________ this trail every day for the past year. *(has walked)*
3. By next year, Zach ____________ this trail over a hundred times. (will have walked)

Introduction

- Read aloud the Introduction and examples. Explain to students that a verb must be in agreement with the subject and the tense of a sentence.

  If something sounds strange in a sentence, check to make sure the number and tense of the verb are correct. A verb can be singular or plural to agree with the subject, and it can be in the present, past, or future tense depending on when the action happens.
- Write the following sentences on a chart or project them on a whiteboard.

  Last year, I __________ every day. *(ran/was running)*

  This year, I __________ three days a week. *(run/am running)*

  Next month, I __________ in the school race. *(will run/will be running)*
- Model for students how to determine which form of the irregular verb *run* to use in each sentence. Demonstrate how to use *run* in the simple tense and in the progressive tense.

Guided Practice

- Read aloud the sentences and Hint.
- Have students complete the activity.
- Remind students that for the helping verb *be*, *am* and *is* are present tense, *was* is past tense, and *will be* is future tense.

English Language Learners

Practice Verb Tenses

Students may not be familiar with English verb tenses. Ask questions that require responses in the simple and progressive tenses to help students practice using the different tenses.

1. *Simple:* What did we do before school? What happens after school?
2. *Progressive:* What were we doing yesterday? What will you be doing later?

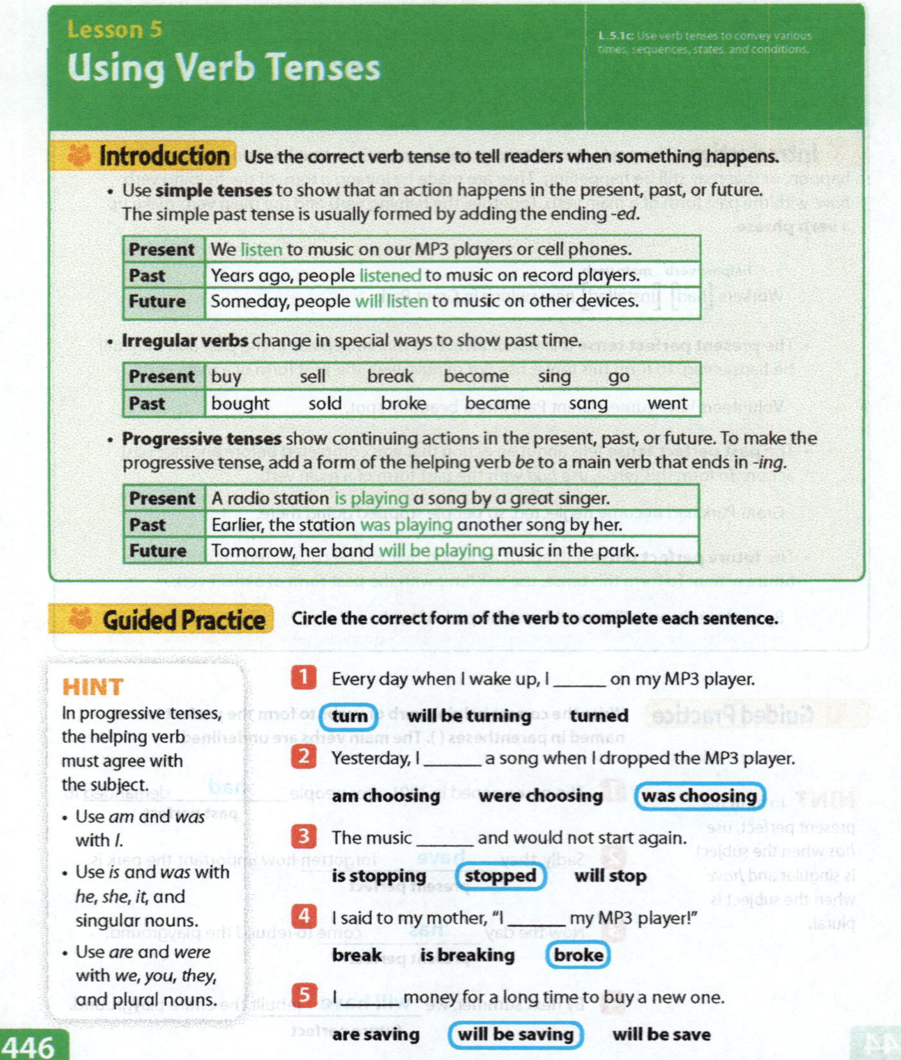

Lesson 5

Using Verb Tenses

L.5.1c: Use verb tenses to convey various times, sequences, states, and conditions.

Introduction Use the correct verb tense to tell readers when something happens.

- Use **simple tenses** to show that an action happens in the present, past, or future. The simple past tense is usually formed by adding the ending *-ed*.

Present	We listen to music on our MP3 players or cell phones.
Past	Years ago, people listened to music on record players.
Future	Someday, people will listen to music on other devices.

- **Irregular verbs** change in special ways to show past time.

Present	buy	sell	break	become	sing	go
Past	bought	sold	broke	became	sang	went

- **Progressive tenses** show continuing actions in the present, past, or future. To make the progressive tense, add a form of the helping verb *be* to a main verb that ends in *-ing*.

Present	A radio station is playing a song by a great singer.
Past	Earlier, the station was playing another song by her.
Future	Tomorrow, her band will be playing music in the park.

Guided Practice Circle the correct form of the verb to complete each sentence.

HINT
In progressive tenses, the helping verb must agree with the subject.
- Use *am* and *was* with *I*.
- Use *is* and *was* with *he, she, it,* and singular nouns.
- Use *are* and *were* with *we, you, they,* and plural nouns.

1. Every day when I wake up, I _____ on my MP3 player.
   turn **will be turning** **turned**
2. Yesterday, I _____ a song when I dropped the MP3 player.
   am choosing **were choosing** **was choosing**
3. The music _____ and would not start again.
   is stopping **stopped** **will stop**
4. I said to my mother, "I _____ my MP3 player!"
   break **is breaking** **broke**
5. I _____ money for a long time to buy a new one.
   are saving **will be saving** **will be save**

446

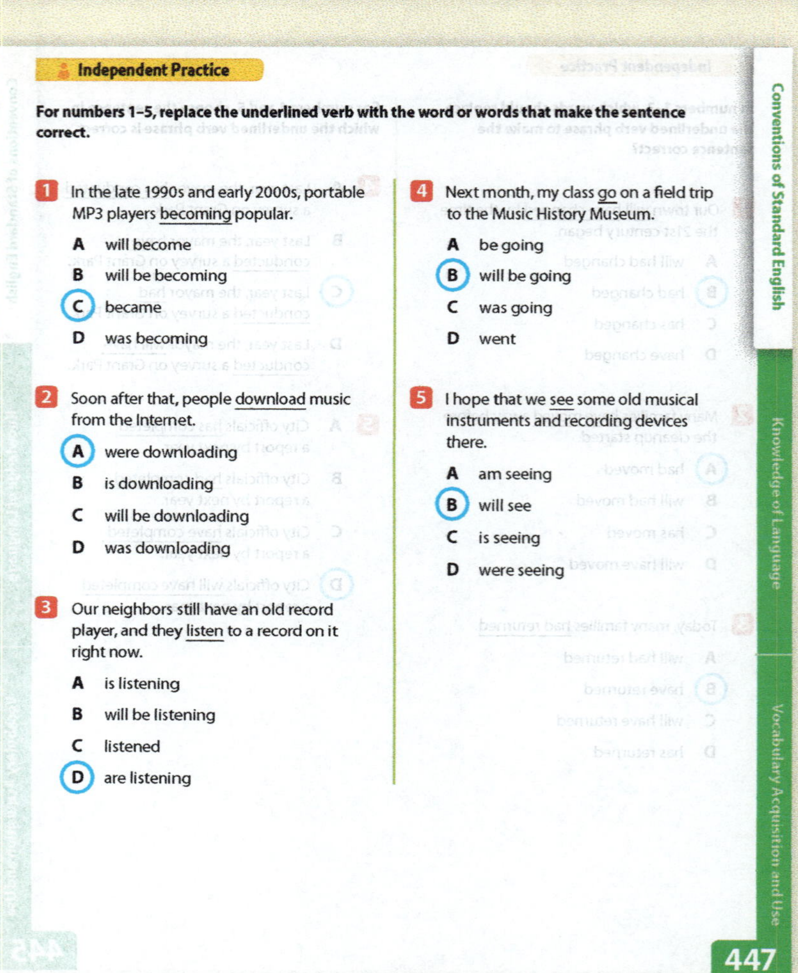

Independent Practice

For numbers 1–5, replace the underlined verb with the word or words that make the sentence correct.

1. In the late 1990s and early 2000s, portable MP3 players becoming popular.
   - A will become
   - B will be becoming
   - C became
   - D was becoming
2. Soon after that, people download music from the Internet.
   - A were downloading
   - B is downloading
   - C will be downloading
   - D was downloading
3. Our neighbors still have an old record player, and they listen to a record on it right now.
   - A is listening
   - B will be listening
   - C listened
   - D are listening
4. Next month, my class go on a field trip to the Music History Museum.
   - A be going
   - B will be going
   - C was going
   - D went
5. I hope that we see some old musical instruments and recording devices there.
   - A am seeing
   - B will see
   - C is seeing
   - D were seeing

Conventions of Standard English

Knowledge of Language

Vocabulary Acquisition and Use

447

Lesson 6
Shifts in Verb Tense

L.5.1d: Recognize and correct inappropriate shifts in verb tense.

Introduction Verbs tell readers that something is happening. **Verb tenses** can show whether an event takes place in the past, in the present, or in the future.

When you write, choose the tense that shows clearly the time of the action. Verb tenses that shift can confuse readers, so change tense only if you want to show a change in time.

Verb Tenses Shifting Incorrectly	Verb Tenses Shifting Correctly
We went to the movies last Saturday. The movie is a comedy and was very funny. We had eaten popcorn during the movie, but we often stop so we will hear every word.	We went to the movies last Saturday. The movie was a comedy and was very funny. We ate popcorn during the movie, but we often stopped so we could hear every word.

Guided Practice **Read the passage. It should be written in the past tense. Cross out each verb that should be changed to make the tenses consistent. Then write the correct verb above each verb you crossed out.**

HINT Look for clues that tell when events happen. Do they occur in the past, present, or future?

Then look at each verb and ask yourself:

- What tense is the verb?
- Does it match the tense of the other verbs?

Jake went to the movies with Mario last week. They ~~see~~ **saw** the film *Frontiers of Space*. Tickets for the show that night were expensive, but Mario ~~has~~ **had** a coupon. He ~~finds~~ **found or had found** the coupon online the day before. Mario ~~will buy~~ **bought** the tickets. Then he looked for seats while Jake ~~purchases~~ **purchased** the snacks. Jake ~~gets~~ **got** popcorn for himself and a pretzel for Mario. They ~~will have sat~~ **sat** in the front row, watched the movie, and ~~enjoy~~ **enjoyed** themselves.

Independent Practice

For numbers 1–5, replace the underlined sentence with the choice that has the correct verb tense.

1. Ari went to the movies last Friday afternoon. She sit in the third row. The screen looked huge from there.
   - A She is sitting in the third row.
   - B She had sat in the third row.
   - C She will sit in the third row.
   - (D) She sat in the third row.

2. My family watched a DVD last weekend. It was a very old movie. We like it anyway.
   - (A) We liked it anyway.
   - B We had liked it anyway.
   - C We will have liked it anyway.
   - D We will like it anyway.

3. The first part of the movie is slow. The action in the second part was really exciting. The end of the movie is a total surprise.
   - A The action in the second part will be really exciting.
   - (B) The action in the second part is really exciting.
   - C The action in the second part will have been really exciting.
   - D The action in the second part had been really exciting.

4. Yesterday I watched *The Secret Garden*. I loved the movie so much, I watch it again. Mom watched it with me, too.
   - A I love the movie so much, I watch it again.
   - B I had loved the movie so much, I will have watched it again.
   - C I loved the movie so much, I had watched it again.
   - (D) I loved the movie so much, I watched it again.

5. My mom and I will go see another movie next weekend. We will go with Chantal and her dad. We meet in front of the theater.
   - A We met in front of the theater.
   - B We were meeting in front of the theater.
   - (C) We will meet in front of the theater.
   - D We had met in front of the theater.

Conventions of Standard English | Knowledge of Language | Vocabulary Acquisition and Use

Introduction

- Read aloud the Introduction and chart. As you discuss the examples, help students label the verbs as past, present, or future tense to help identify the incorrect verb forms.

  The tense of the paragraph should be consistent in each sentence. If the writer is telling about things that have already happened, then all of the verbs should be in the past tense.

- Write the following sentences on a chart or project them on a whiteboard.

  Trent cleans his room before he ate dinner. *(cleaned)*

  Trent completed his homework and then watch a movie. *(watched)*

  Trent finished the movie and go to bed. *(went)*

- Model how to identify the incorrect verb and determine the proper form of the verb based on the tense of the sentence.

Guided Practice

- Read aloud the paragraph and help students identify the errors.
- Have students complete the activity.
- Remind students that the verbs should all be in the past tense.

Access Content

Practice Correct Verb Tenses

Ask students to use context clues to determine which tense of the verb in parentheses to use in each sentence.

1. Lisa will stretch, and then she ______ (run) in the race. *(will run)*
2. Marcus stayed inside and ______ (play) games yesterday. *(played)*
3. Rosa ______ (walk) her dog and practices playing the piano every day. *(walks)*
4. Last weekend, I visited the library, ______ (bake) cookies, and went to my sister's game. *(baked)*

Introduction

- Read aloud the Introduction and examples. Explain to students that correlative conjunctions are used in pairs.

  When the first correlative conjunction is introduced, the thought will not be complete until the second correlative conjunction is used. Each correlative conjunction pair has a different meaning, so pay attention to the purpose of the sentence when choosing which pair to use.

- Write the following sentences on a chart or project them on a whiteboard.

  I am stuck indoors ________ it rains ________ shines. *(whether/or)*

  I can ________ run ________ bike indoors, so I will have to think of something else to do. *(neither/nor)*

  I can ____________ read a book ____________ do a puzzle. *(either/or)*

- Model for students how to determine the correct correlative conjunctions to use in each sentence. Demonstrate how using different correlative conjunctions in the second and third sentences would change the meaning of each.

Guided Practice

- Read aloud the sentences and Hint.
- Have students complete the activity.
- Remind students to think about the purpose of each sentence and choose the pair of correlative conjunctions that fits that purpose.

Scaffolded Instruction

Use Correlative Conjunctions

Display two detailed photographs or paintings. Ask students to write several sentences that use correlative conjunctions to describe the pictures. For example:

***Both** the city **and** the farm have red trucks.*

***Neither** the city **nor** the farm has any snow.*

Lesson 7

Correlative Conjunctions

L.5.1e: Use correlative conjunctions (e.g., either/or, neither/nor).

Introduction Recall that **conjunctions** are connecting words that can join words, phrases, or sentences. **Correlative conjunctions** are conjunctions used in pairs.

Read the chart below to see which correlative conjunctions are used together and how.

Correlative Conjunctions	Example
both . . . and	**Both** my brother **and** I wanted to go rafting on a river.
either . . . or	We were going with **either** a guide **or** my parents.
neither . . . nor	**Neither** my mother **nor** my father knew much about rafting.
not only . . . but also	They **not only** read about it **but also** watched a video.
whether . . . or	The video discussed **whether** rafting was dangerous **or** safe.

Guided Practice **Write a pair of correlative conjunctions from the chart to complete each sentence. Use all five pairs shown in the chart above.**

HINT Use *either/or* to express a choice. Use *neither/nor* to make a negative statement about two choices.

Don't mix up these pairs. Don't use *either* with *nor*. Similarly, don't use *neither* with *or*.

1. My parents said I could ___either___ bring a friend ___or___ go with just the family.
2. I wanted to invite ___not only___ my friend Jake ___but also___ his brother. (or both/and)
3. To my surprise, ___both___ my dad ___and___ my mom said that was fine. (or not only/but also)
4. I was sorry to learn that ___neither___ Jake ___nor___ his brother was available.
5. Still, I knew that I'd have fun ___whether___ I went with friends ___or___ just with my family.

450

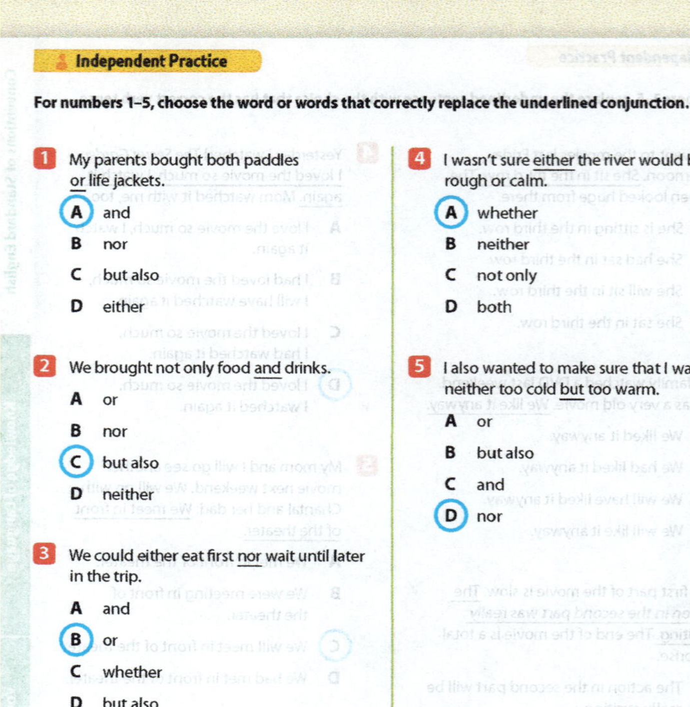

Independent Practice

For numbers 1–5, choose the word or words that correctly replace the underlined conjunction.

1. My parents bought both paddles or life jackets.
   - Ⓐ and
   - B nor
   - C but also
   - D either

2. We brought not only food and drinks.
   - A or
   - B nor
   - Ⓒ but also
   - D neither

3. We could either eat first nor wait until later in the trip.
   - A and
   - Ⓑ or
   - C whether
   - D but also

4. I wasn't sure either the river would be rough or calm.
   - Ⓐ whether
   - B neither
   - C not only
   - D both

5. I also wanted to make sure that I was neither too cold but too warm.
   - A or
   - B but also
   - C and
   - Ⓓ nor

Conventions of Standard English

Knowledge of Language

Vocabulary Acquisition and Use

451

Lesson 8

Punctuating Items in a Series

L.5.2a: Use punctuation to separate items in a series.

Introduction Use a **comma** (,) to separate three or more items in a **series**, or list. Place a comma after each item in the series except the last one.

- Use commas when you list three or more words in a series.

  Many murals decorate buildings in Philadelphia, Chicago, and Boston.

- Use commas when you list three or more phrases in a series.

  People paint murals on buildings, in tunnels, and even along roadsides.

- Use commas when you list three or more clauses in a series.

  You might see a mural when visiting a museum, driving on a highway, or walking around your neighborhood.

Without commas, the items in these lists would run together, making the sentences unclear.

Guided Practice Read the passage. Then add commas where they are needed.

HINT When you use commas to separate items in a series, put a comma before the conjunction *and* or *or*. Do not put a comma after the conjunction.

Cities around the country are changing. Faded boards, dull concrete, and old bricks are coming to life. Communities are turning the walls of their buildings, roads, and bridges into colorful murals. Painters might show local scenes, honor a hero, or celebrate a culture.

Murals can also be great projects for schools. They encourage teamwork, school spirit, and creativity. What would you paint? Your mural could inspire people to recycle, be a volunteer, or cheer for a team.

Independent Practice

For numbers 1–4, answer the questions.

1 Read this sentence. Then answer the question.

Three famous artists who painted murals were Rivera Orozco and Siquieros.

What is the correct position of commas in the underlined section of the sentence?

A Rivera Orozco, and Siquieros
(B) Rivera, Orozco, and Siquieros
C Rivera Orozco, and, Siquieros
D Rivera, Orozco and, Siquieros

2 Read this sentence. Then answer the question.

They painted murals to educate inspire and unite people across Mexico.

What is the correct position of commas in the underlined section of the sentence?

A educate inspire, and, unite people
B educate inspire and unite people
(C) educate, inspire, and unite people
D educate, inspire, and unite, people

3 Read this sentence. Then answer the question.

Siquieros sprayed paint used bold lines and splattered colors.

What is the correct position of commas in the underlined section of the sentence?

(A) sprayed paint, used bold lines, and
B sprayed, paint used bold lines, and
C sprayed, paint used bold, lines, and
D sprayed paint, used bold lines and,

4 Read this sentence. Then answer the question.

You can see murals painted by Rivera in San Francisco Detroit and Mexico City.

What is the correct position of commas in the underlined section of the sentence?

A San Francisco, Detroit, and, Mexico City
B San Francisco, Detroit and Mexico, City
C San Francisco Detroit, and, Mexico City
(D) San Francisco, Detroit, and Mexico City

Conventions of Standard English | Knowledge of Language | Vocabulary Acquisition and Use

Introduction

- Read aloud the Introduction and examples. Explain to students that commas are used when listing three or more words, phrases, or clauses.

  A comma should be used after each of the items in a series. The final comma comes before the conjunction. There should not be a comma after the conjunction.

- Write the following types of apples on a chart or project them on a whiteboard.

  red delicious
  gala
  pink lady
  (The store carries red delicious, gala, and pink lady apples.)

- Model for students how to write a sentence listing the three items. Explain how you determine where to put the commas.

Guided Practice

- Read the passage aloud.
- Have students complete the activity.
- Remind students that a noun with an adjective is one item in a series and that a comma should never separate an adjective from the noun it describes.

Scaffolded Instruction

Practice Listing Items in a Series

Help students understand how to list items in a series by using concrete items in the classroom with sentence frames.

1. The colors of the whiteboard markers are ______, ______, and ______.
2. The three tallest students in our class are ______, ______, and ______.
3. The items you need for math are a ______, a ______, and a ______.

Introduction

- Read aloud the Introduction and examples. Explain that dependent clauses and prepositional phrases can sometimes be found at the beginning of a sentence.

  When you read a sentence, ask if the beginning word, clause, or phrase can stand on its own. If it cannot, you should put a comma after the word, clause, or phrase.
- Write the following sentences on a chart or project them on a whiteboard.

  No, I have never gone overseas.

  Even though I have never gone overseas, I love to think about traveling.

  When I go overseas, I want to see as many places as I can.
- Model for students how to determine where to add a comma in each sentence. Explain why you are adding each comma.

Guided Practice

- Read aloud the passage.
- Have students complete the activity.
- Remind students that a dependent clause is a clause that cannot stand on its own and often begins with a subordinating conjunction. A prepositional phrase begins with a preposition and can tell how, where, when, or what kind.

Access Content

Practice Writing Introductory Elements

Ask students to rewrite the sentences by moving the dependent clause or the prepositional phrase to the beginning of the sentence and adding a comma.

1. I had to stand outside while everyone played indoors. *(While everyone played indoors, I had to stand outside.)*
2. He let out a sigh of relief when he found his keys. *(When he found his keys, he let out a sigh of relief.)*
3. My homework sat untouched in my backpack. *(In my backpack, my homework sat untouched.)*

Lesson 9

Commas After Introductory Elements

L.5.2b: Use a comma to separate an introductory element from the rest of the sentence.
L.5.2c: Use a comma to set off the words *yes* and *no* (e.g., *Yes, thank you*) . . .

Introduction Good writers vary the beginnings of their sentences to make their writing more interesting. When you write, use a **comma** (,) to set off an introductory word or phrase from the rest of the sentence.

- Use a comma after introductory words such as *yes* and *no.*

  Yes, Victor was looking forward to the race in Chile.

  No, it wouldn't be easy to run across the Atacama Desert.
- Use a comma after a dependent clause that comes at the beginning of a sentence. A dependent clause can begin with a subordinating conjunction such as *while* or *because.*

  While on the plane ride to Chile, Victor thought about the race.

  Because he had trained hard, he was in great shape.
- Use a comma after a prepositional phrase that comes at the beginning of a sentence.

  Under the blazing sun, more than 100 people would race for seven days.

Guided Practice **Read the passage. Then add commas where they are needed.**

HINT Some sentences begin with two prepositional phrases in a row. There is usually a comma only after the second prepositional phrase.

Example:
Under the shade of a tree, the runner rested.

Victor was standing in the driest place on Earth. In some parts of the Atacama Desert, not a single drop of water had been seen for decades. On his back, Victor's gear seemed especially heavy. He had food, clothes, and water for the next 250 kilometers. Could he make it? Yes, he could.

While he waited for the race to begin, Victor's heart pounded. Above the desert, wispy clouds crossed the deep blue sky.

Independent Practice

For numbers 1–5, choose the correct way to rewrite the underlined part of each sentence.

1. At the end of the first day Victor collapsed in his tent.
   - A At the end, of the first day Victor
   - B At the end of the first day, Victor ✓
   - C At the end, of the first day, Victor,
   - D At the end, of the first day, Victor
2. Before the sun rose the runners set out across the plains.
   - A Before the sun rose, the runners ✓
   - B Before the sun, rose the runners
   - C Before, the sun rose, the runners
   - D Before the sun rose, the runners,
3. Although sand stung his face Victor kept running.
   - A Although, sand stung his face, Victor
   - B Although, sand stung his face Victor
   - C Although sand stung his face, Victor ✓
   - D Although sand stung his face Victor,
4. When he finally reached the finish line he was thrilled.
   - A When he finally, reached the finish line he
   - B When he finally reached, the finish line, he
   - C When, he finally reached the finish line he
   - D When he finally reached the finish line, he ✓
5. Yes he had achieved the goal of a lifetime.
   - A Yes he had, achieved
   - B Yes, he had achieved,
   - C Yes, he had achieved ✓
   - D Yes, he had, achieved

Conventions of Standard English
Knowledge of Language
Vocabulary Acquisition and Use

Lesson 10

More Uses for Commas

L.5.2c: Use a comma to set off … a tag question from the rest of the sentence (e.g., *It's true, isn't it?*), and to indicate direct address (e.g., *Is that you, Steve?*).

Introduction When you write, use a **comma** (,) to set off the part of a sentence that asks a tag question or addresses a person by name.

- A **tag question** comes at the end of a sentence that makes a statement. It is a way of asking someone to think about or agree with what you have just said. Use a comma to set off a tag question from the rest of the sentence.

  This is a big game for us, isn't it?

  You don't want to lose, do you?

- A noun of **direct address** names a person being spoken to. The noun may come at the beginning, in the middle, or at the end of a sentence. Use a comma or commas to set off a noun of direct address from the rest of the sentence.

  Daria, I know how hard you've worked this season.

  What do you think, Coach Cody, about our chances of winning?

  I think we're ready for the game, Daria.

Guided Practice **Read the passage. Then add commas where they are needed.**

HINT When a noun of direct address comes in the middle of a sentence, put a comma before *and* after the name.

"This is a really important game, Daria," Olivia said. The two girls stood on the basketball court. The gym was packed.

Daria saw the Cougars' star player walking toward her. "You missed all your free throws last week, didn't you?" said the girl.

Daria replied, "I know who you are, Izzy James, and I'm not listening to you."

Olivia said, "Daria, just relax. Izzy's just teasing us, you know?"

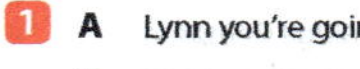

Independent Practice

For numbers 1–5, choose the sentence in each group that is punctuated correctly.

1
- A Lynn you're going to jump for the ball.
- B Lynn, you're, going to jump for the ball.
- (C) Lynn, you're going to jump for the ball.
- D Lynn, you're going to jump, for the ball.

2
- A Thanks, for giving me this chance, Coach Cody.
- B Thanks for giving me this chance Coach Cody.
- C Thanks, for giving me this chance Coach Cody.
- (D) Thanks for giving me this chance, Coach Cody.

3
- A I think you, Olivia should guard their forward.
- B I think you Olivia should guard their forward.
- (C) I think you, Olivia, should guard their forward.
- D I think you Olivia, should guard their forward.

4
- A I'd love to see this team, win, wouldn't you?
- (B) I'd love to see this team win, wouldn't you?
- C I'd love to see this team win wouldn't you?
- D I'd love to see this team win wouldn't, you?

5
- (A) They didn't win any games last year, did they?
- B They didn't win any games, last year, did they?
- C They didn't win any games last year did they?
- D They didn't win any games last, year did they?

Introduction

- Read aloud the Introduction and examples. Explain that a tag question comes at the end of a sentence to turn a statement into a question. Then explain that a noun of direct address names the person that the speaker of a sentence is talking to.
- Write the following sentences on a chart or project them on a whiteboard.

  I didn't forget anything, did I?

  Jack, have you seen my backpack?

  Lora is a very fast runner, isn't she?

  I think, Daniel, that she is the fastest runner on the team.
- Model for students how to identify tag questions and nouns of direct address and set them off with commas. Point out the difference between a noun of direct address and the subject of a sentence.

Guided Practice

- Read aloud the passage.
- Have students complete the activity.
- Remind students that they will add two commas if a noun of direct address is in the middle of a sentence.

Extend Learning

Using Commas

Ask students to think of someone, real or make-believe, that they would like to interview. Have students write several questions to ask the person. Make sure the questions include a direct address and/or a tag question. For example: *Mr. Jordan, you played baseball in grade school, didn't you?*

Introduction

- Read aloud the Introduction and examples. Explain to students that the way a title is written gives a clue to the length of the work.

  The title of a short work is placed in quotation marks. The title of a longer work can be underlined or set in italics. When written by hand, the title is underlined; when using a computer, the title is set in italics.
- Write the following sentences on a chart or project them on a whiteboard.

  Each student in our class chose a poem to recite, so I chose "The Long Summer."

  Monsters Everywhere is one of the scariest movies I have ever seen.

  The article "A Guitar Legend" in this month's issue of My Music was about my favorite artist.
- Model for students how to determine whether to underline or place quotation marks around each title.

Guided Practice

- Read aloud the passage.
- Have students complete the activity.
- Remind students to look for clues in the sentences to help them determine the type of work that is being referenced.

Extend Learning

Practice Writing Titles

Ask students to write three sentences about their favorite movie, book, and song or poem. Then have students exchange papers and check to make sure each title is written correctly.

Lesson 11

Punctuating Titles of Works

L.5.2d: Use underlining, quotation marks, or italics to indicate titles of works.

Introduction When you write, you might include the title of a creative work, such as a book or a poem. Titles of creative works are written in special ways.

- Use **quotation marks (" ")** around the titles of short works, such as stories, poems, songs, articles, and chapters of books.

  Have you read the article "Mountain Time"?

  The poem "Blue Ridge" was quoted in it.

  The writer also mentioned the song "The Long Way."
- When writing by hand, **underline** the titles of longer works such as books, magazines, newspapers, plays, and movies. If you are using a computer, show these titles in ***italic type***.

  The magazine Mountain Days Monthly just arrived at our house. (if handwritten)

  The magazine *Mountain Days Monthly* just arrived at our house. (if on a computer)

Guided Practice **Read the movie review. Correct the titles of short and long works by adding quotation marks and underlining.**

HINT When you write the name of a longer work, either underline or italicize it. Do not do both.

Correct: Ozma of Oz
Correct: *Ozma of Oz*
Incorrect: *Ozma of Oz* (underlined)

Rockville Gorge is unlike any movie you have ever seen. It is about a group of hikers who get lost in a dense forest. The main character is a newspaper reporter who works for The Daily Tribune. The other hikers are doing research for a book called Black Bears of the County. Did I mention that they all sing? Without warning, the characters start singing "I'm So Lost I Feel Alone." Have you ever heard of the poem "Turkeys Are for Gobbling"? The main character reads that poem out loud for no reason I can figure out. The movie reminded me of my least favorite short story, "It's Just a Bad Dream."

Independent Practice

For numbers 1–5, choose the correct way to rewrite the title of each work.

1. Climbing Grandfather Mountain is a great book.
   - A "Climbing Grandfather Mountain"
   - B *"Climbing Grandfather Mountain"*
   - C *Climbing Grandfather Mountain* (underlined)
   - **(D)** *Climbing Grandfather Mountain*

2. The first chapter of the book is called Navigating the Trail.
   - A Navigating the Trail (underlined)
   - **(B)** "Navigating the Trail"
   - C "Navigating the Trail" (underlined)
   - D *Navigating the Trail*

3. During my hike, I hummed a tune called Clear Days.
   - **(A)** "Clear Days"
   - B Clear Days (underlined)
   - C *Clear Days*
   - D *"Clear Days"*

4. Every issue of Blue Ridge Camping Magazine has amazing photography.
   - A "Blue Ridge" Camping Magazine
   - B "Blue Ridge Camping Magazine" (underlined)
   - C "Blue Ridge Camping Magazine"
   - **(D)** *Blue Ridge Camping Magazine*

5. Mountain Years is a funny play with a surprise ending.
   - A "Mountain Years"
   - B *"Mountain Years"*
   - **(C)** *Mountain Years*
   - D "Mountain" Years

Conventions of Standard English · Knowledge of Language · Vocabulary Acquisition and Use

Lesson 12

Revising Sentences

L.5.3a: Expand . . . and reduce sentences for meaning, reader/listener interest, and style.

Introduction Good writers revise their writing to make sure their ideas grab and hold a reader's attention. There are many ways to revise sentences to improve them.

- You can **expand** a sentence by adding details that make the sentence more interesting.

Add Details	*Weak:* Hula is a beautiful Hawaiian dance. *Better:* With its pulsing drums and flowing steps, hula is a beautiful Hawaiian dance.

- You can **shorten** a sentence by deleting unnecessary words or cutting repetition. Short sentences get to the point. They also create rhythm when mixed with longer sentences.

Delete Words	*Weak:* I'll start by saying that I think the dancers move like swaying palm trees. *Better:* The dancers move like swaying palm trees.
Avoid Repetition	*Weak:* Hula is fairly simple and not difficult because it is a dance based on just six basic moves that dancers do. *Better:* Hula is fairly simple because it is based on just six moves.

Guided Practice **Improve each sentence by adding details, deleting words, or avoiding repetition. If you need to add details, use facts from the tables above.**

HINT To decide the best way to revise a sentence, ask yourself: Does it need fewer words or more details?

1. Hula is a dance.
   Hula is a beautiful but simple dance from Hawaii.
2. Now I will tell you that hula is not just for women, but in fact men also dance hula, too.
   Both women and men dance the hula.
3. Modern hula today includes stringed instruments like the ukulele, guitar, and other stringed instruments that are also used in addition to traditional instruments like rattles and gourds.
   Modern hula includes stringed instruments like the ukulele and guitar as well as traditional instruments like rattles and gourds.

Independent Practice

For numbers 1–4, choose the best way to revise the sentence.

1. Hula dancers often wear things they find in nature.
   - A Hula dancers wear costumes.
   - B Hula dancers wear natural things.
   - (C) Hula dancers often wear headbands and bracelets made of leaves.
   - D Hula dancers often wear things from nature such as natural leaves.
2. Some types involve chanting.
   - A Chanting is in some types.
   - (B) Chanting is an important part of some types of hula.
   - C When hula dancers dance the hula, sometimes they chant as they dance.
   - D Sometimes people chant during the hula when they do certain types of hula.
3. Queen Lili'uokalani wrote lots of songs, and one song she wrote was the famous song called "Aloha Oe."
   - (A) Queen Lili'uokalani wrote many songs, including the famous "Aloha Oe."
   - B Queen Lili'uokalani wrote "Aloha Oe."
   - C Queen Lili'uokalani wrote songs, and she wrote "Aloha Oe," a famous song.
   - D Queen Lili'uokalani wrote songs, and one she wrote was famous.
4. Hula means more than entertainment for tourists, and this meaning is the celebration of Hawaiian history.
   - A Hula's meaning is the celebration of Hawaiian history, not only just entertainment.
   - B Hula entertains tourists and it also means the celebration of Hawaiian history.
   - C In addition to entertaining tourists, hula has a lot of meaning.
   - (D) More than just entertainment, hula is the celebration of Hawaiian history.

Introduction

- Read aloud the Introduction and examples. Explain to students that even when a sentence has no errors, it may still be revised to better communicate the message.

  A good writer will deliver a message in the clearest, most concise way possible. Sometimes a writer may add details to a sentence to clarify an idea. A writer may also take out unnecessary words to make a sentence more concise.
- Write the following sentences on a chart or project them on a whiteboard.

  Rock climbing is hard. *(Rock climbing is difficult because it requires a lot of strength and skill.)*

  The dangers and perils involved in rock climbing should not be ignored when considering beginning this risky hobby. *(Consider the risks before you begin rock climbing.)*
- Model for students how to shorten or expand each sentence to make the ideas interesting, clear, and concise.

Guided Practice

- Read aloud each sentence.
- Have students complete the activity.
- Remind students that if a sentence looks short, they may need to add details to clarify an idea; if a sentence looks long, they may need to take out unnecessary words.

Scaffolded Instruction

Practice Expanding Sentences

Ask students to add details to the sentence *The monster moved* using the following prompts:

1. What did the monster look like?
2. How did the monster move?
3. Where did the monster go?

Introduction

- Read aloud the Introduction and examples. Explain to students that combining related sentences will make their writing sound better.

  Combining sentences is a strategy that writers use to make their writing flow more smoothly. One way to combine two sentences is to use a conjunction.
- Write the following sentences on a chart or project them on a whiteboard.

  I don't eat onions. I don't like the smell.
  (I don't eat onions because I don't like the smell.)

  I have to go to the post office. It's closed today.
  (I have to go to the post office, but it's closed today.)
- Model for students how to combine each pair of sentences. Explain why you chose each subordinating or coordinating conjunction.

Guided Practice

- Read aloud the sentences.
- Have students complete the activity.
- Remind students that sentences can be combined in many ways. Encourage them to think of several ways they can combine the sentences and choose the one that sounds best.

Extend Learning

Practice Combining Sentences

Ask students to combine each sentence pair into one sentence.

1. I went to the mall. I bought a new shirt.
   (I went to the mall and bought a new shirt.)
2. I started to feel hungry. I ate at the food court.
   (When I started to feel hungry, I ate at the food court.)
3. The food choices all looked good. I chose to eat tacos.
   (The food choices all looked good, but I chose to eat tacos.)

Lesson 13

Combining Sentences

L.5.3a: [C]ombine . . . sentences for meaning, reader/listener interest, and style.

Introduction Good writers avoid strings of short, choppy sentences. You can **combine sentences** with related ideas to vary sentence style and length.

- When the ideas in sentences are related and equally important, you can join them with a **coordinating conjunction**, such as *and, but, or,* or *so*. Use a comma before the conjunction if each idea is a complete sentence.

Choppy: Our class is putting on a play. I want to be the lion.
Better: Our class is putting on a play, and I want to be the lion.

Choppy: I love to perform. I get nervous. I breathe deeply to relax.
Better: I love to perform but get nervous, so I breathe deeply to relax.

- When one idea is more important than the other, you can join them with a **subordinating conjunction** such as *when, because, although,* or *unless*. If the clause with the conjunction comes first in the new sentence, use a comma after the clause.

Choppy: I'll be very excited tomorrow. I find out which part I got.
Better: I'll be very excited tomorrow when I find out which part I got.

Choppy: Owen usually gets the lead part. He has a great voice.
Better: Because Owen has a great voice, he usually gets the lead part.

Guided Practice **Underline the pairs of sentences you would combine. Then rewrite the paragraph on another sheet of paper. Use all of the conjunctions in the box.** Responses will vary.

HINT You can use a conjunction to combine sentences. You can also use a conjunction to combine just the subjects or the predicates of two sentences.

or	when	although	so	and

We needed a dog to play Toto. My terrier Angus got the part. Angus trotted onto the stage. We all knew a star was born. Angus had never been in a play. I wasn't sure how he would behave. He might follow directions. He might just run off the stage. Luckily, Angus was perfect. He didn't like sitting in Dorothy's basket!

Independent Practice

For numbers 1–5, choose the best way to combine each pair of sentences.

1. Lori is creative. She was in charge of building the set.
   - A Lori is creative, because she was in charge of building the set.
   - B Lori is creative but was in charge of building the set.
   - (C) Lori is creative, so she was in charge of building the set.
   - D Although Lori is creative, she was in charge of building the set.
2. The Emerald City was hard to make. It all had to be green.
   - A The Emerald City was hard to make, so it all had to be green.
   - B When the Emerald City was hard to make, it all had to be green.
   - (C) The Emerald City was hard to make because it all had to be green.
   - D The Emerald City was hard to make, or it all had to be green.
3. The curtain finally rose. The audience gasped.
   - (A) When the curtain finally rose, the audience gasped.
   - B The curtain finally rose, but the audience gasped.
   - C The curtain finally rose, unless the audience gasped.
   - D Although the curtain finally rose, the audience gasped.
4. Green lights cast a strange glow. They made the set look scary.
   - A Green lights cast a strange glow, but they made the set look scary.
   - (B) Green lights cast a strange glow and made the set look scary.
   - C Green lights cast a strange glow or made the set look scary.
   - D Green lights cast a strange glow unless they made the set look scary.
5. Now nothing could go wrong. The set collapsed!
   - A Now nothing could go wrong, and the set collapsed!
   - B Now nothing could go wrong, or the set collapsed!
   - C Now nothing could go wrong when the set collapsed!
   - (D) Now nothing could go wrong unless the set collapsed!

Conventions of Standard English | Knowledge of Language | Vocabulary Acquisition and Use

Lesson 14

Varieties of English: Dialect and Register

L.5.3b: Compare and contrast the varieties of English (e.g., dialects, registers) used in stories, dramas, or poems.

Introduction There are many ways to speak English. You speak informally with your friends but formally to your principal. You use words common to the time and place in which you live. Fiction writers often make their characters speak different varieties of English.

- **Dialect** is how a group in a specific place and time speaks. Below, a young man tells his story in dialect. He uses language spoken in towns along the Mississippi River in the 1800s.

Dialect	Standard English
"You don't know about me without you have read a book by the name of *The Adventures of Tom Sawyer;* but that ain't no matter."	"You wouldn't know about me unless you've read a book called *The Adventures of Tom Sawyer,* but that's all right."

- **Register** is how people speak in different situations. When you talk to a friend, you probably use the informal language of everyday speech. When you give an oral report, however, you are more careful about the language you use. Your language is formal.

Informal	Formal
"Bro, you can't be serious. This experiment is lame. We'll never get it to work!"	"Mrs. Taub, we're having trouble with our experiment. We can't get this circuit to work!"

Guided Practice **With a partner, read aloud the conversation below. Then, on a separate piece of paper, rewrite the dialogue as if it were a formal discussion between Jason and his coach.** Responses will vary.

HINT Informal language includes slang terms such as *dude, ace,* and *ain't.* As you read, **underline** any slang you need to change for a more formal dialogue.

"Okay, dude. You gotta get your head together about the game," Scott said.

"I hear they got a pretty heavy guy pitching today. And there ain't no ties—only one team can win," Jason answered.

"You're not worried, are you? You're an ace hitter!" said Scott.

"I ain't scared, bro," Jason mumbled. "I just need to chill."

464

Independent Practice

This dialogue from *The Adventures of Tom Sawyer* is written in dialect. Tom is whitewashing a fence when his friend Ben Rogers comes along. Rewrite this dialogue as if two friends were talking today.

Conventions of Standard English | Knowledge of Language | Vocabulary Acquisition and Use

1. BEN: Hello, old chap, you got to work today, hey?
TOM: Why, it's you Ben! I warn't noticing.
Ben: Hey buddy. You working today?
Tom: Oh , hey, Ben. I didn't see you there.

2. BEN: Say, I'm going in a-swimming, I am. Don't you wish you could? But of course you'd druther *work*—wouldn't you? Course you would!
BEN: I'm going swimming—aren't you jealous? Of course, you'd rather be working, right?

3. TOM: What do you call work?
BEN: Why, ain't *that* work?
TOM: Well, maybe it is and maybe it ain't. All I know is, it suits Tom Sawyer.
TOM: Work? What's work?
BEN: Well—you're doing work, right?
TOM: Well, maybe it's work and maybe it's not—but I like it.

4. BEN: Oh come on, now, you don't mean to let on that you like it?
TOM: Like it? Why I don't see why I oughtn't to like it. Does a boy get a chance to whitewash a fence every day?
BEN: Oh, come on. You're not saying you like doing that, right?
TOM: Of course I like it! It's not every day you get to whitewash a fence!

465

Introduction

- Read aloud the Introduction and examples. Explain to students that the English language can be spoken differently depending on the time, place, and situation.

  English is used differently in different places and situations. When you are writing, you will usually use standard, formal English.

- Write the following sentences on a chart or project them on a whiteboard.

  I ain't no chicken. *(I am not afraid.)*

  I aced that test! *(I did well on the test.)*

  I'm gonna chill all day. *(I'm going to relax today.)*

- Model for students how to rewrite each sentence using standard, formal English. Explain when you might use informal language and when you might use formal language.

Guided Practice

- Read aloud the sentences.
- Have students complete the activity.
- Remind students that formal language does not include slang. Help students identify the slang words and phrases in the conversation that they will need to rewrite.

English Language Learners

Practice Informal Language

Some words have both formal and informal meanings and may confuse some English language learners. Practice by asking students to use the words in oral sentences that show their formal and then their informal meaning.

1. cool—to make or feel cold/very good
2. ace—a playing card with one figure/expert
3. drag—to pull/boring
4. smooth—flat or even/without problems

Introduction

- Read aloud the Introduction and charts. Explain to students that sometimes readers come across unfamiliar words. A good reader will use context to determine the meaning of the word.

  Writers often include words and explanations that can help readers understand the meanings of unknown words.

- Write the following sentences on a chart or project them on a whiteboard.

  My flower garden thrives in the summer, but the flowers begin to die in the cool fall weather. *(lives and grows)*

  It was a balmy summer day, so I went to the park to enjoy the warm and pleasant weather. *(warm and pleasant)*

- Model for students how to determine the meanings of the underlined words based on context clues in the sentence. Underline the context clues twice.

Guided Practice

- Read aloud the sentences and Hint.
- Have students complete the activity.
- When students are finished, invite partners to compare their definitions and context clues.

Scaffolded Instruction
Practice Using Context Clues

Have students decide which word in parentheses best completes each sentence. Then ask them to explain how the context clues helped them determine the word.

1. It was so (humid/bright) in the room that everyone was sweating. *(humid)*
2. People screamed during the (tragic, frightening) movie. *(frightening)*
3. It was hard work, but the team (failed, managed) to complete the task. *(managed)*

Lesson 15
Using Context Clues

L.5.4a: Use context (e.g., cause/effect relationships and comparisons in text) as a clue to the meaning of a word or phrase.

Introduction You can use **context clues** to figure out the meaning of an unfamiliar word. The chart below gives examples of different types of context clues.

Type of Clue	Example
Definition	Superfoods, or natural foods that may prevent disease, have become popular.
Cause/Effect	Some superfoods, such as blueberries and red beans, contain antioxidants. These can help remove harmful substances from the human body.
Comparison	Some experts look dubiously on claims about superfoods, but other experts believe strongly that these foods can improve health.

Context clues can also help you figure out words with more than one meaning. For example, the table below has two sentences with the word *source*. What does *source* mean in each sentence? You can use the underlined context clues to figure out which meaning of *source* is being used.

Sentence	Context Clues	Definition
Choosing high-sugar drinks can be a source of health problems.	A problem has a cause. Therefore, the source of a problem is its cause.	the cause of something
The website MyPlate.gov is a source for facts about food choices.	A website can have information such as facts. Therefore, a source is something that gives information.	something that gives information

The sentences before and after the sentence with an unfamiliar word can also hold context clues.

Guided Practice **Determine the meanings of *fleeting*, *empirical*, and *panacea*. Then underline the words or phrases that helped you determine their meaning.**

HINT The phrases *as a result of*, *because of*, and *thanks to* all signal cause-and-effect relationships. Words such as *but*, *too*, *also*, and *as well as* all indicate comparisons.

Context clues are underlined.

Some fads are **fleeting**, but more than a few people feel that superfoods are here to stay. The idea of superfoods isn't new, but the amount of **empirical** information we have about them is. Scientific observations and tests offer some evidence that certain foods can help people stay healthy. Nobody claims that these foods are a **panacea**—nothing can guarantee perfect health or cure every disease—but they can be part of a sensible diet.

Independent Practice

For numbers 1 and 2, read the paragraph. Then answer the questions.

For centuries, people in coastal areas of China and Japan have harvested a superfood found in marine environments. Recent studies show that eating seaweed protects against infection. It also might reduce the risk of serious diseases and extend peoples' life spans. If true, these would be important benefits.

1 What does the word marine mean in this paragraph?

A very nutritious
B dark blue in color
C having to do with the ocean
D member of the armed forces

2 Which two words from the paragraph help you understand the meaning of marine?

A "China" and "Japan"
B "coastal" and "seaweed"
C "centuries" and "people"
D "superfood" and "studies"

For numbers 3 and 4, read the paragraph. Then answer the questions.

Closer to home, you can find superfoods right in your garden or local store. Think "crisp and crunchy." Cabbage, broccoli, cauliflower, and kale detoxify harmful substances. As a result, they may help to prevent some forms of cancer. These veggies also are low in calories and have lots of vitamins A, C, and K.

3 What does the word detoxify mean in this paragraph?

A to move in a wide circle
B to chew food slowly
C to make a difficult decision
D to remove bad effects

4 Which two words from the paragraph help you understand the meaning of detoxify?

A "crisp" and "crunchy"
B "prevent" and "cancer"
C "veggies" and "substances"
D "calories" and "vitamins"

Conventions of Standard English | Knowledge of Language | Vocabulary Acquisition and Use

Lesson 16
Greek and Latin Word Parts

L.5.4b: Use common, grade-appropriate Greek and Latin affixes and roots as clues to the meaning of a word (e.g., *photograph*, *photosynthesis*).

Introduction

English words come from many languages, including Greek and Latin.

- A **root** is a word part that usually can't stand alone as a word. Sometimes one root is added to another root to make a word.

Root	Meaning	Root	Meaning
chron	"time"	*port*	"carry, bear"
dict	"say, speak"	*rupt*	"break"
graph	"write"	*scrib, script*	"write"
photo	"light"	*spec, spect*	"look"

- **Affixes** are word parts such as prefixes and suffixes that are added to roots to make words. Knowing what affixes and roots mean can help you figure out the meanings of words.

Prefix	Meaning	Suffix	Meaning
co-	"with"	*-able, -ible*	"able to, worthy of"
contra-	"against"	*-sis*	"action, process"
syn-	"same, together"	*-ity*	"having the quality of"

- As you learn Greek and Latin roots and affixes, your vocabulary will grow.

Guided Practice

Circle the root in the underlined words. Some words have two roots. Write the meaning of each root. Share with a partner.

HINT *Photosynthesis* has several word parts. The word *thesis* means "to place or put." Look to the tables above for what *photo* and *syn-* mean.

1. During science class, our teacher displayed a photograph of a tree.
   ***photo* means "light"; *graph* means "write or written"; *photograph* means "written with light"**
2. Next, she dictated several terms related to plants.
   ***dict* means "say"; *dictated* means "spoke aloud words to be written"**
3. She inspected the notes of some of the students.
   ***spect* means "look"; *inspected* means "looked at"**
4. "How do green plants use air, water, and sunlight to make food during photosynthesis?" our teacher asked.
   ***photo* means "light"; *photosynthesis* means "made with light" or "put together by using light"**

Independent Practice

For numbers 1–4, read each sentence. Then answer the question.

1. Our teacher explained to us that plants are autotrophs.

   The prefix *auto-* means "self," and the root *troph* means "food." What is the meaning of autotroph as it is used in the sentence?

   (A) something that makes its own food
   B something that eats food
   C something that makes food for others
   D something that becomes food

2. Our teacher told us to apply our cognition to that fact.

   The root *cogn* means "know" and the suffix *-tion* means "the state or quality of." What is the meaning of cognition as it is used in the sentence?

   A best efforts
   (B) thinking skills
   C full belief
   D feelings about

3. She told us to check our science books if we doubted the veracity of her claims.

   The root *ver* means "true" and the suffix *-ity* means "to have the quality of." What is the meaning of veracity as it is used in the sentence?

   A greenness
   B intelligence
   (C) truth
   D newness

4. Our teacher's prognosis was that if we studied we would all do fine on the test.

   The prefix *pro-* means "before," and *gnosis* comes from a Greek word meaning "to know." What is the meaning of prognosis as it is used in the sentence?

   (A) prediction
   B advice
   C feeling
   D understanding

Conventions of Standard English | Knowledge of Language | Vocabulary Acquisition and Use

Introduction

- Read aloud the Introduction and charts. Explain to students that paying attention to Greek and Latin roots and affixes is a good way to figure out the meaning of a word.

  If you are unsure of a word's meaning, look for familiar roots and affixes. You can use the meanings of these roots and affixes to figure out the meaning of the word.
- Write the following sentences on a chart or project them on a whiteboard.

  The latest climate report contradicts the theory that the ozone layer is shrinking. *(contra-, dict; "speak against")*

  The newest technology uses easily corruptible software. *(rupt, -ible; "able to be broken")*
- Model for students how to identify the roots and affixes in the underlined words. Then use the meanings of the roots and affixes to determine the meanings of the words.

Guided Practice

- Read aloud the sentences.
- Have students complete the activity.
- Remind students that they can use the charts to help them understand the meanings of the roots and affixes in the words.

Scaffolded Instruction

Use Greek and Latin Roots and Affixes

Explain that students can use words they know to help them determine the meanings of words they do not know that share the same root or affix. Have students answer these questions.

1. If *forewarn* means "warn before," what is a *foreword* in a book? *(a word or section that comes before)*
2. If a *semicircle* is half of a circle, what does *semiweekly* mean? *(every half week)*
3. If *careless* means "without care," what does *merciless* mean? *(without mercy)*

Introduction

- Read aloud the Introduction and examples. Explain to students that some words have more than one meaning or pronunciation.

  You can use a dictionary or glossary to help you determine the meaning or pronunciation of an unfamiliar word.

- Write the following dictionary entry and sentences on a chart or project them on a whiteboard.

  feature (fē-chər) (1) a distinctive attribute of something. (2) a newspaper, magazine, or television news piece. (3) a full-length movie.

  The local paper did a feature on our city's history. *(meaning 2)*

  The city's best feature is its beachfront. *(meaning 1)*

- Model for students how to use the dictionary entry to determine the pronunciation of the word *feature* and to decide which meaning of the word is used in each sentence.

Guided Practice

- Read aloud the passage and questions.
- Have students complete the activity.
- Point out that students can substitute the different meanings of the word in the sentence to help them determine which meaning makes sense in context.

Extend Learning

Use the Dictionary Entry

Ask students to write sentences for each meaning of *feature.* Then have students trade papers and determine which meaning of feature is used in each sentence. *(Seatbelts are a safety feature. [meaning 1] This magazine has a feature on new cars. [meaning 2] The feature tonight is an older movie. [meaning 3])*

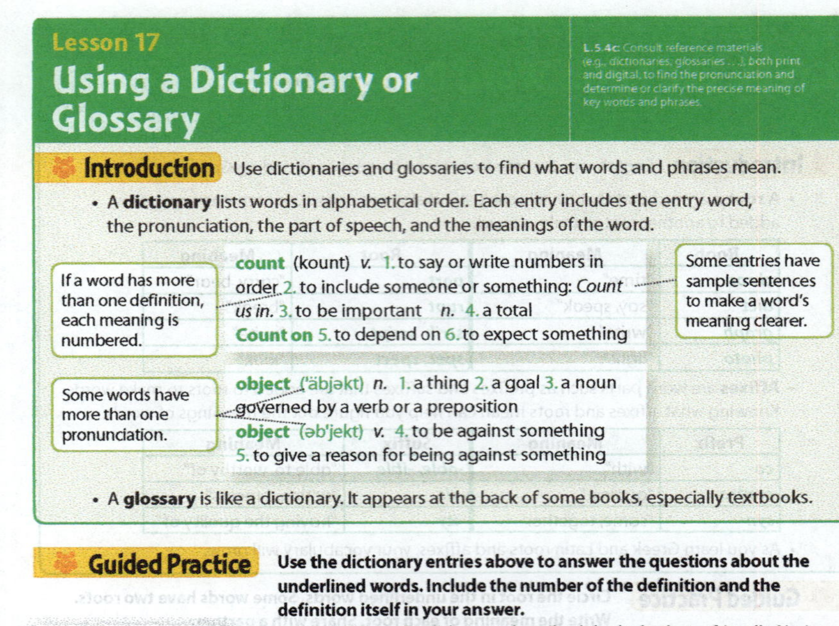

Lesson 17

Using a Dictionary or Glossary

L.5.4c: Consult reference materials (e.g., dictionaries, glossaries . . .), both print and digital, to find the pronunciation and determine or clarify the precise meaning of key words and phrases.

Introduction Use dictionaries and glossaries to find what words and phrases mean.

- A **dictionary** lists words in alphabetical order. Each entry includes the entry word, the pronunciation, the part of speech, and the meanings of the word.

If a word has more than one definition, each meaning is numbered.

count (kount) *v.* 1. to say or write numbers in order 2. to include someone or something: *Count us in.* 3. to be important *n.* 4. a total **Count on** 5. to depend on 6. to expect something

Some entries have sample sentences to make a word's meaning clearer.

Some words have more than one pronunciation.

object ('äbjəkt) *n.* 1. a thing 2. a goal 3. a noun governed by a verb or a preposition **object** (əb'jekt) *v.* 4. to be against something 5. to give a reason for being against something

- A **glossary** is like a dictionary. It appears at the back of some books, especially textbooks.

Guided Practice Use the dictionary entries above to answer the questions about the underlined words. Include the number of the definition and the definition itself in your answer.

HINT When you see two pronunciations for a word, say each one softly to yourself. Hearing the word may help you to figure out its meaning.

In 1584, an English crew described the lush plants, friendly Native Americans, and various objects on Roanoke Island. Roanoke seemed perfect, so colonists from England settled there in 1585. Clearly, they hadn't counted on a lack of food and hostile Native Americans! So the colonists objected to remaining in Roanoke and returned to England.

1. Which definition helps you understand the meaning of *objects?*
   1. a thing
2. Which definition tells you the meaning of the phrase *counted on?*
   6. to expect something
3. Which definition helps you understand the meaning of *objected?*
   4. to be against something
4. Circle the pronunciation that helps you say the word *objected.*
   Students should circle the pronunciation əb'jekt.

470

Independent Practice

Use the dictionary entries to answer numbers 1–4.

embark (em'bärk) *v.* **1.** to cause to go aboard **2.** to recruit someone to invest money in a business **3.** to go aboard **4.** to begin a journey

1. Which definition matches how embarked is used in this sentence?

   A second group of colonists embarked for Roanoke and arrived in 1587.

   A Definition 1
   B Definition 2
   C Definition 3
   (D) Definition 4

fetch (fech) *v.* **1.** to go and get someone or something **2.** to breathe **fetch up 3.** to end up at **4.** to stop

2. Which definition matches how fetch is used in this sentence?

   The leader of the colony sailed to England to fetch supplies, but a war delayed his return to Roanoke.

   (A) Definition 1
   B Definition 2
   C Definition 3
   D Definition 4

record (ri'kôrd) *v.* **1.** to put something into a lasting form, such as writing or film **2.** to make a note of something **record** ('rekərd) *n.* **3.** an account of something, set in writing or other form **4.** a piece of music on a disk

3. Which definition matches how record is used in this sentence?

   Meanwhile, the colonists had vanished, and they left no record of what had happened to them.

   A Definition 1
   B Definition 2
   (C) Definition 3
   D Definition 4

4. Choose the correct pronunciation of record as it is used in this sentence.

   No one had thought to record what had happened, unless the word CROATOAN—carved on a tree—was a clue.

   A ri'kərd
   (B) ri'kôrd
   C 'rekərd
   D 'rekôrd

Conventions of Standard English | Knowledge of Language | Vocabulary Acquisition and Use

471

Lesson 18

Figurative Language

L.5.5a: Interpret figurative language, including similes and metaphors, in context.

Introduction Writers use **figurative language**, including similes and metaphors, to help readers imagine what one thing is like by comparing it to something else.

- A **simile** compares two or more things using the words *like* or *as*. The table below contains two sentences with similes. It then explains what those similes mean.

Simile	What It Means
Noah stood as still as *a rabbit* trying not to be seen.	Noah stood very still.
The *world* around him was like *a beautiful movie*.	Noah saw beautiful things happening all around him.

- A **metaphor** compares two or more things *without* using the words *like* or *as*. In the metaphor below, the clouds are compared to sailing ships.

Metaphor	What It Means
White *clouds* were *ships sailing* across the sky.	The clouds moved like ships across the sky.

Guided Practice **Find the simile or metaphor in each sentence. Underline the two things being compared. Then write the meaning of the simile or metaphor.**

HINT After you find the two things being compared, ask yourself: How are they alike? Use your answer to figure out what each simile or metaphor means.

1. Sunbeams were golden threads piercing the clouds.
   Meaning: Narrow rays of sunlight shone through the clouds.
2. Mountain goats leaped like dancers from rock to rock.
   Meaning: Mountain goats leaped gracefully.
3. The butterflies drifted as lazily as falling leaves.
   Meaning: Butterflies flew slowly and gently.
4. Bright flowers were jewels gleaming in the sunlight.
   Meaning: The colorful flowers were bright.

Independent Practice

For numbers 1–5, choose the correct meaning of the underlined simile or metaphor.

1. The landscape was a patchwork quilt of sights and sounds.
   - A The quilt showed a variety of sights and sounds.
   - B The quilt had a picture of the landscape on it.
   - C The landscape had a blanket covering it.
   - (D) The landscape had a variety of sights and sounds.
2. A waterfall gushed like a faucet down the side of the mountain.
   - (A) The waterfall was powerful.
   - B The waterfall was narrow.
   - C A faucet was on the mountain.
   - D A faucet made the waterfall.
3. The brook gurgled as happily as a well-fed baby.
   - A A baby made pleasant sounds near the brook.
   - (B) The brook made a pleasant sound.
   - C There were many fish in the brook.
   - D The well-fed baby sounded happy.
4. Croaking frogs sounded as loud as a marching band.
   - A The frogs marched as they made croaking sounds.
   - B The frogs were very musical.
   - (C) The frogs croaked very loudly.
   - D The marching band sounded like loud croaking.
5. Noah was a sponge, soaking up the landscape's sights and sounds.
   - A Noah was good at cleaning.
   - B Noah fell into the water and got soaked.
   - C Noah was thirsty as he watched and listened.
   - (D) Noah looked at and listened to everything.

Conventions of Standard English · Knowledge of Language · Vocabulary Acquisition and Use

Introduction

- Read aloud the Introduction and examples. Explain to students that authors use similes and metaphors to make their writing more interesting.

  Figurative language requires readers to use their imaginations. A simile or metaphor helps you to imagine what something or someone is like.
- Write the following sentences on a chart or project them on a whiteboard.

  His room is as cluttered as a garbage dump.
  (He has a messy room.)

  Peter ran like a cheetah around the track.
  (Peter ran fast.)

  The paperwork is a mountain on her desk.
  (There is a lot of paperwork.)
- Model for students how to identify what is being compared in each sentence and then determine the meaning of the simile or metaphor.

Guided Practice

- Read aloud the sentences and Hint.
- Have students complete the activity.
- When students finish, invite partners to compare and discuss their definitions.

Extend Learning

Practice Using Similes and Metaphors

Ask students to rewrite the sentences to include a simile or metaphor.

1. Lily is busy. *(Lily is as busy as a bee.)*
2. Ben is shaking. *(Ben is a trembling leaf.)*
3. Amy is hungry. *(Amy is as hungry as a wolf.)*
4. Jeff moves quietly. *(Jeff moves like a mouse.)*

Introduction

- Read aloud the Introduction and examples. Explain to students that some of these expressions have a meaning that is different than the literal meanings of the words in the phrase.

  When the literal meaning of an expression does not make sense, you can often use context clues to figure out the meaning of the idiom, adage, or proverb.
- Write the following sentences on a chart or project them on a whiteboard.

  Rosa decided to hit the books to prepare for the test. *(study)*

  Even though her brother was mean to her, Marta treated him kindly because two wrongs don't make a right. *(getting revenge doesn't make a situation better)*

  Jim got cold feet and decided not to go to the party. *(lost confidence)*
- Model for students how to determine the meanings of the expressions based on the context. Discuss how the sentences would be different if the literal meanings were used.

Guided Practice

- Read aloud the passage.
- Have students complete the activity.
- Remind students that sometimes the literal meaning will make sense, but other times they will need to use context to figure out the meaning of the idiom, adage, or proverb.

English Language Learners
Practice Idioms, Adages, and Proverbs

Many of these expressions will be new to English language learners. To provide additional support, have students play a matching game. Write common idioms, adages, and proverbs on one set of sentence strips. Write the meanings of the expressions on a second set of strips. Have partners or small groups match each expression with its meaning. Then have students use the idioms, adages, and proverbs in oral sentences.

Lesson 19

Idioms, Adages, and Proverbs

L.5.5b: Recognize and explain the meaning of common idioms, adages, and proverbs.

Introduction **English, like all languages, is full of odd expressions and old sayings.** When you learn their meanings, you'll find that much of what you read becomes more interesting.

- An **idiom** is a common saying with a meaning different from that of its individual words.

Example	Meaning
Ivan looked at the wobbly wheel on my bike. "That will be a piece of cake to fix!" he said.	very easy

- **Adages** and **proverbs** are well-known sayings that have been used for a long time. They often express beliefs. Proverbs usually give practical advice about ways to behave and live.

Example	Meaning
Adage: "I'll help you repair the wheel because two heads are better than one."	It's easier for two people to solve a problem than for one person to do so.
Proverb: "Let's fix that wheel now. After all, a stitch in time saves nine."	It's best to solve a small problem now before it turns into a bigger problem later.

Guided Practice **Read the passage. Underline each idiom, adage, or proverb. Then, above each phrase you underlined, tell what you think it means. One has been done for you.**

HINT If the literal meaning of a phrase doesn't make sense, use context clues to help you understand what the words might mean.

I was down in the dumps (feeling bad) when my new bike broke. The bike had cost an arm and a leg (a lot of money), and it had taken me forever and a day (a long time) to save the money to buy it. I hoped that Ivan could fix my bike. He spends day and night (a lot of time) repairing things and says that practice makes perfect (a person improves by trying). That's why he can fix almost anything. When Ivan fixed my bike, I was on cloud nine! (was really happy)

Independent Practice

For numbers 1–4, answer the questions.

1 Read these sentences.

Ivan and his dad like to fix things. Ivan said, "I guess the apple doesn't fall far from the tree."

What does the underlined adage mean in the second sentence?

- (A) Ivan and his dad have similar interests and abilities.
- B Ivan and his dad spend their time together fixing things.
- C Ivan and his dad are slowly becoming very similar people.
- D Ivan and his dad climb trees to pick and toss down apples.

2 Read this sentence.

I was afraid to tell Mom that I broke the TV, but I know that honesty is the best policy.

What does the underlined proverb mean in this sentence?

- A Telling the truth is difficult to do.
- (B) Telling the truth is the right thing to do.
- C Honesty does not come naturally to most people.
- D Honesty causes problems for people who are close to each other.

3 Read this sentence.

Mom hit the roof when I told her that I broke the TV.

What does the underlined idiom mean in this sentence?

- A Mom thought that the TV had fallen off the roof.
- B Mom jumped happily about the TV being broken.
- C Mom thought the story of the broken TV was a joke.
- (D) Mom was angry when she heard that the TV was broken.

4 Read these sentences.

Ivan fixed our TV, so I am planning a surprise party to thank him. If you see Ivan, don't let the cat out of the bag.

What does the underlined adage mean in the second sentence?

- A Nobody else should plan another party to thank Ivan for fixing the TV.
- (B) Nobody should tell Ivan about the party being secretly planned for him.
- C Only those people specifically invited to the party should come to the party.
- D People should keep the cat away from the party because Ivan is allergic to cats.

Conventions of Standard English | Knowledge of Language | Vocabulary Acquisition and Use

Lesson 20

Synonyms and Antonyms

L.5.5c Use the relationship between particular words (e.g., synonyms, antonyms ...) to better understand each of the words.

Introduction

Words in English can have meanings that are similar or opposite. If you know how two words are related, you can use the meaning of a familiar word to figure out what an unfamiliar word means.

- A **synonym** is a word that has the same or nearly the same meaning as another word.

  Spain established colonies in North America, and other European countries founded colonies as well.

- An **antonym** is a word that has the opposite meaning of another word.

  In 1607, the English started their first permanent settlement in North America. Earlier English colonies had been temporary instead.

- Words and phrases such as *but, instead of, not, rather than,* and *unlike* are clues that a sentence or paragraph might have words that are antonyms.

  Colonists often struggled to survive and not to perish.

  Survival meant overcoming rather than surrendering to challenges.

Guided Practice

Each sentence contains both a synonym and an antonym of the underlined word. Find each one, and then write them on the lines below the sentence.

HINT Words that are synonyms of each other have nearly the same meaning as each other.

1. In Jamestown, for example, colonists faced severe winters—harsh and quite unlike the mild ones they had known in England.

   synonym: harsh antonym: mild

2. Mosquitoes brought illness, and water from the river carried disease, so only a few of the colonists kept their health.

   synonym: illness antonym: health

3. But the colonists soon acquired new skills, shed old ways of thinking, and gained an understanding of their new home.

   synonym: acquired antonym: shed

4. In time, the colony that had threatened to become a disaster like the others instead avoided failure and became a success.

   synonym: disaster antonym: success

476

Independent Practice

For numbers 1–4, answer the questions.

1. Read the sentence below.

   The colonists planted crops that were strange to them, plants that were unlike the comfortably familiar foods that were common in Europe.

   Which word in the sentence is an antonym of familiar?

   A planted
   (B) strange
   C common
   D comfortably

2. Read the sentence below.

   Soon they began concentrating on ways to make money, focusing their efforts on plants and ignoring other possible sources of riches.

   Which word in the sentence is a synonym of concentrating?

   (A) focusing
   B ways
   C efforts
   D ignoring

3. Read the sentence below.

   The colonists tried growing valuable crops for sale, and while many plants were worthless, the tobacco plant proved profitable.

   Which word in the sentence is an antonym of profitable?

   A valuable
   B sale
   (C) worthless
   D tobacco

4. Read the sentence below.

   By 1620, tobacco was the major crop in Jamestown's economy, the chief export that outsold all other, minor goods.

   Which word in the sentence is a synonym of chief?

   A minor
   B crop
   C export
   (D) major

Conventions of Standard English | Knowledge of Language | Vocabulary Acquisition and Use

477

Introduction

- Read aloud the Introduction and examples. Explain to students that many words in the English language have words that are related. One way two words can be related is by having similar or opposite meanings. **Words that have similar meanings are synonyms, and words that have opposite meanings are antonyms.**
- Write the following sentences on a chart or project them on a whiteboard.

  Would you like your usual order or something different? *(antonym: different; typical)*

  The encore was the most thrilling part of the exhilarating show. *(synonym: thrilling; exciting)*

- Model for students how to identify the synonym or antonym for each underlined word. Then use the synonym or antonym to define the word.

Guided Practice

- Read aloud the sentences.
- Have students complete the activity.
- Remind students that synonyms have similar meanings, and antonyms have opposite meanings.

English Language Learners

Identify Synonyms and Antonyms

Students may need support in identifying English synonyms and antonyms. Explain that they can first determine the meanings of the words by drawing or acting them out. Then they can determine whether the meanings are similar or opposite.

bulky/light *(antonyms)*
swift/rapid *(synonyms)*
shout/cheer *(synonyms)*
beneath/above *(antonyms)*

Introduction

- Read aloud the Introduction and examples. Explain to students that homographs can sometimes be confusing to readers because they are spelled the same.

  Sometimes it's difficult to determine the correct homograph while reading. Pay attention to the context of the sentence. The other words in the sentence will often be a clue to the correct homograph.

- Write the following sentences on a chart or project them on a whiteboard.

  I can <u>wind</u> the rope around a tree branch to make a swing. *(to wrap something around another object)*

  The <u>wind</u> was knocked out of me when I fell. *(breath)*

- Model for students how to determine which definition and pronunciation of the word *wind* is correct for each sentence. Use a dictionary or the entry in the Introduction.

Guided Practice

- Read aloud the passage.
- Have partners complete the activity.
- Remind students to try different meanings of a word in the sentence until they find the meaning that makes sense.

Extend Learning

Practice the Language Skill

Ask students to find the homograph *present* in a dictionary and write sentences using different meanings of the word. Then have students trade papers and determine the meaning of *present* in each sentence. For example,

1. Tim gave his sister a <u>present</u> for her birthday. *(gift)*
2. Every student was <u>present</u> for the test. *(being at a place)*
3. I will <u>present</u> my speech to the class tomorrow. *(give)*
4. <u>Present</u> cars are faster than cars from the past. *(at this time)*

Lesson 21

Homographs

L.5.5c: Use the relationship between particular words (e.g., . . . homographs) to better understand each of the words.

Introduction

Homographs are words that have the same spelling but different meanings. Sometimes homographs have different pronunciations from one another.

- The word *wind* is a homograph.

  A brisk wind blew, so I buttoned my coat.

  Then I began to wind my way down the hill to the village.

- You can use a dictionary to check the meaning and pronunciation of homographs. Each homograph is a separate entry in the dictionary.

  wind^{1} (wind) *n.* **1.** moving air **2.** breath, or breathing

  wind^{2} (wīnd) *v.* **1.** to go along a twisty path **2.** to wrap something around another object

  Each homograph has a raised number after the entry word.

  The homograph's pronunciation is in parentheses after the entry word.

- To find the right meaning of a homograph, read the definitions for each entry. Then see which meaning makes sense in the sentence you are reading.

Guided Practice

Read the passage. Find each underlined homograph in a dictionary. With a partner, figure out how to pronounce it. Then write a short definition above each word.

HINT Homographs are spelled the same but are not necessarily pronounced the same.

The village was a perfect place to <u>loaf</u> *(relax in)* for a few hours. I bought a fresh <u>loaf</u> *(large piece of bread)* of bread at a bakery near the beach. A <u>dove</u> *(type of bird)* was eating crumbs on the sidewalk. Across the street, a sea gull <u>dove</u> *(swooped down quickly)* for food as I watched. Then I bought a <u>present</u> *(gift)* for my mom at a store. I planned to <u>present</u> *(give)* it to her tonight at dinner. An old <u>wound</u> *(injury)* in my leg began to ache. So, I <u>wound</u> *(wandered)* my way slowly along the streets.

Independent Practice

For numbers 1–5, choose the correct meaning of the underlined word as it is used in the sentence.

1 I wandered down to the <u>port</u> to watch cargoes being unloaded from boats.

- **(A)** **port**^{1} (pôrt) *n.* a harbor
- **B** **port**^{2} (pôrt) *n.* the left on a ship
- **C** **port**^{3} (pôrt) *n.* a valve, or opening that lets liquid out
- **D** **port**^{4} (pôrt) *n.* a person's manner, or bearing

2 "Your ship looks <u>sound</u>," I said to a fisherman.

- **A** **sound**^{1} (sound) *n.* a noise
- **(B)** **sound**^{2} (sound) *adj.* in good shape
- **C** **sound**^{3} (sound) *n.* a long, wide body of water
- **D** **sound**^{4} (sound) *v.* to measure how deep water is

3 "It has to be," he said. "Tomorrow we're <u>bound</u> for the fishing lanes."

- **A** **bound**^{1} (bound) *v.* to leap or jump forward
- **B** **bound**^{2} (bound) *n.* border
- **C** **bound**^{3} (bound) *adj.* tied
- **(D)** **bound**^{4} (bound) *adj.* on the way to a particular place

4 "High winds and fierce storms are sure to <u>batter</u> us on the open seas," he continued.

- **(A)** **batter**^{1} (ˈbatər) *v.* to hit, pound
- **B** **batter**^{2} (ˈbatər) *n.* a player at bat
- **C** **batter**^{3} (ˈbatər) *n.* a liquid mixture, often of flour, eggs, and milk
- **D** **batter**^{4} (ˈbatər) *n.* a sloping structure

5 "Fortunately, our <u>bow</u> is sturdy and true," he finished.

- **A** **bow**^{1} (bou) *v.* to bend the head or upper body in greeting
- **B** **bow**^{2} (bou) *v.* to be pushed over with age or pressure
- **(C)** **bow**^{3} (bou) *n.* the front of a ship's hull
- **D** **bow**^{4} (bō) *n.* a weapon for shooting arrows

Conventions of Standard English | Knowledge of Language | Vocabulary Acquisition and Use

Lesson 22

Using a Thesaurus

L.5.4c: Consult reference materials (e.g., . . . thesauruses), both print and digital, to find the pronunciation and determine or clarify the precise meaning of key words. . . .

Introduction You can use a **thesaurus** to find synonyms and antonyms for particular words. Words that don't have synonyms are not included in a thesaurus.

- A thesaurus lists words in alphabetical order. Each entry gives the part of speech, definition, and synonyms of the word. Antonyms are listed at the end of the entry.

foreign *adj.* **1.** of or from another place: *Anya is from a foreign city.* distant, faraway *Antonyms: native, local* **2.** introduced into a place where it does not belong: *There's a foreign object in my eye.* odd, abnormal *Antonyms: characteristic, typical*

prompt *v.* **1.** to remind: *Mom prompts me to be nice.* remind, hint, suggest **2.** to cause someone to do something: *The alarm prompted me to get up.* cause, inspire, motivate *Antonyms: caution, discourage*

A sample sentence makes a word's meaning clearer.

Synonyms follow each sample sentence.

When there is more than one meaning, each definition is numbered.

Guided Practice **Read the sentences. Use the thesaurus entries above to answer the questions about the underlined words.**

HINT A *synonym* is similar in meaning to another word. An *antonym* has the opposite meaning of the word.

Today, people come from foreign countries to settle in the United States. Many factors prompt people to leave their homelands.

1. Which words are synonyms for the word *foreign* as it is used above? distant, faraway
2. Which words are antonyms for the word *foreign* as it is used above? native, local
3. Which words are synonyms for the word *prompt* as it is used above? cause, inspire, motivate
4. Which words are antonyms for the word *prompt* as it is used above? deter, discourage

480

Independent Practice

For numbers 1–4, read the sentence. Then use the thesaurus entry to answer the questions.

diverse *adj.* different from one another: *My brother and I have diverse hobbies.* different, varied, unalike *Antonyms: alike, identical, similar*

1. In colonial times, people had diverse reasons for leaving their homelands.

   Which is an antonym for diverse as it is used above?

   A varied
   (B) similar
   C different
   D unalike

please *v.* **1.** to give enjoyment to: *The song pleases me.* delight, gladden *Antonyms: displease, annoy* *v.* **2.** to wish or like: *My cat does as it pleases.* choose, desire, prefer *Antonyms: dislike*

2. In Europe, thousands of people with no religious freedom came to the American colonies to worship as they pleased.

   Which is a synonym for pleased as it is used above?

   A annoyed
   B delighted
   (C) desired
   D disliked

lure *n.* **1.** attraction: *Excitement is the lure of adventure.* attraction, temptation *v.* **2.** to tempt: *The smell of bread lured me.* attract, pull *Antonyms: repel, repulse*

3. The desire for land lured other Europeans to the colonies.

   Which is an antonym for lured as it is used above?

   (A) repulsed
   B attracted
   C pulled
   D tempted

transport *v.* **1.** to bring from one place to another: *Buses transport students to school.* carry, move *n.* **2.** the act of moving something: *A truck is useful for the transport of compost.* hauling, shipment, movement

4. Most Africans were transported to the colonies against their will.

   Which is a synonym for transported as it is used above?

   A hauling
   B movement
   C shipment
   (D) carried

Conventions of Standard English | Knowledge of Language | Vocabulary Acquisition and Use

481

Introduction

- Read aloud the Introduction and examples. Explain to students that a thesaurus shares some of the same features as a dictionary, but it only includes words with synonyms.

  A thesaurus gives information about the parts of speech, meanings, synonyms, and antonyms of a word. You can use a thesaurus to determine a word's meaning or to find a more precise word to use in a sentence.

- Write the following entry and sentences on a chart or project them on a whiteboard.

  field *noun* **1.** open area of land. *Synonyms: land, meadow, pasture* **2.** area of influence, interest, or study. *Synonyms: specialty, discipline, territory*

  He is an expert in the field of environmental science. *(area of study; discipline)*

  The cows grazed in the field. *(open area of land; pasture)*

- Model how to use a thesaurus to determine the meaning of the word *field* in each sentence. Then demonstrate how to choose a word to replace *field* in the sentences.

Guided Practice

- Read aloud the sentences and questions.
- Have students complete the activity.
- Remind students that they should first determine which meaning of the word is used and then find the synonyms and antonyms for that meaning.

Extend Learning

Use a Thesaurus

Ask students to use a thesaurus to find a precise word to use in each sentence.

1. Jenny was _______ (happy) she passed the test. *(thrilled)*
2. The lake is too _______ (cold) to go swimming. *(frigid)*
3. The _______ (big) building towers over the city. *(massive)*
4. I _______ (yell) at the scary parts of a movie. *(shriek)*

Introduction

- Read aloud the Introduction and chart. Explain to students that these words make sentences and paragraphs flow better.

  In most cases, these words can be removed from a sentence or paragraph without changing its meaning. However, by using these words, the writer makes it easier for readers to understand and connect the ideas.

- Write the following paragraph on a chart or project it on a whiteboard.

  The school remodeled its gymnasium. The school remodeled its cafeteria. The school improved its lunch choices. More students are buying school lunches. Many students still prefer to bring their lunches.

  (The school remodeled its gymnasium as well as its cafeteria. The school also improved its lunch choices. Consequently, more students are buying school lunches, although many still prefer to bring their lunches.)

- Model for students how to determine the best words to use to connect the ideas in the paragraph. Rewrite the paragraph using these words.

Guided Practice

- Read aloud the sentences.
- Have students complete the activity.
- Point out to students that sometimes several words or phrases are acceptable and that there can be more than one answer.

Scaffolded Instruction

Identify Connecting Words

Print out a nonfiction selection from a textbook, magazine, or reading anthology that includes good connecting words and phrases. Have students highlight the words that connect ideas. Have them tell the purpose for the words they highlighted in the sentences and paragraphs.

Lesson 23

Words That Connect Ideas

L.5.6: Acquire and use accurately grade-appropriate … words and phrases, including those that signal contrast, addition, and other logical relationships (e.g., however, although, nevertheless, similarly, moreover, in addition).

Introduction Good writers use words and phrases to connect ideas in sentences and paragraphs. Writers who show these connections make their writing easier to understand. A word or phrase can signal an **addition**, a **cause and effect**, a **comparison**, or a **contrast**.

Connection	Words and Phrases	Examples
Addition	additionally, also, as well as, besides, furthermore, in addition, moreover	Jamestown Colony had a deep harbor. In addition, the location seemed easy to defend.
Cause and Effect	as a result, because, consequently, due to, in order that, since	People in London organized the colony because they hoped the colony would make them rich.
Comparison	in the same way, likewise, similarly	Native Americans often gave gifts of food to the colonists. They were likewise friendly when trading.
Contrast	although, but, even so, however, nevertheless, still, yet	Although no Native Americans lived at Jamestown, many lived nearby.

Guided Practice **Complete each sentence by writing a connecting word or phrase that signals the relationship described beneath the blank.**

HINT Choose a connecting word that makes the type of connection specified. Use the chart above for examples of connecting words.

1. At times, the colonists and Native Americans had serious problems. As a result, sometimes there were battles. (cause and effect)
2. The colonists also had other problems. (addition)
3. Much of the water that they found was bad. Consequently, the colonists who drank it became ill. (cause and effect)
4. Similarly, other diseases sickened some colonists. (comparison)
5. Even so, the colonists stayed and grew their town. (contrast)

482

Independent Practice

For numbers 1–5, read each sentence. Then choose the connecting word or phrase that best completes it.

1. _____, the colonists didn't have enough food.

   Which word or phrase that signals **addition** completes the sentence?

   A Moreover (circled)
   B As a result
   C In the same way
   D Still

2. _____, many colonists died of starvation.

   Which word or phrase that signals **cause and effect** completes the sentence?

   A Furthermore
   B Nevertheless
   C Consequently (circled)
   D Similarly

3. _____, some colonists survived.

   Which word or phrase that signals **contrast** completes the sentence?

   A Because
   B Nevertheless (circled)
   C As a result
   D In addition

4. _____, they continued to face challenges.

   Which word or phrase that signals **contrast** completes the sentence?

   A Moreover
   B Consequently
   C Similarly
   D However (circled)

5. But they met those challenges _____ as people do when they move to a new place: They adapted.

   Which word or phrase that signals **comparison** completes the sentence?

   A consequently
   B nevertheless
   C in the same way (circled)
   D yet

Conventions of Standard English | Knowledge of Language | Vocabulary Acquisition and Use

483

Language Handbook Teacher Notes

Glossary of Terms

Academic Talk Words and Phrases

One of the best ways to teach students new vocabulary is by introducing the words through an explicit and consistent instructional sequence (Feldman & Kinsella, 2008) and then applying them in authentic discussions.

Academic Talk introduces and reinforces vocabulary that is aligned to the ELA standards and that students may likely encounter on a standards-based assessment.

In each lesson, a list of key words tied directly to the lesson objective is introduced to students. These terms are strategically revisited in discussion and writing assignments, building familiarity and expanding their use. These terms are introduced and reinforced by the Academic Talk Routine on pp. A48–A49.

academic vocabulary words that are commonly used in written texts but are not generally part of everyday speech

academic words see academic vocabulary

account a written or spoken report of an event or topic

act a main section, or part, of a play

alliteration repetition of initial consonant sounds in a piece of writing to create a special effect

allude to to mention something in an indirect way

analyze to closely and carefully examine a piece of text

background knowledge information that you already know

beginning the start of something; the first part of a text, which introduces the characters and problem in a story or the topic and main idea in an informational text

bold print heavy, dark type; important words in a text are sometimes printed in bold print

caption a phrase or sentence set below a picture in a text that explains something about the picture

cast of characters a list of all the characters in a play, usually in order of appearance

cause something that brings about an effect or a result

cause and effect a relationship between things or events, in which one thing—the cause—brings about, or causes, something else—the effect

cause-and-effect text structure a text organization that tells about events and explains why they happen

central message a lesson about life the author of a story wants to share

challenge a problem or difficulty that needs to be solved

chapters sections, or parts, of stories or books

character person, animal, or made-up creature in a story or play

character traits special qualities of characters, such as shyness or honesty, that makes one character different from another

chronological text structure a text organization in which events are told in the order in which they happen

clues pieces of information that help you figure out something; hints

compare to describe how two or more things are similar

compare-contrast text structure a text organization that describes how two or more things are alike and different

comparison the process of showing how two or more things are alike and different

connected joined or linked together; when two or more things are connected, they are related in some way.

connection how the facts and ideas in a sentence or paragraph relate to each other, for example, some ideas have a cause-and-effect relationship, or connection; causal relations or sequence between two ideas

context clues words, phrases and sentences around an unknown word or phrase in a text that help to determine the word's meaning; context clues may be synonyms, antonyms, examples, or definitions.

contrast to describe how two or more things are different

contribute to add to something; to help bring about a result

demonstrate to show or make clear

describe to tell what something is like or to explain something

details facts, examples, and other pieces of information directly stated in a text

diagram a simple drawing that is used to explain something

dialogue the words the characters say in a story or play

digital source a text on a specific subject area or topic that is located on a computer website or provided in an electronic format

divide to break apart or separate something into smaller sections, or parts

domain-specific words and phrases vocabulary specific to a field of study or subject area

drama a story that is performed on a stage

effect something that happens as a result of something else

end the point at which something is completed; the last part of a text, in which the problem in a story is solved or the main idea in an informational text is summed up

events things that happen in stories and in the natural world

evidence facts, details, quotes, or other pieces of information used to support a claim, point, or an idea

examples things that an author uses to represent an idea or a group of things

experience something that a character in a story or poem does, or that happens to them

explain to describe or give details about something so it can be understood

explicitly clearly stated in a text

explicit meaning an idea or explanation that an author clearly states in a text

figurative language writing that makes comparisons to describe familiar things and events in new and sometimes unusual ways

first before all others in time, order, or importance

firsthand account something written about an event by a person who witnessed the event or who took part in it

first person describes the narrator of a story who is a character in the story and actually experiences what happens; a first-person narrator uses the pronouns *I*, *me*, and *we*

focus a center of interest or attention

genre a type of writing characterized by a particular style, form, or subject area; narrative poems, mysteries, realistic fiction, historical texts, and technical texts are examples of genres

glossary a list at the back of a book of important words from the text and their meanings

graph a chart that is used to show the relationship between two sets of numbers

headings words or a phrase at the beginning of a section of a text that tell what the section is about

historical describes something based on history

historical events important things that happened in the past

historical text an informational piece of writing that tells about people, events, and ideas from the past

hyperlinks features in digital texts that allow you to quickly access additional information

idea a thought, an opinion, or a belief that exists in the mind about what something is like or should be like

illustrations pictures that accompany a text and that often provide additional details about the text

images the pictures, or illustrations and photographs, in a text

implied not directly stated

important points the most important details, facts, examples, and other pieces of information in a text

index a list at the back of a book of all the topics in the book, in alphabetical order, and the page numbers where they can be found

infer to reach a reasonable conclusion about an idea or event not directly stated in a text based on text clues and background knowledge

inference the process of reaching a conclusion based on details in the text and your own background knowledge

influence to have an effect on something or someone

information facts and details about someone or something

integrate to put together or combine information on a topic from more than one source

interaction the way people or things affect each other

interpret to explain the meaning or significance of certain information

key detail an important fact, example, or other piece of information in a text that helps explain a main idea

key facts important ideas in a text that can be proven true

key point an important idea about a topic

key words words in bold print that call attention to something important in a text

knowledgeably in a manner that shows a clear understanding of something or, to speak or write about a topic like an expert

last at the end; after all others; finally

lesson something to be learned—for example, from a story or an experience—that imparts new knowledge

literal describes the usual or most basic meaning of a word

lyric poem a type of poem that uses language in unusual ways to express thoughts and feelings about something

main idea something important that an author wants readers to understand about a topic

main purpose what an author of a text wants to tell, describe, or explain to the reader

main topic what a selection is mostly about

maps drawings that show the cities, roads, rivers, and other details of an area

meaning the thoughts or ideas meant to be conveyed, especially by language

metaphor a kind of figurative language that compares two things that are not alike, without using the words *like* or *as*

meter the regular pattern of stressed and unstressed syllables in a verse, or line, of poetry

middle the central part of something; the part of a text after the beginning and before the end, in which the plot of a story or the main idea of an informational text is developed

mood a feeling a story creates in the reader; setting, word choice, and tone all contribute to mood

motivations the reasons why characters act, think, and feel as they do

mythology a collection of ancient stories belonging to a particular people that tell about their origin, history, gods, goddesses, and heroes

narrator the person who tells a story

nonliteral describes an unusual or unexpected meaning of a word

opposition strong disagreement or conflict; struggle

order the arrangement or sequence of things or events in time

paragraph a group of sentences about a particular idea or topic

personification a kind of figurative language that gives human qualities to animals or objects

persuade to cause someone to do something or to think a certain way about something, by giving them good reasons for it

phrase a short group of words that has meaning

play a story that is performed on stage by actors

plot the sequence of events in a story

points ideas that authors present to convince readers that something is true

point of view
Literary Text the perspective from which a piece of text is written
Informational Text the author's viewpoint that allows the reader to know how the author thinks and feels about a topic

primary source a description of an event from someone who experienced it, such as diaries, speeches, letters, or interviews

print source a text on a specific subject area or topic that is in print form, such as a book or magazine article

prior knowledge see background knowledge

problem a challenge that the main character or characters face

problem-solution text structure a text organization that describes problems and solutions

procedures steps to follow to do something

prompt a writing assignment

prose any form of writing that is not poetry

qualitative measured by the quality of something rather than by quantity

quantitative describes information in the form of numbers or other data or, describes information in the form of quantities, or amounts, of things

quote a short passage, sentence, or phrase of exact wording from a text

reason an explanation for why an idea might be right or true

recount to retell events and details of a story in the order in which they happened using your own words

refer explicitly to use or mention specific details in a story or other text to understand or explain something about it

reflects thinks deeply or speaks seriously about something

regular beat the main rhythm in a piece of music; the main rhythm is created by having an equal amount of time between each occurrence of a beat

relationship the way in which two or more people, events, or things are connected

repetition the use of repeated words or ideas in a piece of writing for emphasis, or to show that something is important

respond to make a reply; to answer; to say or do something in reaction to something else

rhyme the repetition of the same or similar stressed sounds in words

rhythm the regular pattern of sounds in a poem or beats in a piece of music

scene a part of a play in which all the action takes place in the same setting

scientific text a piece of text that explains how or why something happens

script the written text of a drama, which is used by all people putting the drama on stage

search tools Internet utilities that allow users to quickly find information on the Web

secondary source a description of an event based on research that includes key facts such as textbooks, biographies, and newspaper articles

secondhand account something written about an event by a person who did not experience it but rather heard or read about the event

sections smaller parts into which something is divided

setting when and where a story or play takes place

sequence the order in which events in a story or the steps in a procedure occur

sequence of events everything that happens in a story, in the order in which it happens

sidebars short, often boxed, articles included in longer texts that provide additional information related to the main text

significant large enough to be noticed or to have an effect

simile a kind of figurative language that uses the words *like* or *as* to compare two dissimilar things

solution the answer to a problem; or the way the main characters resolve the conflict at the center of a story

solved figured out; worked out a correct solution, or answer, to a problem

source a text on a specific subject area or topic; a source may be in printed or digital form

speaker the character whose "voice" you hear in a poem

stage directions instructions in a script that tell where a scene takes place, what the actors should do, and what should appear or happen on stage

stanza several verses, or lines, of a poem that are grouped together to describe an image, idea, or event

steps in a process a set of actions to do, or directions to make or do something

structural elements special features of texts; they vary from one form of written text to another

structure the particular way a writer organizes a text, such as acts for a drama or stanzas for a poem, that helps the reader understand the writer's meaning

subheading the title of a section, or part, of text; it tells what the section is about

subject a topic; something that is being talked or written about

subject area a specific topic or field of study; science, mathematics, history, outer space, the ancient world, and the environment are examples of subject areas

summarize to briefly retell in your own words the most important ideas, events, and details in a text

summary a short but complete version of a text

support to help explain, or provide evidence for, a main idea in a text

table of contents a list at the front of a book of the sections or chapters of the book in the order in which they appear

technical text a piece of writing that tells how to make or do something

text evidence a detail, fact, or other information in a piece of writing that the author uses to support a point, or an idea

text features special parts of a text that help you locate information, such as specific facts and details, within the text; tables of contents, captions, subheadings, and glossaries are examples of text features

text structure the way an author organizes the ideas and details in a piece of writing; text structures include comparison, cause-effect, chronology, and problem-solution

theme an important message or lesson that an author wants to share either implicitly or explicitly about people or life

third person describes the narrator of a story who is not a character in the story but looks in at events from outside; a third-person narrator uses pronouns, such as *he* and *she*.

time line a chart that shows the dates of important events during a certain time period

tone the general feeling or attitude conveyed by a text

topic the general subject of a text

traditional literature stories, such as fables, fairy tales, and folktales, that were originally passed along by word of mouth and written down much later.

traits special qualities, such as courage, pride, or honesty, that people and characters in stories have

versions descriptions or accounts of the same thing, such as a story or an event, which contain some different details

visual elements pictures that appear with a text

visuals pictures that appear with a text, such as photographs, diagrams, and time lines; visuals are also referred to as *visual elements*.

Name ______________________________ Date ______________

2-Point Writing Rubric

Use this rubric to evaluate your writing.

Points	Focus	Evidence	Organization
2	My answer does exactly what the prompt asked me to do.	My answer is supported with plenty of details from the text.	My ideas are clear and in a logical order.
1	Some of my answer does not relate to the prompt.	My answer is missing some important details from the text.	Some of my ideas are unclear and out of order.
0	My answer does not make sense.	My answer does not have any details from the text.	My ideas are unclear and not in any order.

Name ______________________________ Date ______________

Three-Column Chart: Version A

Name ______________________________ Date ______________

Three-Column Chart: Version B

Name ______________________________ Date ______________

Three-Column Chart: Version C

Name ______________________ Date ____________

Cause and Effect Chart: Version A

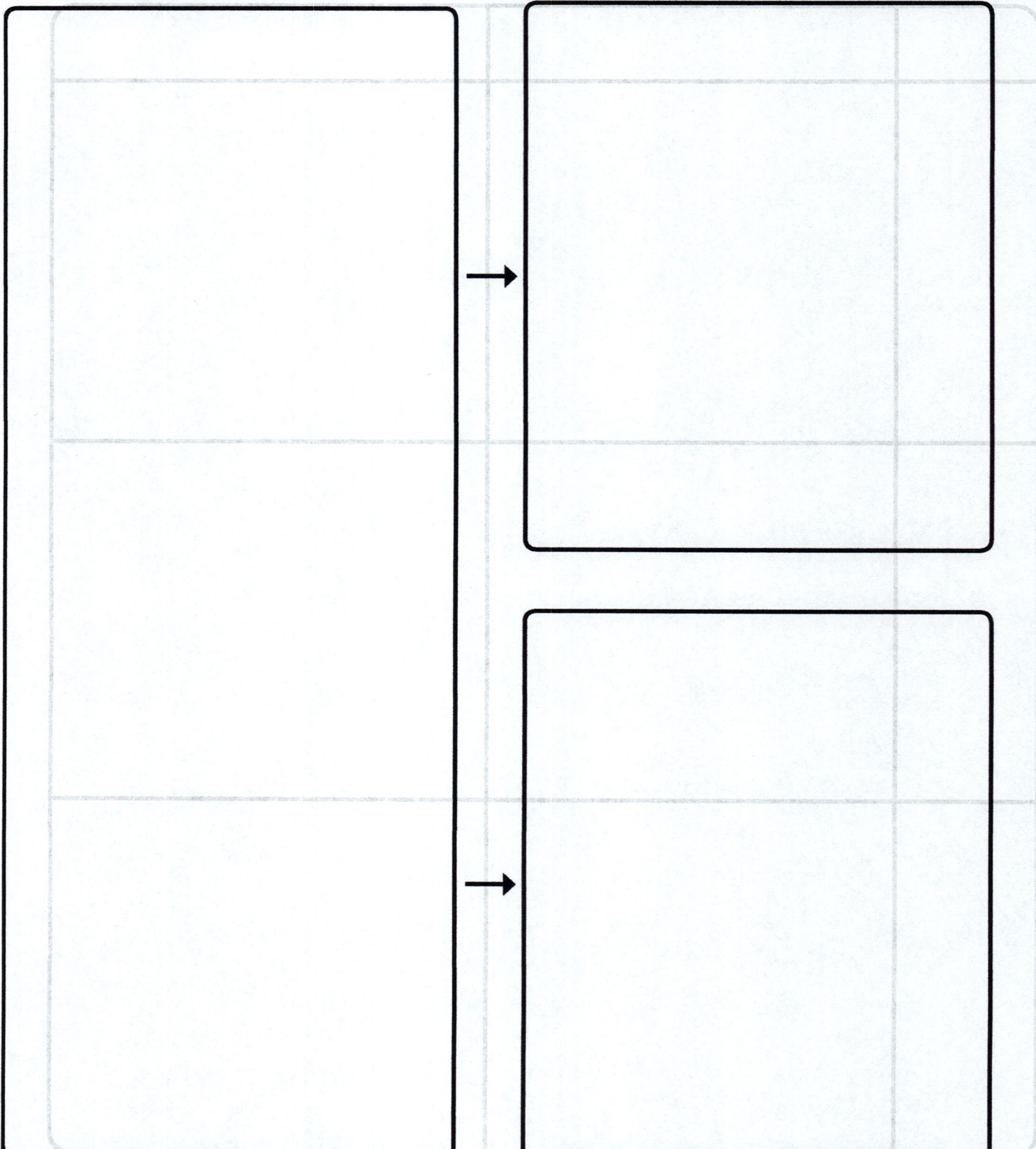

Name ______________________________ Date ______________

Cause and Effect Chart: Version B

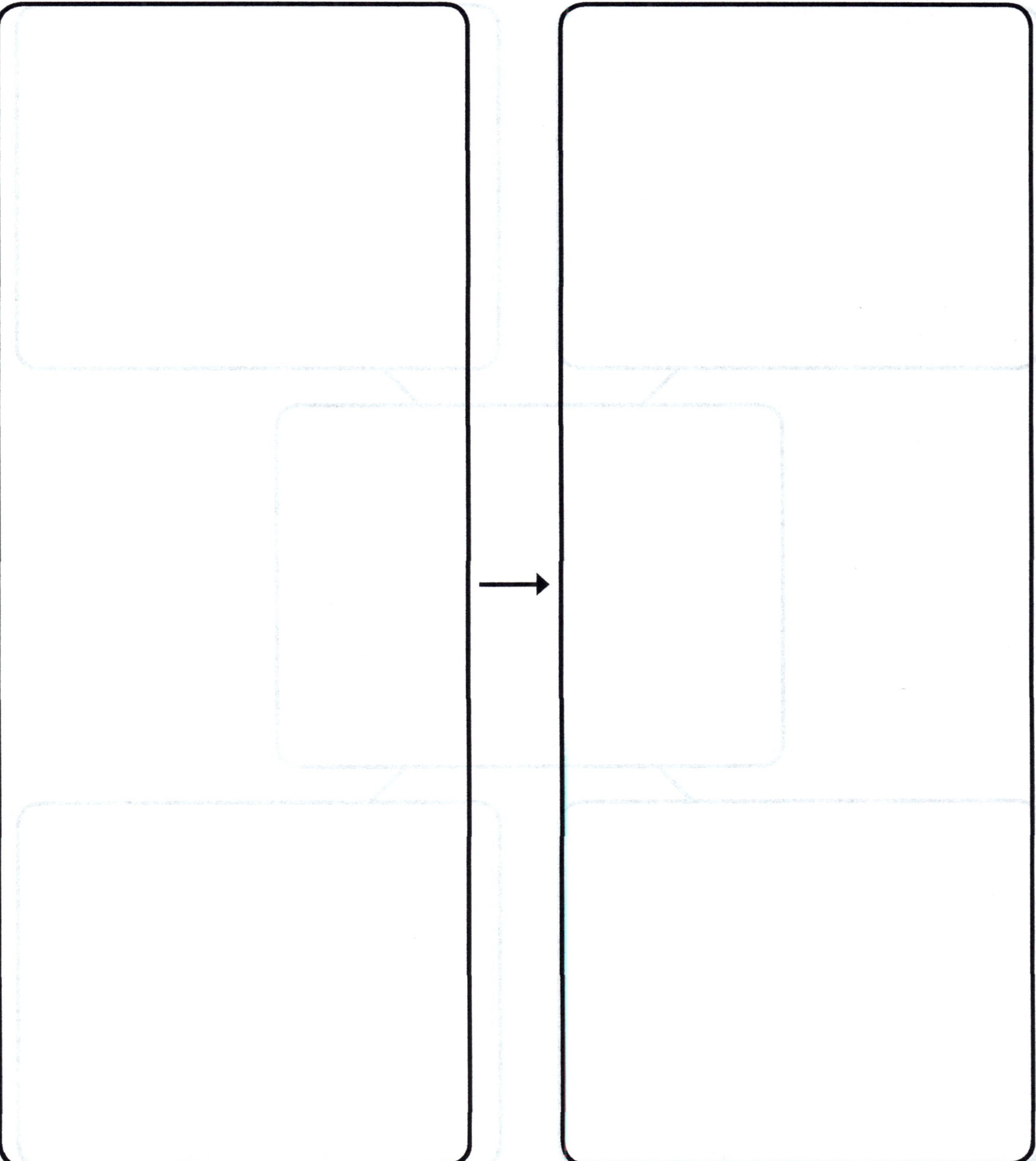

Name ______________________________ Date ______________

Web: Version A

Name ______________________ Date __________

Web: Version B

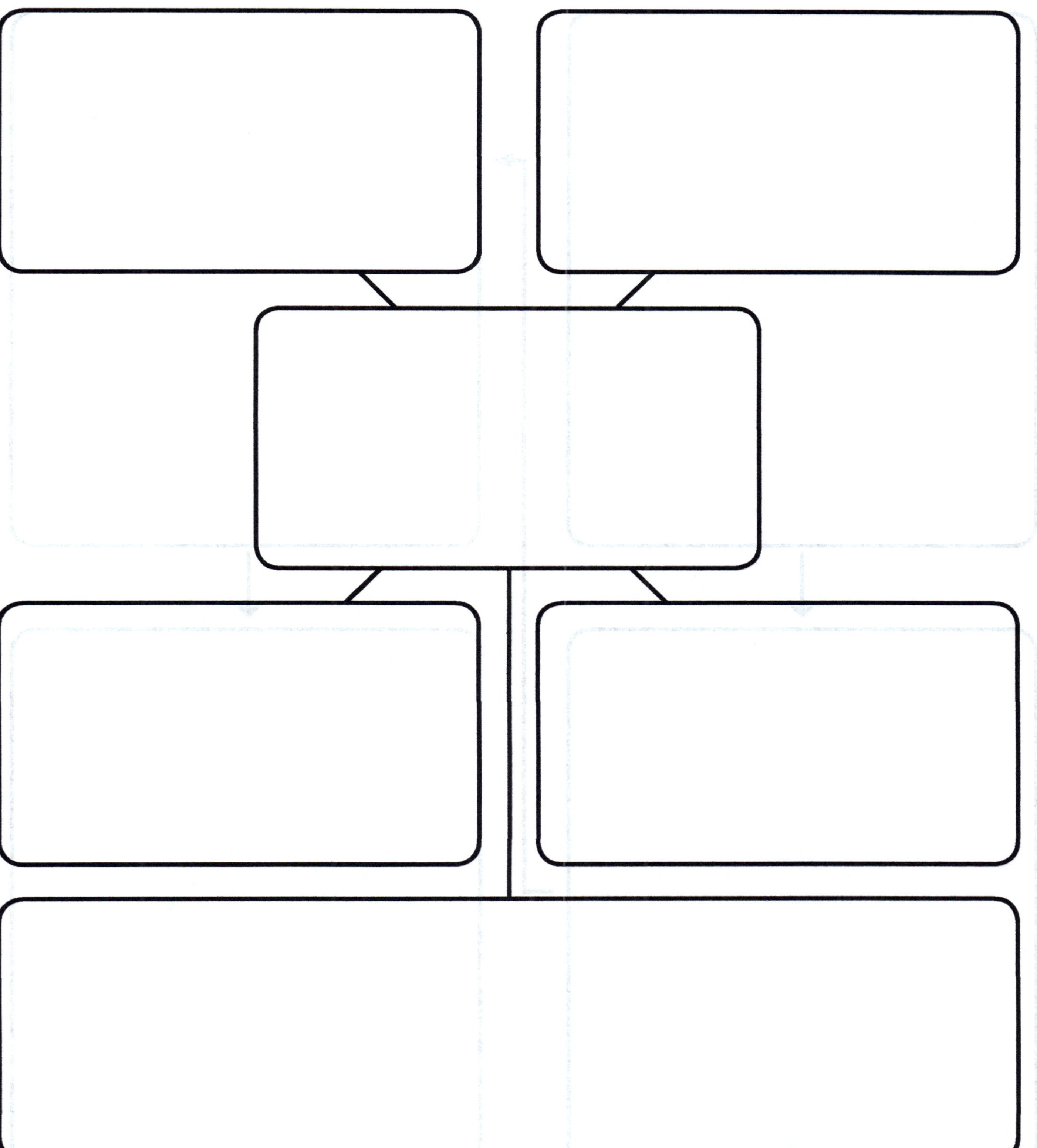

Name ______________________ Date ______________

Four-Square Chart

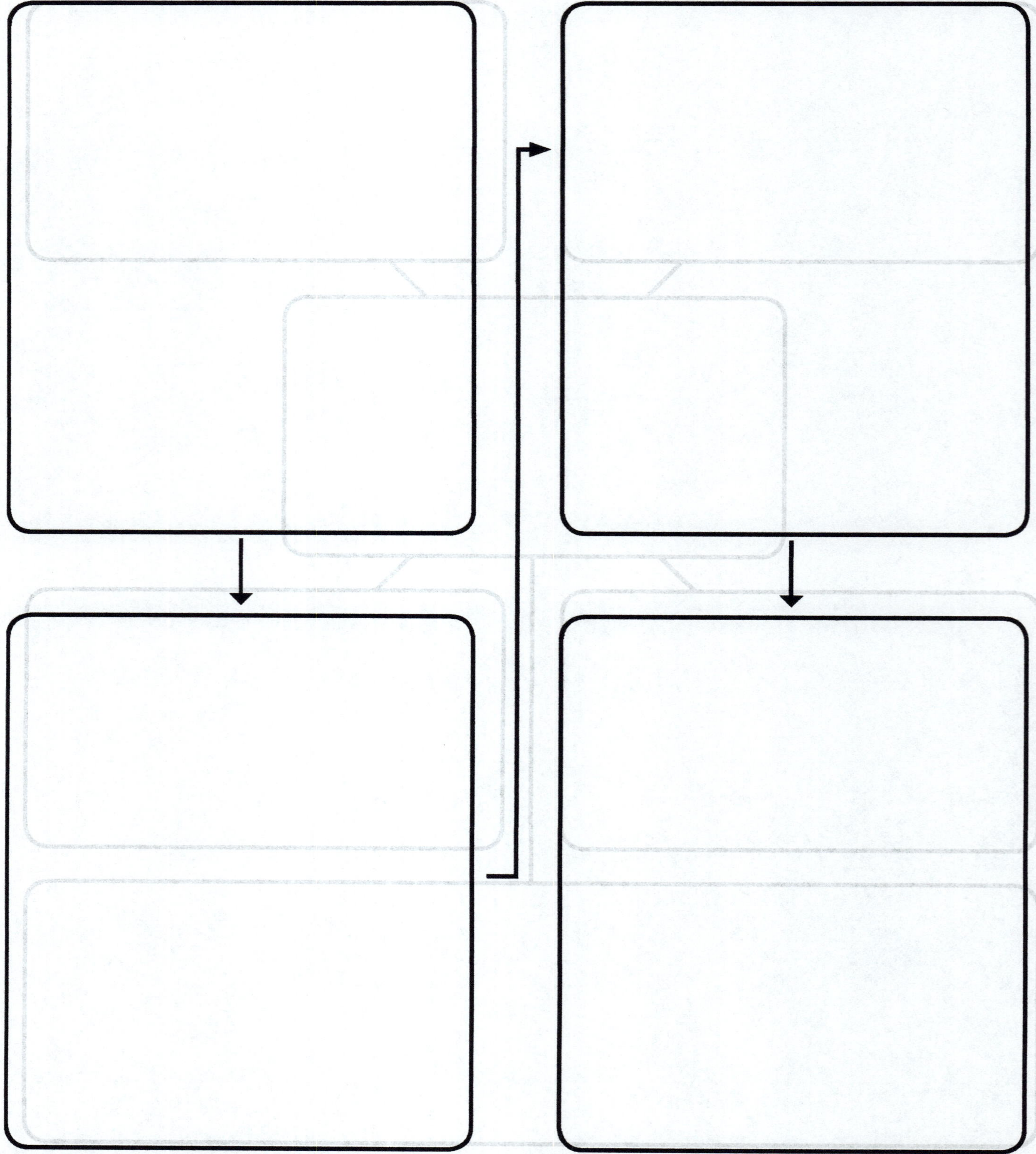

Name ____________________ Date ____________

Main Idea Chart

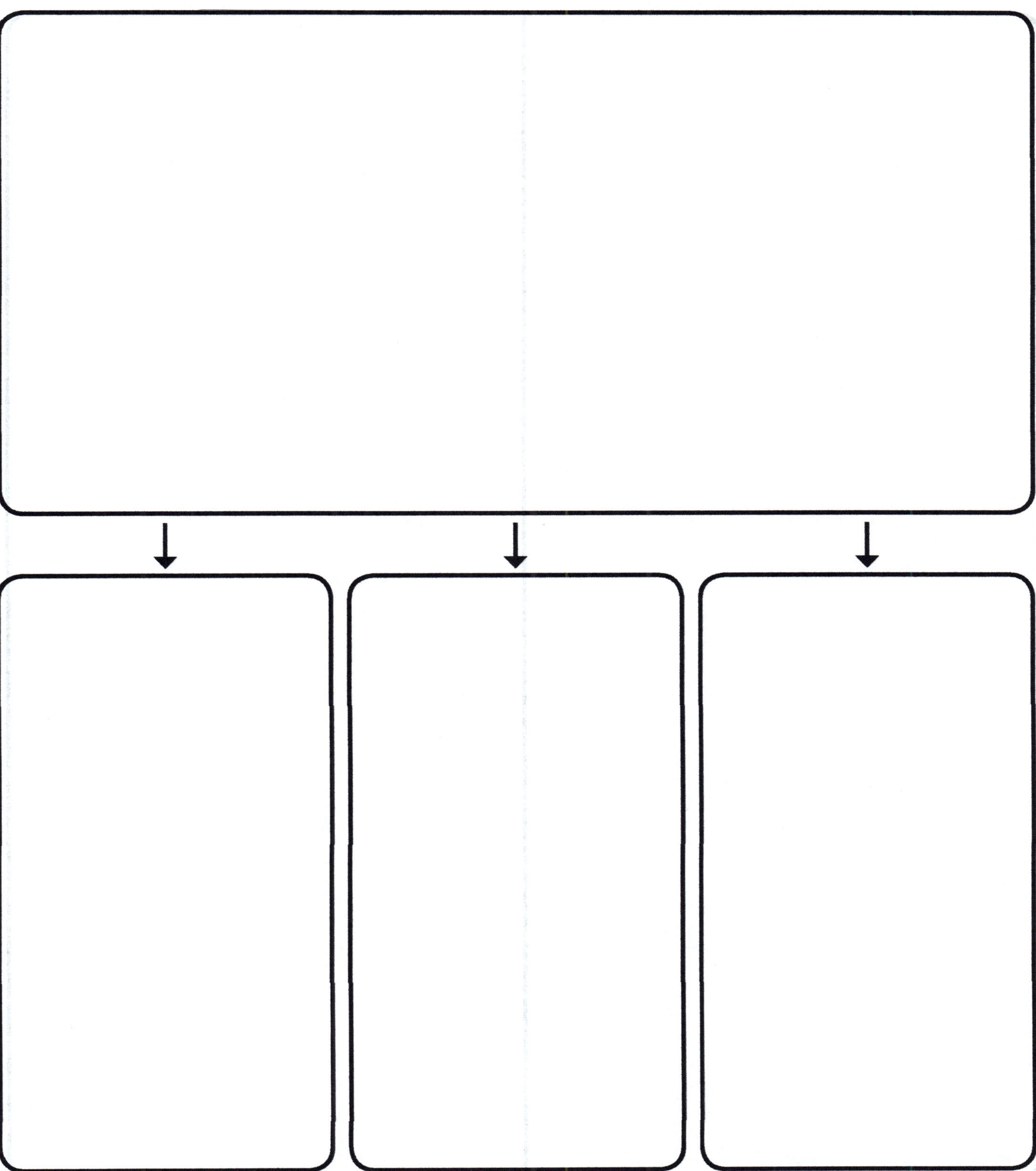

Name ______________________________ Date ______________

Two-Column Chart

Name ______________________________ Date ______________

Problem-Solution Chart

Name ________________________ Date ____________

Sequence Chart

Name ______________________________ Date ______________

Story Structure Chart

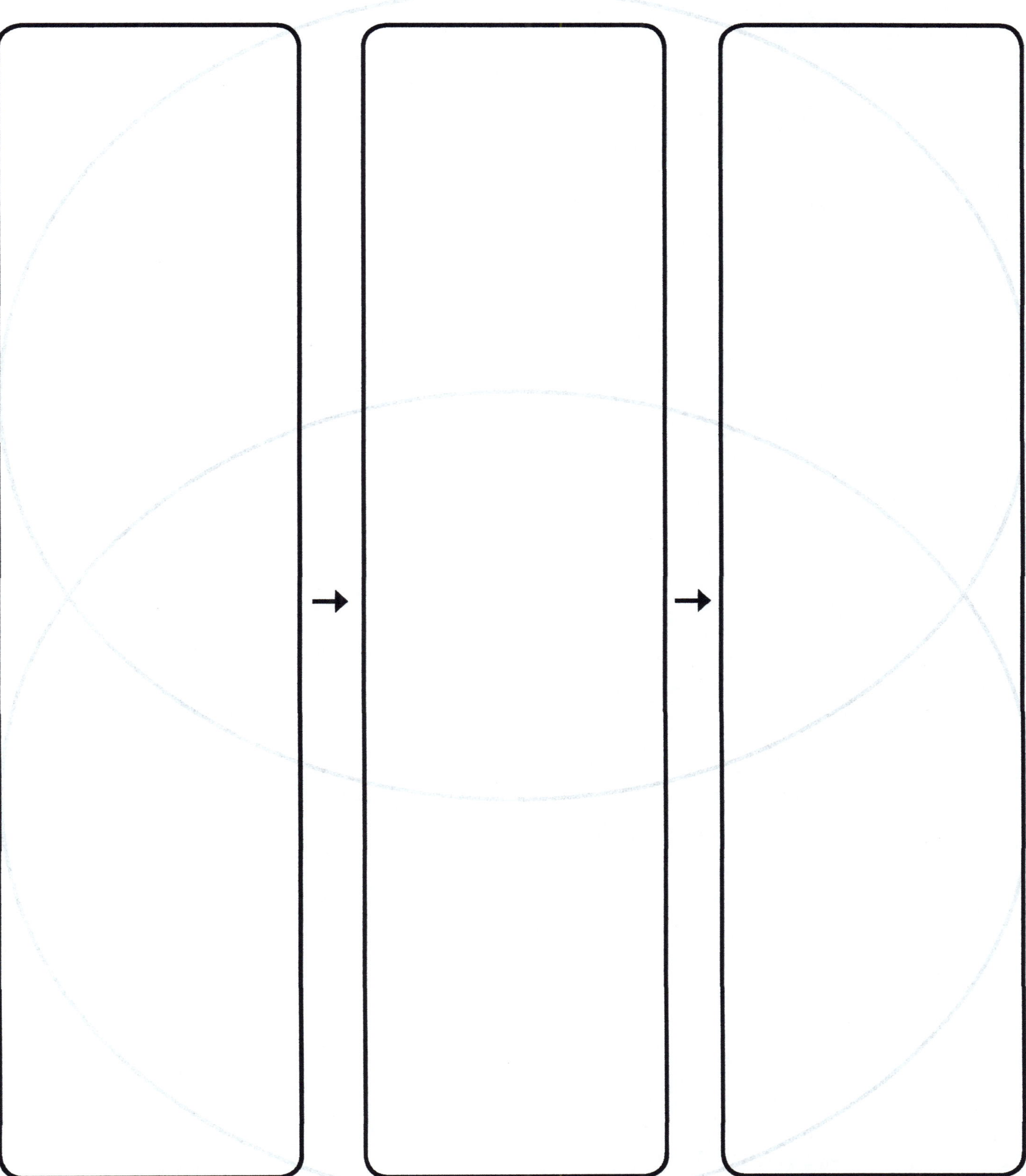

Name ______________________________ Date ______________

Venn Diagram

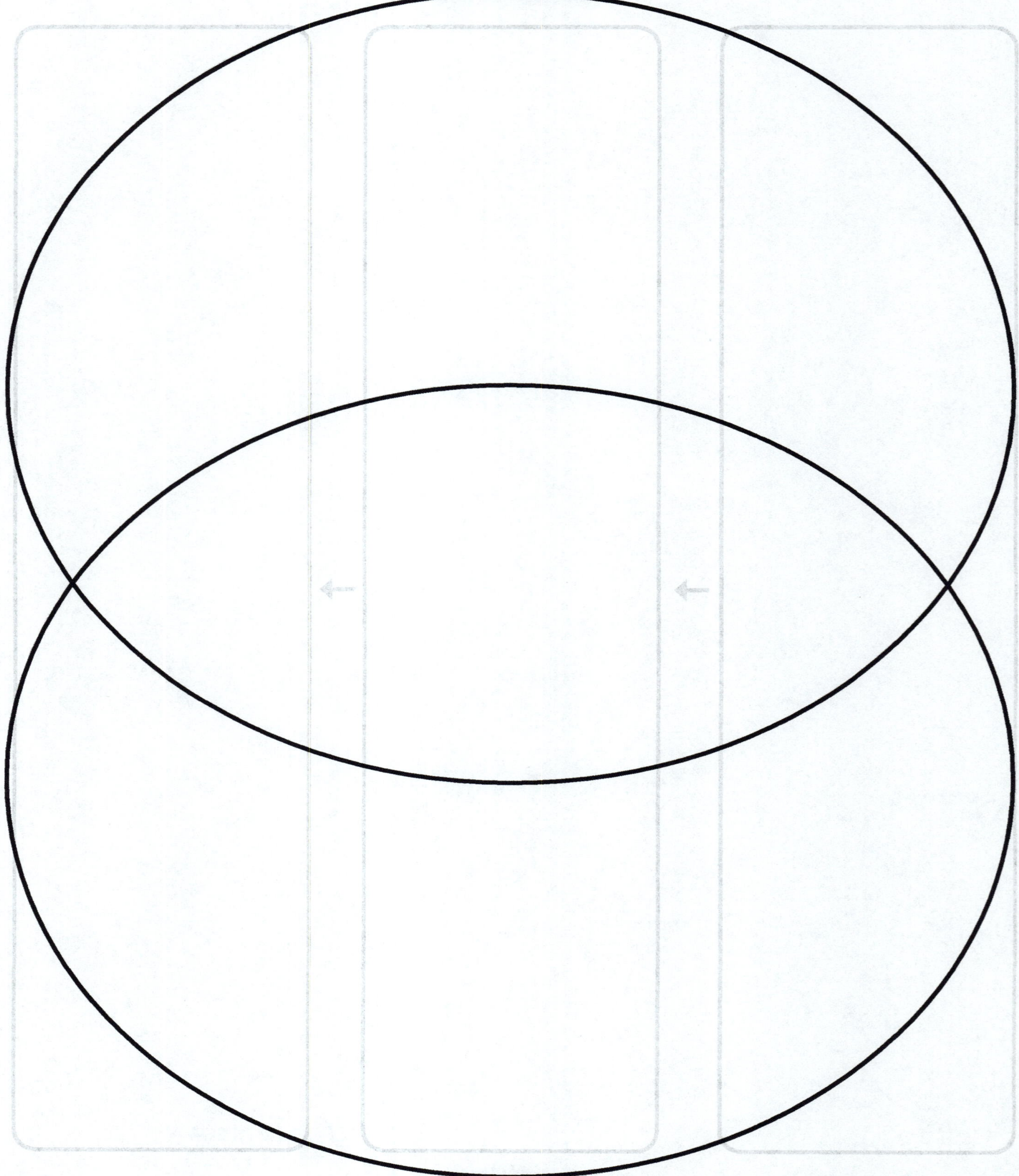

Name ______________________________ Date ______________

Four-Column Chart

Name ______________________________ Date ______________

Six-Row Chart

Name ______________________________ Date ______________

Academic Talk Routine

1. **Read the Academic Talk Words and Phrases.**

   Look at the Academic Talk box in your book. Listen as your teacher explains the words and phrases. Ask for clarification if you don't understand any terms.

2. **Read the Introduction.**

   Circle the Academic Talk words and phrases as you read them in your book.

3. **Practice the Academic Talk Words and Phrases.**

   Challenge yourself to use the words and phrases three to four times in today's discussions.

4. **Use the Academic Talk Words and Phrases.**

   Throughout the lesson, use the words and phrases when you talk or write about a text.

Name ______________________________ Date ______________

Word Learning Routine

Use the following steps to figure out unfamiliar words. If you figure out what the word means, continue reading. If not, then try the next step.

1. **Say the Word or Phrase Aloud.**

   Circle the word or phrase that you find confusing. Read the sentence aloud.

2. **Look Inside the Word or Phrase.**

   Look for familiar word parts, such as prefixes, suffixes, and root words. Try breaking the word into smaller parts. Can you figure out a meaning from the word parts you know?

3. **Look Around the Word or Phrase.**

   Look for clues in the words or sentences around the word you don't know and the context of the paragraph or selection.

4. **Look Beyond the Word or Phrase.**

   Look for the meaning of the word or phrase in a dictionary, glossary, or thesaurus.

5. **Check the Meaning.**

   Ask yourself, "Does this meaning make sense in the sentence?"

Name ______________________________ Date ______________

Talk Routine

1. **Read the Prompt.**

   Take turns with your partner reading the prompt to make sure you understand the topic of your discussion.

2. **Respond and Prove.**

   Use evidence from the text in your response.

3. **Listen and Build.**

   Listen carefully to what your partner says. Ask him or her to explain their thinking and where they found their evidence. Identify connections to their ideas or evidence.

4. **Share Your Understandings.**

   Together with your partner, be prepared to tell your class what you learned from the text and your discussion.

Name ______________________________ Date ______________

Response-Writing Routine

1. **Read and Analyze the Prompt.**

   Identify and circle key words and phrases that tell what you should do. Underline words or phrases that indicate evidence you need to provide. Say the prompt in your own words to be sure you understand it.

2. **Gather Text Evidence.**

   Support your writing with evidence from the text.

3. **Organize Ideas and Evidence.**

   Use a graphic organizer to help you organize your ideas before you begin writing.

4. **Write the Response.**

   Use the information you gathered from the text and talked about with your partner to answer the prompt.

5. **Evaluate Your Response.**

   Revise to make it clearer or to add more text evidence. Fix any mistakes. Together with your partner, tell your class what you learned from the text and your discussion.

Correlation Charts

Common Core State Standards Coverage by *Ready*® *Instruction*

The table below correlates each Common Core State Standard to the *Ready*® Common Core Instruction lesson(s) that offer(s) comprehensive instruction or additional practice on that standard.

Common Core State Standards for Grade 5

Reading Standards for Literature	Comprehensive Instruction	Additional Practice
Key Ideas and Details		
Literature 1. Quote accurately from a text when explaining what the text says explicitly and when drawing inferences from the text.	**Lesson 10:** SB/TRB: pp. 162–175	**Lesson 5:** TRB: pp. 97, 102; **Lesson 6:** TRB: pp. 111, 116; **Lesson 8:** TRB: p. 143; **Lesson 15:** TRB: p. 276; **Lesson 16:** TRB: p. 290; **Lesson 17:** TRB: p. 304; **Lesson 21:** TRB: p. 394; **Lesson 22:** TRB: p. 405
Literature 2. Determine a theme of a story, drama, or poem from details in the text, including how characters in a story or drama respond to challenges or how the speaker in a poem reflects upon a topic; summarize the text.	**Lesson 7:** SB/TRB: pp. 120–133; **Lesson 8:** SB/TRB: pp. 134–147; **Lesson 9:** SB/TRB: pp. 148–161	**Lesson 5:** TRB: pp. 97, 102; **Lesson 6:** TRB: pp. 111, 116; **Lesson 9:** TRB: pp. 158; **Lesson 10:** TRB: pp. 167; **Lesson 15:** TRB: pp. 271, 276; **Lesson 16:** TRB: pp. 290; **Lesson 17:** TRB: pp. 304; **Lesson 21:** TRB: pp. 394; **Lesson 22:** TRB: pp. 411
Literature 3. Compare and contrast two or more characters, settings, or events in a story or drama, drawing on specific details in the text (e.g., how characters interact).	**Lesson 5:** SB/TRB: pp. 92–105; **Lesson 6:** SB/TRB: pp. 106–119	**Lesson 7:** TRB: pp. 125, 130; **Lesson 8:** TRB: p. 143; **Lesson 9:** TRB: p. 158; **Lesson 10:** TRB: p. 172; **Lesson 15:** TRB: p. 276; **Lesson 16:** TRB: p. 290; **Lesson 17:** TRB: p. 299; **Lesson 22:** TRB: p. 411
Craft and Structure		
Literature 4. Determine the meaning of words and phrases as they are used in a text, including figurative language such as metaphors and similes.	**Lesson 15:** SB/TRB: pp. 266–279	**Lesson 5:** TRB: p. 102; **Lesson 6:** TRB: pp. 110, 116, 118; **Lesson 7:** TRB: pp. 130, 132; **Lesson 8:** TRB: pp. 139, 144; **Lesson 9:** TRB: pp. 153, 158; **Lesson 10:** TRB: pp. 172, 173; **Lesson 16:** TRB: pp. 285. 290, 292; **Lesson 17:** TRB: pp. 299, 305: **Lesson 21:** TRB: pp. 389, 394; **Lesson 22:** TRB: pp. 411, 412
Literature 5. Explain how a series of chapters, scenes, or stanzas fits together to provide the overall structure of a particular story, drama, or poem.	**Lesson 16:** SB/TRB: pp. 280–293	**Lesson 5:** TRB: p. 102; **Lesson 7:** TRB: p. 125; **Lesson 9:** TRB: p. 153; **Lesson 17:** TRB: p. 304; **Lesson 22:** TRB: p. 405
Literature 6. Describe how a narrator's or speaker's point of view influences how events are described.	**Lesson 17:** SB/TRB: pp. 294–307	**Lesson 6:** TRB: p. 116; **Lesson 7:** TRB: p. 130; **Lesson 8:** TRB: pp. 139, 143; **Lesson 9:** TRB: p. 158; **Lesson 10:** TRB: p. 172; **Lesson 15:** TRB: p. 276; **Lesson 16:** TRB: p. 285; **Lesson 17:** TRB: p. 304; **Lesson 21:** TRB: pp. 389, 394; **Lesson 22:** TRB: p. 411
Literature 7. Analyze how visual and multimedia elements contribute to the meaning, tone, or beauty of a text (e.g., graphic novel, multimedia presentation of fiction, folktale, myth, poem).	**Lesson 21:** SB/TRB: pp. 384–397	—

Common Core State Standards for Grade 5

Reading Standards for Literature *(continued)*	Comprehensive Instruction	Additional Practice
Integration of Knowledge and Ideas		
Literature 9. Compare and contrast stories in the same genre (e.g., mysteries and adventure stories) on their approaches to similar themes and topics.	**Lesson 22:** SB/TRB: pp. 398–415	**Lesson 10:** TRB: pp. 167, 172
Literature 10. By the end of the year, read and comprehend literature, including stories, dramas, and poetry, at the high end of the grades 4–5 text complexity band independently and proficiently.	**All lessons.** Lessons in *Ready* are structured around direct interaction with high-interest, complex text. Students demonstrate their ability to read grade-appropriate text when they are engaged in reading and rereading to deepen their understanding with appropriate scaffolds when required.	

Reading Standards for Informational Texts	Comprehensive Instruction	Additional Practice
Key Ideas and Details		
Informational Text 1. Quote accurately from a text when explaining what the text says explicitly and when drawing inferences from the text.	**Lesson 3:** SB/TRB: pp. 38–51	**Lesson 2:** TRB: p. 29; **Lesson 4a:** TRB: p. 62; **Lesson 4b:** TRB: pp. 71, 76; **Lesson 11:** TRB: pp. 193, 198; **Lesson 12:** TRB: pp. 214; **Lesson 14:** TRB: pp. 241, 246; **Lesson 18:** TRB: p. 332; **Lesson 19:** TRB: p. 346; **Lesson 20:** TRB: pp. 357, 363
Informational Text 2. Determine two or more main ideas of a text and explain how they are supported by key details; summarize the text.	**Lesson 1:** SB/TRB: pp. 10–23; **Lesson 2:** SB/TRB: pp. 24–37	**Lesson 3:** TRB: p. 48; **Lesson 4a:** TRB: p. 57; **Lesson 11:** TRB: p. 198; **Lesson 12:** TRB: pp. 208, 214; **Lesson 14:** TRB: p. 246; **Lesson 18:** TRB: p. 326; **Lesson 19:** TRB: p. 341, 346; **Lesson 20:** TRB: p. 363
Informational Text 3. Explain the relationships or interactions between two or more individuals, events, ideas, or concepts in a historical, scientific, or technical text based on specific information in the text.	**Lesson 4a:** SB/TRB: pp. 52–65; **Lesson 4b:** SB/TRB: pp. 66–79	**Lesson 1:** TRB: p. 15; **Lesson 2:** TRB: p. 29; **Lesson 11:** TRB: pp. 193, 198; **Lesson 12:** TRB: pp. 208, 214; **Lesson 13:** TRB: p. 224, 230; **Lesson 14:** TRB: p. 241, 246; **Lesson 18:** TRB: p. 326; **Lesson 19:** TRB: pp. 341, 346; **Lesson 20:** TRB: p. 357
Craft and Structure		
Informational Text 4. Determine the meaning of general academic and domain-specific words and phrases in a text relevant to a grade 5 topic or subject area.	**Lesson 11:** SB/TRB: pp. 188–201	**Lesson 1:** TRB: p. 20; **Lesson 2:** TRB: p. 34; **Lesson 3:** TRB: p. 43, 48; **Lesson 4a:** TRB: p. 64; **Lesson 4b:** TRB: p. 76; **Lesson 13:** TRB: p. 230; **Lesson 14:** TRB: p. 246; **Lesson 18:** TRB: p. 332; **Lesson 19:** TRB: pp. 346, 347; **Lesson 20:** TRB: p. 363
Informational Text 5. Compare and contrast the overall structure (e.g., chronology, comparison, cause/effect, problem/solution) of events, ideas, concepts, or information in two or more texts.	**Lesson 12:** SB/TRB: pp. 202–217; **Lesson 13:** SB/TRB: pp. 218–233	**Lesson 3:** TRB: p. 43; **Lesson 4a:** TRB: p. 57; **Lesson 11:** TRB: p. 193; **Lesson 20:** TRB: p. 363
Informational Text 6. Analyze multiple accounts of the same event or topic, noting important similarities and differences in the point of view they represent.	**Lesson 14:** SB/TRB: pp. 234–249	**Lesson 3:** TRB: p. 48; **Lesson 13:** TRB: p. 224
Informational Text 7. Draw on information from multiple print or digital sources, demonstrating the ability to locate an answer to a question quickly or to solve a problem efficiently.	**Lesson 18:** SB/TRB: pp. 320–335	**Lesson 2:** TRB: p. 34; **Lesson 4a:** TRB: p. 62

Common Core State Standards for Grade 5

Reading Standards for Informational Texts *(continued)*	Comprehensive Instruction	Additional Practice
Integration of Knowledge and Ideas		
Informational Text 8. Explain how an author uses reasons and evidence to support particular points in a text, identifying which reasons and evidence support which point(s).	**Lesson 19:** SB/TRB: pp. 336–349	**Lesson 1:** TRB: pp. 15, 20; **Lesson 3:** TRB: p. 48; **Lesson 4a:** TRB: p. 62; **Lesson 4b:** TRB: p. 76; **Lesson 11:** TRB: p. 198; **Lesson 12:** TRB: pp. 208, 214; **Lesson 13:** TRB: p. 230; **Lesson 18:** TRB: p. 332
Informational Text 9. Integrate information from several texts on the same topic in order to write or speak about the subject knowledgeably.	**Lesson 20:** SB/TRB: pp. 350–367	**Lesson 2:** TRB: p. 36; **Lesson 4b:** TRB: p. 71; **Lesson 12:** TRB: p. 214; **Lesson 13:** TRB: pp. 224, 230; **Lesson 14:** TRB: pp. 239, 241; **Lesson 18:** TRB: p. 332
Range of Reading and Level of Text Complexity		
Informational Text 10. By the end of the year, read and comprehend informational texts, including history/ social studies, science, and technical texts, at the high end of the grades 4–5 text complexity band independently and proficiently.	**All lessons.** Lessons in *Ready* are structured around direct interaction with high-interest, complex text. Students demonstrate their ability to read grade-appropriate text when they are engaged in reading and rereading to deepen their understanding with appropriate scaffolds when required.	

Writing	Comprehensive Instruction	Additional Practice
Research to Build and Present Knowledge		
Writing 9.a Apply grade 5 Reading standards to literature (e.g., "Compare and contrast two or more characters, settings, or events in a story or a drama, drawing on specific details in the text [e.g., how characters interact]").	**Lesson 5:** SB/TRB: p. 105; **Lesson 6:** SB/TRB: p. 118; **Lesson 7:** SB/TRB: p. 133; **Lesson 8:** SB/TRB: p. 147; **Lesson 9:** SB/TRB: p. 161; **Lesson 10:** SB/TRB: p. 175; **Lesson 15:** SB/TRB: p. 279; **Lesson 16:** SB/TRB: p. 292; **Lesson 17:** SB/TRB: p. 307; **Lesson 21:** SB/TRB: p. 396; **Lesson 22:** SB/TRB: p. 414	—
Writing 9.b Apply grade 5 Reading standards to informational texts (e.g., "Explain how an author uses reasons and evidence to support particular points in a text, identifying which reasons and evidence support which point[s]").	**Lesson 1:** SB/TRB: p. 23; **Lesson 2:** SB/TRB: p. 37; **Lesson 3:** SB/TRB: p. 51; **Lesson 4a:** SB/TRB: p. 65; **Lesson 4b:** SB/TRB: p. 78; **Lesson 11:** SB/TRB: p. 201; **Lesson 12:** SB/TRB: p. 217; **Lesson 13:** SB/TRB: p. 233; **Lesson 14:** SB/TRB: p. 249; **Lesson 18:** SB/TRB: p. 334; **Lesson 19:** SB/TRB: p. 349; **Lesson 20:** SB/TRB: p. 366	—

Speaking and Listening Standards	Comprehensive Instruction	Additional Practice
Comprehension and Collaboration		
Speaking/Listening 1. Engage effectively in a range of collaborative discussions (one-on-one, in groups, and teacher-led) with diverse partners on grade 5 topics and texts, building on others' ideas and expressing their own clearly.	—	**Lesson 2:** TRB: p. 34; **Lesson 4b:** TRB: p. 76; **Lesson 5:** TRB: p. 102

Common Core State Standards for Grade 5

Speaking and Listening Standards *(continued)*	Comprehensive Instruction	Additional Practice
Comprehension and Collaboration *(continued)*		
Speaking/Listening 1.c Pose and respond to specific questions by making comments that contribute to the discussion and elaborate on the remarks of others.	**All lessons.** This standard is addressed in each lesson through the rich, structured Talk discussions.	
Speaking/Listening 1.d Review the key ideas expressed and draw conclusions in light of information and knowledge gained from the discussions.	**All lessons.** This standard is addressed in each lesson through the rich, structured Talk discussions.	

Language Standards	Comprehensive Instruction	Additional Practice
Conventions in Writing and Speaking		
Language 1.a Explain the function of conjunctions, prepositions, and interjections in general and their function in particular sentences.	**Language Handbook**	**SB:** pp. 438–443 **TRB:** pp. LH438–439, LH440–441, LH442–443
Language 1.b Form and use the perfect (e.g., *I had walked; I have walked; I will have walked*) verb tenses.	**Language Handbook**	**SB:** pp. 444–445 **TRB:** pp. LH444–445
Language 1.c. Use verb tense to convey various times, sequences, states, and conditions.	**Language Handbook**	**SB:** pp. 446–447 **TRB:** pp. LH446–447
Language 1.d. Recognize and correct inappropriate shifts in verb tense.	**Language Handbook**	**SB:** pp. 448–449 **TRB:** pp. LH448–449
Language 1.e. Use correlative conjunctions (e.g., *either/or, neither/nor*).	**Language Handbook**	**SB:** pp. 450–451 **TRB:** pp. LH450–451
Language 2.a Use punctuation to separate items in a series.	**Language Handbook**	**SB:** pp. 452–453 **TRB:** pp. LH452–453
Language 2.b Use a comma to separate an introductory element from the rest of the sentence.	**Language Handbook**	**SB:** pp. 454–457 **TRB:** pp. LH45–455, LH456–475
Language 2.c Use a comma to set off the words *yes* and *no* (e.g., *Yes, thank you*), to set off a tag question from the rest of the sentence (e.g., *It's true, isn't it?*), and to indicate direct address (e.g., *Is that you, Steve?*).	**Language Handbook**	**SB:** pp. 454–455 **TRB:** pp. LH454–455
Language 2.d Use underlining, quotation marks, or italics to indicate titles of works.	**Language Handbook**	**SB:** pp. 458–459 **TRB:** pp. LH458–459
Knowledge of Language		
Language 3.a Expand, combine, and reduce sentences for meaning, reader/ listener interest, and style.	**Language Handbook**	**SB:** pp. 460–463 **TRB:** pp. LH460–461, LH462–463
Language 3.b Compare and contrast the varieties of English (e.g. dialects, registers) used in stories, dramas, or poems.	**Language Handbook**	**SB:** pp. 464-–465 **TRB:** pp. LH464–465

Common Core State Standards for Grade 5

Language Standards *(continued)*	Comprehensive Instruction	Additional Practice
Vocabulary Acquisition and Use		
Language 4.a Use context (e.g., cause/ effect relationships and comparisons in text) as a clue to the meaning of a word or phrase.	**Lesson 1:** SB/TRB: pp. 12, 14; **Lesson 2:** SB/TRB: pp. 26, 28; **Lesson 4a:** SB/TRB: pp. 54, 56; **Lesson 5:** SB/TRB: pp. 94, 96; **Lesson 6:** SB/TRB: pp. 108, 110; **Lesson 7:** SB/TRB: pp. 122, 124; **Lesson 8:** SB/TRB: pp. 136, 144; **Lesson 9:** SB/TRB: pp. 150, 152; **Lesson 10:** SB/TRB: pp. 164, 166; **Lesson 11:** SB/TRB: pp. 190, 192; **Lesson 12:** SB/TRB: pp. 204, 207; **Lesson 14:** SB/TRB: pp. 236, 239; **Lesson 15:** SB/TRB: pp. 268, 270; **Lesson 16:** SB/TRB: pp. 282, 284; **Lesson 17:** SB/TRB: pp. 296, 298; **Lesson 18:** SB/TRB: pp. 322, 325; **Lesson 21:** SB/TRB: pp. 386, 388; **Lesson 22:** SB/TRB: p. 412	**Lesson 3:** TRB: pp. 43, 49; **Lesson 4b:** TRB: p. 76; **Lesson 5:** TRB: pp. 102, 104; **Lesson 7:** TRB: pp. 130, 132; **Lesson 9:** TRB: pp. 153, 158; **Lesson 10:** TRB: p. 173; **Lesson 13:** TRB: pp. 230, 232; **Lesson 16:** TRB: p. 292; **Lesson 17:** TRB: p. 305; **Lesson 18:** TRB: p. 333
	Language Handbook **SB:** pp. 466–467 **TRB:** pp. LH466–467	
Language 4.b Use common, grade-appropriate Greek and Latin affixes and roots as clues to the meaning of a word (e.g., *photograph, photosynthesis*).	**Lesson 2:** SB/TRB: p. 36; **Lesson 3:** SB/TRB: pp.40, 42; **Lesson 4a:** SB/TRB: p. 64; **Lesson 4b:** SB/TRB: pp. 70, 77; **Lesson 8:** SB/TRB: p. 138; **Lesson 9:** SB/TRB: p. 152; **Lesson 13:** SB/TRB: pp. 220, 223; **Lesson 19:** SB/TRB: pp. 338, 340; **Lesson 20:** SB/TRB: pp. 352, 354	**Lesson 3:** TRB: pp. 43, 49; **Lesson 4b:** TRB: pp. 70, 77; **Lesson 5:** TRB: pp. 102, 104; **Lesson 7:** TRB: pp. 130, 132; **Lesson 9:** TRB: pp. 153, 158; **Lesson 12:** TRB: p. 216; **Lesson 13:** TRB: p. 230; **Lesson 18:** TRB: p. 332; **Lesson 20:** TRB: pp. 357, 364
	Language Handbook **SB:** pp. 468–469 **TRB:** pp. LH468–469	
Language 4.c Consult reference materials (e.g., dictionaries, glossaries, thesauruses), both print and digital, to find the pronunciation and determine or clarify the precise meaning of key words and phrases.	**Lesson 4b:** SB/TRB: pp. 68, 70; **Lesson 6:** SB/TRB: p. 118; **Lesson 11:** SB/TRB: p. 200; **Lesson 14:** SB/TRB: p. 247; **Lesson 22:** SB/TRB: pp. 400, 403	—
	Language Handbook **SB:** pp. 470–471 **TRB:** pp. LH470–471	
Language 5.a Interpret figurative language, including similes and metaphors, in context.	—	**Lesson 18:** TRB: p. 332; **Lesson 22:** SB/TRB: p. 411
	Language Handbook **SB:** pp. 472–473 **TRB:** pp. LH472–473	
Language 5.b Recognize and explain the meaning of common idioms, adages, and proverbs.	**Lesson 10:** SB/TRB: p. 164; **Lesson 14:** SB/TRB: p. 236	**Lesson 2:** TRB: p. 34; **Lesson 3:** TRB: p. 48; **Lesson 19:** TRB: p. 346
	Language Handbook **SB:** pp. 476–479 **TRB:** pp. LH476–477, LH478–479	

Common Core State Standards for Grade 5

Language Standards *(continued)*	Comprehensive Instruction		Additional Practice
Vocabulary Acquisition and Use *(continued)*			
Language 5.c Use the relationship between particular words (e.g., synonyms, antonyms, homographs) to better understand each of the words.	**Lesson 5:** SB/TRB: p. 94; **Lesson 14:** SB/TRB: p. 247		**Lesson 19:** TRB: p. 347 ; **Lesson 21:** TRB: p. 396
	Language Handbook	**SB:** pp. 480–481 **TRB:** pp. LH480–481	
Language 6. Acquire and use accurately grade-appropriate general academic and domain-specific words and phrases, including those that signal contrast, addition, and other logical relationships (e.g., *however, although, nevertheless, similarly, moreover, in addition*).	**All lessons.** This standard is addressed in each lesson through the Academic Talk instructional support in the Student Book and Teacher Resource Book.		
	Language Handbook	**SB:** pp. 482–483 **TRB:** pp. LH482–483	

Cognitive Rigor Matrix

The table below combines the hierarchies of learning from both Webb and Bloom. For each level of hierarchy, descriptions of student behaviors that would fulfill expectations at each of the four DOK levels are given. Note that students can show how they evaluate by citing evidence or checking multiple sources, but there isn't a lower-rigor (DOK 1 or 2) way of truly assessing this skill.

Depth of Thinking (Webb) + Type of Thinking (Revised Bloom)	*DOK Level 1* **Recall & Reproduction**	*DOK Level 2* **Basic Skills & Concepts**	*DOK Level 3* **Strategic Thinking & Reasoning**	*DOK Level 4* **Extended Thinking**
Remember	• Recall, locate basic facts, definitions, details, events			
Understand	• Select appropriate words for use when intended meaning is clearly evident	• Specify, explain relationships • Summarize • Identify central ideas	• Explain, generalize, or connect ideas using supporting evidence (quote, text evidence, example . . .)	• Explain how concepts or ideas specifically relate to other content domains or concepts
Apply	• Use language structure (pre/suffix) or word relationships (synonym/antonym) to determine meaning	• Use content to identify word meanings • Obtain and interpret information using text features	• Use concepts to solve non-routine problems	• Devise an approach among many alternatives to research a novel problem
Analyze	• Identify the kind of information contained in a graphic, table, visual, etc.	• Compare literary elements, facts, terms, events • Analyze format, organization, & text structures	• Analyze or interpret author's craft (e.g., literary devices, viewpoint, or potential bias) to critique a text	• Analyze multiple sources or texts • Analyze complex/abstract themes
Evaluate			• Cite evidence and develop a logical argument for conjectures based on one text or problem	• Evaluate relevancy, accuracy, & completeness of information across texts/sources
Create	• Brainstorm ideas, concepts, problems, or perspectives related to a topic or concept	• Generate conjectures or hypotheses based on observations or prior knowledge and experience	• Develop a complex model for a given situation • Develop an alternative solution	• Synthesize information across multiple sources or texts • Articulate a new voice, alternate theme, new knowledge or perspective

Interim Assessment Answer Keys and Correlations

Depth of Knowledge and Standards Coverage by *Ready®* *Instruction*

The table below shows the depth-of-knowledge (DOK) level for the items in the Interim Assessments, as well as the standard(s) addressed, and the corresponding *Ready® Instruction* lesson(s) being assessed by each item. Use this information to adjust lesson plans and focus remediation.

Question	Key	DOK[1]	Standard	*Ready®* Student Lesson(s)
Unit 1: Key Ideas and Details in Informational Text				
1	See page 83.	2	RI.5.2	1
2	See page 84.	3	RI.5.3	4a, 4b
3	See page 84.	2	RI.5.4, L.5.4a	11, L15
4A	B	1	RI.5.2	1
4B	B	1	RI.5.2	1
5	D	3	RI.5.1	3
6	See page 86.	3	RI.5.3	4a, 4b
7A	B	1	RI.5.3	4a, 4b
7B	A	1	RI.5.3	4a, 4b
8	D	2	RI.5.2	1
9	See page 88.	4	RI.5.3	4a, 4b
Unit 2: Key Ideas and Details in Literature				
1	See page 177.	1	RL.5.1	10
2A	B	2	RL.5.2	7
2B	See page 177.	2	RL.5.2	7
3	D	2	RL.5.2	9
4	See page 178.	2	RL.5.2	9
5A	B	1	RL.5.3	5
5B	B	1	RL.5.3	5

Lesson numbers preceded by "L" refer to the Language Handbook.

[1]Depth of Knowledge levels:

1. The item requires superficial knowledge of the standard.
2. The item requires processing beyond recall and observation.
3. The item requires explanation, generalization, and connection to other ideas.

Question	Key	DOK[1]	Standard	*Ready*® Student Lesson(s)
Unit 2: Key Ideas and Details in Literature *continued*				
6	See page 182.	2	RL.5.1	10
7	See page 183.	2	RL.5.3	5
8	C	2	RL.5.4, L.5.4a	15, L15
9	See page 184.	3	RL.5.3	6, 7
Unit 3: Craft and Structure in Informational Text				
1	B	2	RI.5.4	11
2	See page 252.	2	RI.5.4	11
3A	C	2	RI.5.4	11
3B	B	2	RI.5.4	11
4A	A	3	RI.5.6	14
4B	B, D	3	RI.5.6	14
5	See page 257.	3	RI.5.6	14
6	See page 258.	4	RI.5.5, RI.5.6	12, 13
7	A, C	3	RI.5.6	14
8	See page 261.	3	RI.5.6	14
9	See page 262.	4	RI.5.5, RI.5.6	12, 13, 14
Unit 4: Craft and Structure in Literature				
1	D	3	RL.5.4	15
2	B	3	RL.5.6	17
3	See page 310.	2	RL.5.6	17
4	B	2	RL.5.4	15
5	See page 311.	3	RL.5.5	16
6	A, C	2	RL.5.5	16
7A	C	2	RL.5.4	15
7B	A	2	RL.5.4	15
8	See page 315.	3	RL.5.5	16
9	See page 316.	3	RL.5.6	17

Interim Assessment Correlations, *continued*

Question	Key	DOK[1]	Standard	*Ready*® Student Lesson(s)
Unit 5: Integration of Knowledge and Ideas in Informational Text				
1A	C	2	RI.5.8	19
1B	D	2	RI.5.8	19
2	See page 370.	2	RI.5.8	19
3A	A	2	RI.5.8	19
3B	See page 371.	2	RI.5.8	19
4A	D	3	RI.5.7	18
4B	A, C	3	RI.5.7	18
5A	A	2	RI.5.8	19
5B	See page 375.	2	RI.5.8	19
6	C	2	RI.5.7	18
7	See page 378.	3	RI.5.9	20
8	See page 379.	2	RI.5.7	18
9	See page 380.	4	RI.5.9	20
Unit 6: Integration of Knowledge and Ideas in Literature				
1	C	2	RL.5.7	21
2A	B	2	RL.5.7	21
2B	C	2	RL.5.7	21
3	See page 420.	3	RL.5.7	21
4	See page 420.	2	L.5.4c	L17
5	A	3	RL.5.7	21
6	See page 424.	3	RL.5.7	21
7	See page 425.	3	RL.5.9	22
8A	D	3	RL.5.9	22
8B	C, E	3	RL.5.9	22
9A	B	2	L.5.4c	L17
9B	C	2	L.5.4c	L17
10	A	3	RL.5.7	21
11	See page 428.	4	RL.5.9	22

Supporting Research

References

Adams, M. J. (2009). The challenge of advanced texts: The interdependence of reading and learning. In Hiebert, E. H. (ed.), *Reading more, reading better: Are American students reading enough of the right stuff?* (pp. 183–189). New York, NY: Guilford.

Alliance for Excellent Education. (2012). The role of language and literacy in college- and career-ready standards: Rethinking policy and practice in support of English language learners. Retrieved 6/8/2015 from http://www.all4ed.org/files/LangAndLiteracyInStandardsELLs.pdf.

August, D., M. Carlo, C. Dressler, and C. Snow. (2005). The critical role of vocabulary development for English language learners. *Learning Disabilities Research & Practice, 20*(1), 50–57

Beck, I. L., M. G. McKeown, and L. Kucan. (2002). *Bringing Words to Life: Robust Vocabulary Instruction.* New York, NY: Guilford.

Blachowicz, C., Fisher, P., Ogle, D., & Taffe, S. W. (2013). *Teaching Academic Vocabulary K–8: Effective Practices across the Curriculum.* New York, NY: Guilford.

Boyles, Nancy N. (2012). *That's a Great Answer!* Second edition. North Mankato, MN: Maupin House.

CAST. (2011). Universal Design for Learning Guidelines, Version 2.0. Wakefield, MA: CAST. Retrieved 6/8/2015 from http://www.udlcenter.org/aboutudl/udlguidelines.

Cervetti and Hiebert, (2015). "The Sixth Pillar of Reading Instruction: Knowledge Development." *The Reading Teacher*, volume 68, issue 4, January.

Cross, D. R. and Paris, S. G. (1988). "Developmental and instructional analyses of children's metacognition and reading comprehension." *Journal of Educational Psychology, 80*(2), 131–142. Doi: 10. 1037/0022-0663.80.2.131.

Cunningham, Patricia M., and Cunningham, James W. (2015). *Teaching the Common Core English Language Arts Standards: 20 Lesson Frameworks for Elementary Grades*, Solution Tree Press.

Donovan, M. S. and Bransford, J. D. (Eds.) (2005). *How students learn: History, mathematics, and science in the classroom.* Washington, D.C.: National Academic Press.

Duke, Nell K., Pearson, David P., Strachan, Stephanie L., & Billman, Alison K. (2011). "Essential elements of fostering and teaching reading comprehension" in S. Jay Samuels and Alan E. Farstrup (Ed.), *What research has to say about reading instruction.* pp. 51–93 Newark, DE: International Reading Association.

Echevarría, Jana, MaryEllen Vogt, and Deborah Short. (2012). *Making Content Comprehensible for English Learners: The SIOP® Model*. Boston: Pearson.

Edwards, E. C. Font, G., Baumann, J. F., & Boland, E. (2004). Unlocking word meanings: Strategies and guidelines for teaching morphemic and contextual analysis. In J. F. Baumann & E. J. Kame'enui (Eds.), *Vocabulary instruction: Research to practice* (pp. 159–176). New York, NY: Guilford.

Feldman, K. & Kinsella, K. (2008). "Narrowing the language gap: The case for explicit vocabulary instruction in secondary classrooms." In L. Denti and L. Guerin (Eds.) Effective practice for adolescents with reading and literacy challenges. New York, NY: Routledge.

Fisher, Douglas; Frey, Nancy; and Lapp, Diane. (2012). *Text Complexity: Raising Rigor in Reading.* Newark, DE: International Reading Association.

Fisher, Douglas and Frey, Nancy. (2014). *Close Reading and Writing from Sources.* Newark, DE: International Reading Association.

Fisher, Douglas and Frey, Nancy. (2014). *Better Learning Through Structured Teaching: A Framework for the Gradual Release of Responsibility.* Newark, DE: International Reading Association.

Fisher, Douglas and Frey, Nancy. (2015). *Text-Dependent Questions: Pathways to Close and Critical Reading*. Thousand Oaks, CA: Corwin.

Graves, M. F., and Fitzgerald, J. (2003). "Scaffolding Experiences for Multilingual Classrooms" in G. G. Garcia (Ed.), English Learners: Reaching the Highest Levels of English Literacy. pp. 96–124. Newark, DE: International Reading Association.

Graves, M. F. (2006). *The vocabulary book: Learning and instruction.* New York, NY: Teachers College Press.

Hiebert, Elfrieda H. and P. David Pearson. (2014). *Understanding the Common Core State Standards.* (from the Text Project Article Series.) Santa Cruz, CA: TextProject, Inc.

Janzen, J. (2008). Teaching English language learners in the content areas. *Review of Educational Research, 78*(4), 1010–1038.

Kern, L. & Clemens, N. H. (2007). "Antecedent strategies to promote appropriate classroom behavior." *Psychology in the Schools, 44*(1), pages 65–75.

McLaughlin, Maureen. (2012). *Guided Comprehension for English Learners.* Newark, DE: International Reading Association.

McLaughlin, Maureen. (2015). *Inside the Common Core Classroom: Practical ELA Strategies for Grades 6–8.* Boston, MA: Pearson Education.

McLaughlin, M., & Overturf, B. J., (2013). *The Common Core: Teaching K–5 Students to Meet the Reading Standards.* Newark, DE: International Reading Association.

National Reading Panel. (2000). Washington, DC: National Institute of Child Health and Human Development.

Nemecek, D., Adria Klein, A., Briceño, A., and Wray S. (2014) "Students are talking…now what? ASCD Express: *Talking and Listening in Class, 10*(5).

Overturf, Brenda (2015). *Inside the Common Core Classroom: Practical ELA Strategies for Grades 3–5.* Boston, MA: Pearson Education.

Reutzel, D. Ray. (2015) "The Habits of Close Reading." Retrieved June 26, 2015 from www.CurriculumAssociates.com/ReadingThoughtLeaders

Reutzel, D. Ray & Cooter, Robert B. Jr. (2011). *Strategies for Reading Assessment and Instruction.* Boston, MA: Pearson Education, Inc

Reutzel, D. Ray & Cooter, Robert B. Jr. (2012). *Teaching Children to Read: The Teacher Makes the Difference.* Boston, MA: Pearson Education, Inc.

Robb, Laura (2014). *Vocabulary is Comprehension: Getting to the Root of Text Complexity.* Corwin Literacy: Thousand Oaks, CA.

Illustration Credits

pp. 8, 9, 12, 19, 20, 56, 61, 62, 70, 80, 91, 134, 156-158, 176, 180, 251, 294, 309, 313, 319, 330-332, 336, 350, 383, 398, 410-411, 417, 422: QBS Learning
pp. 38, 92, 120, 162, 234, 320: Six Red Marbles
pp. 91, 114-116, 120: Sean O'Neill
pp. 91, 128-130: Veruschka Guerra
p. 138: Yurumi/Shutterstock
pp. 91, 142-143: Dave Shephard
p. 146: Jerome Studer
pp. 91, 170-172: Vladmir Aleksic
p. 254: Library of Congress
p. 260: Yale University Gallery of Art
pp. 265, 288-290: Antonio Vicenti
pp. 265, 302-304: Anni Betts
p. 322: Jenny Nutting Kelchen
p. 373: Mary Jo Heil
pp. 383, 384: Jenny Reynish
pp. 383, 386: Caroline Hu
pp. 383, 388: Matteo Pincelli
pp. 383, 392-394: 208Kevin

Photography Credits

pp. 9, 47: Robert Harding Picture Library Ltd/Alamy
pp. 9, 26: Ken Brown/iStockphoto
pp. 9, 32: Cathy Murphy/Getty Images
pp. 9, 60: Andrew Zarivny/Shutterstock
pp. 9, 66: Michael Rosskothen/Shutterstock
p. 10: godrick/Shutterstock
p. 14: MichaelTaylor/Shutterstock
pp. 18-20 (background): nienora/Shutterstock
p. 18 (bottom left): Kepler/NASA
p. 24: irin-k/Shutterstock
p. 28: Rook76/Shutterstock
p. 33: Bob Parent/contributor/Getty Images
p. 34: Library of Congress
p. 40: LeshaBu/Shutterstock
p. 42: Seita/Shutterstock
p. 46: David Cole/Alamy
p. 48: ClassicStock/Alamy
p. 52: Luis Molinero/Shutterstock
p. 54: Saibarakova Ilona/Shutterstock
pp. 60-62 (background): NRT/Shutterstock
p. 68: Iryna Rasko/Shutterstock
pp. 74-76 (background): R-studio/Shutterstock
p. 74 (left): vvvita/Shutterstock
p. 74 (right): Eli Maier/Shutterstock
p. 76: BnF, Dist. RMN-Grand Palais/Art Resource, NY
p. 81 Leonardo flying machine: Leo Blanchette/Shutterstock
p. 82 Guttenberg press: Jan Schneckenhaus/Shutterstock
pp. 91, 102: New York Times Co/Getty Images
p. 94: vectorkat/Shutterstock
p. 96: Africa Studio/Shutterstock
pp. 100-102 (background): Pakhnyushchy/Shutterstock
p. 100: The Seattle Times/JR Partners/Getty Images
p. 101: Bettmann/CORBIS
p. 106: (left): find info from 2014 program
p. 106: (right): AF archive/Alamy
p. 108: starryvoyage/Shutterstock
p. 122: Ozerina Anna/Shutterstock
p. 124: Baoyan/Shutterstock
p. 136: Vladimir L./Shutterstock
pp. 91, 152: Everett Historical/Shutterstock
p. 164: yyang/Shutterstock
pp. 170-172 (background): © Stapleton Collection/Corbis
pp. 187, 192 (bottom): Ralph Loesche/Shutterstock
pp. 187, 198: Folio/Alamy
pp. 187, 202: Dane Penland, National Air and Space Museum, Smithsonian Institution
pp. 187, 204 (top), 206 (bottom): Courtesy of NASA
pp. 187, 218: Vittorio Bruno/Shutterstock
pp. 187, 238, 244, 245: Library of Congress Prints and Photographs Division Washington, D.C. 20540 USA
pp. 187, 246 (side): Everett Historical/Shutterstock
p. 188: Jagodka/Shutterstock
p. 190: Mega Pixel/Shutterstock
p. 192 (top): BYP/Shutterstock
p. 196: ClassicStock/Alamy
p 197: Universal History Archive/Getty Images
p. 204 (bottom): Johan Swanepoel/Shutterstock
p. 206 (top): nienora/Shutterstock
pp. 212-213: M. Dale-Bannister/NASA
p. 213: NASA/JPL-Caltech
p. 214 (background): HelenField/Shutterstock
p. 214 (side): Roger Ressmeyer/Corbis
p. 228: Tyler Fox/Shutterstock
p. 229: Darren J. Bradley/Shutterstock
p. 230: Poznyakov/Shutterstock
p. 245 (background): Golbay/Shutterstock
p. 245 (book): Jiri Hera/Shutterstock
p. 246 (background): wanchai/Shutterstock
pp. 265, 270: Johnny Adolphson/Shutterstock
pp. 265, 282: Catmando/Shutterstock
pp. 265, 276: Dean Fikar/Shutterstock
p. 266 (top): satit_srihin/Shutterstock
pp 266 (bottom): BOONCHUAY PROMJIAM/Shutterstock
pp. 274-275 (background): Stas Moroz/Shutterstock
p. 274 (side): Potapov Alexander/Shutterstock
p. 275 (center): IR Stone/Shutterstock
pp. 274, 276: ezlock/Shutterstock
p. 275 (top): Monkey Business Images/Shutterstock
p. 324: Vaclav Volrab/Shutterstock
p. 338: wongwean/Shutterstock
pp. 319, 281: Soyka/Shutterstock
pp. 319, 344, 345: Everett Collection Inc/Alamy
pp. 319, 362 (right): Monkey Business Images/Shutterstock
pp. 319, 372: worldswildlifewonders/Shutterstock
pp. 319, 373: reptiles4all/Shutterstock
p. 346: MIKE THEILER/AFP/Getty Images
p. 360 (top): Cienpies Design/Shutterstock
p. 360 (bottom): Horst Petzold/Shutterstock
p. 360 (top): Cienpies Design/Shutterstock
p. 361: GongTo/Shutterstock
p. 369: Quick Shot/Shutterstock
p. 376: sciencepics/Shutterstock
p. 377: sursad/Shutterstock
pp. 383, 409: Debbie Steinhausser/Shutterstock
p. 400: Dn Br/Shutterstock
p. 402: Ozerina Anna/Shutterstock
pp. 408-409 (background): BERNATSKAYA OXANA/Shutterstock
p. 408: Dmitry Naumov/Shutterstock